Electronic Publishing
Avoiding The Output Blues

Taz Tally, Ph.D.

Prentice
Hall

Upper Saddle River, New Jersey 07458

Library of Congress Cataloging-in-Publication Data

Tally, Taz.
   Electronic publishing : avoiding the output blues / Taz Tally.
     p. cm.
   Includes index.
   ISBN 0-13-019465-4
    1. Desktop publishing. I. Title.

Z286.D47 T35 2002
686.2'2544536--dc21

                            00-062439

Director of Production and Manufacturing: Bruce Johnson
Acquisitions Editor: Elizabeth Sugg
Developmental Editor: Judy Casillo
Managing Editor: Mary Carnis
Editorial Assistant: Lara Dugan
Production Editor: Denise Brown
Manufacturing Manager: Ed O'Dougherty
Interior Design and Composition: Taz Tally
Art Director: Marianne Frasco
Cover Design: Miguel Ortiz
Cover Art: Comstock, Inc., www.comstock.com
Printing and Binding: Victor Graphics
Cover Printer: Victor Graphics

Prentice-Hall International (UK) Limited, *London*
Prentice-Hall of Australia Pty. Limited, *Sydney*
Prentice-Hall Canada Inc., *Toronto*
Prentice-Hall Hispanoamericana, S.A., *Mexico*
Prentice-Hall of India Private Limited, *New Delhi*
Prentice-Hall of Japan, Inc., *Tokyo*
Prentice-Hall Singapore Pte. Ltd.
Editora Prentice-Hall do Brasil, Ltda., *Rio de Janeiro*

10 9 8 7 6 5 4 3 2 1
ISBN 0-13-019465-4

Contents

Preface

Many people who are using electronic/desktop publishing systems today are doing so without the benefit of any formal or professional training. Not a few of us have been thrust, dropped, dragged, pulled, pushed, or otherwise cajoled into the world of desktop publishing. However, we have come to enjoy the art, technology, flexibility, and creative tools which are part and parcel of desktop once we figured out how to make it work for us rather than struggle against it.

If you are an instructor in electronic graphic arts you have the dual challenges of trying to update your own graphic arts knowledge and expertise, as well as prepare the next generation of graphics professionals with all the knowledge and skills necessary for them to be successful. In addition, the scope and scale of what needs to be taught has expanded. Skills sets such as scanning, image editing and prepress prep, which used to be relegated to the realm of professional specialists, must now be performed routinely by nearly all of us. And whole new media tools such as the World Wide Web have emerged since we went to school.

If you are a student who is new to the world of electronic publishing, you are faced with the challenges of learning both the creative side of graphic arts, such as typography, design and images, as well as the considerable (though not as bad as you think it is) task of learning the digital world of computers and computer software, scanners, digital cameras, printers, and the Internet. All those bits, Bytes, pixels, and vectors are the building blocks of your future.

The key to success is learning the fundamentals. That our technology will change is a given. Learning the fundamentals of digital publishing will not only provide us with knowledge and skills to satisfy our current needs, but will provide the foundation which will allow us to grow with along with, and adapt to, our changing technology. *Electronic Publishing: Avoiding the Output Blues* is an attempt to provide this fundamental information. This book also includes myriad tips and tricks about desktop publishing. I hope this book helps you become a success!

DEDICATION

To my buddy Jaz for all her love and support!

ACKNOWLEDGEMENTS

Many, many people have contributed to the creation of this book. First I w ant to thank Tim Moore, my editor at Prentice Hall PTR, for opening the door for me at Prentice Hall so that I might reach my dream of publishing a text book which I hope will help mant to learn a field that I enjoy do much. I also want to thank Elizabeth Sugg for agreeing to publish this text book and paving the way for it to happen. Judy Casillo, this project's developmental Editor, deserves untold kudos for putting up with what amounted to nearly a rewite of my original book, when I was supposed to essentially quickly adapt it. Her patience and prodding have resulted in a much more complete, and we hope, helpful and useful text book. I want to also thank Lara Dugan, Judy's Assistant for her valuable help with the project.

To the following content experts I offer a huge THANK YOU for the valuable comments and suggestions you provided. This text book is much stronger for your contributions.

Robert Beaverson, Ferris State University

Paul Davis, DeKalb Technical Institute

Val LeFevre, International Academy of Merchandising and Design

Nancy Ripper, Kellogg Community College

Metha Schuler, Santa Rosa Junior College

And finally, a loving thank you for so many things, to my wonderful buddy Jaz, without whom this book would never have started, never mind finished! In addition to her often unheralded labors of making editing changes, unflagging support, and many suggestions, Jaz kept the rest of our life and business together so that I could steal time away to work on this book.

Electronic Publishing
Avoiding The Output Blues
Walk-Through for...
by Taz Tally

This book is created in four clearly defined parts plus an appendix. While each part and chapter stands alone, the book is designed to be progressive, starting with the fundamentals of electronic imaging in Part 1 and progressing with more detailed concepts and information in the following parts. This book centers around the fundamentals of document construction for print, but includes a chapter on Web graphics and addresses the multipurposing of documents throughout.

• Chapter Objectives

Chapter Objectives are found at the beginning of each chapter. These clearly outline the major points discussed and are useful for both teacher and student as major topic guides to each chapter.

• Key Terms

Key terms are listed at the beginning of each chapter just after the Chapter Objectives. These are the most important terms used in the chapters. Each of these terms will also be found defined in the chapter on terminology, and will be highlighted in the body text.

Chapter Objectives

In this chapter you will learn:
- ◆ **Planning a document**
- ◆ **Using thumbnails**
- ◆ **How print documents are constructed**
- ◆ **Master page elements**
- ◆ **Using style sheets**
- ◆ **Managing your files**
- ◆ **Key Terms**
  - • Thumbnail
  - • Master page
  - • Style sheet
  - • Native file
  - • Paragraph style sheet
  - • Character style sheet
  - • Proofing
  - • Linking
  - • Backup and archive

• Highlighted Key Terms

This feature calls attention to the key terms in a chapter by **highlighting** these terms in the body of the book.

• Terms of Endearment and Terminology Terrorism

Our business of electronic publishing is burdened with a nascent and rapidly evolving lexicon of terms which are often misused and/or poorly understood. Rather than relegating these to a seldom-used glossary at the back of the book, a terminology discussion, along with a comprehensive glossary, has been placed front and center, in Chapter 2. A "Terminology Terrorism" section leads off the chapter discussing the unfortunate reality of misused terms, multiple terms with the same meaning, and similar terms with different meanings.

Terminology Terrorism Example:

bit depth, bit density, pixel depth, color depth

All four terms are used to describe the number of bits of data in an image. For instance a grayscale image commonly has eight bits per pixel. It would therefore have a bit depth or bit density or pixel depth equal to eight.

• Tips

Tips call outs are scattered throughout the book to highlight and call attention to specific key concepts. These serve to reinforce the most important parts of each chapter.

TIP

When organizing your document to send out to a service bureau or printing company for them to output, proper file organization can make everyone's life easier and results in faster service, better turn around time and lower costs. Placing your page layout document in the same folder as the linked graphics will accomplish several key things: 1) Your document and graphics will more likely remain together as they are moved from disk to disk, and 2) whenever your page layout document is launched, by you or by the printing company, the linked graphics will automatically relink to the page layout document.

• Pauline's Tips

At the end of each chapter, all the major points of that chapter are collected together in the form of Pauline E. Prepress Tips. These tips reiterate the key points, tips and tricks of the chapters, and place them all in one place for easy review. There are over 100 tips included.

Pauline's Tip 13.6
To test and final proof your document, collect all document files (Doc. fonts and graphics) to a folder. Activate only the collected fonts; launch your collected document with its linked graphics. Print your final proof from this document. This simulates what your printer will do.

• Review and Concept Questions

This textbook contains two kinds of questions: Review and Concept questions. The Review Questions are objective questions which serve to test the understanding of key points of knowledge in each chapter. The answers to each of the objective questions can be easily found in the chapter.

Review Question Example:

1. Which of the following are required for your documents to print properly?

    A. Page layout document

    B. Linked graphics

    C. Availability of used font files

    D. All of the above

The second kind of question, Concept Questions, 1) test the ability of the student to explain key concepts in their own terms, which greatly aids in the learning process, and 2) test the student's knowledge of concepts and how they are integrated and applied.

Concept Question Example:

10. Review the Dry Run Technique, and explain how it helps us test our document for completeness and create document accurate proofs?

• Projects

At the end of each chapter several projects are suggested for students to complete. These range from interviewing professionals in the field, to completing scans and creating documents. Each one is intended to provide students with an experience which will allow them to explore and apply, in a concrete fashion, the concepts and knowledge they have studied in the chapter just completed. These projects can be modified to suit available resources, and are intended to provide ideas which will generate other projects.

• Illustration Rich

The body of the textbook is richly illustrated throughout with hundreds of graphics to help illustrate the points in the text. The graphics are clearly referenced in the text. In addition the graphic captions contain complete explanations which reemphasize major points made in the text as well as including additional information specific to the figure. Many of the illustrations span a **full page** and some are **two-page spreads**. Complex topics are simplified and clarified through the use of these illustrations.

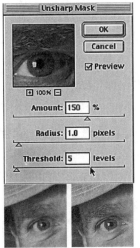

▼ *Figure 12.24 Image Sharpness*
On the left is a portion of an image which has been scanned properly but not sharpened. On the right is the same scanned image, with sharpening applied. Note how the high contrast portions of the right image, such as the eyes, eyebrows, and hat fabric are sharper and appear to be in better focus. This sharpening can be applied either during the scan or in the postscan as it was here in Photoshop. Note the Threshold value is set at 5 to protect the facial skin areas from too much sharpening.

• Screen Grabs from Applications

To help make the book as relevant as possible, dozens of screen grabs for the most common electronic publishing applications such as QuarkXPress, Photoshop, Illustrator, FreeHand, PageMaker, and InDesign, are included as figures to serve as both an introduction, as well as a guide, to the actual applications with which they work.

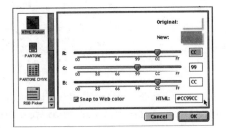

▼ *Figure 14.10 HTML Color Picker for Web Color Assignments*
When assigning colors to an object which will be viewed over the World Wide Web, it is usually best to choose colors from the Web safe color palette of the 216 colors which are common to both the Mac and Windows default system palettes. Assigning the Web safe colors will provide better color consistency and viewing speed.

• Covers Mac and PC

This book is platform independent, and where large differences exist between Mac and PC platforms, such as with font file handling, these differences are highlighted and explained.

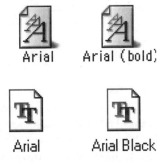

▼ *Figure 11.6 TrueType Font*
A TrueType font file contains both screen and printer font information and is recognized by the triple "*A*" on the icon on a Macintosh and a double "T" in Windows.

• Appendices

Additional information on topics such as bits and Bytes review with ASCII code list, font overview, graphic file formats, questions to ask your printer, preflight lists and forms, Taz's Top Twelve Tips, and DTP Resources, are presented in the appendices.

• Color Section

Important portions of the book which benefit from the use of color, such as the discussion of color images, scanning and separations, are presented in a special color section, Color Plates. Some of the color illustrations span two pages.

FREE Set of Taz's Famous Instructional Videos "Avoiding the Output Blues" Offer to Instructors

For more information about the offer of a free video set, instructors should contact their local Prentice Hall sales representative.

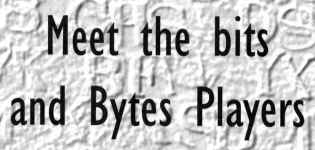

Meet the bits
and Bytes Players

Stars of

"As the BYTE Turns"

Danny D'Ziner

Danny is a very bright, creative artist and designer. Although he never intended to, Danny has started working on a computer. Now Danny does nearly all his work on a computer. Danny bought a great system and started to work. All was rosy until Danny started sending his files to a printer to have them output at high resolution for printing. Danny was used to having everything he handed to the printer work. He was soon to find out that not everything he created on the computer could be output through high resolution PostScript RIP. Danny had to learn how to avoid the perils and pitfalls of PostScript. He needed help.

Sam E. Sales

Like Danny, Sam E. was educated in the old school. He was used to picking up art boards from his clients and delivering them to scheduling, and then on to prepress. He had been doing most of Danny's printing for several years now, and they had a good relationship with few problems. Sam E. Sales has started having problems with client files, though. He gets more disks, and he has no idea what's on them. Prepress has even sent back some clients' disks with strange instructions about parent EPS files and missing fonts. Sam E. no longer feels comfortable answering client questions or even presenting quotes for these electronic jobs. He might just have to learn about that computer after all.

Pauline E. Prepress

Pauline has been with the same printing company for over ten years. She started out in typesetting and then learned stripping (no, not in a night club) and had become quite proficient at assembling film. Pauline likes technology, so when her printing company started getting computers to do typesetting, she learned to use them. Over time Pauline has graduated from typesetting to page layout and, finally, on to scanning and electronic stripping. Pauline's responsibilities now include preflighting incoming client files. Problems with client files have become the biggest bottleneck in prepress. In fact, the problems have become more numerous and severe as clients send in increasingly complex files and more "finished jobs." Sam E.'s problems were coming to her, and worse, he usually refused to inform his clients about their file preparation problems, so the same mistakes reoccurred. Now, Pauline had a secret crush on one of Sam E.'s clients, Danny D'Ziner, but he is one of the worst offenders! Maybe she could help.

Part 1

The Big Picture

The Original DTP System!

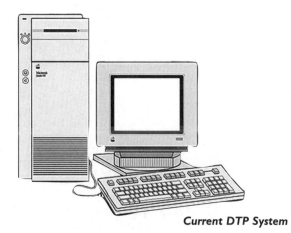

Current DTP System

1
Electronic Document Challenges

As the Byte Turns continues…

Will Danny D'Ziner and Pauline E. Prepress be able to PICT their way through the Perils of PostScript, or will they have one Tiff too many?

Many items on my document look different from the originals, including the photographs, colors, and where images overlap. Why?

That's a good question, but the answer is complicated.

Where do I start? I know part of the answer!

Let's ask Pauline. She can help explain the details.

Many variables affect the printing process. The differences you see boil down to changes in media, image format, and reproduction techniques.

Chapter Objectives

In this chapter you will learn:

◆ **The challenges of printed documents**
◆ **Text and line art challenges**
◆ **Tonal image challenges**
◆ **The need for simplified documents**
◆ **Electronic media challenges**
◆ **Key Terms**
  • Print document
  • Electronic media document
  • Multipurpose document
  • Repurposed document
  • World Wide Web
  • PostScript
  • HTML
  • XML
  • Life-long learning

INTRODUCTION

Whenever we attempt to reproduce images, whether it is in the form of text, line art, or grayscale or color contone images, we are always faced with the challenges inherent with reproducing original materials. Every step or process we apply to an image threatens to change the original nature of, or reduce the quality of, the original image. The history of communications technology has been a struggle to do two things: make the distribution of information and ideas easier and broader, while at the same time maintaining the integrity and quality of the original information or images.

As we all know the invention and subsequent refinement of the printing press has long been considered one of the milestones in the progress of civilization. The advent of the the printed page allowed us to widely distribute information and ideas in an economical fashion. Subsequent development of electronic media such as telegraph, radio, telephone and television further enhanced our ability to communicate. While each of these technologies has been a boon for human communication, most of the technology was controlled by professionals, professional printers, telegraph operators, TV technicians and the like. Each of these communication technologies was a separate discipline which required years of study to master. Control of communications technology was out of reach for the average nonprofessional. The advent of desktop computer technology and the subsequent evolution of the electronic document and the birth, growth, and continued evolution of the Internet and the *World Wide Web* has changed all that. We now have access to many forms of communication through our desktop computers. With access to this control however, we now also share the challenge of controlling the technologies in order to achieve the results we would like.

THE PRINTING CHALLENGE

Pressing problems of putting ink on paper

The basic challenge of printing

The printing process is a challenge in reproduction. There are three challenges in creating a **print document**. The first is to reproduce a document so that it looks as close to the original image fidelity as possible. The second challenge is to provide consistent reproduction of that document over a high volume of prints. The third challenge is to perform the first two challenges in an economically affordable fashion. The second and third requirements, volume and affordability, make the first challenge, image fidelity, most difficult. If price were not an issue, we could reproduce all images as continuous tone photographs. But even then volume would be a problem. How do we quickly create one million photographic copies of a 400-page catalog and then bind it all together for ready distribution and use? Traditional printing technologies (Fig. 1.1) employ many time-consuming steps involving many skills, including: typesetting, photography, engraving, mechanical paste-up, and stripping. These skills require many people with high skill levels to compose and/or reproduce high quality pages. Many of these processes have been changed and simplified with electronic preparation of documents, but much skill is still required, although not always brought to bear. Along with process changes have come changes in people's jobs. Some jobs have changed, others have been eliminated, and new ones have appeared. Chapter 3, "Peaceful Coexistence," Chapter 4, "Electronic Publishing Systems," and Chapter 13, "Document Construction," address how the printing business and process have changed, some of the new tools we are using, and how the nature of the printed document has changed.

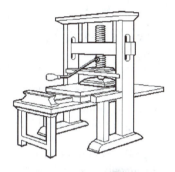

▼ *Figure 1.1 The Original Desktop Printing Press*

Getting many kinds of ideas and information across to many people has always been the role and the challenge of the printing press. New electronic technologies are changing the way we create and produce printed materials. These same technologies are also fundamentally changing the ways in which we communicate and even what we communicate.

New language skills

Along with the new tools and documents, an entirely new language and set of skills has evolved. Terms like "rubylith" and "PMTs" have given way to a digital lexicon more concerned with megabytes, **PostScript**, and file formats. Discussions of photography, film, and enlargers have given way to debates about scanners, Photoshop software, and pixel depth. Chapter 2, "Terms of Endearment," Chapter 5, "Software," Chapter 6, "Bits and Bytes," Chapter 7, "Basic Computer Skills and Habits," and Chapter 11, "Tales of True Typesetting" address the fundamentals of the new languages and skills required to operate an electronic publishing system effectively. Chapter 18, "The Proof Is in the Separation," and Chapter 19, "Managing the Mess," cover some of the new responsibilities which document creators have.

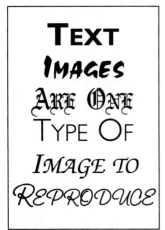

TEXT IMAGES ARE ONE TYPE OF IMAGE TO REPRODUCE

▼ *Figure 1.2 Text Images*

In an electronic document, type is one of the three kinds of images which need to be reproduced in print. There are literally thousands of varieties of type. As you will see, type, which is created with resources called font files, is a special kind of graphics which needs to be carefully managed in order to reproduce correctly.

Typesetting has become easier with electronic publishing, but considerable skill is still required in order to set type properly.

New technical challenges

While the age-old considerations of line screen and dot gain are still with us, a whole new raft of technical issues has appeared which needs to be mastered. The designer and artist and even the secretary now responsible for the monthly newsletter never used to worry about line screens and trapping. Now, they too are having to worry about scanning resolutions, file formats, file preparation, and color calibration. Chapter 8, "Resolving Resolution," Chapter 9, "Grappling with Graphics," Chapter 14, "Color Me Right," Chapter 16, "Screening Your Images," and Chapter 17, "Feeling Trapped?" cover most of the fundamental technical issues involved with producing electronic documents for print.

Image reproduction challenges

We can divide image reproduction challenges into four basic categories: text, line art, tonal (particularly **continuous tone**), and color images. Of these four, text and line art are the easiest to tackle. The ability to reproduce text was initially solved with the invention of the printing press and later facilitated by the invention of movable type. Text has been the easiest of the image reproduction challenges because there is a finite number of character shapes which are constantly reproduced. Both line art and text reproduction were greatly aided through the invention and adaptation of photography to the printing process. Basic text and line art images, because they are constructed out of only black or white areas, can be faithfully reproduced through the photographic process and then directly transferred, again through photography, to plates for high volume reproduction on a printing press. Tonal images, by contrast, are images constructed from shades of gray and (in the case of continuous tone images) constantly varying shades of gray. Shades of gray which characterize tonal images are much more difficult to reproduce than the solid black and white areas inherent in text and line art images. Chapter 13, "Taming Your Scanner," takes you through the depths of image acquisition and editing.

Text and line art

Most graphic images, both line art and tonal, are by their very nature unique. Graphic images, unlike text, cannot be faithfully reproduced through the combination of a set number of basic forms. Words, sentences, and paragraphs are formed through the construction of various combinations of a basic set of characters (Fig. 1.2). In English, we have a basic set of 52 alphabetic characters (upper and lower case), 10 numeric characters, and a variety of punctuation marks: 126 characters in all. These 126 characters are the basis for the ASCII character set discussed in Chapter 3, "Peaceful Coexistence," and listed in the Appendix. So, due to the lack of basic repeatable building blocks, unique graphic image reproduction is, by its very nature, more challenging than reproducing type. Line art reproduction used to be a very time-consuming process because the original image had to be laboriously redrawn by hand. Line art (as well as text reproduction) has been greatly aided through the invention and adaptation of photography to the printing process (Fig. 1.3). Basic line art and text images, because of the continuity of their shapes and their single tone nature (they are either black or white), can be faithfully reproduced through the photographic process and then directly transferred, again through photography, to plates for high volume reproduction on a printing press.

Tonal images

The reproduction of tones in general and continuous tone images (**contones**, Fig. 1.4) in particular has always been a daunting challenge (Fig. 1.4). The challenge has always been how to create a tone or continuous tone out of a solid ink. In some forms of screen printing this was accomplished essentially by smearing the ink out into layers of various thicknesses to create tones or continuous tones. This technique was effective but is a relatively slow and expensive process which does not lend itself to economic, high volume reproduction. The solution to economic, high volume tonal reproduction has been to simulate rather than actually reproduce tones. There have been numerous ingenious methods of tone simulation. Many of the initial contone reproductions were created through the use of line art simulations of contones. Through the use of varying line lengths, thickness, and spacing, the appearance of tone and continuous tone was created. This technique was very effective and many of these original prints are highly valued today. However, this line art technique is very time consuming and requires considerable creative as well as technical skills.

The traditional technique which has been developed to reproduce contone images economically is called halftoning screening, halftoning, or AM (amplitude modulation) screening. In AM screening the size or amplitude of evenly spaced dots is

When faced with the task of reproducing original images, it is always a good idea to begin with the best quality original possible. The higher the quality of the original image the greater your chances of creating a high quality reproduction. The old concept of "garbage in–garbage out" certainly applies here. Don't be afraid to ask for high quality, large format originals. Many of your clients may not know that there is a difference. For instance, many clients will hand you an already printed version of an image, when they have the original version in their possession.

varied to simulate different tones. Patterns of dots of various sizes are created to simulate the appearance of continuous tone. More recently, a process known as FM (frequency modulation) screening has been developed. In FM screening, the position instead of the size of a dot is varied in order to create a contone image. Some screening technologies vary the position as well as the size of the dots to simulate tones. At a distance these dot patterns or screens have the appearance of tones to the human eye. This screening process used to be accomplished photographically and is now performed by a PostScript RIP. Chapter 10, "RIPing Up Your Files," and Chapter 16, "Screening Your Images," tackle the challenges of reproducing contone images on a press.

The problem of dot gain, where the size of a printed dot expands as it is applied during the printing process, is still with us. Instead of adjusting for this ink spread photographically as we used to, we now apply tone correction curves to our images through applications like Photoshop. Refer to Chapters 12, 16, and 18, "Taming Your Scanner," "Screening Your Images," and "The Proof Is in the Separation" for treatment of dot gain issues.

▼ **Figure 1.3 Line Art Images**

Line art images used to be reproduced with cameras and film. Today line art images are routinely captured with digital scanners. Line art images are often the least demanding form of graphic to reproduce because they only have two tonal values which need to be copied. In electronic imaging, issues like path lengths and flatness ratios often need to be addressed.

The challenge of color

The final print reproduction challenge has been and remains the reproduction of color. Similar and related to the challenge we face with reproducing tonal shades, color tests the need to reproduce a very wide range, essentially an infinite one, of colors. If we need to reproduce a solid color, we have the ability to mix up an exact ink color match and print that color separately on the press. This is an effective and even economical solution if we have only one or two colors to reproduce. We do this when we print **spot** colors. However, every separate color which we print requires its own cylinder on a printing press to apply that color. Once we start printing more than six colors, the cost of doing so becomes prohibitively expensive in all but the most demanding color applications. So the real color reproduction challenge becomes apparent when we need to reproduce continuous tone (contone) color which would require the use of dozens or even hundreds or thousands of individual colors in order to reproduce all of the variations of colors in any standard contone image. This practice would clearly involve astronomical costs and is therefore an untenable solution. What is clearly called for is a solution which requires mixing some basic colors to produce a wide variety of other colors. This is precisely the approach which has been taken in the printing process. We use the colors cyan (C), magenta (M), yellow (Y), and black (B) in various combinations to attempt to reproduce the range of colors contained in natural scenes and art productions. This solution is very satisfactory for a wide range of applications. However, there are many colors, particularly those which are bright and rich in white, which cannot be reproduced in the CMYK color gamut. (See Chapters 14, 16, and 18, "Color Me Right," "Screening Your Images," and "The Proof Is in the Separation" for more detailed information.)

It is important to keep in mind that in the case of both tonal and process color reproduction, the results are cost effective approximations of characteristics of the original images. The various screening technologies merely create the appearance of tones and are not actually tonal in nature like the original images they represent. Process color recreations of original colors are approximations and not identical reproductions. The commercial printing process, in an effort to keep the reproduction process affordable, dramatically alters the content and the media of the original image. Hence, even though we have refined and will continue to refine the print reproduction process, and even though there is much we can do to assure as close a match as possible, we should not expect the end results to be identical to the original. Chapter 14, "Color Me Right," covers a wide gamut of issues relating to color reproduction.

Changing printing technologies

So we see that our solutions to these three basic printing challenges of high volume, reasonable cost, and consistent, high fidelity image reproduction have been the development and evolution of three interrelated printing technologies: the offset printing press, screening technologies, and process color. The ways in which these technologies have been implemented have changed only incrementally in the past 200 years – that is, until the advent of open architecture PostScript-based publishing systems. And that is what this book attempts to address: the fundamental challenges of and solutions to preparing PostScript files for print.

▼ **Figure 1.4 Contone Images**

Continuous tone (contone) images are some of the more complex images to reproduce. Contones have a wide range of tonal values which need to be reproduced. Color contone has the additional burden of color as well as tone reproduction. Low cost, easy-to-use desktop scanners have made acquiring these images easy. However, considerable knowledge and skill are required in order to produce a faithful reproduction of an original.

Reduce and simplify: making RIP-ready files

All of the various page elements we create electronically and want to reproduce on a press, including text, line art, and contone images, must be processed through a device called a RIP, or raster image processor. The job of the RIP is to take your electronic document data and convert it into a form, often some kind of a dot pattern, which can be reproduced on a print device. There are many items which we can create on a computer which are difficult or impossible to print. Any print-bound document we are creating on a computer must ultimately be processed through a PostScript RIP, and this RIP is often a tight funnel through which our electronic files must fit before we can image them onto a piece of film or paper. The main emphasis of this book is to help you understand the concepts and help you master the techniques necessary to create RIP-ready files, that is, files which are compatible with processing through a PostScript RIP. Our battle cry for this book, then, is to reduce and simplify all of our documents and images as much as possible. We want to reduce the size of our graphic files and simplify our designs and graphics whenever we can to make them more RIPable.

NEW MEDIA CHALLENGES

The basic challenges of electronic media

Creating an **electronic media document** is easy...creating a useful electronic media document is a challenge which requires attention to a number of key issues. The three top issues which we need to attend to when we create an electronic document are: 1) readability, 2) portability, and 3) printability. Readability refers to the creation of both text and graphic images which are easy to see or read. The portability factor involves creating the document in a format in which it can be transferred to all the places or purposes for which it needs to be used. Printability is still an issue, even with primarily electronic documents, because in many cases we will want our documents ultimately to be printed as as well as transported and viewed.

While most electronic documents are output to monitors and do not have the requirements and challenges of RIPing which print documents have, they have challenges and limitations of their own. Many electronic-based documents do not even employ the same PostScript language commonly found in print based documents. Basic Web page documents commonly use a language known an **HTML** (hypertext markup language) and other languages, such as XHTML (XML), SMIL and SVG, are being developed and evolving all the time. **XML** (Extended Markup Language), which allows more interactivity and cross linking of Web elements, is the likely next evolutionary step in Web language. New languages are being developed and refined as you read these pages.

Creating new documents

When creating documents for electronic media, as with print documents, we must keep the output device in mind. In this case our output device is usually a monitor. Creating a document for output specifically on a monitor has similar but different challenges than creating a document for print. One of the most obvious, and critical, differences between monitor and print based documents is the resolution of your output device. Monitors typically have 72 ppi displays rather than the hundreds or thousands of dots and spots per inch produced by most printing devices. Another difference is the display size available for monitor based documents. While a standard 15" monitor has a viewing area similar to an 8.5" x 11" page (when viewed at 100% size), most Web pages are significantly smaller. Documents equal to or larger than 8.5" x 11" typically require scrolling to be viewed at 100%. Still another difference can be found in the number of viewable colors. While many monitors support the viewing of millions of colors, some only support hundreds of colors. And if your monitor output environment is the World Wide Web then you are dealing with a variable output environment. Your document and images will be viewed on thousand or millions of different monitors. With a printed document once you output a document its characteristics of resolution, size and color are set, while with a document destined for output on the Web, the output/viewing conditions may vary widely from one device to another.

Speed of viewing becomes a key issue with monitor based documents, and particularly when the documents are viewed from a Web page across the Internet. Large, complex print documents with large, high resolution graphics and small complex type usually do not display well or quickly enough when placed on a Web page and viewed over the Internet. Tightly kerned type common found in high quality print documents does not display with the same effect on low resolution monitors.

So when we create documents for use on monitors, and particularly on the World Wide Web, we need to create simpler, lower resolution, more flexible documents which will display well on a variety of output devices. So the construction rules are a bit different for an electronic document which will be viewed primarily on a monitor. Because of the lower resolution and smaller viewing space of our monitors our graphic files should be created at smaller sizes and lower resolution. Type should be larger, simpler, more widely spaced and less voluminous than for a standard print document. When assigning colors we need to keep those eight-bit monitors that can only display hundreds of colors, and the Web safe system palettes, in mind as well. As with print based documents, it is always wise to keep your output device in mind when constructing your document.

Multipurpose documents

Multipurpose documents are documents which are created for more than one use. Repurposing of documents refers to the reuse of a document for a purpose other than the one for which it was initially intended. For instance we now commonly want to be able to view on the World Wide Web a document which was originally created for print, and vice versa. When we create documents which need to be output on a wide variety of devices, the complexity of our task becomes much greater. **Repurposed documents** often must be significantly altered to suit their new use.

The more different the requirements of our various output devices, the more difficult the task of creating a document to meet those multiple needs. It is quite a challenge to create a document which will both print well on a commercial print-

TIP

Prepare yourself for a lifetime of learning. The world of digital electronic media is changing and growing so rapidly that no one person can keep up. Many of the skills we learn in school are often outdated by the time we get into the marketplace. It is wise to focus on learning the fundamental digital imaging principles, as knowledge of these will never be out of date. And it is the knowledge of the fundamentals which will prepare us for our lifelong education to come.

ing press, and view quickly and well from a Web page. Though we are seeking document and graphic file format options which can provide us the flexibility to create documents to meet such disparate output demands, it is currently often necessary to create separate documents for these two specific purposes. And while it is possible to turn just about any PostScript based print document directly into a HTML based Web document, the results are often unsatisfactory. Print documents are often too large, there is too much text, type is often too small and complex with too many typestyles, graphic files are often too large and/or their quality too compromised during the repurposing process.

The key to creating any document is to know as much about the final use of the document before you begin creating that document. Output requirements of a document should control the input or creation characteristics of that document and its text and graphic components. As we will see, new document technologies such as Acrobat PDF and fractal imaging technologies are helping us to multi-purpose and repurpose our documents, but there is no substitute for good job planning and document construction techniques.

Life-long education

The world of electronic media is a constantly and rapidly changing environment, which demands that we continually reeducate ourselves. Gone forever are the days when we learned one set of skills and used them for a lifetime. Our best preparation for a professional life in communications is to learn thoroughly the fundamental principles of digital imaging, because those will never change. The study we do during our formal schooling days is just the start. We need to be prepared for, and indeed excited about, engaging in **life-long learning**. If you stop learning, you will be left behind. The more fully you understand the fundamentals of digital imaging, the easier, and more fun, it will be for you to continue your life-long education.

CHAPTER SUMMARY

The advent and evolution of electronic publishing, also know as desktop publishing, has changed the tools and processes of professional graphic communicators, and brought the capability, power and freedom of widespread communication to the nonprofessional. To create high quality electronic documents we must control the creation and/or reproduction of all the key elements which go into our electronic documents, including, text, line art images and continuous tone images. Print based documents must be created to conform to the high resolution and large grayscale and color data requirements of the PostScript language environment which is the basis of most print oriented documents. Electronic media has its own set of document construction, resolution, size and color characteristics. Increasingly we are creating documents which we want to use for multiple purposes, often for both print and electronic media. The often disparate requirements of print and electronic media can create document construction conundrums. Sometimes separate documents may need to be created for separate uses. The key to high quality document construction, regardless of the use, is preplanning for the final output. Document output requirements should control document input and construction characteristics. Learning digital imaging fundamentals is the key to preparing us for a lifetime of education which is required by the rapidly and constantly changing world of digital imaging.

PAULINE'S DIGITAL IMAGING TIPS

Pauline's Tip 1.1

Take a field trip to your favorite printing company or service bureau and have them take you through and explain the production and printing process in detail. This will be an enlightening experience. Have them show you how they handle customer files and what they check for. By doing this you will more fully understand the challenges printers face when they try to reproduce your work. When you are on your tour, don't be afraid to ask plenty of questions. Make sure you understand the entire production process. This is also a good way to establish a relationship with the folks in the electronic prepress production department, the people who actually output your work.

Pauline's Tip 1.2

Learning the fundamentals of digital imaging is the most important part of your early education in digital communications and electronic media. If you focus too much on current tools and techniques, and fail to learn the basic concepts behind their use, you will be placing yourself at a disadvantage. If you master both fundamental concepts and current tools and techniques, you will be positioning yourself well for both current success, and the lifetime of learning which is demanded by the rapidly and constantly changing world of digital media and electronic communications.

CHAPTER REVIEW

Check Your Comprehension

Multiple Choice Questions

To help you review the topics covered in this chapter, answer the following multiple choice questions.

1. What was the first major technology advance in providing affordable, widespread communication of information and ideas?
   - A. Pony express
   - B. Electronic media
   - C. Laser printers
   - D. Printing

2. Which of the following is a primary goal of printing?
   - A. Accurate image reproduction
   - B. Consistent image reproduction
   - C. Affordable image reproduction
   - D. All of the above

3. Identify the document component which is created by a set of characters.
   - A. Text
   - B. Line art
   - C. Grayscale images
   - D. Color images

4. To what does the word "contone" refer?
   - A. Conditional toning
   - B. Continuous tone
   - C. Constructional toning
   - D. None of the above

5. What is the basic building block which is used in commercial printing to reproduce contone images?
   - A. Photographic building blocks
   - B. Patterns of dots
   - C. Line art patterns
   - D. None of the above

6. _____ are required in order to produce the best image recreations.
   - A. Previously printed images
   - B. Photocopied images
   - C. High quality original images
   - D. Laser printed images

7. Which of the following is used for creating Web page documents?
   - A. PostScript
   - B. HTML
   - C. HPGL
   - D. ASCII

8. Which of the following terms refers to reconstructing a document for another use?
   - A. Repurpose
   - B. Web construction
   - C. Print construction
   - D. Multipurpose

9. Which of the following terms refers to constructing a document for more than one use?
   - A. Repurpose
   - B. Web construction
   - C. Print construction
   - D. Multi-purpose

10. _____ is critical to accurate, efficient document construction.
    - A. Asking about document output requirements
    - B. Preplanning
    - C. Knowing how a document will be used
    - D. All of the above

11. Which of the following is most important to prepare us for our career and future in digital imaging and electronic media?
    - A. Specific techniques
    - B. The skills we learn in school
    - C. Fundamental principles
    - D. None of the above

12. Which of the following best describes how we should view our future in digital imaging?
    - A. A lifetime of learning
    - B. Learn one set of skills very well
    - C. The skills we learn today will suit us for a lifetime
    - D. None of the above

Check Your Understanding

Concept Questions

To help you review and expand your thinking on the topics covered in this chapter, answer the following questions.

1. Briefly explain why the invention of the book was important.

2. What technological development has brought communication technology to the fingertips of the common person? Explain the opportunities and the challenges inherent in the release of this powerful technology.

3. Outline the basic challenges of reproducing images in print.

4. What are the basic challenges in reproducing color in print?

5. Describe three fundamental challenges in creating a useful electronic media document.

6. What do print and electronic media documents have in common?

7. Briefly describe the fundamental differences between print and electronic media documents.

8. What is the difference between a multipurpose document and a repurposed document?

9. Explain the purpose of document preplanning and why it is important.

10. What excites you about electronic publishing? List three goals you would like to accomplish with electronic publishing skills you are acquiring.

PROJECTS

Interview a potential client who needs a brochure created. Make a list of the document project requirements. Ask about the final use/output of the project. Ask them whether they will want to use their brochure for more than one purpose: print, Web, etc. Make a list of those purposes. Also ask them about what kind of document components their brochure will have including: text, line art, grayscale photos, and color photos. Make a list of these components. Ask your new client how they will provide you these document components: as conventional or digital components. Be sure to ask your client for the highest quality samples they have.

2
Terms of Endearment

As the Byte Turns continues…

Will the language barrier of PostScript keep Danny and Pauline at odds forever? Or will they both learn Spanish, move to Costa Rica, and live happily ever after? Hmmm . . . maybe a glossary would help!

What do you mean, your production department told me to save my 1 bit tiffs as vector graphics so that they will RIP faster. What are you talking about???

Well, er, ah…

Oh dear, I don't have the foggiest idea!!

Help !!!

This is difficult – not being able to communicate effectively about these files. Perhaps we should sponsor a seminar on basic PostScript terminology, invite our clients, and have the sales staff sit in too.

Chapter Objectives

In this chapter you will learn:

◆ **The importance of using proper terminology**
◆ **We have multiple words with the same meaning**
◆ **We have some terms with multiple meanings**
◆ **Clarification of terminology problems**
◆ **Use context to determine meaning**
◆ **Glossary of key common DTP terms**
◆ **Key Terms**
  • Resolution terms and units: dpi, ppi, lpi, res
  • Spot vs. dot
  • Bitmapped, raster, pixel
  • Bit depth, pixel depth, color depth
  • Building block vs. alpha channels
  • Halftone vs. contone
  • Font vs. Typeface
  • Composition proof vs. contract proof
  • Many other common terms…

INTRODUCTION

Half the battle

Half of winning the battle in mastering any new discipline is learning the language. The lexicon of desktop or electronic publishing is as specialized and filled with acronyms as any you will encounter. We even have acronyms which can have several different meanings depending upon the context. For instance, ATM may refer to Adobe Type Manager, Asynchronous Transfer Mode, or Automatic Teller Machine, depending upon whether we need to manipulate a **font**, send it over a network, or purchase something! Our catalog of terms is also very new and rapidly evolving. Many of the basic terms such as resolution, screening, **pixel**, vector, and **halftone** are not well understood by most of those who use them. Communication and understanding are not aided when the "experts" misuse terms as well. Confusion about the meaning and use of **dpi**, **ppi**, and **lpi** is a primary example. It is no wonder we are confused about resolution; we can't even agree to use the proper terms!

An increasing number of us in the world of DTP are non-specialists: that is, we use the technology, but our primary job is not publishing. Even if our primary job is publishing, few of us have been afforded the basic training we need to master the all-important fundamentals. With this in mind, I offer up a primer on electronic publishing terms. I have placed it in the beginning of the book, instead of the usual practice of placing it at the end, because of its primary importance in helping us master the tools of our trade.

TERMINOLOGY TERRORISM

Multiple origins

Our terminology in the world of electronic publishing arrives from many different sources. Some of our terms come from the world of design, others from engineering and still others from printing, photography, and even video. As a result of this multiplicity of word sources we often end up with a great deal of confusion about the definition and use of our terms. For instance we often have several words which have the same meaning, such as pixel, **bitmap**, **raster**, all of which refer to images constructed out of pixels. We have words which have multiple meanings, such as ATM. We even have words which can have multiple meanings depending upon how they are used, such as the word trap, which can refer to object or ink trapping. And we have many words which are just plain misused, such as dpi, which seems to be used for any and all types of resolutions. We often have multiple ways of expressing the same concept depending upon what part of the industry we are in. For instance when discussing the size or resolution of a file, a printer will use the terminology of pixels per inch, a photographer will describe the same image in terms of file size in MB, while a video or Web designer will use pixel dimensions such as 800 x 600. All three ways of describing a file are appropriate given the context within which they are used. But get a printer, a photographer and a video technician in the same conversation about the size of an image and you may just see a fistfight break out as a result of all the confusion.

All this confusion of words and meanings makes it at best difficult and often times impossible to communicate with clarity. This confusion leads to miscommunication, misunderstandings, lots of frustration and often costs us valuable time and money. Following is a list and description of some of the commonly used terms and concepts with which we may have problems. Following that is a more complete glossary with definitions.

Mixup of words and meanings

ATM

Can refer to Adobe Type Manager, which is a system level utility which help us utilize PostScript Type 1 fonts. ATM can also refer to Asynchronous Transfer mode which is a networking term which is used to describe the simultaneous transfer of data back and forth across a network. Usually the context within which the the term is used will be the key. If the discussion is on fonts, Adobe Type Manager will be the most likely use, while if the discussion is on networking then Asynchronous Transfer mode will be the best bet.

Bit depth, pixel depth, color depth

All three terms refer to the number of bits per pixel which an image contains. For instance, a black and white image has 1 bit per pixel. This image may be referred to as having a **bit depth** of 1, a **pixel depth** of 1, or a **color depth** of 1. The word color depth is often restricted to use when referring to the total bit depth of a color image such as a 24bit RGB image, a 32bit CMYK image or and 8 bit Index color image. In all cases the terms will refer to the number or density of bits of data which an image contains (see bit depth or density below).

Bit depth, bit density, pixel depth, color depth

All three terms are used to describe the number of bits of data in an image. For instance a grayscale image commonly has eight bits per pixel. It would therefore have a bit depth or bit density or pixel depth equal to eight (8).

24bit, 30bit, 36bit, 42bit scanner/digital camera/image

Lots of confusion about these terms. These three terms refer to the total bit depth which a scanner or digital camera can capture and/or an image can have in RGB mode. RGB, with its three channels, is the reference mode here. A 24bit image has three 8bit channels, a 36bit image has three 12bit channels etc.

Spots vs. dots

Few people ever refer to image **spot**s; we tend to use **dots** (**dpi** for everything). In fact there is an important distinction. The spot, or laser spot, is the smallest mark that a printing device can make. The size of the spot will be determined by the optical or hardware resolution of the printing device. For instance a 2400 "dpi" imagesetter will create spots which are 1/2400" across. The dot, or halftone dot, is much larger than the laser spot, in fact it is constructed out of laser spots. The size and spacing of the halftone dots will be determined by the line screen at which image is printed and the grayscale value being rendered. A 150 lpi printer will produce 150 halftone dots per inch (see dpi, ppi, res, lpi, line screen , screen frequency below).

Resolution

Resolution is often spoken of in a linear fashion, when it fact it is a square function. For example it is common to refer to an image as being 300ppi (pixels per inch). Pixels per inch is a linear description. Because of this when we double an image's resolution from 300 ppi to 600 ppi it would appear that we have doubled the resolution, and therefore the file size of our image. In fact we have quadrupled both the resolution and the file size. Out 300 ppi image is really 300 ppi vertically and horizontally. So a square inch will have 300 ppi x 300 ppi = 90,000 pixels inch^2. when we raise the image's resolution to 600 ppi we are raising both the vertical and horizontal resolution to 600 ppi. Now each square inch of our image will have 600 ppi x 600 ppi = 360,000 pixels inch^2, which is quadruple the number of pixels in the original image. So when ever we "double" the resolution of an image we are quadrupling the file size, opening time, saving time, storage space, printing time, transport time, etc. of that image. We should therefore enhance the resolution of our images with great care and forethought, lest we create enormous unmanageable files.

Input vs. output resolution

Much of the confusion surrounding our understanding of resolution can be removed if we separate input resolution from output resolution. Input resolution refers to images we capture, such as with a scanner or digital camera, or create from scratch, such as in Photoshop. When we discuss image capture or creation we are discussing pixels as our **building blocks**, and therefore should always be using resolution terminology which uses pixels such as ppi (pixels per inch)or **res** (pixels per mm) input resolution. Output resolution refers to the resolution of an output device, such as a printer. Here again when discussing output resolution it is useful to think about the building blocks of the image which is being output, and use these building blocks as your guide to the resolution terminology. When an image is printed we often use spots and dots to print the image, so our output terminology should reflect the use of these building units. For text and line work where edges are being reproduced image spots are used to rebuild those edges. While spots per inch is most accurate, the common terminology used here is dpi (dots per inch). For **contone** images which are rebuilt out of patterns of halftone dots, the terminology is lpi (lines per inch), as in lines of halftone dots per inch. The one circumstance where input and output building blocks, and therefore terminology, match is when our output device is a monitor. A monitor uses the same building blocks as a captured or created image, pixels, and therefore it is appropriate to use ppi in both cases. If we keep out input and output concepts and terminology straight, our understanding and communication about resolution become much clearer.

TIP

Always consider the context in which an term is used in order to figure out its true meaning. Often a term will be misused, but through context you can determine its true meaning. A common example is the use of the units dpi when referring to a scan resolution, or the resolution of a pixel based image. If someone says to scan at 300dpi, you can discern from the context that they are really referring to pixels per inch, which is what will be captured by the scanner. By doing this quick mental determination you will be clear in your own mind that you are discussing input resolution and pixels, and not output resolution with spots or dots. If you are not sure of the proper meaning stop the conversation and ask questions until you are clear.

Dpi, ppi, res, lpi, line screen, screen frequency

It is frightening how much confusion there is on these various resolution terminologies. Dpi tends to be used for everything and usually incorrectly. First we should separate input (scanning and digital cameras) from output resolution (often printing). Use the building blocks of the current image as a guide to the proper terminology. When capturing an image we are creating pixels, therefore ppi (pixels per inch) or res (pixels per mm) should be used. When printing an image we will use dpi (which are actually image spots instead of dots, but we are kind of stuck using dpi instead of spi) for the smallest printing building block (such as 600 dpi) which will refer to the size of the laser spot. We use these small dots (or spots) to recreate text and line art images which require sharp edges. We will use lpi (lines per inch) when discussing the number of halftone dots per inch, such as 150 lpi, which are used to reproduce continuous tone images when we print. Lpi, screen frequency, and line screen all refer to the same things, halftone dots per inch. The term "line" in lines per inch is confusing because we do not really see any lines; rather the halftone dots are usually printed in lines of dots and are thus lined-up in rows.

Vector, line art, object oriented

All three of these terms are used to refer to images which have solid edges, like logos, and use outlines to create images. The term line art is really the more general of the three as it does not refer to any particular type of image building block, such as pixels or vectors, but rather just to the nature of the solid edge. Vector- and object-oriented should refer to the type of building block used to create the image, in this case vectors.

Pixel, raster, bitmap

All three terms are used to refer to images constructed out of pixels. You will see the term rasterization, which refers to the conversion of an image into pixels for some other form such as for vector to pixel.

Densitometer, intensitometer, info tool

All three terms are used to the measurement of grayscale values. Densitometer really measure dot density on film or paper. The term intensitometer is another technical term for a tool which measures the intensity of grayscale value. In software applications it is common to have "Info" tools which measure grayscale value (see grayscale value below).

Measuring grayscale value

There are two common scales which are used to measure grayscale value, the percentage scale and the grayscale unit scale. The percentage scale expresses grayscale value as a percentage of 0% to 100% regardless of the bit depth of the image. The grayscale unit scale expresses grayscale values in terms of the total number of grayscale values in an image. The most common grayscale unit scale is 0-255 (available for 8 bit images), but wider scales extending all the way to 16,384 (available in 14 bit images) shades of gray are not uncommon. As if the various scale were not enough the grayscale percentage and grayscale unit scales read in opposite directions. In the percentage scale 0% = 0% grayscale of pure white, while 100% = 100% grayscale or pure black. In the grayscale unit scale 0 = pure black while 255 = pure white. It is a good idea always to determine the units of measurement being employed by your Info tool prior to using that tool.

File size measurements: 300ppi, 5.4MB, 1200 x 1500, 1.2K x 1.5K

All three terms of the above numbers refer to the same image. The first term, 300 ppi, refers to the linear resolution of the file in terms of pixels per inch. This way of referring to an image is commonly used by printing companies who work with a variety of print sizes. The second term, 5.4 MB, refers to the file size of the a 4" x 5" 300 ppi RGB image. This type of designation is most often used by photographers who typically have a set image size (4" x 5") and use RGB as the standard reference bit depth. The designation of 1200 x 1500 refers to the pixel dimension of this same image, in this case a 300ppi image which is 4" x 5" in size. This image is 1200 pixels down and 1500 pixels across. This type of pixel dimension designation is often used by video and Web folks who work with images which have fixed linear resolutions (generally 72ppi). You may even find some folks, probably photographers, who will refer to this image as a 1.2K x 1.5K image. This "K" designation is short for 1200 x 1500 pixels, where the K refers to thousands.

Optical/hardware vs. interpolated resolution

Scanner and printer manufacturers like to play all sorts of games with the resolutions of their devices. They tout all sorts of wild resolutions in order to help them sell their equipment. The optical or hardware resolution of a device is the actual resolution which a device can achieve. Any resolution above that is interpolated or madeup, and therefore does not represent true capture or reproduction capabilities.

Channels: building block vs alpha channels

This is an especially confusing concept for novices. In a pixel based image editing application like Photoshop, there are typically two type of channels, building black channels and alpha channels. The building block channels determine the basic nature of the image. Black and white images have one 1bit channel, grayscale image have one 8bit channel, RGB images have three channel, CMYK image have four channels and so forth. After some introduction the building block channel concept is easy to grasp. It is with the term alpha channel that we find the problem. First of all, the term alpha channel gives you no clue as to what it is used for, and is therefore slightly intimidating to begin with. An alpha channel is basically a storage location for selections and masks. Selections can be stored and edited in alpha channels, and then reloaded from alpha channels (see selection, mask and alpha channel below).

Selection, mask, alpha channel

These three terms are variations of one entity. Once made, a selection can be saved. The selection,which is not a physical entity, is saved as a physical object known as an alpha channel. An alpha channel is composed of grayscale values which represent transparency or opacity. The opaque (white) portions of the alpha channel represent the saved selection and is therefore the mask within the alpha channel. The black (transparent) portions of the alpha channel are outside of the originally saved selection and are therefore not part of the mask (see transparency, opacity below).

Transparency, opacity

This is the old half full, half empty scenario. Pure white areas of a mask in an alpha channel (see above) can be viewed as 100% opaque or 0% transparent. Similarly the black areas of an alpha channel may be viewed as 100% transparent or 0% opaque. Any shade of gray in between 0% and 100% will represent percentages of opacity or transparency. For instance 50% gray equals 50% transparent/opaque. It is probably wise to visualize one way or the other, and stick to it.

Transparent, translucent

There is some confusion here about the meaning of these terms. Transparent means clear, 100% transparent, all visible light is allowed to pass through. Translucent means partially transparent, or a portion of light will be allowed to pass through. Printers sometimes refer to their inks as transparent, where in reality they are translucent. This is how light commercial printing inks are used to create various colors, by partially absorbing light and allowing some it it to pass through (see Chapter 14, "Color Me Right").

Threshold values vs. threshold tools

The word threshold refers to a value at which something happens. For instance the threshold value in an unsharpmask tool represents the grayscale value differential which must be reached before unsharpmask will be applied. Or the 50% threshold value specified in the "Bitmap" mode change in Photoshop refers to 50% grayscale being the default value at which pixels will be either converted to black or white pixels. Confusion may arise because their are tools called threshold tools, such as the Threshold in the adjust submenu in Photoshop which allows you to alter the black to white threshold value.

File format vs. file content

There is enormous confusion and misinformation about all the various file formats. The easy way to understand file formats is to separate file contents from file containers. There are basically two kinds of file contents pixels and vectors. These pixels and vector contents are placed in various containers. The container which is chosen depends upon the use of the file. For PostScript printing the two preferred file formats (containers) are TIFF and EPS. For Web pages two common file formats are JPEG and GIF for pixels and SWF for vectors. We match up the file content with the nature of the image and select a file container (format) for specific uses.

Highlight values, diffuse vs. specular

The term highlight value is commonly understood to mean the lightest portion of any image. While this is not a wrong definition. it is less useful than it might be. There are two kinds of highlight values, diffuse and specular, with the diffuse value being the one of most interest. The diffuse highlight may be helpfully defined as the lightest portion of an image, which still has detail. A specular highlight is a light area which has no detail. If we adjust the diffuse highlight value properly, the specular will be automatically adjusted. The diffuse highlight is set based upon the minimum highlight dot which an output device can reliably print.

File font vs. typeface

The words **font** and **typeface** are commonly misused and are often used as identical terms, where in fact a font is subset of a typeface. A font is a typeface, like Helvetica, of a specific style, like Bold, of a specific point size, like 12pt so Helvetica Bold 10pt is one font and Helvetica Bold 12 pt is another.

Halftone vs. contone

This mixup leads to all sorts of funny conversations. Printers are notorious for confusing these two in conversations with their clients. A contone is a continuous tone image, like a photograph of someone's face, where there are continuously changing grayscale values. A halftone is a dot pattern simulation of a continuous tone image which is used to recreate contone images during the printing process. Your printer will often refer to a contone as a halftone. He or she is thinking about what the image will eventually become, when they get finished with printing it, rather than what the image is currently. It is important to distinguish between contones and halftones, as their building blocks are completely different and therefore, they will need to be handled differently. For instance, we need to scan and edit contone images using different settings and techniques than already halftoned images. Always be very clear which type of image you are starting with.

Color computer, scanner, etc.

There is no such thing as a color computer or scanner for that matter. Computers and other digital devices only understand 0s and1s or black and white. We create grayscale variations out of black and white, but all color is created by output devices such as monitor and printing devices. Once we understand that computers are only black and white devices, it make our understanding and control of our DTP system easier.

Pantone color ≠ spot color

Pantone is a major manufacturer of color swatch charts and sample books for a standardized color matching system. They make a wide variety of color sample products. Perhaps the most common color sample product is Pantone spot color swatch book. Many have gotten into the bad habit of calling this the Pantone book and the colors contained with THE Pantone colors. While the the colors contained with the Pantone spot color book are certainly Pantone colors, they are not the only Pantone colors, there are many others such as the process and spot to process color books. Spot colors should be called spot colors, not Pantone colors. This removes any ambiguity.

Process color is not necessarily a 4/c process

While four color process (4/c) is by far the most common process color system used in printing, it is by no means the only process color system. There are three, six and seven color systems such as and CMY (3) Pantone's Hexachrome (6), RGB (3 on a monitor) which are process color systems as well. The term process color refers to colors which are built from percentage screens of a specific and limited sets of colors. For clarity always refer to the number of process colors such as 4/c process.

Trapping: object vs. ink

This is a term which has two distinct meaning depending upon context. There is object trapping, and ink trapping. Object trapping, the most common use of the term in DTP, refers to the overlapping relationship of two objects which touch on a printed page. Ink trapping refers to how well one ink will adhere to another when it is applied during the printing process. Be careful when you are discussing trapping with pressmen—they may be talking ink trapping.

Laser ≠ desktop printer

It is common for people to use the word laser print to cover all desktop printers. This is a holdover from the 1980s when most desktop printers were lasers. There are many types of desktop printers including inkjets, dye sublimation and laser printers. Each type of device has its own characteristics, capabilities and limitations. In order to impart as much information as possible and provide the correct impression as to what kind of print will be produced it is best to specify both the color space and type of printing device, such as color inkjet or black and white laser.

MatchPrint ≠ contract proofs

Here is another example were an industry standard tool has become a generic name. Many people use the word MatchPrint to refer to any type of **contract proof** (see contract vs. **composition proof** below). MatchPrint is a very specific type of analog proof made from film with specific dye sheets. There are many other kinds of contract proofs.

Digital dylux or digital blue line

Wow! Talk about an oxymoron! Blue lines, also know as dyluxes, are made from film. Digital proofs by their very nature are not made from film. The term digital blue line or dylux has been adopted by many print company folks because they were used to the word blueline or dylux and they just put the word digital in front of it either to make it seem more familiar or to hide the fact that the proof is usually a large format inkjet print. It is lexicon laziness like this which leads to compound confusion, especially to novices. Use the actual type of printing device to describe the type of proof, such as inkjet. Reserve the terms blue lines and dyluxes for the actual film based proofs. If someone uses a term like digital dylux or digital blue line, stop them and ask them what they are really referring to.

Composition (non-color matching) vs. contract (color matching) proofs

There is a tendency to assume that any color proof you see from a printing company is a contract proof. That is, that the colors which you see in the proof can be matched on press. This is often not the case, and particularly if that proof has been made with one of the many desktop inkjet, laser or dye sublimation printers. Many desktop printing devices can print more vibrant, more highly saturated colors than can be reproduced on a commercial printing press, and particularly in 4/c process. Many color proofs which you are shown are intended to be composition proofs only. These proofs should only be used to check for content not for color fidelity. While your printing company should make it clear to you whether the proof you are looking at is a content or contract proof, it is really up to you to make sure you understand what you are looking at, and what you can expect to see on press.

Proofing

Many folks in DTP think that proofing is only done at the printing company. Nothing could be further from the truth. The proofing cycle starts with you before you hand your file to your printing company or other service bureau to reproduce. It is up to us, the document creators, to make sure that everything is positioned correctly on the page and that all colors are properly assigned. It is also up to us to provide an accurate hard copy composite and color proofs to the printing company so that they know what we expect them to print. (In fact the only way to reliably check to see if all of our colors have been properly assigned is to print color separated proofs.)

Prepress and preflighting

Prepress is defined as the preparation of a file for printing. We can expand this definition to include viewing as well. Preflighting is the process by which we test our file for final output. Like proofing many people believe that prepress and preflighting are only performed at the printing company or other output service bureau. This was generally true back in the days of mechanical art boards. But today in the world of DTP we have so much control, and therefore impact on the printing/output process when we construct our files, that we have to be aware of final output from the moment we begin to create our images and documents. This applies to whether we are outputting to a commercial press, a desktop printer or the Web. It is our responsibility to make sure that, at the very least, all the components of our job, page layout document, graphics, font files, color assignments and accurate proofs are delivered to our output service companies. And if we really care about the quality of our files we will make sure that we have the proper image resolutions, and color spaces, and that our documents are constructed in such as manner that they will print and/or view easily and quickly. The better the job that we do when we construct and hand off our files the better, quicker and less expensively your printing company or other service bureau can process your job.

Press check

The purpose of a press check is to make sure that the printed piece matches the contract proof (see composition vs. contract proofs above) which you had previously signed off on. You should also check for press smears, hickies and registration accuracy. However, this is not the time to try to make that barn redder or grass greener: This should have been done long before in Adobe® Photoshop®. Any color adjustment you make will affect the entire image, not just specific portions of the image. If the press sheet matches the contract proof, let the presses roll. Just because you are there does not mean you have to make adjustments.

Dot gain

Dot gain is the process by which halftone dots grow in size when ink or toner is applied to paper during the printing process. The result of this dot grow is the darkening of our images. We need to adjust for dot gain, particularly with our halftoned images, whenever we print. Dot gain will vary depending upon the printing process and the stock on which we are printing. For instance, uncoated stocks tend to have higher dot gains than coated stocks. One problem arises when we try to communicate dot gain values to one another. For instance, if a halftone dot grows from 40% to 50% some people refer to this as 10% dot gain. In reality, mathematically, this is 25% dot gain because the 10 point increase in grayscale value represents 25% of the original 40% gray value. Add to this confusion the fact that dot gain varies all along the gray scale spectrum, and we can have a real doozy of a communication problem. So…rather than getting mired and frustrated with the moving-target-math, it is easier and better to discuss how far a dot gain correction curve should be moved to accommodate the dot gain which will result.

Color

To many, color is color, what's the big deal, all I want is red. But the more we get into color the more difficult it seems to be to communicate our need properly. First of all there are many descriptions of color. The is RGB, CMYK, CIE, HSV, HSL, and the list goes on. First it is a good idea to make sure that you are using the same color description that your coworkers and service providers are using.

Color separations

Say the word color separation and nearly everyone thinks CMYK separation for print. This is neither wrong nor bad. However, it is important to know that there are many types of color separations. The first color separation usually performed in an image creation and document construction process is when you scan. When you scan an image in RGB mode, you are performing a color separation of your original contone color image into separate red, green and blue components. If you intend to take your scanned images to press, they will have to be reseparated into CMYK before they can be recombined during the printing process. In fact, just about every color mode conversion you put your images through represent a reseparation. It is important to note that each reseparation represents an opportunity for image data loss, and therefore quality reduction. We need to plan and set up our separation carefully.

ELECTRONIC PUBLISHING TERMS

Following is a glossary of some of the terms which we use in electronic publishing, and throughout this book.

Acrobat: Electronic document technology developed by Adobe® as an operating system and application independent, and Internet safe document creation and editing technology. Acrobat technology is used to create and edit PDF documents. See *PDF*.

Active: Currently usable window, application, or document.

Adaptive color: A color palette constructed from the colors contained in an image. Most commonly used when creating an index color palette for use in displaying a color image on a Web page. See *Index color*.

AM dot: Amplitude modulation dot. Image reproduction building block where a pattern of dots with varying sizes, or amplitudes, are used to simulate grayscale values. See *Halftone (AM) dot*.

AM screening: The process of creating an AM screen. See *Screening, Halftone Dot AM*.

Analog: Refers to technologies which employ continuously varying values, often between two end member values. An example would be an analog watch which employs moving hands which vary continuously between 0 and 60 (seconds or minutes) or 0 and 24 (hours). See *Digital*.

AppleShare: Mac-based network file sharing software.

Application file: A computer program with a specific set of capabilities (e.g., page layout, drawing, word processing).

Archiving: Creating copies of a file on separate media with the subsequent removal of those copied files from an active disk. Archive files are often saved and organized for later retrieval.

ASCII: American Standard Code for Information Interchange. This is a standard code for all the alphanumeric characters plus punctuation marks found in the English language. The use of ASCII code allows for easy translation of text files between otherwise incompatible applications and document formats.

ATM: (Adobe Type Manager) A utility which provides background operating system level viewing and printing support for PostScript fonts on both Mac and Windows computers.

ATM Deluxe: (Adobe Type Manager Deluxe) A utility which provides both background operating system level viewing and printing support for PostScript Type 1 fonts on both Mac and Windows computers, and full font file management capabilities as well.

Backup: Creating copies of files on separate storage devices or media as a means of protection against lost, damaged, or destroyed files.

Binary code: The two character code or alphabet consisting of "0" and "1" which forms the foundation of every element created on a digital computer.

bit: The smallest, most fundamental building block of digital computer languages. There are only two bit values, 0 and 1. All computer generated text, and graphic elements, as well as all documents are constructed out of various sequences of bits. For instance, each ASCII character is constructed out of a unique sequence of eight bits. See *Byte* and *ASCII*.

Bit depth: The number of bits of image information in an image. Black and white images have 1 bit per pixel. Grayscale images typically have 8 bits per pixel. RGB images usually have 24 bits per image (eight in each of the three RGB channels) while CMYK images typically have 32 bits per image. If the bit per pixel increases in an image, the total image bit depth increases as well. For instance, an 8-bit per pixel RGB image has a total image bit depth of 24 bits, while a 10-bit per pixel image will have a total image bit depth of 30 bits per image. May also be referred to as bit density, pixel depth or color depth. See *Capture bit depth*.

Bitmap/bitmapped image: A graphic image constructed out of pixels, also known as a raster image, in contrast to vector images, which are constructed out of lines.

Bi-tonal image: Another name for black and white images; meaning two tones, black and white.

Boot disk: The active drive which contains the system software from which the computer has been started up. In the Windows® OS, the boot drive is typically the C: drive. On a Mac, the boot drive is the drive which automatically occurs in the upper right hand corner of the desktop.

Building block: Refers to the building blocks of graphic images. There are two basic building blocks of graphic images, pixels, and vectors.

Built color: Color created and printed using screened combinations of colors rather than a single solid color. Traditionally, built colors have been constructed, or built, from combinations of the basic CMYK process colors. Recently, additional colors, known as Hi-Fi colors, have been added to the four standard process colors (see process color, spot color, and Hi-Fi color).

Byte: A building block of computer language. One Byte is composed of eight bits. Each character in the ASCII character sequence is equal to one Byte. See *Bit* and *ASCII*.

Calibration: Matching of input, display, proof, and final production, especially with regard to color. The adjustment which must be done to make sure that a scanner or digital camera will properly capture an image and that output devices such as monitors and printers properly reproduce images. Fundamental calibration techniques usually involve linearization and neutralization (see *WYSIWYG*).

Capture bit depth: The number of bits per pixel which an image capture device such as a scanner or digital camera can capture. Typical capture bit depths are 8, 10, 12 and 14 bits per pixel. The higher the bit depth the more image information is captured. Often capture bit depth is expressed as the total number of bits captured in a three-channel RGB image, where a 10-bit per pixel capture bit depth is expressed as a 30-bit capture bit depth for the combination of all three channels.

CD-ROM: Compact Disk—Read Only Memory. An optical disk which contains up to 600 MB of information. This information can be accessed (read or copied) but cannot be edited.

Channel: A single, usually 8-bit grayscale portion of an image. There are two kinds of channels, color, and alpha channels. Color channels are the fundamental building blocks of color images, while alpha channels are created from selections.

Character style sheet: - See *Style sheet, Character*

Choke: A color trapping term used to indicate that a surrounding background area containing one color will be overlapped, or choked, into another foreground area containing another, usually darker, color which it encloses (see *Trap* and *Spread*).

Clear: Remove a selection in a document without placing a copy of the selection on the clipboard.

Clipping path: Vector edge added to bitmapped contone images in order to create a clean sharp edge. Often used when creating hard edged silhouettes.

Clipboard: Short-term pasteable storage of copied or cut selections.

Close: Closing a document.

CMYK mode: CMYK mode is a color mode which is constructed out of four grayscale channels, each representing one of the four process colors cyan, magenta, yellow and black. This mode is used for printing color images to color printing devices such as commercial printing presses and desktop color printers. Scanned images must be converted into this mode in order to print them. See *Process colors*.

CMYK separation: The separation of an image into its CMYK components. Required in order to print a contone image. See Separation.

Coat and varnish separation: The separation of the portions of an image which will need to be coated or varnished during the printing process. Required in order to apply a coat or a varnish to a printed image. Each coat or varnish requires its own cylinder on the press. See *Separation*.

Collection: The gathering of all the document components necessary for printing a document. Includes the page layout document, graphic and font files used specifically in that document. See *Preflight* and *FlightCheck*.

Color: 8 bit color = 256 colors or shades of gray. 24 bit color = 16.7 million colors, 32 bit color = 4.3 billion colors.

Color assignment: Various ways of designating how a color should be created and reproduced. In printing, colors are usually designated as either spot, process builds, or tints of spot colors (see *Color matching systems*, *Spot color*, *Process color*, *Built color*, and *Tint*).

Color cast: The presence of color when none should be there. Color cast is typically identified when a neutral or gray portion of an image has unequal amounts of red, green or blue. Fixing a color cast is called neutralization. There are two types of color cast, scanner and image casts, which should be adjusted separately. See *Neutralization*.

Color depth: See bit depth and pixel depth.

Color lookup table: This is file which contains a set of data which describes how the color data in an image from one color space should be converted to color data in another color space. An example of a common color lookup table would be one which contains information on converting RGB to CMYK data. These color lookup tables are often created for specific devices such as a specific printing press.

Color management: The process of controlling color from one device to another through various applications and even computer systems. Color management frequently involves the use of color targets for the creation of color profiles for each device used in an electronic publishing system. The goal of a color management system is to provide consistent and predictable color values. See *Profile* and *ICC*.

Color matching systems: Color assignment and matching systems which utilize specific mixtures of spot and/or process colors to create and reproduce colors. Several of the most common systems include Pantone®, Trumatch®, Focaltone®, and Toyo® (see *PMS color*).

Color Profile: A set of color curves and/or values which are created through a target based calibration process. A color profile contain information about the color gamut of an input or output device or model such as a scanner, monitor, or printer. See *Profile*, *Generic profile*, and *Custom profile*.

Color space or model: Systems for defining and/or describing a spectrum or range of colors:
RGB = Red, green, blue, transmissive, or additive color space
CMYK = Cyan, magenta, yellow, and black, reflective or subtractive color space
CIE = Commission International de l'Éclairage
HSV = Hue, saturation, and value
HSL = Hue, saturation, and lightness or luminance
YCC = Luminance chrominance, chrominance

Common color: Colors which are common to, included in, two touching objects. Assigning common colors to touching objects can minimize trapping requirements and problems. Assigning common colors is a common practice when working with process color images. See *Trap* and *Process colors*.

Composition proof (comp): A proof which shows the accurate content and placement of document page elements, but does not necessarily show image and color quality accurately. Typical examples of comp proofs would be laser printer or blue line print representations of a final commercial print piece (see *Contract proof*).

Compression: The reduction in the size of a file by reducing, through the use of shortcut data recording methods, the space required for storing the information contained in a file (see *JPEG*, *Lossy compression*, and *Lossless compression*).

Computer to plate (CTP): A commercial printing system which bypasses the traditional film creation step on the way to creating plates which will be used to print images on a commercial printing press. CTP is typically faster and higher quality than conventional film-based printing (see *Film to plate*).

Contone/continuous tone : Abbreviation for continuous tone image. An image which contains gradually changing shades of gray. A gradation or blend, and a photograph of a face are examples of contones. Contones contrast with line art images which are typically flat looking with few if any shades of gray. A contone is simulated in printing by the creation of a pattern of various-sized halftone dots.

Contract proof: A proof which shows both the accurate content and placement of document page elements, and accurately shows image and color quality. Typical examples of contract proofs would be MatchPrint (for film-based printing) or color calibrated Inkjet print representations (for computer to plate printing) of a final commercial print piece (see *Composition proof*). Printing companies often show a contract proof to represent what they think they can reproduce on press.

Copy: Copy a selection; places a copy of the selection on the application clipboard. May also apply to text such as the terms "body copy" or "headline copy."

CPU: Central Processing Unit. The primary computing chip in a computer. Speed of a CPU is determined by clock speed and MIPS of the CPU.

CREF Guidelines: An extensive set of file prep guidelines produced by the Scitex Users Group.

Curve: A line graph which controls the ratio of input to output values for grayscale values in an image. A curve is often used to control the brightness and contrast of images and is used to adjust the distribution of grayscale values in individual color channels to accomplish color correction.

Curve tool: A software tool composed of an input/output graph. Used for the adjustment of the distribution of grayscale values in an image. Commonly used for adjusting image brightness and contrast, as well as for color correction.

Custom profile: A set of color curves and/or values which are created through a target based calibration process. A custom (color) profile contains information about the (color) gamut of a specific input or output device such as a scanner, monitor, or printer. See *Profile, Generic profile* and *Color profile.*

Cut: Copies and removes a selection while placing the copy of the selection on the clipboard. Each application is provided its own clipboard by the operating system.

Data block: Digital data is typically stored and transferred in groups of data known as blocks. The size of a data block varies widely from one circumstance to another.

Densitometer: An instrument which measures dot density and/or grayscale value of images.

Desktop: Virtual working or desktop surface on a Mac or Windows monitor. What you see first on your screen when your operating system launches when you start/boot your computer.

Dialog box: A pop-up window, such as a print dialog box, which provides response choices.

Diffuse highlights: Lightest portion of an image which still has detail. This is the most important highlight portion of an image to be captured and preserved. See *Specular highlight.*

Digital: Any equipment, process, or media which utilizes only two values, such as sequences of 0s and 1s, binary numbers, or some facsimile, to create, store, transport, reproduce, or present information, hence the name "digital computer."

Digital image: A digital image is one which is captured and /or edited with the use of a digital scanner, camera, or computer. Digital implies that the image is constructed from two values, 0s and 1s, the only two values a digital computer "understands. These 0s and 1s are used to construct and control pixels and vectors, the basic blocks of digital images.

Digital literacy—The 3 Rs: Refers to the state of being familiar with the fundamental digital concepts, terms, and language of digital technology. The three Rs of the analog world were reading, writing, and arithmetic. The three R of the digital world are RIP, RAM, and Raster.

Digital revolution: Refers to the transformation from analog technology to digital technology. An example is the change from photographic based images to pixel based images. Digital technologies are based on two values, which in current computer technology are the values 0 and 1, known as bits.

Digitize: Convert an analog or continuous format set of data such as a photograph, video, or sound clip to a digital file format. This conversion involves the changing of the image or sound into sequences 0s and 1s so that they may be recognized and manipulated on a digital computer. Images which are digitized are converted into pixels.

Dither / dithering: The creation of intermediate grayscale or color values from preexisting pixels. Dithering is commonly used as a smoothing function along image edges to improve image transitions and within images to reduce posterization, and particularly in index color images. See *Index color*.

DMax (maximum density): Measurement is often used to state the darkest shade of gray which an image capture device can distinguish. Instruments with high dynamic ranges usually have high DMax's as well. See *Dynamic Range*.

Document file: A file created while working in an application containing pages of text and/or graphic elements.

DOS (MS Dos): Disk Operating System. General term for any operating system. Also shorthand for the text based MS DOS, which was the precursor to Windows OF GUI.

Dot (halftone dot): The building block of continuous tone-printed images. Halftone dot resolution is usually commonly referred to as line screen or LPI (lines per inch). Typically line screens in commercial printing vary from 133 lpi to 150 lpi. See *Output resolution*.

Dot gain: The tendency for halftone dots to "grow" or enlarge when they are printed. This dot gain occurs because ink and toner tend to spread out when they are applied to printing substrates. Dot gain results in images which print darker than they scan and view.

Dot gain adjustment: The lightening of an image, usually through the application of a lightening curve, to precompensate for the darkening which will occur when a halftone dot-based image is printed.

Dpi: Dots per inch. A linear measurement of resolution which refers to the number of image dots or spots which a printer can create per linear inch (for example, 300 dpi or 1200 dpi). Dpi is often used when other terms are more accurate and useful. This should not be confused with pixels per inch which is an input resolution term. See *ppi, Spot, Dot,* and *Res*.

Dpi^2: Dots per square inch. An area measurement of resolution which refers to the number of image dots or spots which a printer can create per square inch (for example, a 300 dpi laser printer creates 90,000 dpi^2, a more accurate and useful measurement of resolution than dpi).

Dry run technique: A technique for testing the completeness and integrity of a file which you intend to be used for final output, especially if you intend to send that file out for processing and output. This technique involves using the collected components of a document for the printing of the final proof.

Dynamic media: Media which change. A common example of dynamic media is an interactive Web page. See *Static media.*

Dynamic range: The range of grayscale values, from black to white, which can be captured by a scanner or digital camera. The dynamic range scale is a logarithmic scale ranging from 0 to 4.0, with 4.0 being the highest. Image capture devices which have high dynamic range can distinguish wider range or grayscale values than devices which have low dynamic range. Low dynamic range devices, with dynamic ranges <3.0, typically have a difficult time distinguishing shadow details in images. See DMax

EFIS: Electronic File Information Sheet. Contains information about the creation and content of an electronic document such as number of pages, page size, application and version used, numbers and types of graphics, fonts and colors. May also include printing guidelines or instructions. This information is very useful to service bureau production staff who will be outputting your file.

Edge reproduction: The main focus of scanning line art. Reproducing the edge of line art is the key to good line art scans. Using the optical resolution of the scanner is often a key to accurate reproduction of line art edges.

Electronic media document: A document created electronically with the use of computer hardware and software. An electronic media document may be used for a variety of output purposes, including for print and the World Wide Web.

Electronic publishing: 1) A general term which refers to the use of electronic (usually digital) equipment to create and reproduce text and graphic images of all kinds and combinations. 2) A specific term which refers to the use of digital media, or non-printed media, as the final communication format, examples of which include CD-ROM documents, Acrobat documents, Web pages, on-line publications, and presentation documents.

Electronic publishing culture: The mutually dependent people who are involved with the creation and processing of an electronic document. This culture includes designers, scanner operators, typesetters, photographers, print buyers, prepress production people, Web masters and anyone else involved in the creation, editing and output of an electronic document.

EPS: Encapsulated PostScript files format. File format used for images or documents which are created for PostScript printing. EPS is designed to hold either pixel or vector based image data. Vector files are saved exclusively in EPS format for PostScript printing.

Ethernet: A common networking technology which contains hardware, software, and protocols for sending and receiving digital text and graphics data.

Explorer: Windows system-based application which allows the user to use the operating system and navigate (Create, Name, Locate, Move, Throw Away, and Duplicate Files).

File format: The digital file containers which hold pixel and vector image information or data. File formats vary with the use of an image. EPS and TIFF are used for PostScript printing, while GIF and JPEG are used for World Wide Web transfer and display.

File preparation (file prep): The various steps which must be performed to prepare a file for output. File prep typically involves checking document geometry and content to be sure it matches the requirements of a specific output device. See preflight

File size: File size is a measure of the amount of information contained in a file. Controlling file size is important to both print and Web production processes. Graphic file sizes as controlled by four major variables: 1) Image dimensions, 2) Image Resolution, 3) bit depth, 4) Compression

Film to plate: The traditional commercial printing system which creates a film version of a document on the way to creating plates which will be used to print images on a commercial printing press (see *Computer to plate*).

Final scan: A scan performed at high resolution after an image has been viewed, cropped, analyzed and set up using a low resolution preview scan. See *Preview scan*.

Finder: Macintosh system-based application which allows the user to use the operating system and navigate around (Create, Name, Locate, Move, Throw Away, & Duplicate Files).

FireWire: Very fast and flexible connection to external devices such as scanner and hard drives. Replacing the older SCSI network standard.

Flattening: The simplification and reduction of a document or graphic image through the collapsing and removal of layers and alpha channels. Flattening is usually required for output.

Flatness: The value which controls the number of straight lines which will be used to print a curves path. Lower flatness values (0–2) result in smoother lines but greater RIPing requirements. A flatness value of 3 is recommended for most printing devices.

FlightCheck: An industry standard preflighting utility which is used to preflight documents and the collection of document components prior to printing. See *Preflighting*.

FM dot: Frequency modulation dot. Image reproduction building block where a pattern of dots with varying spacing, or frequency, are used to simulate grayscale values. See *Halftone (FM) dot*.

FM screening: The process of creating an FM screen. See *Screening, Halftone Dot FM*.

Folder: Virtual storage space for applications, documents, and other items.

Font: Typeface of a specific style and size. Example: Helvetica Bold 12pt.

Font file: Physical file which contains the characters information necessary for viewing and printing font characters.
• Screen font - PostScript Font resource used for viewing type on a monitor.
• Printer font - PostScript Font resource used for sending type to a printer.
• TrueType font - Alternative font architecture to PostScript fonts. TrueType font files contain both screen (viewing) and printer font information.

Font suitcase: A handy storage container for PostScript Type 1 screen font and TrueType font files on a Macintosh.

Font set: A set of virtual font files created in a font management utility. A font set typically contains a set of font files for a specific job or sequence of jobs. The virtual font files are linked to actual font files stored on a drive. Font sets are generally activated by themselves, so that only font files used for the job will be active. Use of font sets helps to prevent font conflicts as well as improves speed.

Gamut: The range of reproducible colors which a device has available. A color monitor usually has a larger color gamut than a CMYK printer; therefore there are colors which we can see and produce on a color monitor which we cannot reproduce on the CMYK printer.

Gamut conversion: The image from one color space to another. A common example is the conversion of an RGB gamut image to a CMYK gamut image.

Gang or batch scan: Scanning multiple images in one pass with all images having identical settings.

GCR: Gray component replacement is one of two major descriptions of how black ink (K) is substituted for cyan, magenta and yellow inks in process commercial printing. GCR typically substitutes black ink throughout the gray ramp of an image from the quarter tone through the shadow of an image. See *UCR* and *UCA*.

Generic profile: A generic profile contains information about the average (color) gamut of an input or output model device such as a model of scanner, monitor, or printer. See *Color profile* and *Custom profile*.

Giga- (Gigabit, GigaByte, etc.): Unit prefix which designates 1000 of the following units, such as Gigabit, GigaByte, Gigabits per second, etc.

GIF/GIF89a: Graphic Interchange File format. GIF is an Internet specific file format designed for sending pixel-based image across the Internet. GIF files are limited to a maximum of eight bits per pixel. GIF89a supports transparency.

Graphic formats: File containers which contain the pixel and/or vector building blocks of graphic images. Examples include:
• TIFF - (Tagged Image File Format) Used for high resolution bitmapped graphics and scanned images (PostScript print format).
• PICT - Apple's quick drawing screen display language.

- PCX - MS DOS/Windows-based bitmapped graphic file format.
- BMP – Windows bitmap format.
- EPS - (Encapsulated PostScript) Object oriented or vector based (PostScript print format).
- PAINT- Low resolution (72 dpi) bitmapped.
- POSTSCRIPT - Uneditable (unless you speak PostScript) text-based page description file. This type of file cannot be opened and edited within a page layout or graphics program; PostScript files are downloaded directly to a printer (PostScript print format).
- DCS - Desktop color separation (PostScript print format).
- JPEG - Joint photographic Expert Group (Web pixel format).
- GIF - Graphic interchange format (Web pixel format).
- SWF - ShockWave format (Web vector format).
- ScitexCT - Continuous tone format developed by Scitex® Corporation (PostScript print format).
- Windows Metafile - File used for screen views with windows operating system.
- YCC - PhotoCD native file format.

Gray map: A chart, usually a histogram, which shows the distribution and frequency of the grayscale value in an image.

Grayscale reproduction: The main focus of scanning contone images, such as grayscale and color photographs. Scanner calibration, linearization and neutralization, as well the as setting of proper highlight and shadow points, are keys to accurate reproduction of grayscale values.

Grayscale value: There are generally two scales for measuring grayscale: percentage which varies from 0% (white) to 100% black, and grayscale unit scale which varies from 255 (white) to 0 (black).

GUI: Graphical User Interface. GUI's such as the Mac OF and Windows OF replaced less user-friendly text based operating systems such as MS DOS.

Halftone: An image which is built out of a pattern of halftone dots. Continuous tone images such as photographs cannot be printed as a continuous tone on a printing press, so they are reconstructed out of patterns of dots. These dot patterns are small enough so that they appear as a continuous tone image when viewed at the proper distance. This pattern of dots, usually created by a laser printer or imagesetter, is intended to produce the effect of a continuous tone image. Halftone dots are built out of smaller image dots or spots. The size of the halftone dot varies with the grayscale percentage it is simulating. Traditional halftones were created by taking a high contrast photograph of a continuous tone image through a screen. Digital halftones are created during the RIPing or rasterizing process on a printer or computer (see *Raster image processor*).

Halftone cell: The cell in which a halftone dot is created. The size of the halftone cell is determined by the line screen (lpi) of the output device. The number of building block squares of a halftone cell is determined by the output resolution of the imaging device, which in turn determines the number of shades of gray which can be reproduced.

Halftone Dot (AM): The building block of a printed contone image. A halftone dot is a composite dot created out of one or more laser spots. Halftone dots are variable sized dots which are constructed through the combination of various numbers of laser spots. The size, or amplitude (A), of halftone dots is changed, or modulated (M), to produce a simulated change in grayscale value. A halftone dot is created to serve as a simulation of grayscale or continuous tone. Larger halftone dots are used to create the impression of darker shades of gray and smaller halftone dots are used to simulate lighter shades of gray. A continuous area filled with halftone dots of the same size is known as a tint or screen.

Halftone dot (FM): Similar to the halftone AM dot, but these printed image building blocks are printed with dots whose spacing, or frequency (F), are changed, or modulated (M), to produce a simulated change in grayscale value. This is often called stochastic screening. Like AM dots, FM dots are are fixed size dots which are constructed from a small number of laser spots.

Halftoning / halftone screening: A method of screening for reproducing a continuous tone image which varies the size of the halftone dots to simulate changes in grayscale value (also known as AM [amplitude modulation] screening). With this traditional, nonstochastic method, halftone dots are located in a rigid pattern and only the dot size is varied (see *Screening, Stochastic Screening*).

Hardware RIP: Raster image processor, which is created as a hardware device, usually a CPU. Hardware RIPs are usually less flexible and harder to upgrade than software RIPs and their speed is a set characteristic determined by the CPU and RAM portions of the RIP. See *Software RIP.*

Hexadecimal colors: Colors designated by hexadecimal values. Most commonly used for assigning colors to objects created for display on Web pages.

HI-Fi color: High fidelity color. A color printing system which uses three or four colors in addition to the standard four-color process to produce color images on a printing press. The use of these additional colors dramatically increases the color gamut or range of colors which a printing press can reproduce using built colors. See Process color

High key image: This refers to an image which has an overall bright nature, such as a well lighted room with white walls. See *Low key* and *Medium key images.*

Highlight point–diffuse: The lightest portion of an image which contains details. A diffuse highlight area contains significant grayscale value or information, and will print as a light value of grayscale, which will show details. An example would be the lightest portion of a white shirt. The typical range in which a shadow point will fall is 3% –15% grayscale.

Highlight point–specular: The lightest portion of an image which contains **no** details. A specular highlight area contains little or no grayscale value or information, and will print as pure white with no details. An example would be a reflection off a chrome bumper. A typical grayscale value for a specular highlight is 0% gray.

Histogram: A chart with highlight, mid-tone and shadow sliders which displays the frequency and distribution of grayscale values in an image. A histogram is often used for setting the highlight and shadow points in an image.

HSV/L: Hue, saturation, and value/lightness are used to describe the color of a pixel. Hue is the basic color determined by its frequency or wavelength of light. Saturation is a measure of the the intensity or purity of the color and is controlled by the amount of white color added to the basic color. Value or lightness is a measure of the grayscale value of the color.

HTML: Hypertext Markup Language. HTML is the underlying language code which is the used to create web sites and pages. HTML is to the Web what PostScript is to printed documents and pages.

IBM PC: See *PC/IBM PC.*

ICC: ICC is an acronym for the International Color Consortium. This is a group of industry leading manufacturers who together develop standards for handling color files in open electronic publishing systems. One of the most significant contributions of this group is the creation of the ICC Color Profile system, a set of profile standards which allows all manufacturers of color management product to create mutually compatible profiles.

Icon: Symbol for an item. It can be type or graphic (e.g., Disks, Folders, Applications, Documents).

Image spot: The spot which is generated and imaged on film, paper, or plates by a printing device such as a laser printer or imagesetter. Image dots are combined on film, paper, or plates to create images. The size of the image dot depends upon the resolution of the printing device. For instance, a 600 dpi laser printer creates an image dot which measures 1/600 inch square, while a 2400 dpi imagesetter creates an image dot which measures 1/2,400 inch square. Image dots are combined to create halftone dots (see *Resolution* and *Halftone dots*).

Imagesetter: High resolution (1200 dpi – 5000 dpi), laser-based photographic output device. Imagesetters can often produce both film and paper output. There are basically two types of imagesetters: capstan imagesetters, in which the film is transported during imaging, and drum imagesetters, in which the imaging laser is transported during imaging. Drum imagesetters are considered to be more precise and therefore higher quality and more suitable for reproducing large format and high quality color images.

Imposition: The geometric arrangement of document pages for the commercial printing process where 4, 8, 16, or even 32 pages can be printed at one time.

Index color: A color space limited to a maximum of eight bits of image data and two hundred and fifty six colors. In order to reduce file size, 24 bit color images are often converted into 8 bit index color images for Internet display.

Ink trap: See *Trap.*

Input resolution: Resolution terminology used to refer to images which have been captured or created as pixel-based images. Usually expressed as the number of pixels per inch (ppi) or pixels per millimeter (res). See *Input resolution*.

Intensitometer: A tool, often called a densitometer or Info tool, which is used to measure the grayscale values of pixel-based images.

Internet: The world-wide system of computers linked through a highly integrated and interconnected network. The multimedia portion of the Internet is known as the Web, or World Wide Web.

Interpolation: The creation of new pixels from previously existing pixels. Interpolation commonly occurs when files are resized and/or when their resolution is changed, or a resolution other than the optical resolution of a scanner or digital camera is used to capture an image. See *Optical resolution*.

JPEG: (Joint Photographic Expert Group). A standard Lossy compression scheme and file format used with pixel based Web images and for some print images as well. JPEG compression provides a variety of compression ratios ranging from 2/1 to 100/1. JPEG contains 24 bits per pixel. (see *Compression* and *Lossy compression* and *Progressive JPEG*).

Kerning: The space between two text characters. When used as a verb, kerning refers to the adjustment of space between two text characters.

Keyness: This refers to the overall brightness of an image. See *High key, Medium key,* and *Low key images*.

Kilo- (kilobit, kiloByte, etc): Unit prefix which designates 1000 of the following units, such as kilobit, kiloByte, kilobits per second etc..

Knockout: A color trapping term used to indicate that a background area equal to the size and shape of a foreground area containing a specific color will be removed, or knocked out, during the printing process. This allows the foreground area and color to print without contamination of the background color (see **Overprint**).

Lab mode: Lab mode is a color mode which is constructed out of one grayscale channel—the "L" or luminance channel—and two color channels, the "a" and the "b" channels. This mode is particularly useful for making grayscale only adjustments, such as brightness, contrast and unsharpmask, to color images. By making adjustments only on the "L" channel, color shifts can be completely avoided.

LAN: Local area network. Connection of computers and peripherals within a local environment such as within one building.

Laser printer: Relatively low resolution (300 dpi–1200 dpi) black and white or color desktop printers, which usually print on paper but sometimes on film. Laser printers use toner, a magnetic thermoplastic, rather than a photographic image, which is fused onto the print surface as an imaging medium. Laser printers are generally used as proofing devices in high quality work, but can be used as final output for lower quality work (see **Imagesetter**).

Laser spot: The smallest building block of a printed image. The size of a laser spot is controlled by the resolution of the output device. A 2400 imagesetter produces a laser spot 1/2400" across. Laser spots are printed end to end to reproduce the edges of text and line art. Laser spots are combined to make halftone and stochastic dots, which are used to recreate contone images.

Launch: Startup/activate an application.

Layer: A level or layer in a document or graphics file which can contain document components such as text and graphics. Layers are often found in native file formats. Layers can be activated or deactivated and shuffled. Using layers allows for easier construction and editing of documents and graphic files. Layers are generally removed or collapsed prior to final output in order to simplify and reduce the size of the file.

Leading: The space between lines in a paragraph. When used as a verb, leading refers to the adjustment of space between lines in a paragraph.

Lifelong learning: This concept refers to the fact that technology changes so rapidly that we must engage in education throughout our lives to learn new concepts, techniques and technologies.

Linearization: Adjusting, or calibrating, a scanner so that it will capture grayscale values with their proper values. For instance, a linear scanner will create a 35% pixel when it "sees" a 35% grayscale value. A nonlinear scanner will capture grayscale values other than 35% when it "sees" a 35% grayscale value. Typically, uncalibrated/nonlinear scanners create pixels which are darker than the original grayscale values of an image. For example, an original 50% grayscale area may be captured as 60% gray by a nonlinear scanner.

Line art: Line art images are typically flat looking, monotone images with no shades of gray present. Line art is defined by the shape of the edges of the image. A logo or pencil drawing is a typical example of a line art image. Contrast with *Contone image*.

Line screen: See *Screen frequency*.

Link: The address connection, or link, between a high resolution file stored free on a hard drive to a low resolution preview version placed in a page layout document (see *Linking*).

Linking: Refers to establishing a link between a high resolution external print image and a low resolution preview file placed in a page layout file (see *Link*).

Linux: Simplified operating system used on a variety of types of computers.

Lossless compression: Compression of a file which does not result in the loss of some image data. LZW, Zip, and Stuffit are examples of lossless compression (see *Compression, Lossy compression*, and *JPEG*).

Lossy compression: Compression of a file which results in the loss of some image data. JPEG is an example of lossy compression (see *Compression*, *Lossless compression*, and *JPEG*).

Low key image: This refers to an image which has an overall dark nature, such as a late sunset photo. See *High **key*** and *Medium key images.*

Lpi: Lines per inch. Resolution term used in printing which designates the number of halftone dots per inch which are printed horizontally and vertically. Lpi differs from dpi in that dpi refers to image dots per inch (see *Halftone dot, Image dot, Dpi,* and *Screen frequency*).

Luminance: Luminance refers to the grayscale values of a color image. Luminance adjustments include brightness, contrast and unsharpmask. In Lab mode all of the grayscale or luminance values are contained in the "L" or luminance channel, which makes adjustment of these characteristics easier.

Macintosh: A desktop computer made by Apple Computer. The Macintosh, or Mac as it is commonly referred to, which was developed in 1984, was the first widely available desktop graphics computer and first widely available GUI interface. The Mac has been the standard of the professional graphic arts community. THe Mac has been built around a series of Motorola CPUs. See Mac OS and PC and Windows and GUI.

Mac operating system (OS): Macintosh operating system. The core software used to operate a Macintosh computer. The Mac OS was the first widely available GUI. The Mac OS has been developed in a progressive numeric sequence of versions such as OS 5.2, 8.6, 10.0, etc.

Mainframe: A large computer often occupying a room of its own which serves as a central data processing storage and networking center. Often are linked to a large number of "dumb" terminals which are used to access the mainframe's capabilities.

Master page: A page formatting tool in a page layout application which serves as a template for document pages. Text and graphics items, such as logos and page numbers, occur repetitively on document pages and are placed on master pages so that they will automatically be placed on document pages. Master pages dramatically simplify the creation and editing of multipage documents and help maintain consistency from page to page. Master pages are often used along with style sheets to construct a document (see *Style sheets*).

Medium key image: This refers to an image which has an average overall brightness, such as a well lighted portrait of a person's face. See *Low key* and *High key images.*

Mega- (Megabit, MegaByte, etc.): Unit prefix which designates 1000 of the following units, such as Megabit, MegaByte, Megabits per second etc.

Memory: See *Storage memory*.

Menu: Pop-up and pull-down lists of choices (e.g., application headers, dialog boxes, palettes).

Minimization: Reducing the content of your system and application files and related resources to simplify the complexity and improve the performance of software.

Midtone: Tonal range of an image which centers around 50% gray scale. Grayscale values in an image roughly in the range of 35% to 65% gray scale are considered to be in the midtone region.

Modem: Computer peripheral device used for connecting computers via phone lines. The term "modem" is a compound word derived from the two words "modulate" and "demodulate" (mo-dem), which is what a modem does. The sending computer modulates a digital signal from a computer into an analog signal for transfer over the phone lines. The receiving modem then demodulates the analog signal into a digital signal again for transfer into the receiving computer.

Moiré pattern: A repeating geometric pattern of dots produced when multicolor screened images are printed. This pattern is generated as the result of two colors being printed with slight misregistration at nearly the same angle.

Motherboard: The main component circuit board of a computer which contains many of the key components such as the CPU, and RAM.

Multiple scan: Scanning multiple images in one pass with each image having its own separate scan settings.

Multipurpose image or document: To use an image or document for more than one purpose. The same image may be used for commercial printing, desktop printing, and Web viewing. Multipurposing usually requires that we reconfigure the image to maximize the image characteristics for each use. The changing characteristics include: image dimension, resolution, pixel depth, file format, and color space.

Multitasking: Performing more than one function simultaneously (e.g., printing and typesetting).

Native file: An original editable document file produced by an application, in contrast to some EPS and all PostScript files, which are not easily editable within the application which produced them.

Network: A collection of interconnected devices such as computers, printers, modems, etc. Common examples of networks include AppleTalk: low speed (270KB/sec) network protocol, and Ethernet/EtherTalk: medium speed (10 MB/sec) network hardware and protocol.

Neutralization: Adjusting, or calibrating, a scanner so that neutral portions of an image will be captured as neutral, rather than having a color cast. A neutral area will have equal RGB values. A non-neutral area will have unequal RGB values. For instance, a neutral 5% gray area should have RGB values each equal to

5%. Neutralization if a foundation concept of color scanning, correction, and reproduction.

Object trap: See *Trap*

OCR: (optical character recognition: Digital) Conversion, through scanning, of text as editable characters rather than as graphics.

One bit graphic: Graphic file composed of only two values, usually either black or white.

Open: Refers to activating or opening a closed disk or folder.

Open font: New font file format being developed to replace PostScript and TrueType fonts files. Open fonts are designed to be more cross platform compatible and useful for both print and Internet use.

Optical resolution: The true hardware resolution of an image capture device such as a scanner. Using the hardware resolution of a scanner results in faster and more accurate scans. Scanning at other than the optical resolution of a scanner results in interpolated pixels, which are manufactured and therefore less accurate.

Orphans: Single line sections of paragraphs occurring at the beginning or end of pages. These should be avoided.

Outline graphic: See *Vector graphic*.

Outlining: The process of converting a pixel based image into a vector based image. Typically performed on one bit line art images. Can be accomplished from within most drawing applications, or in dedicated outlining applications such as Adobe Streamline.

Output resolution: Resolution terminology used to refer to images which have been recreated or printed as spot-based and dot-based images. Usually expressed as the number of spots or dots per inch (dpi) or halftone dots per inch or lines per inch (lpi).

Overprint: A color trapping term used to indicate that a foreground area containing a specific color will be printed directly on top of a background area or color without the removal of any of the background color (see *Trap* and *Knockout*).

Partnering: The concept which emphasizes working together with people who are involved with the creation, editing, or output of an electronic document, to ensure a document's output quality. For example, designer and other document creators should partner with their printing companies when they create commercial print documents.

Paragraph style sheet: See *Style sheet, paragraph.*

Paste: Place a copied or cut selection from the clipboard.

PC/IBM PC: PC is short for personal computer, a term coined by IBM in the 1980s for its version of the desktop computer. The IBM PC first utilized a text-based DOS as its operating system, which was later supplanted by the GUI Windows. IBM PCs have been built around a series of Intel CPUs. See *Macintosh*, *GUI*, *Windows*. IBM based PCs are by far the most common desktop computers in the world, with over 85% of the desktop market.

PDF: Portable document format. PDF is the document format created by Acrobat technology. PDF files are operating system and application independent as well as Internet safe. PDF documents can be created from any document which can be saved as a PostScript file through a process known as distilling. PDF documents are used for a variety of purposes including document distribution, display, and printing on a wide variety of computer operating systems.

.pfb file: The outline printer font file of a Windows based PostScript Type 1 font file pair. .pfb files also contain significant screen font information, and are the companion files to .pfm font files. See *.pfm file*.

.pfm file: The font metrics font file of a Windows based PostScript Type 1 font file pair. .pfm files contain the character spacing information and are the companion files to .pfb font files. See *.pfb file*.

Peripheral device: A device which is added onto a computer to expand its capabilities. Common peripheral devices include scanners, digital cameras, storage devices and drives and display devices such as monitors and projectors.

PhotoCD: A range of technologies and services related to a process of scanning, formatting, storage and saving, in a special digital format (YCC), images which have been captured by a camera on film. The PhotoCD process produces a range of image resolutions which can be used for different purposes such as TV, video, and printing at various sizes.

Pixel: Basic square building block of a bitmap or raster image. A pixel can be of various sizes depending upon the resolution of the image. Pixels may contain one or more bits of grayscale information (see *Resolution*, *Ppi*, and *Bit depth/pixel depth*)

Ppi (pixels per inch): the most common term used to express correctly the resolution of a digital image. Ppi refers to the number of pixels per inch both horizontally and vertically in an image. See *Input resolution*.

Pixel depth: The number of bits per pixel (b/p) a graphic image contains. B&W images have 1 b/p; grayscale images typically contain 8 b/p; RGB color images typically contain 24 b/p; and CMYK images typically contain 32 b/p.

Pixel dimension: The size of an image measured in pixels.

PMS color: (Pantone Matching System color). A color assignment and matching system developed by Pantone, Inc., which utilizes specific mixtures of spot and/or process colors to create and reproduce colors. The term PMS is often misused as a general term for spot color (see *Color matching systems*).

PostScript dictionary: A portion of a PostScript RIP dedicated to processing a specific part of a PostScript document. Examples include font, gradient, TIFF and EPS dictionaries.

PostScript error: A break which occurs during the processing of a PostScript based file which is the result of the PostScript RIP, either not understanding some of the PostScript information or because there is too much or too complex information. PostScript errors typically cause the cessation of the RIPing process.

PostScript file: A uneditable, document file which contains all text, graphics, and format information, created specifically to aid in the printing of complex files on a wide variety of PostScript compatible systems. PostScript files are downloaded directly to RIPs without opening the files.

PostScript Interpreter, or RIP: A hardware or software device which interprets, or converts, PostScript language information into printable data. Required for printing PostScript language specific data like that found in EPS and PostScript files and PostScript fonts. See *Hardware* and *Software RIPs*.

PostScript imagesetter: A relatively high resolution printer capable of imaging PostScript image data. Usually contains a built-in or is attached to a PostScript RIP/interpreter. See *PostScript RIP*.

PostScript (language): A page description language standard. This language is particularly useful for describing complex page elements such as scaled text and rotated and/or skewed graphics, or for producing high quality halftones of continuous tone images.

PostScript laser printer: A relatively low resolution desktop printer capable of imaging PostScript image data. Usually contains a built-in PostScript RIP/Interpreter. See *PostScript RIP*.

PostScript printer driver: A printer driver capable of creating PostScript. See *Printer driver*.

PPD: PostScript printer description. A file which contains important information about the characteristics of a specific printing device. Device specific PPDs should be selected prior to printing on a particular device. See *Printer description file*.

PostScript Type 1 font: The preferred standard font files used in the creation and printing of PostScript based print oriented documents. A two-font file font architecture which contains separate font files for screen and printer font data. See *Font files* and *TrueType font*.

Preference file: A file which contains information and instructions concerning the setup and behavior of an application.

PreFlight / preflighting: Check or prepare an electronic file for output. At a minimum, it involves checking for the presence of all the high resolution graphic files and fonts which will be necessary to properly print a file. Two types of preflight are generally recognized: 1) content preflight, which focuses on the collection of document components and 2) technical preflight, which is concerned with the technical condition of a document such as the resolution and color space of linked graphics. See *File prep*.

Prepress: The production process which prepares a document for printing. Typical prepress functions include checking document construction, preflighting, and the creation of film and/or plates.

Preview: The low resolution file used as a proxy, or place holder, or FPO for the high resolution version of a graphic when it is place in a page layout application.

Preview scan: The low resolution overview scan, often 72 ppi, which is performed to create a preview image which is used for the setup for the final high resolution scan.

Print document: A document created for final print output. Contrast with a multipurpose document which will be used for more than one purpose, including, perhaps, display on the World Wide Web.

Printer description files: Small files which contain information about page geometry (size and margins) and sometimes screen angle and frequency for a specific printer. This file is accessed when the Printer Type is selected in the Page Setup or Print dialog boxes. See *PPD*.

Printer driver: Files used to access printers from a computer. Also contains information about page geometry (size and margins) and screen angle and frequency for a specific printer. This file is accessed when the Printer Type is selected in the Page Setup or Print dialog boxes.

Process color: A printed color created from screened, dot pattern, percentages of a preset number of colors. The most common process colors are cyan, magenta, yellow, and black (CMYK). Three, five, six, and seven color process systems are also used (See *CMYK mode*). Process colors are typically used to print color contone images and can be used to build color as well.

Process colors: The four standard colors, cyan, magenta, yellow, and black (CMYK) which create, or build, a wide range of other colors (see *Built colors*, *Hi-Fi color*, and *Spot color*).

Profile or color profile: A file which contains the color gamut information for a particular device. Color profiles can be created for any input or output device we use for capturing, viewing, or printing images including scanners, digital cameras, monitors, and printers. Color profiles are used during the process of moving and and matching an image from one device to another as part of a color management system. See *ICC*.

Progressive JPEG: A JPEG image which will display in in multiple steps with progressively improving image quality. A progressively displayed image will begin to appear more quickly than a nonprogressive image. This is typically used for larger JPEG files (see *JPEG*).

Proof: Refers to a printed piece which is a facsimile of what a document is to look like on final output. There is a wide range of proofs from low to high quality (see *Composition proof* and *Contract proof*, *Proofing*, and *Proof printer*).

Proofing: The process of creating a proof and/or the process of checking the accuracy of a document, including document geometry, checking graphics placement and quality, text formatting and line breaks, as well as color separations.

Proof printer: Commonly used to refer to a low resolution B&W or color output device. But some proofing devices are high resolution and quality (see *Composition proof*, and *Contract proof*).

Quartertone: Tonal range of an image which centers around 25% gray scale. Grayscale values in an image roughly in the range of 15% to 35% gray scale are considered to be in the quartertone region.

Quicktime: A multimedia file format and compression scheme used in video and multimedia files.

Quit: Close an application.

Radio button: A virtual button often contained in dialog buttons.

RAM (random access memory): Fast, short-term volatile memory stored in RAM chips called SIMMS (Single Inline Memory Modules). Serves as fast, active desktop-like work area.

Raster/ raster image: A pixel. Generally used to describe the nature of a graphic, i.e., a raster graphic is one which is composed of pixels. Also know as Pixel based or bitmapped images.

Repurposed image or document: A document which is used for an output purpose different than the purpose for which it was originally intended. A typical repurposed document might be a print document repurposed for display on the World Wide Web. Repurposed documents typically have changes in their size, typesetting, resolution, color space and interface.

Res: A resolution term which is shorthand for pixels per millimeter. More commonly used in place of ppi in high-end scanning and digital camera systems.

Resolution: Number of image building blocks per unit length (e.g., ppi, pixels per inch, dpi dots per inch, dpi) or dots per square area or pixels per square inch) at which an image is either captured (scanned) or printed. Scan resolution is generally stated in pixels per inch (ppi), printing resolution is generally referred to as lines per inch (lpi). Some scanning equipment uses res, which refers to pixels per mm (res 12 = 12 pixels per mm or 12p/mm) (see *Image dot*, *Halftone dot*, *Lpi*, *Pixel*, *Input resolution*, and *Output resolution*).

RGB mode: A color mode constructed out of three grayscale channels. This mode is used for the capture and viewing of color images. Scanners and digital cameras work in RGB mode, as do our monitors. RGB images must be converted into CMYK for printing. See *CMYK mode*.

RGB Separation: The separation of an image into its RGB components. Commonly occurs during the scanning process. See *Separation*.

RIP: Raster Image Processor. An electronic processor, which can be a hardware and/or software device, attached to an output device, such as a laser printer or imagesetter, which converts the PostScript description of a page to dots which will be used to compose the image on the printer's paper or film. All document components, including line art, contone images and text, are processed in order to convert them into printed images. It is the RIP that creates the digital halftone of a continuous tone image.

Router: Device used to connect dissimilar networks (e.g., to connect to AppleTalk and Ethernet).

RTF: Rich text format. A standard text file format which includes basic text formatting information such as character and paragraph formatting. RTF is used for the translation of formatted text from one application or document to another.

Saving: Moving document data from volatile RAM memory to a safer storage memory location on a disk, usually an internal hard drive.

Save As: Creating a new copy of a currently active document.

Scan mode: Determines the pixel depth and color space which an image will be captured or converted into, including: 1-bit (B&W line art), 8-bit (grayscale), 24–42-bit(RGB), 32-bit (CMYK).

Scanners: Image capture devices which converts analog images into pixels. •Transparency scanner: Scans film (drum and CCD). • Reflective scanner: Scans reflective art (hand-held, flatbed, and drum scanners). • CCD scanner: Charge coupled device, low to medium resolution, generally flatbed scanner. • PMT scanner: (Photo multiplier tube) High resolution, generally drum scanner.

Scratch disk: Photoshop's term for virtual memory, which is storage memory used as RAM space. Scratch disk memory use is much slower than RAM.

Screen: A pattern of dots created to simulate a shade of gray in a tint or a continuous tone image.

Screen angle: The angle at which a line of AM halftone dots are printed. The standard angle at which halftone dots are printed in a halftoned grayscale image is 45°. When printing color images, the various inks (CMYK) are printed at different screen angles to discourage the formation of repeating patterns known as a moiré pattern. See *Moiré pattern*.

Screen frequency: The number of lines of halftone dots which are printed per unit distance. Most commonly designated as lines per inch, or lpi. See *Lpi*.

Screening: The conversion of an image into a pattern of spots and dots which will be used to recreate that image during a printing process. This screening process used to be accomplished by placing a screen over an image prior to photographing it. In the digital world screening is accomplished by a RIP and a printer. See *RIP*, *Screen*, and *Halftoning*.

Scrapbook: Permanent storage of copied or cut selections. Can cut, copy and paste Scrapbook items.

Scroll: Used to view the contents of windows which display too small an area to view entire contents.

SCSI: (Small computer system interface). High speed peripheral interface standard.

SCSI 2,3, wide, fast: Improved, newer faster high-speed peripheral interface standard.

Select: Choose an element or object by pointing and clicking.

Selection: An element or object which has been selected or chosen. This is often done with a selection tool such as a pointer, lasso, or magic wand. A selection can be saved as a mask on an alpha channel in an application such as Photoshop.

Separation: Dividing an image into its component colors. Commonly used when referring to spot, process (CMYK), and coats and varnish separations used in the printing process, but also applies to RGB separations which occur during the scanning /image capture process. Each separated print color requires its own cylinder when printing. See *RGB*, *CMYK*, *Process colors*.

Server: A computer which is set up to serve a central, automated, data storage, distribution and processing site for a network. There are many kinds of servers including file servers, print servers, Email, and Internet servers.

Service provider: A company which provides specific output or distribution services for your digital documents and graphics. Common service providers include printing companies, scanning and output service bureaus, and Internet service providers.

Shadow point: The darkest portion of an image which still has details in it. The typical range in which a shadow point will fall is 85% –100% grayscale.

Software RIP: Raster image processor, which is created as a software application. Software RIPs are usually more flexible and easier to upgrade than hardware RIPs and their speed is largely determined by the speed of the computer on which they are loading. See *Hardware RIP*.

Specular highlight: A featureless highlight portion of an image containing no details. See *Diffuse highlight*.

Spot: The smallest building block of a printed text or line art image. Often expressed as dpi (dots per inch). A 300dpi laser printer has spots which are 1/300" across, while a 2400dpi imagesetter has spots which are 1/2400" across. See *Output resolution*.

Spot color: A single, typically solid color, usually a custom mixture of colors, used to create and print an image. Each spot color requires its own separation and its own cylinder on a printing press. Contrast with a process color, which is built from screen percentages of a predetermined set of colors such as CMYK (see *Process color* and *Built color*).

Spot color separation: The separation of an image into its spot color components. Required in order to print the spot colors. Each spot color requires its own separation. See *Separation*.

Spread: An object-trapping term used to indicate that a foreground area containing one color will be overlapped by expanding or spreading that color into a surrounding background area containing another, usually darker, color (see *Trap* and *Choke*).

Static medium: Medium which does not change. A common example of static medium is a printed piece. See *Dynamic media*.

Stochastic screening: A method of screening for reproducing a continuous tone image which varies the placement, and sometimes the size, of the halftone dots to simulate changes in grayscale value. Also known as FM (frequency modulation) screening. With traditional, nonstochastic, halftone screening techniques, halftone dots are located in a rigid pattern and only the dot size is varied. Stochastic screening eliminated moiré patterns and produces more pleasing tonal gradations in some images (see **Halftone screening**).

Storage or memory: Holding or memory locations for data in a computer system. There is both physical storage such as drives and electronic storage such as RAM and cache. Long term safe memory (e.g., hard drives, optical disks, floppy disks) and short term storage such as RAM. Long term storage memory is slower but more secure than short term memory such as RAM.

Streamline: A program from Adobe Inc. which is used to convert pixel-based images into vector-based line art. Sometimes used as a verb as in "streamline an image."

Stroke: Adjusting the thickness of a line. See *Trap*.

Style sheet: A formatting template for type. Style sheets contain a complete set of character and/or paragraph formatting information such as typeface, type style, tracking, leading, and justification instructions. Style sheets are used to format type quickly and consistently in a document. Style sheets are often used along with master pages to construct a document (see *Master pages,* and *Style sheets, character* and *paragraph.*)

Style sheet, character: A style sheet which controls the formatting of individual characters or words within a paragraph. (See *Style sheet* and *Style sheet, paragraph*.)

Style sheet, paragraph: A style sheet which controls the formatting of all of the text in a paragraph. (See *Style sheet* and *Character style sheet*.)

System file: The core component of an operating system.

System resources: Components of a computer operating system which provide specific capabilities to applications which are designed to utilize operating system resources. Common examples of system resources include fonts, sounds, and color palettes.

System software: Fundamental software which provides control of the interaction of hardware, software, and operator with the hardware portion of a computer. System software provides basic disk and file management functions, in addition to basic hardware control. (Examples include System 10 and Windows 2000.)

SWF: Shockwave format. Used for displaying and sending vector based images over the Internet. Commonly used for both static and animated files.

SWOP: An acronym which stands for Specifications Web Offset Press. This is an agreed upon set of industry standard printing conditions used by commercial and publication printers. There are SWOP standards for various kinds of paper such as SWOP Coated, SWOP Uncoated and SWOP Newsprint. Many commercial sheet fed as well as web printers use these standards.

Tera- (Terabit, TeraByte, etc.): Unit prefix which designates 1000 of the following units, such as Terabit, TeraByte, Terabits per second etc.

Three-quartertone: Tonal range of an image which centers around 75% grayscale. Grayscale values in an image roughly in the range of 65% to 85% grayscale are considered to be in the quartertone region.

Thumbnail sketch: A rough sketch of the layout and composition of a document. Frequently contains the size, shape, and orientation of the document as well as a rough layout of the basic text and graphic elements. Detailed thumbnails may also include master page and style sheet elements. See *Master page* and *Style sheet*.

TIFF: Tagged Information File Format. Common file format used used for images which are designed to print. Primarily a pixel-based file format, but can contain vector information.

Tint: A screen of a spot color. In printing, a tint is created by a regularly spaced pattern of equal-sized halftone dots.

Tone compression: Setting the highlight and shadow points of an image which will determine where the captured grayscale values will be placed.

Tone reproduction: The accurate reproduction of tonal values. Usually used in the context of scanning, or other image capture of contone images.

Tracking: The space between multiple text characters or words. Tracking can be divided into character tracking and word tracking. When used as a verb, tracking refers to the adjustment of space between multiple text characters and/or words.

Transparency/opacity: Determines how opaque an image or portion of an image appears. Transparency is controlled by masking or partially masking a selection.

Trap / trapping: There are two types of traps: ink traps and object traps.
• Ink trapping refers to the propensity of one ink to stick to another ink when it is applied on a printing press.
• Object trapping refers to the amount of overlap assigned to two adjacent or touching object colors, a foreground and a background color, which will be printed on a printing press. There are several basic object trapping terms:
- Spread: Color overlap achieved by expansion of a foreground object color into a surrounding background object color. This may be accomplished by stroking the edge of an image.
- Choke: Color overlap achieved by the constriction of a surrounding background color around a foreground object color.
- Knock out: Removal of a background color from underneath a foreground object when no trap is formed.
- Overprint: The direct printing of one color on top of another.
- Trap zone: The area of overlap between two trapped adjacent colors.

TrueType font: The standard font files used in the creation and printing of non-PostScript based print oriented documents. A single-font file architecture which has the screen and printer font data in a single font file. See *Font files* and *PostScript Type 1 font*.

Typeface: The name given to an collection of type characters which are designed as a set. A typeface character set usually contains, at a minimum, all the basic alpha and numeric characters, and may contain many more. Do not confuse with the word font (see *Font*). Examples of common typefaces include Arial, Helvetica, Times and Palatino.

Typesetting: The placement and formatting of type on a page
• Justification: Formatting of lines of text either vertically or horizontally.
• Kerning: Space between two characters.
• Leading: Space between lines of text.
• Tracking: Space between characters and words.

UCA: Under color addition. The addition of extra amounts of cyan, magenta and yellow inks to the shadow region of a CMYK printed image to increase the ink density in the shadow region to produce a denser looking black. See *GCR* and *UCA*.

UCR: Under color removal. One of two major descriptions of how black ink (K) is substituted for cyan, magenta and yellow inks in process commercial printing. UCR typically substitutes black ink primarily in the shadow region of an image. See *GCR* and *UCA*.

UNIX: Operating system used by high powered work stations and servers. UNIX based servers are the most common Internet servers.

Unused colors: Colors which are in a documents color palette, but are not used in that document. Unused colors should be removed prior to output, especially printing.

USB: Universal serial bus. A newer bus architecture utilized by both Macs and Windows machines which allows for more universal connection of external devices such as keyboards, mice, digital cameras, etc.

Unsharpmask / unsharpmasking: A tool for sharpening pixel based images. A good unsharpmask tool will allow you to control the amount, the radius and the threshold of how much and where the sharpening will be applied. Unsharpmasking increases the contrast between adjacent pixels to affect the sharpening of an image.

Utility file: A small application which has a very specific function such as font management, virus protection or file compression.

Vector graphic: A graphic image constructed from lines, also known as an outline graphic. In contrast to a bitmapped or raster image, which is constructed from dots. Also known as an object oriented graphic.

Video / videoboard: The circuits of a computer which contain the memory and display function for providing a signal to a visual display such as a monitor.

Visualization scanning: The process of visualizing what a scanner will do to an image during the scanning process. This visualization helps us make the proper scanner setup decisions.

Virtual memory: Passive storage memory, usually hard drive space used as active RAM space (see *Scratch disk*).

Virus: An exotic, potentially destructive, self-replicating file.

WAN: (Wide area network) Connections of computers and peripherals over a large area such as between buildings, cities, or countries.

Web safe colors: 216 colors which are common to both the Macintosh and Windows operating systems. These colors are used to assign to objects which will be displayed on Web pages. Assigning Web safe colors to Web page items improves the consistency of the colors displayed and the speed of screen redraw.

Window: Viewing area which appears on the desktop. • There are two types of windows on a Mac: Finder windows and Document windows. Finder windows contain icons of folders, applications, and documents. Document windows contain actual text and graphics.

Widow: Single word sentence at the end of a paragraph. These should be avoided as they make the text difficult to read and they look strange.

Windows operating system (OS): Graphically oriented system software for IBM/Intel-based computers. Windows exists in several versions, including Windows 95, 98 and 2000, as well as Windows NT.

World Wide Web: The graphic/multimedia capable portion of the Internet.

WYSIWYG: (What You See Is What You Get). The promise of having what you view on your monitor match what comes out of your printing device.

XHTML (XML): Extended hypertext markup language. XHTML is the evolutionary step from HTML. Like HTML, XML is the underlying language code which is used to create Web sites and pages. XML allows more cross-linking and interactivity than HTML.

ZIP: A lossless compression algorithm.

ZIP disk: Handy removable media for short term backup and exchanging files.

CHAPTER SUMMARY

Misused and inconsistent terminology is a major barrier to becoming fluent in the language of electronic publishing, and communicating clearly with your colleagues. Many concepts have multiple terms, such as bit depth, pixel depth and color depth. Other terms are misused, such as dpi being used for all varieties of resolution. Some terms such as digital dyluxes are oxymoronic, while others such as font and typeface are mistaken for each other. There are some terms such as selection, mask and alpha channel which might seem to be unrelated, but are in fact closely related. We covered many of the terms and concepts which are commonly shrouded in confusion and misinformation.

The first step to defeating terminology terrorism and developing digital fluency is to make sure that you understand the terms and concepts yourself. The second step is to understand that many of your work mates, even very competent practitioners, often use vague and even inaccurate terms. When reading, try to use context to discern the meaning of a word or phase. The third step is to make sure that in any conversation which you are having with someone else that you clearly understand what the other person is talking about. Do not be afraid to ask as many clarifying questions as necessary to make sure you understand. A good example of this is when someone is discussion resolution: Make sure that you know whether they are referring to input or output resolution. Are they talking about pixels or spots and dots? And finally, make sure that you use proper and precise terminology. It will aid communication, and others will begin to improve as well.

PAULINE'S DIGITAL IMAGING TIPS

Pauline's Tip 2.1

It is important to learn the fundamental terms and concepts associated with electronic publishing. Knowing the terms will help you to communicate more effectively with your service companies as well as your colleagues. Knowing the concepts will make you a more effective creator and preparer of electronic documents. Some of the key terms and concepts you need to understand include: resolution, dpi vs. ppi vs. lpi, spot vs. process colors, color gamuts, RIPing, RAM vs. virtual memory, image spot vs. halftone dot, halftone cell, AM vs. FM screening, raster vs. vector, pixel depth, master pages, style sheets, preferences, PostScript, PostScript files vs. document files, paths and clipping paths, flatness and tolerance, splitting paths, Tiff vs. EPS vs. JPEG vs. PhotoCD, document vs. native file, halftoning, screen vs. print fonts, tracking, leading and kerning, compression, SWOP and trapping, and preflighting.

Pauline's Tip 2.2

Always consider the context in which an term is used in order to figure out its true meaning. Often a term will be misused, but through context you can determine the true meaning. A common example is the use of the units dpi when referring to a scan resolution, or the resolution of a pixel based image. If someone says to scan at 300dpi, you can discern from the context that they are really referring to pixels per inch, which is what will be captured by the scanner. By doing this quick mental determination you will be clear in your own mind that you are discussing input resolution and pixels, and not output resolution with spots or dots. If you are not sure of the proper meaning stop the conversation and ask questions until you are clear.

Pauline's Tip 2.3

Even professional production people misuse terminology in our business. Many very competent printing company prepress folks use dpi where they should be using ppi, or use an oxymoronic term such as digital blue line or digital dylux when they should be referring to an ink jet printer. Your job is to make sure that you clearly understand their meanings. It may not be fruitful to correct their terminology, but do not ever be afraid to ask questions until you are clear about what you are discussing. The quality of your work may well hinge on understanding what your service bureaus and other partners are saying. If you consistently use proper terminology, others will pick up on it and improve their use of language as well.

CHAPTER REVIEW

Check Your Comprehension

Multiple Choice Questions

To help you review the topics covered in this chapter, answer the following multiple choice questions.

1. Which of the following is true about our electronic publishing terminology?
   A. We have some terms which have multiple definitions
   B. We have multiple terms which mean the same thing
   C. Our terminology is often misused
   D. All of the above

2. What is one common reason for why we have multiple terms for the same concept?
   A. We want our terminology to be confusing
   B. Our terms are sometimes contributed from multiple industries
   C. So that we don't get tired of using the same terms all the time
   D. Just for the heck of it

3. Which of the following is used to describe the number of bits per pixel which an image may contain?
   A. Bit depth
   B. Pixel depth
   C. Color depth
   D. All of the above

4. Which of the following is the smallest building block which a printing device creates?
   A. Halftone dot
   B. Pixel
   C. Image spot
   D. None of the above

5. Which of the following terms refer to the number of halftone dots per inch which are used to print a halftoned image?
   A. Lpi
   B. Line screen
   C. Screen frequency
   D. All of the above

6. _____ colors are created by combining percentage screens of colors.

   A. Process

   B. Four color process

   C. Seven color process

   D. All of the above

7. Which of the following is used to describe images constructed out of lines?

   A. Vector-based

   B. Line art

   C. Object oriented

   D. All of the above

8. What do densitometers, intensitometers and info tools have in common?

   A. They are all used to measure image resolution

   B. They are all used to measure pixel depth

   C. They all measure gray scale values in one way or another

   D. Nothing

9. Which of the following resolution terms would a photographer most likely use?

   A. 300ppi

   B. 5.4MB

   C. 1200 x 1200

   D. 300dpi

10. _____ is a description of the actual hardware resolution of a scanner.

   A. Interpolated resolution

   B. dpi resolution

   C. Output resolution

   D. Optical resolution

11. Which of the following is the best term to describe the lightest portion of an image which still has detail?

   A. Midtone

   B. Diffuse highlight

   C. Specular highlight

   D. Quartertone

12. An original photograph is best described as a

   A. Contone

   B. Halftone

   C. Quartertone

   D. Midtone

Check Your Understanding

Concept Questions

To help you review and expand your thinking on the topics covered in this chapter, answer the following questions.

1. Why is proper use of terminology important? Give an example of when improper use of terminology may cause problems.

2. What are some of the terminology problems which we have? Detail at least three separate problems.

3. Give an example of incorrect use of resolution terminology.

4. Explain how context can help determine the meaning of a word. Give one example.

5. Give an example of where one DTP term can have two definitions. Explain how could you tell and/or what you might do to determine which meaning is most appropriate in any given circumstance.

6. Explain the difference between spots and dots and how each is used.

7. Distinguish between input and output resolution. Explain which resolution terms go with which concept.

8. What happens to the file size of an image when its resolution is raised from 300ppi to 600ppi? Explain your answer.

9. Explain why the following designations could all refer to the same image: 300ppi, 5.4MB, 1200 x 1500, 1.2K x 1.5K.

10. Explain the difference between a font and a font file?

11. What is the difference between an comp proof and a contract proof?

12. Whose job is it to preflight a file for prepress? Explain your rationale.

PROJECTS

Over the course of one week make a list of all the terms you hear or read whose meaning you are not sure of, or that you think may be incorrectly used. Be sure to note the context. At the end of the week determine the meaning of these terms through the use of the Electronic Publishing Terms section in this book, conversations with your classmates, and your instructor. Compare your list and meanings with other students in your class.

3
Peaceful Coexistence

As the Byte Turns continues…

Will Danny D'Ziner find true happiness with Pauline E. PrePress or will the perils of PostScript keep them apart?

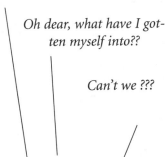

Chapter Objectives

In this chapter you will learn:

♦ **The effects of the digital revolution**

♦ **Who is responsible for file preparation**

♦ **The importance of partnering**

♦ **The need for file preparation**

♦ **How the digital age give us access to many graphics technologies**

♦ **Key Terms**
   • Digital revolution
   • Analog vs. digital
   • Prepress
   • Electronic publishing culture
   • Partnering
   • Convergent technologies
   • PostScript
   • File preparation
   • Digital literacy: The new 3 "Rs"

ELECTRONIC PUBLISHING CULTURE

Effect of the digital revolution

The 10 years from 1985 to 1995 was a period of revolution in the graphic arts industry. This revolution, referred to as the **digital revolution**, involved a shift from analog to digital treatment of information. This was a genuine revolution, a paradigm shift, and not merely a sequence of incremental changes. In the new millennium, we are still in the throes of this revolution with all of the attendant challenges and opportunities which are inherent in any drastic change. The digital revolution involves a fundamental change in how we create, capture, manipulate, store, transfer, and transform information. Indeed, it is forcing us to entirely rethink the ways in which we communicate. For many of us it has even changed how we view and interpret the world around us. To fully understand, adapt to, and take advantage of these changes, one must understand the basic concepts of digital information.

The digital revolution has brought about changes in nearly every aspect of our business. Some of the most obvious changes can be seen in the very tools we use to create, recreate, and reproduce images. Our previous **analog** tools included pencil, pen, brush, crayon, ruler, Xacto knife, camera, engraving tools, rubylith, drafting table, easel, art board, and waxer. All been replaced by **digital** tools such as computer equipment and software applications. Not only have our tools changed, but entire job titles, job descriptions, and responsibilities have been altered. Entire job categories and skill requirements have been changed and, in some cases, have vanished, while new ones have been added. Some jobs and skill sets such as type-

▼ Figure 3.1 Stripping Table Method
The conventional way of compositing film for plate production. With this method, clients would deliver print documents to printers on full-sized mechanical boards. Composite films would then be generated by the printer and assembled on flats. With this method of producing composite films, the full time printing professional had complete control over the construction of the print document. This generally meant less control for the creator of the document, the client, but far fewer production problems.

setting and mechanical art have made the transition to the new tools, while others such as photo engraving have completely disappeared. Many of the jobs which used to be performed by specialists have melded into other roles. For example, few current positions involve only typesetting. Most people setting type are also performing page layout and a variety of **prepress** functions as well. Prepress is rapidly becoming primarily electronic as more and more of the prepress functions such as stripping and trapping are performed digitally. The advent of the electronic document has not only changed the tools of prepress, but has in fact spread the functions and responsibilities of prepress to everyone involved in the creation and processing of a document. This responsibility includes the client who originally creates the document as well as the sales and customer service personnel of the service companies which handle and process these electronic documents. And nearly everyone's job is becoming more technically oriented as a whole new digital awareness and skills sets have to be adopted and mastered. Everyone has been going through retraining, and that retraining will continue.

Typically, when a company or individual begins to adopt an electronic-based publishing system, they focus primarily and often exclusively on short term individual hardware and software requirements and solutions. The question "What size computer and which software do I need to complete a particular job or set of jobs?" is usually the first and often the last question asked. This is a serious mistake. First, there are many issues which need to be addressed which are often overlooked, such as work flow, backup and archiving needs, file management and proper networking, electrical and lighting requirements, and the mix of conventional vs. digital prepress work. Additionally, the viability, productivity, and overall success of an electronic publishing system is dependent upon many variables. Proper integration of compatible hardware and software components, future needs, system expandability and upgradability, and the training needs of production staff members must be addressed early in the planning process.

Equally important is the thorough orientation and proper training of all personnel who will be associated with the electronic publishing system. One of the most important and often overlooked areas of concern is the knowledge, capabilities, and requirements of your publishing business partners, your clients, and service companies. Ultimately, after you have addressed, organized, and streamlined your own in-house electronic publishing skills and procedures, your prepress or publishing productivity will be largely affected by how well you and your partners understand and comply with each other's electronic publishing requirements.

All of these factors contribute to what I call electronic publishing (ETP) culture. The continuing change in communications technology has had a profound effect on our business. These changes affect the products we produce and how we produce them and the entire nature of the service company/client relationship. A smooth transition to, and continued productivity with, an electronic publishing production system requires that all of these variables (equipment and software, people, and procedures) be changed, revised, and updated regularly.

You and/or your company's commitment to electronic publishing means not only substantial additions of equipment and changes in the production processes, but

▼ *Figure 3.2 PostScript Method*
With the advent of desktop PostScript-based systems, print documents are created and composited on a computer by a client and supplied to the printer as completed documents. PostScript systems have dramatically increased the control and flexibility which clients have in creating documents. But this increase in client control has not always been matched by client acceptance or even realization of their responsibility to produce print-ready documents. This situation has led to a wide variety of production problems for printers who must output these files.

some significant adjustments in the way everyone who is even remotely involved in the production process perceives and performs jobs. Everyone, from the sales and marketing and customer service representatives to press operators to clients, must make the adjustment to a new **electronic publishing culture**. One of the consequences of the development and widespread acceptance and use of digital publishing is that customers now have more involvement and control than ever in the publishing process. An increasing percentage of business will involve direct client input into jobs. This involvement started initially with customers beginning to perform their own typesetting and has progressed through page layout. It now includes scanning, manipulation, and placement of final versions of line art and gray scale images and increasingly includes color images as well.

The rapid development of affordable, high-quality digital cameras will guarantee that clients will have even more input and control of their files in the future. The production process used to refer to image and film preparation which occurred once client-created art boards and related pieces reached a printing company or service bureau. Now production starts when a client sits down to work at a computer. Anyone who works with customer-generated files is familiar with the challenges involved. Indeed, solving customer file problems has become a significant production issue both in terms of time and technical expertise. Everyone's job has become more technical. Properly trained sales and customer service people are crucial to developing smooth production links between in-house production staff and customers. Increasingly, there also needs to be direct communication between production staff members of a service company and the clients who generated the documents. And those of us who generate the original files, whether we are designers, photographers, mechanical artists, or desktop publishers working in a bank, all have the responsibility to create files which are appropriately constructed and formatted for their final use.

Like most cultural adjustments, these adjustments will not be made overnight. A progressive process, which gives everyone a chance to learn the opportunities and responsibilities of their new culture, is a prudent course to follow. But the changes must be made. Electronic publishing is a rapidly evolving collection of technologies. The envelope of capabilities is being constantly expanded. As new products and processes evolve along the way, everyone involved must also make adjustments.

File preparation: whose responsibility?

Simply stated, it is we, the generators of electronic files, who are largely responsible for preparing our files for their final purpose or output, be that print or any other media. Preparing files for print is one of the most demanding **file preparation** challenges due to the technical requirements and restricted nature of printed media. Our design capabilities on a computer are far greater than our printing capabilities. This means there are a great many documents and designs which can be created on a computer which cannot be printed. Examples of issues which affect the printability of electronic files include graphics file size, the complexity of graphics, multiple layers, image resolution, and improper formatting. In addition to these basic technical issues, there are component problems involved with files which travel away from their computer of origin. In fact, a large percentage of elec-

▼ *Figure 3.3 Whose Responsibility?*
The pointing match. All too often, when roles and responsibilities for file preparation are not well defined, the client and the printing company end up pointing fingers at each other. This is an unhappy circumstance which can often damage relationships. All three parties – the client, the sales person, and the production staff – need to be well informed. It is the client's job to create and prepare and preflight the files properly. It is the printing company's …

(continued caption on page 67)

tronic prepress problems and delays stem from files which are sent to service companies with missing components, including font and graphic files.

There are still some among us who resist the notion that we should be responsible for preparing our files for output. This is a mistake. The increased control and creative freedom which digital imaging grants us also means that we have enlarged responsibilities for preparing the files which we construct. We must keep in mind the final use of a file when we construct that file. File content and construction requirements for a document which will be shown onscreen are quite different if that same file is to be printed. In the old days of art board preparation, printers were largely in control of the construction of the final composite layout and the content and organization of the production process. Within the **PostScript** realm, much of the construction of the final document is now in the hands of those who originally created that file: we, the clients. How we construct and prepare our documents therefore largely determines how printable a file is. Responsibilities throughout the production process have changed. If files are not prepared accurately, the document designer/creator may be charged for any work that needs to be performed.

(caption continued from page 66) …responsibility to inform and educate their clients as to how best to prepare files for their specific electronic prepress system. It is the responsibility of the sales and customer service representatives to facilitate this communication and to be well enough informed on electronic prepress issues that they may serve as useful conduits for at least basic information. Many successful printing companies employ a technical liaison whose primary responsibility is to help clients with job planning, technical questions, and file prep problems.

> **TIP**
>
> Each output device to which you send a document has its own requirements. It really pays to know the characteristics and requirements for each output device you use. Output devices include printers and monitors both at your facility and at any service provider which you may use. If you have clients who send you files for output, it is a good idea to provide them with information about your output devices, and how they should prepare their files. Some basic file prep variables include page size and orientation, image resolution, preferred applications and file formats.

It is in our best interest to prepare our files properly for the media on or in which they will be ultimately produced. If we are ignorant of the requirements, then we should ask for them. The better we prepare our files, the faster and easier our files will be processed. Sales and customer service representatives for service companies have an enhanced role as well. Sales and CSR staffs need to be knowledgeable about their company's electronic publishing capabilities and limitations. They need to be thoroughly steeped in the file prep requirements which their clients should follow, and they need to be able to interpret those requirements well enough to guide the client through providing an EFIS (electronic file information sheet) which contains information and instructions about the job they would like the service company to output. Production staff members also have new roles in this process. Production's responsibilities include providing regularly updated information and guidelines on supported equipment and software and file prep issues to both the sales and customer service staff as well as to their clients. Production personnel need to communicate more directly with clients, especially with regard to more technical file preparation issues. In general, service companies need to adopt the role of educator. It is in their best interest to do so.

"I never planned on becoming a color separator or a scanner operator, but the technology really allows the individual artist to regain control of their work. Of course, with the control comes an awful lot of responsibility."
Steve Johnson, Digital Photographic Pioneer

Partnering

The result of all this role and relationship migration is that clients and service companies need to work as partners, each with the new and changing responsibilities. Savvy clients will place a high value on service companies which are technically competent, communicate their needs, and are oriented toward education. These clients will also recognize and accept their own need to be technically competent. The best and most successful service companies will promote interactive relationships with their clients and will communicate well and often with their clients about capabilities and requirements. All parties must accept the need for continuing education as technology continues to evolve.

▼ Figure 3.4 Contone Images Continuous tone (contone) images are some of the more complex images to reproduce. Contones have a wide range of tonal values which need to be reproduced. Color contone has the additional burden of color as well as tone reproduction. Low cost, easy-to-use desktop scanners have made acquiring these images easy. However, considerable knowledge and skill are required in order to produce a faithful reproduction of an original.

Another type of **partnering** becoming increasingly common is business-to-business partnerships. Technology is changing so fast that it is impossible for most companies to acquire all of the expertise and equipment necessary to offer all of the services they might like to. A solution is to partner with another communications company which offers different but complementary capabilities and products. A good example of this type of partnering is the emerging relationship between printing companies and service bureaus which offer PhotoCD services. PhotoCD service bureaus can offer inexpensive scanning services for clients, while the printing company can offer the print services from the digital PhotoCD files. Either the service bureau or the printing company can produce the film, depending upon which is better prepared to perform the output, or the files can go directly to plate or press. Myriad partnering opportunities are available and are limited only by our imaginations.

TIP

In the digital age, where much document construction occurs long before it arrives at a printing company or other output service bureau, it is always a good idea to identify your output company as early in the document construction process as possible. More often than not your output service provider can provide you with valuable document construction tips which will allow you to improve the quality of your documents while at the same time making them easier and faster to print and saving you money.

Convergent technologies

Once disparate fields of communications (such as the print, photography, and video industries) which traditionally employed completely separate sets of tools are now beginning to use the same tools to produce their products. I call this

convergent technologies The common tools revolve around computer hardware and software. Digital technology is having the same revolutionizing effect on these other areas of communications as it has been having on print. Grand opportunities, along with startling adjustments, are the norm. Whole new technologies such as CD-ROM, PhotoCD, and Web publishing are emerging to expand and complement our communications tools. The computer chip has been and will continue to be the basic enabling technology in these rapidly evolving and converging revolutions. As other portions of communications industries increasingly utilize these same basic tools, we will experience increasing integration of communications data. The sharing of print, sound, video, animation, and photographic files will become commonplace. Already, electronic documents are being prepared for non-print media distribution and viewing. The development and application independent file formats such as Acrobat, the evolution of more capable and easier to use telecommunications networks and equipment, and the growth of non-print media such as CD-ROMs have opened up whole new channels for communications and business opportunities.

Entire industries are blossoming from these revolutions in communications technology. The opportunities presented by this technological juggernaut are exciting, while at the same time the resources required to keep abreast are daunting. This rapid evolution does not, however, mean that what you learn today will be obsolete in six months to a year. Quite the contrary. After you learn the fundamentals they will provide you with a solid foundation on which you can continually add new information. **Digital literacy** is a must for anyone involved in the communications industry. The three "Rs" of the analog world were reading writing and arithmatic. The three "Rs" of the digital world are RIP, RAM, and Raster :-). Mastering the basics is the first and most important step in the process. Once you have a strong grasp of digital fundamentals, you will have the context within which to place all the refinements which you will continually need to learn. It is these digital fundamentals, and a few refinements, that this book addresses.

CHAPTER SUMMARY

The last 15 years has seen an enormous change in communications technologies as a result of the digital revolution. Tools and capabilities, such as scanning and typesetting, which were once only available to highly trained specialists have, as result of the development of desktop digital technology, been made available to anyone with enough money to purchase a desktop publishing system. Access to these powerful tools has shifted the control and therefore much of the responsibility to those who wield these powerful desktop tools. But access to powerful tools does not create an expert; in fact, power tools in the hands of the uninformed can lead to disaster and high costs. It is the responsibility of every desktop publisher to learn how to prepare their files for output. One way to enhance your education and improve the quality of your digital files is to partner with your output service bureaus, your printing companies and other service providers. Involve them early, even during the document planning process. Better results are usually the result. The digital revolution has given us access to many, once disparate, communication technologies, such as print, photography and video, through one common tool, the computer. While this is very empowering, it is also very demanding in terms of learning the the intricacies of each medium. Get help from those who know, your output service bureaus which specialize in the various communication technologies. As long as you stay in digital imaging you should seek out new sources of information in order to expand your digital literacy. This book will provide you with the important foundation for understanding and mastering digital imaging. And in doing so, it will prepare you to continue your education far beyond the confines of this book…So this is just the beginning of a great and exciting educational journey.

PAULINE'S DIGITAL IMAGING TIPS

Pauline's Tip 3.1

Communicate with your printing company and other output service bureaus. Work with these people during the planning and construction phases of your job, not just when your job is completed. You will want to ask about items such as the press sheet size, which will affect the size and dimensions of your designs, the lpi at which they print (which will determine the resolution at which you scan images), and the file formats which the printer prefers, which will determine how you save your digital files. Working with your printer throughout your job design and creation will help avoid output problems and having to redo things later. In fact, if you have any questions about how to construct your file, ask at any time. An ounce of prevention is truly worth several pounds of cure in the digital world.

Pauline's Tip 3.2

Fundamental digital literacy is the first step to providing you with the ability to compete in the world of digital imaging. Digital literacy is also only the first phase of a lifelong education in digital imaging and communications technology. New technologies, tools and techniques are constantly being developed. If you stop learning you will be left behind. Continue to seek out those partnering relationships discussed in Tip 3.1 as a good way to keep furthering your digital imaging education. The digital imaging business is a constantly changing environment with new information becoming available all the time. Ignorance is not a sin, but staying ignorant is.

CHAPTER REVIEW

Check Your Comprehension

Multiple Choice Questions

To help you review the topics covered in this chapter, answer the following multiple choice questions.

1. What is the name of the big change taking place in the communications industry?
   A. Analog revolution
   B. Digital revolution
   C. PostScript evolution
   D. None of the above

2. What of the following is **not** a digital tool?
   A. Computer
   B. Software application
   C. Pencil
   D. Monitor

3. Who is primarily responsible for file preparation?
   A. The service bureau
   B. The printing company
   C. The document creator
   D. None of the above

4. What is the best way to learn about how to best prepare your electronic files?
   A. Partner with your service provider
   B. Read a book
   C. Use the same techniques all the time
   D. None of the above

5. File preparation is important because
   A. File preparation helps prepare a digital document for output
   B. File preparation prepares a file for storage
   C. File preparation prepares a document for saving
   D. None of the above

6. Convergent technologies refers to which of the following?

   A. Once disparate technologies using similar tools

   B. Technologies running into each other

   C. Technologies being sold at the same place

   D. All of the above

7. Which of the following should be addressed when preparing a file for output?

   A. Page size

   B. File format

   C. Image resolution

   D. All of the above

8. Who among the following need to be digitally literate?

   A. Print sales people

   B. Document creators

   C. Output production people

   D. All of the above

9. Which of the following contains document information and output instructions?

   A. EFIS (electronic file information sheet)

   B. Software manual

   C. Hardware manual

   D. Training manual

10. _____is required in order to keep up with changing technologies.

   A. Digital literacy

   B. Partnering

   C. Willingness to keep learning

   D. All of the above

Check Your Understanding

Concept Questions

To help you review and expand your thinking on the topics covered in this chapter, answer the following questions.

1. Briefly explain what has and is happening during the digital revolution.

2. Explain why file preparation for output is important.

3. Who is primarily responsible for file preparation and why?

4. Explain the concept of partnering and why it is important.

5. What is meant by the term electronic publishing culture?

6. Explain the concept of convergent technologies.

7. What are the opportunities and challenges inherent in convert technologies?

8. What is digital literacy and why is it important?

9. Explain why digital literacy is really only the first step in a lifelong process.

10. Would you rather be a document creator or a document output technician? Explain your preference, why it appeals to you.

PROJECTS

Visit a local printing company or other output service bureau. Interview the production manager and ask the requirements for properly outputting a digital file from you as a customer. Make a list of these requirements and briefly explain the importance of each requirement.

4
Electronic Publishing Systems

As the Byte Turns continues…

Will Pauline have time to help Danny with his conflict and find out that she has interests other than just fixing his SCSI chain or Universal Serial Bus?

I just bought a CD-ROM drive, but it won't work. Someone said I might have a SCSI ID conflict with my scanner or my external Zip drive. Somebody else thought it might be a F.ire-wire or USB drive. What do you think?

Huh?

What the heck did he just ask me?

Can you please take this call?

Sure, and I don't mind helping our clients out, especially when they are willing to ask questions. But I have my hands full just doing production. We really should look into hav-ing a technical liaison to work with customers.

Chapter Objectives

In this chapter you will learn:

◆ **A brief history of desktop hardware**
◆ **The basic components of you computer**
◆ **The function of your computer components**
◆ **The most common computer systems**
◆ **Tips for choosing hardware components**
◆ **Key Terms**

- RAM
- Motherboard
- CPU
- Storage
- Video board
- SCSI, USB, Firewire, Ethernet
- Macintosh
- IBM PC, DOS, Windows
- Mainframe
- Peripheral device
- Server
- Network
- Service provider

INTRODUCTION

Digital computer graphic systems have replaced most previous analog "done-by-hand" systems. This has presented us with a new set of tools and resources to master in order to apply effectively our craft of graphic communications.

Knowledge of your tools and how they work is a critical component of your success. Being familiar with your hardware and software components and how they interact is necessary for you to function effectively in the digital world. While it is not necessary for you to become a computer expert, you should be familiar with the basic components of your computer and how your computer functions. If you view your computer as a mysterious black box about which you know nothing, even the simplest challenges such as allocating memory, or activating a **network** device such as a printer, can be frustrating, costly, and time robbing road blocks to call for repairs. If you have to wait for someone else to remedy all of your technical challenges, you will not be very competitive when it comes to being productive. Even the most creative and artistic people who consider themselves to be completely nontechnical can, and should, master the fundamentals of hardware and software installation and maintenance.

This chapter focuses on the basic hardware components of your system and their functions. Don't just memorize the definition of each component, but rather, make sure that you understand the purpose of each component so that you will be able to visualize its use while you are working. As you will see that most of the components of your computer system have direct analogs in the nondigital world, and by relating these devices and uses, it should be easier to understand their purposes and uses.

Unlike older analog technologies which changed slowly, digital technology changes quickly. But once you have gained an understand of your basic system components and how they work, it will make learning new technology much easier.

DTP HISTORY

Back in the dawn of the desktop publishing age—way back in 1985—there were only a couple of hardware components and a mere handful of software components from which to choose. The hardware choices included the original compact **Macintosh** complete with an 8Mhz **cpu**, a built-in 9-inch B&W screen, 128K of **RAM**, a 400KB floppy disc drive, and no internal hard drive. For **peripheral devices** we had a choice of two printers, a 144dpi Imagewriter and the original 300 dpi LaserWriter (complete with 11 fonts). Application software for the original Mac counted three: MacWrite and MacPaint initially, followed quickly by the first page layout application, PageMaker 1.0. The combination of the Mac, the first LaserWriter, and PageMaker constituted the first complete desktop publishing system. This was the first giant step in the democratization of publishing and the first step in the complete revamping of how print and other documents are created and prepress production is performed. A new language called PostScript had even been developed and many of us have had to learn how to understand and speak this language. This digital revolution has since spread to many other forms of communications media such as photography and video, as well as new forms of communication such as multimedia and the Internet and its graphical component the World Wide Web. But the foundation for this revolution has been laid in print.

The rapid evolution of technology since 1985 has been astounding. Today the range and depth of the tools available for capturing and processing images and the creation, distribution, and reproduction of electronic documents is stunning. Shown in this section is some of the wide variety of these tools. Digital computers, which are the core of this communications technology, have evolved into very different machines with far greater capabilities than their bold but limited ancestors. Today's computers, which can process millions of instructions per second instead of a few thousand per second (typical of the computers in 1985) now boast 500Mhz+ processors, accelerated 21-inch 24-bit color monitors, 500+MB of RAM, multigigabyte hard drives, and a dizzying array of high resolution scanners, cameras, and printers for capturing and reproducing the images processed on these amazing computers. What is additionally amazing and sobering is that this technological juggernaut shows no signs of abating. Just five years from now all the seemingly incredible capabilities which we currently have will pale in contrast to the capabilities we will have then. Tomorrow, our currently impressive equipment will appear to be weak pretenders by comparison. Today's rapidly evolving communications business is not for the weak of heart or for those who resist change.

A modern electronic publishing system can be as simple as one computer, a single page layout application, and a laser printer, or it may contain a network of dozens of image capture and creation devices connected to various types of computer systems which provide for the processing, manipulation, and **storage** of electronic images and documents. These image creation and manipulation devices can in turn be attached to a wide array of output equipment for either the distribution or viewing of documents. All of this work can now be done and shared by many individuals working over farflung networks such as intranets and other wide area networks.

Image capture devices include a spectrum of scanners, which are used primarily to digitize images which have previously been captured or reproduced on either film (slides) or paper (photographs), or original hand-drawn artwork. They include flatbed CCD scanners and PMT drum scanners as well as dedicated slide scanners. Increasingly, images are being captured directly in digital format through the use of digital cameras. Analog video and direct capture digital video are additional tools for image capture. Original fine art art image creation is being increasingly performed directly on computers with the aid of marvelous pressure-sensitive pen tools attached to digitizing tablets.

Computers themselves have become more specialized. The original DTP systems were single station affairs. Today's sophisticated publishing systems consist of networks of computers designated for specific functions such as preflighting, scanning, image editing, page layout, trapping, imposition, RIPing and CD burning. Systems involving many operators with many files often require computers which are dedicated to controlling the flow and management of documents across networks both local and distant. These file management computers are called **servers** and they come in many flavors including file servers, print servers, fax and modem servers, Bulletin Board Servers (BBS), and Web servers. All of these various types of computer stations can be fitted with a variety of storage devices including fixed internal and external hard drives, removable drives such as older Syquest, and Bernoulli drives, and newer Zip, and various optical mechanisms such as optical and CD-ROM drives, and various tape mechanisms and formats.

Output devices span a wide variety of choices ranging from B&W lasers to digital presses. We can choose from among more than a half dozen types of desktop color printer technologies including thermal wax, four-color laser, dye sublimation, phase change, and several varieties of ink jet printers. For high resolution prepress output there is an impressive array of imagesetter devices and sophisticated press proofing systems. Direct to plate and even direct to press imaging is now common. Computers attached to four-color laser printers are increasingly being used as short run on-demand color printing presses.

Although you will read more about technology trends in later chapters, I will mention here that the same personal computer-based open architecture hardware and software systems which have led to the democratization of print-oriented publishing is in the process of opening up a wide variety of other communication technologies to all of us. These technologies include a range of audio, video, and animation, as well as type-oriented media.

COMPUTERS PARTS AND FUNCTIONS

Motherboard (green)

Main circuit board that all other components and peripherals plug into and transmit and receive data through ="Skeleton," "nervous," and "circulatory" systems of the computer.

RAM (random access memory)

Fast, short term, active work space memory = desktop work space. More RAM means larger work space. All system and application software launch into and operate within RAM. Adding RAM is like adding extra leaves to a work table.

Storage memory (large)

Medium to large volumes of permanent storage = file cabinets in an analog office. Examples include hard drives, Zip drives, optical disk drives, CDs and older Syquest, and Bernoulli cartridges.

Storage memory (small)

Small volume, portable storage devices (diskette) = briefcase.

Expansion slot

Plug-in slots which allow for addition of other circuits boards (known as cards), such as video and network cards, which expand a computer's capabilities = adding a radio or air conditioner to your auto.

CPU (central processing unit)

Main computer chip on **motherboard** = brains of the outfit. Most data manipulation occurs here.

Video board

A **video board** converts digital data to a signal which can be used to produce images for display on your monitor. Allows you to see information that is in RAM. Similar to your cable box, which converts unreadable data into readable data.

SCSI, USB, Firewire, Ethernet, printer, and modem ports

Communications/networking ports which allow your computer to communicate locally or over long distance connections with external devices.

Keyboard, mouse, digitizing tablet

Basic tools for entering information/data into your computer = typewriter keyboard, pen/pencil/brush.

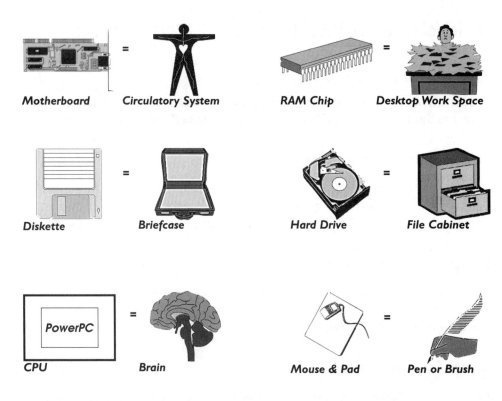

Motherboard = Circulatory System RAM Chip = Desktop Work Space

Diskette = Briefcase Hard Drive = File Cabinet

PowerPC / CPU = Brain Mouse & Pad = Pen or Brush

➠ TIP

To make it easier to understand how the various components of a computer function, try relating each computer component to a specific job, task or function which exists in the analog world. For instance, thinking of our computer RAM as our new desktop help us understand that the function of RAM is similar to that of our previous desktop work spaces. Making these analogous connections helps us not only understand the various computer components, but also helps us understand how these components function together and how they need to be controlled or configured.

▼ *Figure 4.1 Mainframe Computer*
Mainframe computers with their centrally located computing capabilities used "dumb" terminals for access to their power. Mainframes, which are large, expensive, and proprietary, dominated computer use until the 1980s, when the first personal computers arrived on the market.

TYPES OF COMPUTER SYSTEMS

Central computers

Mainframes

For many years the original computing paradigm included a core or central computer to which were connected a number (sometimes hundreds) of "dumb" terminals which operators used to access the computing and storage power of the core or central computer. These types of computers are called "**mainframes**." Mainframe computer systems have all of their computing capabilities located at the central or mainframe computer. Operators access this computing capability from their "dumb" terminals, which have no computational capabilities of their own, over network lines. Mainframes are still heavily used, and some are even used for publishing. But mainframe computers are very expensive and require the operator to be part of a large organization which can afford to purchase one. Each mainframe computer manufacturer also has its own proprietary operating system and application software, which means that software development and utilization of files is restricted to that particular system.

Desktop computers: Work stations

In the late 1970s, the paradigm of the mainframe computer was challenged by the introduction of the first personal computer by IBM, the IBM AT. These were and are called personal computers because they are small (hence the name "desktop") individual computers which have their computational (**cpu**), workspace (RAM), storage (disk drive), and communication (ports) capabilities built in. These machines are not only small and self contained, but also affordable for individual users. These desktop computers are sometimes called work stations. Another major change which occurred with the advent of the personal computer is the development and evolution of what is commonly called open architecture hardware and software. In the previous mainframe model of computing, each manufacturer had its own hardware, operating system, and application software, and there was little if any interchangeability. With open system architecture, many different manufacturers can make competitive hardware and software products to use interchangeably on the same machines. This competition and interchangeability has given consumers much lower costs and a wider range of choices for both hardware and software. Not long ago, computing was accessible to only a few of the technical elite. Computing has now become accessible to almost anyone who has a modest amount of money to spend and the desire to learn.

Macintosh

The first personal computers, the IBM ATs, were designed primarily for manipulating text and numbers; graphics were not a major consideration. The first computer manufacturer to create a personal computer designed specifically for graphics applications was Apple. The first affordable and available personal graphics computer was the 8MHz, 128K Macintosh. This machine had 128K of RAM, a 400K floppy disk drive, a 9-inch 72 dpi screen, and no hard drive. While this is almost unbelievably weak by today's standards, it was a milestone in personal computing. Prior to the first Macintosh, most computers used 64K or less RAM and had monitors with resolutions below 60 dpi.

Macintosh computers, commonly known as Macs, use Motorola CPU (central processing units) chips as their main "brains." Examples of these chips and computer models in which they were used include 68000 (used in the first Macs and MacPluses), 68020 (MacII), 68030 (MacIIci), 68040 (Quadras), and PowerPC (used in PowerMacs). Each progressive generation of chips represents a faster and more capable chip. The early CPU chips performed thousands of instructions per second at clock speeds of 8MHz. Today's machines perform millions of instructions per second (MIPS) at clock speeds of over 500 MHz and growing faster by the month. Each succeeding generation of chip and computer also sported other improvements and capabilities, most notably increases in RAM and disk storage

▼ *Figure 4.2 Macintosh PowerPC*
Significant improvements in performance were realized when Apple adopted for use in their PowerPC computers the same type of RISC (reduced instruction set computing) chips used by traditional high performance computers such as Sun and Silicon Graphics workstations.

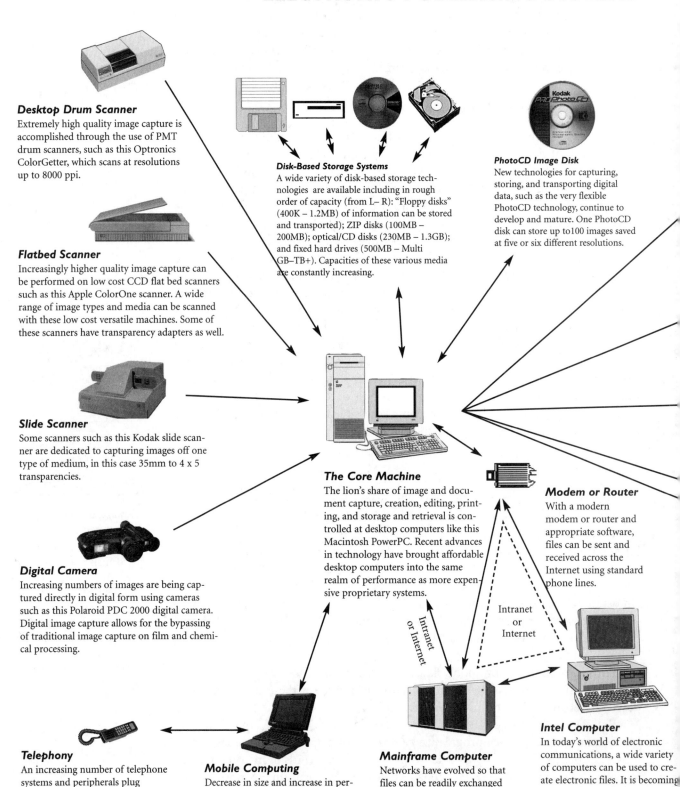

Desktop Drum Scanner
Extremely high quality image capture is accomplished through the use of PMT drum scanners, such as this Optronics ColorGetter, which scans at resolutions up to 8000 ppi.

Flatbed Scanner
Increasingly higher quality image capture can be performed on low cost CCD flat bed scanners such as this Apple ColorOne scanner. A wide range of image types and media can be scanned with these low cost versatile machines. Some of these scanners have transparency adapters as well.

Slide Scanner
Some scanners such as this Kodak slide scanner are dedicated to capturing images off one type of medium, in this case 35mm to 4 x 5 transparencies.

Digital Camera
Increasing numbers of images are being captured directly in digital form using cameras such as this Polaroid PDC 2000 digital camera. Digital image capture allows for the bypassing of traditional image capture on film and chemical processing.

Disk-Based Storage Systems
A wide variety of disk-based storage technologies are available including in rough order of capacity (from L–R): "Floppy disks" (400K – 1.2MB) of information can be stored and transported); ZIP disks (100MB – 200MB); optical/CD disks (230MB – 1.3GB); and fixed hard drives (500MB – Multi GB–TB+). Capacities of these various media are constantly increasing.

PhotoCD Image Disk
New technologies for capturing, storing, and transporting digital data, such as the very flexible PhotoCD technology, continue to develop and mature. One PhotoCD disk can store up to 100 images saved at five or six different resolutions.

The Core Machine
The lion's share of image and document capture, creation, editing, printing, and storage and retrieval is controlled at desktop computers like this Macintosh PowerPC. Recent advances in technology have brought affordable desktop computers into the same realm of performance as more expensive proprietary systems.

Modem or Router
With a modern modem or router and appropriate software, files can be sent and received across the Internet using standard phone lines.

Intranet or Internet

Intranet or Internet

Telephony
An increasing number of telephone systems and peripherals plug directly into computers providing both data and voice communication capabilities.

Mobile Computing
Decrease in size and increase in performance of laptop computers like this Apple PowerBook have made publishing on the road an increasingly viable activity.

Mainframe Computer
Networks have evolved so that files can be readily exchanged between desktop systems and large mainframe computers like this IBM AS400. Online services such as AOL and Compuserve use mainframes.

Intel Computer
In today's world of electronic communications, a wide variety of computers can be used to create electronic files. It is becoming increasingly easier for different types of computers to communicate over networks. Many applications operate on multiple platforms.

COMPONENTS & CAPABILITIES

Projector
The computer video signal can be sent directly to LCD-based projectors for the generation of extremely high quality presentations.

B&W Proof Printer
B&W proofing, and in some cases final output, is handled by toner based laser printers such as this Apple LaserWriter NTX. Formats range from 8.5" x 11" up to 11" x 17" and resolutions from 300 dpi 1800 dpi.

Color Proof Printer
Producing color prints on the desktop used to be an expensive, slow, and low quality exercise. No longer! There are a growing number of affordable, high quality desktop color printers such as this Polaroid dye sublimation PolarPrint printer.

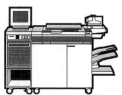

B&W and Four Color Copiers/Printers
Through the use of an intermediary, PostScript RIPs documents can be sent directly from computers to "copy" machines. These machines are rapidly replacing offset presses in the low quality and volume markets.

Fax Machine
With current desktop computer systems and the appropriate software, faxes can be sent directly from design stations to fax machines.

Film Recorder
Direct final output from computer to film is available through the use of film recorders like this ProPalette 8000 film recorder from Polaroid.

Fast RIPs & Large Format Imagesetters
Fast RIPs and larger format imagesetters, like this combination of a Linotronic RIP60 RIP and 3060 Imagesetter, allow for the creation of fully imposed film and even plates directly off the imagesetter. This can save time and money.

Conventional Four-Color Press
Images placed on plates either directly from a computer or created via intermediate film production are placed on press cylinders and used for the reproduction of those images.

The RIP
The RIP (Raster Image Processor) is the business end of a PostScript publishing system. A RIP translates all file information into a printable format. RIPs can be stand-alone hardware modules or software versions which operate on computers like this Macintosh workstation.

Banner Printer
Previously available from machines costing over $100,000, high quality large format prints can now be quickly and affordably made from the desktop using FM screening technologies and inkjet printers like this 50 inch NovaJet Pro printer from NCAD.

Direct Digital Presses
The last few years have seen the introduction of direct imaging presses in which images are sent directly to the press from the computer, thereby skipping the film and plate production steps. The next five years will be a time of rapid proliferation of this direct digital technology.

space. The first Macs supported only 128K of RAM and had no internal hard drives. These capabilities have evolved into today's PowerMacs which now operate at over 500MHz and address up to 4GB (GigaByte) of RAM and multiple GBs of storage space. And these capacities will continue to grow. Soon we will be working at over 1000MHz, addressing many GBs of RAM and accessing TeraBytes of storage space.

Early on, most of the Motorola CPU chips were CISC (complex instruction set computing), the older generation of chips. The PowerPC (or PowerMac computers, as they are sometimes called) use RISC (Reduced Instruction Set Computing) chips, which are the newer and faster generation of chips. These RISC chips are similar to the RISC chips which have long been used by high performance graphics workstations such as Sun Spark stations and Silicon Graphics Indigos (Indys).

Apple currently has a consumer line of Macintoshes called iMacs. These are sold through retail stores like Sears and Best Buy. They are equivalent to other PowerPC Macs, but have names deemed more suitable for the retail market. All Macintosh computers use some version of the Apple Macintosh operating system to provide control of all these Macs.

PCs (Personal Computers)

"PC" or personal computer is a term coined in the 1980s by IBM for their desktop computers. Although all Macintoshes and computers made by IBM, Dell, Compac, and others are literally personal computers, IBM coined the name and registered it as a trademark. At this point in time, however, the colloquial usage of the term "PC" is generally used to refer to all those computers (IBM, Compac, Dell, etc.) which are based upon the Intel standard CPU chip and use **DOS**, **Windows**, or OS2 as an operating system. This distinguishes them from the Macintosh, which uses a Motorola CPU chip and the Mac operating system (OS). And while this distinction may seem arbitrary and somewhat vague, it will become more so as IBM begins producing computers using the same PowerPC chip as that used by the Apple Macintosh, and will in fact operate using the Mac OS as well as its own OS2.

As mentioned above, there is a wide variety of "PC" manufacturers, including IBM (the original), Compaq, Dell, and HP (non-**IBM PC**s are typically called IBM clones). PCs use Intel CPU (central processing unit) chips as their main "brains" rather than the Motorola CPU chips used in Macs. Examples of these chips include the 8086, 286, 386, 486, and Pentium. Like the Macintosh, each progressive generation of chips represents a faster and more capable chip. To date, all of the Intel CPU chips are CISC (complex instruction set computing), which are the older generation of chips. Newer generation PCs use Intel Pentium processors, which like their Mac cousins operate in the 500MHz+ range. Successive generations of Pentium processors are labeled Pentium I, II, III, etc.

PCs use a variety of operating systems. Operating system provide us with the means to control our computers. The early computers, 8086s and 286s, used one called DOS (short for disk operating system), which was a text based OS. DOS was developed by the now famous and titanic Bill Gates of Microsoft Corp. (hence, the

▼ **Figure 4.3 Pentium PC**
The Pentium-based computer represents the highest performance "PC" type of computer. The Pentium replaced the previous 286, 386, and 486 machines.

term MS-DOS). Later, OS2, Windows, Windows NT, and Windows 2000, which are GUIs (graphical user interfaces), were developed to make use of these computers easier. Microsoft makes DOS and Windows which is used by most clone manufacturers. UNIX is the O.S. used on high end work stations and many servers. And new operating systems, such as Linux, are being developed to compete with the established ones. There will be more on operating systems in the next chapter.

TIP

If you have not yet chosen a computer system on which to work, before you do, ask the people with whom you work, such as your printing company and/or service bureaus, what type of computers they recommend. This same advice applies to choosing software as well. If you use the same computer and/or operating system and software as your business partners, it will make it easier to communicate with them and share files. In addition, having similar computer systems will make it easier to help each other troubleshoot problems.

Peripheral devices and software

Along with the evolution of computers themselves, we have seen a parallel evolution of their associated peripheral devices. A peripheral device is one which adds specific capability to the electronic publishing system, such as scanning or printing. The most fundamental of all peripheral devices, the monitor, has gone though a dramatic evolution. Those first built-in 9-inch black and white Mac screens have evolved into 21-inch, 24-bit color monitors supported by 8MB+ of video RAM. Scanners which started out as 200 dpi, 1-bit B&W add-ons to pin printers now boast 8000 dpi of 42-bit color capture capabilities. Storage device choices have evolved from single option 400K floppies to removable storage. Printing device options which began as 180 dpi dot matrix printers are now available in a dizzying array of B&W and color printers spanning a range of resolutions from 300 dpi to 3600 dpi, with a wide choice of output technologies to suit almost any need including laser, die sublimation, thermal wax, phase change ink jet, and electrostatic, in formats ranging from letter to poster size. Telecommunications, while still in its infancy, has already made some dramatic progress as well. Initial modem capabilities included modem to modem speeds of only 300bps (bauds per second). We now have 56Kb (kilobit) network modems, and even faster digital routers which access on-line services and a worldwide telecommunications system. Our image capture capabilities have moved beyond the scanner and now include professional quality direct image capture with digital still and video cameras.

▼ *Figure. 4.4 A Server*
Servers are the key to controlling access to and the storage and distribution of enormous volumes of information being constantly accumulated. Servers often function as the traffic cops for controlling the flow of information around a network of independent electronic publishing stations.

Software has gone through an evolution similar to hardware's. Our initial DTP applications, PageMaker 1.0 and MacPaint, provided us with very basic page layout and painting capabilities without benefit of sophisticated type controls or color capabilities. We now have very sophisticated typesetting and graphics applications which give us type controls to within 1/10,000 of a point and color graphics tools which exceed many of our traditional capabilities. We now also have access to sophisticated digital presentation, animation, sound, and multimedia tools. In addition, we have developed software which affords us complete control over production chores such as trapping, imposition, and work flow.

Servers

Initially, our electronic publishing systems consisted of one computer station attached to a variety of peripheral devices including a scanner and a printer. As we have been asking our publishing systems to perform an even greater number of sophisticated publishing chores, our system have evolved into more complex systems. On larger systems with large work flows, individual tasks such as scanning, page composition, image editing, file management, trapping, imposition, and even telecommunications chores are assigned to individual work stations which are all connected by a network. The core computer in this type of system is the server which is used for file storage and network administration. The server controls the ebb and flow of information around a network and often acts as a repository for large volumes of information such as databases of text and graphic files. There are even specific types of servers such as file servers, print servers, fax servers, and telecommunications servers like the computers which run the global telecommunications network we refer to as the Internet. On larger systems there are even servers to control systems of servers. Servers are becoming the key to the strength of modern electronic publishing systems.

The trend toward the use of servers is somewhat of a return to the original computing paradigm when the computing work was being done on a remote mainframe computer. The difference is that in modern electronic publishing each individual station remains independently capable, turning over only that work which is related to storage or movement of information around a network.

Others: Silicon Graphics and Suns

There are a variety of less common but important high-performance graphics-oriented computers known as "workstations." Two of the better known ones are Silicon Graphics "Indy" and Sun "Spark" stations. The Indy has been used extensively for 3-D modeling and the movie industry, while the Spark stations have long been a mainstay of the engineering CAD/CAM community. Both use very fast RISC-based CPUs, similar to the PowerPC chip discussed above, and are known for their exceptional performance as well as their steep prices. Recently, Indy and Spark stations have been finding their way into electronic publishing systems as file servers and high speed graphic workstations.

Clones

A clone is a copycat hardware manufacturer. Many of the components used in computers today, such as hard drives, floppy disk drives, motherboards, and monitors, are generic and made by many different manufacturers. Any individual with the proper basic knowledge and tools can build a computer by purchasing and assembling components. As mentioned above, the two key components or features which distinguish one computer from another are its "brain" or CPU and the operating system (OS) used to operate and control that computer. While the term clone

▼ Figure 4.5 Sun Spark Station
The Sun Spark station is a very high performance computer workstation. Powerful workstations made by Sun and Silicon Graphics have long utilized RISC-chip technologies and powerful operating systems like UNIX, which offers advantages like multitasking, to provide improved performance over Macintosh and PC-based systems. This performance came with a price, however. Most of these system prices begin at $25,000 and go up, and the operating systems tend to be less user friendly.

or clone manufacturer originally had some negative connotation to it, a number of clone manufacturers have become some of the largest and fastest grow computer manufactures making some of the finest computer systems in the world.

Networks

All these various computers and peripheral devices can be interconnected through systems of wires, cables, radio waves and even satellites. These connections systems are know as networks. Networks can be of any size. A network can be as simple as one connection between a single computer and a printer. A local area network (LAN) may link a large number of computers and devices within one building. Wide area networks (WANs) may link several small networks together. Large companies and other organizations may maintain far flung but integrated networks called intranets. And of course the granddaddy of all networks is the Internet, which is a complex highly integrated network of computer systems all over the world.

What to buy?

Although it is very difficult to make specific recommendations about which system to buy because there are so many variables, here are some general recommendations for a starter electronic system. Remember that a station which uses many graphics usually demands more capabilities than a system which works primarily with text and numbers. A good current choice for a starter Mac or PC publishing system will be a ~500 MHz PowerPC or Pentium CPU, 128MB RAM, 2GB+ HD, 15-17 inch monitor, 20+x CD, extended keyboard, mouse, 56K modem, and page layout, drawing, and painting software, at a cost of about $2,500–$4,000. Add a scanner, with a Dmax of ≥3.2, for $1000 – $1500 and a letter size PostScript printer at a price ranging anywhere from $500 – $2500. If you paint and/or draw or perform a lot of image editing functions, consider purchasing a digitizing tablet for ~$200. Your total cost for this type of system would be between $5000 and $8500. As our development of ever more capable systems progress the specifics and prices of the above configuration recommendations will be quickly out of date, but you will always want a way to capture, manipulate and reproduce images.

CHAPTER SUMMARY

Computer graphic systems have replaced most previously analog "done-by-hand" graphics tools and techniques. To effectively use these new digital tools it is important that we learn how they operate. A good first step is to understand how each component of a computer works. Nearly all the new digital computer components have easy-to-understand analog counterparts. For example, RAM is analogous to desktop work space.

What started out in 1984 with a single computer with a small black and white screen and one laser printer has grown into a vast and continuously expanding array of capturing, editing and output devices. Electronic publishing, sometimes known as desktop publishing, got its start in the world of print and has expanded into just about every aspect of communication technology including video and multimedia. In fact, an entirely new communication medium has been developed which is entirely electronic, the World Wide Web.

There are several types of computers systems including Macintoshes, IBM PCs, Sun, Silicon Graphics and other systems. These various computer systems can be interconnected with and to a wide variety of input and output devices for capturing, manipulating, storing and sharing information. Connections can be made over both local (LAN) and wide area networks (WANs). Don't be afraid to ask your **service provider**s, such as printing companies and service bureaus, for their recommendations on which computer system and configuration to buy. Their professional input can be very valuable.

PAULINE'S DIGITAL IMAGING TIPS

Pauline's Tip 4.1

Know the basic components of your electronic publishing system and how they operate. You definitely need to know what RAM and storage memory are and how to effectively manage both. Be sure that you keep at least 20 percent of the RAM that you assign to any application free so that your application has room into which it can expand. Never assign all of your RAM to open applications, as your system needs RAM space in which to expand. Optimally, your hard drive space should remain at least 50 percent free. The more you know about your system, the more effective an operator you will be and the more troubleshooting skills you will be able to develop.

Pauline's Tip 4.2

Purchase reliable hardware, and most importantly, keep the hardware up to date and tuned up. Make sure your power is clean. Install isolated lines. Use high quality cables from one manufacturer. Keep your publishing environment clean and cool. Imaging equipment hates dirt and high temperatures.

Pauline's Tip 4.3

Ask your service partners, such as your printing companies or other service bureaus, what type of hardware and software they recommend. This type of professional advice is one of your most reliable sources of hardware and software information since these folks actually work with these systems all the time. Having hardware and software components which are compatible with your service bureaus will make sharing files and communicating with them easier and more reliable.

CHAPTER REVIEW

Check Your Comprehension

Multiple Choice Questions

To help you review the topics covered in this chapter, answer the following multiple choice questions.

1. Graphic arts technologies prior to the computer age were mostly
   A. Digital
   B. Electronic
   C. Analog
   D. None of the above

2. As a graphics user, basic knowledge of how a computer works is important because
   A. This knowledge will help us configure and control them
   B. We need to be able to repair them
   C. With it, we can build our own computers
   D. Basic computer knowledge is not really important

3. Computer RAM is analogous to a
   A. file cabinet
   B. briefcase
   C. brain
   D. desktop work space

4. A computer hard drive is analogous to a
   A. file cabinet
   B. briefcase
   C. brain
   D. desktop work space

5. A computer diskette is analogous to a
   A. file cabinet
   B. briefcase
   C. brain
   D. desktop work space

6. A computer CPU is analogous to a

    A. file cabinet

    B. briefcase

    C. brain

    D. desktop work space

7. Which of the following is not considered a desktop computer?

    A. Macintosh

    B. IBM PC

    C. Server

    D. Mainframe

8. A clone manufacture can be described as a?

    A. computer manufacturer

    B. copy cat

    C. computer assembler

    D. all of the above

9. A _____ is used for document storage and network control and administration.

    A. scanner

    B. server

    C. printer

    D. workstation

10. Which of the following would be considered the largest network?

    A. Local area network

    B. Wide area network

    C. Internet

    D. Intranet

11. Which term best describes a network which connects computers systems in one business or organization?

    A. Local area network

    B. Wide area network

    C. Internet

    D. Intranet

12. Who is one of your best sources of professional information on computer equipment?

    A. Local retail computer store

    B. Your graphics services provider

    C. Your library

    D. None of the above

Check Your Understanding

Concept Questions

To help you review and expand your thinking on the topics covered in this chapter, answer the following questions.

1. Briefly explain why having a basic knowledge of how your computer works is important to you as a graphics computer user.

2. Provide a brief overview of the history of DTP.

3. Briefly explain the difference between a mainframe and a desktop computer.

4. Describe the differences between a Macintosh and and IBM PC.

5. What are the functions of a server?

6. What is the purpose of a network?

7. Briefly describe the differences between a local area, wide area network.

8. What are peripheral devices and for what are they used?

9. Distinguish between the terms Intranet and Internet.

10. Describe the basic functionality and components of a desktop publishing system.

PROJECTS

Make a list of all the computer system components in your room or building. Investigate if there is more than one network and if these networks are connected. Ask about how your local networks(s) may be connected to other outside networks. Draw a diagram of how these components are arranged and networks are interconnected. Don't forget to include your connection(s) to the Internet.

5
Software

As the Byte Turns continues…

Will Danny find out that Pauline is a stable Page Maker or will she just just take a Free Hand and XPress herself while she looks out her Windows?

Mac vs. PC, Windows vs. Mac OS vs. UNIX, Pentium vs. Power PC, Zip vs. Jaz, PageMaker vs. XPress. FreeHand vs. Illustrator. What do I buy?

Well, I'm not sure!!!

I wish I knew myself!

Can you help??

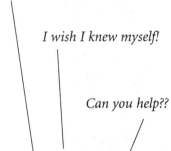

Sure. Have Danny give me a call and I'll advise him. It would be great if Danny had the same type of system components as well as software that we have. That would make file transfer and printing much easier.

Chapter Objectives

In this chapter you will learn about:

◆ **Operating system software**
◆ **Application software**
◆ **Utility software**
◆ **Resource software**
◆ **Acrobat and PDF**
◆ **System minimization**
◆ **Key Terms**
  • Mac OS
  • Windows OS
  • UNIX OS
  • Linux OS
  • DOS (MS DOS)
  • GUI
  • Icon
  • System resources
  • Acrobat
  • PDF

INTRODUCTION

Types of software

In the last chapter we explored some of the basics of the physical hardware which make up a modern electronic publishing system. The other key component of any electronic publishing system is software. Software is the list of instructions, called "code," which provide a computer operator with tools which allow the operator to perform tasks. Software is divided into basically four categories: system software, applications, resources, and utilities. System software provides for basic computer operations such as turning a computer off and on and the look and feel of the interface. Examples of operating systems include various versions of **Windows OS** (3.1, 95, 98, 2000 NT), the various numbered versions of the **Mac OS**, **UNIX OS** which is utilized by high end work stations and many servers, and new operating systems such as **Linux OS** which are rising to challenge the old stalwarts.

Application software provides us with sets of creative tools and capabilities which allow us to create and manipulate text, graphics, and completed documents. Examples of professional graphics applications include QuarkXpress, InDesign, PageMaker, Photoshop, Illustrator and FreeHand. Resources, also known as **System resources**, are items such as fonts, sounds, and color palettes used within applications for the creation of documents. System resources are so called because these are resources which are accessed by the operating system and made available for use by applications. Utilities are really just small applications used for performing specific functions such as disk formatting, troubleshooting, virus protection, and management of resources such as fonts and sounds. The dividing line between applications and utilities is an arbitrary one, vaguely drawn on the basis of size and complexity of the software. Applications, like InDesign, are generally more complex and used in the creation of documents of some sort, while utilities are more focused on the management of a single resource such as fonts.

OPERATING SYSTEMS

Operating systems software

The most fundamental of all software applications is operating system software. Operating system (OS) software provides the basic tools which allow an operator

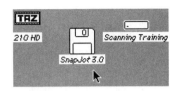

▼ *Figure 5.2 Disk Icons*
Here is a sampling for various disk icons. In the upper left is an icon for an internal hard drive which has been customized with my name. It is common practice to include the size of the disk in its name (as shown here) indicating a 210MB hard drive. The middle icon represents a floppy disk, while the third icon shows a removable disk.

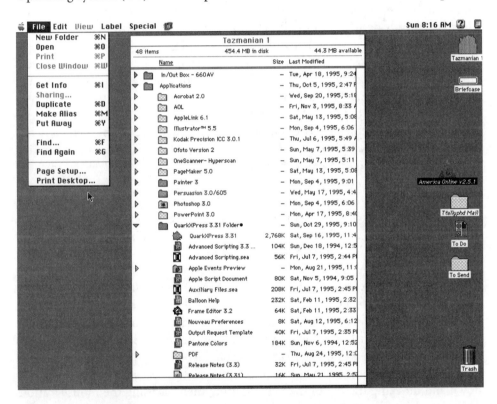

▼ *Figure 5.1 Mac Desktop*
This is an example of a GUI or graphical user interface. All items are represented by logical icons; controls are provided by mouse movements and activation of menu choices, in addition to optional keyboard commands. This is a view of the Macintosh "Desktop." This view all of the icons and menus is created by the Finder, a part of the operating system (Mac OS). The two icons labeled "Tazmanian I" and "Briefcase" in the upper right corner below the Day and Time indicator are the icons for disks. Tazmanian I is the primary or "Boot" internal hard drive where the active system software is installed. "Briefcase" is the name of a 200MB removable disk which I use for transferring files between offices. The large open window in the center shows some of the contents of "Tazmanian I." A Finder menu appears on the left and various folders, documents, and Alias (in italics) icons are shown on the right side of the Desktop. The cursor control icon, which is controlled by mouse movements, can be found on the Desktop under the File menu. Microsoft Windows and IBM OS2 provide functionally similar, albeit different looking, GUIs. The development of GUIs such as these has greatly simplified the operation of complex and sophisticated computers.

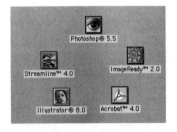

▼ *Figure 5.3 Application Icons*
Shown here is a variety of application icons. Each application has a unique icon which generally bears some graphic resemblance to the purpose for which the application is used. For instance, FreeHand, which is a drawing application, is represented by an icon of a drawing pen.

▼ **Figure 5.4 Document Icons**
Document icons are distinguished from other icons by the little dog ear on the upper right hand corner. Note how each icon has a specific look to it. In order, from top to bottom, are document icons for: PageMaker 5.0, QuarkXPress, Illustrator, and a Photoshop document.

to control the computer. Without an operating system, an operator would have no way to communicate with and control the computer. Most operating systems provide basic functionality tools such as booting (turning the computer on), application launching, disk formatting, file naming, copying, movement and organization, resource management for RAM, fonts, sounds and video, access to peripherals such as monitors, drives, and scanners, and basic communication capabilities such as printing and file sharing. Each operating system has its own specific interface, or way of getting things done. There have historically been two type of interfaces, text and graphic. With a text-based interface one uses sequences of text to complete tasks. With a graphic-based interface, affectionately known as a **GUI** (graphical user interface), **icon**s or symbols are manipulated in order to complete tasks. A common example of a text-based interface is the Microsoft Disk Operating System commonly known as **MS-DOS,** or just plain DOS. MS-DOS was one of the first operating systems used on personal or desktop computers [a personal computer is generally defined as a small self-contained (it has its own RAM, CPU, storage disks and video) affordable computer]. In fact, DOS, while now largely obsolete, has been the most widely used operating system in the world. The problem with text-based operating systems is that they do not operate in the same manner or fashion in which most people think or work. Typing out codes to carry out tasks is foreign to most people's mode of operating. For this reason, text-based operating systems are not considered to be "user friendly." Because of this generally low quotient of "user friendliness," more human-oriented or user-friendly operating systems (such as GUIs) were developed.

The first commonly available GUI was the Mac operating system, or Mac OS. Later, Microsoft, the originator of the original DOS, developed the Windows OS and Windows NT GUIs. These GUI operating systems utilize icons to represent various parts of the system such as disks and files. Icons are manipulated to perform various tasks. A mouse rather than a keyboard is the standard general tool used to manipulate a GUI. A variety of menus as well as keyboard commands can be used to manipulate a GUI. A simple example will illustrate the operational difference between text and graphic-based operating systems. To copy a file from one location on a drive to another would require a command code sequence similar to this: C/COPY D/. The same task in a GUI would involve the operator pointing with a mouse at the file to be moved, clicking on the file to select it, holding the mouse down and dragging the file to the new location, then releasing the mouse button. This second, GUI-based method, is very similar to how an operator would move a physical file from one file cabinet to another and is therefore easier for most operators to relate to and learn, making the GUI more user friendly. The GUI has become the standard interface for other operating systems such as UNIX OS and newer operating systems such as Linux OS.

Desktop views

The desktop view of an operating system is the entry level view of the access and controls available with a particular operating system. Each operating system has its own look and feel. The desktop view shown in Fig. 5.1 is that of the Macintosh. Various icons represent specific functions or features of the computer. For example, in this view, two disks, Tazmanian I and Briefcase, are shown in the upper right hand corner of the "Desktop." Tazmanian I is the primary internal hard disk or "boot" disk which contains the active operating system as well as a variety of applications, utilities, and documents. The main window seen here shows some of the contents of Tazmanian I. Icons for documents, folders, and the Trash can be seen on the Desktop as well. A view of a menu can be seen on the left, as well as the icon for the arrow cursor which is controlled by the movement of a mouse.

Icons

Each operating system which utilizes a GUI uses icons or symbols to represent features and items such as software applications, documents, and storage locations. Fig. 5.3 shows some common icons you will find used in the Mac operating system. Most hardware and software manufacturers develop distinctive icons as a way to make it easy for users to identify their products, as well as to help promote their brand name. Icons are the new logos of the digital age.

Menus

Another control tool common to all GUIs are menus. The operating system, which is itself an application, and each document creation application has its own set of menus, used for utilizing and controlling that application. The Macintosh System File menu, shown in Fig. 5.1, is typical of File menus found in most operating system and

Keeping your operating system, applications and utilities up-to-date is a good idea. However it is also a good idea to test any new updates prior to implementing them. The holy grail of computing is stability, that is working without software or hardware problems. I good modus operandi is to test all updates on a secondary drive prior to installing the software on your main work drive. I configure a secondary drive with the same system, application, utility and resources software as my primary work drive. I boot from the secondary drive to test all updates.

application software. The Apple Menu, shown in Fig. 5.5, is used to access a variety of items and information, including the "About this 'Application Name'" and "About this Macintosh" dialog boxes. When you are working in an application, QuarkXPress, for instance, the first choice under the Apple Menu will be "About QuarkXPress." Menus can be found in many circumstances including most commonly at the top of a window, as in Fig. 5.1, but also as appendages of dialog boxes and floating palettes. Menus within applications often contain a variety of that application's tools.

Windows

Another common feature of many GUIs are windows. Windows provide views of the contents of file storage locations, the contents of documents, and controls of computer functions. There are basically three kinds of windows: location windows, document windows, and dialog boxes. Windows are used extensively in Mac, Windows and Windows NT operating systems.

▼ **Figure 5.5 Application Information**
Knowing and communicating to your service bureau the versions of the applications you use to construct documents is an important help when they output your files.

If you are working on a Macintosh, choose "About the Application" under the Apple Menu. An information plate will appear on the screen showing the name and version of the application you are using. If you hold down the option key when you choose "About QuarkXPress," you will see an even more detailed information plate. Note that in the more detailed information plate it shows a patch level as well as a version number. Knowing this patch or revision level can be very important when trouble shooting specific document creation or output problems.

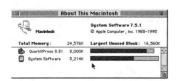

▼ Figure 5.6 RAM Allocation
This Macintosh RAM information dialog box, which is accessed by selecting "About This Macintosh" when you are in the Finder, provides information on how much total RAM a machine has, how much RAM is allocated to each application, and how much is available for further use. Note that in this case there is 24.5MB of total RAM; 3.2MB is allocated to the operating system, 3MB is allocated to QuarkXPress, and there is 16.5MB or RAM available for further use. Note the RAM allocation bar for XPress shows about 20 percent free, a good rule of thumb to follow. Painting applications need 3x the file size of free RAM.

Location windows

The primary view which you have into the contents of a computer is provided through location windows. Location windows, provided by the Finder on a Mac and the File Manager in Windows OS 3.1 and the Explorer in Windows 95 and 98, contain icons of folders, documents, and applications. An example of a location window can be seen in Fig. 5.1, where the Tazmanian I window shows the location of files on the hard drive named Tazmanian I. Location windows usually offer basic manipulation controls such as moving, shaping and sizing to allow for customization of viewing.

Document windows

Document windows are created within page or graphic generation applications like Quark and Illustrator. Document windows contain actual page elements such as text columns and graphics items. These document windows are nearly identical in both the Mac and Windows environments. This page was created in a document window. Document windows usually support the greatest amount of flexibility in terms of control and typically offer sizing, moving, shaping and zooming to allow for maximum page view choices and element creation and editing control options.

Information and dialog boxes

Information and dialog boxes, which often appear in response to a menu choice or keyboard command, provide information and choices. Examples of strictly informational boxes are the "About QuarkXPress" and "About This Macintosh" boxes shown in Figs. 5.5 and 5.6. The "About QuarkXPress" boxes provide information about the QuarkXpress application such as the version and patch or revision numbers of the application being used. The "About This Macintosh" information box supplies information about how much RAM your computer has and how it is being allocated. An example of a dialog box, which provides choices as well as information, is the "QuarkXPress Information" dialog box shown in Fig. 5.7. This dialog box not only shows you how much RAM is allocated to QuarkXPress and recommends suggested and minimum RAM allocations, but also provides you with the response box "Preferred size" which allows you to change the amount of RAM which will be allocated to QuarkXPress the next time it is launched. All of these dialog boxes are important in electronic publishing. The two QuarkXPress information boxes provide you with the version and revision numbers which you need to provide your printer or service bureau when you send them a document created in Xpress. The RAM allocation and setting information and dialog boxes provide you with the means to monitor and control your RAM use. A good rule of thumb for RAM allocation in a page layout application is to have about 20 percent of the "allocation" bar in the "About This Macintosh" information box free. Painting applications should have a RAM allocation equal to about three times the size of the documents which will be manipulated. Information and dialog box windows are often fixed in size and do not usually have the same flexibility of control that a document window will have.

APPLICATIONS

Document creation

The primary tools used for creating, manipulating, and managing electronic documents are applications. Some applications are generalist applications such as Microsoft Works, sometimes referred to as "Swiss Army knife applications," which are designed to provide a wide range of capabilities such as text, graphics, spreadsheet, database, and telecommunications, in one application. Most professional electronic publishers work in applications which are more specific in orientation. Single or narrow focus applications tend to provide more depth and control than the Swiss Army knife applications. In addition, the more focused applications tend to print more easily at higher resolutions. At this point, if you are interested in producing professional quality work, you should generally work in more specific or focused applications. Examples of specific electronic publishing tasks and applications which are designed specifically to address those tasks include:

TASK	APPLICATION(S)	PLATFORM*
Painting	Photoshop, Painter	Mac & Windows
Drawing	Illustrator, FreeHand	Mac & Windows
Drawing	CorelDraw	Mac & Windows
Web graphics	Flash, Fireworks, ImageReady	Mac & Windows
Page layout	QuarkXPress, PageMaker,	
Page layout	InDesign, FrameMaker	Mac & Windows
Web page creation	Dreamweaver, GoLive	Mac & Windows
Multimedia	Director, Authorware	Mac & Windows
Word processing	Microsoft Word	Mac & Windows
Outlining	Streamline	Mac & Windows
Presentation	Acrobat, PowerPoint	Mac & Windows
Cross-platform	Acrobat PDF	Mac & Windows

*Note: Many of these applications also exist on other platforms such as Sun and Silicon Graphics stations, which utilize some version of UNIX OS or other O.S.

It is generally a good idea to use an application for the primary purpose for which it was created. For example, you can set type and lay out pages in drawing applications like Illustrator, FreeHand, and CorelDraw, but typesetting and page layout functions are better handled in commercial print page layout applications like QuarkXPress and PageMaker. Conversely, while you can perform some editing of graphics, such as cropping and rotating, in Quark and PageMaker, you are better off performing those functions in the graphics applications used to create the graphics. Similarly, many basic graphics applications provide some basic Web graphics and multimedia tools; here again dedicated applications such as Fireworks (Web graphics) and Director (multimedia) will generally provide you with better tools and results. There are some emerging trends in applications, such as customization, which may dramatically change the way we choose and work in our applications. Conversely using the wrong tool altogether, such as using a presentation program like PowerPoint to create a commercial print document, can lead not only to poor quality, but often unprintable results. Basically our motto is: Use the right tool, for the right job, to get the best results! If you are unsure what

▼ *Figure 5.7 Application Information*
This Macintosh application information dialog box, which is accessed by selecting an application icon and choosing Get Info under the File menu in the Finder, provides information on how much RAM should be and will be allocated to the application. Setting the "Preferred size" in this dialog box will determine how much RAM will be allocated to QuarkXPress when it is launched. Note that RAM sizes are measured in K (K=1000Bytes), so 3000K = 3MB.

▼ *Figure 5.8 PDF Distiller 3.0 Options*
PDF files are created through Distiller. In order for PDF files to print properly, Distiller Job Options must be properly configured. Attention must be paid to the inclusion of the original font files and high resolution versions of your document's graphics.

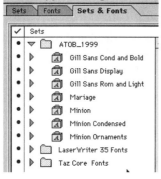

▼ *Figure 5.9 Font Resources*
The font sets dialog box from ATM Deluxe, which is used on both Macs and Windows machines. Shown here is a list of font sets, which are virtual groupings of fonts. Font management utilities like ATM Deluxe allow much more control and flexibility in the management of our font files.

to use, ask a member of your professional service bureau for advice on which applications they prefer to support.

Cross-platform Acrobat PDF

It has become increasingly common for us to need to use our documents onplatforms, operating systems, or applications other than the ones with which we created that document. For instance, we may create a document on a Macintosh, using the Mac OS, in QuarkXpress 4.0, and we want to send this document to someone who is working on a PC in Windows 98, and all they have is Microsoft Word. This need presents many cross-platform conversion problems involving incompatible document formats and the challenges inherent in translating font and graphic information.

The answer to this type of challenge is often found in the use of a document format called Adobe Acrobat PDF. **PDF** is short for Portable Document Format. PDF files are designed to be platform-, operating system-, and application-independent, that is, you need not have the same machine, operating system, or even the same application in order to view, print, and even edit a file.

PDF files are generally created by a program called Adobe Acrobat Distiller. Typically, the original document file is converted into a PostScript file by printing the document file to disk using a PostScript printer driver. This PostScript file is then processed through Distiller. Distiller converts the PostScript file into a PDF document. All that is needed to view and print a PDF document is an Acrobat Reader, which is a free application that can be downloaded from the Adobe Web page. More sophisticated handling and even editing of a PDF file can be accomplished through the use of Adobe applications such as Acrobat Exchange (version 3.0) and Acrobat (version 4.0), as well as excellent third party applications such as PitStop from Enfocus Software.

It is important to know that PDF was originally designed primarily as an on-screen viewing tool, so care should be taken during the creation of a PDF document if you intend to print a PDF file, and particularly if you intend to separate a PDF file for commercial printing. The Job Options in Distiller, Fig 5.8, need to be properly configured for the inclusion of the original font file and high resolution versions of the graphic files. If the original font files are not included with a PDF document, Acrobat will create simulated versions of your font characters, which often do not match the originals. Later versions of Acrobat, 4.0 and above, provide for more editability and better print control functions. I also use PDF files as a handy way to view and proof PostScript files. PDF is also Internet friendly, which means that it can be sent across the Internet without fear of corruption.

RESOURCES

Software resources are files which can be used by many different applications for the creation or editing of files. In most electronic publishing systems, important resources are available and distributed at the system level so that all applications

▼ *Figure 5.10 System Resources*
This dialog box from NOW Utilities shows a view of NOW's Startup Manager dialog box. This utility allows me to turn on only those system resources which I need for a particular job or activity. The check marks indicate those resources which I have activated for my scanning set.

may take advantage of them. Two of the most common and important resources are fonts and sounds. Fonts and sounds can be located in the system where all font-aware applications can access them. This central access to resources has not always been the rule. Prior to the development of the Mac OS and then Windows, fonts had to be supplied for each application. Details of font and font icons are covered in Chapter 11, "Tales of True Typesetting." Examples of other System resources include color profiles, printer drivers, and telecommunication resources.

Utilities

Utilities are small applications which perform specific tasks. Examples of utilities include: virus protection, disk formatting, and font management. Two of the most common and useful examples of utility software are Adobe Type Manager, commonly referred to by its initials ATM, and ATM Deluxe (Fig 5.9). The basic ATM utility is usually a required utility for properly displaying and printing PostScript fonts on both Mac and Windows based computers. ATM Deluxe is a utility which provides the same basic PostScript font viewing and printing functionality as ATM, as well as a full featured set of font management tools. A much more detailed discussion of font management will take place in Chapter 11.

Many utility applications like ATM and ATM Deluxe are also initialization files, commonly called inits. Inits automatically "boot"or start along with your computer's operating system (both Mac and Windows), thereby launching at the same as and working directly with your operating system software. Init icons appear on the bottom of your screen during the start-up process of the Mac operating system. ATM and ATM Deluxe are available for and should be used on both Macintosh and Windows machines. Font management utilities such as ATM Deluxe allow much more control and flexibility over the management of critical resources such as our fonts files.

Drivers, plug-ins and extensions

Drivers, plug-ins, and extensions are add-on programs to larger applications which extend the capabilites of that software. Drivers typically provide us with the ability to access and control external devices. Common drivers include scanner, CD and digital camera drivers. Plug-ins, which tend to provide the ability to perform a special task, are made for a wide variety of applications. For instance, hundreds of plug-ins, such as special effects filters, are made for Photoshop to expand its tools and capabilities. Extensions are very much like plug-ins, and in fact are often indistinguishable from them. Extensions such as table generators and indexing are commonly made for page layout applications as well. All drivers, plug-ins and extensions should be kept up to date and match the version of the application with which they are used. Most device drivers are located in the operating system folder. Plug-ins and extensions are typically stored in specific plug-in or extension folders contained within the application folder with which they work. Old versions of drivers, plug-ins and extensions should be removed after newer version have been added. Failure to keep drivers, plug-ins and extensions up to date may result in those tools no longer working, and failure to remove older versions of these softwares may result in conflicts and crashes.

Minimizing your system

While there are many useful and interesting resources and utilities, it is a good idea to be very selective about what you load onto your computer. Be particularly watchful of resources which you place in your system file, as these files will be constantly accessed by your operating system and therefore take up RAM space and require both CPU and operating system attention to keep them active. Also be aware that some resources may conflict with others. For instance, a font management utility may interfere with a scanner plug-in module you may be using.

To minimize the conflicts and system overloads which may result from having too many resources open, I try to limit the resources I have loaded to the ones I really need. I also divide the resources I use into groups and access them only as I need them. To manage my system, I use resource management tools, such as "Extension Manager" on my Mac, which allow me to create groups of System resources and access them as I need them. Fig. 5.8 shows you a font management tool, ATM Deluxe, which I use to access fonts, on both my Mac and Windows systems, as I need them. In Fig. 5.10 you see an example of how I organize my system resources into task-specific groups such as scanning, presentation, and networking. Taking the time and energy to manage your system this way will dramatically improve your productivity and reduce your stress level and the loss of hair commonly associated with system and application software problems such as software conflicts, updating and speed.

One final word of advice. Before I update my system and applications software on my main boot drive, I always try out new versions on a copy of the system or application that I have placed on a separate disk. I boot my computer from the updated copy and use it while I work out the inevitable bugs prior to updating my primary drive. This is a good and inexpensive insurance policy to have.

CHAPTER SUMMARY

There are two primary components of a desktop computer system, hardware and software. Software can be organized into four categories: operating system, application, resource and utility software. Most modern operating systems use graphical user interfaces (GUIs), rather than text interfaces, which enhances the useability of computers. Icons, menus and windows are all standard components of GUIs which provide access to and control over a wide variety of hardware and software functions. A wide variety of application software has been create to tackle just about any task imaginable, including commercial printing, video, multimedia and Web needs. There are some general purpose, "Swiss army knife," applications which attempt to provide access to multiple sets of tools. However, the most control and the best results usually result from learning and using dedicated tools. Our motto is: Use the right tool, for the right job, to get the best results!

Utility programs are small-job-specific applications which are designed to perform single functions such as virus protection or font management. Drivers, plug-ins, and extensions are created to extend the capabilities of our basic applications. All applications, utilities, drivers, plug-ins and extensions should be kept up to date.

New technologies such as Acrobat are making moving a document cross platform much easier. Utility programs such as font management utilities provide us better control over our system and application resources. Minimizing our operating system and application files will generally result in faster, easier to manage and update software systems.

PAULINE'S DIGITAL IMAGING TIPS

Pauline's Tip 5.1

Know the versions of all the applications which you use to create files. Be sure to supply version numbers to your service bureau when you send your files out to be printed. Each version of an application has its own quirks, and knowing the version numbers of the creating applications can be a big help when setting up and troubleshooting files. It is a good idea to keep up to date on your applications versions. You don't have to buy the latest version as soon as it is available, but don't get more than one application version behind. You should, however, have the latest revision (r.) of whatever version you use. Revisions are generally brought out to fix problems which become apparent after a version is released.

Pauline's Tip 5.2

Keeping your operating system, applications and utilities up to date is a good idea. It is also a good idea to test any new updates prior to implementing them. The holy grail of computing is stability, that is, working without software or hardware problems. One good modus operandi is to test all updates on a secondary drive prior to installing the software on your main work drive. I configure a secondary drive with the same system, application, utility and resources software as my primary work drive. I boot from the secondary drive to test all updates.

Pauline's Tip 5.3

Use the right tool for the right job. There is a dizzying array of applications which have been created for just about any graphics communication challenge you can imagine. Using general purpose tools which try to please too many masters often produces less than desirable results. If you are not sure which applications you should be using, ask a professional user at one of your local service providers who offers services in your area of interest. Especially do this if you intend to be sending your files to this company for manipulation or output.

Pauline's Tip 5.4

Remember that any software which you place on your computer complicates your computer. To help keep your system operating at its peak, limit the amount of software you put on your publishing system. Be especially brutal about removing software which installs files in your system folder. Those are the most intrusive and performance-robbing pieces of software. Yes, that means get rid of those cool screen savers, sounds, and games. Put those on your home computer. Use resource management utilities such as font and system file management tools to help you manage and streamline your system resources.

CHAPTER REVIEW

Check Your Comprehension

Multiple Choice Questions

To help you review the topics covered in this chapter, answer the following multiple choice questions.

1. Which of the following is an example of an application?
   A. Mac OS
   B. Windows 98
   C. InDesign
   D. UNIX

2. Which of the following is a primary purpose of an operating system?
   A. Document creation
   B. Control of the computer
   C. Font management
   D. Virus protection

3. Which of the following is a good example of a utility?
   A. Virus protection software
   B. Page layout software
   C. Drawing application
   D. Operating system

4. Which of the following is not an operating system?
   A. UNIX
   B. LINUX
   C. Windows
   D. ATM Deluxe

5. Icons may represent
   A. Applications
   B. Utilities
   C. Font files
   D. All of the above

6. _____ is (are) primarily used for document creation.
   A. Operating systems
   B. Utility software
   C. Application software
   D. System resources

7. Which of the following is not generally found in a window?
   A. Locations
   B. Documents
   C. Information and dialog boxes
   D. Application tools

8. Which applications would be best used for creating a commercial print document?
   A. QuarkXPress
   B. FreeHand
   C. Dreamweaver
   D. Director

9. The following application was created with cross platform and OS compatibility.
   A. PageMaker
   B. Acrobat
   C. InDesign
   D. Streamline

10. _____ is critical for displaying and printing your PostScript font files.
    A. TIF
    B. USB
    C. SCSI
    D. ATM

11. System minimization refers to
    A. Reducing the number of software elements in your operating system
    B. Making your system files icons smaller
    C. Using fewer operating systems on the same computer
    D. None of the above

12. System minimization will result in
    A. Faster working of your operating system
    B. Fewer software conflicts
    C. Less complicated file management and updating
    D. All of the above

Check Your Understanding

Concept Questions

To help you review and expand your thinking on the topics covered in this chapter, answer the following questions.

1. Briefly explain the difference among operating system, application, and utility software.

2. What is a GUI and why has it been important in promoting the use of computers?

3. What is a system resource? Provide two examples of system resources.

4. What is DOS and how does it differ from most of today's modern operating systems?

5. What are icons and why are they important?

6. How many different kind of windows are there and what are their purposes?

7. What features and/or characteristics does an application window have which other types of windows do not?

8. Explain the motto: Use the right tool for the right job to get the best results. Explain how this applies to digital imaging. Provide two examples.

9. What is PDF and why was it created?

10. Explain the concept of minimization and how it can make your computing life easier.

PROJECTS

Interview a potential client who needs a brochure created for them. Make a list of the document project requirements. Ask about the final use/output of the project. Ask them whether they will want to use their brochure for more than one purpose: print, Web, etc. Make a list of those purposes. Also ask them about what kind of document components their brochure will have, including text, line art, grayscale photos, and color photos. Make a list of these components. Ask your new client how they will provide you these document components: as conventional or digital components? Be sure to ask your client for the highest quality samples they have.

Part 2

File Fundamentals

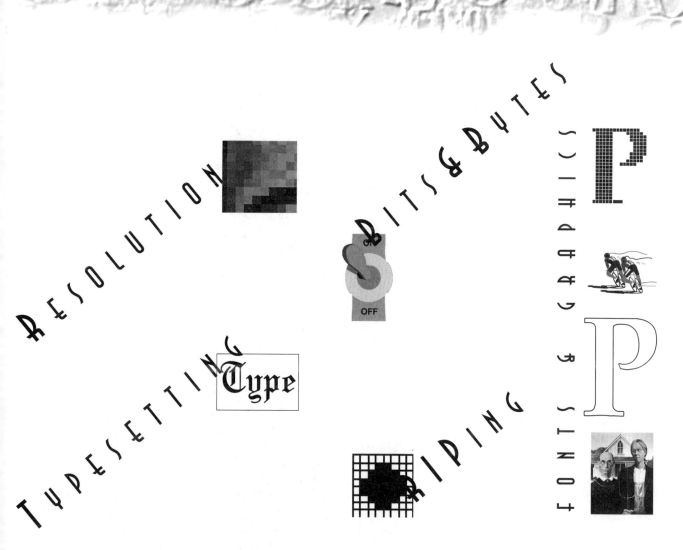

RESOLUTION

TYPESETTING

Type

BITS & BYTES

ON

OFF

RIPPING

GRAPHICS

FONTS

P

P

6
Bits and Bytes

As the Byte Turns continues...

Will Danny and Pauline find a common language format with which to express themselves? Will Danny choose flowery formatting or settle for plain old ASCII??

Here is my Wordstar document with all my formatting!

Oh dear, what have I gotten myself into??

Wordstar... I haven't seen one of those files in a long time...
...I really need to give those salespeople a list of acceptable applications and make sure they use it...

Chapter Objectives

In this chapter you will learn:

◆ **History of communications technology overview**
◆ **Difference between analog and digital devices**
◆ **Building blocks of words**
◆ **Building blocks of graphics**
◆ **Static vs. dynamic media**
◆ **Key Terms**
  • Analog
  • Digital
  • Digitize
  • bit
  • bit depth or pixel depth
  • Bitonal
  • Byte
  • ASCII
  • Kilobit and Megabit
  • KiloByte and MegaByte
  • GigaByte
  • TeraByte
  • Data blocks
  • Static media
  • Dynamic media

INTRODUCTION

Whenever we attempt to reproduce images, whether it is in the form of text, line art, or grayscale or color contone images, we are always faced with the challenges inherent with reproducing original materials. Every step or process we apply to an image threatens to change the original nature of, or reduce the quality of the original image. The history of communications technology has been a struggle to do two things, make the distribution of information and ideas easier and more widely distributed, while at the same time maintaining the integrity and quality of the original information or images.

As we all know the invention and subsequent refinement of the printing press has long been considered one of the hallmarks of civilization. The printed page allowed us to widely distribute information and ideas in an economical fashion. Subsequent development of electronic media such as telegraph, radio, telephone and television further enhanced our ability to communicate. While each of these technologies has been a boon for human communication, most of the technology was controlled by professionals: professional printers, telegraph operators, TV technicians and the like. Each of these communication technologies was a separate discipline which required years of study to master. Control of communications technology was out of reach for the average nonprofessional. The advent of desktop computer technology and the subsequent evolution of the electronic document and the birth, growth and continued evolution of the Internet and the World Wide Web has changed all that. We now have access to many forms of communications technologies through our desktop computers. With access to this control however, we now also share the challenge of controlling the technologies in order to achieve the results we would like.

TWO WORLDS

Analog vs. digital devices and data

The key to understanding how a computer works is to appreciate how a computer manipulates and stores information. A computer is a **digital** device; that is, it only understands information which is represented or recorded in a two-part code like "off and on" or "up and down." A computer does not understand continuous uninterrupted streams of information like light waves, sound waves, or a continuous tone photograph. These are **analog** or continuous forms of information or data. For information to be comprehensible to a computer, it must first be placed in a two-part code of information, or what is commonly referred to as "**digitized**." Two good examples of pairs of devices which clearly show the difference between analog and digital devices are types of clocks and light switches (see Fig. 6.1). A clock which has sweep second, minute, and hour hands is an analog device. It continuously shows the passage of time. The record of the analog watch can be broken into an infinite number of intermediate data (hand) positions. In contrast, a wristwatch which relies on LCD (liquid crystal display) technology is a digital device. It shows the passage of time in discrete increments, usually seconds, and records only a limited number of data positions. Both clocks perform the same function, recording the passage of time, but one does so in an analog fashion, the other digitally. Another common example of analog vs. digital devices can be seen by comparing an on-off light switch to a dimmer switch. The on-off switch is a digital device. It has only two positions or data points which it can represent—on or off. By contrast, the dimmer switch is an analog device. It too can be in on and off positions, but it can be in an infinite number of positions or points in between. One of the advantages of recording and manipulating data digitally is that information can be recorded and manipulated with a limited number of discrete data points rather than the infinite number of points required by analog devices.

Data which is in analog form, such as sound, light, text, painted or drawn graphics, must be digitized before it can be recognized, manipulated, and stored in a computer. Hence, we have data such as digital sound on CDs, digital images such as PhotoCDs, and digital video. Each of these forms of data results from the transformation of original analog information to digital data which can be used in a computer. A common analog-to-digital translation which many of us use is the modem. The word "modem" is short for modulate/demodulate. At a computer station which is sending information across phone lines, a modem's job is to translate, or modulate, the outgoing digital "off/on" information. The modem translates this digital information into an analog wave form which much of our present tele-

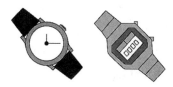

Analog vs. Digital Clocks

Analog vs. Digital Switches

▼ *Figure 6.1 Analog vs. Digital* Analog devices usually have a continuously varying mechanism such as a sweep second hand on a watch or rheostatic dial. Digital devices, in contrast, usually have only two settings, an "On" and an "Off" position. With digital mechanisms, small changes in settings or values are accomplished by creating small differences between the "On" and "Off" positions.

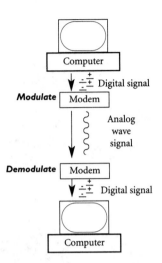

▼ Figure 6.2 Analog to Digital
When we work on digital systems, we are often required to communicate with or transfer information to nondigital, analog systems. A common example of this is when we send files over regular phone lines. The switching equipment used by phone companies is often analog and does not "understand" digital data. When we attempt to send data through these analog systems, we must convert our digital signals into analog signals. These analog signals are then reconverted into digital signals at the other end of the connection. This conversion from digital to analog and back again is accomplished by modems. The word "modem" is shorthand for modulate/demodulate.

phone switching equipment understands. At the receiving end of the phone line the modem's job is to digitize, or demodulate, the incoming signal (see Fig. 6.2). As more of our telephone switching systems become digital, the need for modems will be reduced. One day in the digital future we will look back at these quaint little devices and marvel at how we got along with this complex, slow signal translation, much like we look back at the telegraph today. We have witnessed the gradual transition of one analog communication technology after another being converted into digital form. It started with type, then static graphics, then sound; even video and other multimedia communication technologies have gone digital. Eventually all segments of our communications system will be digital.

One of the the fundamental advantages of a digital format is the enormous increase in flexibility which results once a medium has been digitized. For example, with an image which is on a piece of film, we are very restricted as to what we can easily do with this image. Once that image has been digitized we can easily perform any number of manipulations, such as geometric manipulations, like cropping, scaling, rotating and skewing, and image editing transformations such as brightness, contrast, sharpening, color correction and even image combinations within seconds on a computer. digitizing media also allows us to much more easily combine and interact once-separated media such as graphics, sound and animation.

BASIC COMPUTER LANGUAGE

When someone mentions computer language or programming, many of us recoil because of our perspective that such a language is arcane and difficult. While it is true that the details of some programming may be arcane, the basics of computer language are rather simple. In fact, if you have mastered any other language, including English, then the fundamentals of computerese will be a snap. Don't believe me? Here's proof. How many characters are there in the English language? Twenty six (26), right? Right. Well, there are only two (2), that's right, two, in computerese. In addition, in computer language there are no double meanings or shades of understanding. Computerese is very straightforward: it's all "0s" and "1s! This two character alphabet is known as binary code, and is the foundation for all elements created on a computer. All the applications you work with—the text and graphic images you see on screen and print out, and the operating systems which allow you to operate your computer—are constructed out of sequences of just two characters: zero (0) and one (1). For instance, a simple black and white graphic of a black box surrounded by a white border (Fig. 6.3) is constructed out of dots or pixels which are assigned values of 0 for white pixels and 1 for black pixels. More complex graphics are built the same way, just with more complex sequences of 0s and 1s. Each 0 or 1 is known as a **bit**, designated with a lowercase b. This assignment of 0s and 1s works fine for any solid areas including solid colors. These 0s and 1s can just as easily be assigned to represent Pantone spot colors as they can represent black and white areas. We will discuss how we generate continuous tone grayscale and color images a little later. By the way, our exclusive use of 0s and 1s is why we refer to our computers as being digital and our basic computer code as binary. Both "digital" and "binary" refer to the basic two-character format (0,1) which these computers and their applications understand.

Graphic formats

Basic building blocks: binary code

The most fundamental building block of digital graphic images is a pixel. The simplest kind of pixel is a square which is assigned a single bit value of one (1) or zero (0). These are known as 1-bit pixels because they are only assigned values of either one or zero. The size of a pixel is determined by the resolution of the file of which it is a part. These 1-bit per pixel square building blocks can be assembled, like bricks, to create a wide variety of graphic line art images. Figure 6.3 shows how these simple 1-bit pixels can be assembled to create a black square with a white border. Note how the image is constructed from building blocks which are assigned values of either zero (0) or one (1), the only two values your computer understands. Later we will see how multi-bit per pixel images recreate continuous tone images. The number of bits per pixel which an image has is know as the **bit depth** of that pixel. A simple black and white image, such as that shown in Fig 6.3, has one bit per pixel and therefore has a bit depth of one (1). We will also see, in Chapter 9, "Grappling with Graphics," how pixel-based images can be converted into vector-based images.

> Think of basic graphic images as being like digital brick walls. The basic building bricks are square pixels, or pixel-bricks in this analogy. We assign bits values to these pixels to control their value. For instance we can assign a bit value of "1" for black and bit value of "0" for white. We can build images by constructing walls of these pixel-bricks. Later, in Chapter 9, "Grappling With Graphics," we will see that we can combine multiple rows of these pixel-bricks and assign various numbers of bits to our pixels to create a wide variety of grayscale and color images.

Bit depth

In the above example we created an image which was a simple black and white image. We created this image by assigning a single bit, either "0" or "1," to each pixel. With this simple assignment of either a "0" or "1" to our pixels, we can only create a simple black and white, known as a **bitonal** or two tone, image. If we assign more than one bit per pixel, we can create images with more than two shades of gray. The number of bits per pixel, known as bit depth or **pixel depth**, controls the number of shades of gray which an image can have. We will explore this concept of bit depth vs. shades of gray in more depth in Chapters 8, 9, 12, and 16.

Text formats

Straight text

Assigning bit values to text characters presents a challenge. There are 26 characters plus punctuation marks and other control characters in the English language, but there are only two computer characters, 0 and 1, which can be used to represent all of these characters. The solution to this dilemma has been to assign standardized

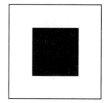

▼ Figure 6.3 Digital Graphic Data
Graphics are captured, created, stored, and transmitted in the form of "0"s and "1"s. This figure shows how a simple black and white graphic would be constructed out of "0"s and"1"s. This type of graphic would be called a 1 bit graphic, because each pixel, or square, is composed of just one bit (0 or 1) of information. More complex graphics will contain multiple bits (8, 24, or 32) per pixel.

sequences of 0s and 1s together in groups of 8. Each standard sequence of 8 bits is equivalent to a specific numeric or alphabetic character, punctuation mark, or control character such as a line break indicator. Each 8-bit sequence is known as a **Byte** and is designated with an uppercase B. An example of this one Byte = one character system can be found by looking at the Byte equivalents of upper- and lowercase "a." Uppercase "A" = 1000001 while lowercase "a" = 1100001. Notice that a substitution of a 1 for a 0 in the second bit position of the Bytes is all that distinguishes "A" for "a" in the code list. So when we type "Shift A" on a computer keyboard, the bit sequence 1000001 is sent to RAM for immediate use and may be stored on a storage drive for later retrieval. This bit sequence is recognized by our application software as uppercase "A" and displayed and printed accordingly on our monitors and printers.

The complete list of sequences which have been assigned to all these characters is known as the **ASCII** character set. ASCII is an acronym for American Standard Code For Information Interchange (a complete list of the ASCII code sequences can be found in the appendix). There are several advantages to using a standard code such as ASCII. First, by having a tiny standard code for each character, we do not need to have a unique code every time we create a character. This keeps text file sizes very small. More importantly, having a standard code for text characters allows us to transport files easily from one computer or application to another and be confident that those files can be recognized. This ASCII code is the format in which raw text files are saved when you save a file as "Text" or "Text Only" or "Text Only with Line Breaks." This raw text file format retains all of the character information, such as numbers, letters, punctuation, and line returns, but discards any other formatting information such as typestyle, size, or paragraph format information. The ASCII text format is the lowest common denominator for text files and is what provides us with the basic text file transfer capabilities which we enjoy.

Formatted text

Each application such as Microsoft Word or QuarkXpress uses its own proprietary formatting code, which is added to the basic ASCII code sequences, for applying character and paragraph formatting to basic text. For instance, the following sequence represents additional code which QuarkXpress uses to assign formatting information:

[@Normal:<*p(7.2,0,0,16,0,3.6,g,"U.S.English")$z14f"Helvetica-Bold">Peaceful Coexistence].

This code indicates that the following formatting will be applied to the words "Peaceful Coexistence:" 14pt B Helvetica Bold with 16pts. of leading, a 7.2 pt. left indent, and a 3.6 pt. space after the paragraph. All of this formatting code is unique to QuarkXpress and cannot be interpreted by other applications without the use of a specific QuarkXpress filter. If this text were saved in straight ASCII format, all that would be saved would be the words "Peaceful Coexistence," but this copy could be imported and interpreted by most other applications without the need for a special filter. So for practical purposes, any time you want to transfer some copy from one computer or application to another and you are not sure if the receiving end will be able to "read" your formatted file, save your text in ASCII or "Text Only" format and you will be assured of transferability.

If you need to send formatted text, another option is to use RTF, or Rich Text Format. RTF is a commonly accepted text file format for formatted text. RTF files can be read by most word processors and many other applications. Ask the person who will be receiving your file if the application can interpret RTF files. Any time you send a formatted text, it is advisable to send along a proof of the formatted copy to show what the text looks like.

COMPUTERESE DEFINED

The basics of Bits, Bytes, and ASCII

bit (b)
The smallest unit of the digital or binary computer language, either a 0 or a 1

Byte (B)
A binary number which defines a computer character such as the number "1" = 8 bits

Kilobit (Kb)
One thousand (1,000) bits or 1000 0s or 1s

Megabit (Mb)
One million (1,000,000) bits = 125,000 bytes
(1,000,000 bits ÷ 8 bits/bytes = 125,000 bytes)

KiloByte (KB)
One thousand (1,000) bytes or characters

MegaByte (MB)
One million (1,000,000) bytes or characters

GigaByte (GB)
One billion (1,000,000,000) bytes or characters

TeraByte (TB)
One trillion (1,000,000,000,000) bytes or characters (a relatively new term used to refer to very large storage drive capacities. This term will become more commonly used in the future.)

Bit depth
Number of bits per pixel (also known as pixel depth and color depth).
- 1 bit per pixel = B&W (bi-tonal image)
- 8 bits per pixel = 256 shades of grayscale 2^8
- 10 bits per pixel = 1,024 shades of grayscale 2^{10}
- 12 bits per pixel = 4,096 shades of grayscale 2^{12}
- 14 bits per pixel = 16,384 shades of grayscale 2^{14}

bits or Bytes/sec (bps or Bps, Kbs, MBs)

Data transfers rate in terms of bits/sec. Bytes/sec., Kilobits/sec., MegaBytes/sec., etc.

ASCII

American Standard Code for Information Interchange. A code which translates binary numbers into number, letter, symbol, or control characters. ASCII or "text only" files is a format in which text files can be saved and nearly universally translated and read on a wide variety of computer platforms, operating systems, and applications. This standardized text character code also allows us to have very small text files because of the standardized repeating characters.

Examples of ASCII code character translations

A = 1000001   a = 1100001   1 = 0110001   ! = 0100001

TIP

When working with the text components of a document, if you want to transfer just the text characters, and retaining the formatting is not important, then save your file as a "Text Only" file. This is also know as an "ASCII" file. Some applications refer to these as "Text Only" and some will actually designate "ASCII" file. By utilizing an ASCII format you are not only creating a minimal sized file, but are creating a file which can be "read" or recognized by most computers, operating systems and applications which we use in electronic publishing. If you want to retain your basic text formatting, then consider using RTF (Rich Text Format). While not quite as universal as ASCII, RTF is still fairly widely accepted by many applications and has the advantage of maintaining basic formatting.

Examples of ASCII code word translations

English Language Words: Avoiding the Output Blues

ASCII equivalent: 1000001 1110110 1101111 1101001 1100100 1101001 1101110 1100111 100000 1010100 1101000 1100101 100000 1001111 1110101 1110100 1110000 1110101 1110100 100000 1000010 1101100 1110101 1100101 1110011 Note that 100000 designates a space.

These make up the 25 characters (including spaces) of *Avoiding The Output Blues.*

A complete list of ASCII characters can be found in the appendix. Remember, even text files can change dramatically when transferred from one computer to another, so your hard copy proof serves as insurance for you.

ASCII, PostScript and HTML

ASCII is not only used as a file format for transferring text, it is used as a standard text format for a variety of other purposes including being used as the standard code text for PostScript (print language) files and HTML (Web language) documents. Following is a typical code string used in an PostScript file to designate a specific document component, in this case a color specification:

```
%%BeginFile: lw8_level1_colorspace-2.0
```

```
/G/setgray ld
/:F1/setgray ld
/:F/setrgbcolor ld
/:F4/setcmykcolor
```

Similarly ASCII is used in HTML documents to designate specific document components of Web pages such as the following sequence which designates the beginning of a Web page:

```
<HTML><HEAD><TITLE>TTALLYHOME<TITLE></HEAD>
<BODY BGCOLOR>="#000000"
BACKGROUND="..images/homerhome.gif">
```

In circumstances such as these, text formatting is completely unimportant and would only represent unwanted code overhead, so the simplest text formatting possible is used, straight ASCII. See the appendix for a complete listing of the 128 basic ASCII binary code sequences and their character equivalents.

Data transfer rates

When digital files are transferred from once place to another, for example from one drive to another on the same computer, or from one computer to another across a local network or even across the Internet, we discuss the transfer of this data in terms of number of **data blocks** bits per unit time. The rate at which data is transferred is often calculated in terms of the bits or Bytes (the data blocks) per second. Typical transfer rates units include Kilobits per second (Kbs), often used for modem transmission, and MegaBytes per second (MBs), often used to refer to drive or fast network file transfers. When discussing transfer rates be sure to keep your bits and Bytes straight. Remember that a Byte is eight time (8x) larger than a bit. If you designate bit (b) when you really mean Byte (B) you will be making a eightfold (8x) error in data transfer rates.

Static vs. dynamic media

Like basic text and graphic images, more complex media such as sound, animation, and video are, once digitized, also rendered into bits of information. Basic text and graphics images are **static media,** that is they do not change over time. Media such as sound, animation, and video are **dynamic media,** which have a time component to them. Once we understand the basic building blocks of our text and graphic static media, it becomes easier for us to understand and then control other forms of digital media such as dynamic media like sound and animation. Sound and animation files, like basic text and graphics, are discussed in terms of their file sizes. In addition to dynamic media we usually refer to some sort of delivery rate such as frames per second. This time-sensitive component is added to our understanding of the the nature and file size of the medium piece when we consider its creation, storage, transfer and use.

CHAPTER SUMMARY

In the world of electronic publishing all document components are rendered into fundamental digital building blocks knows as bits. The word digital refers to two values, in this case "0" and "1." All text and graphics images are ultimately constructed out of only these two values, "0" and "1." Digitizing our media dramatically increases the flexibility of use of our text and images. Having this standardized text sequence allows us to transfer our text file more easily than if each computer had its own text code. Basic graphic images are constructed from square pixel building which are assigned bit values to designate their grayscale values. Simple black and white, or bi-tonal, images will use single "1" and "0" bit assignments to designate black and white values.

More shades of gray can be contained in a pixel-based image by increasing the number of bit per pixel, or bit depth, of the image. Text characters are constructed from standard eight bit sequences of ("0s" and "1s") know as Bytes. The standard set of sequences is know as the ASCII set, which is used to define all the basic alpha and numeric as well as basic punctuation marks used in standard language. ASCII text files can be created when sharing of text files is required. ASCII coded text is nearly universal in acceptance on most computers, operating systems and applications we use in electronic publishing.

We use the number of bits or Bytes which any text element or graphic image has to designate its size. Text files tend to be much smaller than graphic files due to the use of the standardized ASCII characters to designate text characters. Terms such as Kilo, Mega and Giga are typically used to refer to thousands, millions and billions of bits or Bytes contained in a text or graphic file. Static media digital files such as text and graphics are usually discussed in terms of their files sizes. When discussing the transfer of files we usually add a time unit to our file sizes to indicate transfer rates. Typical transfer rates include designating the number of bits or Bytes per second which will be transferred. Examples include Kbps (Kilobits per second) and MBps (MegaBytes per second). It is important to be careful when designating the bits (b) or Bytes (B) per second, because using a "b" (bit) when you really mean to use a "B" (for Byte) will translate into an eightfold (8x) error. On our electronic publishing systems we can work with both static and dynamic media digital files. Dynamic media files such as sound and animation contain critical time components which relate to the delivery of that media file over a period of time.

PAULINE'S DIGITAL IMAGING TIPS

Pauline's Tip 6.1

All text and graphic images in a digital file are constructed out of two values: zeros (0s) and ones (1s). The fundamental building block of graphic images is the pixel which, in its simplest form, is assigned a single bit value of either a zero (0) or one (1). More complex pixels can be assigned multiple bit per pixel values. The basic building block for text is a Byte, which contains eight (8) bits. Each Byte represents one character such as an "A" or a "b." Graphic images and text are composed of combinations of bits and Bytes. It is useful to think of your text and graphic images as combinations of bits and Bytes, as this will facilitate your understanding of how your text and graphic tools work when you are constructing and editing digital documents.

Pauline's Tip 6.2

When sending a text file to be output, be sure that your service bureau or printer can interpret or "read" your text file format. It is best to send an unformatted ASCII or Text Only file which can be universally recognized and interpreted. If you need to send formatted text, be sure to confirm the platform, application name, and version of the application used to create the text file (e.g., Windows WordPerfect, version 5.0). If you are unsure of compatibility, send the text file as an ASCII or Text Only file. Another option is to use RTF, or Rich Text Format, which is a commonly translatable form for formatted text. Even simple formatted text files can change when opened up on another computer, so if you send formatted text, it is a good idea to send a laser proof of the text to provide a visual example of what you intended.

Pauline's Tip 6.3

When referring to the transfer rates of files, we should properly designate both data block size and time unit. It is especially important to be careful about the data block unit size which we designate. If we use bits per second (bps) when we really mean Bytes per second (Bps) we will be making an eightfold error in our transfer speed calculations. Remember that a Byte is constructed out of eight bits and is therefore eight times larger. This is a common mistake which can be avoided by careful attention to the units we use.

CHAPTER REVIEW

Check Your Comprehension

Multiple Choice Questions

To help you review the topics covered in this chapter, answer the following multiple choice questions.

1. Which of the following best describes the transition the communications industry has been going through in the last ten years?
   A. Digital technologies to analog technologies
   B. Analog to digital technologies
   C. Analog to super analog technologies
   D. None of the above

2. Which of the following is an example of an analog device?
   A. A watch with a sweep second hand
   B. A light with a variable control switch
   C. A radio knob which you turn to change radio stations
   D. All of the above

3. Why is computer language easier to learn than English?
   A. Computer language only has 2 characters
   B. English has 26 characters
   C. Computerese is more straightforward
   D. All of the above

4. Which of the following is an example of a digital device?
   A. A watch with a LCD readout
   B. A handle you use to roll up a car window
   C. A rotary dial phone
   D. None of the above

5. A bit is
   A. 0 or 1
   B. The smallest building block unit of digital files
   C. The building block of a Byte
   D. All of the above

6. A Byte is
   A. 11101101
   B. Composed of eight bits
   C. The building block of the ASCII character set
   D. All of the above

7. _____ refers to the number of bits per pixel.
   A. bits
   B. Bytes
   C. bit depth
   D. ASCII characters

8. Which of the following is used in creating universally readable Text Only files?
   A. PostScript
   B. HTML
   C. HPGL
   D. ASCII

9. Which of the following is used in the writing of code for PostScript print files and HTML Web documents where text formatting is unimportant?
   A. Tiff
   B. ASCII
   C. HPGL
   D. EPS

10. Which term would be used to designate a file which was 40 million Bytes in size?
    A. 40TB
    B. 40GB
    C. 40KB
    D. 40MB

11. Which accurately represents a data transfer rate of 28,800 bits per second?
    A. 28.8 Kbs
    B. 28.8 KBs
    C. 28,8000 KBs
    D. 28,8000 MBs

12. An animation file is an example of which of the following?
    A. Static media
    B. Semidynamic media
    C. Dynamic media
    D. None of the above

Check Your Understanding

Concept Questions

To help you review and expand your thinking on the topics covered in this chapter, answer the following questions.

1. Briefly explain the difference between analog and digital devices. Give an example of each.

2. What does the term digitize mean? How does the term modem fit into this discussion?

3. Explain the difference between a bit and a Byte.

4. What do digital images and brick walls have in common?

5. What is ASCII and why is it important?

6. Why are text files usually much smaller than graphic files?

7. To what do the terms Kilo, Mega, Giga, and Terra refer? What are the meanings of these three terms?

8. How is an ASCII text file document different than most documents which contain text? How does an ASCII document differ from an RTF document?

9. When we refer to the transfer of digital data, what must our units of measurements contain, and what must we be careful about?

10. What is the difference between static and dynamic media?

PROJECTS

1. Calculate the amount of time it should take to send a 10MB file via modem at a rate of 28.8Kbs. Hint: You must first calculate the number of bits in the 10MB file.

2. How much faster would the above file be transferred if we sent it at a rate of 1Mbs?

7
Basic Computer Skills

As the Byte Turns continues…

Will Pauline help Danny clean up his system, improve his habits, and find true love in the process, or will she just tick Danny off?

I'm having all sorts of problems with my computer: I keep losing files, my HD crashed, my system bombs, I'm slow, and my wrist hurts!

WOW, it sounds like you have a lemon system.

I knew I didn't want to get a computer!

Does Danny have a lemon?

No. But it does sound like Danny needs to clean up his system folder, manage his files better, institute backups, and start working more from his keyboard.

Chapter Objectives

In this chapter you will learn:

- ◆ **Basic computer control skills**
- ◆ **The advantage of keyboard control**
- ◆ **Thinking in layers**
- ◆ **The importance of keeping organized**
- ◆ **Good file management skills**
- ◆ **Performance tips**
- ◆ **The importance of a boot disk**
- ◆ **Key Terms**
  - G.U.I.
  - Layers
  - System file
  - Boot disk
  - Minimization
  - Application file vs. document files
  - Font files vs. utility files
  - Saving
  - Backup vs. archive
  - Virus
  - Scratch disk and virtual memory
  - Preference file

INTRODUCTION

Computers are only as good as the people who run them. As fast and wonderful as our modern computers are, they still depend upon us for instructions on what to do and how to do it. Computers may eventually inherit the Earth, but for now they still depend upon us. To get the most out of our computers we need to learn how to operate and manage them as quickly and efficiently as possible.

When first learning to operate a computer the use of a mouse and menus is essential. Mousing around through menus is a great way to become familiar with and learn how to use a computer or an application. However, once you become familiar with a particular operating system or application, it is best to learn how to control your computer through the use of the keyboard. Keyboard control is many times faster than mousing around.

Nearly all applications provide layers of items for us to work with, whether it is layers of windows in our operating system or layers of text and graphics in a page layout application. Unfortunately our monitors only provide us with mostly a two dimensional (2D) view of our three dimensional(3D) layers. Our applications use overlapping windows and opacity to help us "view" the third dimension, but it is not entirely satisfactory. Therefore we have to provide the third dimension in our our minds.

One key to efficient work on a computer is good organization. A well organized computer with a complete and consistent file organization and naming system is the key to being able to locate your documents quickly and easily. It is well worth the time you spend to develop a file management system, and then stick to it.

About thirty percent (30%) of the files which come automatically loaded on your computer when you purchase it you will never use. Many applications load all sorts of extra files which you do not need and will never use. All these extra files, particularly those which end up in your operating system folders, not only take up space but they slow down the performance of your computer, sometimes dramatically. Removing unnecessary files also reduces the potential for file conflicts which slow down and often crash our computers. **Minimization**, that is the removal of unwanted or unnecessary files, is one of the keys to speed and smooth operation of your computer-based publishing system.

THE FUNDAMENTALS

Four basic skills

Point

This skill involves moving your mouse, which in turn moves a cursor across your computer monitor/desktop. This movement of the cursor allows you to point at any icon or file you wish to manipulate. This skill is also used as a first step toward accessing menus and responding to dialog boxes.

Point and single-click

This skill is used for selecting any icon, file, or response button. After moving your cursor to a desired location by pointing, single-clicking on an icon or file allows you to select or activate that item. If the item you are pointing at happens to be a dialog box, clicking on the button will complete a response to that button. Some common examples include clicking the "OK" button found in many dialog boxes and accessing menus.

Point and double-click

This skill is used for opening or launching items such as disks, applications, and document files. In the case of type, double-clicking on text will usually select that text. When you double-click on an application it will launch. When you double click on a document this will first launch the application which was used to create the document and then the document itself.

Point, click, hold, and drag

This skill is used for many purposes including moving items, accessing menu choices, resizing items, selecting areas, and drawing items. The context determines the results. Dragging an item on the same disk will move an item, while dragging from one disk to another will result in the copying of that item to the second disk.

Advanced skills

Back to the keyboard

Many of the skills and manipulations discussed above can be accomplished more quickly and easily through the use of keyboard commands. It may seem contradictory for me to send you back to the keyboard after the last chapter, when I made such a point about how easy it is to use a **GUI** with a mouse and menus, but that's exactly what I'm going to do. While using the mouse, menus and icons to navigate around and manipulate your computer is a terrific way to learn how to use your computer, it is also a relatively slow way to operate it. After you have become comfortable with your computer interface, begin to leave your mouse behind and learn keyboard shortcuts. Keyboard manipulation is two to four times faster than mouse manipulations in many circumstances. And you do not have to be a touch typist to be fast with keyboard manipulations, though it really helps to develop efficient and consistent hand positions. Many applications such as Photoshop and QuarkXPress include a keyboard shortcut reference card which contains most of the keyboard

▼ *Figure 7.1 ShortCut Home Position*
The fastest way to control your computer is from the keyboard rather than with the mouse. As with touch typing, a standard home position with finger placement and movement helps increase the speed and accuracy of keyboard controls. Shown here is a Macintosh keyboard. A Windows keyboard is similar but instead of COMMAND and OPTION keys, a Windows keyboard has CONTROL and ALT keys. The COMMAND and CONTROL and OPTION and ALT keys usually match up in terms of their use between the Mac and Windows platform. Shown here is a good HOME position for your hands when using keyboard shortcuts for controlling your applications. Index = Index finger; M = Middle finger; Ring = Ring finger; Thumb = Thumb.

shortcuts for those applications. Many applications have an organization or structure to their keyboard shortcuts. Take some time to figure out the keyboard shortcut structure and it will make learning them less tedious. Programs such as Photoshop allow you to assign, using Actions, your own Photoshop keyboard short cuts. Programs such as "QuickKeys" allow you to make your own keyboard shortcuts in any applications.

Keyboard position

While it is not possible in the space available here to teach you the entire Tazmanian Whirlwind keyboard method, I can at least get you started down the right path. I use a home position, similar to the idea of a home position used in touch typing for characters. Specific fingers are assigned to specific ShortCut keys. The ShortCut keys include the command (ALT key on Windows) OPTION, CONTROL, SHIFT, RETURN, ENTER, ARROW, and LOCATION keys (located above the ARROW keys).

Macintosh and Windows-based keyboards are very similar with the exception that Windows keyboards have an ALT rather than an OPTION key, and a CONTROL rather than a COMMAND key. The CONTROL key on a Windows keyboard generally performs the same function as the COMMAND or APPLE key on a Macintosh keyboard. Figure 7.1 shows the basic keyboard ShortCut home position

 **TIP**

Using your mouse and menus is a good way to learn how to use an application. But after you ar familiar with how an application works, graduate to using keyboard shortcuts to control as many tools, menus and dialog boxes as possible. Using keyboard shortcuts is much faster than using mouse and menu controls and far less frustrating, particularly for controls which reside in submenus! Many applications such as QuarkXPress, PageMaker, InDesign and others contain extensive built-in series of keyboard shortcuts. Other applications like Photoshop provide you with easy ways to make your own shortcuts.

with the fingers in their proper places. Using home keys allows you to work much more quickly and accurately without having to look down at the keyboard. The ShortCut home position can be used along with the typing home position by just shifting back and forth between the two home positions. (Note: I've developed a special Tazmanian Whirlwind keyboard method which you can learn on my video "Speed Techniques and Keyboard Shortcuts," which will speed you up noticeably in all your applications. See the resource list in the back of this book for information on how to obtain this training video.)

Think layers

Window layers

Many windows can be open at the same time but only one at a time can be active. A window can be activated—that is, brought to the front—by pointing and clicking on that window.

Graphics layers

Multiple **layers** in graphic creation and editing applications such as painting and drawing applications such Photoshop and Illustrator provide great flexibility when constructing and editing graphic images. Layer palettes within these applications

▼ **Figure 7.2 Layers**
Most applications support the use of layers. Layers such as those found in this multilayered Photoshop image allow us to construct and edit complex images and documents much more easily. Though we can really only see in two dimensions on our monitors, we must visualize the third dimension so that we can effectively take advantage of its construction and editing advantages. Palettes such as this Layers palette in Photoshop help us visualize as well as create and manipulate these layers.

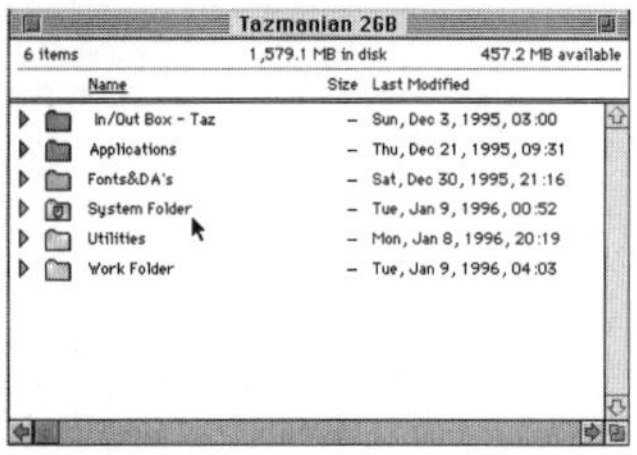

▼ *Figure 7.3 The System Folder*
The system folder holds all of the files which are essential to you allowing you to interact with and control your computer. The system folder should be modified only after careful deliberation.

▼ *Figure 7.4 Application Icons*
In both Windows (top) and Mac (bottom) each application has its own icon. The icon symbols tend to reflect the type of tool that it is. For instance the Photoshop icon shows an image, indicating that it is an image editing application. Notice the name shortcut at the beginning of the two lower Windows icons, and the italicized name on the Mac InDesign icon, indicating that these are proxy shortcut or alias icons which are linked to the actual application file located somewhere else on the computer.

allow us to view, select and reorder and control the interaction between the various layers (see Fig 7.2).

Page element layers

Each element (whether text or graphic) you place on a document page in a page layout application such as QuarkXpress, InDesign or PageMaker, is essentially on its own layer. You need to think of your document page as a three-dimensional document with each graphics or text page construction element on its own layer. You can control the order of the items or layers on the page. Some applications (like many drawing and painting programs) allow you to actually create and manipulate distinct structural layers within a document file. Creating and using these layers can dramatically simplify both the creation and editing of documents.

FILE AND DISK MANAGEMENT

Keep organized

System files

Your system, or operating system, folder contains the software necessary for operating your computer as well as support software for many of the other applications with which you will work. On a Macintosh these **system file**s are contained in the System folder. On a Windows-based computer the system files are contained within the Windows folder. System files controls, which are mostly transparent to us, provide all of the interface controls which we use. The interface controls include the desktop, windows, folders, various icons, and dialog boxes. Your system/Windows folder should be kept as clean as possible. The system/Windows folder also commonly contains a variety of system resources such as fonts, peripheral access files (commonly known as drivers), and printing-related resources. Do not add any files to your system folder unless you are sure of what you are doing. Every file you add to your system folder which is accessed by your system requires resources such as RAM and CPU power. The more system resources your computer supports, the slower your computer will operate and the more likely you are to have operating problems. As I mentioned in Chapter 5, "Software," I organize my system extension resources into job-specific groups, such as scanning and telecommunications, and only load the resources I need for that particular job I am performing. This minimizes the utilization of CPU and RAM resources and reduces the number of system software conflicts which may occur (see Fig. 7.3).

Application files, aliases, and shortcuts

Most modern computer operating systems offer a G.U.I. (Graphical User Interface) which uses icons to represent various items stored on a computer. As part of any G.U.I. each software application has its own distinct icon, which often has a graphic symbol representing the type of tool for which the application is used. Some applications like Claris Works are generalized applications which per-

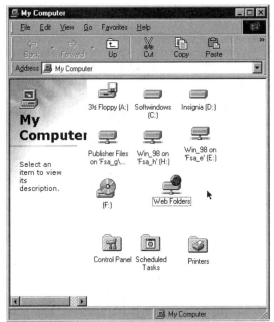

▼ *Figure 7.5 Windows Disk Icons*

Most of the operating systems used today provide a G.U.I. interface which offers the use of icons to represent various items found on the computer. Here we see Windows OS disk and folder icons.

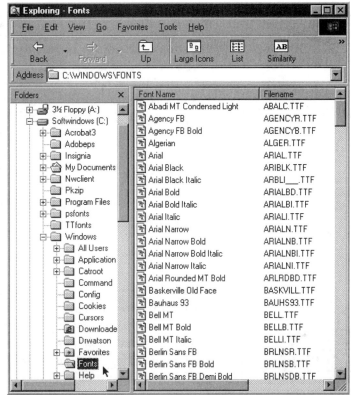

▼ *Figure 7.6 Windows System and Default Font Folders*

The Windows system folder labeled "Windows" holds all of the files which are essential to you allowing you to interact with and control your computer, including the default TrueType (.TTF) Font folder. On a Windows system PostScript fonts are stored in a separate font folder, the ps fonts folder (see Chapter 11 for more information on TrueType and PostScript fonts and their management).

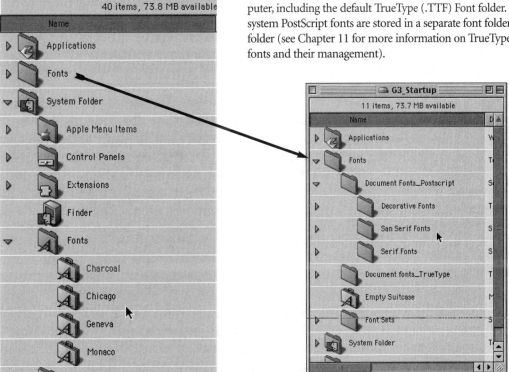

▼ *Figure 7.7 Document Construction fonts outside of the System folder.*

Shown here is an external fonts folder with font files which will be used in document construction taken out of the system folder and placed in an external folder labeled Fonts. See Chapter 11 for more information on font management.

File and Disk Management 131

form multiple functions such as word processing, database and spreadsheet, manipulation telecommunications, and drawing. Most applications used in professional electronic publishing are more narrowly focused, with sophisticated tool sets devoted to a particular set of functions such as page layout (QuarkXpress), image editing, (Photoshop), drawing (Illustrator), or Mail (Microsoft Outlook). Some icons represent the actual application, while others are merely proxies for the applications. These proxies are called aliases on the Macintosh and shortcuts in Windows. Mac aliases can be recognized by the the word alias added to the end of the application name and/or italicized type styling of the name. In Windows, shortcuts are labeled as such. Aliases and shortcuts are tiny placeholder files which are linked to the actual files located somewhere else on the computer. These proxies allow us to access the same file from multiple locations without duplicating the entire original file (see Fig. 7.4).

Font files

Font files are resources used to create type of various styles. The more fonts you have, the more varieties of ways you will have to display your text message. On most modern electronic publishing systems, fonts (like sounds) are system-wide resources; that is, they are not application-specific resources. They are available to all applications. By default font files are stored in your operating system folder, Windows folder on a Windows computer (see Fig 7.6), and the System folder on a Mac (see Fig 7.7). The font files you use to create your documents should be stored in a separate fonts folder outside of the default system font folders (see Fig. 7.8). Storing document construction fonts outside of their default system fonts folder will allow you to manage them much more easily, thereby preventing font conflicts and increasing the consistency of font use within your documents. Individual font file have icons as well (see Fig. 7.9). (See Chapter 11, "Tales of True Typesetting," for more detailed information on managing your font files.)

Document files

Document files are files created while working within applications. A simple example would be a page of text created in a word processor. Many document files show a "dog ear" on one corner of the icon. This dog ear is meant to simulate the corner of a page. Since the iconic symbols for an application file and the document file created by that application may be similar, this dog ear convention is used to make it easy to distinguishing application files from document files at a glance. Like application files, document files may be accessed though the use of aliases and shortcuts as well (see Fig. 7.9).

Utility files

Utility files are small applications which perform very specific tasks. Examples of utilities include: drive formatting, **virus** protection, disk copying, and font management software. Some utilities applications, such as Norton Utilities, may have several components to them, such as troubleshooting and disk optimization. The boundary between an application and a utility becomes blurred with multifunction utilities such as these (see Fig. 7.10).

Safety habits

Saving

Save it or lose It! Save! Save! Save! Any document which you create or any document to which you make additions or changes is not truly created or made in a physical sense until you save that document. The reason is that we work in RAM (Random Access Memory), which is an electronic environment only. If we turn off the computer, or the computer "crashes" and we have not saved creations or changes, our electronic creations will be lost. The act of **saving** a file copies the information for RAM onto a disk, usually a hard drive, which creates a magnetic copy of the information. This is not a bomb-proof version of the document, either, but at least it gives our information a physical presence. It is important that you develop good saving habits. Get in the habit of saving your file every few minutes; it is as simple as holding down the CONTROL key (Windows) / COMMAND key (Mac) and typing the character "S." This SAVING action will save whatever creations or changes which you have in RAM to a physical location on your hard drive. This same action can be initiated from the FILE menu, but is more quickly handled through the use of the keyboard shortcut. Some applications, such as QuarkXPress, have "Auto Save" functions which will automatically save your work to specified files and locations at preset intervals.

Backup and archiving

It is a smart idea to make extra copies of the files on your drives. Remember that the information on your drives is in magnetic form and is therefore susceptible to damage and loss. Backing up involves making a copy of an active file onto another disk. Archiving involves making a copy of an inactive file, one which you will not need to use in the near future, which is then removed from your active disk. Removing inactive files from your active disk helps keep your hard drive free for the use of active files. It is a good practice to have automatic **backups** made every day of your active files. Specific backup and archiving utilities are available designed specifically to help with these tasks. Manual backups are always time consuming, often inconsistent, and prone to error. An alternating sequence of M, W, F and T, Th, Sat backups on two separate media provides for multiple copies of your active data. **Archive** data on a monthly or at least a quarterly basis. Archived files can be retrieved from their stored locations. For best performance your active drives should have 50% free space. Archiving inactive files is a key to maintaining this.

Viruses

Computer viruses are usually small self-replicating files which reproduce every time they are accessed. Many computer viruses "live" in the system files where they are constantly accessed and therefore encouraged to multiply. A multiplying computer virus rapidly consumes RAM and storage space and dominates your CPU resources, bringing the operation of your computer to a crawl. Viruses are the computer version of sickness. And just like with diseases, some viruses are more dangerous than others. Infection by a computer virus can be prevented by checking every foreign file (that is, a file received via a disk or modem) with a virus-

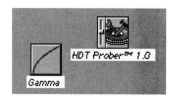

▼ *Figure 7.10 Utility Software*
Utility software is usually a single focus application intended to perform a very specific task. Shown here are icons for two utilities: Gamma, used for calibrating monitors, and HDT Prober, used for locating and mounting disks.

checking application/utility prior to launching the file. Your virus protection utility should be configured to scan and fix all files, including files on your active drives, as well as files on any removable media, other drives which you may mount over a network, and the files that arrive at your computer via Email from your local area network or the Internet.

Virus protection definitions should be updated regularly (at least monthly) so as to keep your protection current against the latest viral invasion. Most virus protection applications provide automatic updating service via the Internet.

Keep the contents of your operating system folder (System folder on a Mac, Windows folder on Windows) as lean and as clean as possible. Remove any extraneous files which are not necessary. Keeping your system folder small and clean will allow your computer to operate much faster and with fewer conflicts. Whenever a new application is loaded, beware that files are often added to your system folder. To see which files are added to my system folder, prior to installation, I paint all my current system files a color. After the installation I can easily see which files have been added to my system folder. Then I can evaluate which file to keep.

Performance tips

Be a minimalist

Less is more, or at least faster and more trouble free. It is easy to load all sorts of sounds, screen savers, and games on your computer. Many of these files add additional resources to your system folder. Each additional system resource, while adding a capability, also adds a burden by taking up RAM space, CPU time, and storage space. To help maintain a healthy and top performing computer, be ruthless about restricting the addition of unnecessary resources. If you have three rows of startup files which appear on your screen when you boot your computer, you are guilty of system abuse, and you will be punished! Resist the temptation to add those cool screen savers and nifty games. Keep your working computer pared down as much as possible. Be a minimalist!

Keep file sizes small

Graphic images often account for the lion's share of space consumed by documents on your drives. The three variables which affect the file size of an graphic images are: 1) image dimension, 2) pixel depth, and 3) resolution. When capturing or creating graphic images, keep their file size as small as possible by minimizing these variables as much as possible. Image dimension can be minimized by proper cropping. Pixel depth is the least flexible variable, but some space can be saved by not converting your RGB files to CMYK images until absolutely necessary. File resolution, the most flexible variable, can often be lowered to dramatically reduce file sizes (see Chapters 8, "Resolving Resolution," and 9, "Grappling with Graphics," for more detailed information on the relationship of image dimensions, resolution and pixel depth on file size. Also see Chapter 15, "Weaving Web Graphics," for a discussion of and tips on reducing file sizes for graphic images used on the Web).

Never work off removable media

Always copy work from removable media, such as floppy disks, Zip disks, Jaz drives, Syquests, opticals, Bernoullis (Wow, there's an old one!), and the like, to your internal hard drive before launching an application or opening a file contained on the removable disk. Most removable disks are much slower (up to 300 percent in the case of floppies) than your internal hard drive, both in terms of read/write access to and throughput of data. Also, removable media tend to be less stable than fixed hard drives, and therefore more prone to file damage and loss. This warning about working off removable media applies to using these media as **scratch disks** or **virtual memory** as well. Copying original files from removable media which you receive from a client allows you to preserve an original, untouched version of those files. This is an important C.Y.A. maneuver!

Virtual memory or scratch disk

Virtual memory is the use of storage memory, such as a hard drive, RAM or active work space. In Photoshop this is called scratch disk space. Scratch disk space is used when an application does not have enough RAM memory to perform all the tasks required. The advantage of having the ability to use scratch disk space is that if an application runs out of RAM space, instead of just quitting, the application expands into the use of the scratch disk or virtual memory space. This is an obvious advantage for systems which have limited amounts of RAM space. Not all applications can take advantage of a scratch disk. RAM-hungry applications such as most pixel editing applications (like Photoshop) are commonly built with the ability to use a scratch disk.

Using a scratch disk, however, means that you will pay a performance penalty, and often a substantial one. Reading and writing data to and from a scratch disk, which is normally meant to store data only, is usually many times slower than working in RAM. When working in virtual memory, all of an application's functions slow down. The greater the percentage of virtual memory use, the slower your application will operate. Therefore, it is generally a good idea to limit the use of virtual memory and keep most of your application functions operating in RAM.

Most graphics applications such as Photoshop, Illustrator, and FreeHand are required to use virtual memory/scratch disk space. To obtain the best possible performance and eliminate the dreaded "Sorry, out of Scratch disk space" error messages, it is preferable to assign a separate hard drive volume to be used as scratch disk space. This scratch disk volume should be at least 1GB in size on a local, fixed

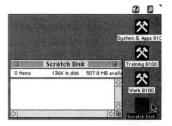

▼ *Figure 7.11 Scratch Disk Volume*
To speed up the function of virtual memory-capable applications such as Photoshop, it is advisable to dedicate a specific hard drive volume for that use. This can be either a separate individual hard drive or a separate partition of a larger drive. In either case, I always label my dedicated volume as "Scratch Disk" so that no one is tempted to store any files there. Note that the 500 MB scratch disk volume is completely empty. Do not use removable media for scratch disks, as they are generally too slow for the job.

Use a separate, fixed local hard drive as a virtual memory scratch disk for your graphics applications to use for file swapping. Using a clean dedicated scratch disk will provide better performance and minimize scratch disk errors.

media hard drive which has no other files located on it. This separate scratch disk will provide your graphics application with plenty of contiguous free space with which to work for swapping file data back and forth (see Fig 7.11). While virtual memory use can rarely be eliminated entirely, it can be reduced by utilizing plenty of RAM, and by lowering your file sizes as much as possible

In the real world of digital imaging, few of us have enough RAM to satisfy our ever-growing needs. (The digital imager's lament: You can never have too much RAM or too much hard drive space.) While it is certainly prudent to have enough RAM to meet your everyday needs, there are always times when we end up using virtual memory. Applications, whether they are utilizing real or virtual RAM, require contiguous RAM space. That is another way to say that the memory space cannot be fragmented. To be sure that you always have enough contiguous hard drive space for Photoshop and similar applications to utilize for their scratch disk needs, it is best to dedicate specific hard drive volumes for use as virtual memory—I recommend a minimum of 1GB—by either assigning a separate hard drive for use as virtual memory or to partition a larger drive and dedicate one of the partitions as a scratch disk. I actually label my virtual memory partition as "Scratch Disk" so that I do not use this drive for data storage by mistake. Either way the object is to keep a large, clean, contiguous volume of storage space available for your virtual memory-capable applications to use. Do not use removable media such as Syquests or opticals for scratch disk space as they are too slow. Dedicating a volume to scratch disk use will speed up your applications and prevent dialog boxes such as the dreaded "Can't complete this; ran out of scratch disk space" from occurring.

Preference files

One other important time-saving habit to adopt has two parts. First, always take the time to set your application preferences before you begin creating images or documents. Setting your preferences customizes your application to behave the way you want it to. Doing so can dramatically improve your efficiency. Initially set your preferences without a document open. Doing so will set the default preferences the way you want them. These defaults will be automatically used with every document you create thereafter. Your default preferences can be altered to suit the needs of any specific document once you have opened up that document. After you set your default preferences for each application you use, make copies of these files and save them in a separate folder or directory. Preference, or default, files may be found in either the same folder as the application, or in the system folder, depending upon the application. Later, if any of your **Preference files** become corrupted,

Create copies of your preference files for all your applications. When a preference file becomes corrupted, you can delete the corrupted preference file, and replace it with a copy of your backup preference file for that application. Having and using these backup replacement copies of your preference files prevents you from having to reconfigure your preferences every time one of your preference files gets corrupted. Update your backup preference files every time you make a permanent change to your application preferences.

as they are wont to do from time to time, forcing you to throw the preference file away, you can just drag a copy of the backup reference file into the appropriate preference file folder or directory, thereby saving you the time and hassle of recreating the preference file. Each time you reset your default preference file for any application, be sure to replace the copy of the preference file with a new copy.

Boot disk

One of your most valuable tools in times of computer system trouble will be a separate **Boot disk** from which you may boot or start your computer. This boot disk should contain a minimized system folder, separated document font files and a utilities folder. If you boot disk is large enough you can keep a copy of your more critical applications as well. Your utilities folder should contain disk management utilities such as Norton's Utilities as well as an up-to-date copy of your virus protection software and definitions. These utilities will be used to troubleshoot and fix disk or files problems which may arise. I also usually keep copies of most critical active files on this disk as an extra protective measure.

▼ Figure 7.12 Backup Boot Drive
It is always good to create and keep a backup boot drive handy. This drive should contain at a minimum a minimized system folder and a utility folder which contains disk and file management utilities such as Norton's Utilities, and virus protection software. If space allows, you may want to create a copy of your basic working environment with a separate fonts folder, your most critical applications and a copy of your most active files. I like to use my boot disk as a short term storage space for my most critical active files. As you can see in this figure, I also use this as one of my file backup disks.

CHAPTER SUMMARY

A computer is only as good or as fast as the person who operates it. Mice and menus are fine for learning to use a computer or application, but keyboard control is the key to control speed on a computer. Our applications provide the ability to work in three dimensional layers; we just need to visualize clearly the third dimension to take full advantage of it. Our modern operating systems which utilize G.U.I.s (Graphical User Interfaces) to display the contents of our computers make extensive use of icons to represent the various items we store on our computer drives. Items such as operating system files, font files, applications, utilities and documents all have distinctive icons which make recognizing and managing them easier. Aliases (Macintosh) and Shortcuts (Windows) provide us with small file size proxies which allow us to access applications, documents, and other elements from multiple locations without having to duplicate the original file. Organization is the key to efficient operation of your computer. Well organized and named files are a must for easy file access and retrieval.

Minimizing the number of files we have on our computer, particularly those that reside in our operating systems, can dramatically improve the speed at which our computers operate, and reduce the operating system conflicts which often plague our computers. Font files used in the construction of documents should be stored outside of the default system fonts folder to allow for easier and better font management. Save your work to a hard drive often. Unless you save your work, it will only exist in RAM and will not be retrievable if your computer freezes or crashes. Never work off removable media; copy all working files to an internal hard drive first. Perform daily backups of all your active drive files. Perform monthly archives to remove files which are not currently in use. Use and frequently update your virus protection. Use a separate hard drive volume as a dedicated scratch disk for your graphic applications like Photoshop and Illustrator. This will increase performance and decrease scratch disk errors. Creating a separate boot disk with critical system, application, and utility files is a must for providing you a way to troubleshoot and fix and disk or file problems which arise.

Pauline's Digital Imaging Tips

Pauline's Tip 7.1

Don't be a mouser; work from your keyboard. It's faster and less stress-ful. Working from the keyboard is 100 – 400 percent faster than mousing around. Working more from the keyboard will also help reduce the incidence of carpal tunnel syndrome.

Pauline's Tip 7.2

Think and work in layers. Working in layers will improve your control during the creation and editing of your graphics and page layout documents. But remember that layers also add files size, so don't get too carried away! :-)

Pauline's Tip 7.3

A computer is a great tool, but it needs management and maintenance like any other system. Keep your system up to date and be a minimalist; remove unnecessary software from your system. Be sure to save regularly and perform Save As documents several times per day. Save copies of your preference files after you configure your computer, perform regular backups to protect your data, and archive regularly to remove inactive files to keep your active drive free for current use.

Pauline's Tip 7.4

To assure the safety of your files and to maintain ample working space on your active hard drives, back up your files daily and archive your inactive files each month.

Pauline's Tip 7.5

To prevent damaging infections, use active virus protection and update your virus definitions at least each month and/or during virus outbreaks.

Pauline's Tip 7.6

Removable media like floppy disks, Zips, optical disks, and Syquest cartridges are too slow and undependable to be used for active work. Use them for storage only. So don't work off floppies and do not use removable media such as scratch disk space.

Pauline's Tip 7.7

Use a separate, local, fixed hard drive as a virtual memory scratch disk for your graphics applications. Having a separate dedicated scratch disk will improve performance and minimize out-of-scratch-disk error messages.

Pauline's Tip 7.8

Fonts files which are to be used in the creation of documents should be taken out of their default font storage folders, which are generally in the System folder, and placed in a separate folder outside of the system folder. Creating a separate fonts folder will allow for easier font management and decrease font problems.

Pauline's Tip 7.9

Create a separate boot disk with critical system, application, and utility files. This boot disk can be used to help you troubleshoot and fix any disk or file problems which arise. Being able to boot, or start, your computer from a separate disk is critical if your system becomes too damaged to start and/or fix your computer disk or files.

CHAPTER REVIEW

Check Your Comprehension

Multiple Choice Questions

To help you review the topics covered in this chapter, answer the following multiple choice questions.

1. What is generally the fastest method for controlling your computer and its applications?

    A. Mouse

    B. Menus

    C. Keyboard

    D. All about the same

2. Which of the following increases your control and flexibility when creating and editing graphics and documents?

    A. Working in multiple layers

    B. Working in one layer

    C. Type on one layer, graphics one layer

    D. None of the above

3. Which of the following are important parts of organizing and managing your files?

    A. Folder organization

    B. Complete and consistent naming system

    C. Regular backups and archives

    D. All of the above

4. Font files which are used for document creation should be stored

    A. In their default system font folders

    B. In the application folders

    C. In the active document folders

    D. In a separate fonts folder outside of the system

5. The following is (are) true about backing up and archiving.

    A. Backing up copies files to another medium storage site

    B. Archiving copies and removes files

    C. Both should be done regularly

    D. All of the above

6. _____ is required in order to actually create a physical file.

    A. Working in RAM

    B. Saving the file to a drive

    C. Working in layers

    D. Virus protecting files

7. _____ will help increase the speed of your operating system and reduce conflicts.

    A. Filling up your hard drives

    B. Minimization of system files

    C. Maximizing system software

    D. None of the above

8. Scratch disk virtual memory is best managed by

    A. Using your boot drive as a scratch disk

    B. Creating a separate hard drive scratch disk volume

    C. Using the application folder as the scratch disk

    D. Using a separate removable drive as a scratch disk

9. What should we do with preference files once we have configured them?

    A. Make backup copies

    B. Leave them alone

    C. Move them to the scratch disk

    D. Delete them

10. _____ is critical to protecting all of our computer files.

    A. Virus protection

    B. Saving our work

    C. Backing up and archiving

    D. All of the above

11. G.U.I is short for

    A. Gigabyte Utilization Instrumentation

    B. Giant Underwater Insect

    C. Graphical Utility Information

    D. Graphical User Interface

12. What do Macintosh Aliases and Windows ShortCuts have in common?

    A. They are both applications

    B. They are both small proxy files which can be used to access larger original files

    C. They are spelled the same

    D. Nothing!

13. A separate _____ is used for troubleshooting and fixing disk and file problems

    A. Scratch disk

    B. Applications disk

    C. Backup disk

    D. Boot disk

Check Your Understanding

Concept Questions

To help you review and expand your thinking on the topics covered in this chapter, answer the following questions.

1. What is the fastest way to learn how to use a computer versus the fastest way to operate a computer or software application once you have leaned how to use it?

2. Outline a good file management strategy which will allow you to easily find, access and protect all of your files.

3. Outline the advantages of working in layers.

4. What are preference files and how should they be managed?

5. What is a G.U.I and why is it important?

6. Describe at least three performance tips which you could employ to help your computer operate faster and more efficiently.

7. Define the concept of virtual memory scratch disks and explain how scratch disks should be managed.

8. What are font files? Where are they found by default on Windows and Macintosh computers? Where should document creation fonts be stored, and why?

9. Distinguish between backing up and archiving. What is the purpose of each?

10. Is it a good idea to work on files which are located on removable media? Explain why or why not.

11. What is a boot disk used for? Which files should a be boot disk contain?

PROJECTS

1. On a separate disk, create backup copy of your operating system which can be used to boot your computer. Minimize your system folder and organize your font files properly. Be sure to include a utility folder which contains file management utilities such as Norton's Utilities, and virus protection which will allow you to troubleshoot and fix any disk or file problems. Also set up a folder which can be used for backing up your files on a daily basis. Note: Using removable media is OK here since this will be an emergence disk.

2. Use a backup and archiving application to configure a file backup routine which will back up files every day of the week from Monday through Friday. Have the Monday, Wednesday, and Friday backups save the files to one disk. Have the Tuesday and Thursday backups saved to a separate disk.

3. Configure a virus protection utility so that it will scan all volumes on your computer included any removable media and any folders which receive files via your local area network or Internet.

4. Reformat and partition a drive and assign one of the partitions as a scratch disk volume which can be used by your graphics applications for swapping file back and forth into and out of virtual memory. It will be best to use a fixed media hard drive for this. After creating the scratch disk volume, be sure to assign that volume as the scratch disk in your various graphics applications such as Photoshop and Illustrator.

8
Resolving Resolution

As the Byte Turns continues…

Will Danny and Pauline be able to Resolve their differences, or will their budding relationship be RIPed apart?

My files printed fine on my 300 dpi laser printer. Why are you having problems outputting my files?

We should be able to.

Can't we print his file?

Just because a file prints at 300 dpi does not mean it will print at 2450 dpi. High resolution RIPing is much more demanding.

Chapter Objectives

In this chapter you will learn:

- ◆ **What resolution is**
- ◆ **Input and output resolution**
- ◆ **The relationship of resolution to file size**
- ◆ **The difference between spots, dots and pixels**
- ◆ **Dpi and Lpi, and shades of gray**
- ◆ **Optical vs. interpolated resolution**
- ◆ **Key Terms**
  - • Pixel
  - • Spot
  - • Dot
  - • LPI
  - • bit depth, pixel depth
  - • Input resolution and output resolution
  - • Halftone dot
  - • Halftone cell
  - • Optical resolution
  - • Interpolation

INTRODUCTION

Image resolution is one of the key characteristics of an image which determines the quality of an image during reproduction. Resolution is essentially a measure or description of how many building blocks there are in an image. Different types of image capture and output devices require different types and numbers of building blocks. We should use resolution as a concept to help us distinguish and therefore communicate about the various types and numbers of image building blocks. As critical as resolution is, there is much confusion which surrounds this topic. Confusion and misunderstanding about resolution exists mostly because we often fail to distinguish different kinds of building blocks and therefore resolutions. We tend to lump all types of image building blocks, and therefore resolution, into one big basket. Part of this lumping problem is the tendency to use the term and unit "dpi" when referring to any kind of resolution. Clarity begins to emerge when we start to separate the various building blocks and therefore types of resolution. The first and most important step in this process of resolution clarification is to separate **input resolution** from **output resolution.**

As we will see resolution requirements in electronic publishing vary widely. Input resolution ranges from a low of 72 ppi for Web images to a high of 8000 ppi for scanned images which will be scaled a large amount. Output resolution typically varies from a low of 300 dpi at 65 lpi to a high of 3600 dpi at 200 lpi. For the best results and greatest efficiency and performance it is usually critical that we match the proper input and output resolutions of the various devices with which we work. It is nearly always helpful to know how an image will be used prior to creating that image. The use of the image will usually provide us with information about both the input and output resolution requirements for that image.

RESOLVING RESOLUTION

What is resolution?

The term "resolution" has its origin in the word "resolve," which means to distinguish or discern. To resolve a difference between two opinions, we take a close look at both opinions to distinguish how they are similar or different. When we look closely at an object, we often see that it is composed of smaller building blocks. The more closely we look, the more we magnify an object or issue, the more detail we can generally see or resolve. When we look at a house from a half mile away we see only the entire object, the house. As we move closer, we see that it is composed of walls, a roof, and windows. When we look closely at one of the walls, we see that it may be made up of a repeating pattern of small bricks separated by mortar between each brick. An even closer look at the mortar reveals that it is composed of grains of sand, and so forth. In each step we have a more enlarged or magnified view of the house, and we see more detail. By resolving the components of the house, we can understand the composition of the house and how it was constructed. A close look at the brick wall can help us see how it was constructed and have a good idea how to construct one like it.

A digital image, like the brick wall, is composed of building blocks. Some images, like the brick wall, are composed of a repeating pattern of the same building blocks, such as bricks. Other images, like the house, are composed of several types of construction components such as wood and bricks. Similarly, some digital graphic images are simple and composed of one type of building block, while others are more complex and contain several varieties of building materials. Graphic images, like walls, can be made up of various sized building blocks. Some walls are composed of small bricks, others of larger cinderblocks, and some of even larger flagstones. With graphic images, the size of the building blocks determines the resolution of an image. The smaller the building block, the higher the resolution, and the finer the detail which can be shown. Some of the lowest resolution images are constructed out of **pixels** which are only 1/72 inch on each side. These images are said to have a resolution of 72 pixels per inch (ppi) and are simply referred to as 72 ppi images. Image resolutions from 72 ppi to 1200 ppi are common in electronic publishing. 72 ppi images are used for output on low resolution output devices such as monitors. Web images which will be viewed on monitors are constructed at 72 ppi. 300 ppi to 1200 ppi images are used for output to printing devices. The highest resolution images may have as many as 2400 to 3600 ppi (pixels per inch), and sometime even higher, which resolve very fine detail and can often be scaled up in size significantly. These kinds of high resolution images are generally created for output at a commercial print facility and are usually scaled prior to printing. It is important to pay attention to the final resolution of an image, after scaling, and match it to the final output device.

RESOLUTION TERMINOLOGY

Dots, spots, and pixels

There is much confusion surrounding the meaning and use of **dots, spots,** and pixels. All three terms are used when discussing resolution. All three terms refer to the building blocks of images. To sort out these terms, we need to think along the lines of two separate types of resolution, input resolution (scan or capture or input) and output resolution (print).

Input resolution

We should use the nature of the building blocks of our images to guide our use of terminology. Input resolution is used when discussing image capture, such as with scanners and digital cameras. Here we are working with pixels, not spots or dots. There is not a dot to be seen in any scanned image; nothing but pixels for as far as the eye can see! So, when discussing the resolution of pixel-based images, we should always use pixel-based terminology, such as ppi (pixels per inch) or res (pixels per mm). The term ppi is the most commonly used correct terminology, and will be used here. (Note: Some drum scanners and digital camera software use the term res, which equals pixels per mm.) The term 200 ppi refers to 200 pixels per inch. This means that our image is composed of 200 pixels in every inch, horizontally and vertically. This also means that each pixel will be 1/200th inch on a side. Many software programs, including scanning software, will use dpi when referring to their input resolution. This is wrong and confusing, but we know better! The higher the resolution of an image, the smaller and more numerous the pixels. Smaller pixels generally lead to sharper images. Smaller pixels also lead to larger file sizes and longer printing times. We usually try to strike a balance between resolution and file sizes/printing times. There are diminishing returns when we use too much resolution.

Output resolution

When we reproduce our images by printing them on laser printers, imagesetters, or other print devices, the nature of an image's building blocks changes, as should our terminology. During the printing process, our pixel-based images are converted into patterns of spots and dots. (This transformation is the job of the RIP. See Chapter 10, "RIPing Up Your File," for more details on this process.)

A dot or a spot is the building block which is used by printers to reconstruct images. So when we print we are discussing output resolution, and the proper terminology should by dots, or spots, per inch. While I prefer the term spot per inch (spi) because it is unambiguous, the commonly used terminology is dpi, although this can be easily confused with **halftone dots** per inch (more on that later). Whether you use dpi or spi the key point to remember is that this terminology refers to the size of the smallest building block which is used to print an image. The size of these spot/dot building blocks is measured in fractions of inches or mm. The smallest size dot/spot which a printer can produce determines its resolution. Hence, a printer which can produce a dot or spot which is 1/600 inch x 1/600 inch

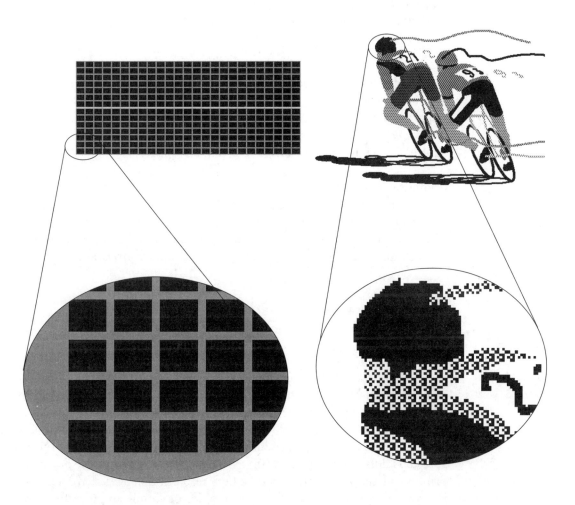

▼ *Figure 8.1 Digital File Construction*

Electronic graphic images are constructed out of either lines (vectors) or dots (bitmaps). Like a brick wall, digital bitmapped or raster graphic images are constructed out of smaller components. In the case of the wall, the construction materials are bricks. In the case of the graphic, the construction components are dots or pixels. The picture of the bicyclist above is a low resolution, 72 dpi image (paint file format) where each pixel is 1/72 inch on a side. In this image, each pixel is either black or white. The greater the number of pixels an image has, the higher its resolution. Higher resolution images are generally higher quality, but they are also more demanding in terms of processing. The key to good file preparation is to reduce the file size of an image without adversely affecting the quality of the image.

is a 600 dpi printer. Imagesetters, which are high resolution imaging devices used in printing companies to produce film and plates, typically use spots/dots which range from 1/2400" to 1/3600" across, so their resolution would be expressed as 2400 dpi/spi to 3600 dpi/spi. Here again the terminology we use coincides with the nature of the building block used to create the image.

Confusion arises when we mix up input resolution with output resolution. Match the terminology to the building blocks. Scanners don't capture spots or dots; they capture pixels. Therefore we will use ppi (pixels per inch) or res (pixels per mm). But when these pixels are printed, they are reproduced as dots or spots, so we use dots per inch for output resolution. In summary, we capture pixels, and we print dots.

RESOLUTION ISSUES

Resolution vs. file size

Most people think that a 600 dpi laser printer is twice as good as a 300 dpi laser printer. In reality, it is four times better. The reason is that dpi, dots per inch, is not as important as dpi^2, dots per square inch. A 300 dpi laser printer has 90,000 dots per square inch, whereas a 600 dpi laser printer has 360,000 dots per square inch. This is a quadruple amount of information. A 1200 dpi imagesetter must process 1,440,000 dots per square inch (in^2). This accounts for why some documents may print on a laser printer, but not on a high resolution imagesetter. Therefore, keeping your documents, especially your graphics, as simple and therefore as small as possible is important to keep in mind. See Figure 8.2 for a review of the effects of resolution on file size.

Another word used to refer to the concept of input resolution is the term "res." You may hear the terms res 12 or res 14. Res is shorthand for pixels per mm. Res 12 is equivalent to 304.8 ppi. Conversion from res to ppi is accomplished by multiplying the res number, in this case 12, by 25.4. The term res is most frequently used by people who work with high-end propriety publishing and scanning systems made by companies such as Scitex and Linotype-Hell.

RESOLUTION COMPARISON

Resolution is a square function, not a linear one. Therefore, as the line resolution doubles, the amount of data increases by a factor of four (4). For example:

• A 300 dpi laser printer prints 300 dpi x 300 dpi = 90,000 dpi2

• A 600 dpi laser printer prints 600 dpi x 600 dpi = 360,000 dpi2

This means that a 600 dpi laser creates four (4) times as much information as a 300 dpi laser.

• Calculate how much more information a 2400 dpi imagesetter must process than a 300 dpi laser.

       A 2400 dpi imagesetter produces_____dpi^2.

       This is_____times as much information as the 300dpi laser.

• Calculate the file size of an 8x10 B&W image scanned at 600 dpi.

bits(b) _____, Megabits (Mb) _____, Bytes(B) _____, MegaBytes (MB) _____

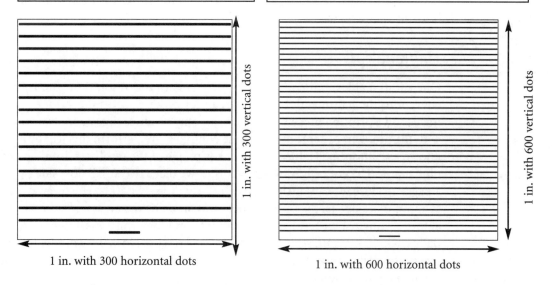

| 300 dpi Laser Printer Resolution
300 dpi x 300 dpi
This square inch represents 300 dpi horizontal x 300 dpi vertical | 600 dpi Laser Printer Resolution
600 dpi x 600 dpi
This square inch represents 600 dpi horizontal x 600 dpi vertical |

1 in. with 300 vertical dots

1 in. with 600 vertical dots

1 in. with 300 horizontal dots   1 in. with 600 horizontal dots

▼ *Figure 8.2 Resolution Comparison*

Resolution is a square, not a linear, function. As the linear resolution doubles, the square resolution, and therefore the file size, quadruples. A 300 dpi image is actually a 300 dpi x 300 dpi image with 90,000 dots per square inch. A 600 dpi image is 600 dpi x 600 dpi or 360,000 dpi^2, or four times the resolution *and file size* of the 300 dpi image.

Single and Multi-bit contone images

Besides having shape and size, pixels also contain grayscale information in the form of bits of data. A pixel can contain one or more bits of information. The number of bits of information in a pixel is know as **bit depth** or **pixel depth**. Black and white (bitonal) images have one (1) bit of information per pixel. Continuous tone (contone) images such as grayscale and color photographs, screens, and blends all require more than one bit per pixel to create them. All contone images contain one or more shades of gray. The human eye can distinguish several thousand shades of gray. In PostScript Level 1 and 2, we are limited to working with 256 shades of gray (PostScript Level 3 supports the output of more than 256 shades of gray). Because a computer is a digital device and can work with only two values, in the case of graphics those are black and white. All continuous tone images whether they are grayscale or color are treated by the computer as grayscale images. Color images like RGB or CMYK images are stored as multiple grayscale channels, three in the case of RGB and four for CMYK. In order for a digital computer to create, manipulate, and store images with multiple levels of grayscale, it must use multiple bits per pixel to create images. Grayscale, with 256 shades of gray, requires eight (8) bits per pixel to record the 256 shades of gray. RGB and CMYK color images require three and four eight (8) bit grayscale channels, respectively (one for each color), for a total of twenty-four (24) and thirty-two (32) bits per pixel, respectively. Because contone images require multiple bits-per-pixel to create, file sizes increase by the factor of the pixel depth. For instance, an eight (8) bit grayscale image is eight times the size of a one (1) bit B&W rendering of the same image. Figure 8.3 shows some examples of how file size is affected by both resolution and pixel depth. See Chapter 9, "Grappling with Graphics," for more information of bit/pixel depth.

Halftone dots

One additional level of complexity which adds to our resolution confusion is the concept of the halftone dot. Since we cannot produce continuous tone (contone) images on a printing press, because we can only produce dots or spots, we are faced with the problem of reproducing these contones. We perform this feat by a process known as halftoning. Halftoning takes advantage of the resolving limitations of the human eye. The concept is basically this: If we place two small dots side by side on a page, up close we can distinguish or resolve those two dots. However, if we begin to move that page farther and farther away, at some distance we will no longer be able to distinguish or resolve those two dots, and they will appear as one. We essentially trick the eye into seeing one dot instead of two. Now, if we gradually vary the size of the dots across an area we will simulate a gradation. It is in this way that we create the impression of tone, using dots.

The technical problem with creating halftone dots is that most laser printers and imagesetters can produce only dots or spots of fixed sizes. The solution is to combine smaller laser spots or dots in order to create halftone dots of various sizes. Figure 8.3 demonstrates this process. A halftone dot is defined by and constructed from a grid of laser spots known as a Halftone cell. Any of the cell sites can be filled in with laser spots or left blank. The greater the number of these cell sites which are filled in with laser spots, the larger the halftone dot and the darker the shade of gray simulated.

RESOLUTION GLOSSARY

Digital computer language
- Binary language has only two characters: 0 and 1
- 1 bit = Either a 0 or a 1
- 1 Byte = A series of 8 bits , 0's and/or 1's. For instance: 1000001 = 8 bits = 1 Byte
- 1-bit graphic = Black and white only
- 8-bit grayscale graphic = 8 bits per pixel = 8x the file size of a 1-bit image
- 24 bit grayscale graphic = 24 bits per pixel = 24 x the file size of a 1-bit image

File size terminology
- Bit = either a 1 or a 0
- Byte = 8 bits = 1 character: 1000001 = 1 Byte = The character A
- Kb = Kilobits = 1000 bits
- KB = KiloBytes = 1000 bytes
- Mb = Megabits = 1,000,000 bits
- MB = MegaBytes = 1,000,000 bytes

Scan or input resolution vs. file size
- 300 ppi scan captures 300 pixels, vertical and horizontal
- 600 ppi scan captures 600 pixels, vertical and horizontal
- 8x10-inch page scanned at 300 pixels (1 bit per pixel) = 7,200,000 bits = 7.2Mb = 900,000 bytes = .9MB
- 8x10-inch page scanned at 600 pixels (1 bit per pixel) = 28,800,000 bits = 28 = 28.8Mb = 3,600,000 bytes=3.6MB

Output or print resolution
- Spots per inch, also known as dots per inch (dpi) = Smallest building block of print image
  300 spots per inch (dpi) = 300 dpi x 300 dpi (horizontally and vertically)
  600 spots per inch (dpi) = 600 dpi x 600 dpi (horizontally and vertically)
  2400 spots per inch (dpi) = 2400 dpi x 2400 dpi (horizontally and vertically)
- Halftone dots per inch, also known as lines per inch or lpi = Number of halftone dots printed in every inch
  300-dpi laser printer = 60 lpi
  600-dpi laser printer = 85 lpi
  2400-dpi imagesetter = 133–200 lpi
- FM (large-format inkjet) printers ≠ lpi = Random dot patterns whose size depends upon the image size and viewing distance
- Line art and text images are converted into small spots to create sharp edges
- Continuous tone images are converted into halftone (AM) or stochastic (FM) dots to simulate grayscale values
- Halftone and stochastic dots are constructed from patterns of spots

▼ *Figure 8.3 Resolution Glossary*
Above is an overview of resolution terms and concepts. For clarity and to remove confusion, separate input/scanning resolution (pixels) from output/printing resolution (spots and dots). Line art and text are reproduced with small spots, while contone images are reproduced with patterns of larger halftone dots.

Halftoning: where it occurs

A RIP is a raster image processor. This is the portion of your computer-based publishing system which converts the images you generate on your computer into a form which can be reproduced on a piece of paper or film. To "rasterize" means to create dots, and that is what a RIP does. It generates dots. All elements on your page, text, line art graphics, and contone graphics must be converted by a RIP into a series of dots in order to be printed. In a PostScript publishing system, halftoning of contone images occurs at the RIP, not at the design or scanning station. All contone graphic images printed from a computer to a laser printer or imagesetter must be constructed out of a series of dots. In order for a continuous tone image to be rendered by these printers, the image must first be converted into a special series of dots known as halftone dots or cells. Halftone dots are composed of a series of smaller dots known as image dots. The number of image dots which make up halftone dots determines the number of shades of gray which can be rendered. The number of image dots available to construct a **halftone cell** of a particular size is determined by the dpi of the printer or imagesetter being used. The number of halftone dots per inch determines the resolution or sharpness of the rendered image. Here are some numbers to think about.

The number of halftone dots per inch is equivalent to the line screen of the printed image. That is: **lpi** = halftone dots per inch (hdpi)

\# shades of gray = dpi ÷ lpi (hdpi)

Example: (1600 dpi ÷ 100 lpi)= 16 dot cell : 16 x16 = 256 shades of gray

Example: (1200 dpi ÷ 100 lpi)= 12 dot cell: 12x12 = 144 shades of gray

Problem: If you want to be able to reproduce 256 shades of gray @ 133 lpi, what minimum dpi will be required on your imagesetter? (See Fig. 8.4)

Output resolution controlling input resolution

When we are deciding what resolutions to use when we capture images with scanners or digital cameras, or deciding at what resolution to create an image when painting, it is generally best to know the output resolution at which the images will be reproduced. Stated simply and specifically, the output resolution at which we print should control the input resolution at which we scan. The general rule of thumb for print is to scan at no more than two times [2 x lpi] the line screen at which the image will be printed. In fact we can scan at 1.5 times the line screen [1.5 x lpi] and have enough image resolution to print. As we will discuss in Chapter 12, "Taming Your Scanner," scaling must always be considered when an image is being created. For now we will use the formula 1.5 x lpi and make the provision that the image will be reproduced at the size at which it will be created.

Dpi vs. lpi vs. shades of gray

The size of the halftone dot is limited by the line screen at which the image is printed. In fact, the side dimensions of the halftone cell are determined by the line screen of the printer. Therefore, lpi (lines per inch) is equivalent to hdpi (halftone

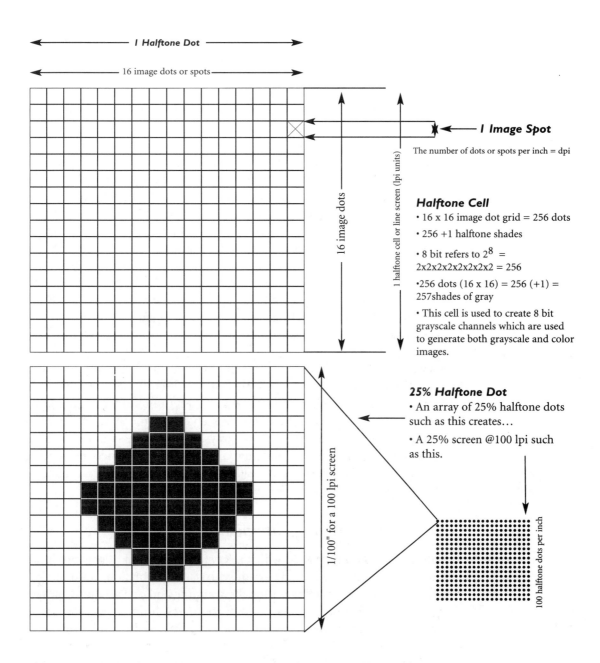

I Halftone Dot

16 image dots or spots

16 image dots

1 halftone cell or line screen (lpi units)

I Image Spot

The number of dots or spots per inch = dpi

Halftone Cell
- 16 x 16 image dot grid = 256 dots
- 256 +1 halftone shades
- 8 bit refers to 2^8 = $2 \times 2 \times 2 \times 2 \times 2 \times 2 \times 2 \times 2$ = 256
- 256 dots (16 x 16) = 256 (+1) = 257 shades of gray
- This cell is used to create 8 bit grayscale channels which are used to generate both grayscale and color images.

25% Halftone Dot
- An array of 25% halftone dots such as this creates…
- A 25% screen @100 lpi such as this.

1/100" for a 100 lpi screen

100 halftone dots per inch

▼ Figure 8.4 Halftone Cells and Dots

Traditional halftone dot patterns are created in set patterns determined by halftone cells. Laser printers and imagesetters use this cell pattern to determine spot placement on film or paper. Collections of image spots are used to create halftone dots. Halftone dots of various sizes simulate various grayscale percentages. Patterns of small and large halftone dots create the impression of light and dark grayscale, respectively. Patterns of variably sized halftone dots are used to simulate the appearance of continuous tone grayscale.

dots per inch). Since halftone dots are created by a grid of laser dots or spots which fill in the halftone cell, the relationship of lpi to dpi is set by the grid dimensions of the halftone cell. If a halftone cell is composed of 256 cell sites, the dimensions of the cell will be 16 x 16 (16 x 16 = 256). Note that the number of cell sites in each halftone cell also determines the number of shades of gray which can be reproduced. If the halftone cell is composed of 144 cell sites, then the halftone cell will be composed of a 12 x 12 grid of potential laser spots. Remember that the laser spots are the smallest dots which can be created by the printer, and that these laser spots build the halftone dots.

Therefore, the dpi of the printer required to create any given halftone dot is determined by the line screen (which controls the physical size of the halftone dots) and the number of cell sites required in each cell (which will determine the number of shades of gray which can be reproduced). For example, if we want to print a photograph at 100 lpi which will reproduce 144 shades of gray, we will need to create 100 halftone dots per inch with cell dimensions of 12 x 12 laser spots. This would require an imagesetter which can produce 1200 laser spots per inch (100 halftone dots per inch x 12 laser spots per halftone dot). If we want to reproduce this same photograph at 150 lpi, we will need an imagesetter which can produce 1800 dpi (150 lpi x 12 spots per halftone dot = 1800 dpi). Figure 8.4 shows you a graphical representation of these relationships.

As we will see in Chapter 16, "Screening Your Images" there are actually two types of halftoning techniques which are used to recreate contone images in print. Conventional halftoning, also known as AM (amplitude modulation) printing which we have discussed here, involves changing the size, or amplitude of the halftone dots to simulate changes in grayscale values. A second type of halftoning known as FM (frequency modulation) printing way varies the spacing, or frequency, of the halftone dots, instead of their size, in order to simulate changes in grayscale values.

Optical resolution vs. interpolation

Interpolation is fancy word which refers to the creation of new pixels based upon the information from already existing pixels. Interpolation can occur in a variety of circumstances including during the scanning and image editing processes. Most scanners can capture images at a variety of resolutions but they have only one hardware or **optical resolution**. The optical or hardware resolution of a scanner is the resolution, in pixels per inch, at which the scanner will capture an image. The scanner's interpolated resolution will be any resolution to which the scanner converts the image after it captures the image. If a scanner has an optical resolution of

Image quality in general and line art edge quality in particular will be improved by capturing images at the optical resolution of the capture device (scanner or digital camera). Any time an image is interpolated either during image capture or after, image quality will suffer. Interpolation should be avoided whenever possible.

RESOLUTION AND INTERPOLATION

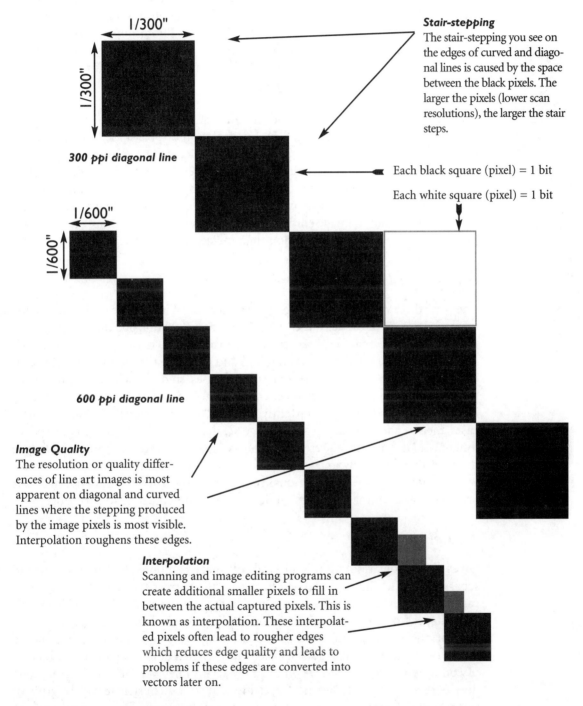

Stair-stepping
The stair-stepping you see on the edges of curved and diagonal lines is caused by the space between the black pixels. The larger the pixels (lower scan resolutions), the larger the stair steps.

Each black square (pixel) = 1 bit

Each white square (pixel) = 1 bit

1/300"

1/300"

300 ppi diagonal line

1/600"

1/600"

600 ppi diagonal line

Image Quality
The resolution or quality differences of line art images is most apparent on diagonal and curved lines where the stepping produced by the image pixels is most visible. Interpolation roughens these edges.

Interpolation
Scanning and image editing programs can create additional smaller pixels to fill in between the actual captured pixels. This is known as interpolation. These interpolated pixels often lead to rougher edges which reduces edge quality and leads to problems if these edges are converted into vectors later on.

▼ *Figure 8.5 Interpolated Resolution*
Shown here is a simplified view of how an interpolated edge can be constructed out of previously existing pixels. While higher resolution images can be created through interpolation, the tradeoff usually involves reduced image quality as a result of the creation of the "made up" or interpolated pixels.

600 ppi, it will capture pixels which are 1/600" on a side. If you choose a scan resolution of 1000 ppi, the scanner will first capture the image at 600ppi and then rebuild the pixels at 1/1000" The interpolation process involves rebuilding the pixels at a new size (see Fig. 8.6). This same process of interpolation can occur when we resample or resize an image in an image editing application like Photoshop. If we resize a 200 ppi image from 4" x 5" to 8" x 10" in Photoshop and keep the resolution at 200 ppi, Photoshop will be forced to create a wide variety of pixels through interpolation, because the new 8" x 10" image will have four times as many pixels as the original image (see Fig. 8.5).

This interpolation process often leads to lower quality edges in line art images and fuzzier contone images (see Fig. 8.5). Interpolation of pixel-based images should be avoided whenever possible. Line art images which will be converted into vector should be scanned at 100% size using the optical resolution of the scanner. Scaling should be performed after the image is converted into vectors. Contone images, such as photographs, which require scaling, should be scaled during the scanning process rather than in image editing applications such as Photoshop. Scanners will perform higher quality interpolation than image editing applications.

A final word about file sizes

There are three variables which affect the file size of an image: the dimension of the image (5" x 7", 8" x 10" etc.), the image resolution (300 dpi, 600 dpi, etc.), and the pixel depth of the image (1, 8, 24, or 32 bits/pixel). An increase in any of these variables will increase the file size of an image and therefore the requirements for processing that image. As an image's file size increases, so does its RAM requirements for opening the image, storage space for storing the image, CPU time for processing the image and, most importantly, the RIP time to print the image. In most cases, the size and pixel depth of an image are determined by the design of the document, and are therefore preset. The one variable which we can control to reduce the overhead which any image imposes is to keep its resolution as low as possible without adversely affecting the quality of the image. Chapter 12, "Taming Your Scanner," has a complete discussion of the resolution guideline for printing.

A final resolution

Given the various resolutions and kinds of image components which we need to separate, it is helpful to understand and use the correct terminology. For image capture and viewing, scanning and digital image capture, and monitor viewing, we should speak of resolution in terms or pixels/in or pixels/mm. For printing to a laser printer or imagesetter, we should use two terms: dpi and lpi. The building blocks of all images will be dots per inch(dpi)*. When describing the reproduction of continuous tone images, we will use the terms lines per inch (lpi) or halftone dots per inch (hdpi), knowing that halftone dots are constructed from grids of image dots or spots.

* **Terminology terrorism note:** Some prefer the use of the word "spot" to "dot." Using the terms "spot" and "spot-per-inch" (spi) instead of "dot" and "dot-per-inch" (dpi) is desirable for a number of reasons. If we use spot instead of dot it

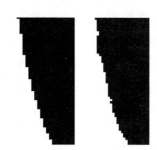

▼ *Figure 8.6 Optical vs. Interpolated Resolution*
On the left is a line art edge captured using the optical resolution of the scanner (600ppi). On the right is the same edge captured using an interpolated resolution (1000ppi.) Note the greater "raggedness" of the lower quality, interpolated edge.

makes the difference between spots and halftone dots less ambiguous. However, the terminology dpi is so ingrained in our industry that it might prove more difficult and confusing to try and substitute the word "spot" for "dot" in our lexicon. As an alternative, I suggest that we can accomplish our communication goals if we clearly distinguish between dots per inch (dpi) and halftone dots per inch (hdpi). We will also need to recognize that hdpi and lpi (another ingrained term) are equivalent terms.

CHAPTER SUMMARY

Much confusion exists about resolution and the use of resolution units and terms. The first and most important step in our battle to resolve this resolution confusion is to separate input resolution from output resolution. When discussing input resolution we should always use pixel, such as ppi (pixels per inch). The number of bits of information per pixel, known as bit depth or pixel depth, determines the number of shades of gray which an image can contain. When discussing output resolution we should use spots, dots or line screen to refer to the output resolution building blocks. Image spots or dots are the smallest building blocks of printed images. An image's file size is determined by a combination of three variables: the physical size of the image, the resolution of the image and the bit depth of the image. All three of these image size variables are directly proportional to file size. Halftone dots are constructed from these smaller image spots or dots, and are used to simulate grayscale values of contone images. Halftone dots can either be varied in size or spacing in order to change the simulation of grayscale value. The number of image spots in a halftone cell determines the number of shades of gray which can be printed. It is nearly always preferable to capture an image using the optical resolution of the scanner or digital camera. Using nonoptical resolutions results in the interpolation of pixel values, which in turn leads to lower image quality.

PAULINE'S DIGITAL IMAGING TIPS

Pauline's Tip 8.1

Keep your resolution concepts and terminology straight. This will help reduce the confusion which surrounds us when we discuss resolution. We capture, create, and view pixels, but we print dots. Therefore, all input resolution, such as when we paint in Photoshop or capture images with scanners and digital cameras, should be discussed in terms of pixel per unit area, such as ppi (pixels per inch) or res (pixels per mm). By contrast, we print with dots, both single dots (more correctly called "spots") and compound dots, which are created through the combination of groups of the smaller spots, called halftone dots. Individual dots or spots are used to recreate single tone text and line art images. The larger halftone dots are used to recreate contone images.

Pauline's Tip 8.2

Three variables affect file size of an image: image dimensions, pixel depth, and resolution. Increases in any of these variables will increase an image's file size and therefore increase the production demands of a number of variables. These include: storage space, CPU resources, RIP time, and transportation and storage resources. Image dimension and pixel depth are determined by the document design, so resolution is often the only variable which we can adjust to decrease a file's size. The goal is to decrease file size as small as possible without affecting the output quality of the image. Understanding the basic concepts of resolution helps us understand that resolution is a square and not a linear function. Therefore, whenever we double the linear resolution of a file, for example, from 300 ppi to 600 ppi, we quadruple the file size.

Pauline's Tip 8.3

When discussing resolution with your printer, distinguish between input resolution (ppi) and output resolutions (dpi and lpi). Find out at what resolution your files will be output and create or adjust your file resolutions accordingly. Resolutions for pixel-based line art images should be between 600 ppi and 1200 ppi. Final resolutions of contone images should never exceed 2 x lpi (see Chapter 12, "Taming Your Scanner," for more advice on this topic).

Pauline's Tip 8.4

Whenever possible capture images at the optical resolution of the scanner or digital camera. Capturing images at nonoptical resolutions will result in the interpolation of the image's pixels and a lowering of image quality in general and edge quality in particular. Adjusting the size and/or resolution of an image in an image editing application such as Photoshop after it has been captured can result in interpolation as well. Be sure that interpolation of your images is kept to a minimum.

CHAPTER REVIEW

Check Your Comprehension

Multiple Choice Questions

To help you review the topics covered in this chapter, answer the following multiple choice questions.

1. _____ can be defined as the number of building blocks in an image.
   A. Bit depth
   B. Resolution
   C. Pixel depth
   D. Shades of gray

2. Which of the following is **not** a resolution term?
   A. Pixels per inch
   B. Dots per inch
   C. Bits per pixel
   D. Lines per inch

3. Into what two categories should we divide resolution in order to improve our understanding of and communication about resolution?
   A. Input and output
   B. Optical and interpolated
   C. Bit depth and pixel depth
   D. Dpi and lpi

4. Which of the following is an input resolution term?
   A. Dpi
   B. Lpi
   C. Spot per inch
   D. Pixel per inch

5. Which of the following is the building block of scanned images?
   A. Spots
   B. Dots
   C. Halftone dots
   D. Pixels

6. Which formula best represents the relationship between input and output resolution?

   A. Input resolution = 1 x lpi

   B. Input resolution = 1.5 x lpi

   C. Input resolution = 2.5 x lpi

   D. Input resolution = 3 x lpi

7. Which of the following controls the number of grayscale values in an image?

   A. Dpi

   B. Lpi

   C. bit depth

   D. None of the above

8. A _____ is constructed out of image spots.

   A. halftone dot

   B. image dot

   C. pixel

   D. pixel depth

9. If we change an image resolution from 300 ppi to 600 ppi, what will happen to its file size?

   A. It will double

   B. It will triple

   C. It will quadruple

   D. It will remain the same

10. The size of a halftone cell is controlled by

   A. The dpi of the imaging device

   B. The lpi of the imaging device

   C. The ppi of the imaging device

   D. The bit depth of the imaging device

11. Which of the following would be the best choice for capturing the best edge quality?

   A. Interpolated resolution

   B. Optical resolution

   C. Higher bit depth

   D. None of the above

12. _____ will usually result in reducing the quality of an image.

   A. Using nonoptical resolution

   B. Scaling of images

   C. Interpolation of pixels

   D. All of the above

Check Your Understanding

Concept Questions

To help you review and expand your thinking on the topics covered in this chapter, please answer the following questions.

1. Briefly explain the difference between input and output resolution.

2. What are the three factors which control files size? Give three numeric examples of how changing each of these variables will affect file size of an image.

3. What happens to file size of a pixel-based image when its resolution is changed from 300 ppi to 600 ppi? Explain why.

4. What is the basic difference between an image pixel and an image spot or dot?

5. What is the difference between a halftone dot and a halftone cell?

6. Explain the relationship between image dots, halftone dots. line screen and shades of gray. Which one(s) can be printed?

7. Explain the relationship between the input resolution at which we scan and the output resolution at which we print.

8. To what does the term bit depth refer and what does it control?

9. What is optical resolution, and why is it important?

10. What is interpolation? Why should we avoid it?

PROJECTS

1. Calculate the file size of a 1 bit black and white 4" x 5" 200 ppi image.

2. Calculate what would happen to the file size of the above 1 bit black and white 4" x 5" 200 ppi image if we enlarged to this image to 8" x 10" and increased the resolution to 300ppi.

3. How many shades of gray can we print if we are printing an image at 100 lpi using a 1200 dpi (spi) imagesetter? Hint: Calculate the maximum number of cells which will be in the halftone cell.

9
Grappling with Graphics

As the Byte Turns continues...

Will Danny and Pauline see the big picture, or will they have one Tiff too many?

You told me to reduce my file size as much as possible. So I saved my graphics in PICT format because I noticed that the PICT format is very small.

Sounds good to me; the smaller the better.

I know small is better. I know Pauline will be happy.

Hey Pauline, guess what?

Oh, no! PICT files should be used only for screen display. They are not made for printing.
This is a perfect example of a little knowledge being dangerous.

Chapter Objectives

In this chapter you will learn:

◆ **Types of graphic files**
◆ **Graphic file formats for print and Web**
◆ **When pixels and vectors should be used**
◆ **Matching file format with use**
◆ **Converting pixels to vectors**
◆ **Preparing graphics for print**
◆ **Compressing images**
◆ **Key Terms**
  • Pixel, bitmap, raster
  • Vector, outline
  • Native file
  • TIFF and EPS
  • GIF, JPEG, and SWF
  • Outlining
  • Bit depth, pixel depth
  • Lossless and lossy compression

INTRODUCTION

There is a lot of confusion about graphic file and graphic file formats. Much of this confusion can be relieved by separating graphic file contents from containers. Graphic file contents are limited to **pixels** and **vectors**, while graphic file formats vary with intended use. Pixel based images are used for high detail images such as contones while vector based images are most often used for simple line art images. Pixel based images can be converted into vector based images in order to take advantage of the reduced file size, editability, and resolution independence of vector based images. Pixels and vectors can be saved in the same file. Images are generally constructed in an applications **native file** format, which is typically a highly editable format. Simplified output formats are used for printing and viewing images for file use. **TIFF** and EPS are the two preferred file format containers used for PostScript printing. **GIF** and **JPEG** are the two preferred file formats for pixel based graphic images used on the Web, while **SWF** is the file format used for Web vector images. Both TIFF and EPS can be taken cross platform, as can GIF and JPEG. To assure maximum transportability it is best to use eight or fewer characters in a file name followed by a three-character lowercase extension. The number of bits of information placed in an image will control the number of shades of gray or color values which can be displayed by that image. When preparing a graphic file for final use it is best to concentrate on reducing file size and complexity to optimize fast and troublefree printing and viewing. For instance, it is best to avoid nesting one image inside another. Blends are best created with pixel based images. There are two types of compression, **lossless** and **lossy**. Lossy compression offers far more file size reduction but increased image quality degradation as well. It is best to avoid high compression ratios for images which will be printed in a high resolution PostScript environment.

TYPES OF GRAPHIC FILES

Contents vs. containers

There are myriad different file formats and even different versions of the same format. There is TIFF, EPS, GIF, JPEG, BMP, WMF, RIFF... and many others, with more being created all the time. In short there is a veritable alphabet soup of file formats. Then there are different types of graphic images. There are pixel-based or raster images, and vector or outline images as well. All these different types of graphic files and graphic file formats can be very confusing. One way to simplify this whole graphic file/file format maze is to separate graphic file contents, or building blocks, from their containers or formats. There are only two basic types of graphic file building blocks, pixels and vectors. But there are myriad types of graphic file containers or file formats. The same graphic file contents can be saved in any number of different graphic file formats. For instance a pixel-based image may be saved in TIFF, EPS, GIF, JPEG just to name a few. Which file format is chosen depends upon how the image will be used. We have created different file formats for different uses.

Bitmap/raster vs. outline/vector images

As we discussed above, there are many different specific graphic file forms which are known as file formats. There are, however, only two basic types of digital building materials: pixels and vectors. Images constructed out of pixels are called bitmapped or **raster** images, while those constructed out of lines are called outline or vector images. **Bitmap** refers to a map or pattern of bits or pixels. The origin of the word "raster" graphic is derived from a line of pixels on a television screen which is known as a raster. Raster and bitmap both refer to images composed of pixels. The word outline refers to graphic images which are composed of lines or outlines. The word vector is used for these images because these line images are made up of line segments geometrically referred to as vectors because, like all vectors, they have magnitude (length) and direction (orientation). There are two basic kinds of vector or outline paths. Open paths, such as straight lines, do not fully enclose an area. Closed paths, such as circles, do enclose areas. Closed paths can be easily filled with patterns, screens, and colors as well as being stroked because they have a boundary. Open paths can be less dependably stroked and filled.

These graphic image terms, bitmap/outline and raster/vector, exist because of two separate professional histories for each pair of terms. The graphically descriptive terms bitmap and outline were developed and used historically in the graphic design community, which has also historically been the Macintosh culture. The more technical terms raster and vector were developed in the physics and engineering community and were used predominantly by engineers and architects who worked with IBM-based computers or PCs or UNIX workstations, and worked in computer-aided design and manufacturing (CAD/CAM).

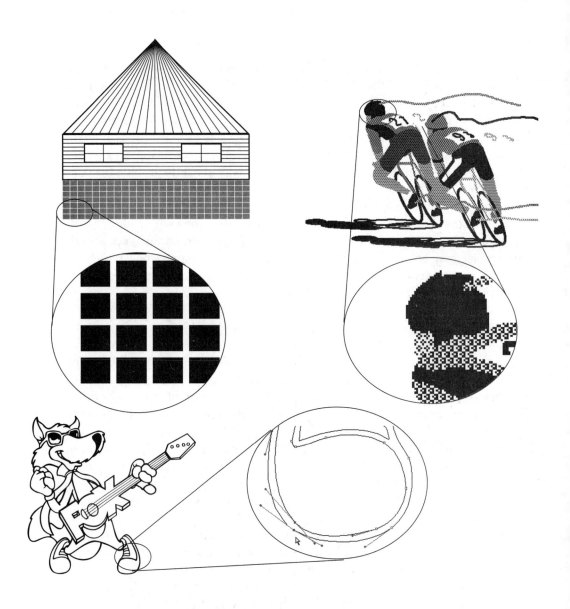

▼ Figure 9.1 Digital Graphic File Construction

There are only two basic types of digital graphic files: pixel-based/raster images and outline/vector images. The file type you use depends upon the kind of image you are constructing. Like a brick wall, digital pixel or raster graphic images, (sometimes referred to as bitmapped graphics) are constructed out of repeating patterns of smaller component building blocks. In the case of the wall, the materials are bricks. In the case of the graphic, the components are pixels. Shown on the right is a bitmapped image of a biker. This is a low resolution, 72 ppi image where each pixel is 1/72" on a side and is either black or white. Shown on the left, the upper portion of the house is like an outline or vector image. Instead of being constructed out of building block components like bricks (or pixels), both the house and vector images are made up of outline components which are linked. In the case of the house, the outline components are boards. In a vector graphic, such as the fox, outline components are lines or vectors instead of pixels.

Painting and drawing

Bitmapped images, which I think of as painted images, are created during the digital capture of images with scanners and digital cameras, or during the creation of graphics in painting and pixel-based image editing applications such as Adobe Photoshop or Painter®. Vector-based images, which I relate to illustration or drafting types of images, are created in drawing applications such as Adobe Illustrator, Macromedia FreeHand, or CorelDraw. Images can be transformed from one type of format to another. For instance, bitmapped images can be converted into vector-based images using an application called Adobe Streamline, while vector-based images can be converted into pixels or rasterized in applications like Photoshop. Images with fine details, such as multitone images (photographs or bitonal images which exhibit fine details) are best saved as pixel based images.

Compound images

Complex images which contain both pixel and vector characteristics can also be created. A common example would be a contone photograph which contains a hard edged silhouette, where the edge of the silhouette is created through the addition of a vector path, known as a clipping path, in a pixel-based application such as Photoshop (see Figure 9.7). Other compound images can be created by placing

> **To help you simplify and understand the myriad types of graphic files and file formats, separate graphic file contents, or building blocks, from their containers. There are really only two kinds of graphics file contents or building blocks, pixels and vectors. There are however many different types of graphic file containers or formats. Graphic file formats are created for specific uses. TIFF and EPS graphic file formats are the two containers in which we place pixels and vectors for use in the world of PostScript printing, while GIF, JPEG are SWF are the preferred file formats for saving images which will be used over the World Wide Web.**

pixel based images in a predominantly vector-based image constructed in a drawing application such as Illustrator. Both TIFF and EPS file formats support clipping paths, although EPS is more commonly used on Macintosh, while TIFFs with clipping paths are more common on Windows. Ask your printing company for their advice on which format to use with their RIPs and workflow.

GRAPHIC FILE FORMATS

While there are only two basic file types, raster and vector, there are numerous file formats in which those two image types can be saved. File formats are usually use-specific; that is, you choose a file format based upon how you will use it. For instance, TIFF and EPS are the preferred file formats for images which will be printed using a PostScript printer. GIF, JPEG and SWF are the preferred file formats for use on the World Wide Web (WWW). PICT, PCX, and BMP file formats are used for images which will primarily be displayed on a monitor or printed to

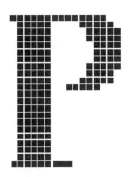

▼ *Figure 9.2 Bitmap/Raster Graphic*
Bitmap and raster both refer to graphics constructed out of pixels. The preferred print file format is generally TIFF, while the Web file format will be either GIF or JPEG. Compare the file size of these two "Ps." This bitmapped graphic is larger (1MB) because the entire graphic form must be built out of pixels.

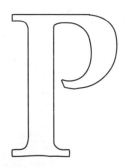

▼ *Figure 9.3 Outline/Vector Graphic*
The terms outline and vector both refer to graphics constructed out of lines. The preferred print file format is EPS, while the Web format will be SWF (ShockWave). Compare the file sizes of this and the above "P." This graphic is smaller (100KB) because only the border between the black and white areas need to be recorded as lines.

GRAPHIC FILE TYPES

▼ *Figure 9.4 1 Bit B&W Bitmap*

This 1 bit B&W image is the simplest form of a bitmap graphic. The butterfly image is constructed out of black and white pixels, each containing 1 bit of information. Fine detail images are best left as bitmaps rather than converted to outlines. This image can be edited by changing, adding, or removing pixels. The preferred print file format is usually TIFF although EPS may be used if a transparent background is preferred. Web formats include GIF and JPEG, although for a simple one or two color graphic such as this, GIF would be the better of the two.

▼ *Figure 9.5 1 Bit Outline Graphic*

This is an outline graphic file constructed of lines instead of dots. The larger version on the left shows the finished product. The smaller version on the right shows the screen view of the outlines. Note the location of the control points which can be moved and edited to resize and reform the image. The preferred print file format is EPS.

▼ *Figure 9.6 8 Bit Grayscale Bitmap Graphic*

This image is a multibit bitmapped image. There are 8 bits for every pixel, instead of 1 bit/pixel, to record the grayscale information. Like the 1 bit B&W bitmap image above, this image is composed of pixels. Each pixel is assigned a shade of gray which can be edited. This image should be saved as a TIFF for use in printing purposes. Web formats include GIF and JPEG.

Interior Bitmap Contone (TIFF)

Outline Clipping Path (EPS)

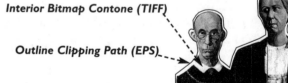

▼ *Figure 9.7 Compound Image Bitmap and Outline Graphic*

This graphic image is a compound image because it contains continuous tone bitmapped information from the original image, plus an outline vector component, known as a clipping path, around the edge where the silhouette was made. The outline, shown here as a black line, is invisible but it encases the entire contone. The outline forms a smooth boundary around the jagged bitmap portion of the image. Both TIFF and EPS file formats support clipping paths.

non-PostScript printers. There are specific file formats for nearly every conceivable use including multimedia, digital video, and the Internet/Web. And new file formats are constantly being created. There are even file format variations between platforms. For instance, Photoshop Tiffs can be saved in either Mac or PC format as can EPS image previews.

Native vs. output file format

There are basically two categories of graphic file formats: native graphic file format and output graphic file formats. Native graphic files formats, also called parent file formats, are application specific file formats, that is they are associated specifically with the graphic application which is used to create or edit a graphic file. Native graphic file formats are unique to each graphics application, and can usually only be opened and edited by that particular application. Output file formats are more more general graphic file formats which are used when we want to access and output our graphic files from other, usually page layout, applications.

Native or application file formats

Most graphics applications have their own proprietary format(s) which may be used during file creation. For instance, you may want to work in Photoshop's proprietary format, which is recognized by its unique extension (.psd), for performing extensive image editing chores (the Photoshop format is more flexible than output file formats such as TIFF or EPS). Application-specific file formats often allow you to work in layers, channels, and with transparent backgrounds. Examples of other application specific file formats include RIFF (raster image file format: .rif) for Painter files, (.ai) for Adobe Illustrator and (.fh) for Macromedia FreeHand native files. After you are done constructing and editing your images, most applications allow you to, and in fact we are generally required to, save files in either output formats such TIFF, EPS, GIF and JPEG, if we intend to use these graphics for output. In general, you will want to send TIFFs and EPSs files to your printer or service bureau, rather than, or in addition to, the application-specific files. Send the application-specific files along if you think the printing company may need or want to edit your file.

Output file formats

Following is a detailed description of some of the more common file formats used in PostScript printing and for use on the World Wide Web. See the appendix for a more complete list of files formats which you may encounter.

TIFF: Pixel-based

The most common, one of the most flexible, and often the most desirable file format for bitmapped graphics which you intend to RIP and print is the TIFF (Tagged Information File Format) (see Figure 9.9). You will typically create and save TIFF files when you capture an image with a scanner or digital camera, or create or edit an image in a bitmap editing applications such as Photoshop, Painter, or Picture Publisher. Line art images which are captured as scanned images will almost always

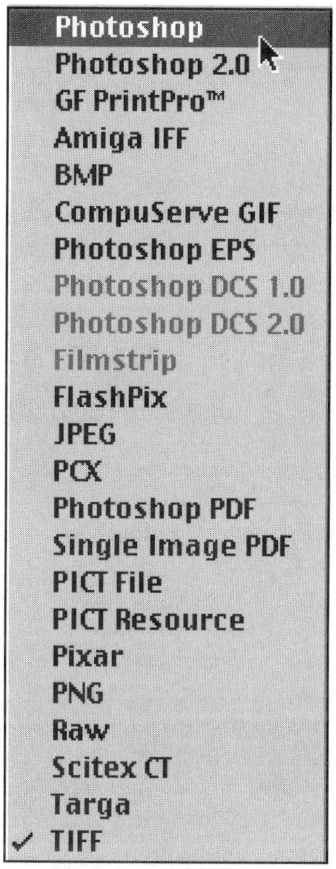

Photoshop
Photoshop 2.0
GF PrintPro™
Amiga IFF
BMP
CompuServe GIF
Photoshop EPS
Photoshop DCS 1.0
Photoshop DCS 2.0
Filmstrip
FlashPix
JPEG
PCX
Photoshop PDF
Single Image PDF
PICT File
PICT Resource
Pixar
PNG
Raw
Scitex CT
Targa
✓ TIFF

▼ *Fig. 9.8: Graphic File Formats*
Shown here is a list of the some of the graphic file formats in which an image can be saved. Although there are only two basic kinds of images, pixel and vector, there are numerous different file formats in which these two image types can be saved. The file formats have been devised to suit specific purposes. TIFF and EPS are formats in which images should be saved for print, while GIF and JPEG should be used for the Internet. The top two formats Photoshop (Ver 5.5 here and 2.0) are examples of native file formats for Photoshop which allow you to retain full editing functions such as layers and transparent backgrounds. Photoshop 4.0 and above allows for the inclusion of layers and layer effects.

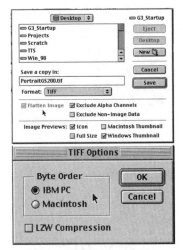

▼ Figure 9.9 Creating TIFFs
TIFFs are used in printing. Using the Save As dialog box allows you to flatten and remove alpha channels on the fly as you save your image. I generally save my TIFFs in IBM PC format, to enhance cross platform compatibility, and without any compression to reduce printing problems.

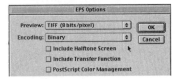

▼ Figure 9.10 Creating EPSs
Like TIFFs, EPSs are used in printing. EPS files require previews in order for them to be viewed in a page layout application. Choose the screen view which is appropriate for your image, keeping in mind that lower pixel depth previews will display and redraw more quickly. Choose either a Mac or PC (TIFF) header. Most printing companies prefer binary encoding. Use ASCII encoding if you are working on a Windows network and are having problems transferring/printing binary files. Keep the Halftone Screen, Transfer Function and PostScript Color Management unchecked unless you are informed otherwise.

be saved initially as TIFFs because scanners create bitmapped images, and TIFF is usually the default format. Line art images which are too complex to be converted to EPS format through **outlining** (see EPS line art and EPS graphics below) should remain as TIFFs. The TIFF bitmap format is best used for line art when there is a great deal of detail to be reproduced. Outlining can sometimes ruin or alter the details of complex images. Grayscale and color contone images, which are always constructed from multibit pixels, are very often saved in TIFF format. When in doubt, save your contones as TIFFs.

EPS: Vector/Line art

The most common and desirable format for printing outline or vector based graphics is EPS (Encapsulated PostScript). You will use drawing applications such as Illustrator, FreeHand, or CorelDraw for creating outline-based EPS files. When you export an image from a drawing application it should be saved in the EPS format, as this is the format which allows page layout applications like QuarkXPress and PageMaker to import them as placed images to use in layouts. When converting bitmapped line art images into vector-based outlines in applications like Adobe Streamline, those outline images should be saved in EPS format. In general, vector-based EPS files usually have the advantage of being smaller, simpler, and more scalable than their bitmapped TIFF cousins. This, however, does not hold true for contone EPS files, which are discussed below. Because EPS files are sealed or encapsulated, a page layout application cannot construct a low resolution screen preview from the high resolution EPS image. Therefore, when exported, all EPS files should be saved with a low resolution screen view image which can be placed as a viewable image in a page layout application. Pay close attention when you export an EPS file, for it is during the export process that the EPS generating application will give you a variety of screen preview choices. If you fail to save an EPS image with a screen preview, your page layout application will be able to place and print the image but you will not be able to preview the image in the page layout application. See Figure 9.10 for an EPS screen preview creation dialog box.

EPS: Pixel/Contone

In some circumstances, you will want to save images which are composed primarily of multibit pixels, such as photographs, in EPS format instead of the simpler TIFF format discussed above. If you perform image editing chores such as creating hard edge silhouettes of continuous tone images by adding vector-based clipping paths to contone images, you may end up creating a compound file, one which has dual characteristics; that is, it contains both pixels and vectors. A clipping path silhouetted image, for instance, has variable tone pixels (bitmapped) information surrounded by a clipping path (vector) outline which forms a smooth, sharp border. These types of compound images have traditionally been saved as compound EPS files out of applications like Photoshop. Unlike their simpler outline EPS cousins created in object-oriented applications like Streamline, FreeHand, or CorelDraw (which are smaller and simpler than their bitmapped TIFF counterparts), compound EPS files are larger and more complicated, and therefore more difficult to RIP than either of their contone bitmapped or outline components. *Note:* It is now possible to save these types of compound images as

1 Bit B&W Image

A 1 bit line art image such as this contains only one layer of pixels with 1 bit of data per pixel. Each pixel is either Black (1) or White (0). These are the smallest and simplest types of bitmapped images. File size = 285KB at 300 dpi

8 Bit Gray Scale Image

An 8 bit grayscale image such as this contains only one layer of pixels, but with 8 bits of data per pixel (8 b/p), and has the capacity to store and display 256 shades of gray. Contrast this to the 1 bit per pixel used to create the line art image above. This grayscale file size is eight times larger than the 1bit images discussed above. This 8 b/p file is also the basic building block for the RGB and CMYK color files discussed below. File size = 2.2MB at 300 dpi

24 Bit RGB Color (Screen) Image

A 24 bit color image such as this contains three layers of pixels with 24 bits of data per pixel, or three 8 b/p grayscale files, one for each color (RGB). Each color can be shown in 256 shades. Therefore, the total number of colors possible is 256 R x 256 G x 256 B = 16.7 million colors. This RGB image file size is 24 times larger than the 1 bit line art image. These images are used for displaying color images on monitors and printing to color film. File size = 6.6MB at 300 dpi

32 Bit CMYK Color (Print) Image

A 32 bit grayscale image contains four layers of pixels with 32 bits per pixel or four 8 bit grayscale files, one for each color. A 32 bit CMYK image produces the same number of colors as the 24 bit RGB image above (16.7 million). The fourth black channel (K) is substituted for various portions of the three color channels (CMY). This K channel improves contrast and shadow detail and reduces ink coverage but does not add any colors. This CMYK image file is used for printing and is 33 percent larger than the equivalent RGB file, and 32 times larger than a similar 1 bit image. File size = 8.8MB at 300 dpi

▼ *Figure 9.11 Pixel Depth of Images*

Electronic images can be divided into three basic categories: B&W, grayscale, and color. B&W images only require 1 bit per pixel for creation and display. Grayscale images require 8 bits per pixel to display 256 shades of gray. Color images require either 24 or 32 bits per pixel depending upon whether they are RGB or CMYK images. File size, storage space, and RIPing time increase as pixel depth increases. You will find a color version of this figure (Fig. C.2) in the color plate section in the center of the book (see page C-4).

TIFFS (Photoshop 3.0+) with clipping paths rather than as EPS files. The primary advantage of the TIFF format here will be reduced image file size. Various page layout applications may have preferences for the use of either the TIFF or EPS with a clipping path. Ask about and/or experiment with your application and version (see Chapter 12, "Taming Your Scanner," for more detailed information on outlining and silhouetting).

Contone images may also be saved as EPS files when you wish to include a Transfer Function which may contain image altering instructions, such as dot gain adjustment or screening instructions, which will be applied to the image when it is RIPed. In these cases the EPS format is required because these kind of Transfer Functions cannot be saved with a TIFF file. The EPS format forms a little storage packet or capsule (hence, the name EnCAPsulated PostScript) around the image which contains both the image data and the transfer function. Contone files saved in EPS format are nearly always larger than those saved in TIFF format because of the additional formatting information required to accomplish the encapsulation (see file format vs. file size on page 174 and Fig. 9.13). Like the line art EPS images discussed above, contone images need to be saved with screen previews if you intend to place and view these EPSs in a page layout application.

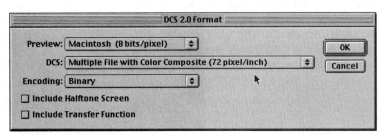

▼ *Figure 9.12 Creating DCSs*
Like regular EPSs, DCSs are used in printing. And like regular EPSs, DCS files require previews in order for them to be viewed in a page layout application. Choose either a Mac or PC (TIFF) header.

When saving your image as a DCS file you will have several DCS options which will determine the number of files, and the type of composite file which will be created. Ask your printing company for specific instructions as to whether they use DCS files and how they prefer to have them set up.

As with other EPS graphic files, most printing companies prefer binary encoding. Use ASCII encoding if you are working on a Windows network and are have problems transferring/printing binary files. Keep the Halftone Screen, Transfer Function and PostScript Color Management unchecked unless you are specifically informed otherwise.

Five-file EPS (DCS) format

There is a special version of the EPS format called a five-file EPS or, as it is also known, DCS (desktop color separation) format. The DCS format was developed specifically for working with and printing color separated spot and process color files. There are two versions of this format, DCS 1.0 and DCS 2.0. DCS 1.0 is used for contone images which have only the four standard process colors (C,M,Y,K). DCS 2.0 is used for images which contain spot colors in addition to the four process colors. DCS format literally creates five or more separate files. A standard DCS 1.0 file will have four separate high resolution images, one for each of the process colors, plus a separate low resolution composite file which can be distributed as a separate file and imported for use in a page layout file. Figure 9.8 shows the EPS preview dialog box where you instruct Photoshop as to what kind of an EPS file you would like to create. Note the pull-down menu section for DCS file creation. This option will only appear when you are saving CMYK files, as the DCS format is designed specifically for use with color separated files. The advantage of the DCS format over the single file EPS is that with the single file EPS the entire image must be sent four times to a RIP to be imaged because the color separation information for all four colors is contained in the EPS which, because of its encapsulated nature, cannot be segmented on the fly during printing. After the creation of the five-file DCS, each high resolution color file can be sent separately, which reduces printing time by as much as 75 percent. The other advantage to the DCS format is that the fifth, low resolution file can be used separately for inclusion in a page layout file, thereby reducing the network and storage space overhead associated with working with the entire composite file. When a document using DCS images is RIPed, the low resolution composite image is merged back with the four high resolution separation files which are then sent to the RIP for processing. If you are ever sent a low resolution DCS composite file, do not rename this file, as its name will be used to remerge this low resolution image with its high resolution cousins at the printing location (see Figure 9.12 for a file view of a set of DCS files).

JPEG

JPEG format is a compressed file format used to reduce the storage file size of an image. Compressed file formats like JPEG should primarily be used for archiving, transportation, or telecommunication (Web) purposes. The use of JPEG images in print production should be avoided because the file compression lowers image quality, and decompression of files takes time. More details of JPEG are discussed later in this chapter under the section on compression (see Chapter 15, "Weaving Web Graphics," for more information).

SWF

SWF (shock wave format) is a vector-based format commonly used on the Web for animation graphics. This type of image file format can be grayscale, 8 or 24 bit RGB images. SWF can also be used for printing at high resolution, but should be converted into a spot or CMYK color space, TIFF, or EPS prior to printing (see Chapter 15, "Weaving Web Graphics" for more information).

PhotoCD (PCD)

The PhotoCD format is a special, very flexible, multiresolution, CIE color space compressed bitmapped file format developed by Kodak for saving scanned images. PCD format was originally a proprietary format which could only be created on a Kodak Photo Imaging Workstation (PIW). Be careful to distinguish between digital photos on CD, which can be photos of any format which happen to be stored on a CD (compact disk), and PhotoCD which is a specific file format. More details about the PhotoCD format are contained near the end of Chapter 12, "Taming Your Scanner."

PICT, PCX, WMF, and others

PICT, PCX, BMP, and WMF file formats are commonly found on DTP systems. These file formats produce files which are often significantly smaller than TIFF and EPS files, so they are seductive. But resist the use of these files for PostScript printing. These files are made for screen viewing (PICT, PCX, and WMF) or for printing (BMP and PCX) on non-PostScript printers. If you have an image in a file format other than TIFF or EPS and you are having trouble converting it, try opening it in Photoshop first and saving it as a TIFF or EPS out of Photoshop. If Photoshop won't open the image, try one of the dedicated file conversion utilities like Debabelizer; these will nearly always work.

File Format vs File Size		
14 items	406.6 MB in disk	101.3 MB available
Name	Size	La
▽ 🗀 5-File DCS (eps) – UCR	–	
🗋 Portrait CMYK–UCR 300.C	2.2 MB	
🗋 Portrait CMYK–UCR 300.eps	808K	
🗋 Portrait CMYK–UCR 300.K	2.2 MB	
🗋 Portrait CMYK–UCR 300.M	2.2 MB	
🗋 Portrait CMYK–UCR 300.Y	2.2 MB	
🗋 Portrait CMYK 300.EPS	11.2 MB	
🗋 Portrait CMYK 300.JPEG(L)	264K	
🗋 Portrait CMYK 300.JPEG(M)	888K	
🗋 Portrait CMYK 300.Tiff	8.9 MB	
🗋 Portrait RGB 300.Tiff	6.6 MB	
🗋 Portrait RGB 72.eps	680K	
🗋 Portrait RGB 72.Tiff	416K	

▼ *Figure 9.13 File Format, Size and Names*

This screen grab shows the same image saved in a variety of file formats, TIFF, EPS and JPEG. At the top of the list you see a folder containing a five-file DCS version of the image which contains four larger, high resolution files, one for each process color, and a smaller low resolution composite image. The EPS versions of the image are significantly larger than the TIFF versions. The JPEG(M) is compressed less with maximum quality, while the JPEG(L) is more compressed but with the lowest quality. Each image name contains four elements (Item, Pixel depth, Resolution, and File format). This naming scheme makes for unambiguous file names and easy recognition, especially for images with multiple versions.

Right format for the right use

There is truly an alphabet soup of file formats in the world of electronic publishing, and more are created every day. There are formats for multimedia, digital video, music, sound, and the Internet. For final images intended to be processed through a PostScript imagesetter, your choices should nearly always be TIFF or EPS. Ask your printing company which versions of the two formats they recommend and/or prefer before you send in your files.

GRAPHICS ISSUES

File format vs. file size

When you convert an image from one file format into another, the file size will often change. Converting one bit TIFF files to EPS vector files will almost always significantly lower the file size of the image because you are often converting hundreds of thousands or millions of pixels to a few vector paths. Converting a multi-bit contone image into a contone EPS in Photoshop usually results in the opposite effect–the files size will grow significantly, because you are adding an EPS portion to the image rather than converting pixel data. Fig. 9.13 contains some examples of an image which has been saved in various file formats. If you know what is happening to your image during a file format conversion, you will generally be able to predict if a significant size change will occur as well. The compression of an image, such as saving in JPEG format, will dramatically reduce the disk storage size of the image, but when you open the image it will generally decompress back to a larger size. The amount of difference between the disk saved file and the open file will be determined by the amount or ratio of compression.

Cross platform file exchange

The two most common computer operating system platforms used in desktop publishing are Apple Macintoshes and Microsoft Windows, so we will focus our discussion on these two platforms. For PostScript printing, the good news is that Macintosh and Windows applications both support TIFF and EPS file formats. The bad news is that the two systems organize the data in these two formats slightly differently, so applications on one platform will not as readily read file formats from the other. But there is more good news–applications on both platforms generally allow you to save TIFF and EPS in either format. So all you have to do is pay attention when you save your files. In Photoshop, for instance, when you save a TIFF file it will ask you if you want to save your image in Mac or PC format; choose the one you need (see Fig. 9.9). If you are sending your file to a service bureau who uses a different platform than you do, you may want to save a separate set of images in their format and send those along with your files. So find out which platform your printing company or service bureau uses, and be sure to discuss all cross platform image transfers with your printer or service bureau before you send your files. If you are having troubles getting EPS files to transfer from one platform to another, try saving your drawing files in Illustrator 1.0 or 1.1 format, transport them to the other platform, and then create the EPS on the other platform. It is worth noting that Macintosh computers will generally be able to read PC formats easier than Windows machines can read the Mac format so if you have to save for both, save your TIFF and EPS images in Windows/PC format. GIF and JPEG are both cross platform file formats.

File naming system

One of the least glamorous but potentially the most time- and frustration-saving habit you can acquire is to adopt a good file naming system and use it consistently. A good file naming system can save you hours of time when you are trying to find an image. This is particularly true if, like me, you tend to save several versions of a file. A complete graphic file name should include item name, **pixel depth**, resolution, and file format. An example is Trees CMYK 200.tiff. This type of attention to detail in file naming, while perhaps a bit cumbersome, will make your file management and finding chores much easier. In addition, it will make it easier for your printing company to identify your graphic images. I also use this file naming scheme to help me remember to change my nonprint file format to printable ones. The most common example is reminders to change my PICT screen grabs to TIFFs before I send my image out for printing (see Figure 9.8 for some file naming examples).

For most flexible, cross platform use, it is a good idea to place a proper three character, lowercase format identification extension or suffix at the end of your file names. Examples include .tif for TIFF, .eps for EPS files, .gif for GIF files, and .jpg for JPEG files. This three character extension is not only important for the visual recognition of the file format, but is necessary for some computers to recognize the file format. Windows computers require the three character extension, and Macs do not. Regardless, it is useful to have that three character extension as it helps to quickly and easily identify the file format of a graphic file at a glance.

If you are sharing your images with others on other platforms and/or across the Internet it is good practice to get in the habit of limiting your file names to eight (8) alpha and/or numeric characters with no spaces followed by a lowercase three character file format extension. If you do not, the other platforms and/or Internet will do the limiting for you, indiscriminantly.

Use the 8.3 convention, a maximum upper limit of eight character alpha-numeric file names, with no spaces, plus a "dot" followed by a lowercase three character file format extension to increase the cross platform compatibility of your graphic images.

Pixel depth

Various images require different amounts of information in order to create, view, and print those images. In electronic images, this information is referred to as pixel depth. Pixel depth is a measure of the number of bits of digital information per image pixel required to completely render that image for its final use. For instance, a black and white line art image only requires one (1) bit of information per pixel in order to completely create, display, and print that image. Only one bit per pixel (1 b/p) is required because any individual pixel only needs to represent either black or white, which can be done by assigning that pixel a value of either 0 for black or 1 for white. This is why black and white images are called 1-bit images.

Grayscale images, on the other hand, need to be able to store 256 tonal variations or shades in every pixel. This requires eight (8) bits of data per pixel in order to completely represent one of the possible 256 shades of gray in each pixel. Since grayscale image pixels hold eight times (8x) as many bits per pixel as a one bit (1 bit) black and white image, 8 b/p grayscale images will have eight times larger file sizes as 1 b/p black and white of the same size and resolution.

Color images require even more information to represent them than grayscale images. Because your computer is digital, that is, it only understands two values, 0 and 1, your computer can't really capture, manipulate, and store true color data. All color data is actually stored as groups of grayscale information called channels. Your computer produces grayscale information to which color is applied when the information leaves the computer, most commonly to a monitor, color printer, or printing press. The grayscale channel information is converted into color by activating color phosphors on your monitor's screen. During the printing process, color inks and dyes are applied to grayscale channel information in order to produce final color images. Because your computer is truly only a black and white device, it is useful to think of your color images as collections of grayscale channels.

In electronic publishing we typically work with two kinds of color images: RGB (Red, Green, and Blue) and CMYK (Cyan, Magenta, Yellow, and Black) images. RGB images and files are used to display color images on monitors and print onto color film, while CMYK images and files are used for reproduction of color images in most printing applications (see Chapter 14, "Color Me Right," for a more complete discussion of these two color spaces). RGB images require the creation of three eight bit per pixel (8 b/p) grayscale channels, one for each color, R,G, and B. Since each pixel has eight bits of information for each of three colors, this requires that each pixel have a total of 24 bits of data for each pixel. This means that each RGB image contains three times (3x) as much data per pixel as a grayscale image, and twenty four times (24x) as much information per pixel as a 1 bit black and white image. This of course also means that RGB images will be eight times larger than grayscale and twenty four times larger than black and white images of the same dimensions and resolution. This also means that RGB images will require that much more RAM to open, disk space to store, and RIP time for processing. In RGB color images, each 8 b/p channel has the capacity to store a total of 256 shades of that color, so that there are 256 shades each of red, green, and blue. This means

▼ *Figure 9.14 Simple Line Art*

This simple 1 bit graphic is an excellent candidate for outlining. It is simple with large areas of black and white which will create only a few (4) short, simple paths. This outline form of this graphic was created in two steps:

1) Scanned at 600 dpi and saved as a TIFF with a file size = 250KB.

2) Outlined in Streamline and saved as an EPS, EPS/outline file size = 50KB.

Note the dramatic 80 percent savings in file size.

▼ *Figure 9.15 Intermediate Complexity Line Art*

This graphic is more complex but still very convertible to paths. Many more paths (41) are created, but all the paths are relatively short and not very complex. This image was scanned at 600 dpi and saved as a 200KB TIFF. It was outlined and centerlined in Streamline, and saved as a 40KB EPS file which equals an 80 percent reduction in file size. Fine lines such as those that divide the sections of the butterfly's wings have been centerlined instead of outlined to preserve their delicacy.

▼ *Figure 9.16 Complex Line Art*

This complex graphic creates a series of long complex paths when outlined. This image was originally scanned at 550 dpi and saved as a 200KB TIFF. It was outlined and centerlined in Streamline, and saved as a 60KB EPS file size which equals a 90 percent reduction in file size. The length, number, and complexity of the paths may offset any file size advantage in terms of RIP time. This image could cause RIPing problems. Care must be taken to split and simplify these paths, and increase flatness ratio of these lines prior to RIPing.

▼ *Figure 9.17 High Detail Line Art*

This highly complex graphic is an example of a poor outlining candidate. In addition to destroying the fine dot details, outlining this image makes a far too complex outline graphic. While the files size savings is moderate, original TIFF = 242K, outline = 100K, or 60 percent of the original size, the number and complexity of the paths definitely offsets any file size advantage in terms of RIP time. It took me 15 minutes just to outline this file and I never could get it through a RIP. This kind of file is much better left as a TIFF both for image quality and RIPing purposes.

that when we multiply these three channels of 256 shades each together, we can have 256(R) x 256(G) x 256(B) = 16.7 million total possible color combinations.

CYMK images are treated very much like RGB images, with the difference that there are four 8 b/p grayscale channels instead of only three. During the preparation of an RGB screen image file to a printable format, the RGB colors are converted into the closest CMYK equivalents available. Black, or K, is then substituted for various percentages of C, M, and Y in order to improve contrast and detail, as well as reduce total ink density. This black substitution is accomplished using one of two substitution processes, under color removal (UCR) or gray component replacement (GCR). UCR generally replaces CMY in neutral shadow regions, while UCR replaces neutral CMY values throughout a broader tonal range of the image. Because CMYK files have a fourth 8 b/p grayscale channel, these files are 33 percent larger than their RGB equivalents (see Figure 9.11 for an overview of pixel depth).

WORKING WITH GRAPHICS

Pixel/raster graphics

Printing pixels

As we have mentioned, TIFF is the preferred general file format for pixel-based or raster image graphics which will be processed by a PostScript RIP and printed. Pixels can also be saved in EPS format. Which format we use usually depends upon the preference of the RIP being used to print the images. Ask your printing company for their preference, either TIFF or EPS, for pixel-based images. The primary file preparation issue, besides image quality, with pixel-based images is file size. Raster images, and particularly multibit per pixel images, can become huge files. The three variables affected are image dimension (e.g., 5"x 7"), pixel depth (e.g., 1, 8, 24, 32 bits/pixel), and resolution. Image dimension and pixel depth are generally determined by the document design and are therefore set. Resolution is therefore the one variable which can be altered to control the file size of an image. For multibit contone images, a good rule of thumb is generally not to exceed a resolution which is greater than two times (2x) the line screen at which the image will be printed. For instance, if an image will be printed at 150 lpi, then your image need not be greater than 300 dpi for a gray scale or color contone image. In most instances, even lower resolutions (1.5 x lpi) will actually suffice, but at least use the 2x lpi rule as an upper limit. One bit bitmapped line art images generally need to be created and saved at high resolutions (600 dpi+) due to their dependence on edge sharpness for image quality (see Chapter 12, "Taming Your Scanner," for a complete discussion of image resolution and line screen).

Viewing pixels

Pixel-based images which will be used for viewing of transporting over the Web should be saved in either GIF or JPEG format. The primary issue here is obtaining as small as file size as possible by reducing the pixel dimensions, resolution and/or **bit depth** of the images. See Chapter 15, "Weaving Web Graphics" for a more thorough discussion of creating graphic images for the Web. Other pixel-based viewing formats include WMF in in Windows and PICT on the Macintosh, both of which may be used in presentation programs such as PowerPoint. Be advised, however, that these file formats are not recommended for PostScript printing.

Vector graphics

Printing vectors

As previously noted, EPS is the preferred file format for outline/vector graphics which will be printed in a PostScript environment. Because of the outline rather than pixel composition, vector EPS graphic images are inherently more difficult to RIP and print. With pixel-based images we are converting pixels to other dots in the RIPing process, but with EPS graphics we must convert lines to dots, which is a more demanding task computationally. There are three factors which control the RIPability of an EPS graphic. They are path length, number of control points, and flatness ratio. Path length is measured from the start to the end of any closed path. A PostScript RIP must process an entire path, so the longer a path is, the more difficult it is to process. The number of control points along a path determines how complex the path is. The more control points there are, the greater a path's complexity and the more difficult it is to RIP.

Digital computers only "understand" straight lines. They do not understand curves, so all curved lines must be constructed out of progressive sequences of straight lines. Flatness ratio controls the number of line segments which will be used to construct a curved line. Flatness ratios generally vary from 1 to 10. A flatness ratio of 0 will require that a RIP create a large number of line segments to construct a curve, while a ratio of 10 will require very few lines. Both extremes are to be avoided.

Controlling path lengths, number of control points, and flatness ratios is important for all outline files. This includes EPS graphics created in drawing applications like FreeHand, Illustrator, and CorelDraw; outlining applications such as Streamline; and clipping-type outline paths created in applications like Photoshop. Generally speaking, you will want to minimize all three variables as much as possible without adversely affecting image quality. Path lengths should be split to reduce their length. The number of control points should be reduced by either manually removing them or through filters such as the simplification filter found in FreeHand. The optimum flatness ratio depends upon the path characteristics, the printing resolution, and the RIP being used. However, a good rule of thumb is to assign flatness ratios of between two and five (2–5). Nesting grouped objects and/or files inside of one another should also be avoided. Nested files can be created by Placing a previously created graphic inside a new graphic document. Copy and paste vector graphic elements between vector documents to avoid nesting. All final graphic elements should be editable. On the following page is a list of some common EPS guidelines. (See Chapter 16, "Application-Specific Tips," for more details. Also see Chapter 20, "Managing the Mess," for some specific EPS file prep procedures.)

▼ *Figure 9.18 Complex Line Art*
This is a complex line art graphic which has been saved as an EPS file. This graphic will benefit from the conversion from bitmap to outline format. The EPS format is smaller in file size than a TIFF file, and much easier to scale due to the line vs. bitmap construction of the image.

▼ *Figure 9.19 Complex Paths*
While converting this image into an outline image has advantages in file size and editability. This process also creates a fairly complex outline with long paths and many control points. After conversion, this image should be opened in a drawing application and have its long paths split and simplified, and flatness set to 2 or 3 to improve its RIPability.

▼ *Figure 9.20 Tight Fit Conversion*
This image shows the results of setting the conversion preferences in Streamline to Tight during conversion to an outline from a bitmap. As a result, these paths have many more control points than the image shown in Fig. 9.21. Each extra control point demands more processing time at the RIP.

▼ *Figure 9.21 Loose Fit Conversion*
This image shows the results when setting the conversion preferences in Streamline to Loose. These paths have far fewer points than the image shown in Fig. 9.20. This image, with its fewer control points, will be much easier to RIP.

Vector EPS file preparation for printing guidelines

- Simplify all path lengths prior to export of EPS from drawing applications.
- Split all paths prior to exporting EPS graphics from drawing applications.
- Set flatness ratio for paths between 2 and 5 for all exported EPS graphics.
- Simplify paths of outline graphics which have been created through an outline application.
- Set Tolerance preference to Loose prior to outlining a graphic in an outlining application such as Streamline.
- When creating paths from selections in Photoshop, and particularly if those selections have been defined through the use of the Magic Wand tool, be sure to set as high a tolerance as possible, usually greater than 1 when creating the path. This will reduce the number of control nodes which will be created when the path is drawn. I usually err on the side of simplicity and then fine tune the curves with the pen tool.
- Copy and paste, rather than Place, vector graphic elements between vector graphic documents to avoid nesting of graphic files
- When creating a clipping path from a path, always set the flatness to greater than 1, usually between 3 and 5 to reduce the number of individual vectors or straight lines which will be used to recreate curved lines.

Viewing vectors

For displaying vector-based images over the Web the preferred, at at this time only supported, file format is the ShockWave format (SWF). Using the Shockwave format allows us to take advantage of the small files sizes, crisp edges and scalability which vector images provide on the Web. Please see Chapter 15, "Weaving Web Graphics," for a more thorough discussion of creating graphic images for the Web.

Other vector-based viewing formats include WMF in in Windows and PICT on the Macintosh, both of which may be used in presentation programs such as PowerPoint. Be advised however, that these file formats are not recommended for PostScript printing.

TIP

Convert simple, low detail, one-bit pixel based line art images into vector/outline graphics in EPS format. Vector EPSs have smaller file sizes than pixel-based images and are resolution-independent and scalable as well. Use vector EPS file to reduce file size and improve editability (especially scaling and skewing) of line art files.

Outlining pixel-based graphics

Consider converting the original pixel-based image of scanned 1-bit line art graphics (logos for example) into outlined vector graphics using an outlining application such as Streamline. (Note: while drawing applications such as FreeHand, Illustrator and CorelDraw have their own outlining tools, a dedicated outlining tool, such as Streamline, will typically provide better control and results). Original images should be of high quality and scanned at moderate to high optical resolution (see Chapter 12, "Taming Your Scanner") to avoid jagged edges. Outlining can save 50–90 percent on file size. Outlining an image will allow you to scale, rotate, and skew images without any loss of image edge quality. Spot/Pantone color original images should generally be scanned as black and white images, converted to outline/vector EPS files, and have the color built within a drawing program. This approach will net you smaller, more editable and color correct files. Don't use PICT or WMF files for PostScript printed material. These are mainly for on-screen, video, and multimedia creations.

While outlining is often a good idea for simple and intermediate complexity line art images, there are some potential problems to be aware of. Outlining may create paths which are very long and complex, which make them more difficult to RIP. There are several procedures you can follow to help eliminate or reduce these characteristics. It is generally a good idea to set the Fit preference to Loose in an outlining application like Streamline, as tighter settings tend to create paths which are too complex. Also consider running your outlined graphic through a drawing application like FreeHand, Illustrator, or CorelDraw so that you can simplify and split the paths, and set the best flatness ratios (see Figs. 9.16–9.19 for examples of various line art images which lend themselves in various degrees to outlining). There are some images, such as that shown in Fig. 9.16, which should never be converted to outlines, but should be left as bitmapped images (see Chapter 12, "Taming Your Scanner," for a complete discussion of evaluating a graphic image for outlining. Also, see Chapter 15, "Application-Specific Tips," for examples of applications such as FreeHand and Streamline). All the above tips for reducing the complexity of vector based images through control of the number of control points and flatness ratios are important tools in our struggle to *Reduce and Simplify*!

Blends

Always use blends, fills, and patterns judiciously. One problem which commonly occurs when creating blends is banding. Banding occurs most frequently in long blends containing a wide gray scale spectrum. Banding is caused by the PostScript limitation of 256 gray scale steps. When working with blends, choose the minimum number of steps necessary to create a smooth blend. Use a formula or a utility like Blender. Smooth, band-free blends, and especially large ones, are best created in bitmap-oriented applications like PhotoShop, rather than in object-oriented drawing programs like Illustrator, FreeHand or CorelDraw. Unlike drawing applications, in bitmap-oriented applications, where you will create a blend between the foreground and background layers, you can redistribute pixels. The banding problem can be overcoming applications like Photoshop if you apply 3–4 units of Gaussian blur or dither the blend which redistributes pixels across blend borders. The

Gaussian blur mainly affects midtones. This is an especially effective technique for blending large areas.

Imported or placed graphics

Graphic files are imported into page layout applications as low resolution versions unless they are imbedded. (This is why your Quark or PageMaker documents are not as large as they they would be if they included the entire hi-res file.). The layout application links the low resolution placed image to the external high resolution graphic file for printing. Do not change a graphic file's name after importing the graphic into another application because the links are maintained through name recognition. The importing (page layout) application will not be able to find and link to the renamed file. If you make a change to the graphic which you have imported into a page layout application, and you are not using publish and subscribe capabilities, be sure to update your screen view in the page layout application. If you do not do so, you may be surprised at what you get when you print out the document.

Precropped, scaled, and rotated TIFF and EPS graphics print faster than those cropped, scaled, and rotated within a layout program. During the image creation process, plan to precrop, rotate, and scale the original or scanned image to the exact size you will ultimately need for printing. Doing so, particularly for graphic-intensive documents like catalogs, will save you hours of manipulation and RIPing time during the document construction and printing processes. If you are unsure of what the final crop and size will be, use your layout program as a design and iteration tool, but perform final graphic manipulations on the high resolution images in the original graphic applications prior to printing. Remember that images placed in page layout applications are only low resolution proxies for the high resolution images which are external to the layout document (see Chapter 13, "Document Construction," for a review of this concept). When a placed image is cropped, rotated, or resized in a page layout document, only the low resolution proxy is being manipulated. If you do not perform the final manipulations to the high resolution files, these changes will need to be processed on the fly during the RIPing process, which will dramatically increase processing times. This precropping, rotating, and resizing of images is particularly crucial with graphic-intensive documents such as catalogs where on the fly processing of hundreds of images can lead to unacceptably long RIPing times.

One other issue to be addressed is the imbedding of high resolution graphics in page layout documents. Some applications such as PageMaker give you the option of including (imbedding) the high resolution version of a placed graphic image, as well as the low resolution proxy, which is always included. In most circumstances, it is better to **not** include the high resolution of a placed graphic. Imbedding the high resolution versions of placed graphics files will significantly increase the file size of the page layout document, making it more difficult to manage. Imbedding also makes editing and updating the graphic image much more difficult. It is better to keep the high resolution versions of your graphic images as separate files which will be sent along with the page layout document file.

Avoiding nesting graphics

PostScripts RIPs have a difficult time finding graphics files which have been placed one-inside-the-other. Avoid nesting graphics such as Placing one EPS graphic into a drawing application document and then constructing additional graphic elements around it. Always Open a previously created EPS so that it is editable, then you can add additional graphic elements to the same file without creating a nested file. It is also dangerous to create EPS files out of a document which already contains EPS or TIFF files, such as a page layout document.

Type (fonts), which are just special kinds of graphic files set in an exported EPS file as editable text, may not be found by a RIP, or the entire file may not print at all. It is always best to limit the amount of type which you set in a graphic file which you know will be exported as an EPS file. Any type which is created in the outline graphic should be converted to paths prior to exporting it as an EPS file. If type characters need to remain as editable type, due to the amount of type and/or poor outlining results, limiting the number of typeface and styles used will improve printing speed as well. Remember that it is usually preferable to set large amounts of type in page layout program such as QuarkXPress, PageMaker or InDesign.

Some miscellaneous graphical do's and don'ts

Here is a brief list of a few other separate but important guidelines for working with graphics.

- Logo sheets with several (6 or more) logos on them will print fastest from the programs in which they were created, for example, FreeHand or Illustrator. Imported logo graphics will generally print but will take longer and cost more money at the service bureau. Cut paths in drawn (object-oriented) graphics. Keep auto-trace paths as simple as possible.

- Don't use Hairline widths for lines: always assign a specific value to a line's width. Hairline values are inconsistent from one application to another and many are too thin to print properly at high resolution. Don't assign line values below 0.25 pt., as they will often not print properly at high resolution.

- Use graphics boxes instead of text boxes to create borders. Don't specify hairline rules or lines for files to be printed on an imagesetter, they may disappear. Specify a specific line weight, e.g., 0.5 or 0.25. Don't assign dot percentage on a small line. For files to be printed on an imagesetter, don't use an outlined Zapf Dingbats "n" to specify a check box (☐); its outline stroke is too thin. Instead, use another font's box or try the Zapf Dingbat "o"(❑).

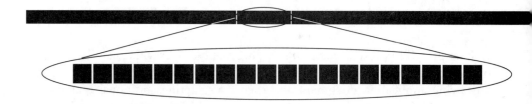

▼ *Figure 9.22 Compression Scheme*
One technique used by nearly all compression schemes is to record and then remove redundant pixels when the file is compressed. The compression of a black line shows how this works. The black line above may require 2,500 black pixels stacked end to end, like the pixels in the expanded view, to construct it. This would require 2,500 bits of file space to record. We will use a redundant pixel record and remove compression technique to compress this 2,500 pixel line segment above. The first pixel is located and stored in the file. The compression software will note that the next 2499 pixels are the same, but instead recording each pixel, the software makes a notation like [+2499] which indicates that the next 2499 pi are identical to the first black one. In this example, the compressed version of the file requires 56 bits space for the notation (7 ASCII characters x 8 bits/pixel), plus one bit for the original black pixel, for a total of 57 bits of information. Compared to the 2,500 bits required to store the uncompressed version the file, the compressed version achieves a 44/1 compression ratio with a reduction of 97 percent file s

FEELING COMPRESSED

What is compression?

Compression is the reduction in the size of a file by reducing, through the use of shortcut data recording methods, the space required for storing the information contained in a file. Compressing a file is somewhat like squeezing a sponge. You can squeeze a sponge in your hand to 1/10th of its original size, but all the sponge information is still there, it's just in a more compact form. When you release your grip on the sponge, you decompress the sponge, and the sponge reassumes its original form. The sponge had a built-in memory of its original size and shape. This is similar to what happens with the compression of digital files. Some types of digital file compression retain all of the original information, like our sponge, and some do not.

Need for compression

As we have seen in this chapter and in Chapter 8, "Resolving Resolution," graphic files can take up huge volumes of digital space. Graphic file pages are hundreds to thousands of times the size of pages filled with text alone. A standard 8.5" x 11" page filled margin to margin with 12 point type requires a mere 5KB (kilobytes) of storage space. An 8.5" x 11," 300 dpi, 1 bit (bitonal, B&W) graphic takes up 1.05MB (MegaBytes) of space, two hundred times (200x) the room required for the text only page. That same page at 600 dpi requires 4.2MB of space or eight hundred times (800x) the size of the text only page. And that same page created as a 32 bit/pixel CMYK image @ 600 dpi demands 135 MB of room, which is over twenty five thousand times (25,000x) the room required by the text only page!

As file sizes grow, so does the need for RAM space to work on those images, storage space to physically store and transport those images, and time to process those images. And sending these huge graphic images around our local area networks (LANs) and wide area telecommunications networks (WANs) becomes a daunting task indeed. The mushrooming image demands of digital video and multimedia are also driving the development of compression technologies. The practical storage and transportation of large graphic files has required the development and use of increasingly sophisticated compression schemes which provide continually improving decompressed image quality with increasing amounts of compression.

The need for fast transport/transfer times for images which are sent and viewed across the Internet on the World Wide Web makes compression of images, even extensive compression, not only acceptable, but a necessity (see Chapter 15, "Weaving Web Graphics," for more information on creating Web images).

How compression works

There are many different varieties of compression schemes and some are quite ingenious and sophisticated, such as the nifty Huffman compression used in PhotoCD. One common routine used by most compression schemes is the removal of redundant information. Most images have large numbers of pixels which have the same, that is, redundant, values. When a file is compressed, instead of recording each identical pixel in a graphic format, shortcut notations can be made about the presence of these redundant pixels instead of actually storing the pixels. These shortcut notations require far less space to record than the actual pixel data. An example may help here. Redundant pixel compression of a long straight black line, like the one shown in Fig. 9.17, will illustrate how this type of compression works.

The more redundant pixels an image has, the easier it is to achieve large high quality compression files. In general, bitonal or black and white images are easier to compress than contone images because, with only two tone values, they have greater numbers of identical or redundant pixels.

Types of compression

There are basically two compression technologies: lossless and lossy. With lossless compression technologies, examples of which include LZW, ZIP and Stuffit, an image does not lose any information during the compression/decompression process. Lossless compression generally does not provide greater than fifty percent (50%), that is, 2/1, compression. With lossy compression, a common example of which is JPEG, we can achieve from 20 to 90 percent (5/1 to 90/1) image compression. With this type of compression we always affect some loss of information and therefore quality. The amount of quality loss depends largely upon the amount of compression. As a rule, the more an image is compressed beyond 50 percent, the more information we can expect to lose. Figure 9.23 shows a sequence from uncompressed, slightly compressed to highly compressed.

▼ *Figure 9.23 Compressed vs. Uncompressed Images*
Shown here are three files of the same image:
Top: Uncompressed 200 ppi TIFF image
Middle: Minimum JPEG compression (5/1)
Bottom: Maximum JPEG compression (50/1)
In terms of their quality, the top and middle images are similar to each other as there is little apparent image degradation due to the modest (5/1) compression. The bottom image however, which has been compressed significantly (50/1), shows major damage to the image. Note the posterization which results from the extreme compression.

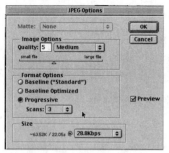

▼ Figure 9.24 Creating JPEGs
JPEGs are best used for Web images, for storage and sometimes low quality printing. The quality of the image can be controlled through the amount of compression. Because of compression related quality reduction, it is best to avoid using JPEG compressed images for high resolution PostScript printing.

Lossy compression is required if we are to achieve significant amounts of file size reductions. A 135MB CMYK file would only be reduced to 67.2MB with a 50 percent, 2/1 lossless compression. And while this will halve our storage space and transmission time demands, it is often not enough. A 67MB file is still a monster. Conversely, a 40/1 compression of our 135MB file yields a 3.3MB file which is exceedingly smaller and therefore more manageable. As we will see in Chapter 15, "Weaving Web Graphics," significantly reduced file sizes are a must for displaying and even sending images over the World Wide Web.

Compression and printing

Because of the potential loss of significant image quality, it is generally a good idea to refrain from applying lossy type compressions, such as JPEG, to images which will be printed on PostScript printing devices, and particularly if they are to be imaged on high resolution imaging devices such as on an image or platesetter at a commercial print company. Image quality problems can show up during the RIPing and printing process which may not have been obvious when the compressed image are viewed on screen.

Compression formats

Compression file formats are proliferating like rabbits. Entire volumes are now being written and rewritten on compression file formats. There is a great deal of confusion and disagreement about compression file format standards. Luckily, in the general print and Web arenas, we have some standards. GIF files, used for the Web, employ lossless (2/1 maximum) LZW compression. JPEG is also commonly used on the Web. JPEG was developed by a group of industry experts as a way of setting a high quality, predictable compression standard which all could use. But, as we have discussed, lossy compression is required in order to achieve significant file size reduction. Other compression schemes like QuickTime are used for digital video and multimedia files. In general, images which are primarily intended for viewing can accept more image compression before unacceptable image quality degradation occurs, than can those images which will be used for print.

Limit the amount of compression—use lossless compression if any at all—that you apply to image which will be printed, especially in a high resolution PostScript environment. High compression, lossy, of image which will be used for viewing over the Web is more acceptable and in fact many times necessary in order to achieve reasonable Internet transport times.

Working with compressed files

If you need to compress image files to free up storage space or facilitate transmission over networks (local or wide area), be sure to be aware of whether the compression is lossless or lossy. If your compression is lossy, make sure you choose a compression ratio which does not degrade your image too much. Remember that some compression applications will allow you to compress selectively various portions of your image by varying amounts. Also, if you intend to send your compressed files to someone else, be sure that the receiving party has the ability to decompress your images. Many compression applications provide decompression

TIP

Always resave lossy compressed images, such as JPEGs, as uncompressed or lossless compressed images. If lossy compressed images are recompressed in a lossy manner, severe image quality damage is likely to occur.

utilities which you are free to send along with your compressed files. Using JPEG compression is generally a safe bet because most major applications like Photoshop, QuarkXpress, and PageMaker have extensions or plug-ins for accessing JPEG compressed files.

Compare and contrast the images in Fig. 9.23. The first image is a 200 ppi Photoshop image which has been saved as a Tiff file with no compression. The second file is the same image saved as a JPEG file out of Photoshop with minimum JPEG compression, and the third image has been saved with maximum JPEG compression. The file size for the first, uncompressed image is 320K, while the maximum JPEG compressed image is only 64K. This represents a 40/1 compression, which is highly compressed, with a 80 percent decrease in file size. As you can see, the difference between the two images is very subtle. Generally, JPEG compression ratios of 5/1 to 10/1 produce very good quality images which are often difficult to distinguish from the original images. The third image saved with maximum compression shows much more noticeable image quality degradation. There is one rule of thumb which you should try to follow: Avoid compressing a graphic file more than once. My modus operandi is that while an image is in print production, I keep it in an uncompressed format like TIFF or EPS. When I am ready to archive an image or send it via modem or I am preparing it for viewing on the Internet, then I will compress it.

Never double compress an image, as severe image quality degradation will likely occur. An example of double degradation of an image would be to perform a Save As on an JPEG image and save it as another JPEG image. This would apply another round of image resampling and averaging during the second compression process.

CHAPTER SUMMARY

Much of the complexity and confusion surrounding graphic files can be relieved by separating graphic file contents from containers. Contents include pixels and vectors. Graphic file formats are use specific. Pixel-based images are used with high detail images such as contones, while vector based images are most often used with low detail images such as logos. Pixel based images can be converted into vector based images in order to take advantage of the reduced file size, editability, and resolution independence of vector based images. Compound images contain both pixels and vectors in the same file. Graphic images are constructed in highly editable native file formats and then saved for final use in output formats for printing and viewing. TIFF and EPS are best used for PostScript printing. GIF and JPEG are the two preferred file formats for pixel based Web images, while the SWF file format is used for Web vector images. TIFF, EPS GIF and JPEG can be taken cross platform. To assure maximum transportability it is best to use eight or fewer characters in a file name followed by a three character lowercase extension. The number of shades of gray or color values in an image is controlled by its bit depth. Reducing file size and complexity are keys to fast and trouble free printing and viewing. Avoid nesting images inside one another. Blends are best created with pixel based images. There are two types of compression, lossless and lossy. Lossy compression offers far more file size reduction but increased likelihood of image quality damage as well. It is best to avoid lossy compression, or even avoid compression altogether, for images which will be printed in a high resolution PostScript environment. Compression, even extensive compression, is acceptable and even necessary for images which are transferred and displayed over the Web.

PAULINE'S DIGITAL IMAGING TIPS

Pauline's Tip 9.1

There are two basic types of electronic graphic images, bitmapped/raster images which are constructed out of pixels, and vector/outline images which are constructed out of lines. Choose the type of image which best suits your needs. Vector images are preferred for simple line art which needs to be rendered with sharp edges. Vector based images have the benefit of scalability without alteration of their resolution. The raster basis for an image is preferred when great detail is present, such as in complex line art and contone images.

Pauline's Tip 9.2

Match graphic file format with end use. TIFF and EPS are the preferred file formats for use in PostScript printing. Use TIFF format for high detail and continuous tone images. Use EPS format for low detail images and for scalability or for contone images which have additional information stored with them such as clipping paths and transfer function data. Do not use PICT or PCX files for print pieces. These are screen format files. Stick to using EPS and TIFF file formats whenever possible for files to be printed in a PostScript environment. GIF, JPEG and SWF are the preferred file format for Web images.

Pauline's Tip 9.3

Convert simple, low detail, one-bit pixel based line art images into vector/outline graphics in EPS format. Vector EPSs have smaller file sizes than pixel-based images and are resolution-independent and scalable as well. Use vector EPS file to reduce file size and improve editability (especially scaling and skewing) of line art files. Use dedicated outlining applications, such as Adobe Streamline, to accomplish this task; your control and results will be better than using the built-in outlining capabilities of your drawing application.

Pauline's Tip 9.4

Create blends in pixel based editing applications like Photoshop instead of in vector based drawing or page layout applications. You will have more control over your blends and they will print faster and better. A pixel-based application like Photoshop allows you to add noise to your blends, which helps reduce banding upon output.

PAULINE'S DIGITAL IMAGING TIPS

Pauline's Tip 9.5

Choose the proper pixel depth of your image depending upon how it will be used. Remember, increasing pixel depth increases file size. Use 1 bit for line art images, 8 bit for grayscale images, 24 bit for RGB screen images, and 32 bit for CMYK process color images.

Pauline's Tip 9.6

Vector images are inherently more difficult to RIP than pixel-based images. Vector-based EPS files need to be specially prepared. Simplify (reduce the number of control points), split long or complex paths, and set Flatness ratio for paths between 2 and 5 prior to creation of an EPS file. Attention to these three variables will make your vector-based images much easier to RIP.

Pauline's Tip 9.7

Exercise care when creating outline paths. When creating an outline in applications like Streamline, set Fit Tolerance preference to Loose prior to conversion to assure a simpler file with fewer nodes. This will make it easier for a PostScript RIP to process the paths created.

Pauline's Tip 9.8

When converting paths from selections in Photoshop, be sure to choose a tolerance which results in a low number of path control points, usually ≥ 2. Also, when converting a path to a clipping path in Photoshop, select a flatness ratio ≥ 3; this will reduce the number of line segments used when the path is drawn during printing. This is similar to what we discussed in File Prep Hints 18 and 19, and will help simplify the vector-based portion of these primarily contone images for easier RIPing.

Pauline's Digital Imaging Tips

Pauline's Tip 9.9

Do not assign Hairline widths for lines; they are inconsistent and usually too thin. Always assign a specific, unambiguous, thickness value to a line. Do not assign any line thickness values less than 0.25 points.

Pauline's Tip 9.10

Do not assign patterns or grayscale values to thin lines (≤4pts.), as these patterns or values will be rendered as halftone dots during RIPing and printing and will be displayed as discontinuous blotches on paper.

Pauline's Tip # 9.11

Find out in which file formats your printer or service bureau prefers to receive your files. While TIFF and EPS are certainly the universal formats, there are often several choices for saving a file within these two general formats. For instance, 1 bit line art images can be saved as TIFFs or converted to vector-based EPSs. Color contone images are perhaps the most variable. Find out if you should send in your file as a CMYK TIFF or a 5-file DCS. You should avoid creating single file CMYK EPS files, as these are very time consuming to RIP.

Pauline's Tip 9.12

Use these tips to increase the likelihood that your graphic images can be shared cross platform. Use the TIFF file format for pixel based images. Use generic EPSs or Illustrator files for vector based images. Limit file names to eight characters. Place a three character lowercase extension, such as .tif, on the end of each file name to make sure that the file format will be recognized regardless of which platform on which it is used. GIF, JPEG and SWF file formats are by their nature cross platform capable file formats.

Pauline's Digital Imaging Tips

Pauline's Tip 9.12

If your printing company or service bureau performs scans for you or otherwise creates original graphics, be sure that when they send the file back to you that you know if it is a high or low resolution version of the graphic. If you intend to edit, correct, or otherwise perform pixel level alterations of the image, be sure you receive the high resolution version, as the low resolution version is useless for this purpose. A low resolution version will only be useful for placement purposes. In either case, and particularly if you receive a low resolution FPO (for placement only) image, do not change the name in any way. If the printing company has sent you a low resolution image, they have the high resolution image (which will be used during the the actual RIPing) stored on their drive. If you change the name your FPO image will not be recognized as a match for the high resolution print version when you return the image, and a low quality image will result during printing.

Pauline's Tip 9.14

Avoiding using highly compressed (lossy compressed) images in printing. In fact it is a good idea to stay away from placing compression of images in documents which are intended for printing. This is especially true for any documents and images which are to be printed in a high resolution PostScript environment. If compression is to be used at all, lossless compression ($\leq$ 50%) is best used for images which will be printed. Be aware that the greater the compression, the greater the likelihood of significant image quality reduction. Also be aware that image quality problems may not be obvious when viewing the image on a monitor, but may show up during printing.

Pauline's Tip 9.15

Never resave a lossy compressed image as another lossy compressed image. For example never open a JPEG image and then resave it as another JPEG image. This will force a double compression of the image which will lead to severe image degradation. Always save compressed image in uncompressed or lossless compressed formats to prevent further image degradation.

CHAPTER REVIEW

Check Your Comprehension

Multiple Choice Questions

To help you review the topics covered in this chapter, answer the following multiple choice questions.

1. What concept helps us simplify and understand graphic files and formats?
   A. Print and Web formats are the same
   B. Use vectors for all images
   C. All graphics are bitmaps
   D. Separate graphic file contents and containers

2. Which of the following is a graphic file content building block?
   A. TIFF
   B. JPEG
   C. Vector
   D. GIF

3. Which of the following would be considered a graphic file format?
   A. GIF
   B. Vector
   C. Pixel
   D. Compound image

4. Choose the pair which is contains the best file format for PostScript printing.
   A. GIF and JPEG
   B. TIFF and EPS
   C. Pixel and vector
   D. TIFF and SWF

5. Choose the pair which contains the best file format for Web use.
   A. GIF and JPEG
   B. TIFF and EPS
   C. Pixel and vector
   D. TIFF and SWF

6. Which of the following is smaller, more scalable and easier to edit than the others?
   A. Vector image
   B. Pixel image
   C. JPEG image
   D. GIF image

7. _____ is used to convert pixel based images into vector based images
   A. Photoshop
   B. Scanner
   C. Streamline
   D. Compression program

8. Compound images have
   A. GIF and JPEG components
   B. Compressed and uncompressed portions
   C. Pixels and vectors
   D. All of the above

9. Which of the following terms is a native file format?
   A. Photoshop
   B. TIFF
   C. GIF
   D. SWF

10. _____ are generally used to create high detail images.
   A. Raster images
   B. Bitmapped images
   C. Pixel based images
   D. All of the above

11. Which of the following adheres to the 8.3 cross platform file naming convention?
   A. Red Bird Image
   B. Redbird.TIF
   C. Redbird.tif
   D. Redbird

12. Blends or gradients are best constructed in
   A. Photoshop
   B. Illustrator
   C. FreeHand
   D. QuarkXPress

Check Your Understanding

Concept Questions

To help you review and expand your thinking on the topics covered in this chapter, answer the following questions.

1. Briefly explain the difference between graphic file contents and containers.

2. Describe the difference between pixel and vector based images. Explain when should each be used.

3. Explain the concept of matching file format with use. Provide two examples of this matching concept.

4. What is the difference between a native file and an output file format?

5. What are the advantages of converting a pixel based image into a vector image?

6. What type of images do not lend themselves to conversion into vector? Explain why.

7. Briefly explain the concept of bit depth. What does bit depth control? Give two examples.

8. What can we do to help provide cross platform compatibility for our graphic files?

9. Outline the specific details to which we must attend in order to properly prepare a vector EPS file for print.

10. Describe the two basic types of compression, how each affects image quality and where each should and should not be used.

PROJECTS

1. Open a 200–300 ppi pixel based image in Photoshop. Make four duplicate copies of this image and save them out as TIFF, EPS, GIF and JPEG. How do the dialog boxes vary from one file format to another. Arrange them in order of file size. Describe where you would use each file format type.

2. Create a bitmapped image and convert an image in Streamline using the guidelines set forth in this chapter. Open this new vector image up in a drawing application and scale the image. Does the edge quality change as a result of scaling?

3. Open a 200–300 ppi contone image in Photoshop. Perform a Save As on this image five different times to create five JPEG formatted images, using progressively higher compression amounts each time. Be sure to return to the original image each time you create another JPEG. Describe the changes which you see in the image from the lowest to the highest compression amounts. Be sure to include both file size and image quality in your description.

10
RIPing Up Your Files

As the Byte Turns continues…

Will Danny's plans to get together with Pauline have a chance,
or will Pauline RIP his plans to shreds?

My file printed fine on my 300 dpi laser. What's wrong with you and your equipment?

Well, ah, I don't know.

We can't have Danny upset !

Can't we make his file print?

What do you think I am, a Magician? To process these files at high resolution requires millions of more calculations than his 300 dpi laser!

Chapter Objectives

In this chapter you will learn:

◆ **How PostScript RIPs work**
◆ **PostScript Language**
◆ **Resolution and RIPing**
◆ **The need for smaller, simplified documents**
◆ **PostScript dictionaries**
◆ **Levels of PostScript**
◆ **RIP once, print many times**
◆ **Key Terms**
  • RIP
  • PostScript
  • PostScript interpreter
  • Software RIP
  • Hardware RIP
  • PostScript laser printer
  • PostScript imagesetter
  • PostScript printer driver
  • Spots
  • Dots (halftone dots)
  • PostScript dictionary
  • PostScript error

INTRODUCTION

Whenever we print an image or a document, our files are passed through a processor know as a **RIP**. RIP is short for raster image processor. The job of a RIP is to convert your image into printable building blocks. There are many types of RIPs which understand a variety of document languages, but the types of RIPs with which we are most concerned are **PostScript** RIPs. PostScript RIPS process our pixel and PostScript image and document data into spot and dot data which can be imaged on one of our PostScript printers. RIPs can be either hardware or software based. High resolution RIPing requires more computing power than low resolution RIPing. Text and line art images are RIPed into patterns of **spots** while contone images are RIPped into halftone dot patterns (see Chapter 17, "Screening Your Images" for a more thorough examination of spots and dots). If you are working in a PostScript environment it is very important to be using both **PostScript printer drivers** and PostScript printing devices, i.e., printing devices with PostScript RIPs. Creating and printing PostScript based documents without the use of PostScript printer drivers and printers will result in inaccurate printing at best, or **PostScript errors** and no printing at all. In fact it is always best to have a PostScript printer driver chosen prior to beginning the construction of a PostScript based document.

It is useful to think of your PostScript RIP as a funnel through which all your digital document components must be processed. If our document components are too large or complex, it can significantly slow down, or even prevent, the RIPing process. PostScript RIPs contain PostScript dictionaries where various portions of a digital document are processed. If any one of these PostScript dictionaries is overwhelmed with data, a PostScript error may result, which usually results in the termination of the RIPing and therefore the printing process. There have been progressively improving levels of PostScript starting with PostScript Level 1, then Level 2, and now there is PostScript Level 3. Each level includes more capabilities than the one before. It is important that you match up the level of PostScript you generate from your documents and printer drivers with the PostScript level of the RIP. If you try to print PostScript Level 3 data on a PostScript Level 1 or 2 RIP your document will not RIP and print properly, if at all.

POSTSCRIPT LANGUAGE AND DRIVERS

PostScript language

PostScript is a page description language, also called a "code," developed by Adobe, which was specifically designed to enhance the creation and integration of complex text and graphics for printing. The PostScript language is used to describe the page geometry as well as the size, shape, placement, content and characteristics of text and graphic elements of electronic documents. Fig. 10.1 shows an example of a section of PostScript code. Although it is unnecessary for you to learn to write PostScript code, it is very helpful to be at least familiar with how PostScript works. I highly recommend *PostScript: A Visual Approach* by Ross Smith as a good, understandable introduction to PostScript and how it works. In order to create and print PostScript based documents we must have a tool box of PostScript based tools including PostScript savvy applications, printer drivers and RIPs.

PostScript Printer drivers

Along with PostScript capable applications we need to use PostScript printer drivers when we create and print our documents. PostScript printer drivers are the critical link between our page layout documents and our PostScript RIPs. Printer drivers contain important information, such as page geometry, resolution, page margins, image area, and screening information, about the device to which we will be printing. This information is used in both the creation and the printing of our documents. A PostScript printer driver creates a stream of PostScript formatted document information which the RIP can recognize and process into spots and dots. It is even critical that we have a PostScript printer driver available and selected on our computers even before we begin to create a PostScript based document. If we change from a non-PostScript printer driver to a PostScript printer driver after we have begun to construct our document, we will usually see dramatic changes in the such as page geometry and the placement and /or orientation of our text and image components. Of course the PostScript printer driver is a critical component during the printing process itself.

PostScript Code

```
0 0 F 4 (I___Copperplate32bc)
T F
/I_____CopperplateThirtyTwoB
C 0 T dfnt
0 18 18 f
246 48 135 96 m .55 0 14 149
.5 (PostScript Code)d
end
```

▼ *Figure 10.1 PostScript Code*
This is a small portion, text formatting information of the PostScript language description of the bordered text box shown above with the words **PostScript Code** set in Copperplate 32bc. The entire length of code for an 8.5" x 11" page with just this one bordered text box runs into 22 pages.

THE POSTSCRIPT RIP

The generation of spots and dots

What is a RIP anyway? The word RIP is not really a word at all but an acronym, or shortcut, for raster image processor. This sounds like a complex, intimidating term but in reality the basic concept of the RIP is quite simple. Let's break the phrase down into its components. First of all, a raster is just a fancy word for dot or line of dots. Image is self explanatory. Processor is a device which alters the characteristics of something or changes one thing into another. Now let's read the phrase backward. Processor image raster, or more simply – a RIP processes images into spots and **dots (halftone dots)**(see Chapter 17, "Screening Your Images," for more detailed information on spots and dots).

Every element on a page which is sent to a RIP is converted into spots and/or dots. That is, all page geometry, text, line art, and contone graphics are converted into spots and dots. This is the sole function of a RIP. While there are certain advantages to working with some graphic images which are constructed out of lines (vector line art and printer fonts) and others out of pixels (contone raster images and screen fonts) while we manipulate them on the computer, all of these elements must ultimately be converted into spots and dots when we want to print them.

PostScript printers and RIPs

Nearly all printers which are used in electronic publishing systems work in tandem with a RIP. Digital documents created on a computer are sent to a RIP. The RIP then processes this information so that your printing device can recreate your document out of spots and dots, the building blocks which the printer then images onto a piece of film or paper. The printer itself is merely the spot/dot generation, or imaging, instrument. It is the RIP's job to translate all of the page information coming from the computer, which does all of the heavy work. While there is a wide variety of RIPs and associated printers, the vast majority of printers which are used with current open electronic publishing systems are PostScript printers. This means that these printers are matched with and connected to RIPs which "understand" or can interpret and process PostScript code into patterns of dots. PostScript RIPs are often called **PostScript interpreters** because they interpret PostScript code into patterns of dots which the printer hardware can work with. Whether you are printing to a 300 dpi laser printer or a 5000 dpi imagesetter, a RIP is used to translate or interpret the information you create on your computer into a pattern of dots which the printer places on a sheet of film or paper.

▼ *Figure 10.2 PostScript Laser Printer*
Desktop laser printers such as this Apple LaserWriter have a PostScript RIP, or interpreter, built onto an internal board which is built into their cases. The print engine itself would not work without this built-in RIP.
Desktop laser printers have resolutions ranging from 300 dpi to as high as 1200 dpi. Laser printers generally produce lower resolution images than imagesetters and therefore produce far fewer dots which require far less data processing by the RIP.

CREATION, RIPING AND PRINTING OF IMAGES

From Pixels, to spots and dots, to print

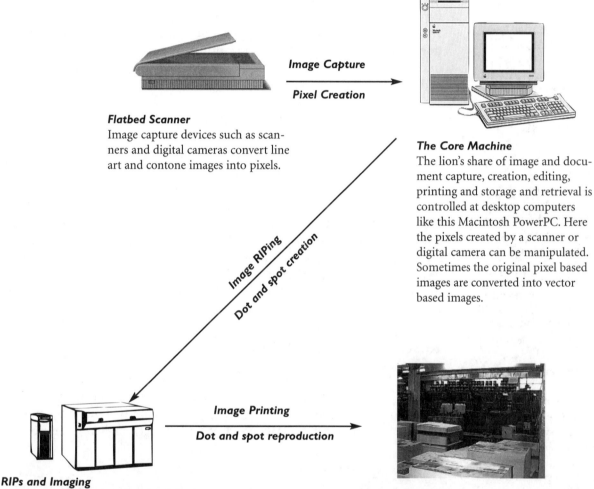

Image Capture

Pixel Creation

Image RIPing

Dot and spot creation

Image Printing

Dot and spot reproduction

Flatbed Scanner
Image capture devices such as scanners and digital cameras convert line art and contone images into pixels.

The Core Machine
The lion's share of image and document capture, creation, editing, printing and storage and retrieval is controlled at desktop computers like this Macintosh PowerPC. Here the pixels created by a scanner or digital camera can be manipulated. Sometimes the original pixel based images are converted into vector based images.

RIPs and Imaging
RIPs (raster image processors) attached to imaging devices such as imagesetters and laser printers convert vector and pixel based images into patterns of spots and dots. In commercial printing digital documents are sometimes imaged to film first, then reimaged into plates. Increasingly digital documents are being imaged directly onto plates, which bypasses the filmmaking process. Printing direct to plates, known as CTP (computer to plate), results in reduced processing times and high quality results, but also places a premium on accurate document construction and file prep.

Conventional Four-Color Press
Images, now in the form of spots and dots, are formed on plates, either directly from a computer or created via intermediate film production, are placed on press cylinders and used for the reproduction of those images.

There are two kinds of RIPs: **hardware RIPs** and **software RIPS**. Hardware RIPs are really just very specialized computers that have a motherboard just like a desktop computer. Sometimes the RIP motherboard is housed in its own separate case, as is often the case with imagesetter RIPs, or the RIP may be built into the printer box itself, as it usually is in most desktop printers. On a RIP motherboard, the normal CPU chip is replaced by a PostScript processing chip. Hardware RIPs have their own RAM, storage capabilities, and communication ports just like any other desktop computer. And just like desktop computers, there are slow RIPs and fast RIPs, and fast RIPs cost more money. Built into the PostScript processing chip is a set of interpretation instructions which are designed to read PostScript instructions sent from an application and/or printer driver and convert that information into sequences of dots, which is the only kind of information that laser printers and imagesetters understand.

Software RIPs perform the same function as hardware RIPs, that is, they convert PostScript information into dots, but instead of having a dedicated processor chip, a software RIP operates on a standard desktop computer. A software RIP uses the computer's CPU, RAM, and storage for its processing chores. The conversion or interpretation instructions are contained in the form of software instead of being hard-wired into a hardware chip. The advantage of software RIPs is that they are more flexible, easier, and less expensive to upgrade. A wide variety of printing devices, including laser printers, ink jets, dye sublimation and image and platesetters can be PostScript capable. But regardless of the type of printing device you have, it should be a PostScript capable device if you expect your documents and images to print accurately. Without a PostScript RIP capable printer many portions of your documents may image with low quality if at all.

Resolution and RIPing

RIPs, be they hardware or software, that perform PostScript interpretation chores for high resolution imagesetters are required to generate vastly greater numbers of image dots per unit area than for a laser printer. Figure 10.4 shows the tremendous increase in dot generation required at increasingly higher resolutions. These

TIP

The speed at which a RIP will process images depends upon the capabilities of the CPU which is being used by the RIP, the amount of RAM available to the RIP and the size and complexity of the files being processed. To maximize RIP performance provide your RIP with a fast CPU, plenty of RAM and reduce the files size and complexity of you image as much as possible.

greater processing (RIPing) requirements of high resolution printing often result in increased printing times for many files compared with lower resolution printing of the same file. Many files which print quickly on a 300 dpi laser may take much longer to print at 2540 dpi or, in some cases, they may not print at all

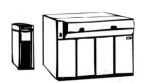

▼ *Figure 10.3 PostScript Imagesetter*
PostScript imagesetters such as this Linotronic 3060 are high resolution cousins of laser printers. Imagesetters usually have RIPs which are separate from the actual imaging unit. The RIP may be a hardware version with its own RAM, CPU, and storage space, or software which operates on a separate computer station and utilizes the RAM, CPU, and storage capacity of the computer.
Imagesetters range in resolution from 1200 dpi to 6000 dpi. High resolutions require RIPs to generate from 16x to 200x the number of image dots generated by 300 dpi laser printers. This large number of dots means longer and more complex RIPing.

Dots per Square Inch

Based on an 8" x 10" Image

300 DPI	7,200,000	BASE
600 DPI	28,800,000	4 x
1200 DPI	115,200,000	16 x
2540 DPI	516,128,000	72 x

▼ *Figure 10.4 File Size vs. Resolution*

This chart shows the dramatic increase in the number of dots which need to be generated to fill a B&W 8" x 10" page as resolution increases. Note that as the linear resolution doubles, the number of dots quadruples. Seventy two times as many dots need to be generated to fill an 8"x10" page at 2540 dpi compared with the same page at 72 dpi. (See Chapter 8, "Resolving Resolution," for more detailed background information on resolution.)

TIP

Many files which RIP fine on a 300 dpi laser will take much longer to RIP at 2400 dpi or in some cases they may not print at all. If a file will not RIP at 300 dpi, don't expect it to RIP and print at 2400 dpi. This is why it is so important to simplify our images and documents, so that they will be able to print reliably on a wide variety of printing devices.

because there is seventy two times (72x) as much information to process. If a file will not print at 300 dpi, don't expect it to print at 2400 or 3600 dpi: It won't (see Chapter 8, "Resolving Resolution," for more detailed background information on resolution).

IMAGE RIPING

Text and line art images

Text and line art images are formed from combinations of continuous lines with well defined boundaries or edges, unlike contone images, which are composed of areas which blend into one another with indistinct edges. As a result of this difference, RIPs handle text and line art images differently than they do contone images. Text and line art images are reproduced as sequences of touching spots. Refer to our discussion of halftone dots and image spots in Chapter 8, "Resolving Resolution," to remember that an image spot is the smallest dot which a printer can

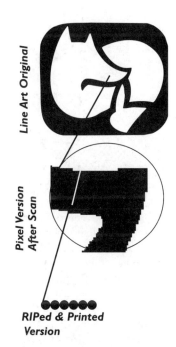

Line Art Original

Pixel Version After Scan

RIPed & Printed Version

▼ *Figure 10.5 Line Art RIPing*

This sequence shows how a line art image is captured and converted into dots at a RIP. An original line art image (top image) may be scanned and converted into pixels (middle image). This pixelized version is then converted into image spots or dots by the RIP/Printer combination (bottom image). The RIP determines the placement, and the resolution of the printer determines the size of the individual dots or spots. As shown above, the straight line of black pixels which compose a portion of the black background between the nose and the body of the fox are RIPed into a series of touching image spots. Text images are reproduced in a similar fashion.

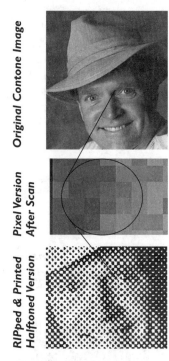

Original Contone Image

**Pixel Version
After Scan**

**RIPped & Printed
Halftoned Version**

▼ *Figure 10.6 Contone RIPing*
In contrast to line art images
which are recreated directly
out of individual image spots
lined up sequentially, contone
images are reproduced
through the generation of
halftone dots which are constructed from collections of
image spots grouped together
to create the halftone dot. The
above sequence shows the
stages a contone image goes
through during the print production process. The original
contone image (top) is captured by scanning and converted into pixels (middle),
The pixels are then converted
into halftone dots by the RIP
and printer (bottom). The size
and placement of the halftone
dots are controlled at the RIP,
whose values are constrained
by the dpi and lpi capabilities
of the output device .

create. The crispness or sharpness of line art and text images depends upon the size
and sharpness of the image spots which a printer produces. A 300 dpi laser printer creates image spots or dots which are 1/300" across, while a 2400 dpi imagesetter generates image spots or dots which are 1/2400" across. Consequently, text
and line art images reproduced with a 2400 dpi imagesetter will be far sharper than
those reproduced with the laser printer. Text and line art images are captured or
created as pixels on your computer and then converted to sequences of image spots
on your printer. The placement of the image spots is determined by the RIP. Figure
10.5 shows the processing sequence a line art image goes through on its way to
being printed. Note how the RIPing/printing process converts the pixel-based version of the original line art images into spots.

Digital halftones

As described in Chapter 8, halftone dots are used to simulate continuous tone
images. The job of the PostScript RIP is to convert the tonal information contained
in pixels into halftone dots, which as we know are collections of smaller image
dots. Depending upon the resolution of the image, that is, the number of pixels per
inch used to create the image, what generally happens is that the tonal values from
a group of pixels will be averaged to create the information which is used to create
a single halftone dot. The higher the resolution of the original image, the greater
the number of pixels which will be averaged to create a halftone dot. In contrast to
line art images which are recreated directly out of individual image spots lined up
sequentially, contone images are reproduced through the generation of halftone
dots which are constructed from collections of image spots grouped together to
create the halftone dot (see Chapter 17, "Screening Your Images," for more information on the generation of halftone screens). Figure 10.6 shows the sequence a
contone image goes through during scanning RIPing and printing. Note how the
size of the halftone dots varies depending upon the grayscale percentage they are
representing, while the spacing of the halftone dots remain the same regardless of
the grayscale percentage presented.

Unlike line art images where precisely capturing edges is of utmost importance,
with contone images one need only capture areas of tone rather than edges. The
proper pixel size of the captured areas, that is, the input or scan resolution, will
depend upon the line screen at which the final image will be reproduced. Because
RIPs convert areas of tonal information into halftone dots, and higher image resolutions necessarily mean more RIP processing, one needs to be cognizant of the
resolution at which contones images are created or captured (see Chapter 12,
"Taming Your Scanner," for a complete discussion of scanning variables and rules).

POSTSCRIPT DETAILS

The RIP as a funnel or filter

In order to be reproduced or printed on a PostScript device, all elements within a
document, text line art, and contone images must be rasterized or RIPed. All the
fancy text and graphics which we can create on a computer must be renderable as

dots (RIPed). Simple text and graphics are easier to RIP than more complex text and graphics. In fact, there are many types of text and graphic images which are very difficult or impossible to RIP. While the speed and capabilities of PostScript RIPs are always improving, the capabilities of creative software applications and the people who use them seem to be improving faster.

It is useful to think of a PostScript RIP as a funnel through which all document information must pass and be converted into dots. Like all funnels, the RIP funnel is a point of restriction, the publishing process slows down, and in some cases stops here. Whenever we are constructing a document which will be used for print, we should keep this PostScript funnel in mind and remember that whatever we are creating must fit through that funnel. It is a fact of PostScript life that there are many images we can create on a computer and view without problems on a monitor which may not fit through our PostScript RIP. Examples of these items include: large page sizes, too many and/or very long paths, complex paths with too many control points, nested EPS graphics and fonts, multiple font architectures and non-PostScript fonts, complex compound graphics with multiple clipping paths, overlapping gradations or multiple masks, and many out-of-gamut colors. We should always try to reduce the size of files and simplify files which we intend to print.

PostScript dictionaries and errors

One key concept to understanding how a PostScript RIP works is understanding some of the basic parts of the RIP. While the entire RIPing process is multistepped and complex, there is one concept which I keep in mind when I think about trying to make my files "RIP Ready," and that is the concept of the **PostScript dictionary**. A PostScript RIP contains a series of dictionaries, each of which is devoted to processing a certain part of a document. There are font dictionaries, page geometry dictionaries, line art dictionaries, and bitmap art dictionaries. I think of these dictionaries as being storage and processing areas within the RIP. When a PostScript file is received by the RIP, it sends the font portion of the file to the font dictionary, the line art graphics to the line art dictionary, and so forth. The size of the dictionary depends upon how much RAM is assigned to that dictionary. If more information is sent to a dictionary than it can hold, you will receive a PostScript error, the dreaded: POSTSCRIPT ERROR: STATUS-DICTFUL. This means that the dictionary is too full to receive any more information. This kind of error is common with long complex outline files such as clipping paths and line art that has been converted to vectors using Streamline. A PostScript RIP must be able to process the entire length of a line art file in order to continue. If the line art dictionary becomes full prior to completing the processing of an entire line or line segment, a PostScript error will be generated and the RIPing will come to an end, that is, the RIP will "bomb." Dictionary overflow errors can be prevented with line art by decreasing the length of and complexity of line art files. This is why we split paths, increase flatness ratios, and simplify path lengths of line art files (see Chapter 9, "Grappling with Graphics," and Chapter 16, "Application-Specific Tips" for a more complete discussion of line art files and how to treat them). Missing elements like fonts can cause PostScript errors as well. Attention to reducing size and complexity of, and checking the presence of all page elements will help reduce the probability of PostScript errors, particularly when printing to a high resolution device.

Levels of PostScript

PostScript was first introduced to the desktop publishing market in 1984, through the sale of the first Apple LaserWriter printer and driver. This first PostScript printer and driver pair was designated a PostScript Level 1 printing system. Since 1984 there have been progressively improving levels of PostScript starting with PostScript Level 1, then Level 2, and now there is PostScript Level 3. Each level includes more capabilities than the one before. It is important that you match up the level of PostScript you generate from your documents and printer drivers with the PostScript Level of the RIP to which you are printing. If you try to print PostScript Level 3 data on a PostScript Level 1 or 2 RIP, your document will not RIP and print properly, if at all.

RIP once, print many times

In the early days of desktop publishing we generally had one output device, and that was the one we prepared our files for. Even printing companies had one primary output device, usually an imagesetter to which they printed, and most proofs were still analog. Today, however, it is not uncommon for us to be creating composition proofs on a black and white laser or low resolution inkjet printer, color contract proofs on a high quality inkjet printer, and final output on an imagesetter or plate setter. If each of these devices has a different RIP which processes these files, we could end up with three different print interpretations of the same file. So in circumstances where print fidelity is critical from one device to another, it is best to look for and use production systems which allow you to RIP a file once and image it to multiple output devices. This is known as RIP once, print many times. These RIP once systems remove one of the variables which can cause inconsistency, RIP interpretation. In addition most of the RIP once print many times system allow you to store already RIPped files for reprinting, which, by eliminating RIPing time, can save time and money on multiple prints or proofs if they are necessary or desired for any reason.

CHAPTER SUMMARY

PostScript is a powerful computer based page layout description language. Whenever we create, view and print PostScript based documents we need to have a number of PostScript components including a PostScript printer driver and RIP. The PostScript printer driver creates a stream of PostScript code which the RIP and printer then convert into patterns of spots and dots. Creating and printing PostScript based documents without the use of PostScript printer drivers and printers will result in inaccurate printing at best, or no printing at all. High resolution RIPing requires more computing power than low resolution RIPing. Text and line art images are RIPped into patterns of spots while contone images are RIPped into halftone dot patterns.

It is useful to think of your PostScript RIP as a funnel through which all your digital document components must be processed. If our document components are too large or complex, we can significantly slow down, or even prevent, the RIPing process. PostScript RIPs contain PostScript dictionaries where various portions of a digital document are processed. If any one of these PostScript dictionaries is overwhelmed with data, a PostScript error may result, which usually results in the termination of the RIPing and therefore the printing process. Reducing the size and complexity of our documents, as well as making sure that all of our document components are present, such as their associated fonts and graphics files, will help reduce PostScript errors during printing and ensure higher quality printing.

There have been progressively improving levels of PostScript starting with PostScript Level 1, then Level 2, and now there is PostScript Level 3. Each level includes more capabilities than the one before. It is important that you match up the level of PostScript you generate from your documents and printer drivers with the PostScript level of the RIP. If you try to print PostScript Level 3 data on a PostScript Level 1 or 2 RIP, your document will not RIP and print properly, if at all. RIP once, print many times production systems prevent interdevice print inconsistency, and reduce time and costs on reprints.

PAULINE'S DIGITAL IMAGING TIPS

Pauline's Tip 10.1

Remove unnecessary elements from your document pages. Don't just cover them up. All elements within active margins will be processed by a RIP which processes a page from the bottom up, and it has no idea what is on top. The concept of out of sight but not out of RIP applies here. To help find extraneous items, I set my view on Fit Spread in Window so that I can see my entire page as well as the pasteboard. Then I scroll through the document and check for items on the pasteboard. Another trick is to select all the items on a page. This will activate the handles of any extra items which are underneath foreground items.

Pauline's Tip 10.2

Always have a PostScript printer driver selected when you construct and print a PostScript based document. Without a proper PostScript printer driver your document will not be properly formatted. If you change from a non-PostScript printer driver to a PostScript printer driver after you have begun constructing your document, your page geometry and component placed will likely change.

Pauline's Tip 10.3

Always have a PostScript printer available for proofing and printing. If you print your PostScript based documents on a non-PostScript printer your page geometry and elements will print incorrectly, poorly, or not at all.

Pauline's Tip 10.4

Create complex graphics (especially line art EPS graphics created in drawing applications) in separate layers. Doing so will allow you to create the graphics more efficiently and will let your printer troubleshoot and edit them more easily.

Pauline's Tip 10.5

Make sure you can RIP and print every graphic you create on your low resolution desktop laser printer before you send it out to be RIPed by someone else on a higher resolution RIP. If it won't RIP and print at low resolution on your laser printer, it certainly won't RIP and print on a more demanding higher resolution RIP. However, be aware that just because an image

PAULINE'S DIGITAL IMAGING TIPS

RIPs and prints on your system does not guarantee that it will be able to be RIPed and print-ed, or print the same on another system. Each RIP has its own specific requirements and its own way of interpreting image and document data (see Tip 10.9 below).

Pauline's Tip 10.6

Avoid including the high resolution version of graphic images in your page layout documents. Including the high resolution images makes the page layout document much larger and more unwieldy. It also makes troubleshooting, editing, and updating the file while it is imbedded impos-sible. Send along the high resolution images as separate files.

Pauline's Tip 10.7

Nesting is for the birds! Be conscious of not nesting text and graphic ele-ments in your documents, as nested elements are difficult for RIPs to locate and process. Avoid placing previously created EPS graphics inside of a drawing document when you intend to export that document later as an EPS file. Type set in a drawing document to be exported as an EPS should be out-lined/converted to a graphic prior to creation of the EPS. Saving entire document pages as EPS files will generally create nested elements, and should be avoided when possible.

Pauline's Tip 10.8

Make sure you match the level of the PostScript driver and document data with the level of the PostScript which the RIP can process. There are three levels of PostScript: Level 1, 2, and 3. If you send higher level PostScript to a lower level RIP, your document and images may not RIP properly or at all.

Pauline's Tip 10.9

When you are working in an production system, such as a commercial printing company, which requires that you use multiple printing devices to proof and output a job, it is advisable to use a RIP once print many times production system. This eliminates interdevice RIPing inconsistencies and can save time and money on multiple proofs or prints.

CHAPTER REVIEW

Check Your Comprehension

Multiple Choice Questions

To help you review the topics covered in this chapter, answer the following multiple choice questions.

1. _____ is a document page description language which describes the page geometry as well as the content, position and orientation of the text and graphic elements.
   A. A printer driver
   B. PostScript
   C. A RIP
   D. Screening technology

2. The acronym RIP is short for
   A. Resolution image printing
   B. Resolution image processing
   C. Raster image processor
   D. Rotten image processor

3. Which of the following is a primary role of a PostScript RIP?
   A. Rasterize vector images
   B. Rasterize pixel images
   C. Convert document components into spots and dots
   D. Convert document components into pixels and vectors

4. Which of the following is the critical software link between a document and a RIP?
   A. PostScript interpreter
   B. Printer driver
   C. Halftoning engine
   D. Network

5. What is the basic building block which is used in commercial printing to reproduce contone images?
   A. Photographic building blocks
   B. Patterns of halftone dots
   C. Line art patterns
   D. Pixels

6. Which of the following would be considered the smallest building block of a printed image which is produced by RIPing?

    A. Halftone dot

    B. Image spot

    C. Pixel

    D. Vector

7. What is another name for a PostScript RIP?

    A. PostScript printer

    B. PostScript error

    C. PostScript interpreter

    D. PostScript dictionary

8. A _____ is a part of a RIP which is dedicated to processing a certain portion of a PostScript document.

    A. PostScript driver

    B. PostScript printer

    C. PostScript glossary

    D. PostScript dictionary

9. What often results when we try to RIP documents which contain elements which are too large and/or complex?

    A. Image compression

    B. PostScript interpolation

    C. PostScript errors

    D. Smoke and fire leap from our PostScript printing devices.

10. We should make sure that the output of PostScript from our PostScript drivers matches the _____ of our PostScript RIP.

    A. Resolution

    B. Bit depth

    C. Level

    D. Hardware

Check Your Understanding

Concept Questions

To help you review and expand your thinking on the topics covered in this chapter, answer the following questions.

1. Briefly explain what a PostScript RIP does.

2. What is the relationship between the resolution of a graphic files and the performance of a RIP to which it is sent?

3. What is the difference between a laser printer and and imagesetter? Why will some files print on a laser printer but not an imagesetter?

4. Distinguish between spots and dots. What are spots and dots used for?

5. What is a PostScript printer driver and what function does it perform?

6. Why is it important for you to have a PostScript desktop printer, even if you intend to ultimately print your documents on a high resolution imagesetter at someone else's location?

7. What is a PostScript dictionary and what is its function?

8. What kind of problems result in PostScript errors? List three document characteristics to which you should pay attention which will help prevent PostScript errors during RIPing.

9. To what does the term Level of PostScript refer, and how is the Level of PostScript related to a printer driver?

10. What does the phase "RIP once, print many times" refer? Why would we want to use such a system and what are its advantages? Can you think of any disadvantages?

PROJECTS

1. Locate the various printer drivers on your computer. Identify at least one PostScript printer driver and one non-PostScript printer driver. Create a document which contains at least one complex vector EPS graphic. Print this document which contains the vector EPS graphic to a PostScript printer using both printer drivers. Report the results of each printing.

2. Try printing the above document which contains a vector EPS file to both a PostScript printer and a non-PostScript printer. Report the results.

11
Tales of True Typesetting

As the Byte Turns continues...

What type of setting will Pauline find when she visits Danny to teach him about her style ... sheets?

You charged me a bundle for editing my copy in that catalog you printed for me last month. Why was it so much?

Apparently, it took us a long time!

I wonder why it took so long ?

Why did Danny's last catalog job take so long and cost so much?

We had to reformat and proof 400 pages of text with five different levels of heads and subheads by hand. If Danny had used style sheets, we could have accomplished the reformatting in minutes instead of hours.

Chapter Objectives

In this chapter you will learn:

- ◆ **What fonts and type are**
- ◆ **Identification of Windows and Mac font files**
- ◆ **Default location of Windows and Mac font files**
- ◆ **PostScript and TrueType fonts**
- ◆ **Font management tips**
- ◆ **Using font management utilities**
- ◆ **Typesetting tips**
- ◆ **Key Terms**
  - Font
  - PostScript Type 1 font
  - TrueType font
  - OpenType font
  - Font suitcase
  - ATM
  - Font set
  - Screen font and printer font files
  - .pfb and .pfm font files
  - Tracking, leading and kerning
  - Style sheet

INTRODUCTION

The two most common font architectures are **TrueType fonts** and **PostScript Type 1 fonts. Font** files contain both **screen font** and **printer font** information which provide on-screen viewing as well as the printing of type characters. Typesetting involves the selection of a font and the control of size, **tracking**, **leading**, and **kerning** as well as its paragraph formatting. Both Mac and Windows computers provide default font locations where these font files are stored and accessed for use. Font file used in document construction should be stored outside of these default locations to allow for easier font management. Font file mishaps are the single biggest problem in customer supplied files to printing companies and service bureaus. Effective type management involves the utilization of proper font management procedures and a good font management utility. A good font management utility should provide the ability to activate and deactivate fonts, create and manage font sets, and troubleshoot font files. Current PostScript and TrueType fonts are not easily used cross platform and have limited font character sets. New font technologies such as **Open Type** and Unicode fonts should provide for better cross platform utilization of fonts and more flexible and universal character sets. Typesetting is not typewriting. There is a number of well established guidelines for formatting type which should be followed in order to create properly formatted, readable type. **Style sheets** should be used to format type which repeats in a document such as heads, subheads and body copy.

WHAT ARE FONTS AND TYPE?

Font characteristics

The terms typeface and font are often used interchangeably and while they are related, they are not the same. The classical definitions of font and typeface, which come from the days of hot and cold type, are still useful. Type is defined by three basic terms: typeface or typeface family, style, and size. For instance, the body copy of this paragraph is set in 12 point Minion Regular (or Roman). The typeface is Minion, the style is plain or Roman or Regular, and its size is 12 points. Varieties of this font are:

Minion Regular (Plain or Roman) 18 pts
Minion Italic 18 pts
Minion Bold 18 pts
Minion SemiBold Italic18 pts

All four lines of type are set in the same typeface, StoneSerifMedium, and all are the same point size,18 points. But their styles differ from Roman, to Italic, to Bold, to BoldItalic. Therefore, each line is set in a different font. If we just changed the point size, would we have a different font?

Type characteristics

Type is the characters we create with data contained in font files. Type is normally created in sentences and paragraphs. In addition to adjusting the point size of type, we routinely adjust the space between lines of type (leading), the general space between multiple words and characters (tracking), and the specific space between two characters (kerning). We also control the placement of type on a page by controlling the indent of lines and the spacing between paragraphs.

TYPE CHARACTERISTICS

Font: StoneSerif-ITC (Roman/Plain) 60pts

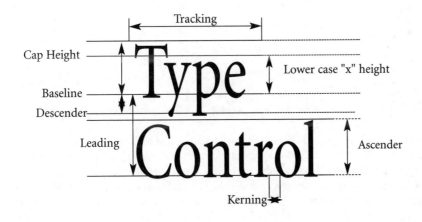

FONT FILE LOCATIONS

Windows

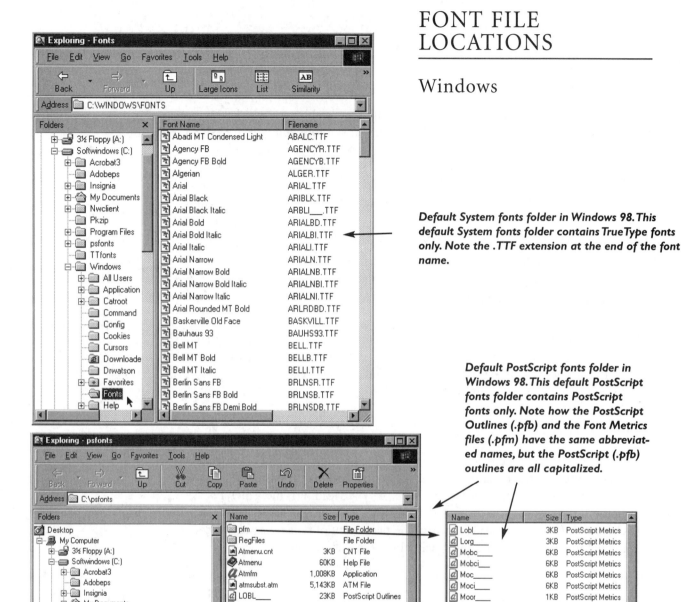

Default System fonts folder in Windows 98. This default System fonts folder contains TrueType fonts only. Note the .TTF extension at the end of the font name.

Default PostScript fonts folder in Windows 98. This default PostScript fonts folder contains PostScript fonts only. Note how the PostScript Outlines (.pfb) and the Font Metrics files (.pfm) have the same abbreviated names, but the PostScript (.pfb) outlines are all capitalized.

▼ *Figure 11.1 Windows System and Default Font Folders*

In Windows (Ver. 98 here), the default System fonts folder named Fonts (top) is in located in a folder labeled Windows located on the "C:" drive. This default fonts folder holds contains TrueType (.TTF) fonts only, including all of the default System font files which are essential to allowing you to control your computer. On a Windows System, PostScript fonts (labeled PostScript Outlines; these PostScript outline files are also called .pfb files) are stored in a separate font folder, the ps fonts folder (bottom left). Notice that the PostScript font names are abbreviated. Window's PostScript fonts are made up of pairs of font files which work together, including PostScript Outline files (bottom middle) and a matching set of font Metrics files which are found in the .pfm folder (bottom right).

FONT FILE LOCATIONS

Macintosh

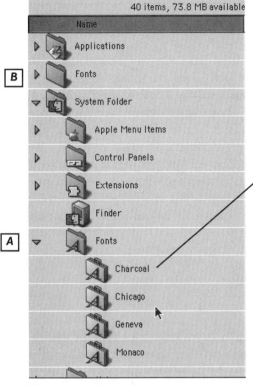

▼ *Figure 11.4 Screen Font Suitcase*
On a Mac screen fonts can be stored in a suitcase (above) to make transporting easier and access quicker. Inside the suitcase you will find either screen fonts or, as seen here (right), TrueType fonts. Helpful hint: You can put a "(" before the suitcase name to keep it at the top of your view list for easy access.

Note: City named fonts, such as Chicago, should not be used for document construction as they are mono-spaced fonts which do not look or read as well as variable spaced fonts.

▼ **Figure 11.2 Two Locations of Fonts on a Macintosh**
On a Macintosh, fonts are located in either the Fonts folder in the System folder (A), the default location, or in a separate folder outside of the System folder (B). System fonts, Chicago, Geneva, and Monaco are stored in the default System font folder (A). Generally, it is best to keep your document creation fonts outside of the System folder (B) so that the font files can be readily activated, deactivated and otherwise managed.

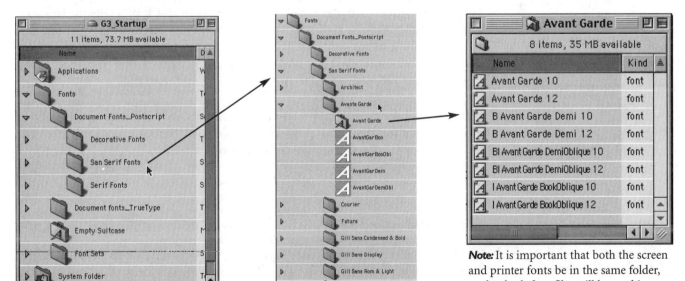

Note: It is important that both the screen and printer fonts be in the same folder, so that both font files will be working together when activated.

▼ **Figure 11.3 Document construction fonts outside of the System folder**
Shown here is an external fonts folder with font files which will be used in document construction taken out of the System folder and placed in an external folder labeled Fonts. Inside this external fonts folder fonts are organized by architecture, PostScript and TrueType, and then by font class (Serif, San Serif, etc.), and then by typeface family, Avant Garde, Futura, etc. This type of strict font organization helps prevent font management problems.

▼ *Figure 11.5 Mac Type 1 Fonts*
Screen font files (top) are named using full names and have point sizes beside them. Printer fonts have PostScript abbreviated names with no point sizes. Both font files must be present for characters to be properly viewed and printed.

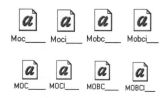

▼ *Figure 11.56 Windows Type 1 Fonts*
Font Metric files .pfm (top) have upper- and lowercase abbreviated names. PostScript outline fonts (.pfb) have all uppercase abbreviated names. Both font files must be present for characters to be properly viewed and printed.

▼ *Figure 11.7 TrueType Font*
A TrueType font file contains both screen and printer font information and is recognized by the triple "A" on the icon on a Macintosh and a double "T" in Windows.

FINDING YOUR FONTS

Font locations

On a Mac, fonts are by default placed in a fonts folder inside your System folder. On a Windows computer there are two default font folder locations: 1) the primary default font folder—labeled Fonts, located inside of the Windows folder on the C: drive—contains only TrueType fonts, and 2) The ps fonts folder which is located on the first level of the C: drive, which is the default location for PostScript font files. Fonts placed in their default folder locations are automatically made available to any application which is launched, but these font files are much more difficult to manage. I prefer to keep all of my document construction font files outside my System folder and access them indirectly through a font utility such as **ATM** Deluxe or Suitcase. This indirect access allows me quickly and easily to control which fonts are accessible or "open" and which are not.

Font file structure

PostScript vs. TrueType

The two most common types of font architectures are PostScript Type 1 fonts and TrueType fonts. Type 1 fonts are constructed of two files, a screen font and a printer font. Screen font files are low resolution, fixed size, bitmapped font files used for displaying font characters on your screen or monitor. Printer fonts are high resolution, scalable, outline, or PostScript font files accessed when characters are printed. TrueType fonts consist of a single file which contains both the screen and printer font information. While TrueType fonts are easier to manage because they are a single file, PostScript Type 1 fonts are preferred for printing on high resolution lasers, imagesetters, and platesetters because the RIPs which process font files during the printing process are PostScript-based and therefore more compatible with the PostScript information contained in the Type 1 files. See Figs. 11.1–11.7 for detailed information on recognizing and locating both PostScript Type 1 and TrueType font files on both Mac and Windows computers.

Unfortunately Mac and Windows font architectures are different enough to make cross platform font file transfer difficult. While both Windows and Mac have two-font PostScript architectures, the **.pfm** and **.pfb** Windows font files are not Mac screen and printer font equivalents. TrueType fonts, while simpler with their single font architecture, do not readily translate cross platform either.

MultipleMaster Fonts

There is a special version of PostScript Type 1 fonts known as MultipleMaster fonts. MultipleMaster fonts contain two or more master fonts which provide the ability to create versions or iterations of font by adjusting axes such as width, height or the optical size. While the creative control provided by MultipleMaster fonts is impressive, output service bureaus discourage their clients from using them due to output problems which can arise with their use. Be sure to consult with your service bureau before using and sending them MultipleMaster font files.

ATM (Adobe Type Manager)

If you use PostScript Type 1 fonts on either a Macintosh or a Windows computer you must have a font utility program called ATM (Adobe Type Manager) installed in your operating system. ATM provides basic font viewing and printing capabilities for PostScript Type 1 fonts. ATM provides us with WYSIWYG (what you see is what you get) font character viewing and printing by using scalable PostScript printer font information to create more precise on-screen characters. Without ATM PostScript Type 1 font files will not view properly on screen.

Font naming

The font naming schemes which have evolved on computers are among the most diabolical naming systems ever conceived. On the Mac, the screen and printer fonts use different naming formats. Adobe Type 1 Screen fonts are named using full names and have point sizes beside them, e.g., Helvetica 12. Printer fonts have abbreviated PostScript names with no point sizes next to the name, e.g., Helve is the printer font match for the screen font Helvetica 12. Screen fonts are designated with point sizes because they are bitmapped and therefore a specific size. Printer fonts are not designated with point sizes because they are PostScript outline files and therefore inherently scalable. TrueType fonts are single font files which have

> The first step is properly managing your font files is to separate your operating system fonts files from your document creation font files. Your operating system fonts files should be kept in the default font folders so that they will always be available for use by your operating system for its basic requirements of lists, menus and dialog boxes. Your document creation fonts should be placed outside of your operating system so that they can be managed through the use of a font management utility. If you do not isolate your document creation font files, you will not be able to effectively control and manage your font files.

both screen and printer font data in one file and have a naming scheme which utilizes characteristics of both screen and printer fonts. A TrueType font has a full name, like screen fonts, but has no point sizes like the printer fonts, e.g., Helvetica.

FONDLING YOUR FONTS

Fonts files: the number one problem

The number one problem associated with incoming customer files mentioned by virtually every service bureau is fonts, or more accurately font files. Customer routinely send in their documents with some sort of font file problems. These font file problems include missing fonts, the wrong fonts, and corrupted fonts. The most powerful tools we have in combating the problems we have with fonts are good font management practices and the proper use of font management utilities. Following are some effective font management procedures.

Tips for managing your fonts

Following are some core font management guidelines.

- Separate System font files from document construction fonts files. Only install font files which are required for use by your operating system in default System font folders: Mac: Chicago, Geneva, Monaco (± Charcoal); Windows 95/98: Minimum = MS Serif and San Serif (.fon) files, Bitmap font files. Recommend: TTF versions of Arial, Times New Roman and Courier families, plus Wingdings and Symbol. Windows 2000 uses TTF versions of MS Sans Serif and Tahoma Regular and Bold for its user interface rather than bitmapped (.fon) versions. All font files which will be used in the construction of documents should be located outside of the default fonts folders, and managed with a font management utility.

- Use font management utilities like ATM Deluxe (Mac and Windows) Suitcase (Mac) and MasterJuggler (Mac), Font Reserve (Mac) to help you identify, organize, activate/deactivate, troubleshoot and otherwise manage your document construction fonts.

- Keep the number of fonts used in a document to a minimum. This is both good technical advice and a good design habit to have. On the technical side, the greater the number of fonts you have in a document, the longer the processing time will be. It is easy to complicate and clutter a document's message with too many different fonts.

- Be sure to send both screen and printer fonts for Mac Files, and Font Metric (.pfm) and Outline font files (.pfb) for Windows files for all the fonts in a document.

- Screen fonts can and should be stored in a screen **font suitcase** for ease of transportation and rapid access. Keep an empty suitcase handy in your fonts folder on your hard drive to copy to your output disks. This will make organizing screen fonts easier when you are sending out fonts.

- Both screen and printer fonts should be placed in the same folder on your hard drive and when traveling on a disk so that they will automatically be linked to each other for screen display and printing.

- Due to naming convention inconsistencies on the Mac and name abbreviations in Windows, there is often some confusion about which members of a typeface family need to be sent along with a document file. Send the entire font family (Roman, Italic, Bold, and BoldItalic faces) if there is any question about which members of a typeface family need to be sent with your document file.

- As mentioned in the Chapter 13, "Document Construction," don't mix TrueType and Type 1 PostScript fonts in the same document. Using more than one font architecture in the same document will, at the very least, slow down the printing process and can lead to the failure of RIPing.

- Avoid using bitmapped city name fonts such as New York and Chicago. City named fonts are meant to be used for monitor display by the Mac and for non-PostScript printing. Also avoid using pseudo-condensed laser printer specific fonts such as Helvetica Narrow.

- Test your font files on a regular basis (weekly) for missing or corrupt font files. One corrupt font file can cause your system to crash on a regular basis.

- Prior to printing or creating PostScript files, check for and remove miscellaneous fonts, as these extra fonts will just make a large file even bigger. Also be sure that when you create your PostScript file that all of the fonts files used in the document are included in the PostScript file. See Chapter 16, "Application-Specific Tips," for more information on creating PostScript files.

- When creating an Acrobat PDF file, be sure that all of the fonts files used in the document are included in the PDF file. See Chapter 16 for more information on creating PDF files.

- Set as much type as possible in the parent printing program (usually Quark, PageMaker Frame, or InDesign) rather than in graphics applications such as Illustrator, FreeHand, or CorelDraw.

- If you do set type in a drawing application such as FreeHand, Illustrator or CorelDraw, and you intend to export this document as an EPS graphic which will placed in a page layout application document: 1) Minimize the amount of type which you set, as well as the number of typefaces and style you use, and 2) whenever possible, convert your type to graphics prior to final export as an EPS file. Remember that small serif type may not convert to outline accurately. Note: If you outline your type characters, be sure to save an original editable native file for character editing later on.

- To speed up printing on your own system, download nonresident fonts to your printer prior to multiple printing sessions.

- Note font type or manufacturer used in your documents when you send them out to be printed: e.g., Adobe, Bitstream, Font Haus, etc.

- Don't buy cheap fonts. Also avoid using TrueType fonts if you are printing to high resolution imagesetters. There are some items you should not skimp on and fonts are one of them. Avoid the too-good-to-be-true font offers: 75 fonts for $50.00. These cheap fonts are often poorly constructed and do not always print well on high resolution printers. Stick with high quality Adobe Type 1 fonts to help minimize font problems during output.

- Create font sets which match specific jobs. Only activate the fonts you need for a specific job on which you are presently working. This will dramatically reduce the likelihood of font conflicts.

- Use a font collection utility to collect your font files prior to sending out your documents for printing or before archiving. Manual collection of font files is tedious and too error prone. Many applications such as FreeHand and InDesign offer their own font collection utilities. Or you may use the preflighting and file component collection capabilities of tools such as FlightCheck from Markzware. See Chapters 16 and 20 ("Managing the Mess") for more detailed information on these preflighting and collection tools.

▼ *Figure 11.8 ATM Deluxe Font Info and Sample Page*
Here we see the font sample page found in ATM Deluxe. At the top of the page we see a wealth of information about the font file selected, Bookman. ATM provides us with the menu name (large type), the font type (PostScript), the PostScript name (Bookman Light), the version number, the suitcase name, the printer font name and font foundry information.

▼ *Figure 11.9 ATM Deluxe Sets and Fonts Window*
This is the combined window which allows us to see and manage at a glance all the sets we have created (left) and fonts we have recognized and either activated or deactivated (right).

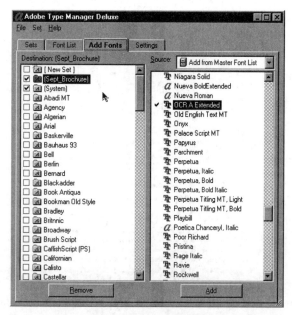

▼ *Figure 11.10 ATM Deluxe for Windows*
This combined window allows us to see a master font list, and create and manage our font sets we have created. At a glance we see all the sets we have created and fonts we have activated or deactivated.

FONT MANAGEMENT UTILITIES

If we isolate our document construction font files out away from our System folder, as we have recommended, then these font files will not be available for use through our applications. In order to make our isolated document construction font files accessible to our application, we must access them indirectly through the use of a font management utility. While adding a font management utility to our operating system does increase the complexity of our operating system, the benefits provided by having isolated font files and a utility to manage them far outweigh this increase in system complexity. Font management utilities allow us to manage our font files quickly and flexibly. Proper font file management with a utility depends upon having your document creation font files located outside of your System folder on a Mac or Windows fonts folder and PS fonts folder on a Windows computer.

Font utility uses

Following is a list of some of the fundamental capabilities which a good font management utility should provide:

▶ Font identification and information
▶ Font organization
▶ **Font set** creation
▶ Opening and closing font files
▶ Testing and troubleshooting font files
▶ Collecting font files
▶ Auto launching fonts (suspect activity in some utilities)
▶ Printing examples

Font organization schemes

Good document font management begins with well organized font files. Your fonts can be organized in many ways, including:

▶ By architecture: PostScript vs. TrueType vs. Open
▶ By kind: Serif, Sans Serif, Decorative, etc.
▶ By manufacturer: Adobe, Bitstream, Font House, etc.
▶ By client: ABC Marketing, Acme Art, etc.

- By job: Annual report, quarterly catalog
- By use: Core fonts, corp internal, advertising, etc.

Once your font files are organized they can be easily and reliably accessed through your font management utility.

Font identities

One of the confusing issues with working with font files is that they may have as many as five different names as well as other identifying characteristics. Font file characteristics include: menu name, suitcase name, screen font name (.pfb), printer font name (.pfm), version number, PostScript name, Kern checksum, Fond number, and font foundry. Confusion of font file identities by applications, operating systems and even the system operators, you and me, is one of the most common font problems we have in the creation, viewing and printing of electronic documents.

Font sets

The core tool in any font management system is the creation and use of font sets. A font set is a virtual set of fonts created within a font management utility. **Font sets**, when activated, always link to the same actual font files. When used properly, font sets eliminate font substitution and conflicts during document creation and printing (see Figs. 11.9 and 11.10).

Font utilities

- ATM Deluxe: Cross platform font management tool
- Master Juggler: Mac only
- Font Reserve: Mac only, planning a Windows version
- Suitcase: Mac only, being discontinued
- Fontographer: Cross platform font creation and conversion

Cross platform font issues

Unfortunately Mac and Windows font architectures are different enough so as to make cross platform font file transfer difficult. While both Windows and Mac have two-font PostScript architectures, the .pfm and .pfb Windows font files are not Mac screen and printer font equivalents. Even the single font architecture of the TrueType fonts do not transfer easily without a file translation step. Font file conversion applications such as MacroMedia's Fontographer can be used to translate font file between Mac and Windows. This is an inelegant, time consuming process. There are other solutions to moving font files cross platform. Following is a list of the most common cross platform font solutions:

- Font file translation e.g., with Fontographer
- Purchasing fonts on both platforms

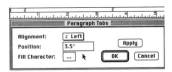

▼ *Figure 11.11 Tab Settings Dialog Box*
Tabs, instead of spaces, should be used to control the horizontal spacing. Using tabs provides you with flexibility, precision, and editability. The use of tabs is particularly important when you need to align variable spaced type. Tabs can also be assigned as a portion of style sheet formatting.

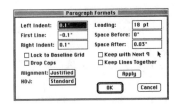

▼ *Figure 11.12 Paragraph Formatting Dialog Box*
This is a paragraph formatting dialog box in QuarkXPress, similar to controls in other applications such as PageMaker. Think of typesetting in terms of paragraphs, defined by the presence of a hard return, when planning the placement and spacing of your type. Paragraph controls should be used for controlling the vertical placement of type. Paragraph formatting of type provides for greater accuracy, speed, and editability than manual formatting.

The·space·control·for·this·type·is·done·incorrectly…¶
········Note·that·the·indents·for·these·lines↵
········are·controlled·by·multiple·spaces·instead¶
········of·by·tabs…And·note·the·double·spaces·at¶
········the·end·each·sentence··¶
¶
¶
¶
Also·not·the·use·of·multiple·returns¶
···This·should·also·be·avoided¶
···Also·note·the·use·of·hard·returns¶
···where·there·should·be·soft·returns··¶

▼ *Figure 11.13 Improper Type Formatting*
This is an example of all the wrong ways to control type. Errors include: multiple spaces to move type horizontally, hard returns used for line breaks instead of soft returns, double spaces placed at the end of sentences, and multiple hard returns used after a paragraph to control space between paragraphs. See Fig. 11.12 to see the proper methods for these type controls.

The·space·control·for·this·type·is·done·correctly↵
→ Note·that·the·indents·for·these·lines↵
→ are·controlled·by·tabs·instead↵
→ of·by·multiple·spaces.·Also·note·the·single·spaces·↵
→ instead·of·two·at·the·end·of·each·sentence.¶

Also·not·the·use·of·one·return↵
→ between·the·two·paragraphs,↵
→ and·the·use·of·soft·returns·to↵
→ control·line·breaks·

▼ *Figure 11.14 Proper Type Formatting*
Here we see correct methods for the control of type. These include use of tabs to control horizontal placement of text, soft returns to place line breaks, single spaces used at the end of sentences, and the placement of only one hard return between paragraphs.

❧ PostScript file creation including the font files
❧ PDF file creation including the font files

See Chapter 16, "Application-Specific Tips," for more information on properly creating PostScript and PDF files.

Future fonts

OpenType and Unicode fonts

An evolving solution to the inherent incompatibility problems we have between platforms, and the increasing demands for multicultural fonts, is the development of a new font architecture know as the OpenType font architecture. OpenType fonts are cross platform and support both TrueType and PostScript font data in a single format. OpenType also supports the Unicode character set which supports 65,356 font characters as opposed to the standard 256 characters supported by the ASCII standard used by most previous font architectures. While the OpenType architecture has yet to be proven in practice and is not yet widely used, it is a font technology worth watching.

TIP

Use style sheets when formatting type. Style sheets should especially be used to control type formatting when the formatted type appears repeatedly throughout a document, such as with repeated heads, subheads, body copy and running heads. Using style sheets allows you to create and format your document type much faster and with far greater consistency with fewer mistakes. The use of style sheets also make the reformatting and editing of type much faster and easier.

TYPESETTING VS. TYPEWRITING

Different techniques and capabilities

Perhaps the most marvelous book ever written on typesetting is called *The Mac Is Not a Typewriter*, by Robin Williams (marvelous for its clarity, brevity, and insight as well as for its completeness). Robin's book is a "must read" for anyone who sets type on a computer of any sort. Her basic thesis is that typesetting and typewriting are two related but ultimately very different endeavors. Basically, typewriting is a very crude and imprecise way of placing text on a page. Typesetting, in contrast, provides us with the tools to elegantly and precisely control the look and placement of type on a page. Typesetting is an art as well as a set of skills. I encourage everyone to own and read and reread *The Mac Is Not a Typewriter* every once in a while. Until you do, here are some basic typesetting guidelines which will help you create more professional looking type and allow you more control over its formatting and reformatting.

Some typesetting guidelines

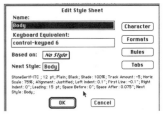

- Don't use multiple em (space bar) spaces to control text placement horizontally. Use tabs instead. On a computer which uses PostScript typefaces, each character has its own character width. This approach contrasts with typewriter characters, which are monospaced, that is, all characters have the same width. Trying to align variable spaced type with the space key is a losing battle. In addition, type placement which is controlled with tabs is infinitely more editable than space bar controlled type. Don't place two spaces at the end of a line; PostScript type automatically recognizes periods and places additional space at the ends of lines. As a general rule, if you need more than one space, set it with a tab.

- Don't use multiple paragraph returns to control text placement vertically. Use paragraph format settings instead: Space Before and Space After. The rationale here is similar to our discussion of tabs above. The accuracy, flexibility, and editability of paragraphs is severely limited through the use of multiple paragraph returns. You should never have more than one paragraph return. If you need more than one paragraph return, adjust the paragraph formatting.

- Don't use automatic leading; set absolute leading values. This practice will eliminate uneven line spacing (leading) problems which can result from applying superscript, subscript, or superior formatting to individual characters in a line of type.

- The proper control of horizontal and vertical placement of text, especially through the use of style sheets, makes for easier, faster, and more consistent and accurate text formatting and editing of text.

- Avoid false type styling by making font choices from a font, rather than a style menu.

- Use style sheets to format recurring text.

- Use the correct typesetter versions of '…' and "…" instead of '…' and "…".

Typesetting with style

Controlling type formatting is best accomplished through what are known as style sheets. **Style sheets** allow you to consistently and easily assign a comprehensive set of formatting instructions and to create a template of these instructions which can be applied to any new or previously created text. It is preferable to use style sheets for consistency of repetitively formatted type, such as heads, subheads and body copy, and running heads, just to name a few examples. Examples of the use of style sheets appear on this page. Figure 11.16 shows a list of some the style sheets used in this book and indicates the location of the the style sheet formatted text on this page. You will note that I use style sheets to format all of my copy. This helps improve the speed and consistency of my typesetting and makes any text formatting changes quick and easy. Any time I want to edit the formatting of any text, all I have to do is edit one style sheet instead of manually selecting and reformatting dozens or even hundreds of individual sections of text. See Chapter 13, "Document Construction," for more details on style sheets.

▼ *Figure 11.15 Style Sheet Dialog*
This is the basic style sheet dialog box in QuarkXPress. Similar ones can be found in other applications such as PageMaker. Note all of the type formatting controls available in one location. Any characteristics which are set in a style sheet can be applied as a template to automatically format any new or previously created text.

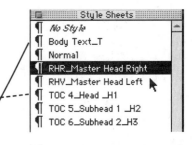

▼ *Figure 11.16 Style Sheets*
This is a list of some of the style sheets used in this book. There are several style sheets used on this page. They are shown by arrows. The use of style sheets helps improve the speed and consistency of your typesetting and dramatically improves the editability of the text after it has been initially set. *All of* the subhead text in this entire book was formatted with the style sheet labeled "Sub Head 2," with just a few clicks of the mouse.

Setting type in drawing applications

In general, you should avoid setting much type in outline graphics applications such as Illustrator, FreeHand, and CorelDraw, particularly if you intend to export the graphic as an EPS for inclusion in a page layout application. Most type elements which will be part of an exported EPS file should be converted to graphic outlines to facilitate the RIPing of the file. See the discussion and file prep hints in Chapter 10, "RIPing Up Your Files" and specific instructions on type conversion in Chapter 16, "Application-Specific Tips" under the section on drawing programs. Also see Chapter 20, "Managing the Mess," for some suggestions on when and how to create a finished exportable EPS file.

CHAPTER SUMMARY

TrueType and PostScript Type 1 fonts are the two most common font architectures. Font files contain screen and printer font information. Size, tracking, leading, kerning, and paragraph formatting are controlled using type characters. Mac and Windows computers provide default font locations. Font files used in document construction should be stored outside these default locations to allow for easier font management. Font file mishaps are the single biggest problem in customer supplied files to printing companies and service bureaus. Effective type management involves proper font management procedures and utility. Current PostScript and TrueType fonts are not easily used cross platform and have limited font character sets. Consider creating and using PDF files when you take a document across platforms. New font technologies such as OpenType and Unicode fonts should provide for better cross platform utilization of fonts and more flexible and universal character sets. Typesetting is not typewriting. There is a number of well established guidelines for formatting type which should be followed in order to create properly formatted, readable type. Style sheets should be used to format type which repeats in a document, such as heads, subheads, and body copy.

PAULINE'S DIGITAL IMAGING TIPS

Pauline's Tip 11.1

Separate System font files from document construction font files. Locate the document construction font file outside of the default system font folders to allow for easier and more effective font management.

Pauline's Tip 11.2

Use PostScript Type 1 rather than TrueType fonts in documents which will be printed on a high resolution PostScript imaging device such as an imagesetter. If you use TrueType fonts, use them exclusively; don't mix TrueType with Type 1 in the same document.

Pauline's Tip 11.3

When working with PostScript Type 1 font files, make sure that both of the required font files, screen and printer font files on the Mac and .pfb and .pfm font files in Windows, are in the same folder, so the screen and printer font information will both be available to use together.

File Prep Tip 11.4

Choose typeface styles from the font menu rather than from keyboard shortcuts or font style palettes. This will prevent the on-screen creation of fonts which do not exist.

File Prep Tip 11.5

Be careful about adding too many fonts to your documents. This is both good design and good technical advice. Each font increases the complexity of your document.

File Prep Tip 11.6

Avoid reversing small and serif typefaces, as the character shapes are difficult to create and maintain when they are printed.

PAULINE'S DIGITAL IMAGING TIPS

File Prep Tip 11.7

Do not baseline-shift large blocks of text; move the entire text box or area. Baseline-shift should be used to adjust individual characters or words.

File Prep Tip 11.8

Use a font management utility to manage your font files after they have been isolated outside of their default system font locations.

File Prep Tip 11.9

Create and use virtual font sets to control which fonts are active. This will prevent font substitution and conflict errors.

File Prep Tip 11.10

Assign leading absolute values rather than using autoleading. Autoleading may create inconsistent leading when individual characters are baseline-shifted, such as when using superscripts and subscripts.

File Prep Tip 11.11

Your computer is not a typewriter; it is a sophisticated typesetting tool. Don't use multiple spaces and returns to control the horizontal and vertical placement of type. Use paragraph formatting and tabs to position type. Read Robin William's book, *The Mac Is Not a Typewriter.* I think this is the best introduction to typesetting written.

File Prep Tip 11.12

Snap body copy type to baseline grids when working with multicolumn text pages. This will keep the baselines of your body copy consistent from one column to another.

File Prep Tip 11.13

Use style sheets to control any type formatting which is repeated throughout a document. Style sheets provide fast, accurate and easy to edit type formatting.

CHAPTER REVIEW

Check Your Comprehension

Multiple Choice Questions

To help you review the topics covered in this chapter, answer the following multiple choice questions.

1. Which of the following is the minimum set of characteristics required to define a font?
   A. Typeface
   B. Typeface and style
   C. Typeface, style, and size
   D. Typeface, style, size, architecture

2. Which of the following pairs represent a Mac PostScript Type 1 font?
   A. Screen and printer font files
   B. .pfb and .pfm font files
   C. .TTF and .pfm
   D. All of the above

3. Which of the following pairs represent a Windows PostScript Type 1 font?
   A. Screen and printer font files
   B. .pfb and .pfm font files
   C. .TTF and .pfm
   D. All of the above

4. Which of the following is the default Windows TrueType font location folder.?
   A. System font folder
   B. psfont folder
   C. Windows font folder
   D. None of the above

5. Which of the following is a good place to store screen fonts on a Macintosh?
   A. Font suitcase
   B. Font folder
   C. Font extension folder
   D. None of the above

6. _____ is (are) required in order for PostScript Type one fonts to display and print properly.

   A. Screen and printer fonts on a Mac

   B. .pfm and .pfb file in Windows

   C. ATM

   D. All of the above

7. Which of the following should a font management utility provide?

   A. Font file identification

   B. Font activation and deactivation

   C. Font file trouble shooting

   D. All of the above

8. Creating and using virtual _____ are the best way to avoid font ID conflicts.

   A. memory sets

   B. font sets

   C. font utilities

   D. system files

9. Identify the default Macintosh operating system font.

   A. Chicago

   B. Geneva

   C. Monaco

   D. All of the above

10. _____ is critical to dependable font management.

   A. Use of a font management tool

   B. Having all of your document creation fonts accessible in the system font folder

   C. Mix your TrueType and PostScript font file together in the system font folder

   D. All of the above

11. Which of the following is generally the best tool to use for setting type?

   A. Drawing application

   B. Painting application

   C. Page layout application

   D. The above are about equal

12. Which tool provide us with fast, accurate, editable type formatting?

   A. ATM

   B. Style sheet

   C. Font management utility

   D. None of the above

Check Your Understanding

Concept Questions

To help you review and expand your thinking on the topics covered in this chapter, answer the following questions.

1. Briefly explain why operating system fonts and document creation fonts should be separated from each other.

2. Explain the difference between PostScript Type 1 and TrueType font files.

3. Describe the fundamental differences between Windows and Macintosh PostScript Type 1 font files.

4. Explain why we have problems transferring our font files cross platform. Identify three different solutions to these cross platform font problems.

5. What is the basic function of a font management utility? Discuss at least four characteristics of a good font management utility.

6. What are virtual font sets and why are they so valuable?

7. Outline the characteristics of an effective font management program.

8. Explain the difference between typewriting and typesetting. Describe at least four fundamental typesetting principles.

9. Explain the purpose of document preplanning and why it is important.

10. What is the number one problem with client files which arrive at printing companies and service bureaus? Outline an approach to avoid having these problems.

PROJECTS

1. Make a backup copy of your operating system on a separate hard drive. On the backup, locate the default system font folder (Windows or Mac). Make a list of all the fonts found in this folder. Identify the font files which are required for use by your version of the operating system (ask your instructor for a list). Now remove all the nonessential operating system fonts and place in a separate fonts folder outside of the System folder. These will be your document creation font files

2. Organize the document creation font files isolated in Project 1 above. Organize these fonts into folders by class and type face families.

3. With a font management utility create three virtual font sets for three different documents. Activate one of the font sets and launch its associated document. Now check to make sure that all the fonts needed for that document are active.

Part 3

Project Construction

STYLE SHEETS

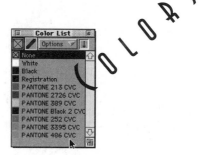

COLORS

APPLICATION

MASTER PAGES

FoxRun

12
Taming Your Scanner

As the Byte Turns continues…

Can Danny capture Pauline's imagination, or will Pauline just give him a one-pass scan?

I have a 1200 dpi scanner! Now I can scan all my images at high resolution and get great results!

Yeah, go for it! That'll make all your images print great!

Oh dear, what have I gotten myself into?

Shouldn't he?

You told him to go ahead and scan at WHAT resolution? …By the way Danny, get your resolution terminology straight!

Chapter Objectives

In this chapter you will learn:

- ◆ **Visualization scanning**
- ◆ **Scanning challenges**
- ◆ **Scanner calibration**
- ◆ **Image analysis and scan modes**
- ◆ **Scan setups for line art and contones**
- ◆ **Postscan image manipulation**
- ◆ **Choosing the best resolution**
- ◆ **Selecting file formats**
- ◆ **Setting scanning resolutions**
- ◆ **PhotoCD scanning**
- ◆ **Scanner limitations**
- ◆ **Scanning for multipurpose image use**
- ◆ **Key Terms**
  - Visualization scanning
  - Preview scanning
  - Tone reproduction
  - Dynamic range and DMax
  - Multipurposed and repurposed images
  - Dot gain
  - Gamut conversion
  - Linearization and neutralization
  - Tone compression
  - Highlight, midtone and shadow areas and points
  - Unsharpmasking
  - PhotoCD

INTRODUCTION

Visualizing the scanning process and the postscan manipulation of your scanned images allows you to make better scanning choices. Know the challenges of scanning such as how your image changes, the image data which can be lost, the limitations of the **Dynamic range** of your scanner, the impact of **Dot gain**, and how your image will be converted after the scan all provide valueable insight into how you should scan and manipulate your images in order to capture and maintain the highest image quality possible. Calibration, **linearization** for grayscale images and **neutralization** for color images, are key to high quality consistent scanning. Allowing your scanner to perform most of your basic image adjustments such as applying **tone compression** to set **highlight** and **shadow** points, performing gray map adjustment for brightness and contrast as well as scaling and resolution adjustments, rather than performing these chores in the postscan will result in higher quality images. Image sharpening should be performed last. In general the input resolution at which we scan should be controlled by the output resolution at which we use our images. We will typically choose higher resolution (600–1200 ppi) for line art images and lower resolutions 150 ppi–400 ppi for contone images. Automated scanning technologies such as **PhotoCD** can speed up the scanning process and reduce costs, but be aware that more postscan image manipulation may be needed to adjust these images. Multipurposing of image requires that we consider all the uses for which a scanned image will be needed. In general we will scan for the highest resolution, quality and size requirements, which is often commercial printing. It is a good idea to create and save general purpose, large gamut archive images which can then be copied and used for many other purposes.

VISUALIZATION IN SCANNING

History

Traditionally, those of us who created images which were to be reproduced for printing relied upon professional photographers and scanner operators to capture and reproduce our images. Typically, we would leave a blank area on our composite page where the photographed or scanned and imageset image would be placed. Even with the advent of desktop scanners, most of us choose to use our scanners primarily for FPO (for position only) work and leave the final image capture and manipulation to the professionals. There are, however, many reasons, including creative control, experimentation, and cost and time savings, for wanting to take control of the capture and production of our final art images. So over time as the resolution, tonal range, and quality and capabilities of available scanning and image manipulation software improved, we have become bolder, more adventurous scanner operators. We have become more interested and more willing to take on the challenges of capturing, manipulating, and preparing our own graphic images for output. The dawn and growth of direct digital image capture through the use of digital cameras has emboldened us even more. Most of us started with simple B&W line art images and progressively tested our mettle on more complicated and demanding images such as detailed line art, grayscale, and then color images. I remember my first introduction to scanning, circa 1985, way back in the dawn of the desktop publishing age. I bought one of the first "desktop" scanners, called a Thunderscan. It was a small plastic unit which fit on my dot matrix imagewriter printer. The scanning unit took advantage of the transport mechanism of the printer to move the image during scanning. It took 20 minutes to capture a 3" x 5" image at 200 ppi. I waited patiently for the image to be captured and transported through the serial port to my hard drive. I was thrilled when the first image popped up on my 9" B&W screen. Today, 15 years later, we work with desktop scanners which can capture 11" x 17" 10 bit color images at 2400 ppi or more at amazing speeds.

How scanners work

It is always helpful to know how an instrument works if you want to learn how to control it more effectively. In concept, color scanners are relatively simple devices. All scanners have at least four basic components in common: a light source, an image holder or carrier, a filter system, and a light capturing and converting device.

▼ *Figure 12.1 Types of Images*
There are three basic categories of images: line art (top), grayscale contones (middle), and color contones (bottom). Each type of image has its own scanning challenges. Line art images usually involve capturing edge detail. With grayscale and color images, the challenges revolve around reproducing tonal ranges accurately and completely. Color contone images have the added requirement of reproducing color values as well as tonal ranges accurately. There are some images which contain characteristics and challenges of all three types of images.

Note: A color version of this image (Fig. C.2) can be found on page C-4 in the color plate section in the center of this book.

The basic scanning process proceeds like this. Light, usually produced from a bulb-based light source, is either passed through or reflected off of a secured image. This light is then filtered through red, green, and blue filters which separate an image into three different channels (R, G, and B) of light. These three channels of light are then collected by a light capturing mechanism. There are basically two kinds of light capturing devices in common use. One is the photomultiplier tubes (PMT) which are typically used in high quality drum scanners. The other is the charge couple device (CCD), typically used in flatbed scanners and digital cameras. PMTs and CCDs not only capture the light, but convert the light into electricity, a form of energy your computer understands. In this way, your image is captured and converted into a sequence of on and off electrical signals stored as bits on your computer. It is important to realize that all images, even continuous tone (contone) color images, are captured and stored as black and white or grayscale images. Your computer, being a digital device, understands only two data values, on and off, 0 and 1, black and white. Color images are stored and manipulated as black and white or grayscale images on your computer. The three RGB color channels you capture with your computer are really three grayscale channels to which color is added when those images are sent to output devices. Examples include the red, green, and blue phosphors on your monitor or the colored inks on a printing press.

Goals for scanning

Your scanner can be used as a tool for either recreating and reproducing an image or for altering an image. In scanning for reproduction, our goal is to match the final version of the image as closely as possible to the original. A scanner can also be used as a tool to alter images, such as changing contone images into line art or color into grayscale or B&W. In this chapter we will concentrate on scanning to reproduce originals. Once you master scanning for reproduction, you can more confidently and predictably use your scanner as an instrument of change.

Types of images

There are three basic types of images: line art, grayscale contones, and color contones. A fourth category could include complex images which have the characteristics of two or three of the basic types. Examples of line art include images, such as logos, which are constructed from line-based drawings. Pure line art images do not contain continuous tone information; that is, they are composed of lines or areas which can be rendered as either black or white. Colored line art can be captured by your scanner as areas of black and white. Grayscale and color contones are similar to each other in that both are composed of areas of continuous tones. Grayscale images are captured by your scanner as one grayscale channel. Color images are captured as three grayscale channels, one for each color (R, G, B). An example of a complex image would be an image which contains a combination of line art and continuous tone images such as a piece of cloth with a logo label on it.

Parts of an image

When your goal is to reproduce an image, you often have a range of image characteristics which need to be reproduced. These include image size, image area, shapes, tones, contrast, color, detail, and edges. Different images may have different characteristics. For instance, line art images usually have edges which need to be captured. With contone images, edge capture is not nearly as important as **Tone reproduction**. Not all scanners do an equally good job of capturing all of these characteristics, and few scanners can maximize the capture of all these characteristics at one time. Your job as a scanner operator is to evaluate the characteristics of your images, determine what are the most crucial components of your images, and adjust your scanner to concentrate on those characteristics.

SCANNING GOALS AND CHALLENGES

Reproducing images and particularly continuous tone color images for print is one of the most technically demanding challenges we face in electronic publishing. Scanning for reproduction involves trying to match the tones, contrast, color, and detail of an original image. Scanned images are often too dark or light or have altered contrast and color balance when compared to the original. These changes can be related to five basic challenges which we face when we try to reproduce an original image through scanning and printing. They are: changes in the image, loss of data, media changes and Dot gain, **Gamut conversion**, and impure image inks.

Challenge 1: changes in image

During scanning, viewing, and printing, an image is transformed quite dramatically. For instance, a continuous tone grayscale or color photograph is digitized into a sequence of 0s and 1s during scanning, converted into pixels for viewing on a monitor, and finally RIPed into a pattern of dots known as halftone screen dots for reproduction during the printing process. Halftoning, rendering a contone image as a pattern of dots, is required in order to reproduce contone images on a printing press because a printing press cannot print continuous tone information. They can print only solid areas and dots.

This halftoning process is the most dramatic of the three transformations because at this point your image no longer contains any true contone information. Halftone screen dots are "sleight of the eye" impostors for the areas of continuous tones which make up the original photograph. The technique of using halftone dots to reproduce original continuous tones is nearly as old as the printing process itself. The halftone concept takes advantage of the human eye's limited capacity to resolve small dots at a distance. Halftone dots are so small and so closely spaced that at normal reading distances the human eye does not see individual dots but rather a blur of the dot patterns which our mind interprets as grayscale or continuous tone information. The larger or more closely spaced the dots are, the darker the image appears and the darker the shade of gray the eye "sees" (Fig. 12.2).

It is important to realize and remember that it is the job of the PostScript RIP and not of the scanner to perform this miracle of translation from grayscale pixels to halftone dots. These dots are then placed on various kinds of paper or film by a laser printer, image setter, printing press, or other printing device. In fact, an image may go through several generations of printing reproduction, film, and plates.

Scanning: Digitizing

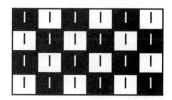

Viewing: Pixels on screen

RIPing: Halftone dots for printing

▼ *Figure 12.2 The Changed Image*
The process of scanning, viewing, and printing an image changes it significantly. Here you see how an original continuous tone image is transformed into 0s and 1s during the scanning process, then into grayscale pixels for screen view, and finally into a pattern of halftone dots for printing.

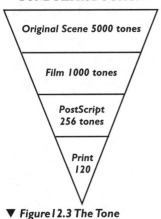

▼ *Figure 12.3 The Tone Pyramid*
Over 90 percent of tonal information is lost from an image during its transformation from its original screen to printed piece. Our eyes can recognize approximately 5000 tonal gradations. High quality positive photo film captures 20 percent of the original, while in PostScript we are limited to 256 shades of gray.

▼ *Figure 12.4 Calibration*
On the left is an image scanned on an uncalibrated scanner. On the right is the same image scanned on the same scanner with the same settings, but this time after linearization. Notice how overall image brightness, contrast, and shadow details are improved through calibration.

Clearly, any image is significantly transformed during this process of scanning, viewing, RIPing, and printing. It helps to understand and visualize what happens to an image as it goes through these various stages and processes if you want to be able to predict what any given image will look like when it emerges at the end of this process.

One of the consequences of this scan, view, and print process is that nearly all con-tone images appear flatter or in lower contrast than their originals after they have been scanned. This contrast must be replaced if you want to come close to reproducing the original image.

Challenge 2: loss of data

The human eye can distinguish about 5000 tonal shades. High quality film can capture about 20 percent, or 1000, of those 5000 tonal shades. In PostScript we are limited to working with 256 tonal values, a mere five percent of the original 5000. On a printing press we can reproduce between 80 and 120 tonal gradations (~2%) of the original scene. Our challenge is to capture the best possible 256 shades for use in PostScript and then distribute that information to the most important parts of the image. Images which are too light or dark are often the result of not properly reproducing the best 256 shades of gray (Figure 12.3). This loss of data is referred to as tone compression, the loss of tonal range from the original image to the printed product.

Challenge 3: calibration and dynamic range

Calibration

Every image capture device (including scanners), no matter what their cost or capabilities, needs to be calibrated to assure consistent results. Nearly all scanners tend to capture images darker than they actually are. Each device is different and is affected over time by variables such as temperature and bulb age. Calibration helps to standardize the capture response of the scanner and is accomplished by scanning a target with known grayscale values (see Figure 12.4). The values which the scanner "sees" are then compared with the actual values of the target. The scanner is then adjusted or corrected so that it captures the target values correctly. To assure accurate and consistent scanning of your images, calibration should be performed prior to each scan session. See the section on how to calibrate your scanner later in this chapter and the offer in the back of the book on how to obtain your own calibration target.

Dynamic range

The measure of a scanner's ability to capture a range of grayscale values, or densities, is known as its dynamic range. Dynamic range varies on a scale from 0 to 4.0 with each integer step being a tenfold increase in grayscale density recognition capacity, and with 4.0 being the most capable. A scanner's dynamic range is most noticeable in the shadow, or maximum density, regions of an image. Scanners with good dynamic range, and therefore high maximum densities (**DMax**) can see a lot

Color
Plates

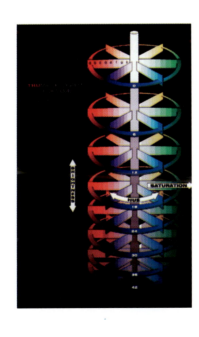

DOCUMENT
Low Resolution Screen Images vs.

Low Resolution Screen Font File
- Low resolution (72 ppi)
- Bitmapped file and image
- Used to display text on screen
- *Not* included in page layout document
- Must be sent along with document on disk
- *Linked* to external scalable outline printer font file

Screen Font Name
Palatino

Link to Screen Font ➡

Quark, PageMaker, InDesign, FrameMaker, Document

PAGE LAYOUT DOCUMENT

➡ *Link to High Resolution Print Graphic File* ➡

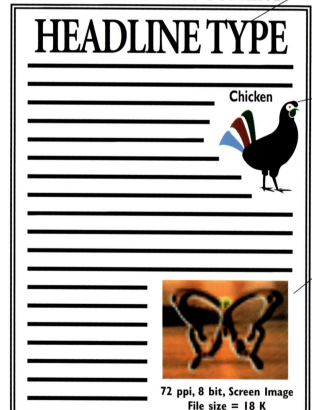

HEADLINE TYPE

Chicken

Low Resolution Screen Preview Image PICT (Mac) or Tiff (Win)
- Low Resolution (72 ppi) *view* image
- *Included* in page layout document
- *Linked* to external high resolution vector EPS *print* image

➡ Link to High Resolution Print Graphic File ➡

**72 ppi, 8 bit, Screen Image
File size = 18 K**

Low Resolution Screen Preview Image PICT (Mac) or Tiff (Win)
- Low resolution (36 or 72 ppi) *view* image
- ~18 K @ 72 ppi
- Low res bitmapped PICT (Mac) or TIFF (Win)
- Used to display graphic images on screen
- *Included* in page layout document
- *Linked* to external high resolution *print* image

▼ *Figure C.1 Document Construction*
Page layout documents are shells into which proxies for type and graphics are placed. Low resolution versions of graphic images are stored in the page layout document itself. High resolution versions, used for printing, are stored externally to the page layout document. Font information is entirely external. All the external files need to be sent to your printer along with the page layout document itself (See Fig. 13.9).

CONSTRUCTION
High Resolution Printing Images

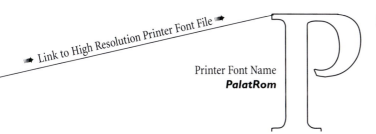

Link to High Resolution Printer Font File ➡

Printer Font Name
PalatRom

High Resolution Printer Font File
- High resolution Postscript/Outline file
- Scalable
- *Not* included in page layout document pages
- *Linked* to external low resolution screen font file
- *Not* seen on screen, but used to print document
- Must be sent along with document on disk

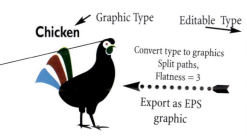

Graphic Type

Editable Type

Chicken

Convert type to graphics
Split paths,
Flatness = 3

Export as EPS
graphic

Drawing Document
- FreeHand
- Illustrator
- CorelDraw

Exported EPS Print Image
- Encapsulated Postscript
- Vector /Outline: Resolution independent
- For importing into page layout file
- *Not* included in page layout document
- Must be sent along with document on disk
- *Linked* to low resolution preview

Original Parent/Native Documents
- Original Photoshop or drawing file
- High resolution pixel and/or vector image
- May contain layers, channels and/or editable type
- *Not* included in page layout file
- Should be sent as separate unlinked graphic file along with page layout document and linked graphics on disk. Place this native file in a separate folder for use in case editing is required. Use same name as print graphic file, but with different three character extension, such as .psd for Photoshop.

Flatten layers, remove alpha channels, and convert to CMYK. Export as TIFF or EPS Graphic

**200 ppi 4.34MB
Multi-layered, 24bit
RGB Photoshop (.psd) image**

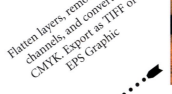

High Resolution TIFF or EPS CMYK Printing Image
- High resolution (200 ppi – 300 ppi)
- 370 KB @ 200 ppi (No layers or channels)
- High resolution bitmapped TIFF or EPS
- Used for *printing* graphic images
- *Not* Included in page layout document
- *Linked* to low resolution graphic file
- Sent along with document on disk

**200 ppi 370KB
Flattened 32bit, CMYK
Print (.tif or .eps) Image**

1 Bit Black & White Image

1 bit line art images such as these contain only one layer of pixels with 1 bit of data per pixel. Each pixel is either Black (1) or White (0). These are the smallest and simplest types of bitmapped images. File size = 285KB at 300 ppi.

8 Bit Gray Scale Image

8 bit grayscale images contain only one layer of 8 bit pixels which has the capacity to store and display 256 shades of gray. Contrast this to the 1 bit per pixel used to create the line art image above. This grayscale file size is eight times (8x) larger than the 1bit images discussed above. This 8 b/p file is also the basic building block for the RGB and CMYK images shown below.
File size = 2.2MB at 300ppi.

24 Bit RGB Color (Screen) Image

24 bit color images contain three layers of 8 bit grayscale pixels, one for each color (RGB). Each color can be shown in 256 shades. Therefore, the total number of colors possible is 256 Red x 256 Green x 256 Blue = 16.7 million colors. This RGB image file size is twenty-four times larger than the 1bit line art image. File size = 6.6MB at 300 ppi.

32 Bit CMYK Color (Print) Image

A 32 bit grayscale image contains four layers of 8 bit grayscale pixels, one for each color. Note: A 32 bit CMYK image produces the same number of colors as the 24 bit RGB image above (16.7 million). The fourth black channel (K) is substituted for various portions of the three color channels (CMY). This K channel improves contrast and shadow detail and reduces ink coverage but does not add any colors. This CMYK image file is used for printing and is 33% larger than the equivalent RGB file, and 32 times larger than a similar 1 bit image. File size = 8.8MB at 300 dpi.

▼ *Figure C.2 Pixel Depth of Images*

Electronic images can be divided into three basic categories: B&W, grayscale, and color. B&W images only require 1 bit per pixel for creation and display. Grayscale images require 8 bits per pixel to display 256 shades of gray. Color images require either 24 or 32 bits per pixel depending upon whether they are RGB or CMYK images. File size, storage space, and RIPing time increase as pixel depth increases.

Basic Color Theory

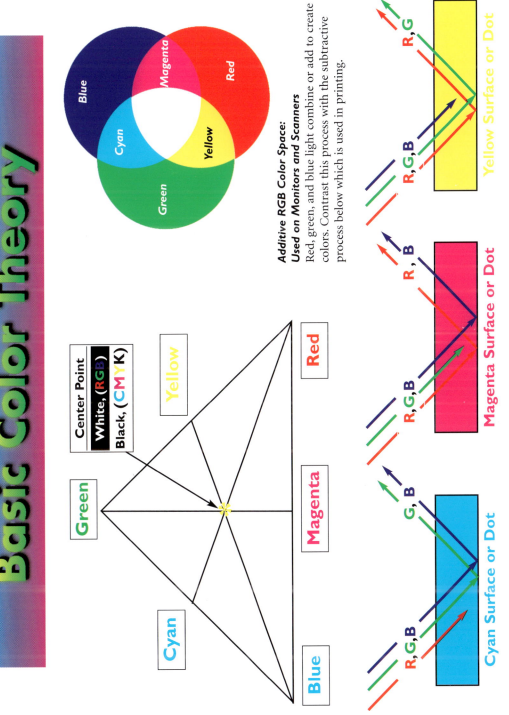

Additive RGB Color Space:
Used on Monitors and Scanners

Red, green, and blue light combine or add to create colors. Contrast this process with the subtractive process below which is used in printing.

Center Point
White, (RGB)
Black, (CMYK)

Green
Yellow
Cyan
Magenta
Blue
Red

Cyan Surface or Dot
Magenta Surface or Dot
Yellow Surface or Dot

R,G,B   G, B
R,G,B   R , B
R,G,B   R,G

▼ **Figure C.3 Subtractive CMYK Color Space Used In Printing**
Transmitted (RGB) light is selectively absorbed by various combinations of the three process colors (C, M, and Y). The color(s) we see on a printed piece comes from the light which is transmitted and reflected rather than absorbed by the process colors.

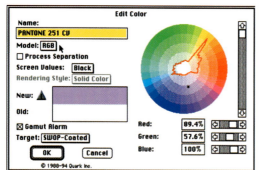

▼ *Figure C.4 RGB/HSV Color Picker*

To the left is the HSV color picker. By manipulating the sliders in this dialog box, you can create all of the colors which this monitor can display.

• The Hue, or basic color, is represented by the colors on the *outside* edge of the color circle. We are working in RGB color space so the values are recorded in percent of RGB.

• The Saturation is represented by all of the colors *inside* of the rim of the color circle. As you can see, the colors nearer the center of the circle are lighter, that is, less saturated, than the colors nearer the rim.

Progressive amounts of white are added to any Hue (rim color) at positions tending away from the rim toward the center. The center is pure white or 100% Red + 100% Blue + 100% Green.

• Value is a measure of the percentage of grayscale which a color contains. Value ranges from 0% to 100% and is controlled (added or subtracted) by sliding the large vertical slider up and down. In its current position, the value of this color is 0% grayscale. If the slider were moved all the way to the bottom of its track, 100% gray would be added to the color and it would be pure black.

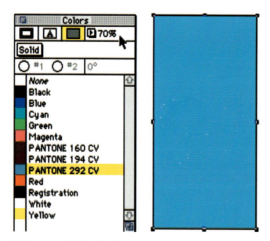

▼ *Figure C.5 Color Assignment Palette*

In most applications colors can be stored in and applied through a palette such as this QuarkXPress color palette. The three Pantone colors are spot colors. RGB colors are monitor colors and should not be used for printing. CMYK colors are used for building and printing process colors. The Registration color is assigned to page elements such as crop, registration, and fold marks which should occur on every separation.

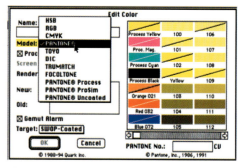

▼ *Figure C.6 Color Models*

This shows a list of the more common color matching systems which are used in graphics applications. The Pantone System is the most widely used. The system labeled Pantone contains the spot color guide colors. The Pantone Process system contains the process color guide colors, and the Pantone ProSim contains the closest simulated process color matches for the spot colors. The Focoltone, TruMatch, Toyo, and DIC systems offer process color matching guides similar to the Pantone Process system.

**Pantone Spot
Color (CV) Guide
Solid Color**

Pantone 250CV
1 pt. Purple
31 pts. Trans. White

Pantone 251CV
2 pts. Purple
14 pts. Trans. White

Pantone 252CV
8 pts. Purple
8 pts. Trans. White

Pantone Purple
1 pt. purple

Pantone 253CV
16 pts. Purple
1/4 pt. Black

Pantone 254CV
16 pt. Purple
1 pt. Black

Pantone 255CV
16 pt. Purple
4 pts. Black

**Pantone Process
(S) Color Guide
4/C Process**

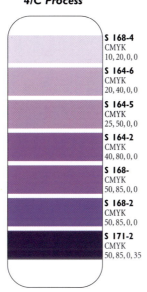

S 168-4
CMYK
10, 20, 0, 0

S 164-6
CMYK
20, 40, 0, 0

S 164-5
CMYK
25, 50, 0, 0

S 164-2
CMYK
40, 80, 0, 0

S 168-
CMYK
50, 85, 0, 0

S 168-2
CMYK
50, 85, 0, 0

S 171-2
CMYK
50, 85, 0, 35

**Pantone Spot (CV) & Process
Simulation/ProSim (CVP)
Comparison Guide**

ProSim
250CVP
6C, 18.5M, 0Y, 0K

ProSim
251CVP
C15, M43, Y0, K0

ProSim
252CVP
C23, M56, Y0, K0

ProSim
Purple CVP
C43, M91, Y0, K0

ProSim
253CVP
C47, M91, Y0, K0

ProSim
254CVP
C51, M94, Y0, K0

ProSim
255CVP
C51, M91, Y0, K34

Pantone 250CV
1 pt. Purple
31 pts. Trans. White

Pantone 251CV
2 pts. Purple
14 pts. Trans. White

Pantone 252CV
8 pts. Purple
8 pts. Trans. White

Pantone PurpleCV
1 pt. Purple

Pantone 253CV
16 pts. Purple
1/4 pt. Black

Pantone 254CV
16 pt. Purple
1 pt. Black

Pantone 255CV
16 pt. Purple
4 pts. Black

Color Assignment - Spot Color

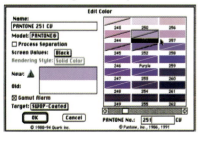

*Color Assignment -
4/C Process (164-6)*

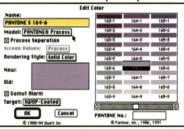

*Color Assignment - Solid to Process
/ Process Simulation (251CVP)*

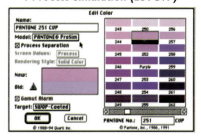

▼ *Figure C.7 Color Choice Guides*

Three basic types of color swatch book guides appear here. From left to right they are: 1) Pantone spot/solid color guide, 2) Pantone CMYK process color guide, and 3) Pantone Solid to Process color guide (previously known as ProSim or Process simulation). The spot color guide shows a range of spot colors 250CV to 255CV. ("CV" means printed on coated stock and "U" means uncoated stock.) They are the same color but look different because of the printing substrate. CVP designates process simulation of a spot color, while the S prefix indicates a color chosen from the Process color swatch chart. The process guide shows the closest regular Pantone process colors to these spot colors. As you can see, the match is not good, especially in the lighter, more saturated colors. The Solid to Process guide is a special collection of process colors built specifically to simulate, as close as possible, the Pantone spot colors. Look closely and you will see that the Solid to process guide has color values designated by single and even half percent values rather than the standard 10% and 15% value changes. Even this specific, focused attempt to match the spot colors with process colors fails with the more saturated colors. *Note: All spot colors shown on this page are printed with process colors and are therefore not accurate. The above charts are meant to show the differences between the spot and process values for the same colors.

▼ **Figure C.8 Color Space Model**
This is a three-dimensional model of HSV (Hue, Saturation and Value) color space created by TruMatch Corp. Hue is represented by the outside rim of the cylinder. Saturation, color purity or intensity, varies across any cross section of the cylinder with maximum saturation on the outside rim and minimum at the center. Value, which is a measure of grayscale value or brightness, varies along the vertical axis of the model cylinder, with 100% gray at one end and 0% gray at the other. The color picker diagram (Fig. C.4) on page C-6 is a cross section view through the cylinder. The slider to the right of the pie changes the value or view position along the vertical axis.

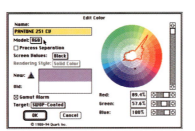

▼ **Figure C.9 Color Gamut Comparison**
The entire color picker circle shows the gamut of the RGB colors which can be seen on the monitor. The roughly triangular Red area inside of the color picker circle is the limited range of those colors which can be reproduced by CMYK. The black dot in the lower half of the color circle shows the position of the Pantone spot color 251 CV, which is well out of gamut and will not be reproducible in CMYK.

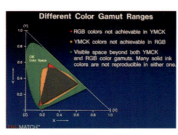

▼ **Figure C.10 Color Gamuts**
Color gamut describes the range of color that a particular device can capture or reproduce. This diagram is a two-dimensional slice through three-dimensional color space. Note how much larger the visual gamut of the human eye is (CIE area) than either the RGB (monitor) or CMYK (printer) gamuts. You will also see that there are RGB colors that will not reproduce in CMYK and vice versa. In this two-dimensional slice the gamut ranges of RGB and CMYK gamuts are of similar extent, but in the entire three-dimensional space the practical CMYK gamut is much smaller than RGB due to pigment impurities and ink density limitations. Figure C.9 shows a clearer representation of the difference between the extents of the RGB and CMYK color gamuts.

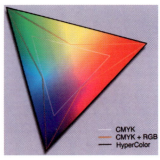

▼ **Figure C.11 Color Gamuts**
This diagram shows the color gamuts for three different color spaces: HyperColor, RGB, and CMYK. Note how the gamuts for RGB color space and the human eye are much more extensive than the gamut for CMYK printing gamut. HyperColor is a version of HiFi color which utilizes double hits of CMYK to increase the process color gamut. Other HiFi color systems use additional process colors to increase the gamut range of process color. Pantone Hexachrome adds green and orange to CMYK to achieve an enhanced gamut.

▼ **Figure C.12 Q 60 IT8 Chart**
This industry standard chart is used as a scanning target. During a calibration sequence this target would be scanned, viewed, and output. The monitor image can be measured with a spectrophotometer and adjusted. The printed image can be measured with a densitometer and colorimeter. These measurements are then used to create transfer functions or curves which will be used for adjusting future output to that specific printer. Similar calibration curves can be constructed for each scanner printer combination.

Cyan (C)   Magenta (M)   Yellow (Y)   Black (K)

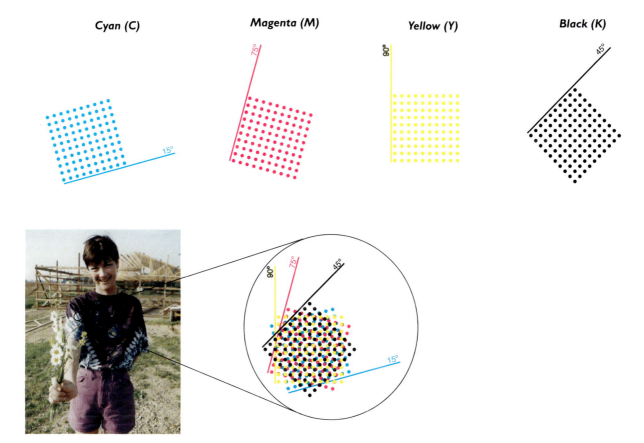

▼ *Figure C.13 Color Contone Images: Overlapping Four Color Process Halftone Screens*
Complex color contones such as this photograph are reproduced using a complex pattern of four overlapping screens of halftone dots. There is one screen pattern for each process color. Each color is printed at a different angle to avoid the generation of moiré patterns. Colors are separated as much as possible across the available 90°. The three strongest colors – Black, Cyan, and Magenta – are each separated by 30°. The fourth and weakest color, Yellow, is separated from two of the other colors, in this case Cyan and Magenta, by only 15°. When all four color screens are combined, a continuous tone color image simulation is produced. Note the rosette pattern which results when the four screens are in perfect registration.

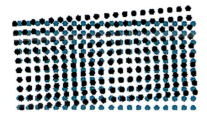

▼ *Figure C.14 Moiré Pattern Generation*
When two or more overlapping screens are printed out of registration, repeating geometric patterns known as a moiré pattern can result. Printing each screened color at a different and optimum angle helps reduce the occurrence of moiré patterns. It is the repeating pattern of halftone dots which makes conventional screening technology prone to the development of moiré patterns. The use of frequency modulation screening technology, where image dots are more randomly placed, can mitigate this problem of moiré pattern development.

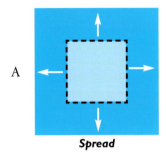

Spread

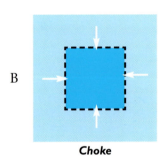

Choke

A

B

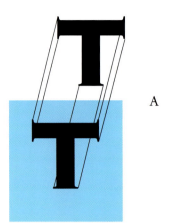

A

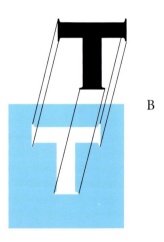

B

▼ *Figure C.17 Trap Example*
Different applications use different methods for applying trap, but they all spread, choke, knockout, and overprint in one way or another. The Freehand trap dialog box shows the foreground T being spread by 1 pt. If the reversed button were activated, then the background would choke.

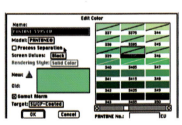

▼ *Figure C.18 Spot Color Separation*
This edit color dialog box in QuarkXPress demonstrates how to designate a spot color to separate as a spot color. Here the spot color 3395 is assigned from the Pantone spot color swatch chart mode. Note that the Process Separation check box near the upper lefthand corner is *not* checked. If this box is checked, QuarkXPress will separate all items assigned to this color on the four process color plates.

▼ *Figure C.15 Spread vs. choke*
This figure shows the difference between a spread and a choke. A spread (A) is generally applied where an inclosed lighter object (dashed edge) is expanded or spread out into a surrounding darker area. A Choke (B) is typically applied where a lighter surrounding area is brought in around, or choked, a darker object (dashed edge). By moving lighter objects into darker objects any changes in the sizes of the trapped objects tend to be less apparent.

▼ *Figure C.16 Overprint vs. Knockout*
This figure shows the difference between an overprint and a knockout. In the overprint (A) the black "T" is printed directly on top of the lighter Cyan area without removing any of the Cyan. In the knockout, the Cyan area under the black T is removed or knocked out from behind the T. Overprinting is the safest way to trap because there are few alignment problems. However, overprinting will usually result in darker objects and color alterations of the overprinted object unless it is very dark (>95 grayscale value). To trap this pair, would you spread the black "T" or choke the cyan background?

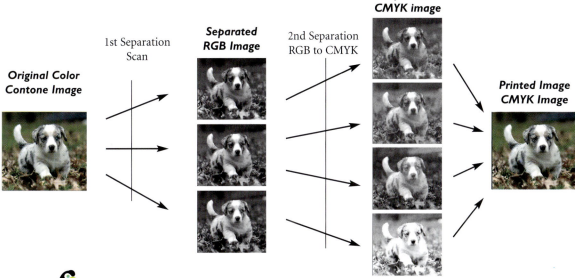

Original Color Contone Image

1st Separation Scan

Separated RGB Image

2nd Separation RGB to CMYK

Separated CMYK image

Printed Image CMYK Image

7/C Chicken built with 7 Spot Colors

▼ *Figure C.19 Twin Separation process*
This digital imaging process involves two different separation events on the way to creating a printed image. The first separation is from color contone image to RGB. If your final output device is a monitor you will stop here. If printing is your final destination a second separation is required converting from RGB to CMYK.

Pantone 213 Plate

Pantone 2726 Plate

Pantone 389 Plate

Pantone Black Plate

Pantone 252 Plate

Pantone 3395 Plate

Pantone 486 Plate

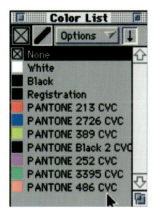

▼ *Figure C.20a Spot Color Palette*
Each of the assigned spot colors seen in this palette will be printed on its own plate. Each differently colored portion of the image is separated and has a specific spot color applied to it from a different press cylinder. Note that all the extraneous colors have been removed from this palette. While multicolor spot color printing like this allows you to use vivid custom colors, it is far more expensive than using combinations of process colors to produce the many color variations.

7/C Chicken built with 4 Process Colors

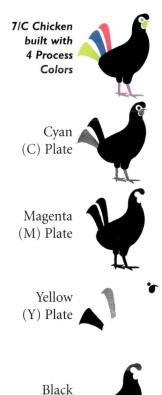

Cyan (C) Plate

Magenta (M) Plate

Yellow (Y) Plate

Black (K) Plate

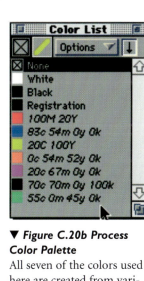

▼ *Figure C.20b Process Color Palette*
All seven of the colors used here are created from various combinations of CMYK. Since only four sets of separations, film, plates, and cylinders are required to print this image, it is much less expensive to print than its spot color "equivalent." Note that all the extraneous colors have been removed from this palette to avoid confusion.

▼ *Figure C.20a and b Spot vs. Process Separations*
This seven-color chicken is built and separated first with seven spot and then with four process colors. Note how the spot colors require the use of seven separations, sheets of film, and press cylinders, while the process build requires only four of each.

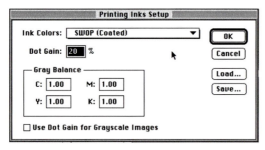

▼ *Figure C.21 Printing Ink Setup (SWOP)*

Prior to converting an RGB image into a CMYK image in Photoshop, you should pay close attention to: 1) the ink color set chosen, and 2) the dot gain percentage. Contact your printer to obtain both pieces of information. The dot gain percentage, 20% here, should be for the dot gain at 50%. The values set here will affect the appearance of the Separation Setup dialog box shown below. Note: This dialog box is from Photoshop 4.0. See Fig. C.24 for the combined (Printing Ink and Separation) CMYK Setup dialog box found in Photoshop 5.0 and 5.5.

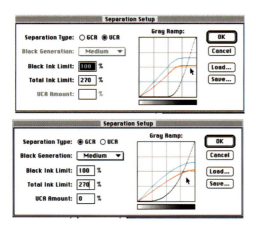

▼ *Figure C.22 Separation Setup*

The values set in the Printing Inks setup dialog box above affect the curves shown here. Your choice of UCR or GCR will also affect the separation curves. The Black generation begins at the three quarter tone for the UCR and at the quarter tone for the UCR curve. The overall placement of the UCR curves is lower due to the differences in the beginning of the Black generation. Compare and contrast these curves with those used for other types of printing devices. Note: This dialog box is from Photoshop 4.0. See Fig. C.24 for the combined (Printing Ink and Separation) CMYK Setup dialog box found in Photoshop 5.0/5.5.

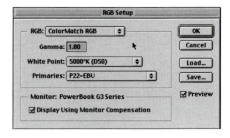

▼ *Figure C.23 RGB Setup*

Here the RGB Setup is being set for a match with commercial printing. It is important to set this RGB setting properly as it will dramatically affect the results of the RGB to CMYK conversion. sRGB should be avoided here if you are printing.

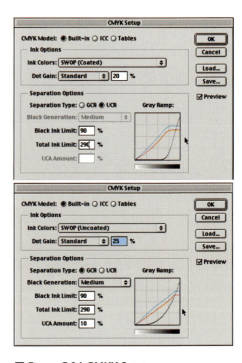

▼ *Figure C.24 CMYK Setup*

These curves show the Separation Setup curves applied to an image to be color separated for printing on a SWOP commercial printing press. Note the difference in the starting positions and the effects of the Black generation curves in the UCR and GCR variations. Obtain values for ink colors, dot gain, Black Ink Limit and Total Ink Limit from your printer. These curves will be applied to an RGB file when it is converted to a CMYK image, so be sure to make and set the correct choices and values in both dialog boxes prior to performing that conversion.

▼ **Figure C.25 UCR Separations**
Four separations are created here. Top to bottom, C, M, Y, and K using UCR black generation. Note how the black plate does not have as much tonal range as does the GCR black separation in Figure C.26. Also note how the C, M, and Y plates are darker than their GCR counterparts.

▼ **Figure C.26 GCR Separations**
Four separations created, top to bottom, C, M, Y, and K using GCR black generation. Note how the black plate has a much broader tonal range compared with the UCR black separation in Figure C.25. Also note how the C, M, and Y plates are lighter than their UCR counterparts.

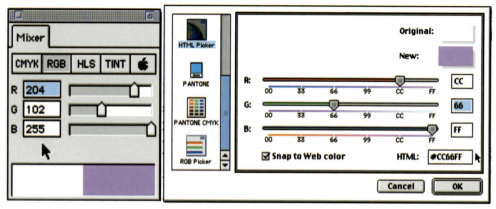

▼ Figure C.27 RGB vs. HTML Color Values

We are used to using RGB (left) or CMYK values when we work in applications such as Photoshop, Illustrator, or FreeHand. When assigning colors to objects which will be used on the Web, HTML values (right), instead of RGB values, are used to designate colors. THe HTML designation of CC 66 FF would be the HTML equivalent of RGB values of 204, 102, 255. Most HTML color pickers, such as the one shown here (right) will allow you to restrict your HTML color value choices to the Web safe colors. In this Freehand dialog box the color choices are restricted to Web safe colors by clicking on the "snap to Web color" check box in the lower left hand corner.

▼ Figure C.28 Color Palette

This is a color palette from QuarkXPress showing the four process colors; a Pantone process color, and a custom process color build, using the four process colors, one Pantone spot color, and a varnish. There will be six individual separations printed on their own individual pieces of film from this list of ten (10) colors. Note that the RGB colors have been removed from the color palette because they should not be used in the printing process. Also notice that the varnish is listed and will be applied and separated, like a spot color. The process colors will be combined together during the printing process. The registration color (generally a composite black) should be applied only to items such as crop, trim, registration, and fold marks which need to be placed on each film separation.

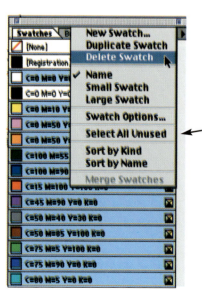

▼ Figure C.29 Deleting Colors

Deleting unused colors should be done prior to exporting a document as an EPS graphic or printing. For example in Illustrator 8.0, first choose "Select All Unused" from the color palette menu. Then choose "Delete Swatch" from the same menu. This same procedure can be performed in all the major drawing type applications.

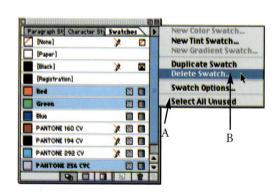

▼ Figure C.30 InDesign Color Tool

InDesign provides the color Swatches Palette which allows:

A) Selection of unused colors

B) Deletion of those unused colors.

These unused color ID and removal tools should be used prior to printing the final version of your document.

▼ *Figure C.31 Obtaining Neutral Densities*

These images show how adjustments in the RGB or CMY percentages of highlight dots change the appearance of an image. We want this highlight dot to print as a white area without cast. The top image has a CMY color mix of 19/2/5 and prints too blue. The second image which shows a color mix of 3/2/3 is closer to a castless white, but the dot percentages are too low and cannot be reproduced on most presses. The result is that large areas of the white will be reproduced without any dot detail and will appear "blown out." The final image, shows a CMY color mix of 5/3/3, has enough dot density to be printed and therefore shows detail and the right mix of CM&Y to compensate for the impure image inks. The highlight range of 5/3/3 to 6/4/4 works well for most printing presses. Try CMYK color mix of 55/40/40/20 to obtain a neutral midtone gray and a CMYK color mix of 95/85/85/75 for a neutral shadow dot. Ask your printer which percentage values work best on their presses for obtaining neutral highlight, midtone, and shadow values.

▼ *Figure C.32 Sharpening*

All scanners reduce the contrast of images when they capture and digitize them. In order to reproduce the look of the original image, contrast must be added back in. With digital images, this is accomplished by increasing the difference in tonal values between adjacent pixels, thereby giving the image more contrast. This process is known as "sharpening," sometimes referred to as "unsharpmasking." Above are four examples of sharpening applied to a strawberry image. Too little sharpening results in a flat, unclear image. Too much removes too much tonal gradation and begins to create edges and posterizes the image. A 50 percent sharpening is a good place to start. If your scanning application allows you to preview the effects of sharpening, try several amounts and pick the one you like best.

Composite RGB Image

Red

Green

Blue

▼ *Figure C.33 RGB "Color" Image*

A 24bit RGB "color" image such as this is essentially composed of a sandwich of three (3) grayscale images. The color we produce or output through either viewing or printing is provided by the output devices to which we send these images.

RGB images contain three channels of grayscale pixels with 24 bits of data per image, or three 8 b/p grayscale files, one for each color (RGB). Each color can be shown in 256 shades. Therefore, the total number of colors possible is 256 R x 256 G x 256 B = 16.7 million colors. This RGB image file size is 24 times larger than the 1bit line art image. These images are used for displaying color images on monitors and printing to color film.

To control the color in this image we control the grayscale values which in turn control the color.

of shadow details, while those with poor dynamic range can see little. A scanner's dynamic range is largely determined by the quality of the CCD used in the scanner, which is not an adjustable feature. However, a properly calibrated scanner allows us to take full advantage of its dynamic range. Increased dynamic range is one of the capabilities you pay for when you purchase more expensive scanners. Your scanner should have a dynamic range of at least 3.0 to be an effective tool for capturing good shadow details. The DMax, or maximum density, of the scanner is a common reference value for measuring the quality of a scanner. Higher DMaxs correlate to enhanced ability to distinguish shadow detail.

▼ *Figure 12.5 Dynamic Range (Dmax)*
On the left is an image scanned with a scanner which had a dynamic range of 2.5. On the right is the same image scanned with a scanner (PowerLook III) with a DMax, or maximum density of 3.4. Note the much improved shadow details captured by the PowerLook III. Look specifically at the hair, and you will see how much farther along the hair you can see.

Challenge 4: media changes and dot gain

Another challenge involves knowing what happens to an image when it is reproduced on different types of media. The appearance of any image will change if it is rendered on different kinds of media. For example, a photographic image reproduced on a tee shirt looks very different from that same image reproduced on paper. In print-oriented electronic publishing, an image may be displayed on several types of media. An original contone may start out as an image on photographic paper, be viewed as pixels on a glass monitor, printed on film, reproduced onto a metal, fabric, or paper plate, and then finally printed on paper stock. An image will look different on each of these media and the appearance of the final printed image will vary depending upon what kind of paper is used.

Dot gain

The inks which we use in the printing process react differently on different media. An image printed on coated stock will be much sharper and brighter than an image printed on uncoated stock. Inks applied to uncoated paper are absorbed more and tend to spread out more than inks applied to coated paper. This spreading out of ink is known as "dot gain." Dot gain can vary from as little as five percent on hard glossy stock to as much as 30 percent on porous news print (see Figure 12.6). Dot gain tends to be greatest in the midtones of an image and decreases toward the highlight and shadow portions of an image. The more an ink spreads out, the larger the area it covers, resulting in darker and duller images, especially in the midtone region. Dot gain must be compensated for before an image is printed on film. Here again, knowing the process through which an image is transformed, the various media on which that image will be rendered, and particularly the final media on which the image will rest, will help you predict how that image will look.

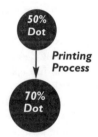

▼ *Figure 12.6 Dot Gain*
During the printing process the size of halftone dots tends to increase as ink spreads out, causing photographs to darken. Dot gain tends to be greatest in the midtone region, where the percentage of dot gain may be 20 percent or more.

Challenge 5: gamut conversion

Some of the colors we capture in the original RGB scan are not reproducible with CMYK ink and will be lost during the conversion from RGB color space to CMYK color space. To print a colored image which has been scanned into RGB color space, we must first convert that image into CMYK color space. The range of colors which are reproducible in RGB color space, the RGB capture and viewing gamut, is generally much larger than the CMYK printing gamut. This means that some of the original RGB colors are not reproducible with CMYK ink and will be lost during the conversion from RGB color space to CMYK color space. This color

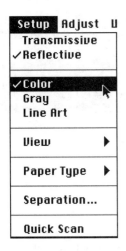

▼ Figure 12.7 Scan Mode Choices

A scan mode setup dialog box should provide at least three scan mode choices: line art, grayscale, and color. If your scanner has the ability to capture images from film (slides and negatives), then you will select either a transmissive (film) or reflective (paper) mode as well as an image type. Line art mode, which captures 1 bit per pixel, should be used when scanning B&W line art and for color line art as well if you can assign the color values (spot or CMYK) during the postscan process. Grayscale mode should be used for capturing grayscale contones and detailed line art. The color mode should be used when capturing color contone images. The halftone option, which creates a halftone version of your image during the scanning process, should be avoided in most cases.

space transformation is known as a gamut conversion. To predict how our images will print, it is therefore very helpful to know the gamuts of our various printing devices to which we will be printing. We must be aware of which colors will be transformed and which will not. In addition, we cannot depend upon our color monitor to provide us with a faithful view of what the printed piece will look like because it is an RGB device (see Chapter 14, "Color Me Right," for a full discussion of color, color spaces, gamuts, and color calibration).

Challenge 6: impure image inks

The process inks (CMYK) we use to reproduce contone images are not pure. Magenta and yellow both contaminate cyan and each other. Because our inks are not pure, we must not only contend with the challenge of translating an image from one color space (RGB) into another (CMYK), but also adjust the color of our images to compensate for impure image inks. Most cyan (C) inks are actually about 60 percent C and 40 percent M and Y. Our magenta inks are 55 percent M and 40 percent Y, and Yellow, the purest of all, usually about 90 percent Y and 10 percent M. The reasons for using impure inks is that pure ink colors, while attainable, would be very expensive. Obviously, magenta and yellow are found in all the inks. The overabundance of these two inks, and particularly of magenta, because it is more visually dominant than yellow, must be compensated for when we print an image. Failure to compensate for the overabundance of magenta will typically result in images which appear to have a overall red cast to them. We must adjust for the overabundance of these two inks to avoid unwanted red color casts. Scanners capture color images in RGB mode and then convert the images into CMYK after the scan is completed.

So, any scanned images and particularly contone images go through significant reconstitution on their way from scanner to monitor to various printers. No final image will ever exactly match the original. Our challenge is to get our final image as close as possible to the original.

Visualization

It is these format and media changes which demand the most attention. My basic conceptual approach to scanning images for print is to apply a technique I learned in photography years ago. As photographers we were taught to "see like the camera sees." Similarly, I try to view my images as a scanner would see them and as a laser printer or imagesetter or printing press would reproduce them. I find it very helpful to visualize the process which occurs when an image is digitized during scanning, then the conversion of these digital images to dots during the RIPing and printing processes. Whenever I look at an image which I am about to scan, I try to visualize what that image will look like in digital form and then how that digitized image will be transformed again when it is halftoned and printed. Of course, the more you understand about the scanning and halftoning process, the easier this **visualization** process is. This process of visualization has been very important in helping me understand why I need to capture and manipulate my images.

SCANNING APPROACH

The original image

Start out with a good quality original. While there is a number of image enhancement tools available in most image editing applications, creating good quality images from poor originals is, at best, very time consuming, costly, and often impossible. The old adage "garbage in, garbage out" applies here.

Original line art images such as logos need to be clean, high contrast, sharp, and of reasonable size (larger than 2" x 2"). The more complex the original image, the larger, sharper, and higher contrast it should be. It is very difficult to capture detail from small, low contrast, and fuzzy line art images. In general, contone images such as grayscale and color continuous tone photographs should be in focus, have good contrast, and have a wide range of tonal values. The larger the original image is, the better the quality of the scan will be. Enlargement of images usually involves interpolation of image data, which leads to a reduction of image quality.

Image analysis and scan modes

Assuming I have been able to acquire a high quality original, the next step is to determine how I want to capture the image at hand. Most scanners provide us with at least three or four scanning modes or options. The most common ones are line art (which will produce a 1 bit bitmapped file), grayscale (which will produce an 8 bit bitmapped file), and color (which will generally produce a 24 bit RGB or 32 bit CMYK bitmapped file). Many scanners offer a halftoning option. This option should generally be ignored when working with PostScript printers. When you print a contone image scanned in halftone mode, the result is a horribly moiréd (patterned) image. The descreen option is used for scanning previously screened (printed) images. Some scanners provide on the fly RGB to CMYK conversion, but the original capture will be done in RGB. One important point to make is that all scanned images start off as bitmapped as opposed to outline images. Some images can be converted to outlines, but they must be captured as bitmaps first. Scanners capture images pixel by pixel, so they naturally produce pixel based bitmapped or raster images.

While any of these scan modes can be used creatively on any type of image (using line art mode to capture and convert a multibit contone image into a one bit line art file), we will restrict this discussion to scanning for reproduction of originals. For line art such as logos which will be reproduced in B&W, spot colors, tints, or gradations, I will typically scan in one of two modes, line art or grayscale. I use line art scanning mode for the simplest and cleanest images. I employ grayscale mode when I have line art images which have many fine lines and/or fine line detail. Contone images I scan either in grayscale or color depending upon the nature of the original. For color images which I wish to convert to grayscale, I generally scan the original in color mode and then convert the image to grayscale. Regardless of which mode I decide on, I always visualize how each mode would affect the image to help me decide which mode and process will best serve my needs.

Before I scan any image, I try to make four determinations: 1) What kind of image do I have—line art, grayscale contone, color contone, or a compound image? 2) What scan mode should I work in? 3) What, if any, editing or manipulations will I have to perform on this image? and 4) Into what file format will I ultimately save my image? 5) What will the final output be? These five items largely determines how I will scan my image.

For line art images, I analyze how sharp the edges of an image are as this will affect the final resolution that I choose. For line art with sharp edges, I will generally scan at high resolution, while images with fuzzy boundaries will permit lower resolution scanning. Simple line art images will generally dictate line art scan mode, while complex or detailed images may require grayscale scan mode. Grayscale contones should be scanned in grayscale mode, and color contones require color mode. If you have the option of saving your images in RGB or CMYK format, you should initially choose RGB; this will be a smaller and more versatile file format. But remember that your images will need to be converted into CMYK format prior to printing.

SCANNING PROCESS

Prescanning

Standard scanning procedures for most desktop publishers have been to scan in an image and then perform all of the editing and corrections in an application like Photoshop. This process is both time consuming and robs the image of quality. Every time you alter an image in Photoshop using curves or levels, you remove information from that image. Perform five or six alterations and you have significantly reduced the quality of that image because so much data will have been lost. A far more efficient and higher quality approach to scanning is to perform nearly all of the image correction functions during the scanning process by performing a quick low resolution (72 ppi) prescan of an image prior to performing a high resolution final scan. With this prescan method, the low resolution image is analyzed to determine appropriate corrections which will be performed during the final high resolution scan. This process is faster than performing the same functions in Photoshop and results in less loss of data from the image. The use of prescan image analysis for final scan setup has long been used by professional scanner operators for the efficient creation of high quality scans.

▼ *Figure12.8 Bitmap Image*
This graphic image of the character "P" is constructed out of dots and should be saved as a TIFF.

▼ *Figure12.9 An Outline Image*
This graphic image of the character "P" is constructed out of lines and should be saved as an EPS.

▼ *Figure12.10 Compound Image*
This silhouetted image contains two parts. Part one is a contone TIFF of the two people. Part two is an invisible EPS outline called a clipping path. The clipping path defines a sharp border around the silhouette, which cleanly removes the background of the photo. Note: The addition of the clipping path increases the file size from 160K to 288K.

▼ *Figure 12.11:Three Scanning Modes*
Here is the same image shown in three different modes: Black and white, continuous tone (contone) grayscale, and contone color. (See Fig. C.2 on page C-4 in the color plate section of this book for a color version of this image.) When scanned, the black and white mode image will be a 1 bit B&W image, the grayscale image will have 8 bits per pixel, and the color image will have either 24 bits per pixel (or 32 bits per pixel if you want the scanner to convert your image into a CMYK image for printing, depending upon whether it is saved in an RGB or a CMYK format).
Note: CMYK is not really a scan mode: RGB is the color scan mode. But some scanners have the ability to convert images from RGB to CMYK on the fly after they have been captured in RGB mode.

Calibrating your scanner

Calibrating your scanner is the first step to the creation of scanned continuous tone images like photographs with good quality. Without calibration you will rarely experience consistent results from your scanner. The fundamental calibration procedure for grayscale and color images is linearization. Following is a 9-step linearization procedure. This is performed on one channel for grayscale images, and on three channels for color contone images.

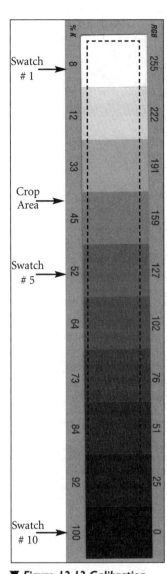

Swatch
1

Crop
Area

Swatch
5

Swatch
10

▼ *Figure 12.12 Calibration*
Scanner calibration requires
the use of a multiswatch
grayscale target with known
values, such as this ten-step
target developed by the author.
Note that the GS values are
conveniently listed on the right
side. (See the calibration offer
in the back of the book to find
out where to obtain Taz's Ten
Step calibration target.)

Simple linearization procedure for grayscale images

Clean your scanner bed and place your 10-step calibration target (see the back of
this book for ordering information) and your first images squarely side by side on
the scanner bed (see Fig. 12.12).

Simple step-by-step linearization calibration for grayscale images:

1. Set the Preview size of your scanner to its maximum area. Then prescan the
   target in 8-bit mode (grayscale mode).
2. Select the 10-step grayscale portion of the calibration target, including the
   pure white and pure black end swatches.
3. Select an editable histogram tool in your scanning software. A histogram will
   show you the frequency and distribution of grayscale values in an image. An
   editable histogram will allow you to adjust highlight, shadow, and **midtone**
   values (see Fig. 12.14).
4. Adjustment: Move the highlight and shadow pointers so that they are at the
   beginning and the end of the data peaks. This can be confirmed by measuring
   the grayscale values of the pure white (255) and pure black (0) swatches.
5. Zoom in a bit on the middle portion of the grayscale target so that you have a
   good view of the middle swatches. Use swatch 5 (127) to start (counting down
   from the white swatch).
6. Now with a built-in Info tool, measure the grayscale value of the 5th target
   swatch. Swatch 5 will probably register a grayscale value lower (darker) than its
   actual value of 127 (see Fig. 12.13).
7. To make a quick overall correction of your scanner's response to grayscale values, adjust the midpoint of the gamma curve value for your scanner until the
   scanner measures the 5 target swatch at about 127. The default gamma value in
   many scanners is in the range of = 1.0 – 1.5. Adjust the gamma curve midtone
   value up until the 5 grayscale swatch = 127 (see Fig. 12.13). Perform this change
   incrementally, 0.1 per change, and watch how the Info tool readings gradually
   increase. You may have to jiggle the info tool slightly (move the cursor) after each
   adjustment to make sure the software registers the change in grayscale value. A
   typical adjusted midpoint in the gamma curves may be 1.7–2.0. Note how the
   curve arches up and the entire image lightens when you make this adjustment.
   Don't worry if the Info tool doesn't read exactly 127, or if the value varies slightly (by one or two points) as you move the Info tool around the swatch.
   Remember that a one unit movement only represents a 0.4 percent change!

➠ TIP

Calibrating your scanner is a simple way to improve the performance and consistency of your scanner. Nearly all scanning capture images darker than they really are,
and particularly in the midtone to shadow portions of your images. Even a simple
two-step (highlight/shadow + midtone) calibration as shown here can dramatically
improve the quality and consistency of your scanned images. Perform a simple calibration at the beginning of each scan session. See the offer at the back of this book to
find out how you can obtain your own scanner calibration target.

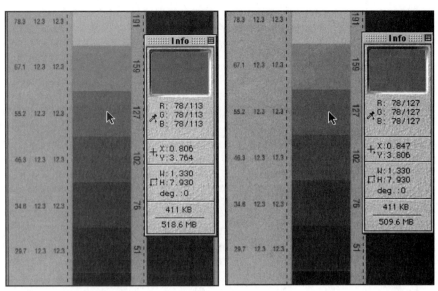
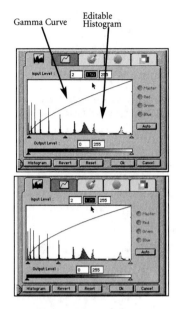

Gamma Curve   Editable Histogram

▼ Figure 12.13 Info Tool
An Info tool is used to measure grayscale values on targets and images. Note the starting (113) and ending (127) values before and after gamma curve adjustment calibration. See Fig. 12.4 on page 240 to see the difference between an image scanned with a calibrated and an un alibrated scanner.

8. Save the corrected scanner settings as default settings, so that they will automatically be applied to each image scanned. The gamma curve should not be touched again while adjusting individual images. To do so would destroy the calibration you have just performed.

9. For best results, this linearization calibration should be performed at the beginning of each scan session.

Color contone calibration: neutralization

Calibration for scanning color contone images will proceed like the nine step grayscale linearization calibration detailed above, but will be done on all three color (RGB) channels instead of just on the one grayscale channel as in grayscale contone image scanning. When linearization is performed on all three channels in an RGB image, this type of three-channel calibration is know as neutralization. Once neutralized, your scanner will measure equal RGB values on any grayscale swatch on the calibration target.

Note: Protect your targets. When not in use, keep your targets in moisture-proof light-tight containers. Constant exposure to light and humidity will progressively degrade the target, and it will no longer be consistent with its published data sheet values.

Note: This simple linearization adjustment provides you with an easy way to make noticeable improvements in the overall quality and consistency of your scanned images without drowning you in technical details, long procedures, or costly purchases. Remember, once you have set the gamma curve midpoint, do not adjust it when you are scanning individual images, or you will destroy the calibration setup.

▼ Figure 12.14 Gamma Curve Linearization
Seen here are an editable histogram and gamma curve. The top curve box shows the default settings. The bottom dialog box shows the calibrated settings. Compare the top and bottom boxes for: 1) positions of the highlight and shadow pointers; 2) shapes and positions of the gamma curves; 3) the position of the midpoint and the midpoint numbers (1.5 and 1.75). The calibrated settings are obtained by setting the shadow pointer (far left) and highlight pointer (far right) so that the first (white) and last (black) grayscale swatches measure 255 and 0, respectively. Then adjust the position of the midtone number so that the fourth grayscale swatch measures 127 when measured with the scanner's info tool. The midtone gamma curve number will generally be between 1.9 and 2.0 after the adjustment.

Scanning Process   247

▼ *Figure 12.15 Simple Line Art Image*
A simple image like this is well suited for outlining. The file size decreases from 240K to 60K when it is converted from a TIFF to an EPS.

▼ *Figure 12.16 Intermediate Complexity Line Art Image*
This is the type of image that should be scanned at high resolution in 1 bit line art mode, then converted to an outline image.

▼ *Figure 12.17 More Complex Line Art Image*
This is the type of image which should be scanned as a grayscale (8 bit mode) and then converted to a 1 bit bitmapped image.

Any tool, such as the gamma curve tool which is used for calibration, should not be used for any other purpose.

Line art scanning

Line art images, even colored line art, should generally be captured as B&W or grayscale images. If the original line art image is colored and built from known spot or process color builds, the color can be applied in postscan process. There are two big advantages to this method. The first is that you are able to capture and manipulate much smaller 1 bit black and white files as opposed to having to manage 24 bit RGB color files which are 24 times larger than the black and white versions. Second, by assigning the exact color values after the image is captured, you need not worry about having to capture the color accurately; you can very accurately assign the color during postscan editing.

Remember that your digital computer really captures, stores, and manipulates B&W images because it only comprehends two values, 0 and 1. Therefore, your scanner only sees areas as black or white anyway. On your electronic publishing system primary output from your computer is black and white or grayscale; color is added at your monitor, at your color printer, or on a printing press. Scan characteristics which should be set during the analysis of the prescan of a line art image include: cropping, scaling, rotating, thresholding, and resolution.

Postscan image editing may include pixel editing of the bitmapped image (addition or removal), conversion to outline format in an application like Streamline (for simple line art), editing the outline, and finally, addition of color as spot color, process color builds, or tints. Color assignments for the line art file will usually be performed by opening and editing the converted line art file in a vector-based drawing application like Illustrator, FreeHand, or CorelDraw.

Simple line art images should be converted to outlines and saved in EPS format using an outlining application such as Adobe's Streamline. Outlining reduces file size, makes editing easier, and permits resolution-independent scaling. Complex line art can be better captured in grayscale mode and then converted to a B&W image after resolution enhancement, sharpening, and thresholding. Complex line art should generally remain as a bitmapped image. Converting complex or detailed line art to outlines may ruin the look of the image and create very complex files which are difficult to RIP and print. Outlined images can be colored and edited in drawing applications such as Illustrator, FreeHand, or CorelDraw.

Complex line art

Complex line art images which contain much detail, such as reproductions of wood carvings, are often difficult to capture effectively in 1 bit line art scanning mode. Closely spaced lines and dots often merge, while fine lines and small dots may be lost altogether. A good procedure to use with complex line art is to scan the original image in 8 bit/grayscale mode. This allows the scanner to act as a more sensitive instrument and gives your scanner a broader range of choices for capturing an image. In grayscale mode, the scanner has 8 bits instead of 1 bit of information for each area which it samples. Once captured, this 8 bit image can be manipulated with resolution enhancement, **unsharpmasking**, and thresholding in an image editing application such as Photoshop to develop the detail of the image effectively.

Contones: grayscale and color

Contone images require the same attention to scan geometry, cropping, scaling, and rotating as line art images do. In addition, with contones we must worry about tone, contrast, and color reproduction. The grayscale and color modes will generally scan original grayscale and color contones. Grayscale and color images have many similar requirements. Grayscale and color contones both demand accurate tonal reproduction. Color images have the added requirements of color correction. For contone scan settings include scan geometry, cropping, scaling, rotating, tonal compression (setting highlight, midtone, and shadow points), gray map adjustments, color correction, and sharpening as keys to producing high quality final images. Again, we should perform a low resolution prescan of the image to be scanned and then set the final scan parameters.

Scan geometry

Determine the exact size, shape, and orientation which the image needs to be before you perform the final scan. Cropping, scaling, and rotating an image during the scan process will allow you to capture the exact area, size, position, and file size of the image you need. This will save you a considerable amount of time during the page layout and RIPing/printing processes. These production time savers can be significant with contones because of the large file sizes associated with these 8, 24 and 32 bit images. Performing these geometric manipulations during the scan rather than after the scan in an image editing application such as Photoshop will also produce superior quality images.

Tone compression and gray map adjustment

The problem of lost and altered data which we discussed earlier in Challenge 2 can be largely addressed through obtaining the proper tone compression and gray map adjustment of an image. Tone compression involves taking all of the tonal values contained in an image (256 for grayscale and 256/color for RGB images) and distributing them properly between the highlight, midtone, and shadow points. More detailed controls on some scanners even allow for control of the quarter and three-quarter tone points. Setting the highlight involves finding the lightest point on your image which still has detail and setting a pixel value for that point. Setting the shadow point involves a similar process for the darkest point of detail. Adjusting where the midtone value occurs controls where the 50 percent gray point should fall on your image. Improper adjustment of highlight, midtone, and shadow points on an image can result in images which are too light or too dark.

Setting these points should happen during the prescan phase with the use of an on-screen info tool/densitometer. This tool, provided with your scanning software, allows you to measure the grayscale and color values of any pixel on the screen. You choose your highlight, midtone, and shadow points on your low resolution pres-

▼ *Figure 12.18 Tone Compression*
Tone compression, or setting the highlight and shadow points of an image, is one of the most important basic scan parameters you choose. The highlight point, known as the diffuse highlight, should be set on the lightest area of your image which shows detail. Your diffuse highlight point should not be set on an area which shows no detail such as a gleam off of a bumper. Such an area, known as a specular highlight, will be reproduced as a pure white area with no detail. Similarly, the shadow point should be set on that area which is the darkest image area to show detail.

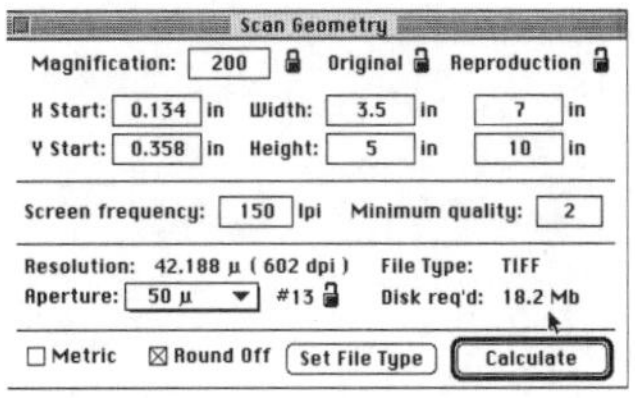

▼ *Figure 12.19 Scan Geometry*
Configure the scan geometry to select the exact cropping and enlargement you will need for the final image. This will save you editing time later and reduce file size as well. Here a 3.5" x 5" area will be scanned and enlarged 200 percent to a 7" x 10." The enlargement you choose will also affect the resolution you choose and the resulting file size.

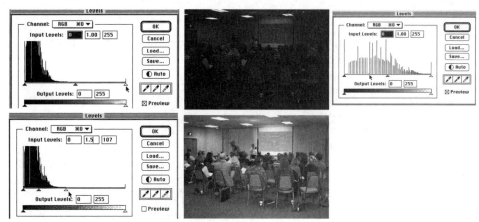

▼ *Figure 12.20 Incorrect Tone Compression*

The dark image (top) shows the result of initial incorrect tonal compression. The first diagram shows the distribution of tonal values in this image. The tonal values are grouped near the shadow end of the histogram. The tonal grouping at the shadow end is due to location of highlight point on the very bright florescent lights. Most of the tonal values in the image are much darker than the pixels in the lights. The lights represent a specular highlight. The second histogram shows how the tonal compression would be adjusted in Photoshop using levels. The highlight point is adjusted down to a diffuse highlight position. The second image shows the visual results of the third adjusted tone compression. The third histogram shows the consequences (lost data) of making the tonal corrections as postscan adjustments. Each blank level indicates a missing tonal value. Primary tone compression should be performed during the scan.

canned image and set the grayscale values you want for each of those points. During the final high resolution scan, these points will be set as the high, medium, and low points of your images and all the rest of the image tonal data will be distributed between them.

Brightness and contrast

After the highlight and shadow portions of an image are set using an editable histogram, overall brightness and contrast should be controlled through the use of a curve control (see Fig. 12.21). Overall image brightness is adjusted by moving the midpoint of a curve up or down. Image contrast is controlled by altering the slope of the curve in various sections of the curve. Grayscale is concentrated wherever a curve is lowered (flattened). Performing these brightness and contrast adjustments during the scanning process, rather than after the scan is completed, will result in higher quality images. Avoid using the brightness and contrast sliders in Photoshop, as using this tool will usually result in upsetting your highlight and shadow points.

Because of the limited tonal information you have to work with in PostScript, you may want to distribute your tonal information into one area of your image or another depending upon the requirements of your image. If the highlight and midtone areas of your image are more important, such as in an image of a light skinned person or a fruit basket, you may want to distribute tonal data there.

Alternatively, for a dark-skinned individual or an image of furniture which contains dark wood grain, you may want to concentrate tonal data more toward the shadow region. This type of data redistribution is known as "gray map adjustment," accomplished through the use of a gamma curve type of adjustment as in Photoshop. Your scanning application should provide you with a similar type of adjustment tool.

Global Color Cast Correction

With color contone images you want to make sure that your colors are properly balanced so that your final image has the same appearance as your original. Having an unwanted color cast or abundance of one color is a common problem with color images. Color cast may come from several sources: incorrect initial exposure, lighting, scanner color, and color bias imposed by the use of impure image inks. Not all color cast is bad. For instance, an image of a sunset should have an overall red color cast, and its removal would destroy the appearance of the image. Neutralization of your image capture device through neutralization calibration, discussed earlier in this chapter, will remove any color cast which might be imposed by the scanner or digital camera.

Global color cast removal involves neutralizing any color cast from the highlight, midtone, and shadow areas of your image, making them neutral gray. Remove the color cast by measuring, on your prescanned image, each neutral area with your on-screen densitometer to determine their color values. Then adjust the color at those three points to neutralize them. Each scanning application has its own tools for making these adjustments. Some use gamma curve adjustments, others use slider type adjustment tools such as those shown in Figure 12.22, while others allow you to set numbers. The results of these adjustments, however, should be the same: your highlight, midtone, and shadow areas should all be neutral grays. Don't measure a single point or pixel, but rather measure an average of an area of at least five square pixels to perform your color measurements.

Neutralization can be performed initially in RGB mode for the scanning process. Neutralization of a neutral area of an RGB image, such as a white highlight, is accomplished by making all three (RGB) values the same. For instance, a five percent (5%) highlight area would register at five percent (5%) values for the red, green, and blue channels of the image. A neutral midtone in RGB would have all three values equal to fifty percent (50%). For print images, it is also a good idea to think in terms of CMYK values in addition to RGB values. Here are some values to get you started. A neutral white point should have dot values of 6% cyan, 4% magenta, and 4% yellow; neutral midtones should be 60% cyan, 45% magenta, and 45% yellow; neutral shadows should print with 95% cyan, 80% magenta, and 80% yellow (black will also be substituted into the midtone and shadow regions).

This abundance of cyan ink values in all three areas will compensate for the contamination of magenta and yellow in the printing inks used in the printing process. Adjustment of the color values at the highlight, midtone, and shadow points will assure a good color balance throughout the image. (If you are sending your images out to be printed, you may want to consult your printer concerning the neutral ink

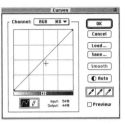

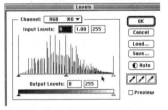

▼ **Figure 12:21 Curves Adjustments**
The Curves dialog box above shows the tones adjustments made in Fig. 12.20 performed in Curves. Curve adjustments of midtone grayscale values to adjust overall image brightness and contrast are generally superior to Levels adjustments because, as shown here, the entire tonal curve is adjusted with gradual changes along the entire gray map occurring, rather than only adjusting the tonal values at the highlight, midtone, and shadow points as in Levels. Contrast the Curves histogram shown here with the last levels-generated histogram shown in Fig. 12.20.

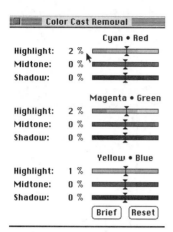

		Cyan • Red	
Highlight:	2 %		
Midtone:	0 %		
Shadow:	0 %		

		Magenta • Green	
Highlight:	2 %		
Midtone:	0 %		
Shadow:	0 %		

		Yellow • Blue	
Highlight:	1 %		
Midtone:	0 %		
Shadow:	0 %		

[Brief] [Reset]

▼ Figure 12:22 Color Cast Removal

Color cast adjustments are accomplished through the adjustments of color values at the highlight, midtone, and shadow points through the use of dialog boxes like this one in Optronics ColorRight scanning software. When working with print-bound images, it is useful to work with CMYK percentages as well as RGB. Always use a densitometer to measure the impact of the color values of an area; never depend upon the "look" of your image on screen.

RGB and/or CMYK values are adjusted so that neutral areas of an image, such as the white highlight areas in this piña colada, obtain a 5% highlight. The RGB values would all equal 5%. The CMYK values might be C=6%, M=4%, Y=4%.

▼ Figure 12.23 Obtaining Neutral Densities

These images show how adjustments in the RGB or CMY percentages of highlight dots change the appearance of an image. We want this highlight dot to print as a white area without cast. The top image has a CMY color mix of 19/2/5 and prints too blue. The second image which shows a color mix of 3/2/3 is closer to a castless white, but the dot percentages are too low and cannot be reproduced on most presses. The result is that large areas of the white will be reproduced without any dot detail and will appear "blown out." The final image shows a CMY color mix of 5/3/3, has enough dot density to be printed and therefore show detail and the right mix of CM and Y to compensate for the impure image inks. The highlight range of 5/3/3 to 6/4/4 works well for most printing presses. Try CMYK color mix of 55/40/40/20 to obtain a neutral midtone gray and a CMYK color mix of 95/85/85/75 for a neutral shadow dot. Ask your printer which percentage values work best on their presses for obtaining neutral highlight, midtone, and shadow values.

Note: Fig. C.33, the color version of this image, can be found on page C-15 in the color plate section of this book

values they recommend for their specific inks and presses.) As mentioned in Challenge 5, Gamut Conversion, you are always viewing your image in RGB mode, but you print in CMYK mode. So make all your color measurements with your densitometer. Don't base any color move or make any changes based upon how your image looks on screen.

Sharpening

All scanners reduce the contrast of an image when they digitize them. This is one of the image changes we discussed in Challenge 1, Changes in Image. This contrast reduction is an unavoidable artifact of the digitizing process. This problem can be easily corrected, however, through the use of sharpening tools. Sharpening tools come in various forms and names. Sometimes sharpening is called "unsharpmasking," sometimes "edge sharpening," and sometimes just "sharpening." The result of sharpening is to increase the difference in grayscale value between two adjacent pixels. Increasing contrast between pixels will result in an overall increase in contrast and therefore sharpness across your entire image. A word of warning here, however: Over-sharpening an image removes too much tonal variation and your edges may begin to look too abrupt and develop white halos along some edges (see Figs. 12.24 and 12.25).

The sharpening tools built into many low-end scanning applications are not very sophisticated, with most providing you only with a simple linear scale with one composite variable. Many do not distinguish edge areas from non-edge areas, as do more robust unsharpmasking tools. Experiment with your scanning application and compare the results against those you can produce in Photoshop. If you perform unsharpmasking in Photoshop, I suggest starting with an amount of 50 percent, a radius of 1.5 – 2, and a threshold of 3 – 4. It's easy to add more sharpening, but you can't easily remove it once it's applied. After you have worked with your scanner and your software for a while, you will develop a sense of how much sharpening is required.

Dot gain

As we discussed under Challenge 4, Media Changes and Dot Gain, images print differently when they are reproduced on various types of media. Dot gain is one of the variables which changes from medium to medium. Dot gain is a description of how much inks spread out when they are applied to paper. Dot gain percentages vary from 10 percent on glossy stock to 30 percent on some porous newspapers. Images printed without dot gain compensation will print darker than they should, so dot gain must be compensated for in the printing process. One good rule of thumb to follow is to increase dot gain compensation in the midtones because dot gain tends to be greater in the midtones than it is in the highlight and shadow regions. Increasing midtone dot gain will lighten up the midtone region, giving your image better overall contrast. Ask your printer how much dot gain to expect on their presses and where dot gain should be controlled. The printer may have you control it, or may want to control it in the production process.

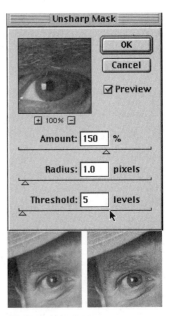

▼ *Figure 12.25 Image Sharpness*
On the left is a portion of an image which has been scanned properly but not sharpened. On the right is the same scanned image, with sharpening applied. Note how the high contrast portions of the right image, such as the eyes, eyebrows, and hat fabric are sharper and appear to be in better focus. This sharpening can be applied either during the scan or in the postscan as it was here in Photoshop. Note the Threshold value is set at 5 to protect the facial skin areas from too much sharpening.

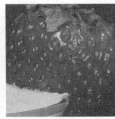

▼ *Figure 12.24 Sharpening*
All scanners reduce the contrast of images when they capture and digitize them. In order to reproduce the look of the original image, contrast must be added back in. With digital images, this is accomplished by increasing the difference in tonal values between adjacent pixels, thereby giving the image more contrast. This process is known as "sharpening," sometimes referred to as "unsharpmasking." Above are four examples of sharpening applied to a strawberry image. Too little sharpening results in a flat, unclear image. Too much removes too much tonal gradation and begins to create edges and posterize the image. A 50 percent sharpening is a good place to start. If your scanning application allows you to preview the effects of sharpening, try several amounts and pick the one you like best (see C-15 for a color version of this figure).

RIPing considerations

Two important variables which control the "RIPablility" of a file are a file's size and its complexity. File size is determined by image dimension, pixel depth, and resolution. As linear resolution doubles, file size quadruples. As file size increases, so does the time required to RIP that image. Image dimension and pixel depth are usually fixed by the design requirements of the document; therefore, we need to minimize a scan file's resolution without adversely affecting the quality of the image. Following are some guidelines for helping you decide your input scan resolution (see Chapter 8 "Resolving Resolution," and Chapter 9, "Grappling with Graphics," for more detailed information on these file size and complexity characteristics).

Resolution guidelines

Setting the proper resolution of your scanned images is crucial to obtaining high quality and RIPable results. In general the output resolution at which you will be using your image should control the input resolution at which you scan. The key is to scan at the lowest resolution possible without degrading the quality of the image. Higher resolution is not always better. Here are some guidelines.

Line art scanning resolutions

Original line art with crisp, sharp edges should generally be scanned at high resolution in order to capture the precise, crisp edges of the lines accurately. My definition of high resolution starts at 800 ppi and goes up. Resolution settings of 1000–1200 ppi are appropriate for high detail line art image. An image captured at anything less than 800 ppi will show visible stair-stepping on curves and diagonals. Low detail line or line art which has rough edges and low detail can often be effectively scanned at resolutions as low as 500–600 ppi, with good results, particularly if you intend to convert your image into vectors after the scan. Scanning rough-edged line art at high resolution will generate large file sizes without necessarily producing any better results than 500–600 ppi scans.

Contone scanning resolutions

Unlike line art, where edge capture is the key concern, with contone images we are concerned with capturing areas of grayscale pixels which will be recreated as halftone dots. For this reason, continuous tone images can generally be scanned at a relatively low resolution of 200 to 300 ppi. Your choice of input/scan resolution is dependent on the line screen at which the image will ultimately be printed and the amount of scaling which will occur. Input scan resolution = lpi x (1.5 to 2.0) x scaling factor. The lpi, or lines per inch is set by your printer. The range of 1.5 to 2.0 is known as the quality factor which you will set depending upon the type of image you are scanning. The scaling factor is determined by how much you intend to enlarge or reduce your image. For example, the scan resolution for a 5" x 7" image to be printed at 150 lpi with no scaling would be: 150 lpi x 1.5 x 1 = 225 ppi. A quality factor of 2.0 would yield a scan resolution of 300 ppi. Using a quality factor near 1.5 will work well for images which are of a completely continuous tone in nature. A higher quality factor should be used for images which have areas of high contrast, such as product shots which have dark type on lighter backgrounds or where detail needs to be captured from dark shadow areas. Keeping input resolution (particularly of multibit contone images) as low as possible is a key tool in our battle to *reduce and simplify*!

If we need to scale that 5" x 7" image up 2x to an 8" x 10" for printing, the scan resolution will also double from 225 ppi to 450 ppi [150 lpi x 1.5 x 2 = 450 ppi]. With experience you will learn which quality factors work best with your images, equipment, and software setup.

POSTSCAN MANIPULATIONS

Postscan manipulation of line art images

After you have scanned your image, you will need to decide what, if any, corrections and/or editing need to be performed. With 1 bit line art images you basically need to choose whether you will leave your line work as a bitmap file or convert it to an outline file. Conversion to an outline image, through the use of an outlining application like Adobe Streamline, has several advantages. Outline images are constructed out of lines; these contrast with bitmap images, which are composed of pixels. Outline images, compared with their bitmapped counterparts, tend to be smaller in size by as much as 90 percent, easier to edit and add or build colors, and more suited for editing, rotating and scaling. Bitmapped images tend to be more appropriate for more complex images and those which contain fine detail. Images with the highest complexity, such as very fine and closely spaced lines, I choose to scan as an 8 bit grayscale image and convert to a 1 bit image after resolution enhancement and sharpening. I use threshold adjustments during the grayscale to bitmap conversion to control detail rendering.

Pre-/postscan manipulation of contone images

As mentioned earlier, contone images will be scanned and captured as either 8 bit grayscale or 24 or 32 bit color images depending upon the nature of the original, the scanner used. As with the line art images, after you have scanned your contone image, you will need to decide what, if any, corrections and/or editing need to be performed. Contone images will generally remain as bitmap files unless you are silhouetting or performing extensive image editing. Although it is always preferable to perform your basic image correction manipulations during the scanning process, you may occasionally need to perform these functions on images which have already been scanned.

There are four major manipulations you will generally perform on contone images which you intend to reproduce: tonal compression, tone curve adjustment (also known as gray map adjustments), color cast correction, and sharpening. These adjustments can be made either during the scanning process or in postscan manipulations in image editing applications like Photoshop. The most efficient procedure is to perform these adjustments during scanning. Tonal compression is necessary to

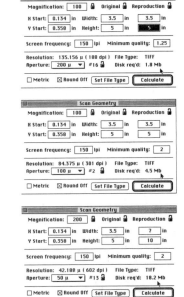

▼ *Figure 12.26 Resolution Guidelines*
These three Scan Geometry dialog boxes show how Resizing (Magnification), Original image size (Width and Height), Quality factor (Minimum quality), and Printing or output resolution (Screen frequency– lpi) affect the Scan or input resolution (Resolution) and Image File Size (Disk req'd). The first dialog box shows a scan set up for a 3" x 5" image with no scaling, a quality factor of 1.25, and an lpi of 150. The file size becomes 1.8MB. The second box shows the effect of increasing the quality to 2.0. The file size increases to 4.5 MB. In the third scan setup we have scaled the image 200% which results in a quadrupling of the file size to 18.2 MB.

distribute all of the limited grayscale information across the entire 256 shades of gray available to an image in PostScript.

Tone curve adjustment is important to setting the general distribution of tones and contrast in an image. Most scanned images are too dark, particularly in the midtones, resulting in images which look muddy, flat, and lack detail in shadow. Many people use contrast and brightness controls to adjust how light or dark their images look, but this is generally a bad approach. Brightness and contrast controls affect all portions of an image equally, that is, in a linear fashion, which causes large shifts in tonal values across the entire image. This approach generally results in loss of detail at one end of the tonal range or the other. Nonlinear correction using tools like the Curves dialog box in Photoshop are preferable. It is also possible to perform these manipulations in a Levels type of tool, but with only three points available for adjustment, highlight, midtone, and shadow, the transitions are not as smooth as those made in Curves, where all the points along the gray map are gradually adjusted. Figures 12.20 and 12.21 show a comparison of the use of Curves and Levels to manipulate the gray map of an image. You should note that the Levels-adjusted image shows a more abrupt change in the image map around the midtone point than the Curves-adjusted image which shows a more gradual transition. In either case, when Curves or Levels are used to adjust an image in a postscan environment, there is a significant loss of image data (see Fig. 12.20 for a comparison of the histogram of an image both before and after a postscan manipulation of an image has been performed in Photoshop). This is one obvious reason for performing these manipulations during the scan.

Color cast correction is used to remove any image-wide color cast. The presence of significant color cast can be easily seen as an overall tint of a particular color. A quantitative measurement of color cast can be gained by measuring the color values of an image area which should be neutral gray with the on-screen densitometer. This measurement can be performed after a prescan in your scanning software or on a final scan in Photoshop. The quality and quantity of needed shift can be judged by either the RGB or CYMK values which compose the neutral gray area. Once you have determined the shift which needs to be made, these adjustments can be made in either the Color Balance or Hue/Saturation controls found under the Adjust submenu of the main Image menu in Photoshop.

The final adjustment is image sharpening or unsharpmasking. Sharpening is necessary to counteract the general softening which usually occurs when an image is processed through digital scanning. A wide range of sharpening capabilities exist depending upon the application used. Some applications allow you to apply different amounts of unsharpmasking to various tonal levels, while others provide only overall unsharpmasking. In Photoshop there are three possible adjustments: Radius, Amount, and Threshold. The Radius affects the width of the zone over which the unsharpmasking will be applied. Amount determines the percent of shift which will be applied to adjacent pixels, and Threshold determines the difference in tonal values which must exist between adjacent pixels before unsharp mask will be applied to those pixels. Setting any of these values too high will result in too much increase in contrast and the development of halos on edges of items in the image. Here are some starting values for you: Radius = 1.5, Amount = 50 (the

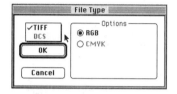

▼ **Figure 12.27 File Saving Option**
Most scanner interfaces will provide you with several file options for saving a scanned image. For images which you intend to take to press, you should save all of your images as TIFFs. You may decide to convert some of your line art TIFFs to line art EPSs after you scan them, but they should initially be saved as TIFFs. As shown here, some scanners give you the choice of saving a color image in RGB or CMYK format. A scanner always captures color images in RGB format, then converts them to CMYK format. Initially, save your image in RGB format if you intend to use the image for anything other than printing. CMYK is a much more restricted color space than RGB. Saving an image in RGB format preserves a wider range of color information, and allows for more flexible use of the file for media such as a monitor display, transparency film, or for presentations which can reproduce a wider range of colors than offset printing.

default), and Threshold = 4. Others have recommended high values for Amount up to 200, but I prefer to start lower and build; you can always add more. After I apply my final unsharp mask, I usually have one more look at my tone histogram in levels to see if any of my pixels have been pushed too far toward black or white. I may make final tiny adjustments in my highlight and shadow points if my histogram shows some open ends.

Image and file formats

There are basically three kinds of images found in digital imaging: 1) bitmapped or raster images, 2) outline or vector, and 3) compound images which are combinations of the first two. Bitmapped images are constructed out of pixels. Outline images are constructed out of lines or vectors. Compound images such as hard edged silhouettes are often bitmapped images surrounded by smooth outlines known as clipping paths. All scanned images start out as bitmaps; this is how they are captured by a scanner, as pixels.

As explained in Chapter 9, "Grappling with Graphics," file formats are the containers into which the pixel and vector graphic file components are stored and transported. Among all file formats which exist including PICT, PCX, Paint, BMP, EPS, WMF, GIF, RIFF, TIFF, JPEG and others, two formats – TIFF and EPS – are the preferable file formats to be used for files to be printed. Nearly all scanners save their images, or at least provide you with an option of saving, in a TIFF format. TIFF is one of the most flexible bitmapped file formats, and it is designed to be used for printing. File formats such as PICT are not designed for printing. Most of your contone images should be saved in TIFF format as should your complex or detailed line art files. The EPS file format should be used primarily for line art files which have been converted from original scanned TIFFs to outline files through an application like Streamline. Most compound images are saved as EPS images out of Photoshop which contains both contone and outline line art components. It is possible to also save TIFF files with integrated clipping paths out of Photoshop 3.0 and above. Check with you service bureau to see which they prefer.

If you are thinking of saving your images in some file format other than TIFF or EPS, call your printer or service bureau and ask for their guidance. If you will need to transfer your files from Mac to PC or vice versa, there are a number of options, but two standards will work for most files. To translate bitmapped files on either platform, convert your file to a TIFF first and then open the TIFF in Photoshop and save it as a TIFF in the platform you want. For outline files, the most compatible format is to save the EPS in Illustrator 1.1 format, which has consistently been a very compatible cross platform EPS format.

Pixel based images can be resaved as GIF and JPEG format files for use as graphics which are placed in Web pages. Images converted into vectors can be resaved as Shockwave SWF format images for use over the Web. See Chapter 9, "Grappling With Graphics," for more information on graphics and graphic file formats.

PHOTOCD IMAGES

▼ *Figure 12.28 Master PhotoCD*
This is the disk produced from the Master PhotoCD station which handles 35mm film images exclusively. It can hold up to 100 scans in Image Pacs with five (5) different resolution files for each image.

There are many circumstances in which you will be working with images you have not personally scanned but someone else has. If an image you are using has been scanned on a drum scanner by a highly trained professional scanner operator, the chances are good that your image will be at least reasonably well prepared for printing. Good scanner operators know about tone compression, gray map adjustments, print-specific color correction, and sharpening. With other images you may not be so lucky. One source of outside scans will probably be **PhotoCD**.

What is PhotoCD?

PhotoCD is an inexpensive and flexible way to capture, store, and distribute digital images which originally were captured on photographic film. PhotoCD is not just one product, but rather a collection of related imaging technologies and products (see Figure 12.30). This collection currently includes two special film scanners with related scanning stations and associated software, a color proofing system, a CD writer, a unique image compression scheme for storing the PhotoCD images, some third party production software products, and several software products offered by Kodak. The two primary PhotoCD products from which you are most likely to acquire images are Master and Pro PhotoCD.

▼ *Figure 12.29 Pro Photo CD*
This is the disk produced from the Pro PhotoCD station which handles 35mm film images exclusively. It can hold up to 100 scans in Image Pacs with six (6) different resolution files for each image.

❥ Master PhotoCD is the original PhotoCD consumer product (Fig. 12.28). This product is produced from 35mm slides and provides an image pack which contains five (5) images at five different resolutions for each slide. Each Master PhotoCD disk holds about 100 images.

❥ Pro PhotoCD is the professional version (Fig. 12.29), which offers the ability to scan 4"x 5" film as well as 35mm and many film sizes in between. Pro PhotoCD offers the same five resolutions as those offered by the Master PhotoCD, but also provides a sixth high resolution format which is attractive to professional photographers who want to work with higher quality images. Each Pro PhotoCD disk holds between 25 and 100 images depending upon the image's resolutions.

Multiple resolutions: why and how?

The core of the uniqueness and flexibility of PhotoCD technology is in how images are sampled and stored. Current PhotoCD disks have either five (Master) or six (Pro) different files for each scanned image, each with a different resolution. Each resolution is useful for reproduction of different sized images. If you need to reproduce an image as an 8" x 10" one day and as a 3" x 5" the next, each size should use a different resolution. The 8" x 10" reproduction requires 5.6 times more information, or resolution, than the 3" x 5" image does. If you use the highest resolution to reproduce all of your images, you waste too much time in processing, hence the need for the various image resolutions which PhotoCD provides. Each resolution contains a specific number of pixels of information, has a specific file size, and is useful for the reproduction of different sizes or kinds of images.

These are the six possible resolutions currently available and their characteristics:

Level	Resolution	File Size(RGB)	Screen Use and Print Size
base/16	128 x 192	72K	Thumbnails & Screen / Web
base/4	256 x 384	288K	CD Catalog and 1.3" x 1.9"
base	512 x 768	1.13MB	TV and 2.5" x 3.8"
4base	1536 x 1024	4.5MB	HDTV and 5.0" x 7.5"
16base	3072 x 2048	18MB	Full resolution and 10" x 15"
*64base	4096 x 6144	72MB	20" x 30"
256base	8192 x 12,288	288MB	40" x 60" (Future)
1024base	16,384 x 24,576	1152MB	80" x 120" (Future)

*Pro PhotoCD only

Note that the various levels of PhotoCD are designated as a base that is multiplied or divided by a 4, 16, or 64. The original images (35mm to 4" x 5") are scanned at the highest resolution (3072 x 2048 for Master and 4096 x 6144 for Pro PhotoCD) and then sampled down, either two or three times, to the base level. This base level is then used to construct, through either sampling up or down, the other resolutions which PhotoCD offers.

PhotoCD utilizes a unique lossless compression scheme called Huffman compression, which uses a series of interpolations, comparisons, and residuals to create the base image and then recreate the other resolutions without any loss of data. This same Huffman compression scheme is also used as the basis for lossy JPEG compression.

PhotoCD file format

The PhotoCD file format is a special one called YCC, which is very similar to Lab in that it maintains a separate luminance channel, the "Y" channel in this case, which contains all the grayscale or luminance information. The YCC format is a generic color format easily transformed for a variety of uses including video, TV, and even print. The origin of YCC is in television. The Y is a luminance or brightness channel; the two Cs contain the color information, channels, one for hue and one for saturation. If you are familiar with the HSV hue saturation and value) model for describing color, then the YCC format will be an easy transition. The YCC format is similar to an RGB file, but is organized into an HSV file format so that V (brightness or value, such as brightness contrast and unsharpmask) can be adjusted separately from the chrominance (hue and saturation) channels.

Challenges of PhotoCD print production

The PhotoCD technology was originally developed for on-screen viewing and was not intended to be used for commercial print purposes. The YCC format is an excellent general format for viewing images on a wide variety of screens. After all, the YCC format was adopted from a TV format. This original orientation toward screen viewing created two problems related to using PhotoCD images for high quality offset-press print reproduction. One problem has been solved, while the other remains.

▼ *Figure 12.30 PhotoCD Station*
This is the Master PhotoCD station. The 35 mm PCD 2000 scanner is behind the operator. The Spark20 cpu (bottom), the PCD Writer (middle), and a CD reader (top) are to the left of the scanner.

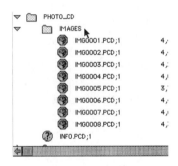

▼ *Figure 12.31 PhotoCD Image Pacs*
These are the Image Pac files which were produced on the Photo Imaging Workstation (PIW). Image Pacs contain the compressed image information for all of the Pro PhotoCD images. There is one Image Pac for each scanned image stored on the disk.

PhotoCD Images   259

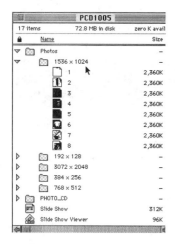

PCD1005		
17 items	72.8 MB in disk	zero K avail
Name		Size
▽ 📁 Photos		–
▽ 📁 1536 × 1024		–
📄 1		2,360K
📄 2		2,360K
📄 3		2,360K
📄 4		2,360K
📄 5		2,360K
📄 6		2,360K
📄 7		2,360K
📄 8		2,360K
▷ 📁 192 × 128		–
▷ 📁 3072 × 2048		–
▷ 📁 384 × 256		–
▷ 📁 768 × 512		–
▷ 📁 PHOTO_CD		–
📄 Slide Show		312K
📄 Slide Show Viewer		96K

▼ Figure 12.32 PhotoCD Folders
The Photo folder contains five folders, one for each set of different resolution files. Each folder contains a specific resolution file for each scanned image. This disk indicates that it has eight images recorded on it. The file data is contained in the Image Pac as above.

The first problem involves file formats. In order to use PhotoCD images for print, they must be converted into CMYK format. Initially, this was a problem because the YCC images had to first be converted to RGB images prior to the final conversion to CMYK. This double conversion resulted in too much loss of image quality and significant calibration problems as well. As with most conditions in the world, if there is a void, nature moves to fill that void. And so it was that several third party companies, most notably Parrup with its PhotoImpress product, developed applications which would allow for the direct conversion of YCC images into their CMYK equivalents with minimal loss of image quality. Others have evolved as well.

The second issue is the quality of the original scan. One good yardstick of scanner quality is the dynamic range of the scanner. Dynamic range is a logarithmic scale which measures the range of tonal values which a scanner can "see" and capture. The dynamic range scale starts at zero (0) and goes to (4), with four being the best tonal range capture. The best drum (PMT) scanners have dynamic ranges between 3.5 and 4.0. High quality flatbed (CCD) scanners generally sport dynamic ranges of 2.8 to 3.5. Both PhotoCD scanners have dynamic ranges of 2.8, which is equivalent to many high quality CCD scanners but well below the best drum scanners. The high dynamic range of drum scanners is mostly required for capturing fine detail in shadow areas. So, for the highest quality scanning requirements such as high quality ads and high line screen color reproductions, PhotoCD images fall a bit short. However, all is not doom and gloom, because 75 percent to 80 percent of all color scan jobs do not require the highest tonal range reproductions. There is a growing number of service bureaus who are making very successful livings providing scanning services for commercial printers and their clients. The technology exists to increase the dynamic range of the PhotoCD scanners. I think that in the near future we will see PhotoCD scanners with dynamic ranges well above 3.0.

Access to PhotoCD is provided through an increasing number of applications including Photoshop 3.0 and above and PageMaker 6.0 and above. Whichever route you use to access and utilize PhotoCD images, be sure that you treat them with at least as much attention as you would a normal scanned image. Be sure to start out with good quality originals. During the initial scan, be sure that the proper film type information is used by the PIW site performing the scan. Remember that PhotoCD scans are not automatically optimized for print production. Make sure that you properly adjust tone compression, gray map adjustments, and global color correction, as well as apply proper sharpening for print. These adjustments can all be made manually in Photoshop. But this process takes more time than some applications which are designed specifically for working with PhotoCD images. If you really like the PhotoCD format, you can even take non-PhotoCD images and create your own Image Pacs. PhotoCD is an inexpensive and highly flexible technology which will be increasingly used in multitudes of imaging applications. If you have not yet worked with this technology, it is worthwhile getting familiar with it.

SCANNER LIMITATIONS

Keep in mind that if you use a desktop CCD scanner there are some images which you will not be able to capture effectively. The dynamic range, that is, the range of tonal capture, of most desktop scanners is significantly lower (2.5 – 2.9) than that of PMT drum scanners (3.6 – 4.0). This means that images which have large tonal ranges and deep shadow detail may be beyond the ability of your scanner to capture completely. So be prepared to send images of black cats on white wedding dresses out to a service bureau which has a PMT drum scanner.

Scanning software

Good scanning software that gives you good control is the most important feature of a desktop scanner. Most scanners ship with at least some type of image acquisition software. Some provide you with only basic controls such as mode and resolution and the ability to save the image to disk with no view at all. Others are very sophisticated and provide preview with complete prescan image control. While I have not used all the scanning applications available (there are many good ones), here is a sampling of a few applications which I recommend. If you use an older Apple scanner and you want to scan directly into Photoshop, I recommend Scantastic. MagicScan for UMAX scanners is also excellent. It provides you with a full range of prescan controls. If your scanning software does not provide you with robust scanning controls, there are several good third-party scanning software products. Here are a few that are available: ScanPrep Pro is an amazing "intelligent" automated scanning application which produces excellent results, supports a wide variety of scanners, and provides built-in calibration abilities; Binuscan's ColorPerfect is also excellent, as is ArtScan Pro. Whenever you can, perform all of the image adjustments we have discussed on a prescanned image and let the scanner and its software apply them during the scanning process. This will save you much postscanning image editing in Photoshop or other image editing software. Adjustments you should make to a prescanned line art image include assignment of cropping, sizing, and resolution values. If you choose grayscale mode for detailed line art, you may also perform sharpening during the scanning process. The conversion to B&W through resolution enhancement and thresholdings will generally be done in in the postscan through Photoshop, unless you use an automatic scanning application like ScanPrepPro which will perform these functions for you.

Multipurposing of images

Although our discussions in this book center mainly on the preparation of files for prepress uses, we would be remiss if we did not briefly address some scanning guidelines for images which will be used for two or more output device, that is, multipurposed. The more purposes for which you intend to use an image, the more general your scan settings should be. If you intend to use your images to output to RGB film and place them as well in WEB pages, then you may not want to perform some of the prepress-specific manipulations such as gamut conversion, dot gain adjustments, and unsharpmasking. The more manipulation you intend to perform in the postscan environment, the less restrictive your scan should be. If you intend to **multipurpose** or **repurpose** your images, here are a few quick guidelines:

Multipurpose guidelines

1. Scan into a device-independent CIE color space like Lab.
2. Keep the original image unaltered in this form.
3. Make copies of this image to convert into other device-specific color spaces and graphic file formats.
4. Make prepress-specific adjustments such as RGB to CMYK gamut conversion, dot gain adjustments, and unsharpmasking on a copy of the image.
5. Images which will go to the Internet need to be kept in CIE space to retain their color saturation.
6. Limit all your gamut conversions to one step if possible to reduce loss of image data and color saturation.
7. Compress images only as a final step before sending or archiving, and never compress an image more than once.

A final word

The more you work with scanned and RIPed images, the more you will develop a feel for how they work. Get in the habit of looking at your digital images on screen at high magnification. See how your scanning choices affect the pixels and their relationships. Before you scan, contact your printer to obtain the values they recommend for such items as neutral ink percentages, line screen, and dot gain. Also keep in mind the final use of your image, and realize that any image you scan is likely to be used used in more than one way. So scan your images for the largest size and highest quality for which for your image will be used. This is typically commercial printing. And remember that controlling resolution (and therefore file size), particularly of multibit per pixel contone images, is a critical tool in helping us to *reduce and simplify*!

CHAPTER SUMMARY

A key to high quality scanning is being able to visualize the scanning process and the postscan manipulation of your scanned images. Be always mindful of the challenges of scanning and manipulating images. Understand how your image will change, protect your scanned images from data loss, be aware of the dynamic range limitations of your scanner, then be prepared for the impact of dot gain. Know in advance how your image will be gamut converted after the scan. Being aware of these critical variables will provide valuable insight and guidance into how you should scan and manipulate your images in order to capture and maintain the highest image quality possible. Frequent calibration, linearization for grayscale images and neutralization for color images, is a key to high quality consistent scanning. Allowing your scanner to perform most of your basic image adjustments such as applying tone compression to set highlight and shadow points, performing gray map adjustment for brightness and contrast as well as scaling and resolution adjustments rather than performing these chores in the postscan will result in higher quality images. In general the input resolution at which we scan should be controlled by the output resolution at which we use our images. We will typically choose higher resolution (600–1200 ppi) for line art images and lower resolutions (150 ppi–400 ppi) for contone images. Image sharpening should be performed last. Automated scanning technologies such as PhotoCD can speed up the scanning process and reduce costs, but be aware that more postscan image manipulation may be needed to adjust these images. Multipurposing of images requires that we consider all the uses for which a scanned image will be needed. In general we will scan for the highest resolution, quality and size requirements, which is often commercial printing. It is a good idea to create and save general purpose, large gamut archive images which can then be copied and used for many other purposes.

PAULINE'S DIGITAL IMAGING TIPS

Pauline's Tip 12.1

Image data changes during scanning from original image to 0s and 1s in RAM, to pixels on screen, to dots on paper. Original data is not 100 percent reproducible. All print images are constructed out of dots. Line art is constructed out of small touching dots or spots, while contones are formed from patterns of larger separated dots (constructed from groups of the smaller spots) called halftone dots. It is useful to imagine the changes which happen to your images because being able to visualize the changes will help you decide the best way to scan your images.

Pauline's Tip 12.2

Up to 95 percent of data is lost (from 5000 visible tones down to 100 printed tones) during the transition from original scene to film to digital data to PostScript to print. We must capture and save the best possible 256 shades of gray or tones during the scanning process. Proper tone compression, setting the highlight and shadow points, is crucial for this. Be aware of the difference between setting your highlight dot on a specular versus diffuse highlight area. Specular areas are pure white and have no tonal values; therefore, they should be avoided as highlight choices. Tone compression should be primarily performed during the scanning process and not during the postscan in applications such as Photoshop.

Pauline's Tip 12.3

Brightness and contrast adjustments through alteration of tonal curves can be used to correct your images and concentrate limited tonal data in those portions of the image which are most important.

PAULINE'S DIGITAL IMAGING TIPS

Pauline's Tip 12.4

Make sure your scanner is linearized and neutralized so that you know that it will properly reproduce all values of grayscale and color. Use a gray scale target with known values to calibrate your scanner.

Pauline's Tip 12.5

To remove the color cast imposed on your images by your scanner, scan a target which contains a variety of neutral tones. Measure the neutral areas with an on-screen densitometer and create correction curves which can be applied to all scanned images.

Pauline's Tip 12.6

Don't forget to compensate for dot gain before you print your final image. Compensate for dot gain during the scanning process. But if you intend to multipurpose your images, scan without dot gain compensation, make copies of your original images, and apply dot gain only to those images which will be used for print. Also, be sure to apply dot gain corrections which are specific to each print device you will use.

Pauline's Tip 12.7

We print with impure process inks. This flaw must be compensated for when setting gray balance. In highlight: C/M/Y = 6/4/4; in midtone: C/M/Y = 60/45/45. This correction can be, and often is, done during the scan process, but if you intend to multipurpose your images, you should scan your images neutral, make copies of the original scan, and apply the correction for impure printing inks only to images which you intend to print. This color correction can be performed during the RGB to CMYK gamut conversion and should be specific to each printer you use.

Pauline's Tip 12.8

All scanners soften images as they sample images when they capture them. In order to return an image to its original sharpness or even improve it, a scanned image must be sharpened.

PAULINE'S DIGITAL IMAGING TIPS

Always choose a sharpening tool such as unsharpmasking, which preferentially sharpens higher contrast areas of an image. Sharpening can be, and often is, applied during the scan process; however, if you intend to significantly modify an image after it is scanned, save the sharpening for last.

Pauline's Tip 12.9

We work in various color gamuts in electronic prepress such as CIE (Lab or YCC), RGB on scanners and monitors, and CMYK on press. This means color data is lost during the gamut conversion process from RGB to CMYK. In general, and particularly when we will be multipurposing images, we want to capture an image into as large a color space as possible (usually a CIE color space) and then convert copies of the original images into whichever color space we intend to use them. Limit your image gamut conversions to one step whenever possible to reduce color saturation loss which inevitably occurs during gamut conversions.

Pauline's Tip 12.10

Don't judge color visually on a monitor. Always use an on-screen densitometer to measure tone and color data.

Pauline's Tip 12.11

Be aware of the tonal capture range (dynamic range) of your scanner. Your desktop scanner may not be able to capture the entire tonal range of some images.

Pauline's Tip 12.12

Most image adjustments should be performed during the scanning process, not afterward. Use a low resolution prescan technique to set cropping, scaling, tone compression, gray map adjustments, global color corrections, and sharpening to save time and preserve image quality.

Pauline's Tip 12.13

Simple, crisp line art images should be scanned at high resolution 500–600 ppi or greater and then converted to outline files in a dedicated outlining application like Streamline. Rough line art can be scanned as low resolution (300 ppi).

PAULINE'S DIGITAL IMAGING TIPS

Pauline's Tip 12.14

Scanning resolutions for unscaled continuous tone images, which will be two times (2x) the lpi at which the images will be printed. A 1.5 – 2.0 (quality factor) x the lpi is sufficient for most unscaled images. Use the following formula to determine the input scan resolutions for contone images: [1.5 – 2.0 x lpi times scaling factor]. Using smaller quality factors of 1.5 will dramatically reduce the file size of the image. High quality factors approaching 2.0 need only be used for images with high contrast areas or when trying to capture subtle shadow detail.

Pauline's Tip 12.15

Final resolutions (after scaling) for contone images which will be reproduced with FM, or stochastic screening methods such as on banner printers, need not exceed 100 ppi, as FM screening processing does not require as much pixel information as AM screening.

Pauline's Tip 12.16

Complex and fine detail line art images can be scanned as 8 bit grayscale images and then converted to 1 bit line art using sharpening and thresholding.

Pauline's Tip 12.17

Visualize the effect of the entire scanning and production process on your image before you start. Scan with a final purpose in mind. For multipurpose images, create neutral uncorrected scans, but always tone compress and map during the scan.

Pauline's Tip # 12.18

Pixel-based images should be saved in either TIFF or EPS format for use in a PostScript printing environment. For use on the World Wide Web pixel based images can be saved in either GIF of JPEG format, while vector images can be saved as Shockwave SWF format.

CHAPTER REVIEW

Check Your Comprehension

Multiple Choice Questions

To help you review the topics covered in this chapter, answer the following multiple choice questions.

1. _____ is the technique we use to help us predict and understand what will happen to our scanned images, and therefore make better scanning setup choices.
   A. Calibration
   B. Visualization
   C. Linearization
   D. Neutralization

2. Which of the following is a primary challenge of scanning?
   A. Loss of image data
   B. Shadow detail capture
   C. Potential dot gain adjustment
   D. All of the above

3. Which of the following will result in higher quality and more consistent scanning?
   A. Neutralization
   B. Linearization
   C. Calibration
   D. All of the above

4. Tone compression refers to
   A. Reducing the tonal range of an image
   B. Setting highlight and shadow values
   C. Constructional toning
   D. Compressing images to reduce file size

5. Overall image brightness and contrast are best controlled using
   A. Curve tool during the scan
   B. Histogram in Photoshop
   C. Dodge and burn tool
   D. Brightness and contrast sliders in Photoshop

6. High detail line art images should be scanned at which of the following resolution ranges?

   A. 300 ppi–500 ppi

   B. 500 ppi–600 ppi

   C. 1000 ppi–1200 ppi

   D. Any of the above

7. Which of the following formulas works well for determining contone image resolution?

   A. 1.0 x lpi x scaling ratio

   B. 1.5 x lpi x scaling ratio

   C. 2.5 x lpi x scaling ratio

   D. 3.5 x lpi x scaling ratio

8. Which application is used to convert pixel-based line art into vector-based line art?

   A. Photoshop

   B. PageMaker

   C. Scanning application

   D. Streamline

9. Which of the following terms refers to constructing a document for more than one use?

   A. Repurpose

   B. Web construction

   C. Print construction

   D. Multipurpose

10. Having high scanner _____ is critical in order to capture contone shadow detail.

    A. dot gain

    B. dynamic range

    C. capture bit depth

    D. resolution

11. Which of the following could cause an image to print too dark?

    A. Improper tone compression

    B. Noncalibrated scanner

    C. Dot gain

    D. All of the above

12. When is generally the best time to apply unsharp mask to an image?

    A. Before tone compression

    B. Before brightness and contrast adjustments

    C. After all other image adjustments have been made

    D. It doesn't make any difference

Check Your Understanding

Concept Questions

To help you review and expand your thinking on the topics covered in this chapter, answer the following questions.

1. Explain why visualization is important in the scanning process

2. Outline the four basic challenges we have when we set out to scan an image.

3. Explain what calibration is and why it is important in the scanning process.

4. Describe six key scanner settings we should configure prior to scanning a contone color image.

5. What are the three basic scan modes we have to choose from? Describe the differences between each of these scan modes in terms of the image building block which will be created when each mode is used.

6. Which of the above three scan modes would you choose to scan the following types of images? Describe why you choose each image/mode match: 1) Simple line art, 2) detailed line art, 3) grayscale contone, 4) color contone.

7. Define the scan resolutions you would choose for each of the following images if they were to be printed at 150 lpi on a commercial printing press: 1) Simple line art, 2) detailed line art, 3) grayscale contone, 4) color contone.

8. Explain the statement: CMYK is not a scanning mode, it is a conversion mode.

9. Describe your approach to scanning and how you would handle a color contone image that you wanted to output on a 175 lpi commercial printing press, an 85 lpi desktop laser printer, and a Web page. Do not forget to describe where, when, and how much unsharpmasking you would apply.

10. Explain the benefits and challenges of using an automated scanning technology like Kodak PhotoCD.

PROJECTS

1. Get samples of the following: Simple line art, detailed line art. a grayscale contone photograph and a color contone photograph. Scan each of these images for use printing specifically on a 150 lpi commercial printing press. Which of these images might you convert to vectors and why?

2. Detail the changes you would make in your scanning decisions and procedures if you knew you were multipurposing for use on a Web page as well as commercial printing. Rescan for multiple use.

13
Document Construction

As the Byte Turns continues…

Will Pauline only help Danny make the connection to his high-res files, or will they make another connection as well?

I copied my page layout file to the disk I sent you. All the graphics and fonts showed up fine just before I copied it. Why can't you print my document correctly? I have a proof to prove it right here!

Well, I don't know.

I wish I did know.

So why can't we print his file?

I can't print his files because the high resolution graphics and his fonts are not there. Danny needs to understand how his documents are constructed and linked.

Chapter Objectives

In this chapter you will learn:

◆ **Planning document**
◆ **How to use thumbnails**
◆ **How print documents are constructed**
◆ **Master page elements**
◆ **How to use style sheets**
◆ **Managing your files**
◆ **Key Terms**
  • Thumbnail sketch
  • Masterpage
  • Style sheet
  • Native file
  • Paragraph style sheet
  • Character style sheet
  • Proofs, Proofreading, and Proofing
  • Linking
  • Backing up and archiving

INTRODUCTION

The goal of any document construction process is to create a document which is easy to construct, consistent and easy to edit. Document planning is a key to creating well constructed documents. Using **thumbnail sketches** to try out various document designs as well as lay out the basic document page parameters such as page size, orientation and margins and making critical decisions such as whether the document will be a facing or nonfacing page document and whether or not it will have automatic text boxes are key decisions to make early on in the document construction process. Making the proper decision early on can help prevent costly, time consuming reworks later on. Be sure to use graphic file formats which are consistent with the end use or output of your document. For example, use TIFF and EPS graphic file formats for PostScript printing. Leave time for the **proofing** process to occur and let someone else take a look at the document. Be sure to clean up your document by removing unnecessary document elements prior to final output. Keep in mind that there are some things you can create on a computer that you may not be able to print. Examples include highly complex graphics or highly saturated colors.

Remember to use the right tool for the right job. Use graphics applications, such as Illustrator or FreeHand for vector graphics and Photoshop for pixel-based images, for creating and editing graphics, and use page layout applications such as QuarkXPress, PageMaker and InDesign for setting type and composing pages. Final documents need to have all their text and graphic elements linked to print properly, including screen and printer fonts as well as high resolution graphics. Name and organize your files to maintain links and regularly **backup** and **archive** your files.

DOCUMENT PLANNING

Planning

Planning your print project should be your first priority. With proper planning you can eliminate unnecessary mistakes as well as minimize the complexity of your document and the number of changes you need to make by having a standard set of guidelines to go by. Design and produce your document with the final output in mind. The tried and true practice of using **thumbnail sketches** (Fig. 13.1) is still very useful. In fact, with all the document construction and typesetting controls available to us, the use of thumbnailing has become even more important.

Here are some general planning guidelines:

❥ Plan your document with thumbnails before you start laying out your document on the computer. On your thumbnails include characteristics such as page size and orientation, margins, facing or nonfacing page design, flowing vs. nonflowing text areas, number of columns as well as width of and gutter between them, and list of master page and style sheet elements.

❥ Use **Masterpage** items to create an page element which repeats from page to page such as text boxes, page numbers, running headers and footers, etc.

❥ Use **style sheets** to format and control and type formats which occur repeatedly throughout the document, such as heads, subheads, body copy, page numbers, captions, etc.

❥ Plan to use graphic file formats which are appropriate for your project's final media. For most print projects use TIFF and EPS graphics whenever possible (more on this later).

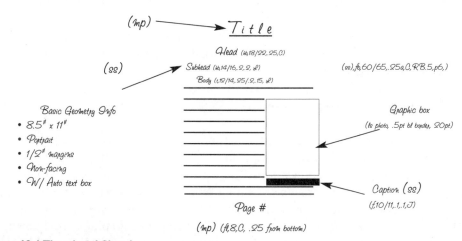

▼ **Figure 13.1 Thumbnail Sketch**
Creating rough thumbnail sketches before you begin work on the computer can save you time and editing. Notice that in addition to basic document information such as page size, orientation, margins, page facing, and auto text information, Master Page items (mp) and Style Sheets (ss) are marked and notated with formatting information. Even though I may ultimately adjust some of the formatting, this process helps to get me organized and dramatically speeds up my work.

▼ *Figure 13.2 Screen Font*
This is a low resolution bitmapped screen font. The character is built out of dots, like a bitmapped graphic. Contrast this with the outline printer font in Figure 13.3, which is constructed out of lines instead of dots. The screen font file is used for the display of type on screen. Screen fonts are not imbedded in a page layout document and must be sent with its printer font partner, as a separate file to accompany the page layout document in which it is used.

▼ *Figure 13.3 Printer Font*
This is a high resolution outline printer font built out of lines, unlike the screen font in Figure 13.2. The printer font file is used for scaling and printing. Printer fonts are not imbedded in the document and must be sent with the screen font partner as a separate file to accompany the page layout document. Printer fonts are like outline graphic files.

❧ Plan to set aside some time to **proofread** your copy. It also helps to have more than one person **proof** the job. You can never proof a job too often. More on this in Chapter 19, "The Proof is in the Separation."

❧ Keep your document as clean as possible. Do not leave unnecessary boxes, lines, colors etc., lying around. Do not try to use white boxes to knock out an area. Be "code conscious" when creating your document. Choose the simplest way to accomplish your task; for example, move a text box instead of using the baseline shift to reposition an entire section of text.

❧ There are many graphics and documents which you can create on a computer which are difficult or impossible to print. Examples include complex masks, complex paths, bright spot colors printed in CMYK, and complex overlapping blends. As a document designer and creator, you must keep this in mind as you prepare your files. The freedom you have as a computer-oriented designer must be tempered by your responsibilities to create files which are compatible with their final use.

We will be discussing all of the above topics in more detail throughout the book.

DOCUMENT COMPOSITION

Composite page layout

The composite document is the document which contains all of the various text and graphic elements which make up the final document. The composite application is used for formatting, arranging, and organizing all of these text and graphic elements, and is usually used for printing as well. The most common composite applications are page layout programs such as PageMaker, InDesign, Framemaker, and QuarkXpress. These applications are well suited for precise control of type as well as compositing pages. Some composite pages are produced in drawing applications such as Illustrator, FreeHand, or CorelDraw. Using a drawing application for compositing single-page, graphic-intensive documents is acceptable, but one can construct longer, more text-intensive documents more effectively in a page layout application.

Graphics applications

Just as page composition and typesetting is best performed in page layout applications like QuarkXpress, InDesign and PageMaker, most graphic elements are best created in graphics applications. There are basically two types of graphics applications: painting and drawing. Painting type graphics, also known as bitmapped or raster graphics, are created in applications like Photoshop or Painter. Paint images are constructed out of patterns of dots. Drawing type graphics, also known as outline or vector graphics, are created in applications such as Illustrator, FreeHand, or CorelDraw. These graphics are constructed out of lines. Graphics are generally created in one of these graphics applications and then imported into page layout applications as elements for final document composition.

Page elements

Type

Text on a page is created through the use of fonts. As discussed in Chapter 11, "Tales of True Typesetting," it is usually best to use PostScript Type 1 fonts for PostScript printing, rather than TrueType fonts. While there are several varieties of fonts (more on this later), most contain two types of information, and PostScript fonts actually have two separate font files (See Chapter 11 for more detailed info on fonts). First is screen font information (Fig. 13.2), which is used for displaying type on a monitor; second is printer font information (Fig. 13.3), which is used for printing the font. Screen font files are generally bitmapped files of low resolution (low resolution is all that is required for viewing on a screen). Printer font files are high resolution outline files which can be scaled to a wide range of sizes for printing. The screen font file and printer font files are linked to each other and to the document where they are placed. Both the low resolution screen font files and the high resolution printer font are necessary for creating, viewing, and printing type in a document. It is important to note that both the screen fonts and printer fonts are external files which are not automatically included within a page layout document when you copy or move the document to another disk. If you attempt to view

At the outset of your document construction process use pencil sketch thumbnails to sketch out your document. This is a fast and easy process which allows you quickly and easily to designate the basic document geometric parameters such as size, orientation, and margins, as well as other document characteristics such as numbers of columns and baselines. I also place designate masterpage elements, and initial style sheets lists as well. Using thumbnails also allows you to test out various design ideas in much less time than a more formal representation. Just because we are working mainly on the computer to implement our final work does not mean that the old fashioned pencil and paper thumbnail cannot be used with some great benefits.

or print a document which does not have access to the proper font files, the copy will generally be rendered on screen and printed as a default font, most often Courier. Therefore, when you move a document from one computer to another you must make sure that you send the font files, both screen and printer, for all of the fonts which you have used along with the document.

There is one concept which has helped me understand fonts and has removed some of the confusion and complexity surrounding them. Fonts are often discussed as if they are file types or document elements completely separate from graphics. I prefer to think of fonts as being special types of graphic files. The bitmapped screen fonts are special types of paint or bitmapped graphics, and printer fonts are special versions of outline or vector files. Keep this comparison in mind as you work your way through the chapters on graphics and typesetting.

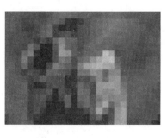

▼ *Figure 13.4 Low Resolution Screen Image*
This is the low resolution (72 ppi) screen image (55K) used for viewing an imported image. This low resolution file is imbedded in the page layout document and should be linked to an external high resolution file which will be used during printing. It looks pixilated when it is printed. Compare with the sharper high resolution image in Figure 13.5

▼ *Figure 13.5 High Resolution Print Image*
This is the high resolution partner to the file shown in Figure 13.4. This is a 300 ppi image (1.3MB) and is linked to the low resolution image when imported into a document. This image is used for printing. This high resolution file is not imbedded in the document, so it must be sent separately and linked to the internal low resolution image.

(Note: In Windows the PostScript screen and printer font file equivalents are called .pfm and .pfb files. Also, this discussion of screen and printer fonts does not apply to TrueType fonts which combine these two components into one file. See Chapter 11 for a more complete discussion.)

Graphics

Graphic elements are generally created within a graphics application and then imported into a page layout document for combination with type and other graphic elements. Most graphics are constructed in their native file formats, such as Photoshop (.psd) format. These native file formats support layers and alpha channels and transparency which is terrific for creating and editing graphics but consume memory and are not good for printing. Native files typically need to be flattened and resaved in a file format more appropriate for output such as TIFF or EPS for PostScript printing or GIF or JPEG for use on the Web. While some page layout applications, such as InDesign, allow for the import and editing of native graphic files, it is still smarter and safer to ultimately place flattened and simplified graphics in your page layout applications prior to printing.

▼ **Figure 13.6 Native Document**
Original outline graphic is created as a document in a drawing application such as Illustrator, FreeHand, or CorelDraw.

Like fonts, graphic elements have two components: a low resolution screen view component (Fig. 13.4) and a high resolution print file component (Fig. 13.5). The low resolution screen view component of the graphic file is, unlike fonts, actually embedded in the page layout document. This means that when you move a page layout document which contains an imported graphic file to another disk or computer, the low resolution graphic file moves along with the document. So the screen view will always be there unless you remove it intentionally. The continual presence of the the low resolution screen view file can lead you to believe that the entire graphic file is present. But, in order to print properly, the high resolution graphic file component must also be present and **linked** to its low resolution graphic file partner. Because the low resolution screen view image is always visible, it is easy to forget, when copying or moving a document to another disk or computer, that the high resolution version of imported graphic files is not part of the page layout document itself. What will happen if you try to print a document for which you have forgotten to send along the linked high resolution versions of the imported graphic files? You will see the graphic on screen, but only the low resolution screen preview will be present. In preview mode the graphic box often shows no graphic image but appears as a box with an "X" through it like this ⊠. When you print this image only this low resolution data will be available for imaging. This generally results in the image being rendered with large pixels and much lower quality (see Fig. 13.9 for a visual guide to flattening and linking of graphics).

▼ **Figure 13.7 Exported EPS File**
This graphic is exported as an EPS file, which is then suitable for importing into a page layout application such as QuarkXpress or PageMaker.

Native files

Most graphic application documents, such as FreeHand or CorelDraw documents, are not directly importable into other applications in their original or native document format. Therefore, some types of graphic files, most notably EPS graphics which are produced in drawing applications, must be specifically exported as EPS files in order for us to be able to import them into other applications such as PageMaker or QuarkXpress (see Figs. 13.6 and 13.7 for examples). The EPS file is sometimes not as editable as the original parent or native document from which it

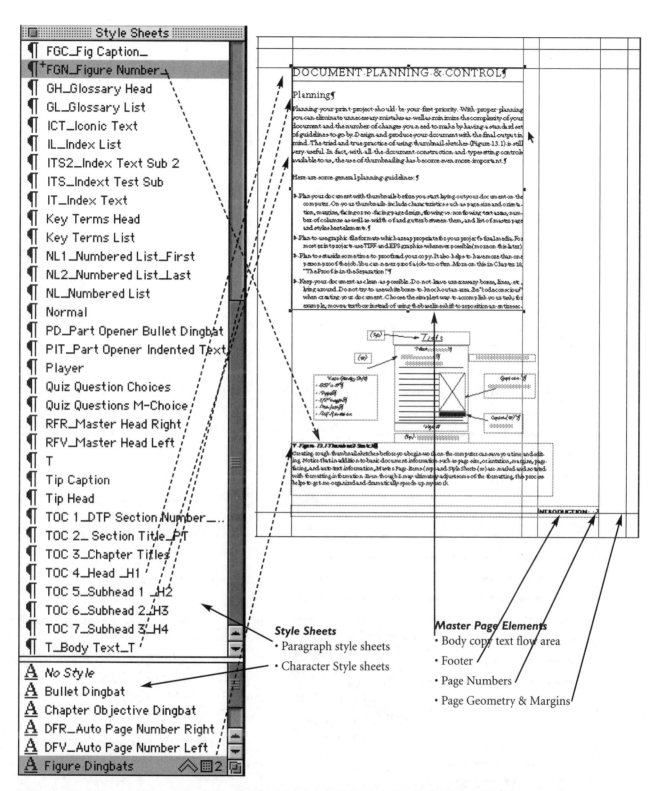

Style Sheets
- Paragraph style sheets
- Character Style sheets

Master Page Elements
- Body copy text flow area
- Footer
- Page Numbers
- Page Geometry & Margins

▼ *Figure 13.8 Master Page and Style Sheet Elements for Some of the Elements Used in This Book*
Any repeating page element such page geometry and margins, main text box areas, chapter headers and footers, and page numbers should be set up on master pages. Each chapter of a book will typically has its own master page. All formatted type is controlled by style sheets. Style sheets can control either whole paragraphs (paragraph style sheets) such as the HI head above, or selected text within a paragraph (character style sheets) such as the Figure Dingbats above. Using master page elements for repeating page elements and style sheets for repeating type formatting make document construction and editing easier, faster and far more consistent.

DOCUMENT
Low Resolution Screen Images vs.

Low Resolution Screen Font File
- Low resolution (72 ppi)
- Bitmapped file and image
- Used to display text on screen
- Not included in page layout document
- Must be sent along with document on disk
- Linked to external scalable outline
  printer font file

Screen Font Name
Palatino

***QuarkXPress, PageMaker,
InDesign, Framemaker,
etc., Document***

PAGE LAYOUT DOCUMENT

HEADLINE TYPE

Chicken

➠ *Link to Screen Font* ➠

➠ *Link to High Resolution Print Graphic File* ➠

Low Resolution Screen PreviewImage PICT (Mac) or Tiff (Win)
- Low resolution (72ppi) <u>view</u> image
- <u>Included</u> in page layout document
- <u>Linked</u> to external high resolution
  vector EPS <u>print</u> image

➠ Link to High Resolution Print Graphic File ➠

**72 ppi, 8 bit, Screen Image
File size = 18 K**

Low Resolution Screen PreviewImage PICT (Mac) or Tiff (Win)
- Low resolution (36 or 72 ppi) <u>view</u> image
- ~18 K @ 72 ppi
- Low res bitmapped PICT (Mac) or TIFF (Win)
- Used to display graphic images on screen
- <u>Included</u> in page layout document.
- <u>Linked</u> to external high resolution <u>print</u> image

▼ *Figure 13.9 Document Construction*
Page layout documents are shells into which proxies for type and graphics are placed. Low resolution versions of graphic images are stored in the page layout document itself. High resolution versions, used for printing, are stored externally to the page layout docume Font information is entirely external. All the external files need to be sent to your printer along with the page layout document itself. Note: A color version of this image can be found in the Color Plate section in the center of this book (see Fig. C.1, page C-2 of the color section of this book).

278 Document Construction

CONSTRUCTION
High Resolution Printing Images

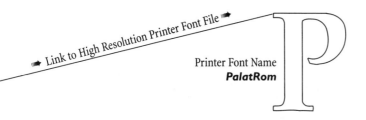

High Resolution Printer Font File
- High resolution PostScript/Outline file
- Scalable
- Not included in page layout document pages
- Linked to external low resolution screen font file
- Not seen on screen, but used to print document
- Must be sent along with document on disk

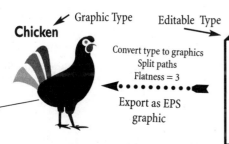

Original Parent/Native Documents
- Original Photoshop or drawing file
- High resolution pixel and/or vector image
- May contain layers, channels and/or editable type
- *Not* included in page layout file
- Should be sent as separate unlinked graphic file along with page layout document and linked graphics on disk. Place this native file in a separate folder for use in case editing is required. Use same name as print graphic file, but with different three charter extension, such as .psd for Photoshop.

Exported EPS Print Image
- Encapsulated PostScript
- Vector /Outline: Resolution independent
- For importing into page layout file
- *Not* included in page layout document
- Must be sent along with document on disk
- *Linked* to low resolution preview

Drawing Document
- FreeHand
- Illustrator
- CorelDraw

**200 ppi 4.34MB
Multilayered, 24bit
RGB Photoshop (.psd) image**

High Resolution TIFF or EPS CMYK Printing Image
- High resolution (200 ppi–300 ppi)
- 370 KB @ 200 ppi (no layers or channels)
- High resolution bitmapped TIFF or EPS
- Used for *printing* graphic images
- *Not* included in page layout document
- *Linked* to low resolution graphic file
- Sent along with document on disk

**200 ppi 370KB
Flattened 32bit, CMYK
Print (.tif or .eps) Image**

was produced and exported. As a result, when you are copying documents to a new computer or sending your files out to be printed, it is good practice to send along the native or parent graphic document as well as the exported EPS graphic file. This will allow whoever is printing the file to edit any aspect of the graphics file if it becomes necessary.

DOCUMENT CONSTRUCTION

Master pages

Master pages are templates for placement of document elements (see Fig. 13.8). Master pages automatically place repetitive text and graphic elements and are especially useful for longer documents. Repetitive page elements such as page numbers and mastheads can be constructed in master pages and then applied to multiple document pages. Using master pages to locate repetitive document elements saves a tremendous amount of time and improves the consistency of element placement. The use of master pages also dramatically improves the editability of a document. Note that in the thumbnail sketch shown at the beginning of this chapter I have Master Page elements designated. (See Chapter 11 for a more complete discussion of master pages.)

Style sheets

A style sheet is a template for type formatting (see Fig. 13.8). A style sheet should be used to format any type which occurs repetitively throughout a document. As with the use of master pages, using style sheets saves time, improves consistency, and dramatically aids in the editing process. When I am sketching my thumbnails, I always include at least the initial names and basic formatting characteristics of the style sheets I intend to use. For more details on style sheets, see the "Typesetting with Style" section in Chapter 11.

▼ *Figure 13.10 "Save as" Menu Choice*
"Save as..." allows you to create a new document with a different name.

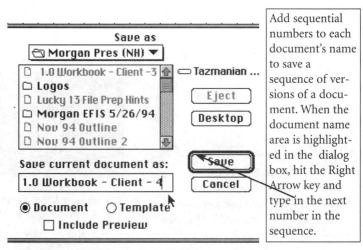

Add sequential numbers to each document's name to save a sequence of versions of a document. When the document name area is highlighted in the dialog box, hit the Right Arrow key and type in the next number in the sequence.

▼ *Figure 13.11 "Save as..." Dialog Box*
Use this to create multiple copies of working documents. Be sure to appropriately name and place each new document you create.

TIP

The use of master pages and style sheets is the at the foundation of all well constructed multipage documents. Any page elements which occur on multiple pages, such as running heads and footers, page numbers, logos, text boxes etc., should be placed on a master page. Any text formats which occur more than once such as heads and body copy should be formatted with the use of style sheets. Using master pages and style sheets makes document creation and editing faster, easier and far more consistent and more mistake free.

Style sheets can be designated as **paragraph style sheets** to control all of the type in a paragraph, or as character based style sheets which will be applied only to selected type within a paragraph, such as a bullet symbol at the beginning of a caption. See Fig 13.8 for a look at some paragraph and **character style sheets**.

DOCUMENT MANAGEMENT

Raise your hand if you have never lost a file. If you have your hand in the air, you are either a blatant liar or a computer neophyte. In either case, lost or temporarily misplaced files are a pain in the rear and something to be avoided. One often overlooked and crucial aspect of electronic publishing is the proper management of files. Here are some file management tips.

1. Develop a consistent folder and file naming system and use it. Always name a file properly and know where you are placing your files when you first save them. This consistent naming system will also come in handy when you establish **backup** and archiving routines (see 5 and 6 below).

2. A good way to make sure that your page layout documents and their associated graphics always remain linked is to place the high resolution graphics in the same folder as the page layout documents in which they have been placed. Organizing your files in this manner will ensure that your page layout documents and associated high resolution graphics always remain together and that whenever the page layout document is launched it will automatically relink to its high resolution graphics (see Fig. 13.10 for a visual guide to linking).

3. It is a good idea to send your output service companies the editable, native graphic files, as well as the high resolution graphics which are linked to their associated page layout documents prior to output. Having the native files handy will allow for easier editing if needed.

4. A good habit to have when working on documents is to periodically save multiple copies of your documents. This should be done in addition to or as a supplement to daily backup procedure. One of the easiest ways to accomplish this is to use the "Save as…" command (see Figure 13.10 for menu location) to create new sequentially named or numbered versions of documents. There are many advantages to using this procedure consistently. Most important, if your document becomes corrupted through a system crash or other mishap, you will

have only lost a few hours of work rather than a whole day (or many days, if you haven't done a recent backup). I always perform a "Save as..." prior to printing. I do this to protect my document from the intrusive printing process and to simplify my files. Figure 13.11 shows the dialog box you will see when doing a "Save as...." Simplifying files helps to make printing go smoother and faster.

5. One other speed-enhancing suggestion is to consider reducing your long documents into smaller, more manageable ones. This is extremely important if your document is graphic-intensive.

6. Make daily **backups** of your files in case of computer crashes or lost data. If you have sensitive data which cannot be lost under any circumstances you may want to make multiple backups and keep one of them off site. Most page layout applications will allow you to establish and maintain pages numbers across several related documents.

7. **Archive** images, that is make copies of them and remove them from your active hard drives, to make room for new files on your computer.

Note: Backups and archives are most effectively performed using dedicated applications such as Retrospect or Norton utilities.

CHAPTER SUMMARY

High quality document construction involves creating documents which are easy to construct, consistent and easy to edit. Document planning is a key tool when creating well constructed documents. Use of thumbnail sketches allows testing of various document designs as well as specifications; layout; the basic document page parameters such as page size orientation and margins; and help in making decisions such as whether the document will be a facing or nonfacing page document and whether or not to include automatic text boxes. Proper decisions early can help prevent costly, time consuming reworks later on. Be sure to use graphic file formats which are consistent with the end use or output of your document, such as TIFF and EPS for print and GIF and JPEG for the Web. Proofing, especially by someone else, is a key function to perform on documents. Clean up your document by removing unnecessary document elements prior to final output. Keep in mind that there are some things you can create on a computer that you may not be able to print. Examples include complex gradients and/or bright, saturated colors.

Use the right tool for the right job. Use graphics applications, such as Illustrator for vector graphics and Photoshop for pixel-based images, for creating and editing graphics. Page layout applications such as QuarkXPress, PageMaker and InDesign should be used for setting type and composing final pages. Final documents need to have all their text and graphic elements linked in order to view and print properly. These elements include screen and printer fonts as well as high resolution graphics. I will typically send native as well as print graphic files into my service companies. Having the native graphic files allows for easier file editing. Name and organize your files to maintain links. Regularly back up and archive your files to prevent lost files and make room for new documents.

PAULINE'S DIGITAL IMAGING TIPS

Pauline's Tip 13.1

Use thumbnails to plan your documents. Include basic document geometry characteristics, master page elements, and initial style sheet lists. Thumbnails can also be used to speed up the design process.

Pauline's Tip 13.2

The use of master pages and style sheets is at the foundation of all well constructed multipage documents. Any page elements which occur on multiple pages, such as running heads and footers, page numbers, logos, text boxes, etc., should be placed on a master page. Any text formats which occurs more than once such as heads and body copy should be formatted with the use of style sheets. Using master pages and style sheets makes document creation and editing faster, easier and far more consistent and more mistake free.

Pauline's Tip 13.3

In addition to sending a composite page layout document such as an Quark or PageMaker document, send all of the high resolution versions of any graphic images you have included (placed or imported) in your document. Remember that graphic images which are visible in page layout documents are only small, low resolution screen versions of the larger, high resolution graphic files. The high resolution graphic files exist as separate files from the page layout document.

Pauline's Tip 13.4

Send original or parent document versions of EPS and TIFF graphic files as well as the exported EPS graphics themselves which have been exported from drawing applications such as FreeHand, Illustrator, or CorelDraw documents.

Pauline's Tip 13.5

Send font files for all fonts used in your documents. Send both the screen and printer font files. Both are required for the proper viewing and printing of your file. View your fonts as special types of preformed graphics.

PAULINE'S DIGITAL IMAGING TIPS

Pauline's Tip 13.6

Do not embed the high resolution graphic images in a page layout document. Keep the high resolution files separate for easy access and editing.

Pauline's Tip 13.7

Avoid setting type in drawing programs and then exporting as a vector EPS graphics file with embedded type. Set type whenever possible in the page layout program form which you will be printing. If you do have nested type be sure to inform your output service company of its existence and send these fonts to your printer.

Pauline's Tip 13.8

Avoid applying geometric adjustments such as scaling and rotation to graphic images placed in page layout documents. These adjustments should be done in the original graphics applications such as Photoshop, Illustrator and FreeHand.

Pauline's Tip 13.9

Allow time for someone else to proof your documents prior to final output. It is very tough to see your own mistakes.

Pauline's Tip 13.10

Place high resolution graphics in the same folder as their associated page layout documents. This will help keep the document and graphics together and facilitate linking any time the page layout document is launched.

Pauline's Tip 13.11

Back up your files daily to prevent lost files. Archive your inactive files to make room for more recent documents and graphics.

CHAPTER REVIEW

Check Your Comprehension

Multiple Choice Questions

To help you review the topics covered in this chapter, answer the following multiple choice questions.

1. Thumbnails can be used for which of the following?
   A. Sketching document geometry
   B. Designating masterpage elements
   C. Making lists of initial style sheets
   D. All of the above

2. Which of the following is used for formatting text?
   A. Masterpage
   B. Style sheet
   C. Thumbnail
   D. File format designation

3. Which of the following is typically the most editable?
   A. TIFF
   B. Print file
   C. native file
   D. EPS file

4. A _____ format is usually preferred for PostScript printing
   A. JPEG file
   B. GIF file
   C. native file
   D. TIFF file

5. Which of the following might typically be placed on a master page?
   A. Running read
   B. Automatic page number
   C. Margin guides
   D. All of the above

6. _____ is required in order to print images properly from a page layout document.
   A. Compression
   B. Linking
   C. Backing up
   D. Style sheet formatting

7. Which would you use to format a portion of a paragraph of type?
   A. Paragraph style sheet
   B. Character style sheet
   C. Masterpage
   D. Backup program

8. When should you always have someone else take good look at your document?
   A. Proofing
   B. Scanning
   C. Backing up
   D. Archiving

9. Which of the following needs to be included when you send out a file for printing?
   A. Linked graphics
   B. Screen and printer fonts
   C. Native files
   D. All of the above

10. _____ is critical saving copies of your files for safe keeping.
    A. Making "Save as" copies of files
    B. Backing up your files
    C. Archiving your files
    D. All of the above

11. Where is the best place to put your high resolution graphics so that they will remain linked to their low resolution pairs in a page layout document?
    A. In a separate folder from the page layout document
    B. In a backup folder
    C. In the same folder from the page layout document
    D. None of the above

12. Which would be the best application for setting type and composing a page?
    A. InDesign
    B. CorelDraw
    C. Illustrator
    D. Photoshop

Check Your Understanding

Concept Questions

To help you review and expand your thinking on the topics covered in this chapter, answer the following questions.

1. Explain the concept of thumbnailing and explain how it can be used to speed up both the document design and the document construction processes.

2. What are master pages and why is it important to use them? Provide a list of typical master page elements.

3. What sort of page elements would you *not* want to place on a master page? Name three elements and explain why it would not be a good idea to place them on a masterpage.

4. Describe the usefulness of style sheets. Why should we use them?

5. Describe the concept of linking and explain why it is important.

6. Distinguish between native files and output files. When should we use each one?

7. Distinguish between and give examples of a paragraph and character based style sheet.

8. What is the best way to organize your page layout documents and their linked graphics? Explain Why?

9. Explain why it is poor practice to rotate a graphic file in a page layout document.

10. What is the difference between backing up and archiving? When should each be done?

PROJECTS

1. Create a thumbnail of a brochure document you would like to construct. Be sure to include the basic page geometry elements, columns, masterpage items and a list of initial style sheets.

2. Now create the document you thumbnailed in question one above. Use a page lay out application. Be sure to use master pages and style sheets for this document construction.

3. Import some ASCII text and some graphics. Format the text using your style sheets. Place the high resolution graphics in the same folder as the page layout document.

4. Perform a "Save as" on this first page layout document and create a sequentially labeled second document. Edit your style sheets in this second document. Compare the second document with the first one. Make a backup copy of the entire job using a backup application such as Retrospect or Norton Utilities.

14
Color Me Right

As the Byte Turns continues…

*Will Danny and Sam E. Paint themselves into
a corner that Pauline can't PICT them out of?*

*Can you match this
metallic Pantone
with 4/c process?*

We can do it!

*Oh dear, what have I got-
ten myself into?*

Can't we ?

*You told them we could
reproduce what with
4/c process !
I'm gonna kill both
of them.
Just wait and see!*

Chapter Objectives

In this chapter you will learn:

◆ **The fundamentals of color**
◆ **Color assignment for print**
◆ **Color assignment for the Web**
◆ **The basics of calibration**
◆ **Color management**
◆ **Key Terms**
  • Color definition: HSV, etc.
  • Color assignment: RGB, CMYK, Spot
  • Spot color
  • Process color
  • Hexadecimal color
  • Color gamut
  • HiFi color
  • Web safe color
  • Color space
  • Color management
  • Generic profile
  • Custom profile

INTRODUCTION

There is no color on a computer. This is because your computer is a digital device which really only works directly with black and white. All color created by our color output devices such as monitors and printers. Each color device we work with has its own gamut, or range of reproducible color. There are numerous was to describe color. One very useful way to describe color is hue, saturation, and value (grayscale or luminance value) **HSV**, which can be visualized in the form of a color cylinder.

When assigning colors to objects it is important to know the **Color gamut** capabilities of the output devices you are using. When assigning colors for commercial printing be sure to assign spot and **Process color**s properly. When printing on desktop color printers, process colors should be assigned, as most of these devices are not **Spot color** capable. When assigning colors for displaying on monitors it is appropriate to use **RGB** values. And when assigning colors to be displayed on a Web page, use the 216 color Web safe palette.

Calibration of your system components is essential in order to maintain consistent performance of our capture and output devices. Fundamental calibration involves making sure each device is linear and neutral through the use of simple grayscale targets. More sophisticated forms of calibration, known as **color management**, involve the the use of more complex targets, measuring devices and analytical software which results in the creation and use of average **generic profiles** for models and **custom profiles** for specific devices.

COLOR BASICS

No such thing as a color computer!

You may be shocked to find out that you do not own a color computer! That's right. Although your computer was advertised as an 8 bit/256 color or 24 bit/16.7 million color machine, your computer, in fact, only truly understands two values: black and white. This is because you work on a digital computer and the digital nature of your computer restricts it to understanding only two signals, 0 and 1, or black and white. But wait! Before you rush indignantly back to your computer store to demand a refund for false advertising, think about this: having only two color values to worry about is a lot less complicated than keeping track of 16.7 million. The RGB and **CMYK** images you capture, create, and work with on your computer are really composed of grayscale channels, which in turn are composed of groups of black and white values. Color is always added outside of your computer. The color you see on your monitor is the result of the stimulation of red, green, and blue phosphors embedded inside your monitor glass. The color variations you see on screen are the result of different intensities of off and on signals (0s and 1s) sent from your computer to each of the colored screen phosphors. Similarly, all hard copy output from a computer is black and white, with the color being added by an external device. Take a look at the film output from a "color imagesetter." It is four different sheets of black and white film, one for each of the **process colors**. The color in this case is applied through the application of cyan, magenta, yellow, and black (K) printing inks on a printing press. If you are still not quite convinced about the black and white nature of your computer, open up an RGB image in Photoshop. Look at each channel (R, G, and B) individually. You will see that each "color" channel is actually a grayscale channel with 8 bits or 256 shades of grayscale information contained in each pixel. Enlarge the image so that you can see the component pixels (see Fig. 14.1). Now bring up your on-screen densitometer/image information palette (F8) and explore the field of pixels from which the image is constructed. Keep track of the K values in the image information palette as you survey the image. Note that the values will vary from 0 to 256. This concept of working in black and white can really simplify working with color graphics. Instead of trying to relate to 16.7 million colors, it is easier and more accurate to think about and work with our color images as combinations of several grayscale images whose tonal values we will manipulate to adjust the final color output.

Basic color issues

Several related issues need to be kept in mind when you are working with color images on an electronic publishing system and preparing files for print. The first is that we work in at least two different **color spaces**: RGB for our scanners and monitors, and CMYK when we go to press. The second issue is that we print with various combinations of inks, such as **Spot color** inks and Process color inks. Each color space or ink set has its own distinctive color values or gamuts, some of which are not reproducible in the other color systems. Because we work with different color systems, we must be very careful when we assign our color values as we create our electronic documents. We must always be mindful that the colors we create on screen can be recreated in the final output color space and media.

Composite RGB Image

Red
Green
Blue

▼ **Figure 14.1 RGB "Color" Image**
A 24bit RGB "color" image such as this is essentially composed of a sandwich of three (3) grayscale images. The color we produce or output either through viewing or printing is provided by the output devices to which we send these images. RGB images contain three channel of grayscale pixels with 24 bits of data per image, or three 8 b/p grayscale files, one for each color (RGB). Each color can be shown in 256 shades. Therefore, the total number of colors possible is 256 R x 256 G x 256 B = 16.7 million colors. This RGB image file size is 24 times larger than the 1bit line art image. These images are used for displaying color images on monitors and printing to color film.

To control the color in this image we control the grayscale values, which in turn control the color. You will find a color version of this figure on page C-15 in the color plate section in the center of the book (Fig. C.33).

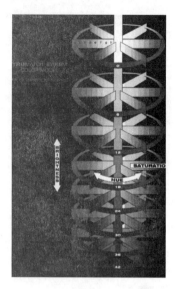

▼ *Figure 14.2 Percent Color Space Model*

This is a three-dimensional model of HSV (Hue, Saturation & Value) color space. Hue is represented by the outside rim of the cylinder. Saturation, or color purity or intensity, varies across any cross section of the cylinder with maximum saturation on the outside rim and minimum at the center. Value, which is a measure of gray scale value or brightness, varies along the vertical axis of the model cylinder, with 100 percent gray at one end and 0 percent gray at the other. The color picker diagram on the facing page is a cross-section view through the cylinder. The slider to the right of the pie changes the value or view position along the vertical axis.

Note: A color version of this figure, Fig. C.8 on page C-8 can be found in the color plate section of this book.

Color concepts terminology

- Color space: Color spaces are models we use to describe or define color. Color spaces generally involve ranges of color which occur within the visible spectrum. The volume of a specific color space depends upon how that color is produced. The two most common color spaces we work with are RGB color space, for scanning and viewing on monitors, and CMYK color space for printing.

- Color gamut: The range of colors which a device such as a color printer or monitor can reproduce. Printers, which work in CMYK color space, typically have far smaller color gamuts than those captured by color scanners and reproduced by color monitors. This difference in color gamut often results in printed colors which look significantly different, usually darker and less vivid, than those captured by scanners and viewed on monitors.

- Bit depth: The number of bits per pixel used to create the various grayscale values in an image. One bit images are black and white, 8 bit images have 28 or 256 shades of gray, 24 bit RGB images have 224, or 16.7 million colors. These are constructed out of three 8 bit grayscale channels, one for each color, red, green, and blue. CMYK images have four 8 bit grayscale channels and are therefore 32 bit per pixel images.

- RGB color space: The range of visible colors produced by adding various combinations of transmitted red, green, and blue light together. RGB values are used to define images, and other objects, which are used for viewing on monitors, such as for viewing images on the World Wide Web over the Internet, and must be converted to CMYK for printing.

- CMYK color space: The range of visible colors produced by subtracting various portions of red, green, and blue light when it is reflected off of a media such as paper with CMYK color applied to its surface. CMYK color space is utilized in printing, both commercial and desktop.

- Process colors: Colors created through the combination of various percentages, or screens, of a specific set of colors. The most common set of process colors and inks used to recreate images on a printing press comprises cyan, magenta, yellow, and black (CMYK). Additional process colors, such as green, violet, and orange can be added to expand the normally small process color gamut. Process colors are typically used to reproduce continuous tone color images, but can be used for building colors to fill objects as well. The four-color process color gamut is much smaller than the Spot color gamut and should not be used to attempt to produce exact matches with spot colors. A wide range of print colors can be created with only four print cylinders used on a press.

- Spot colors: Spot colors are special mixtures of various combinations of 14 standard colors plus a transparent white. The 14 standard Pantone spot colors include: Pantone Yellow, Pantone Yellow 012, Pantone Orange, Pantone Warm Red, Pantone Red 032, Pantone Rubine Red, Pantone Rhodamine Red, Pantone Purple, Pantone Violet, Pantone Blue 072, Pantone Reflex Blue, Pantone Process Blue, Pantone Green, and Pantone Black C. Spot colors are commonly referred to as PMS colors (PMS is short for Pantone Matching System). Spot colors found on the PMS swatch charts are usually specific mixtures of only three of these colors, one of which is usually either transparent

Basic Color Theory

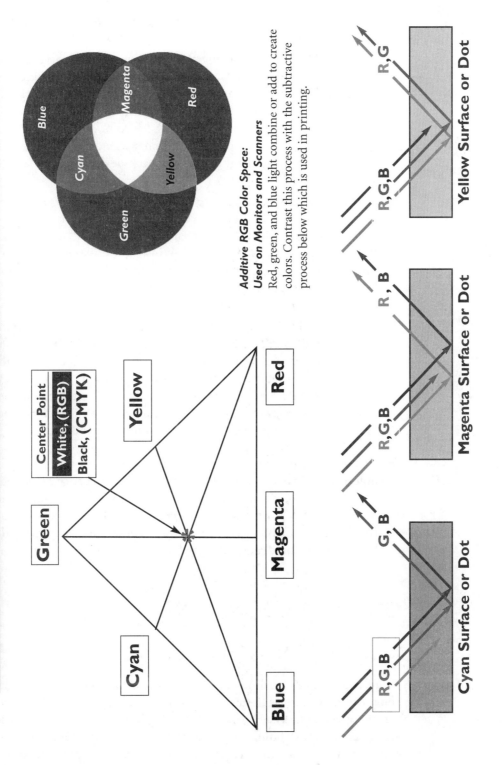

Center Point
White, (RGB)
Black, (CMYK)

Green

Cyan

Blue

Yellow

Magenta

Red

Blue

Cyan

Green

Magenta

Red

Yellow

Additive RGB Color Space:
Used on Monitors and Scanners

Red, green, and blue light combine or add to create colors. Contrast this process with the subtractive process below which is used in printing.

R,G,B

G, B

Cyan Surface or Dot

R,G,B

R , B

Magenta Surface or Dot

R,G,B

R,G

Yellow Surface or Dot

▼ *Figure 14.3 Subtractive CMYK Color Space Used In Printing*

Transmitted (RGB) light is selectively absorbed by various combinations of the three process colors (C,M, and Y). The color(s) we see on a printed piece comes from the light which is transmitted and reflected rather than absorbed by the process colors (see Fig. C.3 on page C-5 of the color plate section of this book for a color version of this figure).

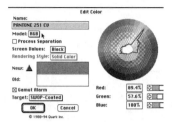

Edit Color
Name:
PANTONE 251 CV
Model: RGB
☐ Process Separation
Screen Values: Black
Rendering Style: Solid Color
New: ▲
Old:
☒ Gamut Alarm
Target: SWOP-Coated
Red: 89.4%
Green: 57.6%
Blue: 100%
OK   Cancel
© 1988-94 Quark Inc.

▼ *Figure 14.4 Color Gamut Comparison*

The entire color picker circle shows the gamut of the RGB colors which can be seen on the monitor. The roughly triangular red area inside of the color picker circle is the limited range of those RGB colors which can be reproduced in the CMYK space. The black dot in the lower half of the color circle shows the position of the Pantone spot color 251CV. Pantone 251CV is well out of gamut and will not be reproducible in CMYK.

Note: Figure C.9 shows a color version of this image and can be found in the color plate section on page C-8.

white or Pantone Black. The spot color gamut is much larger than the process color gamut. Each spot color assigned requires that a separate print cylinder be assigned on press. (Note: Pantone has a wide variety of matching system books, including process and spot [solid] to process simulation, but it has become common practice to refer to the spot colors as PMS colors)

➥ Color calibration: The matching of color values from an original image to those captured by a scanner or other digital imaging device, viewed on a monitor, and printed on one or more printing devices. Each device in the link will capture, display, or reproduce color differently. The challenge is to adjust each device so that they will match each other's color reproduction. The three primary issues involved in color calibration are color space of each device, color gamut of each device, and the drift of each device's color characteristics over time.

➥ Assigning colors: When choosing your working colors, choose colors which will be consistent with the final use of those colors. For instance, if you plan to print all of your colors in CMYK, use a CMYK color swatch book such as the Pantone Process Color System book instead of a spot color chart. Choosing initial spot colors which are later approximated with process colors can often lead to very disappointing results. RGB values are used for assigning colors for viewing (see **Web safe colors** below).

➥ Gamut conversion: Converting the colors in an image from one color space into another. RGB color files need to be converted into CMYK color files for printing. RGB color files work fine on your monitor, which uses the RGB color space to create and display colors on your monitor, but the printing process requires CMYK files. Files left as RGB images will often end up being printed as spot colors or grayscale images. The RGB to CMYK conversion/gamut mapping should be done specifically for each individual device.

➥ Web Safe color palette: The best or safest colors to use when assigning colors to objects which are to be used for display on a Web page over the Internet. There two hundred and sixteen (216) colors which are common to both the Macintosh and Windows system color spaces. These colors will display more consistently and faster than other colors. These colors are usually designated as **hexadecimal** color values and are known as the Web Safe colors.

COLOR ASSIGNMENT

Describing colors: models

There is a number of different models which have been developed to describe color. Defining color is not as easy at it may seem at first. We know what the colors red, green, and blue generally look like, but when we get down to the nitty-gritty of precisely defining colors, we run into problems. One reason for our difficulties is that evaluation of color is heavily dependent upon human perception of color. Our perception of color depends upon a wide range of variables including lighting conditions, context (surrounding colors), and even what we have eaten. On top of all this we all have different social and cultural color values.

▼ Figure 14.5 RGB/HSV Color Picker

To the right is the HSV color picker. By manipulating the sliders, you can create all of the colors which this monitor can display.

• The hue, or basic color, is represented by the colors on the outside edge of the color circle. The values are recorded in percent of RGB.

• The saturation is represented by the colors inside the rim of the color circle. The colors nearer the center of the circle are lighter, that is, less saturated, than the colors nearer the rim. Progressive amounts of white are added to any hue (rim color) at positions tending away from the rim toward the center. The center is pure white or 100% Red + 100% Blue + 100% Green.

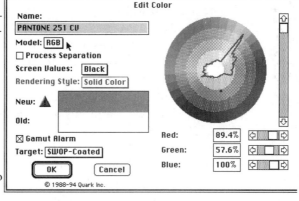

• Value is a measure of the percentage of grayscale which a color contains. Value ranges from 0% to 100% and is controlled (added or subtracted) by sliding the large vertical slider up and down. In its current position, the value of this color is 0% grayscale. If the slider were moved all the way to the bottom of its track, 100% gray would be added to the color and it would be pure black.

Note: A color version of this image can be found in the color plate section in the center of this book (see Fig. C.4 on page C-6 for a color version of this figure).

Color Models Available

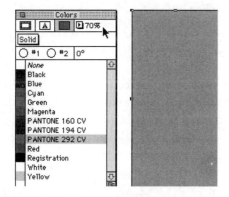

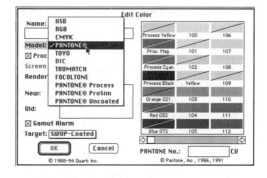

▼ Figure 14.6 Color Assignment Palette

In most applications colors can be stored in and applied through a palette such as this QuarkXPress color palette. The three Pantone colors are spot colors. RGB colors are monitor colors and should not be used for printing. CMYK colors are used for building and printing process colors. The Registration color is assigned to page elements such as crop, registration, and fold marks which should occur on every separation.

Note: A color version of this image and Fig. 14.5 can be found in the color plate section in the center of this book (see Fig.C.5 on page C-6 for a color version of this figure).

▼ Figure 14.7 Color Models

This is a list of the more common color matching systems which are used in graphics applications. The Pantone System is the most widely used. The system labeled Pantone contains the spot color guide colors. The Pantone Process system contains the process color guide colors. And the Pantone ProSim (also known as Solid to Process) contains the closest simulated process color matches for the spot colors. The Focoltone, TruMatch, Toyo, and DIC systems offer process color matching guides similar to the Pantone Process system (see Fig. C.6 on page C-6 for a color version of this figure).

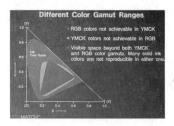

▼ *Figure 14.8 Color Gamuts*
Color gamut describes the
range of color that a particular
device can capture or reproduce. This diagram is a two-
dimensional slice through
three-dimensional color space.
Note how much larger the
visual gamut of the human eye
is (CIE area) than either the
RGB (monitor) or CMYK
(printer) gamuts. You will also
see that there are RGB colors
that will not reproduce in
CMYK and vice versa. In this
two-dimensional slice the
gamut ranges of RGB and
CMYK gamuts are of similar
extent, but in the entire three-
dimensional space the practical
CMYK gamut is much smaller
than RGB due to pigment
impurities and ink density limitations. Figure 14.9 shows a
clearer representation of the
difference between the extents
of the RGB and CMYK color
gamuts.

Note: A color version of this
image can be found in the
Color Plate section in the center of this book (see Fig. C.11
on page C-8 for a color version
of this figure).

In the digital printing world we typically work in two related but different color
spaces: RGB and CMYK. RGB space is used when we are working with devices such
as monitors and scanners, which generate their own light. CMYK is used when we
work with light which is reflected off of a surface, such as with printed material.
When we work on a computer, we work in RGB color space. When we print and
view our results, we work in CMYK color space. Regardless of the color model in
which we work, we commonly define a color by describing its hue, saturation, and
value (**HSV**). Hue is the basic color, such as red, green or blue, and is defined by
the wavelength or frequency of light. Saturation is the purity of the color and is a
measure of the amount of white which has been added to a hue. The less saturated a color is, the more white has been added, and the lighter the color appears.
Value is a measure of the amount of grayscale which has been added to the color.
The greater the value of a color, the darker it is. Most current "color pickers" use
this HSV model or some variation to define colors. RGB colors tend to be more

When assigning colors in a document, pay particular attention to the color capabilities (gamut) of your output device(s). Commercial printing presses can print either
spot or process colors. But not all print jobs include the use of spot colors. The
assignment of spot colors which ultimately print as process can result in unsatisfactory results. For assigning colors to images and objects which will be viewed over the
World Wide Web it is advantageous to use colors from the 216 color Web safe palette.
Determine the output color gamut before you begin assigning colors.

saturated and therefore brighter than colors reproduced through the CMYK
process. Note: A more universal color model known as CIE color space is gradually being adopted and will probably eventually replace HSV for many definition
applications.

Types of colors

There are generally three basic types of colors which you work with in an electronic
document: spot colors, process colors, and tints. Spot colors are solid colors made
up of specific mixtures of inks. Process colors, also known as built colors, are made
up of screen combinations of between four and seven process colors. Currently,
most process colors are built out of the traditional four process colors: cyan,
magenta, yellow, and black (CMYK). Recently, an expanded set of process colors
(violet, red, and green) known as Hi-Fi colors has been added to the process color
tool box. This expanded set of process colors allows us to print an expanded and
richer gamut of process colors. Tints are screens of single solid colors. An example
would be the 70 percent screen of spot color Pantone 292 shown in Fig. 14.4. All
three of these types of colors are generally viewed in RGB space and printed CMYK
color space.

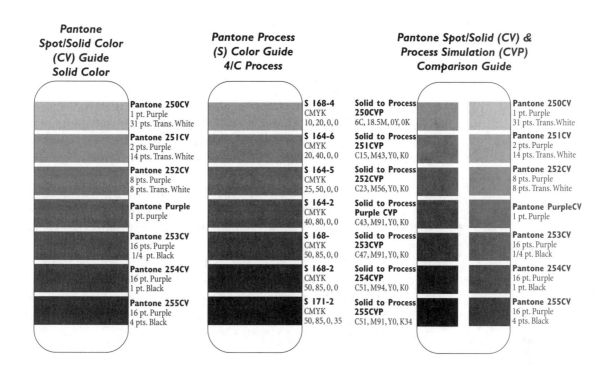

Pantone Spot/Solid Color (CV) Guide — Solid Color

	Pantone 250CV 1 pt. Purple 31 pts. Trans. White
	Pantone 251CV 2 pts. Purple 14 pts. Trans. White
	Pantone 252CV 8 pts. Purple 8 pts. Trans. White
	Pantone Purple 1 pt. purple
	Pantone 253CV 16 pts. Purple 1/4 pt. Black
	Pantone 254CV 16 pt. Purple 1 pt. Black
	Pantone 255CV 16 pt. Purple 4 pts. Black

Pantone Process (S) Color Guide — 4/C Process

	S 168-4 CMYK 10, 20, 0, 0
	S 164-6 CMYK 20, 40, 0, 0
	S 164-5 CMYK 25, 50, 0, 0
	S 164-2 CMYK 40, 80, 0, 0
	S 168- CMYK 50, 85, 0, 0
	S 168-2 CMYK 50, 85, 0, 0
	S 171-2 CMYK 50, 85, 0, 35

Pantone Spot/Solid (CV) & Process Simulation (CVP) Comparison Guide

Solid to Process 250CVP 6C, 18.5M, 0Y, 0K			**Pantone 250CV** 1 pt. Purple 31 pts. Trans. White
Solid to Process 251CVP C15, M43, Y0, K0			**Pantone 251CV** 2 pts. Purple 14 pts. Trans. White
Solid to Process 252CVP C23, M56, Y0, K0			**Pantone 252CV** 8 pts. Purple 8 pts. Trans. White
Solid to Process Purple CVP C43, M91, Y0, K0			**Pantone PurpleCV** 1 pt. Purple
Solid to Process 253CVP C47, M91, Y0, K0			**Pantone 253CV** 16 pts. Purple 1/4 pt. Black
Solid to Process 254CVP C51, M94, Y0, K0			**Pantone 254CV** 16 pt. Purple 1 pt. Black
Solid to Process 255CVP C51, M91, Y0, K34			**Pantone 255CV** 16 pt. Purple 4 pts. Black

Color Assignment - Spot Color

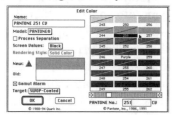

Color Assignment - 4/C Process (164-6)

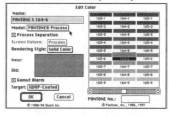

Color Assignment - Process Simulation (251CVP)

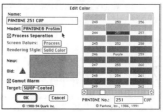

▼ *Figure 14.9 Color Choice Guides*

Three basic types of color swatch book guides appear here. From left to right they are: 1) Pantone spot/solid color guide, 2) Pantone CMYK process color guide, and 3) Pantone Solid to Process color guide (previously known as ProSim or Process simulation). The spot color guide shows a range of spot colors 250CV to 255CV. ("CV" means printed on coated stock and "U" means uncoated stock.) They are the same color but look different because of the printing substrate. CVP designates process simulation of a spot color, while the "S" prefix indicates a color chosen from the Process color swatch chart. The process guide shows the closest regular Pantone process colors to these spot colors. As you can see, the match is not good, especially in the lighter, more saturated colors. The Solid to Process guide is a special collection of process colors built specifically to simulate, as close as possible, the Pantone spot colors. Look closely and you will see that the Solid to process guide has color values designated by single and even half percent values rather than the standard 10% and 15% value changes. Even this specific, focused attempt to match the spot colors with process colors fails with the more saturated colors. Note: All spot colors shown on this page are printed with process colors and are therefore not accurate. The charts are meant to show the difference between the spot and process values for the same colors. A color version of this figure can be found in the color plate section (see Fig. C.7 on page C-7 in the color plate section of this book for a color version of this figure).

Color selections

Print color selections

The most reliable way to choose a color which will be used in the printing process is to use a color guide or swatch book. Examples of three common guides appear in Fig. 14.9. The first guide shown is the spot color guide, the second is the process color guide, and the third is a process color simulation guide. The spot color guide should be used if you intend ultimately to have your colors printed as spot colors. Many people use this guide even if they intend to print them as process colors. This approach is wrong. When you choose a spot color and ask your printer to "match that color," you will often be disappointed with the results. The spot color guide contains a far wider range of saturated colors than the CMYK process colors spectrum can reproduce. Many of the spot colors which you find in the spot color guides (such as Pantone's *Color Formula Guide 1000*) cannot be reproduced in CMYK printing; that is, they are out of gamut. If you intend your colors to print as process colors, then you should assign the color values from a process color guide (such as Pantone's *Process Color System Guide*). Doing so will give you a clearer idea of how your color will look and reduce your disappointment with your final printed results.

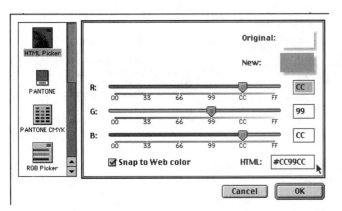

▼ **Figure 14.10 HTML Color Picker for Web Color Assignments**
When assigning colors to an object which will be viewed over the World Wide Web, it is usually best to choose colors from the Web safe color palette of the 216 colors which are common to both the Mac and Windows default system palettes. Assigning the Web safe colors will provide better color consistency and viewing speed.

Do not use your monitor to judge color unless you have a well calibrated monitor, and even then be very careful. Several factors work against a proper screen representation of colors which will be printed. First, your monitor works in RGB color space and you print in CMYK color space. RGB color space on your monitor is significantly larger than CMYK color space, so it is very easy to assign colors which look great on screen but will never print. Secondly, most high quality color monitors are 20–30 percent brighter than they should be, so even colors which can be reproduced on press will appear differently on screen.

Monitor and Web color selections

When we assign colors to be used for viewing on a monitor it is appropriate to assign RGB values to objects and images. RGB values are by default assigned to images which are captured by scanners and digital cameras. RGB values can also be assigned to objects which will be viewed on monitors. When you are assigning color values for objects which will be viewed over the World Wide Web it is advantageous to to choose colors form the 216 color Web safe palette. These 216 colors are common to both the Macintosh and Windows default system color palettes. Instead of the standard 0-255 RGB values which are commonly used in scanning and video, RGB values are assigned using HTML values, which are also known as hexadecimal values (see Fig. 14.10). Using these 216 RGB colors will produce more consistent and faster viewing of Web objects. See page 295 in this chapter and Chapter

15, "Weaving Web Graphics," for more information on Web graphics, color spaces, and color assignment.

COLOR GAMUT CONVERSION

Because we scan and view our colors in RGB color space and print our colors in CMYK color space, the colors which we create and view in RGB space must be converted into CMYK equivalents. Although RGB and CMYK color spaces are theoretically similar, the RGB color space which we view on our monitors is usually much larger than the CMYK color space we print in (see Fig. 14.6). That is, RGB has a larger color gamut than CMYK. Impurities in ink pigments and limitations on ink densities on press significantly reduce the practical CMYK gamut. If we choose RGB colors which are outside of the CMYK color gamut, those out-of-gamut RGB colors will be significantly changed when they are converted to their CMYK equivalents. The color gamut diagram in Fig. 14.11. shows the vast practical difference between RGB monitor space and CMYK printing space. red, green, and blue should not be assigned for printing colors.

Hi Fi color

Because of the practical limitations of color reproduction imposed by the use of standard 4/c process inks and techniques, many people have tried various ways of enhancing the process color gamut. One such approach is called **HiFi color**. HiFi color is actually a variety of color-enhancing technologies. These include, but are not limited to, new screening technologies, such as the stochastic screens discussed in the screening chapter, and the use of more than four process colors or four passes of process colors. Some companies, such as Pantone, which developed its Hexachrome system use two extra colors in addition to the four process colors. Others have seven-color systems which employ the use of three additional colors— usually orange, violet, and green—which are added to the four process colors. Dupont has taken a different approach to the HiFi color ink process. They use the standard four process colors, but they apply them twice, thereby increasing ink density. All of these approaches enlarge the standard process color gamut. Figure 14.11 shows the qualitative increase in color gamut which results from the use of the Dupont HyperColor system.

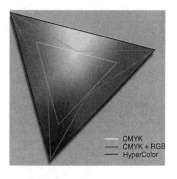

▼ *Figure 14.11 Color Gamuts*
This diagram shows the color gamuts for three different color spaces: HyperColor, RGB, and CMYK. Note how the gamuts for RGB color space and the human eye are much more extensive than the gamut for CMYK printing. HyperColor is a version of HiFi color which utilizes double hits of CMYK to increase the process color gamut. Other HiFi color systems use additional process colors to increase the gamut of process color. Pantone Hexachrome adds green and orange to CMYK to achieve an enhanced gamut.

Note: A color version of this image (Fig. C.11) can be found in the color late section in the center of this book (see page C-8).

▼ *Figure 14.12 DTP System*
Each component of a DTP system treats color differently. As an image is transferred from scanner to computer to printer, its color values may change. The object of calibration and color management system is to adjust all of the devices and the files so that the image is rendered as equally as possible on each system component.

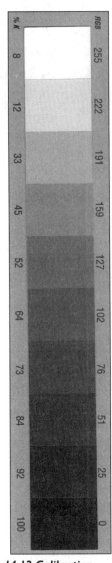

Consider the final use

Always consider the final use of your electronic document. If you are preparing your document for viewing only on screen, you have a great deal more latitude in your color choices than if you intend to print your document. Particularly if you are printing your documents, be sure to use the proper color guide to designate your colors. For maximum accuracy, your color guide should use the pigmented

Fundamental control of your grayscale and color values in your grayscale and color images and objects begins with the calibration of your system components. Basic calibration involves the linearization and neutralization of your capture, viewing and output devices. Linearization and neutralization can be accomplished with the use of a simple multistep grayscale calibration target like the one seen in Fig.14.13. More sophisticated calibration, known as color management, involves the use of more complex targets, such as the IT8 target seen in Fig. 14.14, as well as sophisticated measuring equipment and dedicated profiling software. Without calibration your capture, viewing and printing of images is inconsistent and unpredictable.

colors you intend to print with, should be printed at the same line frequency, use the same screening method you intend to employ, and should be printed on a paper similar to the one you will be using. Using the proper guide will help you minimize color gamut conversion problems and improve your calibration attempts.

COLOR MANAGEMENT

The need for color management

Proper assignment of colors is the first step to controlling color in a either a video or a print environment. To truly have control of your color reproduction, you must manage your color from start to finish, from image acquisition to the final printed piece. Controlling color on the desktop has always been a challenge. Unlike integrated proprietary systems such as Scitex and Barco (which have matched components and software from the start), open desktop systems frequently have hardware and software components from a dozen or more manufacturers all working, or not working as the case may be, together. While open systems provide us with the blessing of choice and upgradability, they also challenge us with the requirements of controlling tone and color in images which must pass through all of these unmatched components. The matching of images across these unrelated components is called calibration. Each component of an electronic publishing system captures, displays, or prints color differently. One of the more significant challenges is that some components work in entirely different color spaces. This means that color has to be translated from one color space to another. This is known as gamut mapping. The most common gamut mapping hurdle is from the RGB color space, in which scanners capture and monitors display color, into CMYK color space, in which most printers reproduce color. Because RGB and CMYK gamuts

▼ *Figure 14.13 Calibration*
Scanner calibration requires the use of a multi-swatch grayscale target with known values, such as this ten-step target developed by the author. Note that the grayscale values are conveniently listed on the right side.

Note: See page 445 in the back of this book for information on how to obtain the 10-step calibration target shown here.

are inherently different, there will never be complete fidelity between them. The tonal range compression alone, compressed from about 1000 tones in a 35mm transparency to around 100 on a printing press, guarantees that, at best, a printed image will be an approximation of the original. The tonal compression is even greater with digital image capture (see Chapter 12, "Taming Your Scanner," for a more complete treatment of tonal compression). To make matters even more interesting, we are always adding new gamut mapping challenges. The use of PhotoCD technology as a prepress tool requires that we gamut map from YCC color space to CMYK (see pages 259–261 in Chapter 12, PhotoCD, for a discussion of YCC color space).

Calibration

Linearization and neutralization

Fundamental control of your grayscale and color values in your grayscale and color images and objects begins with the calibration of your system components. Basic calibration involves the linearization and neutralization of your capture, viewing and output devices. Linearization and neutralization can be accomplished with the use of a simple multistep grayscale calibration target like the one seen in Fig. 14.13. More sophisticated calibration, known as color management, involves the use of more complex targets, such as the IT8 target seen in Fig. 14.14, as well as sophisticated measuring equipment and dedicated profiling software. Without calibration your capture, viewing and printing of images is inconsistent and unpredictable (see Chapter 12 for more information on linearization and neutralization of scanners).

Color management

Sometimes basic linearization and neutralization is not enough. If you are outputting to multiple devices, there may be significant differences in the color gamuts of all these devices. In these cases more sophisticated targets, measuring devices and analytical software is needed in order to create color profiles of each device in your system. The object of color management is to adjust your hardware and software so that you will be able to pass images from one to the other without significantly altering the image. Once set up to do this, the equipment should not be altered except for periodic adjustments to keep the components in line with each other. There are many variables which can affect the way color looks. But for us, all of these variables can be grouped into three categories of concern:

1. Each device and software application captures, displays, reproduces, or handles color differently.
2. Colors must be gamut mapped as they move from one device to another, most importantly from the scanner or digital camera to the printer.
3. All hardware devices drift with time. Scanner bulbs age and their output spectrum changes. Monitor phosphors age and change. Printer toners, inks, and other variables change.

All three of these issues must be addressed for effective color management. There

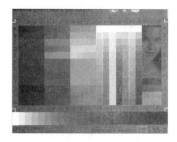

▼ Figure 14.14 Q 60 IT8 Chart
This industry standard chart is used as a scanning target. During a calibration sequence this target would be scanned, viewed, and output. The monitor image can be measured with a spectrophotometer and adjusted. The printed image can be measured with a densitometer and colorimeter. These measurements are then used to create transfer functions or curves which will be used for adjusting future output to that specific printer. Similar calibration curves can be constructed for each scanner printer combination.

Note: A color version of this image (Fig. C.12) can be found in the color plate section in this book on page C-8.

are basically two types of calibration systems, open and closed. Open calibration involves the use of general device characterization files or profiles to control output for a specific model of printer. These device profiles are constructed from a series of test prints which are made on a large number of printers of that model to determine the average output characteristics of that specific model of printer. These characterization files are then used to adjust and control the printing of images to this model of printer. The beauty of these profiles is that they are easy to use and do not require a great deal of operator knowledge to use them. The short-comings of this type of calibration are that they often do not include the scanner in the calibration system and the profiles are model- but not device-specific. These are known as generic profiles. So if you happen to have a nonaverage printer, the general device profile would not help very much. Some model profile systems allow the operator to adjust the profile to account for the peculiar characteristics of specific machines. However, if one is going to go to the trouble of "tweaking" the profiles, which is generally a time consuming process demanding color measurements of printouts, you might as well use the second type of calibration system, the closed loop.

Closed loop calibration is system- and device-specific. There is a number of closed loop systems. Ofoto was one of the first widely available desktop solutions, but they all have one characteristic in common. All closed loop calibration systems or procedures start with targets of known values–grayscale, color or both–which are scanned, printed, and then measured. The measurements of the prints are then compared with the original known target values. The differences between the orig-

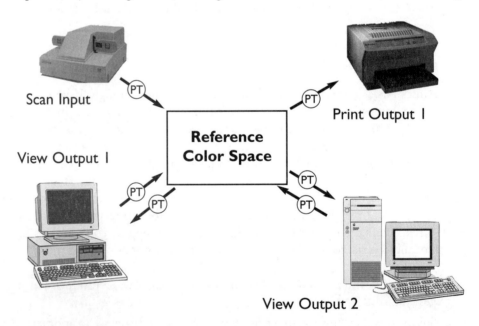

▼ *Figure 14.15 CMS*

In a closed loop color management system (CMS), color transforms or profiles are created through analysis of scanned, viewed, and printed targets with known values, like a Kodak Q60 IT8 target series. Images and profiles are transformed back and forth through a device-independent reference color space (RCS), usually some variant of the CIE color space. The RCS serves as the primary point of reference or touchstone for images as they move back and forth across the system. The image is always referred to the RCS regardless of where it is in the system.

inals and the prints are used to construct color lookup tables or calibration curves, known as transfer curves or transfer functions. These tables and curves are then used to adjust any images scanned and printed on those devices. These curves are similar in function to the model characterization curves used in the open system described above. The difference is that the closed loop system functions are developed for a specific combination of scanner, software, and printer. A different curve or custom profile is developed for each scanner printer combination used. Over time, as equipment drifts or components and consumables are replaced or changed, the transfer functions can be changed to match those specific changes. All that is involved is a rescanning and printing of the known target with subsequent measurement and color profile creation (see Fig. 14.15 for a diagram of how profiles are used).

CHAPTER SUMMARY

All color on a computer is ultimately controlled by grayscale. You computer is a digital device which really only works directly with black and white values which make up grayscale. All color associated with computer graphics and other objects is supplied by color output devices such as monitors and printers. Each color device has its own range of reproducible color, or gamut. There are numerous ways to describe color, but one very useful one is to use hue, saturation and value (grayscale or luminance value) HSV, which can be visualized in the form of a color cylinder.

Knowing the color gamut output devices you are using is critical when you start assigning colors which will be output on that device. When assigning colors for commercial printing use swatch books to make sure that you are assigning the proper spot and process colors. When printing on desktop color printers, process colors should be assigned, as most of these devices are not spot color capable. It is also a good idea to make your own swatch books for your desktop printing devices, as the colorants (inks) and substrates used in the creation of the commercial printing swatch books may deviate significantly from the colorants and papers you use for printing. When assigning colors for displaying on monitors it is appropriate to use RGB values. And when assigning colors to be displayed on a Web page, use the 216 color Web safe palette.

Calibration of your system components is required in order to maintain consistent performance of our capture and output devices. Basic calibration involves making sure each device is linear and neutral through the use of simple grayscale targets. More sophisticated forms of calibration, known as color management, utilize more complex targets, measuring devices and analytical software which results in the creation and use of device specific color profiles.

PAULINE'S DIGITAL IMAGING TIPS

Pauline's Tip 14.1

Assign color properly when designating colors for printing. Use spot and process color designations properly. Assign spot color only to those items which will actually be separated as separate colors and printed as spot colors on the press cylinder. Assign process colors names to items which will print as process colors. Do not assign an item or area a spot color name and then ask the application or printer to convert it to process colors.

Pauline's Tip 14.2

When assigning colors to be used on objects which will be displayed on monitors over the World Wide Web, assign Web safe colors from the 216 color palette which is common to both the Mac and Windows system palettes.

Pauline's Tip 14.3

Use color swatch books to judge and assign colors values. Do not use your monitor! Use a spot color swatch book to assign spot colors, a process color swatch book to assign process colors, and the ProSim (process simulation) book to assign process colors which are the closest approximations to the various spot colors. Always note the difference between the spot color and its closest approximation. It is usually not too close. If you are printing to a desktop color printer you may want to create your own swatch books, as the colorants and printing substrates are so different from commercial printing.

Pauline's Tip 14.4

Be sure that colors assigned to portions of imported graphics are included in the output application. Also be sure that any imported colors have names identical to the same colors used in the importing application. Also check to be sure that each color has its correct spot or process color designations. Use imported colors for assignment to prevent any duplication of colors either in the palette or during printing.

Pauline's Tip 14.5

Delete unused colors in color palettes in all applications used—page layout as well as graphic applications. Delete colors from the color palettes of vector graphics before they are exported as EPS files from their parent applications.

PAULINE'S DIGITAL IMAGING TIPS

Pauline's Tip 14.6

Be aware of color gamut limitations when you assign colors. Remember that RGB and spot color spaces are far more extensive than CMYK color spaces. Therefore, many of the colors you can create on your computer and view on your monitor cannot be reproduced in CMYK printing.

Pauline's Tip 14.7

Remember that RGB files must be converted into CMYK for printing. Your RGB-to-CMYK gamut conversion must be controlled and set as specifically as possible to produce CMYK images which match the gamut of every output device on which the image will ultimately be printed.

Pauline's Tip 14.8

In order to create and maintain the performance and consisitency of your capture, display and viewing devices you will need to perform at least basic calibration procedures. The foundation of calibration in an electronic publishing system is linearization and neutralization. Creating and maintaining a linear and neutral work flow requires the scanning, viewing and printing of a grayscale target with know values. This basic calibration needs to be performed on a regular schedule in order to maintain a calibrated system.

Pauline's Tip 14.9

In order to establish and maintain the best color fidelity possible throughout the design and creation process, you will need to calibrate your system with a color management system. Color management is best achieved through the use of a closed loop calibration process. This process utilizes targets with known values which can be compared with scanned, viewed, and printed results and analyzed to create custom device-specific profiles for each component of your production system.

CHAPTER REVIEW

Check Your Comprehension

Multiple Choice Questions

To help you review the topics covered in this chapter, answer the following multiple choice questions.

1. Which of the following controls both RGB and CMYK values in color images on your computer?
   A. Grayscale values
   B. 0s and 1s
   C. Bits of information
   D. All of the above

2. When assigning colors for use in commercial printing which pairs of colors can we use?
   A. RGB and CMYK
   B. Spot and process
   C. RGB and process
   D. RGB and spot

3. Which set of print colors requires that we have a separate print cylinder for each color assigned?
   A. Spot
   B. Process
   C. RGB
   D. CMYK

4. In the acronym HSV to what do the H, S, and V refer?
   A. Halftone, saturation, version
   B. Halftone, scripting, version
   C. Hue, saturation, value
   D. None of the above

5. What is the best tool to use for judging and assigning colors for printing?
   A. Monitor view of colors
   B. Swatch books
   C. Color palettes in applications
   D. All of the above

6. RGB images must be converted into _____ for printing.

   A. CMYK images

   B. HSV images

   C. Web safe colors

   D. CIE images

7. Which of the following is used for assigning colors for use in Web Pages?

   A. PostScript color values

   B. HTML color values

   C. HPGL color values

   D. CMYK color values

8. Color _____ defines the range of reproducible colors for a device.

   A. gamut

   B. space

   C. swatch

   D. calibration

9. Which of the following terms refers to process colors printed with more than four process colors?

   A. Spot colors

   B. Web safe colors

   C. HiFi colors

   D. Pantone colors

10. How many colors are there in the Web safe color palette?

    A. 16.7 million

    B. 16 thousand

    C. 256

    D. 216

11. What are the basic components of calibration?

    A. Linearization

    B. Neutralization

    C. Matching input and output values

    D. All of the above

12. Which of the following is a component of a color management system?

    A. Sophisticated color targets

    B. Analytical hardware and software

    C. Color profiles

    D. All of the above

Check Your Understanding

Concept Questions

To help you review and expand your thinking on the topics covered in this chapter, answer the following questions.

1. What is meant by the statement: "There is no such thing as a color computer?"

2. Explain the difference between spot and process color. Which colors are usually used to print contone images and why?

3. What are Web Safe colors? When should we use them and why?

4. What is HSV is for?

5. What are the differences between RGB and CMYK color spaces? Explain where each color space is typically used.

6. What are the best tools to use for choosing colors to assign to objects for printing? Explain briefly how these tools are used.

7. To what does the term "gamut conversion" refer? Give an example of a typical gamut conversion.

8. What are linearization and neutralization? Why are they important?

9. What is color management and why is it necessary?

10. What is meant by "closed loop calibration? What tools are necessary to accomplish this?

PROJECTS

1. Create a new one page document in a page layout application like QuarkXPress, PageMaker or InDesign. Create three rectangles in this document. Using swatch books, assign a spot color (185) to the first rectangle, a process color to the second rectangle, and a 185 ProSim or solid to process color to the third rectangle. Print this document as separations to a desktop black and white laser printer. Note how many separations print.

2. Create a new vector graphic in a drawing application such as Illustrator or FreeHand. Create a circle. Using a spot color swatch book, assign the spot color 2577 to the circle. Save this document out as a vector Eps graphic file. Place this graphic in the one page document you created above. Look at the page layout document color palette. Note any changes. Print this document as separations to a desktop black and white laser printer. Note how many separations print now. Compare and contrast these separations with those you printed in Project 1.

15
Weaving Web Graphics

As the Byte Turns continues…

Will Danny D'Ziner and Pauline E. Prepress weave their way through the wonderland of Web graphics…or will they get waylaid in the spider Web of too much file size and not enough speed?

Woah! What happened to the images I put on my Web page? Why do they take so long for me to be able to see them…? What do you mean that my bit depth and resolution are too high, and my pixel dimension is too large??

Well let's see now, UMM?

Well you see…it's like this…

Oh heck I don't know. Pauline…HELP!

Creating images for use on the Web is a whole different proposition than creating print images. Our focus needs to be on creating "fast" images, while trying to preserve image quality.

Chapter Objectives

In this chapter you will learn:

- ◆ **Similarities and differences between print and Web graphics**
- ◆ **Converting print graphics into Web graphics**
- ◆ **Creating Web graphics**
- ◆ **Using index and Web safe colors**
- ◆ **The need for speed**
- ◆ **Key Terms**
  - • File size
  - • Pixel dimensions
  - • Resolution
  - • Index color
  - • GIF
  - • JPEG
  - • Progressive JPEG
  - • ShockWave
  - • Lossy and lossless compression
  - • Web safe colors
  - • Adaptive color
  - • Dithering

INTRODUCTION

Increasingly we are creating graphics for multiple uses, including print and Web. While the topic of Web graphics is worthy of an entire book, this chapter will serve as an introduction to the topic, so that you can understand the requirements and know the techniques for creating Web and print graphics. The Internet, and its multimedia component the World Wide Web, is a constantly and rapidly changing, highly integrated world wide network. While originally designed for text transmissions only, the recent and rapidly expanding multimedia demands we are placing on this network have been and continue to represent a challenge. The requirements for outputting Web graphics are quite different than producing graphics for print. Web graphics requirements are governed by the requirements of transmitting graphics across the Internet followed by output on a monitor. The joint Internet/monitor requirements usually involve creation or recreation of our graphics utilizing: 1) smaller sizes, 2) lower **resolutions**, 3) reduced bit depth, 4) the application of image compression and 5) saving images in Web compatible formats. Image transmission and viewing speed are of utmost concern when we create a Web graphic. Until the bandwidth of the Internet and our compression technologies improve significantly we are often faced with making speed vs. quality judgments. The techniques we employ and the order in which we apply them can often have significant impact on the final quality of our images. When we create our graphics files for one purpose, it usually behooves us to keep in mind the other uses for which an image may be used.

THE WEB CHALLENGE

The basic challenge of Web graphics

When creating or converting graphics for use on the World Wide Web we must always keep in mind how our Web graphics are being delivered or output. Instead of being printed, our graphics are being sent across the Internet and displayed or output on someone's monitor. This represents a far different challenge than outputting to a printing device. So there are really two fundamental parts to the challenge of Web graphics. The first challenge is getting your images across the Internet and into someone's computer. The second challenge is controlling how these images will display when they arrive. Our emphasis on the first challenge has to be speed. Our focus needs to be on preparing our images so that they can be rapidly transferred across the Internet. For the second challenge, we want to maintain the original quality and appearance of our images as much as possible.

Internet and the World Wide Web

The word Internet grew out of the general concept of networks. A network is a series of computers linked together. A network can be as simple as two computer devices connected by one cable, or can contain thousands of computers with various types of connections. The first networks were primarily limited to connecting various computers and peripherals to each other in a single office. This was known as a local area network, or LAN. Then we began to connect several local area networks and we called those wide area networks, or WANs. As we began to connect even more widely spaced networks, such as a network which connected all the computers in an individual organization or company which might be located in various places around the world, we devised the name intranet. The logical evolution of this process of network growth and integration was to eventually begin connecting computers all over the world. This world wide network began mostly as a network for the U.S. government and universities to exchange information, and was designed primarily to transmit text files. This loose connection of government and university networks eventually evolved into what we call the Internet.

Once the Internet started growing out into the private sector, we began to want to do more with the Internet. We wanted to transfer more than just text files. We wanted to be able to send and share graphics and sounds and multimedia. To accommodate this growing request to handle other media besides text, servers and protocol were developed to handle graphics and sounds. This multiple media portion of the Internet became the fastest growing portion. We call this the World Wide Web. The reason for this quick history lesson is to point out that the original purpose and use of the Internet was to transfer text files. It has rapidly grown into a multiple media network. As we learned in Chapter 6, "Bits and Bytes," graphics files are much larger than text files and therefore will take longer to transfer across a network. Therein lies the basis for our first fundamental challenge, getting graphics and sound files across a network which was originally designed primarily to handle text files. Our desire to send large files has rapidly outrun our ability to upgrade the speed of our networks.

The Internet/World Wide Web "super highway"

The Internet is often referred to a the digital highway or super highway. This analogy is useful from the standpoint of the Internet as an information pathway, but a bit misleading, at least now, in terms of the images which the words highway or super highway conger up. In terms of speed, for the average Web user, the Internet is more like a back country road rather than a super highway, great for a leisurely Sunday drive, but not very conducive to getting somewhere fast.

As mentioned, the Internet is a collection of thousands of interconnected networks, each one being controlled by a different network server. The World Wide Web is a Web of connections between these computer networks which are capable of exchanging multiple media files. There are typically many different ways to get to the same destination on the Internet. While it is true that some portions of the Internet are very fast, there are many pathways which are very slow. The path which your images take across the Internet will vary with each time they are sent. Sometimes they travel along fast pathways; other times they may encounter slow sections. The path is unpredictable (see Fig. 15.1).

Add to this uncertainty the impact of other network traffic. Like any road or highway the more traffic you put on it, the more slowly the individual pieces move. In rush hour, speeds diminish to a crawl. This is true for computer networks as well as automobiles. The speed at which a file is transferred will largely be controlled by the slowest link in the network chain and the other demands being placed on the network. It is because of this wide variability in network speed and the uncertainty of the network route and traffic that we must pay close attention to the time it takes to send our files across the Internet.

▼ Figure 15.1 Web Connections

The World Wide Web is an interconnected Web of servers and computer networks which are connected in a variety of ways with various speed connections. One time your Web graphic file may take a straight line path from your Web server directly to your client/viewer. Another time it may take a more circuitous path through other Internet servers.

The speed with which your graphic file can be transferred across the Web will depend upon the size of the graphic, the route that it takes and the other network traffic which is already there. It therefore behooves us to reduce the size of our graphics as much as possible.

The Web lexicon

When we begin working with Web graphics we add a few new terms and concepts to our electronic publishing lexicon. But don't despair: All the older terms and concepts of resolution, file formats, the building blocks of pixels and vectors, etc., still apply. In fact the fundamentals that you learned in print publishing form a terrific foundation for learning Web graphics terms and concepts. When we work with Web graphics we will use a new color space term called **index color** space. We add a few new file formats, **GIF**, **JPEG** and **SWF** to our list. We will be compressing our files more with both **lossy** and **lossless** compression. We will be working with Web color palettes and using file smoothing techniques like **dithering**. All of these concepts will build on the digital fundamental base that you already have.

Web site server   Web client/viewer computer

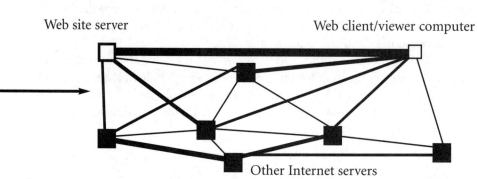

Other Internet servers

PRINT VS. WEB GRAPHICS

The need for speed

There are several key differences between preparing graphics for print and the WEB. These key differences include: physical dimension, resolution, file format, compression, color space (bit depth), image quality, and **file size**. These differences are largely determined by the nature of the devices on which the images are output, and the network over which we send those graphics to be output.

WEB output devices

When we output print graphics they are typically output on devices that have resolutions which range from hundreds to thousands of spots/dots per inch. Web graphics by contrast are output on monitors which are comparatively low resolution, usually in the range of 72 ppi to 96 ppi, with 72 ppi being the most common (see Fig. 15.2). A 72 ppi monitor requires a much lower resolution graphic than the higher resolution print devices. Here again, we use the concept of the resolution of the output device controlling the resolution of the input device. Monitors also tend to be less demanding in terms of image quality than high resolution printing devices, so we can often get by with displaying lower quality images on our monitors than we we would find acceptable for print. Because monitors tend to have smaller viewing areas than many printing devices, and also because larger graphics take much longer to transfer than smaller images, our Web graphic images tend to be smaller than print images.

WEB network

The networks over which we send Web graphics tend to have much less bandwidth and are therefore much slower than networks over which we print our images. As we discussed earlier the bandwidth and speed of the Internet varies widely, but an average practical speed which we can count on seems to be about 28,800 bits/sec (kb/s). Local area print networks, while they also vary in bandwidth and speed, tend to average at least 1,000,000 bits/sec (1MB/sec). This means that on average transferring files over the Internet is about thirty five times (35x) slower than local area print networks. Add to this enormous speed difference the fact that the person who is accessing our Web site is sitting there waiting for one of our Web pages to appear on their screen, and we have a real incentive to get our images there as fast as possible.

WEB color space: index color

The color space we use for both RGB monitor viewing and CMYK printing contains 16.7 million colors (24 bit color space). While many monitors can display millions of colors, some monitors cannot: They can only displays hundreds or thousands of colors. The operating systems of our desktop computers have the built-in ability to display 256, or 8 bits of color. Therefore, the current preferred color space for the WEB is restricted to 256 colors. This 256 (8 bit) value color space is known as index color. Index color gets its name from the 256 value color tables which are built in to the operating systems of all Mac- and Windows-based

▼ *Figure 15.2 Monitor Output*

The concept of preparing graphics for the device on which they will be output works just as well for the Web as is does for print. When preparing graphics for use in a Web page remember that the typical output device is a 72 ppi monitor which typically displays thousands of colors. Older monitors may only display 256 colors, but those are being rapidly replaced by devices which display thousands or millions of colors.

computers. These Mac and Windows palettes are known as system palettes. To display larger color space images, such as RGB images, as fast and as consistently as possible, they may need to be indexed to the 256 color system palettes of the computers on which they display. While many of our images which we display over the Web, such as color contones, may have thousands or millions of colors and be saved in a 24 bit color space file format such as JPEG, we need to be aware that these colors may be forced into a smaller 8 bit 256 color space, or take longer to display as the image colors outside of the built-in 256 color 8 bit system palette will need to be generated on the fly. Often the additional time requirement is worth the increase in quality for contone images but rarely for line art or other flat color images. There is often a tradeoff between speed and quality over the Web.

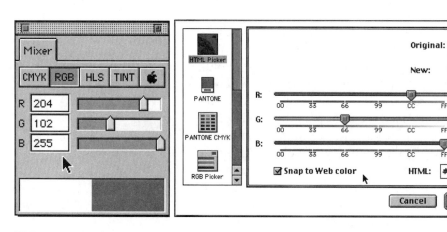

▼ **Figure 15.3 RGB vs. HTML Color Values**

We are used to using RGB (left) or CMYK values when we work in applications such as Photoshop, Illustrator, or FreeHand. When assigning colors to objects which will be used on the Web, HTML values (right), instead of RGB values, are used to designate colors. THe HTML designation of CC 66 FF would be the HTML equivalent of RGB values of 204, 102, 255. Most HTML color pickers, such as the one shown here will allow you to restrict your HTML color value choices to the Web safe colors. In this FreeHand dialog box the color choices are restricted to Web safe colors by clicking on the Snap to Web color check box in the lower left hand corner (see Fig. C.27 on page C-14 in the color plates section of this book for a color version of this figure).

To add a bit more confusion to this concept of 8bit system palettes, we need to keep in mind that Mac and Windows operating systems do not have the same 256 colors in their system palettes. So we are faced with the decision of assigning colors by choosing either the Macintosh or Windows based 256 index color palette. Luckily, there are 216 colors which are common to both the Windows and the Mac system palette. This Mac and Windows common palette is commonly called the Web or **Web safe color** palette or sometimes the Netscape palette. So, if we want to assign colors which will redraw quickly and dependably on both Mac and Windows computers we can assign colors which are on common Web safe palettes(see Fig. 15.3).

Rather than using standard RGB values for colors that we assign for use on the Web, we use hexadecimal color values that we assign through HTML code values. We still have a three part naming system as in RGB, but we use HTML designations instead of RGB values. For instance, a color with RGB values of R=204, B=102, G=165 would have HTML designations of CC66FF. See Fig 15.3 for an example of Web color palette. Most HTML color pickers, such as the Macromedia FreeHand color picker shown in Fig 15.3, allow you to restrict your HTML color designation to the Web safe colors. The use of Web safe colors is often used to assign colors to flat colored objects such as logos, graphs and line art. The Web safe colors are less commonly used to rebuild color contone images, because the the 216 color palette often proves to be too restrictive for all the color values found in a typical color contone image. Use of the Web safe colors to build color images often results in posterization.

File formats for the WEB

Web graphic images have the same choice of image building blocks or contents that print images do, that is pixels and vectors. But the output devices and networks over which we transfer and view our images require different containers, or file formats, for the image building blocks. Whereas print images will usually be packaged in TIFF or EPS file formats, Web graphics are stored in GIF (Graphic Interchange Format), JPEG (Joint Photographic Expert Group), PNG (Portable Network Graphic) and SWF (Shock Wave) formats. Just as TIFF and EPS formats are optimized for PostScript printing, GIF, JPEG, PNG and SWF are optimized for Web transfer. Images stored in in formats other than GIF, JPEG, PNG or SWF tend not to work well when used over the Internet/Web. Browsers such as Netscape Navigator, Internet Explore and AOL are designed to accept the Web formats and will usually not accept other file formats. Even transferring graphic images in non-Web graphic file formats can result in corruption of the images.

 **TIP**

The key to creating effective and useful Web graphic images is to reduce the size of the graphics so that they will transfer and view quickly over the Web. Reducing image dimension, resolution, and bit depth, while employing compression, can effectively lower the file size of an image to affect rapid Internet transfer. However, lower file sizes using these methods often result in image quality degradation. We must decide how much image quality we are willing to sacrifice in order to enhance speed of transfer.

GIF and JPEG file formats are the two most commonly used graphics file formats for pixel based images. The SWF format is used for vector based images and is commonly used in animations as well. PNG can be used for pixel-based images, but as of the writing of this book is used less commonly than GIF and JPEG. The GIF format is limited to a maximum of eight bits per pixel (8b/p) and therefore can store a maximum of 256 colors. This 8 bit maximum color space known as index color JPEG can store a full twenty four bits per pixel (24b/p) and can therefore store up to a full 16.7 million colors. Because of its 256 color restriction, the GIF file format is used most commonly for holding flat color images such as logos, graphs and line art images. The JPEG file format, with its full color capabilities, is used most commonly for RGB continuous tone images such as color photographs and gradient colors. JPEG is less often used for flat color images as the additional color bit depth, and therefore file size, is not needed, and the JPEG compression algorithm creates unwanted artifacts along high contrast edges in line art and type.

Compression

When we work with print images we usually try to avoid compressing our images. Compressing our print images often interferes with the viewing and printing of our images, and can also unacceptably lower their quality. With Web-based images the reverse is true: We nearly always compress our images. Image compression offers the enormous benefit of significantly reducing image file size, which in turn reduces transfer times.

(A)

0% Compression 2.0 MB
Transmit time = 556 sec*

(B)

2/1 LZW Compression 1.0 MB
Transmit time = 278 sec*

(C)

5/1 JPEG Compression 400KB
Transmit time = 111 sec*

 (D)

50/1 JPEG Compression 40KB
Transmit time = 11 sec*

▼ *Figure 15.4 Image Compression*

Image compression is used to reduce large image file sizes (A) and transmission times. Two types of image compression are available, lossless and lossy. Lossless image compression, such as LZW, has no image data loss, but a maximum of 2/1 compression (B).

With lossy compression, such as JPEG, image data is lost, but much greater image compression ratios are possible. JPEG typically offer a range of 5/1 (C) to 100/1 compression (D).

Higher compression ratios create smaller file sizes, which allow for faster transmission time, but also result in greater loss of image data . Transmit times are calculated at 28,000b/sec.

There are two kinds of compression, lossless and lossy. Lossless compression guarantees that there will be no loss of image content or quality during the compression and decompression process. Lossless compression is limited to a maximum of 2 to 1, or 50% compression. With lossy compression, as the name implies, there will be loss of image data and therefore quality. But the tradeoff benefit is that much more compression is possible. The GIF format employs a lossless compression called LZW compression. Gif files can have up to 50% compression and therefore as much as a 50% reduction in file size. This maximum compression can usually only be realized in one or two color images where there are many redundant pixel values. Contone images such as grayscale and color photographs, which do not have a large percentage of redundant or identical pixels, will typically exhibit only 10–15% lossless compression. The JPEG format offers an extensive range of lossy compression. JPEG compression varies between 5/1 and 100/1 compression. Higher compression ratios result in smaller file size, and therefore faster file transfer over the Internet. However, higher compression ratios also result in greater image quality degradation (see Fig. 15.4).

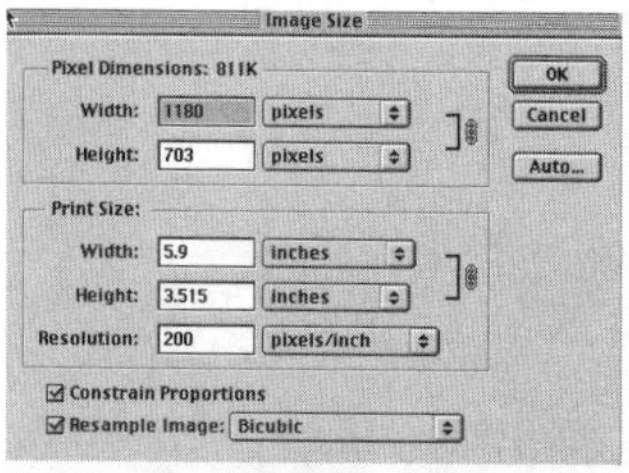

Quality vs. Speed

There is definitely a tradeoff between image quality and the speed at which an image can be transferred over the Internet. In the world of print, image quality nearly always takes precedent over the speed of output. We are typically willing to wait a bit longer for an image to print, if it means that we will have better quality. Plus, we can do something else while our image is printing. In the world of the Web the emphasis is the opposite. In order to enhance the speed of transfer we are typically willing to sacrifice some image quality. The rationale is simple: We would rather have thousands of people look at and enjoy our B to B+ quality images rather than a few dozen people who are willing to wait around to see our A to A+ images. We each have to decide how much image quality degradation we are willing to accept. The key then is to maximize the speed of image transfer while minimizing the loss of image quality.

TIP

Reducing file size is a key to creating images which rapidly transmit across the Internet and redraw quickly on screen. Reducing file size usually involves a combination of the reduction of image size, resolution and pixel depth, as well as the application of some form of compression. The order in which these various adjustments is applied is critical to maintaining as much image quality as possible. Image size and resolution adjustment should be made first, prior to the application of any bit depth reduction or compression application, in order to keep as much image quality as possible.

PREPARING GRAPHICS FOR THE WEB

Many of the images you use on your Web pages will be converted from images used for printing. When we convert an image which is also used for printing we need to customize the image for use on the Web. As discussed above, our emphasis is usu

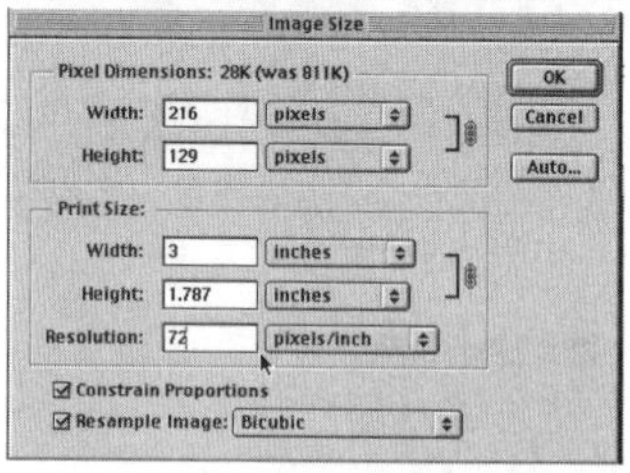

▼ Figure 15.5 Image File Size Reduction

Print quality images usually need to have their **pixel dimensions** and resolution reduced for preparation for use on the Web.

Reducing image size and resolution can significantly decrease the file size of an image, thereby making it more Web compatible. As seen above the starting image (A) above was 811K with a image dimension of 5.9" x 3.5 " at 200 ppi.

After lowering the image dimension of 3.0" x 1.8" and the resolution to 72 ppi, the file size is reduced to a more manageable 28K (B).

For best image quality, when adjusting images for the Web, reduce image dimension and resolution of an image first, prior to reducing the pixel depth or applying unsharpmask or compression to the image.

ally on reducing file size to promote rapid file transfer across the Internet. This customization usually involves a combination of image adjustments which involve adjusting several if not all of the following.

- Physical dimensions: Usually reduced to $\leq 6^2$" (2" x 3") (see Fig. 15.4)
- Resolution: Reduce to 72 ppi (see Fig. 15.4)
- Color space (bit depth): Lower to 8 b/p or below for flat color images
- Compression: Significant compression especially for color contone images
- File format: Change to a Web friendly format such as GIF, JPEG, PNG or SWF. Note: At the time of the writing of this book the PNG is not widely recognized by most browsers, but it is a very flexible format which may be used more in the future. It is a good candidate to replace the GIF format.

Web file formats

The file format you choose for your Web graphics images depends upon the type of image you have. Following is an overview of Web graphics file formats, their characteristics, and their common image type uses:

- GIF: Graphic Interchange Format (.gif)
  - ≤8 bits pixel based
  - LZW compression (lossless)
  - 72–96ppi
  - Used for flat color line art and grayscale contone images

- GIF89a: Graphic Interchange Format version 89a (.gif)
  - Similar to basic GIF, but also supports transparency
  - ≤8 bits pixel based
  - LZW compression (lossless)
  - 72–96 ppi
  - Used for flat color line art and grayscale contone images

- JPEG: Joint Photographic Expert Group (.jpg)
  - 24 bits pixel based
  - Various compressions (lossy)
  - 72 – 96 ppi
  - Used for grayscale and color contone images

- PNG: Portable Network Graphics (.png)
  - 2 to 32 bits pixel based (including 8 bit alpha channel)
  - Various compressions (lossless)
  - 72 – 96 ppi
  - Used for flat color line art, grayscale and color contone images (less widely used than GIF and JPEG)

- Flash: **ShockWave** Format (.swf)
  - 2–32 bits per pixel
  - Vector images
  - Resolution independent
  - Low files size images
  - Animation

Note: See the appendix in the back of this book for a complete description of the various file formats used in electronic publishing.

Index color space

The pixel/bit depth (bits per pixel) of an image controls numbers of colors or shades of gray which an image will contain. As bit depth decreases so does file size. Our object is usually to reduce bit depth as much as possible without reducing the visible image quality below an acceptable amount. Image quality is subjective, so you will need to make your own judgment as to what is acceptable. Below is a list of bit depth vs. numbers of shades of gray/colors supported.

- Conversion to index color maps 24-bit, 16.7 million to 8-bit, 256 colors
- 8 bit = 256 colors
- 7 bit =128 colors
- 6 bit color = 64 colors
- 5 bit colors = 32 colors
- 8 bit Netscape colors = 216 common to Mac and Windows palettes (6 x 6 x 6)

Adaptive color palettes

When you create an index color image you will usually have a choice of color spaces to choose from. Common color space choices include Mac, Windows, Web safe, and **Adaptive colors**. The Mac and Windows color spaces contain the predetermined 256 colors built in to each operating system. The Web safe palette includes the 216 colors which are common to both the Mac and Windows color palettes. If you choose a common color palette, the Web safe palette would be the best choice since it contains colors common to both the Mac and Windows operating systems. The advantage to using colors common to both operating systems is more consistent color display and faster screen redraw. The adaptive color palette will force your application to create a custom color palette using the colors which already exist in the image which is being indexed. The advantage of using the adaptive color palette is two-fold. First, the colors in the final indexed color image will be truer to the original image. Second, the use of an adaptive color palette will allow a reduced pixel depth while still maintaing good image quality, and therefore smaller file size. When creating a flat colored line art Web image from scratch for the Web, it is best to use Web safe colors. When indexing previously created multicolor contone images, such as color photographic type images and even multicolor line art images, it is best to use adaptive color palettes.

▼ **Figure 15.6 Flat Colored Images**

Logos and other flat colored images typically have few colors and are therefore good candidates for being converted into index colored images. These image are commonly saved in GIF format for use on the Web. Use of the Web safe colors is often appropriate here.

This screen capture is a portion of Photoshop's "Save for Web" dialog box. This, and similar Web graphic specific tools in other applications, allows you to experiment with various file variables such as file formats, color spaces, compression ratios, and dithering options, and view the effects of these choices on the fly. These Web graphic specific tools and dialog boxes will often also provide you with estimated download times as well, so you can evaluate the tradeoffs of image quality vs. download speed.

CONVERTING PIXEL IMAGES

Following are some guidelines for converting various kinds of pixel-based print images for use in Web pages.

Flat color image conversions steps

Examples of flat colored images include: Logos, many line art images, cartoons, type-based images, consistent backgrounds, low detail images in general.

Conversion tips:

1. Open a pixel-based image in Photoshop or other pixel-based image editing application. (See section below about original vector-based flat art images.)
2. Create a working duplicated copy of image for conversion
3. Resize image to small size (≤2x3)
4. Set resolution to 72–96 ppi
5. Convert to index color
6. Assign Web palette colors (216 colors), or small bit depth adaptive. If you use **adaptive colors** try adaptive mode with 2–5 bit (see Fig. 15.6).
7. Do not use **dithering** (see Fig. 15.6)
8. Save as GIF
9. Select Normal row order in GIF options dialog box

Vector line art image note

If your line art or logo image is a vector image you can save the image as a GIF file directly out of a drawing application such as FreeHand and Illustrator, which will often result in good, sharp-edged images. You also may convert this image into a pixel-based image by opening it in an application such as Photoshop. This image can then be prepared for Web use, using the steps and techniques described above. Alternatively, vector-based images can be converted directly into ShockWave format (.swf) files. The SWF format supports the display of vector-based images over the Web. See the section on converting vector based images for Web use later in this chapter.

Grayscale contone conversion steps

1. Open image in Photoshop or other pixel-based image editing application
2. Create a working duplicated copy of image for conversion
3. Resize image to small size: Create your images at the size you will use them and try to keep their sizes below 2" x 3".
4. Set resolution to 72–96 ppi
5. Reduce number of shades of gray to 32 (5 bit) (see Fig. 15.7)
6. Deselect Interlacing

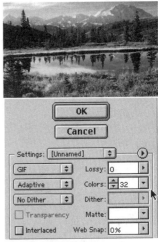

▼ *Figure 15.7 Grayscale Images*

Grayscale images can be converted into 5 bit GIF (32 shades of gray) with little noticeable reduction in on-screen image quality. JPEG is also an option but not always necessary for grayscale contone images.

7. Save as GIF

8. Save without low preview

Grayscale contone conversion option

Option: Consider saving your images as 1 bit (B&W) images with diffusion dither. Again GIF is the best format to use here.

Note: All contones do not have to be saved as 24 bit JPEG images. Using GIFs reduces file size and improves speed of viewing performance. And, in the case of grayscale contone images, we do not suffer any noticeable image degradation problems when we view the images.

Color contone conversion steps

1. Open image in Photoshop or other pixel-based image editing application

2. Create a working duplicated copy of image for conversion

3. Crop the image to optimal content

4. Resize image to small size ($\leq$2 x 3)

5. Set resolution to 72 ppi

6. Choose Save as JPEG

7. Experiment with quality level (average approximately 5 out of 12 or 30 out of 100) Larger higher detail images require higher quality levels (see Fig. 15.8)

8. Assign **Progressive JPEG** with three steps

Note: I generally convert color contones to JPEG format due to their higher bit depth and therefore higher quality. This higher bit depth means larger file size and slower redraw. The file size can be reduced by using a higher compression ratio. Experiment with compression ratios to see where the quality drops too low during viewing.

Color contone image conversion option

1. Create another working duplicated copy of image for conversion

2. Crop the image to optimal content

3. Resize image to small size ($\leq$2 x 3)

4. Set resolution to 72–96 ppi

5. Instead of JPEG we will choose GIF

6. Assign adaptive palette colors (256 colors taken from image. This will give us a better color match of the original image)

7. Reduce the bit depth of the image until the image begins to degrade, usually 5–6 bits per pixel (32-64 colors)

8. Applying diffusion dithering here may will improve tone and color transitions in the image but can also increase the redraw time. Experiment.

9. Choose Save As GIF

10. Select Interlaced row order in GIF options dialog box

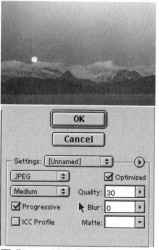

▼ *Figure 15.8 Color Image*

Color images can be saved as 24 bit JPEG with medium to medium-high compression while still maintaining high enough on-screen viewing quality. On the fly results of your choice of format, compression, dithering, etc., can be seen in Photoshop's Save for Web option dialog box shown here.

Tip: If one portion of a color contone image is more important than other portions, such as a face in a portrait, select that portion of the image prior to bit depth reduction. Colors from the selected area will be more densely represented in the final reduced color palette, thereby reducing posterization of that critical image area. This allows for lower bit depths, while greatly enhancing the final quality of critical image areas.

Tool Note: Use of the Save For Web tool in Photoshop (Fig. 15.8) allows you to see the results of your choices of file format, compression amount, dithering and other variables on the fly. Tools such as this, which can also be found in applications such as Macromedia's Fireworks and Adobe's ImageReady, take much of the guesswork out of creating Web images.

Image with transparent background

🔸 Open an image with a solid background in Photoshop or other pixel-based image editing application

🔸 Resize image to small size (2" x 3")

🔸 Set resolution to 72–96 ppi

🔸 Convert to index color. Use index color w/ 2–5 bit adaptive palette, no dithering

🔸 Export as GIF 89a

🔸 Select transparent area with eye dropper

Masking alternative

🔸 Open image in Photoshop

🔸 Select areas you want to become transparent in Web image

🔸 Save the selection as an alpha channel mask

🔸 Export as GIF 89a

🔸 Load mask of areas to define transparency (see Fig. 15.9)

🔸 Assign transparency index color

🔸 Netscape = 192R, 192G and 192B

🔸 Try this with a color contone with a mask using adaptive index colors

Tool note: Photoshop 5.5 also offers a background eraser tool and an Extract Command tool which are very useful in removing backgrounds.

Assigning Colors for the Web

If you are constructing a graphic such as a logo or line art graphic which will be used specifically for viewing on the Web, it is generally advantageous to assign colors from the 216 color Web safe palette. See Fig. 15.3 for an example of a Web Safe color palette. Using the Web safe color set to assign your colors will provide you with more consistent color reproduction and faster screen viewing of your images. If the color of a logo or other image is too different than the colors available in the 216 Web safe palette, you may want to use an adaptive palette instead. The adaptive palette will use colors from the image and provide a better match, but still may not appear consistently on multiple monitors.

▼ *Figure 15.9 Controlling Transparency*

One way to control transparency is to export an image as a GIF89a, which supports transparent image area in an image. The transparent areas can be controlled either by selecting the areas using a magic wand in the Export dialog box, or by creating and applying a transparency mask, as shown above. Using the transparency mask to control image transparency usually provides you with more flexibility, better control and higher quality results.

CONVERTING VECTOR IMAGES

Shockwave and Flash vs. pixels and GIF

Many line art and logo images are originally constructed as vector-based images in order to take advantage of the scalability and editability of vectors. As described earlier, you may convert these vector images into a pixel-based image by opening it in a pixel-based application such as Photoshop. An image so converted can then be prepared for Web use using the steps and techniques described earlier in the Flat colored image conversions steps section. Alternatively, vector-based images can be converted directly into ShockWave format (.swf) files. The SWF format supports the display of vector based images over the Web. SWF was developed by Macromedia Corporation specifically for using vector-based images on the Web. Historically, nearly all Web page images were pixel based, because Web browsers did not support the viewing of vector-based images. The development of the Shockwave format allows us to take advantage of the small size, and therefore transmission and viewing speed, of vector-based images over the Web.

Shockwave format image can be exported out of traditional drawing applications such as Macromedia FreeHand or created directly in an application called Flash®, also produced by Macromedia. Flash and .swf format files are increasingly being used to create vector-based Web graphics and becoming the application and file format of choice for creating animated files for display over the Web. The small size and scalability of the vector-based .swf file makes it a perfect vehicle for delivering animation files over the Web.

Note: One word of caution. While SWF files are rapidly becoming the file format of choice for flat colored line art images and animated graphics on the Web, many earlier versions of Web browsers do not support the viewing of SWF files. Web browsers that do not support the SWF format can be enhanced to accept SWF files through the downloading of SWF plug-ins. This downloading can be a time-consuming process. If you use SWF files, be sure your audience will be able to view them. A good Web page construction plan, at least until the older versions of browsers are retired, is to provide a combination of pixel-based images which nearly everyone can view, and some SWF files which viewers with more recent browsers can view and enjoy.

Testing your images

Low bit depth viewing

You should get into the habit of testing your images before final placement in your Web site pages. Remember, while most monitors used to view Web images now support at least thousands of colors, a significant number of older monitors only support the display of a maximum of 8 bits per pixel, or 256 colors. So for maximum flexibility you might want to test viewing your Web images at 8 bits per pixel.

Browser and platform testing

You can expect that your Web pages will not appear exactly the same from one computer and/or browser to another. Art work can shift and font characteristics may change. These variations should be taken into account during the design process, and it is one of the reasons why keeping your Web pages simple is a good idea. It is also a good idea to test view your images on both Mac and PC computers and with a variety of browsers. It is a good idea to test the viewability of your images on the top three Web browsers, which currently include: Netscape Navigator, Windows Internet Explorer, and AOL. Keep in mind that earlier versions of browsers do not support all of the most recent Web graphics file format versions and functions. To ensure that the maximum number of people can load and view your images, it is best to construct the core parts of your Web pages with simple universally compatible Web images and components.

Image conversion fundamentals review

Web image fundamentals overview

- Keep image dimension ≤ 2" x 3", set resolution = 72 ppi
- Keep pixel depth ≤ 8 bit whenever possible
- Use 216 Web safe palette for new images, but use adaptive 5 bit to lower file size and improve image quality for many flat color conversions
- No dithering on flat colors, but may improve tonal transitions in contones
- Use 5 bit GIF (32 gray shades) for saving grayscale contones
- Use JPEG for most high detail color contone images (experiment with compression and go as low as you can). JPEG will usually produce smaller file sizes than GIG for contone images. But also try 5 bit adaptive GIFs to increase image quality and improve image speed, especially on 8 bit monitors
- Select the most critical portion of contone images prior to bit reduction to allow lower bit depths and improve the quality of critical image areas
- Use GIF 89a to preserve transparency in images
- Remember, *do not* save image previews when creating Web graphics
- View graphics in 8-bit video and the three major browsers to test images

MULTIPURPOSE GRAPHICS

If you create or capture images which you intend to use with multiple output devices, it is best to create images for the most demanding output device, and then create copies of those images and reconfigure them for the additional uses. The most demanding use, that is highest quality, resolution and bit depth, will often be commercial printing. As we have seen throughout this book, commercial print images demand uncompressed 200–300 ppi, 32 bit/pixel images. When creating images to be used for both print and Web you may find the following list helpful.

1. Create 200–300 ppi uncompressed RGB images as core images
2. Create a copy which will be converted to CMYK TIFF or EPS format for print
3. Create a copy which will be sized, resolution sampled, and compressed down for use as GIF, JPEG or SWF format images on the Web
4. Save the original uncompressed RGB image as an archive image for later use

CHAPTER SUMMARY

The World Wide Web is a constantly and rapidly changing highly integrated world wide network. The Internet was originally designed just for transmission of small text files. With the recent development and rapid growth of the multimedia Web, these constantly increasing demands have been and continue to represent a challenge. The requirements for outputting graphics are quite different than producing graphics for print. Web graphics requirements are governed by the requirements of transmitting graphics across the Internet followed by output on a monitor. The joint Internet/monitor requirements usually involve creation or recreation of our graphics utilizing: 1) smaller sizes (typically 2" x 3" or smaller), 2) lower resolutions (generally 72 ppi), 3) reduced bit depth (index color, ≤ 8 bits/pixel, for flat color and grayscale images), 4) the application of image compression (LZW and JPEG) and 5) saving images in Web compatible formats (GIF, PNG, JPEG, SWF). Image transmission and viewing speed are of utmost concern when we create a Web graphic. Until the Internet bandwidth and compression technologies improve significantly, we are often faced with making speed vs. quality judgments. The techniques we employ and order in which we apply them can often have significant impact on the final quality of our images. When we create our graphic files for one purpose, it usually behooves us to keep in mind the other uses for which an image may be used. As a general rule, we should create graphics for the highest quality and highest resolution use, which is often commercial printing, and then repurpose our images by customizing them for other uses, such as for display on the Web.

PAULINE'S DIGITAL IMAGING TIPS

Pauline's Tip 15.1

The key to creating effective and useful Web graphic images is to reduce the size of the graphics so that they will transfer and view quickly over the Web. Reducing image dimension, resolution, and bit depth while employing compression can effectively lower the file size of an image to affect rapid Internet transfer. However, lower file size using these methods often results in image quality degradation. We must each decide how much image quality we are willing to sacrifice in order to enhance speed of transfer.

Pauline's Tip 15.2

Reducing file size is a key to creating images which rapidly transmit across the Internet and redraw on screen. Reducing file size usually involves a combination deduction of image size, resolution and pixel depth as well as the application of some form of compression. The order in which these various adjustments are applied is critical to maintaining as much image quality as possible. Image size and resolution adjustment should be made first prior to the application of any bit depth reduction of compression application, in order to keep as much image quality as possible.

Pauline's Tip 15.3

It is a good habit to test your images prior to final placement in your Web pages on your Web site. Image testing should involve: 1) Testing the image quality at low viewing bit depths (8 bits per pixel), 2) viewing your images on both Mac and Windows computers, and 3) testing the loading and viewing of your images on at least the three most commonly used browsers: Netscape Navigator, Windows Internet Explorer, and AOL. A good rule of thumb is to build the core of your Web pages with simple, universally compatible Web page components.

Pauline's Tip 15.4

If you create or capture images you intend to use with multiple output devices, it is best to create images for the most demanding output device, and then create copies of those images and reformat them for the other uses. The most demanding use, that is highest quality, resolution and bit depth will often be commercial printing requiring uncompressed 200–300 ppi, 32 bits/pixel images. Web images can be reformatted from the higher quality images to accommodate the typically compressed, 72 ppi, often ≤ 8 bits/pixel images.

CHAPTER REVIEW

Check Your Comprehension

Multiple Choice Questions

To help you review the topics covered in this chapter answer the following multiple choice questions.

1. The Internet was originally designed to transmit
   A. Graphics files
   B. Multimedia files
   C. Text files
   D. Sound files

2. Which of the following do print and Web graphics have in common?
   A. File size
   B. Resolution
   C. Pixel depth
   D. Pixel and vector components

3. In which of the following do print and Web graphics differ?
   A. File size
   B. Resolution
   C. Pixel depth
   D. All of the above

4. Which of the following has only 8 bits/pixel or fewer?
   A. RGB color
   B. Index color
   C. CMYK color
   D.   Print graphics

5. Pixel-based flat color line art images are typically saved as which of the following formats for use on the Web?
   A. EPS
   B. GIF
   C. JPEG
   D. SWF

6. _____ can be saved as 5 bit/pixel GIF files with little loss of monitor image quality.

    A. RGB color contone images

    B. CMYK color contone images

    C. Grayscale contone images

    D. None of the above

7. Color contone images are typically saved in which of the following formats for Web use?

    A. JPEG

    B. GIF

    C. SWF

    D. None of the above

8. Which of the following formats supports display of transparency?

    A. JPEG

    B. GIF

    C. GIF89a

    D. None of the above

9. Which of the following has lossless compression?

    A. LZW

    B. JPEG

    C. Both of the above

    D. None of the above

10. _____ contains only the 216 colors common to both Mac and Windows system palettes.

    A. 8 bit index palette

    B. JPEG

    C. 24 bit RGB palette

    D. Web safe palette

11. If you save a contone color image in 8 bit GIF format, which color set should you pick?

    A. Web safe palette

    B. Adaptive palette

    C. RGB palette

    D. CMYK palette

12. After we create a Web graphic, on which of the following should we test it?

    A. Mac monitor

    B. Windows monitors

    C. Multiple Web browsers

    D. All of the above

Check Your Understanding

Concept Questions

To help you review and expand your thinking on the topics covered in this chapter, please answer the following questions.

1. Describe the fundamental differences between graphics which we create for print and those we create for display on the Web.

2. Briefly explain why we have to pay careful attention to the size of Web graphics.

3. What is index color and how does it differ from RGB color? What are the advantages of index color, and its challenges?

4. Explain the differences between lossy and lossless compression. Give examples of each.

5. Discuss the tradeoffs of using lossy compression.

6. Explain why we tend to use JPEG format rather than GIF format when saving color contone images for display on the Web.

7. Explain why grayscale contone images can be effectively saved in 5 bit GIF format but color contone images will usually suffer too much in terms of image quality.

8. What is the SWF format? For what kind of images would we use this format, and what are the advantages and disadvantages of its use?

9. Outline a good testing program for your Web images.

10. Outline a good approach and procedure for creating graphics which will be used for both commercial printing and Web display. Be sure to include considerations of image dimensions, resolution, bit depth, compression and file format and later reuse.

PROJECTS

1. Convert a 600–1200 ppi flat colored pixel-based line art TIFF image to a Web graphic that is less than 5K in size.

2. Convert a 200–300 ppi grayscale contone TIFF EPS image to a 5 bit/pixel Web graphic that is less than 10K in size.

3. Convert a 200–300 ppi color contone TIFF or EPS image to a 24 bit/pixel Web graphic that is ≤ 10K in size.

16
Application-Specific Tips

As the Byte Turns continues…

Oh woe is me! With all these different applications and updates to learn and keep up with, will there be any time left for Danny D'Ziner and Pauline E. Prepress to go Beyond Press?

You said you could take all of my files. You're the professionals. You're responsible for making them print !

We can do it!

Oh dear, what have I gotten myself into?

Can't we ?

I can't process these files. They are too complicated and pieces are missing. It's the customer's responsibility to prepare the file properly !!

Chapter Objectives

In this chapter you will learn:

◆ **Application specific file prep tips**
◆ **Application preflight tools**
◆ **Application document component collection tools**
◆ **Dedicated preflight tools**
◆ **File simplification tips**
◆ **Key Terms**
  • Preflighting
  • Flatness
  • Unused colors
  • PPD
  • Printer driver
  • PostScript file
  • PDF
  • FlightCheck

INTRODUCTION

Our ultimate goal when creating any document is to be able to reproduce this document on an output device of our choice. Outputting, and especially printing, our documents usually requires some sort of processing. For printing this processing usually involves the RIPing of a file. The two most important tasks we can perform to prepare an electronic document for output are to 1) make sure all the components of that document are present and linked, and 2) reduce and simplify the complexity of those components as much as possible.

Most applications have some built-in tools which can help you prepare your files for final output. Tools such as the font and graphic utilities in QuarkXPress, the Prepare For Service Provider in PageMaker, and the PreFlight tool on InDesign all provide useful tools to help use prepare and collect our components. There are also tools included in our graphics creation applications such as the Simplify tool in FreeHand and the Delete colors tools in Illustrator which help us reduce and simplify our individual graphics prior to linking them to a page layout document. In addition there are many decision we make while we are constructing our graphics and documents which can have dramatic effects on how easily we can output our files in the future. The resolution choices we make when we scan an image profoundly impact both the quality and the printability of our images. The threshold values and **flatness** ratios we assign in Photoshop can make or break our ability to output a clipping path. There are dedicated preflight tools such as Markzware's **FlightCheck** which provide invaluable help in **preflighting**, troubleshooting and collecting out document components. Whenever we construct any graphic or document we need to keep the final output in mind.

This section is designed to introduce you to some of the the more commonly used applications and some of their file preparation specific tools. Some of the details of the dialog boxes may vary from one version of an application to another. I have tried to include tools which have been consistently included in the applications, as well as some new ones which I think will stay around for awhile. All these application-specific tools help us to satisfy our battle cry of *collect* the components and *reduce and simplify*!

QUARKXPRESS

Font usage utility

Use the Font Usage utility (Utilities Menu) shown in Fig. 16.1 to check your fonts usage prior to collecting your files for output. The Font Usage utility will allow you to see which fonts are being used in your document. The Font Usage utility also has a search and replace capability which is a useful tool for changing the font assignments of large sections of text or as a tool for locating and replacing any stray characters such as spaces or punctuation marks which may have been incorrectly assigned. Using the Font Usage utility will simplify and clean up your font assignments in your document and help preempt any font problems during output. After you have imported text files, especially those translated from another operating system like Windows to Mac, check and use the the Font Usage utility for Courier or other substituted fonts. You can use the Find/Change utility (Edit menu) to remove unwanted spaces, tabs, and line returns from imported text files.

Picture usage utility

Use the Picture Usage utility (Utilities Menu) shown in Fig. 16.2 to make sure that all of your graphics are ready for output. The Picture Usage dialog box can make sure that your imported graphics are all linked to their high resolution versions, that they are of the proper file format, and that they are assigned to print. Picture Usage can also be used to find the location of a high resolution graphic file component. I also use the Picture Usage utility to check for PICT files which I have not yet converted to TIFF files. Specific font usage and graphics can even be identified and located within a QuarkXPress document.

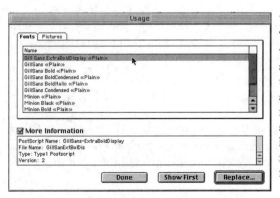

▼ *Figure 16.1 Font Usage Dialog Box*
This QuarkXPress dialog box can be used to see which fonts are being used in a document. The search and replace capabilities of the Font Usage utility is a useful tool for changing the font assignments of large sections of type or as a tool for locating and replacing any stray characters, such as spaces or punctuation marks which may have been incorrectly assigned. The Utilities menu where the Picture Usage dialog box is found is shown highlighted above the dialog box.

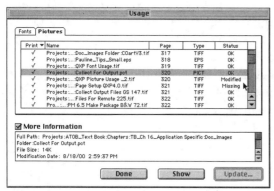

▼ *Figure 16.2 Pictures Usage Dialog Box*
This dialog box can be used to make sure that all low resolution imported graphics are linked to their high resolution partners, are in the proper file format, and are set to print. It can even be used to find the location of a high resolution graphic file, although the entire location path is rarely shown. Note that one of the imported TIFF files is missing and therefore the document is not properly linked to its high resolution graphic file. Also note that the the highlighted graphic file is a PICT file, which should be converted into a TIFF file to facilitate printing. This dialog also shows any graphics which have been modified (one seen here) and allows updating from this dialog box. The Utilities menu where the Picture Usage dialog box is found appears highlighted above the dialog box.

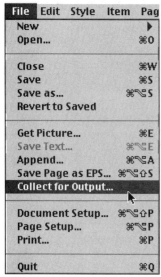

▼ *Figure 16.3 Collect for Output*
The Collect for Output dialog utility, which is included in XPress, is located under the File menu in XPress. Collect for Output helps facilitate the collection of document components which need to be transferred to another site. Collect for Output will gather a copy of the document, the high resolution graphic files, and a document info file. The fonts are not collected.

Collect for output

As an aid in helping you collect file components use the Font and Picture Usage utilities and Collect for Output extension (under File menu) shown in Fig. 16.3 to help collect files on a disk. These will help save a copy of the document, all associated graphics files, and a document data sheet to any folder which is designated. An example of the kinds of files collected when using Collect for Output can be seen in Fig. 16.4. Remember, you will still have to collect the fonts separately, but the document data sheet will tell you which fonts to collect. Also, Collect for Output does not find and save the original or parent files from which an EPS was created. The EPS parent should be included along with Exported/Imported EPS graphics. This is particularly important when sending FreeHand EPS files prior to version 3.11 to the service bureau in case the file needs to be altered. This procedure is most important for time critical jobs. One step better is to use a preflighting utility such as FlightCheck or PreflightPro which will troubleshoot your documents and collect font files as well. See Figs. 16.41 and 16.42 at the end of this chapter and Appendix I: File Prep Utilities for more information on these utilities.

Keep graphics out of gutters in facing page documents unless you mean for that element to bleed from one page to the other. Crossover elements will sometimes cause a double download of graphics for both pages. Use filled graphics boxes instead of filled text boxes when creating tinted or screened boxes.

Blends in XPress

For the best quality blends, use the blend tool in QuarkXPress as an iteration tool only. Use the XPress blend creation tool to try out various blend variations. Create your final gradations and two color (CMYK) blends, especially long ones, in a painting, bitmap editing program like Adobe Photoshop using dithering and adding noise (see Photoshop section below). Blends created in painting programs are generally higher quality and they print faster.

Color assignments and separations

Be sure to check process separations in the colors dialog box (Edit – Colors+New or Edit) for each color you want to print as a process separated color even if you use the CMYK palette to create a color. Delete red, green, and blue from the colors dialog box (Edit – Colors+Delete) when printing 4-color separations, unless you are using one of these colors as a spot color. Printing will be much faster. Illustrator and FreeHand files brought into XPress with custom Pantone spot colors will separate those colors as process colors. If custom spot colors are to be maintained, the custom spot colors must be recreated in Quark using the colors dialog box (Edit – Colors) with exactly the same names as the colors in the Illustrator file. Send or request QuarkXPress preference file if custom traps have been set. (You should send it with your file anyway for versions prior to 3.2). QuarkXPress Version 3.3 and later will automatically update your color palette to include the color names of files which you import, but check to make sure anyway, particularly if the imported spot colors are to be printed as process colors.

Printing

A complete range of printing options and controls are available in QuarkXPress's Print Dialog box. Before creating a **PostScript file** of a QuarkXPress document, be sure to choose the proper **PPD** on a Mac (Printer Description File) or PostScript **printer driver** in Windows in the Pages Setup and/or print dialog boxes. The **PPD**/printer driver you choose should be for the printer on which the final output will be done. If you are sending your file to a printing company or service bureau, this will generally be an imagesetter. Having the proper PPD/printer driver will ensure that the page geometry of your file will match that of the device on which your file will be printed. See Fig. 16.5 for the XPress Print Setup dialog box.

PAGEMAKER

Save for service provider

The Save for Service Provider utility, found under the Plug-ins menu, is a useful and intuitive file component checking and collection utility included in PageMaker Version 6.5. It will not only provide you with a complete list of file components (document, graphics, and fonts), but also will help you gather them up as well (see Fig. 16.6 a and b). It will work with both application and PostScript files generated from PageMaker 6.5. Save for Service Provider has a Package-making submenu which allows you to customize the collection of fonts and graphics. Even more extensive file troubleshooting and file component collection capabilities can be found in preflighting utilities such as FlightCheck and PreflightPro. See Figs. 16.41 and 16.42 at the end of this chapter and Appendix I: File Prep Utilities for more information on these utilities.

Save As: copy files for remote printing

In PageMaker 6.0, if you perform a Save As from the File menu and choose Copy: Files for remote printing (6.0) or All linked Files (6.5) (Fig. 16.7), PageMaker will save a copy of your document in its present state as well as copies of all the high resolution graphics linked to the document. In addition, PageMaker will create a tracking settings file which can be used by your service bureau when they launch your document. This Save As function is similar to

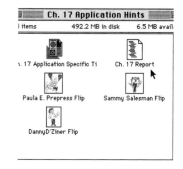

▼ Figure 16.4 Collected Output
This is the collected output from this chapter. Copies of the document and the high resolution graphics, as well as a report document, have been created. The PICT files were not collected. Can you identify which graphic files in this document were still PICTs when this collection was made?

▼ Figure 16.5 XPress Page Setup
In QuarkXPress the proper PPD, or PostScript Printer Description, file is chosen in the Page Setup dialog box. Before you send your file out as a PostScript file, be sure you have the PPD for the output device at the location where the file will be output. Note that in the dialog box the Printer Type is an Agfa Selectset 5000, which in this case is an imagesetter at a printing company where the file will be output. The file can now be saved as a PostScript file by clicking on the Options button and choosing the print as a PostScript file option. Saving a file as a PostScript file should be done with care, as it is an essentially uneditable file in which changes are very difficult to make.

▼ *Figure 16.6a Save for Service Provider*
This Plug-in utility provides detailed information about a PageMaker 6.5 document and provides component checking and gathering capabilities (including fonts). It is much more powerful than the built-in Display Pub Info Addition/Plug-in utility.

▼ *Figure 16.6b Package Making*
This subset utility portion of the "Save For Service Provider" Plug-in allows you to customize the collection of file components such as the types of fonts, the updating of graphics, and the format of a document components information report.

▼ *Figure 16.7 Files for Remote Printing*
Use this Selection in the Save As dialog box in PageMaker to save a copy of the document and high resolution copies of all linked graphics. Tracking tables for that document are saved as well.

XPress' Collect for Output utility, with the exception that PageMaker does not create a document information file. You can save the Display Publication information as a text file to create a document information file which you can send along with your files to your service bureau.

Display Publication Information

As a basic aid in helping you identify file components you can use the Aldus Addition or Adobe Plug-in Display Publication Information (under Utilities—Aldus Additions / Adobe Plug-ins menu and submenu shown in Fig. 16.8) to provide you with a list of all the fonts and graphics as well as other document components such as style sheets and colors used. Display Publication Information will provide you with a list of components, but not the components themselves. One item to note is that Display Publication Information will generally list the system fonts, as well as fonts actually used in the document, whether the system fonts are used in the document or not. I prefer using Save for Service Provider as a file information tool for PageMaker documents. It is more complete and less confusing.

Embedded vs. linked graphic files

Graphic files should be linked to (attached to), but not embedded in (included within) page layout documents. In PageMaker do not select Store Copy in Publication when prompted by a dialog box. Keep graphics as separate external linked files. Use File–Links (Fig. 16.9) to check the linked status of external graphics. Keeping graphics as separate files will: 1) Keep your PM document smaller, 2) allow your service company access to this graphic file if they need to edit the file during preparation for printing, and 3) allow for far easier updating of graphic files if you choose to edit them after they are placed in PageMaker. You can prevent PageMaker from including or attempting to include the high resolution versions of graphic images inside a PageMaker document. Launch PageMaker, but do not open a document. Choose Link Options under the Element menu (see Fig 16.10). Disable (uncheck) the Store Copy in the publication dialog box that appears. This will discourage PageMaker from attempting to store copies of the high resolution versions of graphics when you place a graphic in a document. If PageMaker ever presents you with a dialog box asking you if you want to store a copy in the application, just say no.

Removing unused colors

Removing unused or not to be used colors from your color palette is a good idea for several reasons. First, removing unwanted colors simplifies your color palette. Second, by removing colors which you do not want to use inadvertently, such as red, green, and blue, you can prevent some color assignment mistakes. And, most importantly, removing **unused colors** in a document prior to printing will prevent the printing of unnecessary film during the separation process.

I remove red, green, and blue from my color palette even before I begin construction of a document. Prior to printing access the Define Colors (Fig. 16.11) dialog box (Elements menu) and click the Remove Unused button. Any colors not assigned to a document element will be removed from the list and therefore be prevented from printing. This is also a good time to check for duplicate colors (such as the same spot color being used with two different names, one assigned in PageMaker, and one assigned in an imported graphic).

Printing PostScript

Before creating a PostScript file of a PageMaker document, be sure to choose the proper PPD (PostScript Printer Description) file in the Print Setup dialog box. The PPD you choose should be for the printer on which the final output will be done. If you are sending your file to a printing company or service bureau, this will generally be an imagesetter. Having the proper PPD will ensure that the page geometry of your file will match that of the device on which your file will be printed. See Fig. 16.12 for an example of the PageMaker Print Setup dialog box.

▼ *Figure 16.8 Display Publication Info*
The Display Publication Info utility is a PageMaker Addition, found under the Utilities menu, which helps you create a list of all the document components contained in a PageMaker document. Display Pub Info will not gather any file components together.

▼ *Figure 16.12 PageMaker Print Dialog Box*
In PageMaker the proper PPD or PostScript Printer Description file is chosen in the Print dialog box. Before you send your file out as a PostScript file, be sure you have the PPD for the output device at the location where the file will be output. Note that in the above dialog box the Print to: is a QMS 410, which is the local network printer, but the Type: is an imagesetter, which in this case is the imagesetter at a printing company where the file will be output. The file can now be saved as a PostScript file by clicking on the Options button and choosing the Print as a PostScript file option.

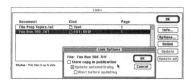

▼ *Figure 16.9 Link Information*
The Link Information dialog box displays information about all linked graphics. It shows whether a high resolution version is stored in the PageMaker document. It is generally best *not* to store any high resolution graphics inside of PageMaker documents. Leave this option unchecked.

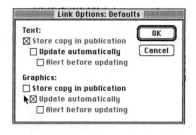

▼ *Figure 16.10 Link Options Defaults*
Be sure the Store copy in the publication check box is disabled. This will discourage PageMaker from including high resolution versions of graphics in its documents.

▼ *Figure 16.11 Removing Colors Dialog*
Prior to printing separations or sending your file out, use the Define Colors dialog box to remove any colors not used in the application.

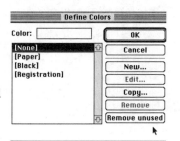

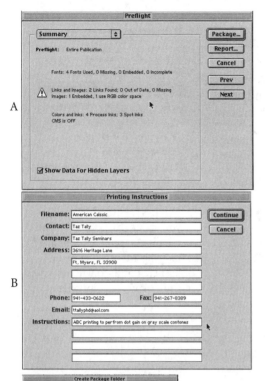

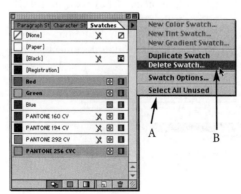

INDESIGN

Preflight and Package tools

Of the top three most popular page layout applications InDesign has the most complete and most dependable preflighting and collection tools. The Preflight utility, found under the File menu, is a useful and intuitive file component checking and collection utility included in InDesign. The Preflight tool will not only look for, and find, all of the graphics, graphic links, and font components within the InDesign document but will find fonts in embedded graphic files as well. This utility provides a summary as well as detailed information on all font, graphics, links, colors and print settings. It even reports on embedded graphic files. It will not only provide you with a complete list of file components (document, graphics, and fonts), but also will help you gather them up as well (see Fig. 16.13 a and b). Included as part of this tool is the Create Package tool which allows you to customize the collection of fonts and graphics. As part of the regular sequence of preflighting and packaging the InDesign Preflight tool even presents you with a Printing Instructions sheet. See Fig. 16.13 for a complete sequence of the InDesign Preflight and Create Package tools. Even more extensive file troubleshooting and file component collection capabilities than these can be found in preflighting utilities such as FlightCheck and PreflightPro. See Figs. 16.41 and 16.42 at the end of this chapter and Appendix I: File Prep Utilities for more information on these utilities.

Deleting unused colors

Just like in other applications removing unused colors from your color palette is a good idea. InDesign provides an easy to access and use duo of tools which allows you to find and then delete unused colors. The Color Swatches Palette allows you to first select unused colors, and then to remove those unused colors (see Fig. 16.14). This unused color detection and removal pair should be used prior to sending your files out for printing.

▼ **Figure 16.13 InDesign Preflight Tools**

InDesign provides a complete content preflight and file component collection tool set. Above is the sequence of dialog boxes encountered in use of this tool.

A) Summary of the preflight analysis

B) Printing instruction sheet

C) Package collection tool

This is a reliable tool which can be used with confidence.

▼ **Figure 16.14 InDesign Color Tool**

InDesign provides the Color Swatches Palette which allows:

A) Selection of unused colors

B) Deletion of those unused colors

These unused color ID and removal tools should be used prior to printing the final version of your document (see C-14 for a color version of this figure).

PHOTOSHOP AND OTHER PAINTING APPLICATIONS

Gradients and blends

Create gradients and blends in a pixel-based application such as Photoshop rather than in page layout or drawing applications. Bitmapped blends tend to print easier, faster, and with better quality. The banding which often occurs when printing gradients and blends at high resolution can be avoided when working in Photoshop by dithering them (check Dither in the Gradient tool palette; see Fig. 16.15). To further reduce the possibility of banding on output, I also like to add one or two pixels of noise followed by an application of a 2 pixel blur (my favorite is Gaussian blur) to help add noise and distribute grayscale values across the entire blended area. In addition, creating gradients and blends in Photoshop, and especially in Photoshop 4.0 and above, also gives you much better control and flexibility than creating them in page layout applications like QuarkXPress.

Clipping paths and silhouettes

The first step in creating a silhouette usually involves selecting a portion of an image which is to be removed from its background. This can be done in Photoshop utilizing a variety of selection tools including the selection marquees, the Lasso, the Magic Wand, and several color selection tools. After a selection is made, this selection must be converted into a path, a vector-based graphic outline, and then further modified into a clipping path. The vector path is used to create a smooth edge around the portion of the image which is to be silhouetted. The creation of the clipping path turns the path into a "cookie cutter" which isolates the selected portion of the image from its background. Paths can be created directly using the pen tool, although this can often be a tedious and time consuming process. Using the Magic Wand to create a selection which you may then convert into a path is often faster, but can be fraught with problems related to the creation of complex paths. I often use several selection tools during this process, but I always have one goal in mind. My goal is to create as smooth and accurate a silhouette as possible with the simplest path possible.

This process of creating a silhouette using a clipping path creates a complex, compound image. This is considered a compound image because it has both

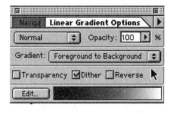

▼ Figure 16.15 Photoshop Gradient Tool
Check "Dither" in the Gradient tool palette when creating gradients in Photoshop to discourage banding from occurring when the gradient is printed at high resolution.

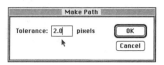

▼ Figure 16.16 Photoshop Path Tolerance Setting
To reduce the RIPing times associated with path creation in Photoshop, pay close attention to the tolerance setting. Create a path to convert a selection into a vector-based line path. Lower tolerance settings result in tighter fits between the selection and the created path. But tighter paths also generally mean more control points, and more complex paths, which results in slower, more difficult RIPing processes. Experiment with various path settings to view the results. Choose a tolerance which creates fewer control points than a perfect fit. Then edit the existing points to correct the line placements.

▼ *Figure 16.17 Photoshop Clipping Path Flatness Ratios*
To reduce the RIPing times associated with clipping paths created and saved in applications like Photoshop, set the flatness ratios to at least 1 and preferably higher. Beware that flatness ratios above 5 often produce visible straight line segments along curved paths. When assigning flatness ratio values, be sure to use whole numbers such as 1 or 3, not fractions of numbers such as 1.5 or 0.75. These values will increase RIPing times.

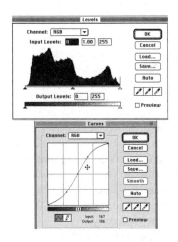

▼ *Figure 16.18 Photoshop Image Control*
When working in Photoshop, select Levels (top) to set highlight and shadow points, and Curves (bottom) to make gray map adjustments, rather than using Brightness and Contrast controls, which tend to dramatically reduce image quality.

bitmapped and vector-based graphic segments in the same image. Compound images are some of the most difficult to RIP because they combine the challenges of RIPing presented by both raster- and vector-based graphics in the same image. During this silhouetting process two decisions you make will determine how easily this clipped image will print. The first involves deciding how closely the path you create matches the original selection. This is determined by assigning a tolerance to the path during the pathmaking step. When you make a path from a selection, the dialog box that you see in Fig. 16.16 will appear. Assigning a low tolerance number such as 0.5 creates a path which closely matches the original selection, but also often results in a path which has a large number of control points. Paths with large numbers of control points are more difficult to RIP. I generally select a tolerance between 1.0 – 2.0 which generates few control points with a fair fit. After the path is created and before I turn the path into a clipping path, I adjust the location of the control points and the curves they control with the pen tools to create a more precise fit. I will often remove unnecessary points during this editing process as well.

Flatness of clipping paths

When a path is converted into a clipping path, be sure to pay attention to the flatness ratio of your path (Fig. 16.17). The flatness ratio controls the number of tangents or line segments used to draw curves along your paths. Small flatness ratios, 0 – 1, create very smooth lines but very complex paths which are difficult to RIP. Larger flatness ratios use fewer line segments and are therefore easier and take less time to RIP. But be aware that a flatness ratio set too high will result in visible straight line segments along paths which should be smooth curves. The best flatness ratio depends upon the RIP being used, the type of curve being drawn, and the output resolution. As a starting place, try setting flatness between 2 and 5. Avoid low flatness ratios of 0 – 1. Experiment with your equipment, but use only whole numbers for flatness values; using fractions, such as 1.5, dramatically increases RIPing times.

Note: While clipping paths can be created and edited in page layout such as QuarkXPress and InDesign, it is usually preferable to create and edit clipping paths in a graphic application such as Photoshop. Output accuracy and precision tends to improve if clipping paths are created around the original graphic.

File resolution

The resolution of any contone bitmapped file which will be used for printing should depend upon the line screen (lpi) at which it will be printed. A good rule of thumb to follow for maximum resolution is that the resolution of an image in ppi should not exceed two times the line screen (2 x lpi) of the final printed image, and often even less resolution. Most often 1x–1.25 x lpi is sufficient. For instance, a Photoshop contone TIFF which will be printed without scaling at 150 lpi need not exceed 300 ppi in resolution, and often 150–188 ppi is fine (see Chapter 8, "Resolving Resolution," and Chapter 12, "Taming Your Scanner," for more information on file resolution). Keeping resolution down is one of the key components of reducing file size in our continual quest to *reduce and simplify*!

Contone color

Remember that scanned images of color continuous tone images which are intended to be used for print need to be globally color corrected to compensate for impure printing inks. A standard white highlight dot is typically corrected to yield the following CMYK values: C=6%, M=4%, Y=4%, K=0%. Corresponding midtone values might be C=60%, M=45%, Y=45%, K=25%.

Tone adjustments in Curves and Levels

When performing tone adjustments in Photoshop, use Levels and Curves rather than Brightness and Contrast. I use Levels to set highlight and shadow points and Curves to make any gray map adjustments after I have set my highlight and shadow points (see Fig. 16.18). Curves adjustments provide a continuous series of linked control points along the Curves graph line. When one point is adjusted, other points along the curve are incrementally adjusted as well, creating smooth tonal adjustments with a minimum loss of data. But be aware that every time you make an adjustment, such as a change in the Curves dialog box to a file in an image editing application, you are not only adjusting the data but also losing data. Keep your number of adjustments to a minimum (see discussion of scanning applications below and in Chapter 12).

SCANNING APPLICATIONS

Prescanning

When scanning images, continuous tone images in particular, it is best to use a low resolution prescan technique (see Fig. 16.19). Use the low resolution prescan image to evaluate your potential scan image. Most of your image adjustments, such as cropping, scaling, tone compression, gray map adjustments, global color corrections, and sharpening, should be performed during the scanning process rather than as postscan adjustments in an application like Photoshop. Evaluation of the low resolution prescan image allows you to decide how the adjustments need to be set during the high resolution scan. Using a prescan evaluation and high resolution scan adjustments save time and preserve image quality, because every postscan adjustment made in Photoshop deletes data from the image.

Line art

Simple, crisp line art images should usually be scanned at high resolution, ≥ 800 ppi, and then converted to outline files in a dedicated outlining application like Streamline. Coarse-edged images with little edge detail can be reproduced very well with low resolution scans (~300 ppi). Complex and fine detail line art images should be scanned as 8 bit grayscale images and then converted to 1 bit line art using sharpening and thresholding. Be sure to scan line art at a multiple of the optical resolution of the scanner. This will result in more consistent edges which will be easier to Streamline.

▼ *Figure 16.19 Scanner Interface*
The screen above shows the Photoshop scanner plug-in interface control of UMAX MagicScan software. Scans should be performed in two steps: an initial low-resolution preview scan followed by a higher resolution final scan. Cropping and other necessary adjustments are made during the preview or prescan and applied during the final scan. Note the final scan resolution is set at 150 lpi. A quality/multiplication factor of 1.5 has been set in a separate scanning preference dialog box, yielding a final scan and image resolution of 225 ppi.

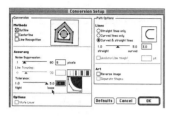

▼ Figure 16.20 Streamline Setup

Streamline is terrific for creating easily editable and scalable outline files from bitmapped images. One of the potential problems with Streamline-created outline files is that Streamline tends to make long, complex paths which are difficult to RIP. To help reduce the complexity (number of control points) of a Streamline file, set the tolerance to loose. In most cases, Streamline will create a very accurate outline without too many control points.

▼ Figure 16.21 Document in Layers

Layers palette in FreeHand shows how a document is constructed in separate layers rather than all in one plane. Each layer can be activated and edited separately.

Contones

Scanning resolutions for unscaled continuous tone images rarely need to exceed two times (2 x) the line screen at which the images will be printed. Often using quality factors of 1.25–1.5 x the lpi is sufficient. If an image is to be scaled up or down either during the scanning process or afterward as a postscan manipulation, be sure to account for this when assigning the scan or input resolution. The resolution of a file, as determined by the above guidelines, needs to be adjusted either up or down by the percentage of the scaling. For example, if a 4" x 5" image is to ultimately be scaled and printed as an 8" x 10" image, the scan resolution will need to be doubled because both sides of the image will be scaled 200%. The following formula can be used to determine input or scan resolution: 1.25–2.0 x lpi x scaling factor. If we use 1.25 as our quality factor, 200 percent as our scaling factor, and 150 lpi as our printing resolution, then our input resolution should be 1.25 x 150 x 2 = 375 ppi (see Chapter 12 for a complete discussion of this issue). Here again the hew and cry is to *reduce and simplify*!

STREAMLINED/OUTLINED FILES

Outlining preferences

When working with line art files, particularly if the line art has been generated as an outline from Streamline, you need to be cognizant of path length and the number of control points along any given path. Streamline tends to: 1) create many control points, particularly if the original outlined graphic was low resolution or very detailed, and 2) create long paths. Both of these conditions increase the RIPing complexity of the graphic file. You can preempt having to perform corrective editing of the Streamlined path in an illustration application by initially creating a simplified version. Figure 16.20 shows how the tolerance can be set to Loose in the Streamline Conversion Setup dialog box. Experiment with the tolerance setting on various types of images to see how it affects the outlining of images. I set the tolerance to maximum for most images. (See Fig. 9.11 and 9.12 in Chapter 9, "Grappling with Graphics" for a comparison of a line art image which was converted using both tight and loose tolerance settings.)

DRAWING APPLICATIONS IN GENERAL

Build graphics in layers (see Figure 16.21) so that they can be constructed, edited, and troubleshot more easily if there are RIPing problems. Often, only a portion of an EPS file may be the cause of an output problem. For instance, one path in an illustration may be too long or complex. If a complex graphic is built in layers which can be individually viewed and activated, isolating and correcting the trouble-making paths can be easy. Editing the image in any way is easier if the graphic is built in layers.

Always adjust the flatness ratio in drawing programs like Illustrator, FreeHand, and CorelDraw prior to printing or creating EPS files. Flatness ratios should always be greater than 0. A flatness range of 2–5 is a good starting place for most line art graphic files.

Use proper printer description files (APDs, PPDs, PDXs, **PDF**s) when printing a file (choice of printer in print setup box). When preparing EPS graphics to export for placement in another application such as a page layout, choose the printer description file of the highest resolution final output machine (imagesetter), even if you will be proofing on a lower resolution printer such as a laser printer. This will have the graphics program include flatness and path lengths which are compatible with the more memory intensive imagesetter RIP. Default PPD selections can also be done through the use of the LaserWriter Driver 8.x in the Chooser (Mac) or through the printer driver dialog in Windows.

Setting type in drawing applications

Avoid setting a lot of type in outline graphics applications such as Illustrator, FreeHand, and CorelDraw if you intend to export the graphic as an EPS for inclusion in a page layout application.

Create outlines of text in EPS files imported in page layout documents. This will improve printing speed and reduce font location problems. (Use ATM in Windows.) Note: Converting text to outlines works well for small amounts of type. Converting large amounts of type to outlines will increase, rather than reduce, the complexity of the file. Text heavy documents should be created in page layout applications. Also note that small serif type may not covert well to outlines.

To create an outline of some text characters, select the copy, make sure printer fonts and ATM are loaded, then choose a convert to paths or outline text option. This is available in nearly all drawing applications. An example is shown in Fig. 16.22.

See Chapter 20, "Managing the Mess," for some suggestions on when and how to create a print-ready exportable EPS file while retaining its editability.

▼ *Figure 16.22 Convert to Paths*
This is the Convert to Paths selection in FreeHand. This command is used to convert type to graphic paths prior to exporting as an EPS, preventing the nesting of font files.

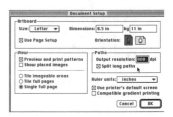

▼ *Figure 16.23 Illustrator Path Control*
Choose Split Long Paths to reduce the length of paths prior to creation of an EPS. Setting the resolution will determine the flatness and the length of split path segments.

▼ *Figure 16.24 Object Control*
The resolution of individual objects can be controlled in Illustrator by selecting an item and choosing Attributes under the Object menu. Controlling the resolution of an object in Illustrator is how the flatness is controlled. The default object resolution is 800 ppi, which results in a flatness of 3 at 2400 dpi output resolution.

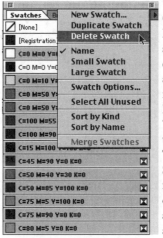

▼ *Figure 16.25 Deleting Colors*
Deleting unused colors should be done prior to exporting a document as an EPS graphic or printing. For example in Illustrator 8.0, first choose "Select All Unused" from the color palette menu. Then choose "Delete Swatch" form the same menu. This same procedure can be performed in all the major drawing type applications.

Note: See Color Plate section C-14 for a color version of this figure.

▼ *Figure 16.26 Change Fonts*
The Find Font utility in Illustrator is useful for making font lists and for finding and removing unwanted fonts.

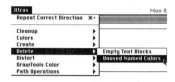

▼ **Figure 16.27 Delete Utility**
Use Delete utilities in
FreeHand to remove unused
colors and text boxes prior to
printing or creating EPS files.

▼ **Figure 16.28 FreeHand**
Output Options
FreeHand allows you to control the splitting and flatness
of all paths through its Output
Options dialog box. Set flatness between 2 and 5.

▼ **Figure 16.29 FreeHand**
Flatness Control
Individual path flatness can be
controlled though the
Inspector Palette in FreeHand
by selecting the path and
choosing the geometric symbols in the palette.

ILLUSTRATOR

To control the document-wide path lengths and flatness ratio in Illustrator use File–Document Setup (Fig. 16.23) and input the resolution of the output device you will be printing to, then check Split Long Paths. The resolution setting will determine the path lengths which Illustrator creates.

In Illustrator the flatness of individual objects may be controlled by adjusting its resolution on an object-by-object basis by selecting an object and choosing Objects–Attributes (Fig. 16.24) and setting a separate individual resolution for the selected graphic.

In Illustrator 8.0 unused colors may be removed from the list of colors in the color palette by selecting and deleting unused colors (Fig. 16.25). Select "All Unused" and then choose "Delete Swatch". This will reduce the size of the color list which allows for faster importing and printing of the graphic file and prevents the printing of unwanted pieces of film during separation output. Illustrator also has a nifty Find Font utility (Fig. 16.26) which allows you to view all the fonts used in the document, select one, and change it to another font globally. This utility is very useful for making font lists when gathering fonts for sending your file out. It is also useful for searching and replacing fonts that you do not want in the document, such as those pesky spaces and paragraph returns which did not get selected when you changed the formatting of some copy.

FREEHAND

FreeHand provides for deletion of unused colors through several avenues; the easiest to access is the Delete submenu under Xtras menu (Fig. 16.27). To remove

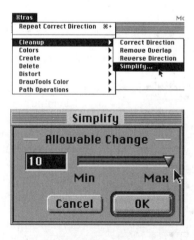

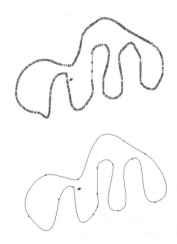

▼ **Figure 16.30 Simplify Paths**
One of the best file prep utilities in FreeHand is the Simplify Control. The Simplify dialog box allows to add or subtract a point from a path. The path on the top is a very complex path with hundreds of trol points. The path on the bottom is the same path after Simplify has been applied with a setting of As you can see, the integrity of the path has been maintained, but the number of control points has b reduced by over 95 percent. The simplified path on the bottom will RIP/print much faster than the unsimplified path on the top.

extraneous colors from the color palette prior to export as an EPS file in older versions of FreeHand (prior to 5.0), select all elements on a page which you wish to export and copy them to another page. Only the colors which you have used will be copied and placed in the new document. Or you may use the Delete Unused Colors tool.

Path length and flatness ratio can be controlled in several locations in FreeHand. Global control can be exercised through the selection of the Output Options choice under the File menu (Fig. 16.28). Check Split Long Paths. Set Flatness to greater than 0 (try 2–5). Control of flatness for individual objects is accomplished through the use of the Inspector Palette (Fig. 16.29). Select your path and then click on the geometry symbols.

One of the most useful and flexible file prep tools available in FreeHand is the Simplify tool (Fig. 16.30). Use Simplify to reduce the complexity of a path created or opened in FreeHand. Simplify gives you complete control over how much simplification (how many control points will be removed) will be applied to a line. This type of control can dramatically reduce the RIPing times required to process a path. This is a good tool for simplifying complex paths which may be created by Streamline or other outlining applications.

FreeHand's Collect for Output tool will collect the FreeHand document as well as all font and graphics file used in that document.

POSTSCRIPT FILES

What is a PostScript File?

When we construct our documents we usually save them, at least initially, as application files in native document formats such as PageMaker, and QuarkXpress files. These native file format documents are full viewable and editable with most of their document components such as high resolution graphics and font files being maintained as linked but separate and easily editable external files. These are made for document creation, viewing, editing, and printing.

An alternative to saving your documents in native file formats is to save your file as a PostScript file. A PostScript file is a text based document which contains, if properly constructed, all the document information, including imbedded font and graphic files, required for printing that document. A PostScript file is a print-oriented document format. PostScript files are not easily viewable without a special PS file viewer or editor, and they are not editable without a special PostScript file editor. The entire object behind creating a PostScript file is the creation of a complete file made primarily for printing, not editing. The greatest strengths of a PostScript file, its completeness and uneditable nature, are also its greatest weaknesses. If you construct a PostScript file correctly it will print correctly no matter who prints it. However, if you make any mistakes in the construction of your document, or the creation of the PostScript file, those mistakes get printed too.

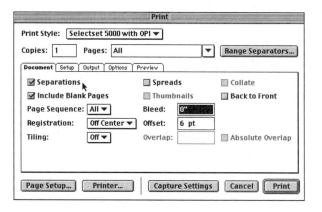

▼ *Figure 16.31 Document Setup Print Dialog Box*

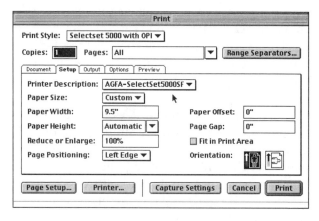

▼ *Figure 16.32 Setup Choices Print Dialog Box*

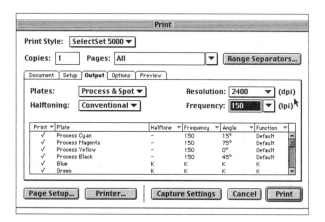

▼ *Figure 16.33 Output Print Dialog Box*

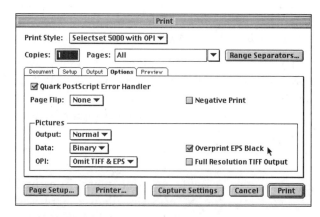

▼ *Figure 16.34 Print Options Dialog Box*

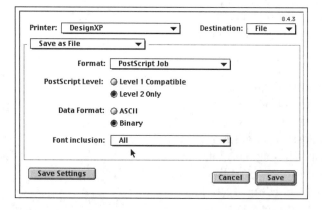

▼ *Figure 16.35 Printer Dialog Box*

Use of PostScript files

PostScript files are often created and used when the the person who creates a document either does not want their document to be edited when they send it out to be printed, or they are sending their document file to someone who needs to print their document but does not have the application which was used to create the document.

PostScript files are created by preparing your file as if you were about to print your document, but instead of printing your document to a printing device, you print your file to a disk.

Once you are sure that your document is constructed properly you must pay close attention to properly configuring the various print setup dialog boxes provided by your application before your actually "print" your PostScript file to your disk.

Creating a proper PostScript file

On the next page you will see some typical print setup dialog boxes. These are from QuarkXPress 4.04, but your application and version will have similar dialog boxes. Different applications and versions have different dialog boxes, but the key variables must always be set for proper printing to occur. Following is a list of typical PostScript file setup variables:

Document setup variables (Fig. 16.31)

- Page range to print: All is typical, but if you want only a portion, you need to specify which pages you want to print
- Separations: "On" for imagesetting or "Off" for composite desktop printers
- Page sequence: "Odd," "Even," or "All"
- Registration: On or Off depending upon whether your file will be separated or not. Turn "On" for separations
- Bleed: If and how much. A typical value here is 0.125"
- Spread: Whether facing pages will print together

Setup choice variables (Fig. 16.32)

❧ PPD for Mac, and Printer Driver for Windows (choose the highest resolution device on which the final document will print). This is a crucial setting.

❧ Paper size and width: Should match the output device.

❧ Enlargement: Usually best set at 100%.

❧ Orientation: Landscape or Portrait.

❧ Paper Offset and Gap: You should get this print device specific information from your printing company.

Output choices (Fig. 16.33)

❧ Type of plates: Spot and/or process separations to print.

❧ Resolution: Choose the resolution of the highest output device. 2400 is typical for many imagesetters. 300–1200 dpi is typical for most desktop printers.

❧ Line screen (lpi), or frequency, at which halftones will be printed: 150 lpi–200 lpi is the typical range for commercial offset presses. 60 lpi for 300 dpi laser printers, 85 lpi for 600 dpi laser printers and 110 lpi for 1200 dpi laser printers.

❧ Screen angles used to print: There are many options here depending upon the RIP which is used.

❧ Spot color screen angles: The default screen angle is generally the same as the K (black) ink angle (generally 45°). Screens or tints of spot colors which overlap should be set at different screen angles to prevent the creation of moiré patterns during printing.

Print options variables (Fig. 16.34)

❧ Picture quality: Usually set to High Resolution or Normal.

❧ Picture data: Usually Binary for imagesetters. Some Windows networks prefer ASCII, which is larger but more compatible.

❧ Overprint options: Generally turned on.

❧ Whether a positive or negative print image is needed.

PostScript file variables (Fig. 16.35)

❧ Destination: File instead of Printer.

❧ Format: Set to PostScript.

❧ PostScript Level: One, Two, or Three, depending upon RIP and work flow.

❧ Data format: Binary for most high resolution imagesetter output. Some Windows networks handle the ASCII file format better, which is a larger but more compatible format.

❧ Font Inclusion: Be sure to select All here. The default is often None. If None is chosen, none of the font files you used to create your document will be included in the PostScript file. Other font files will be substituted, with the result being different looking type and reflowing of type.

Ask your printer

The settings, variations, and options I have discussed and recommended for PostScript files above will work in many circumstances. However, it is always a good idea to check with the printing company or service bureau who will be printing your PostScript files for recommendations which are unique and/or specific to their equipment, RIPs, and/or workflow. Some of the settings we discussed here such as line screen and screen angles may be set or overridden at the RIP. In most print dialog boxes you can save a set of settings and recall them later. This is called a Print Style in these dialog boxes. Print Styles save valuable time and prevent print setup errors.

PDF: PORTABLE DOCUMENT FORMAT

What is PDF?

PDF, or portable document format, is a nonnative file format which is viewable and has limited editability. PDF requires only a PDF viewer in order to see the document. PDF is a file format created by Adobe Systems as a document format which is independent of the platform, application, or computer on which it was created. PDF was designed primarily for viewing and printing of documents without needing the native application installed on a computer. PDF even has font character simulation capabilities to aid in the viewing and printing of documents. PDF has many advantages but also some liabilities. If you are aware of both, and create and use PDF document properly, it is a powerful, flexible, and very useful document technology.

PDF advantages

PDF is portable, that is, it is application-, platform-, and OS-independent and does not require the native application for viewing and printing. A PDF document, like a PostScript file, can contain all fonts and graphics if properly constructed. But unlike a PostScript file it is easily viewable and at least somewhat editable.

Acrobat PDF document files have the best of both worlds. If properly constructed they have the completeness of a PostScript files as well as the viewability and at least some of the editability of a native application document file. As with a properly constructed PostScript file, the keys to good PDF files are completeness and attention to preparing the PDF for the final output device. This second point is most important with PDF files. Whereas PostScript files are nearly always created for printing, a PDF document can be prepared for output on a wide variety of devices, including for viewing on monitors. In fact, the original intent of PDF files was for viewing on monitors and printing on low resolution devices. Pay close attention to the Job Options which are assigned in Distiller prior to creating a PDF. And remember that the quality and completeness of a PDF is limited by the PostScript file from which it is created.

PDF also contains high quality easy-to-RIP and print normalized PostScript information. PDF files also tend to be very compact, with much smaller files sizes. File size reduction of up to 90 percent, compared to a PostScript file, can be obtained. PDF files are also page efficient. PDF documents are built a page at a time and can therefore be processed that way: RIPing, trapping, imposition, etc. PDF can be used for a variety of purposes including: Emailing (due to its small size and Web compatible format), proofing, exchanging, and editing prior to printing. It is also an excellent document archiving and retrieval tool.

For production purposes, PDF documents can contain job ticketing information with document and job information. This is a huge work flow advantage. PDF is also extensible, which means that many extensions can and have been built for PDF and more are on the way. For example, Forms extensions allow variable data input to PDF files. And, finally, PDF is Web safe/compatible, which makes PDF an easy and dependable way to send files across the Internet.

PDF challenges

▼ *Figure 16.36 Distiller Job Options Menu Choice*
Select and configure the Job Options prior to Distilling a document into PDF format.

Most of PDF's challenges relate to printing problems, especially in high resolution separation environments. PDF files are generally created from PostScript files. Therefore the quality and completeness of the PDF document depends upon the quality and completeness of the PostScript file from which it is constructed. PDF was originally designed primarily for viewing documents in an RGB environment, not printing them in a high resolution CMYK-oriented separation environment. Therefore, PDF is not inherently separation compatible, and currently (version3.0) requires the plug-ins in order to work effectively with PDF files in a prepress environment. PDF has a fairly complex print preparation interface, and not all RIPs will process print PDF files. If there are problems with the PDF file, they are not as editable as an application file.

Preparing PDF files for print

Preparing a PDF file for print requires the same attention as creating any print document. We must be aware of missing fonts and graphics, or corrupted components such bad PostScript code, fonts, or graphics. Improper geometric manipulation (resize, crop, rotation) may cause slow RIPing. We should avoid white "cover-ups" and provide the proper graphic file formats for print by using TIFF and EPS graphics and avoiding PICTs, WMF, BMP, CAD formats, etc.

PDF preflight

Like PostScript documents, PDF files need to be set up properly in order to print correctly. Here is a short list of some common PDF page construction bugaboos:

❥ Correct trim size
❥ Fold marks properly defined
❥ Bleeds properly defined
❥ No hairlines
❥ Proper graphic file format

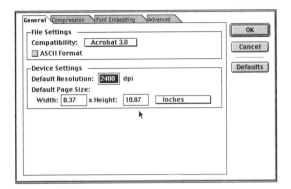

▼ *Figure 16.37 Distiller General Preferences*
In General settings, pay particular attention to the page size. Some printers do not like the default 8.5" x 11" size. Check with your printing company for specific values to place here.

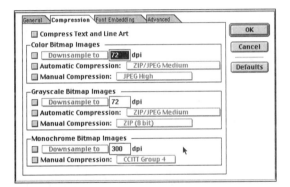

▼ *Figure 16.38 Distiller Compression Preferences*
The safest way to create a PDF file which will print properly and without problems is to turn off all the compression. Doing so, however, will create much larger files.

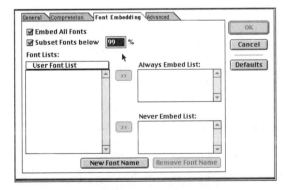

▼ *Figure 16.39 Distiller Font Preferences*
The safest way to create a PDF file which will print properly is to embed all the font files. This will create a larger but more accurate printing document. If you are using your PDF strictly for on-screen proofing or viewing purposes and send your PDF file across the Internet, subsetting is an option.

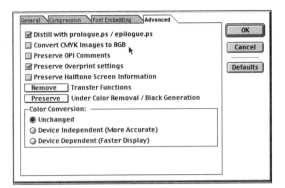

▼ *Figure 16.40 Distiller Advanced Preferences*
These advanced preferences vary from printing company to printing company. I have set this up for a typical output print. You will want to consult your service provider for specific requirements.

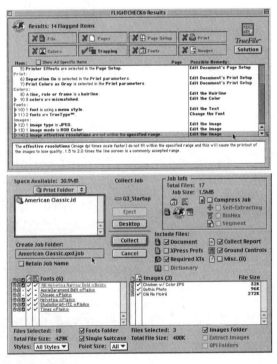

▼ *Figure 16.41 FlightCheck*
Dedicated preflighting utilities such as FlightCheck provide the most complete and dependable preflighting and file collection capabilities. As seen here in the Results screen (top), FlightCheck reviews all aspects of a document including: File characteristics, page configurations, page setup values, print settings, color assignments, trapping settings, font files needed and image linking and characteristics. FlightCheck will check PostScript and PDF files as well as native application document files. The collection portion of this tool is equally impressive as it provides complete control over what is collected and where it will be placed. If you intend to send your collected files over the Internet for delivery, FlightCheck even provides the tools to compress, BinHex convert, and make a self extracting archive from your collected files to assure safe transport over the Internet as well as easy accessibility at the receiving end.

PDF: Portable Document Format 349

- Color space conversions: RGB will not convert to CMYK
- All font files included
- Rules and borders properly positioned
- No blank pages
- Colors properly assigned (spots vs. process, RGB vs. CMYK, removal of unused)
- Trapping properly applied
- Total ink coverage not exceeding 340%

Distiller setup

Distiller is the Adobe application through which a PostScript file is processed in order to create a PDF document. One of the most common errors when creating a PDF document is using the default "Job Option" setting in Distiller. Distiller's defaults settings are RGB view oriented, and most are inappropriate for printing. To have our PDF files print properly we must configure the Distiller Job Options correctly through the PDF "Job Options" dialog box. This is particularly true if you are sending your PDF files out for printing (see Fig. 16.36).

PDF "Job Options"

There are four tabbed subsections of the PDF "Job Options" dialog box. Following are some setting recommendations for print, and particularly for prepress.

General options (Fig. 16.37)

- Usually set Compatibility to Acrobat 3.0; some older versions of the Viewer and Exchange will only read Acrobat 2.1.
- Pay attention to Page Size. Some printing companies prefer a 8 3/8 (8.375)" x 10 7/8 (10.875)" over the default 8.75.
- Only use the ASCII setting when instructed by your printing company or if you are having problems printing your PDF file across your network. The ASCII version is generally more compatible, but is a larger file size.
- Set resolution to the highest output device to which you will be printing. This is usually 2400 dpi for an imagesetter and 600 dpi for a laser printer.

Compression options (Fig. 16.38)

- The safest way to create a PDF file which will print properly and without problems is to turn off all the compression. Doing so, however, will create much larger files. If you are sending your files in on a disk, the file size increase may not be a problem.
- If you are sending your PDF files across the Internet, the large file size created by uncompressed text and images may be a problem. Check with your service bureau or printing company who will be printing your files for compression guidelines.
- If you do compress your images, here are some of the safer suggestions:
- Check Compress Text and Line Art (this is a safer lossless compression).

- *Do not* Down-sample or Subsample your images.
- *Do not* choose Automatic Compression.
- *Do* select Manual Compression and high quality JPEG or 8-bit LZW.
- Check with your service bureau for their RIP specific compression compatabilities.

Font embedding options (Fig. 16.39)

- Part of the advantage of the Acrobat technology is the ability to substitute font proxies for missing fonts. But this also leads to documents which do not print exactly like the original.
- For best results, check the "Embed All Fonts" check box.
- Also, place "99% "in the Subset fonts dialog box.
- Including all the font files will make the resulting PDF document larger—but the text will print more reliably.
- If you are just using the document for on-screen proofing or viewing and/or sending your PDF file across the Internet, you may not want to embed the fonts. In this case, uncheck the "Embed All Fonts" and use the Acrobat default value of 25% in the Subset dialog box.

Advanced options (Fig. 16.40)

The advanced tab in the Distiller Job Options setup is easily the most cryptic and confusing. Here are some guidelines:

- Check/activate the "Distill with prologue.ps / epilog.ps" so that spot colors will separate properly.
- Uncheck "Convert CMYK Images to RGB." This is checked/activated by default and should be deactivated.
- Uncheck "Preserve OPI Comments" unless instructed to turn this on by your printing company.
- Check/activate "Preserve Overprint Settings" to make sure that any colors assigned to overprint will do so.
- Uncheck "Preserve Halftone Screen Information" if the Halftoning is set at the RIP. Check/activate this preference if you have set your halftoning information in Photoshop and want it to be honored.
- Choose the "Remove" "Transfer Functions" option unless you are sure that you want a transfer function you have created in Photoshop to be applied.
- Choose the "Preserve" "Under Color Removal/ Black Generation" option to make sure the the color conversion functions you have chosen in Photoshop will be applied. If these functions are addressed in a different separation application at the RIP, then this function should be set to "Remove" instead of "Preserve."
- Check/activate "Unchanged" button color conversion section.

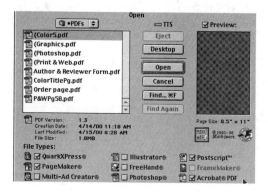

▼ *Figure 16.42 PDF Preflight*

Dedicated preflight tools such as Markzware's FlightCheck can preflight PostScript and PDF files as well as native application files such as QuarkXPress, PageMaker and Indesign document files.

PDF Editing and Preflight

Preflighting of PDF files can be accomplished through the use of dedicated preflighting tools such as FlightCheck (see Figs. 16.41 and 16.42) Other PDF specific tools such as PitStop from Enfocus provide PDF editing and preflighting capabilities. But remember that the editability of PDF files is far less, and more difficult to accomplish, than working with a native application file. So there is no substitution for a properly constructed and preflighted native document file when your ultimate goal is creating a PDF document. Creating a PDF document can simplify a file, but it cannot make up for poor document construction decisions and techniques.

Ask your printer

The settings, variations, and options I have discussed and recommended for either PostScript files or PDF will work in many circumstances. However, it is always a good idea to check with the printing company or service bureau who will be printing your PostScript or PDF files for recommendations which are unique and/or specific to their equipment, RIPs, and workflow.

CHAPTER SUMMARY

When preparing an electronic document for output our two most important tasks are: 1) make sure all the components of that document are present and linked, and 2) reduce and simplify the complexity of those components as much as possible. Most applications have some built-in tools which can help you prepare your files for final output. Tools such as the font and graphic utilities in QuarkXPress, the Prepare for Service Provider in PageMaker, and the PreFlight tool on InDesign all provide useful tools to help use, prepare and collect our components. There are also tools included in our graphics creation applications such as the Simplify tool in FreeHand and the Delete colors tools in Illustrator which help us reduce and simplify our individual graphics prior to linking them to a page layout document. In addition there are many decision we make while we are constructing our graphics and documents which can have dramatic effects on how easily we can output our files in the future. The resolution choices we make when we scan an image profoundly impacts both the quality and the printability of our images. The Threshold values and flatness ratios we assign in Photoshop can make or break our ability to output a clipping path. Dedicated preflight tools such as Markzware's Flightcheck provide invaluable help in preflighting, troubleshooting and collecting our document components for PostScript and PDF as well as native application document files. Always keep the final output in mind whenever we create any graphic or construct and page layout document.

Pauline's Digital Imaging Tips

Pauline's Tip 16.1

Graphic elements placed or imported into page layout documents should be manipulated (scaled, cropped, rotated, or skewed) for design iteration purposes only in those applications. Final editing choices should be applied in the original graphics application. Use Publish and Subscribe to speed up these updating chores.

Pauline's Tip 16.2

In QuarkXPress use Collect for Output and Font and Picture Usage to help identify and collect document components. Extensions such as The Bundler provide even more extensive help.

Pauline's Tip 16.3

In PageMaker use the utility Save for Service Provider and Save as Files for remote printing to help identify and collect document components. Plug-ins such as Document Info may provide additional help.

Pauline's Tip 16.4

In InDesign use the Preflight utility to perform a content preflight on your documents. Use the Create Package portion of this utility to collect all of the file components. Also use the find and delete unused color choices from the Color Swatches palette to find and remove unused colors.

Pauline's Tip 16.5

Use the Link Options menu choice under the Element menu to prevent PageMaker from automatically including high resolution versions of graphic images in its documents.

Pauline's Tip 16.6

Create all blends in bitmapped editing applications like Photoshop. You will have more control, they will be of higher quality, and will print faster. Use Dithering and add Noise and Gaussian blur to blends to prevent banding on output.

PAULINE'S DIGITAL IMAGING TIPS

Pauline's Tip 16.7

When creating clipping paths in Photoshop, be sure to create simple paths with few control nodes by setting tolerance at 2.0 and above during the creation of the path from a selection. Set the flatness ratio to 3.0 or above to facilitate output at high resolution.

Pauline's Tip 16.8

Use Levels and Curves in Photoshop instead of Brightness and Contrast controls to make tonal adjustments on photographic images.

Pauline's Tip 16.9

When adjusting the resolution of a contone image in Photoshop, do not merely add resolution to a file. This will destroy your image. You can safely increase the resolution of a contone image by reducing its dimension while holding the file size constant in the image size dialog box.

Pauline's Tip 16.10

When scanning always use a two-step scanning process which includes an initial low resolution prescan. This scan is used to analyze and adjust settings which will be applied during a second high resolution scan.

Pauline's Tip 16.11

Before converting bitmapped images to vectors using Streamline, set the tolerance to a high number, usually 4–5, to reduce the number of nodes generated by Streamline.

Pauline's Tip 16.12

Construct complex images in layers in both painting and drawing applications. This makes both initial construction and subsequent editing and troubleshooting much easier. Save native copies of the original layered images prior to export as printable TIFFs and EPSs.

Pauline's Digital Imaging Tips

Pauline's Tip 16.13

Convert type set in drawing documents to graphic outlines prior to exporting the file as an EPS document. It is also a advisable to limit the amount of type which is set in any document slated for conversion to an EPS. Avoid converting small (≤20pt.) and serif typefaces.

Pauline's Tip 16.14

Be sure to remember to split long paths and set path flatness ratios to at least 3 prior to export as an EPS in all vector-based documents.

Pauline's Tip 16.15

In general, use applications for the purposes for which they were intended. Perform layout and typesetting with applications like QuarkXPress and PageMaker, draw with applications like Illustrator, FreeHand, or CorelDraw, and paint with applications like Photoshop and Painter.

Pauline's Tip 16.16

For highly complex paths, use your drawing application's ability to decrease the path complexity by reducing the number of control points which occur along the paths.

Pauline's Tip 16.17

Learn a small number of applications very well, rather than trying to learn several varieties of each kind. Become expert at one page layout, one drawing, and one painting application. Experiment with others after you are well grounded in your primary applications.

Pauline's Tip 16.18

Dedicated preflighting utilities such as FlightCheck from Markzware often provide the most complete and dependable preflighting, troubleshooting and file collection capabilities. FlightCheck can be used to preflight PostScript and PDF documents as well as native application document files. And while these tools can be used to preflight PostScript and PDF files, there is no substitution for a properly constructed and preflighted native document file.

CHAPTER REVIEW

Check Your Comprehension

Multiple Choice Questions

To help you review the topics covered in this chapter, answer the following multiple choice questions.

1. What is our battle cry for file prep?
   A. Collect file components
   B. Reduce file size
   C. Simplify file complexity
   D. All of the above

2. Which of the following QuarkXPress tools allows us to check on our fonts and graphics?
   A. Page setup
   B. Font and graphic utility
   C. Print dialog
   D. None of the above

3. What is the name of the preflight tool that comes with PageMaker ?
   A. FlightCheck
   B. Preflight Pro
   C. Save for service provider
   D. Collect for output

4. The preflight tool on InDesign will do the following:
   A. Check for font use
   B. Check graphic use and linking
   C. Collect all the document components
   D. All of the above

5. In Photoshop, which of the following should we use to help gradients print more smoothly?
   A. Thresholding
   B. Dithering
   C. Adjusting flatness
   D. None of the above

6. _____ controls the number of control points along a Photoshop clipping path.

A. Threshold

B. Dithering

C. Resolution

D. Flatness

7. Which of the following controls the printing smoothness of vector paths?

A. Threshold

B. Dithering

C. Resolution

D. Flatness

8. Which of the following should we remove from documents before we print?

A. Linked graphics

B. Font files used in the document

C. Unused colors

D. Used colors

9. Which of the following should be used to adjust brightness and contrast in Photoshop?

A. Brightness and contrast sliders

B. Levels and curves

C. Resolution

D. Dithering

10. _____ files are complete but not very editable.

A. Native document

B. PDF

C. TIFF

D. PostScript

11. PDF files have the following characteristics:

A. Complete if constructed properly

B. Viewable on screen on multiple platforms

C. Editable

D. All of the above

12. Which of the following provides complete preflighting for native QuarkXPress, PageMaker and InDesign documents, PostScript and PDF document files?

A. Collect for output

B. Save for service provider

C. FlightCheck

D. ID Preflight

Check Your Understanding

Concept Questions

To help you review and expand your thinking on the topics covered in this chapter, answer the following questions.

1. What is preflighting and why is it important?

2. What are the key elements which need to be collected and sent to a service company in order for them to output your files properly?

3. What are unused colors and what should be done with them? Explain why.

4. What potential problems do we have with gradients and how can we prevent them?

5. What are clipping paths? Describe the two biggest potential problems with creating, editing and printing clipping paths. What tools do we use to prevent these problems?

6. When converting pixel-based images into vector-based images, what preflight issues do we need to address?

7. Describe the difference between a native document file, a PostScript file and a PDF document. What are their relative strengths and weaknesses?

8. Outline the steps and key setting which must be addressed to create a proper PostScript file document.

9. Detail how we would configure Distiller for creating a PDF for commercial printing.

10. Describe how you would reset the Job Option settings from Question 9 if you intended to prepare the PDF for viewing over the Web.

PROJECTS

1. Open any native page layout document file and do the following:
   A) Check for font and graphic links
   B) Print this native document file to a laser printer
   C) Collect the document and its linked graphics and font files
   D) Set up for printing a PostScript file of this document
   E) Print the PostScript file to disk
   F) Print this PostScript file to the same laser printer as above
   G) Prepare the Job Options setting in Distiller to create a PDF file for commercial print
   H) Create a PDF for the PostScript file you created in E) above
   I) Print this PDF file to the same laser printer as above
   J) Compare and contrast the three printed documents for any variations.

Part 4

Finishing the Project

SCREENING

P

TRAPPING

T

PROOFING

DISK PREP

Client Disk

SEPARATIONS

CYAN

MAGENTA

YELLOW

BLACK

17
Screening Your Images

As the Byte Turns continues...

*Will Danny learn to scan his images for the proper lpi, or
will Pauline screen more than his images the next time Danny calls?*

Why don't the printed versions of my photos look more like the originals?

Well, I'm not sure.

I wish I understood how a scanner worked.

Can't we make them better?

Danny's original images are continuous tone, while the printed versions are halftone dot pattern equivalents. Plus, Danny did the original scans and sent us only raw scan files.

Chapter Objectives

In this chapter you will learn:

- ◆ **Screening technologies**
- ◆ **How AM screens simulate grayscale**
- ◆ **Setting screen angles and frequency**
- ◆ **How FM screens simulate grayscale**
- ◆ **Why dot gain occurs**
- ◆ **Adjusting for dot gain**
- ◆ **Key Terms**
  - • Screening
  - • Halftoning
  - • AM screening
  - • FM screening
  - • Screen angles
  - • Screen frequency
  - • Line screen or lpi
  - • Moiré
  - • Dot gain
  - • Curve and Curve tool

INTRODUCTION

As we have discussed earlier, and particularly in Chapters 9 and 10, your electronic documents and digital images are converted into spots and dots. In this chapter we take a closer look at the patterns of dots, known as screens, which are used to recreate our continuous tone grayscale and color images. There are two basic dot patterns or fabrics which are used to print images, conventional halftone **screening** also known as **halftoning** or **AM screen**ing, and stochastic screening, also known as **FM screening**. AM screens uses changing dot size, with a consistent dot spacing, which are printed at specific **screen angles** and frequencies, to create the impression of changes in grayscale value. FM screening employs changes in dot spacing, rather than dot size, to simulate changes in grayscale values. Most commercial printing companies utilize conventional AM screening technologies, while many desktop and large format inkjet printers employ FM screens, which often have lower resolution, and therefore file size requirements.

The spreading or bleeding of ink which occurs when ink or toner is applied to a substrate is known as **dot gain**. The spreading of ink or toner dots causes the screen dots to grow in size as the ink or toner spreads into and/or across a print surface. This growth on dot size results in the darkening of images. The amount of dot gain which occurs is largely affected by the type of substrate. For instance, uncoated papers typically have larger dot gain characteristics than coated papers. Correction for this dot gain, often through the application of a **curve**, is required in order for images to print with the proper and consistent brightness and contrast. Dot gain correction can occur during the scan, in Photoshop or at a RIP.

Each screening technology and version has its own resolution and dot gain characteristics. For instance with AM screening, higher screen frequencies require higher file resolution requirements. In addition, FM screened images have different dot gain characteristics than AM screened images. Ask your output service provider for guidance on image resolution and dot gain correction requirements.

SCREENING TECHNOLOGIES

Reproducing images with dots

There are four basic kinds of images which need to be reproduced on a printing press: text, line art, tints, and continuous tone images. Most of our current printing technology uses dots to reproduce these images. There are basically three kinds of dots: laser dots, halftone dots, and stochastic dots. Laser dots, sometimes referred to as laser "spots," are the small individual dots created by a laser imaging engine such as a laser printer or an imagesetter. The size of the dot produced by a print engine depends upon the resolution of that particular printer. A 300 dpi desktop laser printer creates laser dots which are 1/300" x 1/300" square. A 1200 dpi imagesetter creates laser dots which are 1/1200" x 1/1200" square. Some printers have the ability to create more than one size of laser dots, which allows them to print at more than one resolution. The density of the dot pattern which a laser printer or imagesetter is capable of producing is determined by the resolution of the device. A 300 dpi laser printer can create a pattern of identical dots using 300 dots arranged vertically and horizontally in every square inch (90,000 dpi^2). Any combination of these 90,000 dots can be placed or "turned on" on a page. If all 90,000 dots are placed, a solid 1" black square will result. If none of the 90,000 dots are placed, a solid 1" white square will result. This is how text and line art images are created, either by placing or not placing dots at various points on a page. Halftone and stochastic dots are used to reproduce tints and contones and are constructed from groups of laser dots.

Reproduction of solid text and line art images, such as the solid "P" shown in Fig. 17.1 is fairly straightforward. Solid images can easily be reproduced by merely placing identically sized laser dots end to end and/or side by side in whatever shapes or sequences are required to recreate the image. The size of the dots used is determined by the resolution of the printer. The smaller the dots used to reproduce an image (that is, the higher the resolution of the printer), the finer the detail and the sharper the images which can be reproduced. The solid black "P" shown in Fig. 17.1 is a good example of how dots can be arranged to create a text character or line art image. Notice how higher resolutions will create images with sharper edge detail. Colors can be applied to those solid dot patterns if required.

Image reproduction gets a bit more challenging when we try to reproduce a tint or tone (an area filled in with one shade of gray), and particularly when we try to reproduce a continuous tone (contone) image where tonal values vary continuously across an image, such as in a blend from one shade of gray to another or in a photograph of a person's face.

Why screens?

To fully appreciate the challenge of reproducing a continuous tone (contone) image, we must remember that we are restricted to the use of dots when we want to reproduce an image on a printing press. We do not have the luxury of directly creating shades of gray or colors as we can in photography. PostScript laser printers and imagesetters are essentially dot production machines. At any given position on a piece of film or paper, an imagesetter will either place a dot or not place a dot.

Since we cannot directly create tints or shades of gray, we are forced to use patterns of dots called screens to simulate grayscale values. This simulation takes advantage of the limited ability of the human eye to resolve or distinguish small dots which sit next to each other. Traditionally, we have created dots of various sizes placed closely beside each other to simulate the impression of a grayscale value. These variable-sized dots are called halftone dots. Halftone dots are composite dots constructed out of combinations of laser dots. By using combinations of laser dots to build halftone dots, we can construct halftone dots of various sizes. Unlike laser dots, most halftone dots are separated by space because they are created in a grid pattern known as a halftone grid. Unless the individual halftone dots are large, they do not touch. We generate patterns of halftone dots to simulate the appearance of shades of gray in printed images. Small halftone dots are used to simulate low grayscale or screen percentages such as 10 or 15 percent. Large halftone dots create high tonal or screen values. Larger halftone dots require greater numbers of laser dots or spots to construct them. An area filled with halftone dots of all the same size will create a tint of one tonal value such as a 25% tint or screen. This area will appear to the human eye as an area filled with 25% gray. An example of a 25% tint and an enlargement of the screen pattern used to create it appears in Fig. 17.1. Color can be applied to this area to create a 25% tint of that color. That same area filled with halftone dots of gradually varying sizes creates a graduated screen such as that seen in the third "P" shown in Fig. 17.1. A constantly varying pattern of dot sizes will simulate a continuous tone image, that is, one where the grayscale values vary across the image. This is how grayscale photographs (such as the girl's image in Figure 17.1) are reproduced through printing. The gradual change in tonal values across in a person's face is constructed from a gradually changing pattern of various size halftone dots (see Chapter 8, "Resolving Resolution," for a detailed discussion and example of how a halftone dot is constructed).

Color contones

Meeting the additional challenge of reproducing color as well as tonal variation is accomplished through the use of four overlapping halftone screen patterns. Figure 17.2 shows how a pattern of four overlapping halftone patterns, which have the four process colors CMYK applied to them, are used to create a halftone simulation of a continuous tone color image. The enlarged view shows a highly magnified view of the four overlapping patterns of halftone dots, each with a separate process color applied to it. Halftone dots can form various shapes—9some are round, others are square, elliptical, or even diamond shaped. Halftone dot size and shape may be controlled either through an application or, more commonly, at a RIP. The halftone dots shown in Fig. 17.2 are round dots.

Image Example **Expanded View of Printed Image**

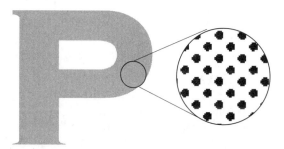

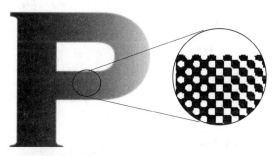

Solid Text and Line Art Images

Text and line art images which are solid, that is 100 percent grayscale or black, can be reproduced by placing solid laser dots end to end with no space in between. Only black and white tones need to be produced. Any solid colors can be assigned to either the black or white area during the printing process. The size of the dots and the stair-steps depend upon the resolution of the image. Higher resolution equals smaller dots.

Screened/Tinted Text and Line Art Images

Images such as this 25 percent grayscale image which are *not* solid images (images of less than 100 percent gray) require the use of spaced halftone dots. These are collections of dots rather than individual dots to simulate the effect of grayscale images. In a halftoning system the halftone dots are equally spaced, and the size of the dots is modified to simulate various shades of gray.

Gradations / Degradés / Blends

A gradation from one shade of gray to another is the simplest kind of contone image. Images such as this 0–100% grayscale blend, known as a gradation, gray ramp, or degradé, are simulated by generating rows of halftone dots of gradually increasing or decreasing sizes. Blends can be created by forming two overlapping gradations. Often a different color will be assigned to each gradation.

Contone Images

This is an example of a complex contone. Complex contones have a wide variety of grayscale areas grading one into another. These areas are reproduced using a complex pattern of equidistant halftone dots of various sizes. The sizes vary according to the lightness or darkness of various parts of the image.

▼ *Figure 17.1 Laser Spots and Halftone Dots*

Small individual dots are all most laser printers and imagesetters have to create images with. Solid areas like the top "P" are fairly easy to construct. A printer lines up laser spots end to end to fill a solid area or create a continuous line. Tones can be reproduced by producing patterns of closely spaced dots, called halftone dots. Traditional halftoning creates patterns of equally spaced dots and varies the size of the dots to produce various shades of gray. Each halftone dot is constructed out of numerous laser spots.

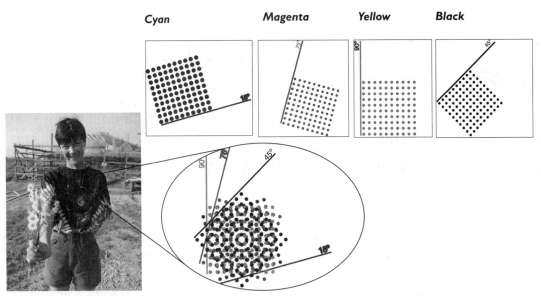

Cyan   **Magenta**   **Yellow**   **Black**

▼ *Figure 17.2 Color Contone Images: Overlapping Four Color Process Halftone Screens*

Complex color contones such as this photograph are reproduced using a complex pattern of four overlapping screens of halftone dots. There is one screen pattern for each process color. Each color is printed at a different angle to avoid the generation of moiré patterns. Colors are separated as much as possible across the available 90°. The three strongest colors—black, cyan, and magenta—are each separated by 30°. The fourth and weakest color, yellow, is separated from two of the other colors, in this case cyan and magenta, by only 15°. When all four color screens are combined, a continuous tone color image simulation is produced. Note the rosette pattern which results when the four screens are in perfect registration.

Note: A color version of this image can be found in the color plate section on page C-9, Fig. C.13.

▼ *Figure 17.3 Moiré Pattern Generation*

When two or more overlapping screens are printed out of registration, repeating geometric patterns known as a moiré pattern can result. Printing each screened color at a different and optimum angle helps reduce the occurrence of moiré patterns. Because yellow is separated from magenta and cyan by only 15°, it tends to form moiré patterns with them. In a dark image any yellow moiré is not very noticeable, but in light images areas such as tans and pastel greens these moirés may be apparent. It is the repeating pattern of halftone dots which makes conventional screening technology prone to the development of moiré patterns. The use of frequency modulation screening technology, where dot placement rather than dot size is used to create tonal variations and the image dots are more randomly placed, removes this problem of moiré pattern development.

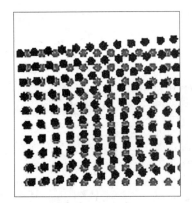

Note: A color version of this image can be found on page C-9 in the color plate section in the center of this book (see Fig. C.14).

This process of creating halftone dots was traditionally accomplished by taking a high contrast photograph of a continuous tone (photographic) image which was covered with a special photographic screen. The photo was then exposed through the screen onto photographic paper resulting in the image being recreated out of this screen generated pattern of dots, known as a halftone screen. The resultant high contrast, pattern of dots image, contains dots which vary in size to correspond to the grayscale value of that portion of the underlying image from which that dot was created. In a PostScript-based electronic publishing system, this screening process is performed by the PostScript RIP (raster image processor). Until a digital contone is actually processed by the RIP, the image information retains grayscale values.

Screening angles

Overlapping patterns of halftone dots are usually printed at varying angles from each other. When contone color images are printed with the process colors Cyan, Magenta, Yellow, and Black, each color is printed at a different angle to help prevent the pattern of dots from interfering with each other. The conventional angles used for printing the four process colors are 90° for yellow, 75° for magenta, 45° for black, and 15° for Cyan. These angles provide the maximum angular distance between each color, which should minimize the geometric interference between them when they overlap during the printing process. This scheme of separating the angles at which colors are printed helps dramatically, but it is not perfect.

If one or more of the screen patterns is misaligned during the imaging of printing process, the screen patterns can interfere with each other. When this interference pattern occurs, it forms a repeating pattern of dot groups called a **moiré** pattern. Figure 17.3 shows a moiré pattern and how it can be produced by two misaligned screens. Moiré patterns tend to be more obvious in lighter areas such as yellows and tans than in darker areas of an image such as browns and dark greens. This is because the misaligned dots forming the repeating pattern tend to be closer together and in some areas form darker sections of the patterns which will be more obvious when applied to a more lightly colored area. Over the years there have been numerous attempts to decrease the occurrence of moiré patterns by developing more sophisticated screening algorithms. Screening technologies such as rational and irrational screening, Adobe Accurate Screens, Linotronic HQS, and Agfa's Balanced screening technologies use custom screen angles to improve upon the quality of halftoned images and reduce the occurrence and impact of moiré patterns. All these technologies, however, use equally spaced halftone dots. Because of the regularity of their placement, they will always be prone to moiré formation.

Conventional screening

Conventional screening, sometimes called halftoning, refers to the use of regularly-spaced halftone dots. The key word here is regularly spaced. In conventional screening we vary the size or amplitude of equally spaced halftone dots to simulate various shades of gray. Technically, this is called amplitude modulation, or AM screening, because we are varying the size or amplitude of the dots to affect our creation of tonal value reproduction. In AM screening technology the center of

▼ **Figure 17.4 Dot Technologies**
These are two different dot manipulation methods for generating tonal values from patterns of dots, AM and FM screening. Here we see magnified views of a tint or screen of one tonal value produced by both methods. On the left is a magnified view of the pattern of equally spaced halftone dots which is characteristic of AM screening technology. On the right is a magnified view of a tint generated by randomly spaced dots used in FM screening technology.

▼ **Figure 17.5 Halftone Tint**
Above is a magnified view of a tint or screen produced by conventional AM screening technology which employs equally spaced halftone dots. Note the regularity of dot pattern. Creation of tonal variations is accomplished by varying dot size. AM screening is prone to the development of moiré patterns due to the regularity of the dot spacing.

▼ Figure 17.6 Stochastic Tint
Above is a magnified view of a tint or screen produced by stochastic or FM screening technology which employs randomly spaced dots. Note the irregularity of dot patterns. In FM screening technology dots is randomly placed within an area. Creation of tonal variations are accomplished by varying the density of the dots rather than their sizes. FM screening technology is less prone to moiré creation.

▼ Figure 17.7 Gradations
Above are two gradations. The one on the left is generated with conventional AM halftone dots where the dot size is varied to create the changing tonal values across the gradation. The gradation on the right was produced with FM screening. Note how the dot density rather than the dot size increases from top to bottom.

each dot is equidistant from all surrounding dots. AM screening works similar to AM radio. With AM radio we are varying the amplitude or size of the radio wave to change a channel. In the case of AM screening we are varying the size of the halftone dot to change the simulated tonal value. As mentioned above, this regular spacing of halftone dots has some inherent problems of moiré pattern development, which are difficult to overcome completely. We are not, however, limited to amplitude modulation for accomplishing our tone reproduction.

Stochastic screening

Stochastic screening, also known as FM or frequency modulated screening, uses irregularly or randomly spaced dot patterns. With FM screening we vary the placement rather than the size of the dots to create tonal variations. Light tonal areas of an image will have widely spaced dots, while darker tonal areas will have more closely spaced dots. One of the several advantages of FM screening is the elimination of moiré patterns created when you have misalignment of two or more regularly spaced dots patterns. We also find the FM screening provides smoother gradations from one tonal value to another. FM screening also requires less image information and therefore lower resolution images as well as smaller file sizes to produce a quality equivalent to that of a conventionally halftoned screened image. Because of these advantages, many of the newer desktop printers use this new FM screening. FM or stochastic screening may eventually replace conventional screening as the standard method for the reproduction of tonal values. Figures 17.4–17.6 show comparisons of AM and FM screening technologies.

Screening frequencies

Conventional halftone (AM) screens can be printed at various output screen resolutions depending upon the nature and capabilities of the output device. Output screen resolutions are referred to by several related names including: **screen frequency**, **line screen**, or lines per inch (**lpi**). 300 dpi lasers create 50–60 lpi screens, 600 dpi laser print at 85 lpi (or below), while 2400–3600 dpi imagesetters can output images up to 133–200 lpi and higher. Higher line screens produce higher quality images, but they also require higher input resolution of our images. See Chapter 8, "Resolving Resolution," and Chapter 12, "Taming Your Scanner," for more information on the relationship between input and output resolution.

FM screening devices have neither predictable line screens nor screen angles, as the placement of the FM dot is random. However, there are various sized FM dots depending upon the resolution capabilities of the FM output device.

There are two basic screening patterns used in printing, AM and FM. It is important to know which screening technology you are using, and the specific details as well. Each screening technology and version has its own resolution and dot gain characteristics. For instance with AM screening, higher screen frequencies require higher file resolution requirements. In addition, FM screened images have different dot gain characteristics than AM screened images. Ask your output service provider for guidance on image resolution and dot gain correction requirements.

DOT GAIN OF SCREENED IMAGES

Any tonal image which is reproduced as patterns of dots will be affected by a phenomenon known as **dot gain**. Dot gain is the tendency for dots to grow in size when they are reproduced on a printing press. Dots of ink grow in size when printed on paper for much the same reason that a drop of colored water will expand when dripped onto a paper towel. The printing ink, like the colored water, is absorbed into the paper and spreads out as it does so. In addition, since the dots of ink are being pressed onto the page by the press, they tend to spread out. Some dot gain can occur during the plate making process, but most of it occurs during the application of the ink onto the page.

Dot gain values and variables

Dot gain values are expressed in percentages and are usually measured at the 50% dot. The 50% dot is used because 50% is generally the point of maximum dot gain, with dot gain values generally decreasing toward the highlight and shadow regions of an image. Dot gain percentage varies with the kind of paper on which you print. Coated papers generally exhibit smaller dot gain values than uncoated papers. Coated stock dot gain values will typically vary from 10% to 20%, while uncoated stocks will exhibit dot gain percentages varying between 20% and 30%. Some newspaper stocks exhibit even higher dot gain values.

There is a number of variables which affect dot gain characteristics: paper surface, texture, and stock, ink characteristics, press setup, screening technology, screen frequency, and paper moisture. Dot gain values often vary with ink type, and may even vary within a set of inks. For example, each of the four process colors (C, M, Y, K) exhibit slightly different dot gain characteristics. Dot gain tends to be greater with FM screened images than with AM screened images due to the larger surface-area-to-volume ratio characteristic of the FM screen's smaller dots. With AM screening technologies, higher screen frequencies also tend to create larger dot gain functions than lower screen frequencies, again due to the smaller dots used. Consult your printer to discuss what dot gain characteristics you can expect with the paper stock, screening, and printing setup to be used with your images.

Controlling dot gain

High quality images can be ruined when affected by dot gain. Images which are not dot gain corrected tend to look dark and have lower contrast than they should. Midtones, in particular, tend to look dark due to the high dot gain characteristics at 50%. A 20% dot gain at 50% will push midtone values up around 70%, thereby darkening the entire image. Figure 17.8 shows the progressive changes a contone image experiences as it proceeds through a digital production process, where dot gain occurs, and the effect dot gain can have on an image. If you are creating your own final high resolution images, you should always adjust for dot gain to help assure that your images look good when they are reproduced on press. A dot gain correction curve can be applied either during the scanning process, after the scan in Photoshop or during the printing process at the RIP. For multipurpose images it is best *not* to apply dot gain during the scan, as this will restrict the use of the image to one device.

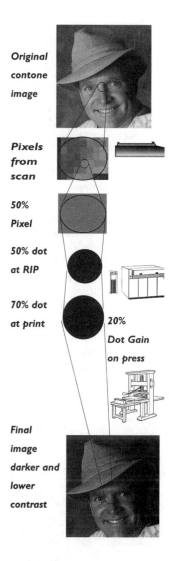

Original contone image

Pixels from scan

50% Pixel

50% dot at RIP

70% dot at print

20% Dot Gain on press

Final image darker and lower contrast

▼ *Figure 17.8 Effects of Dot Gain*
This sequence shows what happens to contone image data as it is scanned, RIPed, and printed. Dot gain occurs during printing. Here, a 20% dot creates a final image which is darker and lower in contrast than the original.

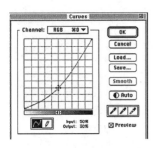

▼ *Figure 17.9 Curves Dialog Box in Photoshop*
Dot gain on a grayscale contone image can be adjusted using the Curves dialog box in Photoshop. Here is a correction for a 20% dot gain at 50%. The midtone point is depressed to 30%. On press this will return to 50%, rendering the image in its proper tones. The percentage of dot gain adjustment decreases toward the highlight and shadow ends of the tone curve.

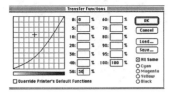

▼ *Figure 17.10 Transfer Functions in Photoshop*
Transfer Functions from Photoshop can help adjust for dot gain on a grayscale contone image. Here is a correction for a 20% dot gain at 50%. The midtone point is again depressed to 30%. On press this will return to 50%, rendering proper tones. The percentage of dot gain adjustment decreases toward the highlight and shadow ends of the tone curve.

Grayscale contones

There is no automatic method in Photoshop of applying a dot gain correction to a grayscale contone. There are two easy ways to adjust for dot gain, however. The first method, making a gamma curve adjustment in the **Curves tool** dialog box, permanently alters the image. The adjustment is easy. Obtain the 50% dot gain figure from your printing company, open the Curves dialog box, then click on the middle of the gamma curve at the 50% mark and pull it down to the 30% mark. Use the In/Out reading at the bottom of the dialog box to help you place the new point. Figure 17.9 shows how a 20% dot gain adjustment would look in Curves. Note how this gamma curve adjustment results in a maximum dot gain compensation at 50% with gradually decreasing values toward the highlight and shadow end of the curve. The advantage of making a dot gain adjustment with Curves is twofold. First, you see the results of the adjustment on screen, and second nothing else has to be done to the image for the dot gain adjustment to be applied. The disadvantage of the Curves adjusted dot gain control is that the change is permanent and specific to that print job. If you use a Curve adjustment to compensate for dot gain you may want to save a copy of the image before you apply the Curve adjustment. It is also a good idea to label the two images differently so you can easily distinguish them. I add a w/C onto my images to indicate they are saved with a Curve correction. For example, an original image may be named Portrait CMYK 200.Tiff and the Curves adjusted image I would name Portrait w/C CMYK 200.Tiff.

If you intend to multipurpose an image (use it for several different purposes), you may want to utilize a second alternative for applying a dot gain correction: Transfer Function. To create a Transfer Function in Photoshop, choose Page Setup from the File menu, then click on the Transfer button in the lower left portion of dialog box. Tab through the grayscale percentage data areas until you reach the 50% box. Enter the dot gain value, 20%, in the 50% box and a gamma curve identical to the one you created in the Curves dialog box will be created. Save this Transfer Function. The next step is to save your image as an EPS file along with the transfer curve you just created. You will notice that your image will not be altered on screen. The transfer Function will be applied only when the image is RIPed. (Refer to Figure 17.10 to see an example of the creation of a Transfer Function curve in Photoshop.)

Again, the advantage of using a Transfer Function is that the curve is applied only when the image is RIPped and does not alter the original image. Another advantage to using a Transfer Function is that if you have more specific dot gain data which you need to apply to percentages other than 50%, it is easier to create these custom curves as Transfer Functions due to the tab-through nature of the Transfer Function dialog box. If you will be printing your image on several different printing devices, such as a desktop printer for proofing, a banner printer for making a poster, and then finally on an offset press, you can apply a different Transfer Function curve for each printer and never alter the original image.

Color contones

The control for dot gain of a color image can take place as early as during the scan of the image, and this may be desirable if an image is only going to press and will be printed only once on a particular paper stock and on a specific press. However,

in the age of multipurposing of images, it is better to adjust for dot gain later in the production process, either when the image is converted from RGB to CMYK, or through the use of a transfer curve when going to press. Photoshop allows you to adjust for dot gain when you convert an image from RGB mode into CMYK mode. Prior to the mode conversion, you can assign a dot gain value in the Printing Inks Setup dialog box, which will then be applied to the image when it is converted from RGB to CMYK. (See Figs. 18.5 and 18.7 in Chapter 20, "The Proof Is in the Separations," for more information on assigning dot gain during separations.)

With color contones, as with grayscale contones, the advantage of using a transfer curve is that the curve is only applied when the image is RIPed and does not alter the original image, and custom curves are easier to construct. Images which utilize transfer curves must be saved in EPS format out of Photoshop in a fashion similar to how we saved the grayscale images in the previous section.

CHAPTER SUMMARY

Two basic patterns of dot, AM and FM, are used to print images. AM screening use changing dot size, with a consistent dot spacing, printed at specific screen angles and frequencies, while FM screening employs changes in dot spacing, to simulated changes in grayscale values. Commercial printing companies most commonly use conventional AM screening technologies, while many desktop and large format inkjet printers frequently employ FM screens, which often have lower resolution, and therefore file size requirements.

Both AM and FM screen dots exhibit dot gain. Dot gain causes darkening of images. The amount of dot gain, and therefore darkening which occurs is largely determined by the nature of the printing substrate. For example, uncoated papers typically have larger dots gain characteristics than coated papers. Dot gain correction, usually through the application of a curve, is required in order to maintain proper image brightness and contrast.

Higher screen frequencies, AM screens, require higher file resolution requirements. FM screened images have different dot gain characteristics than AM screened images. Don't be shy about asking your output service provider for guidance on image resolution and dot gain correction requirements.

PAULINE'S DIGITAL IMAGING TIPS

Pauline's Tips 17.1

Remember that your color images will be separated into individual pieces of film and plates for printing. Be sure to assign your colors properly and print test or proof separations to check your color breaks. Printing separations is really the only way to check to see if your colors will separate properly.

Pauline's Tips 17.2

Be sure that your individual spot colors are assigned different screen angles, particularly if those colors will be overlapped, or moiré patterns will likely result. If you consistently have trouble with moiré patterns when printing colored patterns and images, consider trying an FM screening method rather than conventional AM halftoning.

Pauline's Tips 17.3

Be sure to adjust for dot gain before you send a contone image to press; otherwise, your images will look darker and in lower contrast than you expected. Use Curves or Transfer Functions to adjust for dot gain in grayscale images. For color contones, apply dot gain adjustment during the RGB to CMYK conversion process. For multipurpose images it is best *not* to apply dot gain correction during the scan, as this will restrict the use of the image.

Pauline's Tips 17.4

Contone images and other patterns with tonal values will be printed as a pattern of dots called a screen. Visualize how your image will print as a screen and avoid pattern assignments which cannot be effectively screened. Avoid assigning grayscale values or patterns to thin lines because they will be imaged only as a discontinuous series of dots when printed.

Pauline's Tips 17.5

Choose a screening technology which matches the kinds of images you are trying to reproduce. We will increasingly have choices of different screening technology. Also know which technologies work best on the print device you will be using. Contone images often look better when reproduced with FM screening technology, particularly when printed on desktop banner printers, while solid area images reproduce better with AM screening technologies.

CHAPTER REVIEW

Check Your Comprehension

Multiple Choice Questions

To help you review the topics covered in this chapter, answer the following multiple choice questions.

1. Screening of images can best be described as
   A. The reproduction of image with patterns of dots
   B. The scanning of images into pixels
   C. Evaluation of images by image quality
   D. Yelling at images…or is that screaming? :-)

2. Which screening technology uses AM dots?
   A. Stochastic screening
   B. FM screening
   C. Conventional **halftoning**
   D. All of the above

3. Which pairs of terms match?
   A. AM – stochastic
   B. FM – change in dot size
   C. FM – change in dot spacing
   D. All of the above match

4. In AM screening each _____ prints at a different screen angle.
   A. halftone dot
   B. lpi
   C. color
   D. screen frequency

5. As AM output resolution screen frequency increases…
   A. Input image resolution should decrease
   B. Input image resolution should remain the same
   C. Input image resolution should increase
   D. There is no relationship between input and output resolution

6. The overlapping lines of AM dots when printing multiple colored inks can cause
   A. Dot gain
   B. Dot loss
   C. Moiré patterns
   D. Screen frequency reduction

7. The spreading out of ink and toner during the printing process is known as
   A. Ink trapping
   B. Dot gain
   C. Screening
   D. None of the above

8. Dot gain causes images to
   A. Print darker
   B. Print lighter
   C. Not print
   D. None of the above

9. Which of the following is likely to have the greatest dot gain?
   A. Uncoated paper
   B. Coated paper
   C. A sponge
   D. All of the above will be about the same

10. At which lpi would an commercial printing imagesetter typically print?
    A. 60 lpi
    B. 85 lpi
    C. 150 lpi
    D. All of the above

11. Which of the following would be least likely to exhibit dot gain?
    A. Conventional halftoning
    B. AM screening
    C. FM screening
    D. 150 lpi screening

12. Which of the following tools do we typically use to correct dot gain?
    A. Levels
    B. Curve
    C. Imagesetter
    D. All of the above

Check Your Understanding

Concept Questions

To help you review and expand your thinking on the topics covered in this chapter, answer the following questions.

1. Explain the concept of screening and why it is used in printing.

2. Explain the difference between conventional halftone dot and stochastic dot screening.

3. To what do the screening acronyms AM and FM refer, and how do they describe the screening technologies they represent?

4. Why do we use different screen angles to print different colors? What are the standard angles for the CMYK inks? Can you guess how these angles were chosen?

5. Explain the relationship between screen frequency and input resolution.

6. What are moiré patterns and how are they formed? How can they be prevented?

7. Explain what dot gain is, why it occurs, and its results.

8. How do we compensate for dot gain? What tools do we use, and how do we use them?

9. What are the three common places in the production process where dot gain correction can be applied? Which one should we avoid for multipurpose images; and why?

10. When in the production process do we typically make dot gain adjustments for color contone images? Explain why.

PROJECTS

1. Make a list of all the questions you would ask a printing company before you scanned any images you would send them for printing.

2. Scan an grayscale contone image at 200 ppi. Print this image on a 300 dpi/60 lpi laser, a 600 dpi/85 lpi laser printer and a 2400 dpi/150 lpi imagesetter. Look at each image with a hand lens and report the similarities and differences.

3. From a printing company obtain examples of 133 lpi, 150 lpi,and 200 lpi printed contone images. Examine each image under a hand lens and report the similarities and differences.

4. Scan a grayscale contone image. Print it to a laser printer with no dot gain correction applied. Now make a copy of the image. Apply a 50% to 35% (midtone input/output) dot gain correction curve in Photoshop. Print this image again on your printer. Describe the results.

18
Feeling Trapped

As the Byte Turns continues…

Will Danny D'Ziner and Pauline E Prepress live happily everafter? Or will they begin to feel TRAPPED by their too-numerous PostScript errors?

Why did those lines occur around some of the colored type on my last printed piece?

Looks like the graphics were not trapped.

What a mess!

Why were Danny's files not trapped?

You said he would be responsible for providing us with RIP-ready files and that he would do his own trapping!

Chapter Objectives

In this chapter you will learn:

- ◆ **What is trapping and why do we need it?**
- ◆ **Ink trapping vs. object trapping**
- ◆ **Trapping tools**
- ◆ **Who should perform trapping chores?**
- ◆ **When to use which trapping tool**
- ◆ **Trapping tips**
- ◆ **Key Terms**
  - • Object trapping
  - • Ink trap
  - • Stroke
  - • Choke
  - • Spread
  - • Overprint
  - • Knockout
  - • Common color

INTRODUCTION

In the world and lexicon of commercial printing, there are two types of trapping, **ink trapping** and **object trapping**. Ink trapping is related to how ink dots adhere to each other during the printing process and will not be discussed further here. Object trapping relates to how touching or overlapping objects which are assigned different colors, which therefore may print on separate press cylinders, will be aligned during the printing process. Due to slight shifts in paper alignment during the printing process, touching objects which are printed from different cylinders may become slightly misaligned during printing. When this happens unsightly paper-colored lines may show up between objects which should be touching. To prevent these open spaces between objects we slightly overlap, or trap, these objects. When we discuss object trapping, to avoid confusion, we always refer to foreground objects and background colors. This overlap or trap can be accomplished in several ways. Objects can be **spread** into their backgrounds, **choked** by their backgrounds, overprinted on top of their backgrounds, or even knock out an area in their backgrounds. Which techniques are used depends upon the objects and color involved. In general, in order to preserve the integrity of the size and shape of objects, light colors are moved into, or spread into, darker colors.

In the best of all possible worlds, we would apply trapping values to objects as we created them. However, because trapping values are very specific to individual presses, and proper trapping technique requires a fair amount of skill and experience, and because every print job, press and paper will have a different trap value, it is usually best to leave the object trapping chores to the printing company who will be printing the job. But even if you do not perform most of the trapping functions, you can help mitigate trapping problems by using trapping savvy object creation and color assignment techniques, like assigning **common colors** to touching objects which are built out of process colors.

WHAT IS TRAPPING?

Ink trapping

Originally (and still in some contexts) in the world of print, the phrase "ink trapping" referred to the relative tendency of one ink to stick or "trap" onto another during the printing process. This amount of stick or trap is important to know when determining what size the various printing dots should be when overlapping process colors are being printed on top of each other. Controlling the size of the original image dots on the film and printing plates and being able to predict the amount of increase or decrease in dot size, dot gain, or loss when it is printed by a press is important. The final size of the various color dots affects both the color and the darkness of an image which is being printed. The greater the stickiness of two overlapping inks, the smaller the size of the dots of the overlapping colors needs to be.

Object trapping

The second and currently more common use of the word trap refers to the amount of overlap which occurs between two areas of adjacent touching colors. The trap or overlap of two colors is usually measured in thousandths of an inch, but is sometimes measured in points as well. For the remainder of the discussion on trapping in this book, trapping will refer to this second definition: object trapping.

Why do we need trapping?

Trapping or overlapping of two adjacent colors may be necessary if those adjacent colors, which need to touch and fit snugly against each other, are applied by two separate cylinders on a printing press. Color elements which are supposed to touch on a page can sometimes end up being slightly separated during the printing process. This separation is generally caused by slight misalignments which can occur as paper is transported through a printing press. Other variables such as imprecision of image placement during film making and dimensional stability problems of the film itself can also contribute to misalignment problems. The amount of separation is usually small—only a few thousandths of an inch. But if two dark colors which are supposed to be touching are separated by even the smallest hairline, the generally light colored paper or other media will very obviously show through, ruining the intended nature of the border between the two colors. Preventing this appearance of inappropriate light lines between objects is why we overlap, or trap, objects of different colors on a printed page. Not all touching objects need to be trapped. Only those objects whose inks are applied by different or noncommon press cylinders need to be considered for trap.

Trapping basics

There are four basic ink application and trapping terms and techniques with which you need to be familiar: spread, choke, **overprint**, and **knockout**. But before we define and apply these specific techniques, it will be helpful first to discuss object relationships.

Object relationships

To prevent confusion and facilitate communication about the relationship of overlapping objects and their traps, it is helpful to agree on a frame of reference. The frame of reference we use in trapping is foreground and background objects. Keeping the concept of foreground and background clear is the key to keeping trapping relationships straight, particularly in complex documents with many layers. When determining trapping or overlap relationships, we always choose an object which we designate as the foreground. Then we determine the overlap or trapping relationship which that object has with all of the background objects with which it intersects. If that first object is in turn overlain by any other objects, then it will be considered a background object to all those overlying objects. When two objects meet edge to edge with no clear foreground or background relationship, one will need to be arbitrarily designated as the foreground object. In reality, any object created in a graphics or page layout application is constructed and will exist in its own layer. This construction layer relationship helps determine foreground and background relationships for objects which meet only at the edges.

TRAPPING CONCEPTS

There are four ways in which a foreground colored object can be printed in relationship to a background object. A foreground object can be spread into, choked by, overprinted onto, or knocked out of a background colored object. Trap values are always assigned to foreground objects.

Spreading

Spreading occurs when a foreground object expands or spreads out into or over a background color. Spreading the foreground object slightly increases its size as it spreads out over the background object. Spreading is an appropriate technique when the foreground color is lighter than the background color. Assignment of a spreading relationship between a foreground object and its background results in the assignment of a positive trap value to the foreground object; that is, the foreground object is expanding and its edge is moving out. (See Fig. 18.1.)

Choking

Choking occurs when a background object moves into or chokes the foreground object. Choking the background object slightly increases the area of the background object as it expands over the foreground object. To keep clear as to whether an object is spreading or being choked, always be clear on the foreground and back-

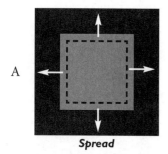

A

Spread

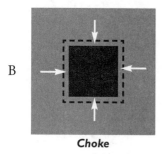

B

Choke

▼ *Figure 18.1 Spread vs. Choke*
This figure shows the difference between a spread and a choke. A spread (A) is generally applied where an enclosed lighter object (dashed edge) is expanded or spread out into a surrounding darker area.
A Choke (B) is typically applied where a lighter surrounding area is brought in around, or chokes, a darker object (dashed edge).
By moving lighter objects into darker objects, any changes in the sizes of the trapped objects tend to be less apparent.
Note: A color version of this image can be found in the color plate section of this book (see Fig. C.15 on page C-10 for the color version).

ground relationship between the objects. Foreground objects can only spread, and background objects can only choke. Assignment of a choking relationship between a foreground object and its background results in the assignment of a negative trap value to the foreground object; that is, the background object is moving into the foreground object. Its edge is moving into the foreground object. Remember that the trap value is always assigned to the foreground object, so even though the background is expanding, the foreground objected is being invaded; hence, the concept of the choke and the assignment of a negative trap value (see Fig. 18.1).

Overprint

Overprinting is the easiest of the trapping concepts to understand and control. With overprinting, a foreground object is printed directly over or on top of the underlying color, hence, the name overprint. This ink application technique is appropriate when you are printing very dark colors with grayscale values above 95 percent. Overprinting colors with grayscale values lighter than 95 percent should generally be avoided, as this will generally make a significant visible change in the color of the overprinted object. The color of the underlying object will be mixed with the overprinting object's color, resulting in the generation of a new and generally darker color. There are, of course, no positive or negative values associated with an overprint because edges do not move (see Fig. 18.2). Overprinting can also be used to create new colors when print colors are limited. For instance a 30% yellow screen overprinted on top of a 10% blue can be used to create a green.

Knockout

Knocking out is not really a trapping technique at all. In fact, knocking out implies an absence of trap or overlap altogether. A foreground object is said to be knocked out of a background area; that is, an area which is the exactly the same size and shape of the foreground layer is knocked out of or removed from the background object. In this way the foreground and background objects will just touch along their borders; they will not overlap. Boundaries between objects formed from knockouts are prone to misalignment problems which result in light media-colored lines showing through along the edges. Knockout can be most effectively applied when one or both the foreground or background object color is very light. If at least one color is very light, a media color which might show through will not be as apparent. Fig. 18.2 shows a knockout.

Trapping rules of thumb

As a general rule, light colors should move into dark colors. Avoid too much trap; it will create edge changes in the trap zone or area of overlap. This is particularly true along edges where light colors overlap. Too much trap along the boundaries between light colors will create darkened edges. Some good trapping applications will allow you to decrease dot percentages of the two overlapping colors within the trap zones to prevent this darkening. Too little trap will result in light lines showing through between the edges of intersecting colors. Ask your printer for the standard trap values and use them.

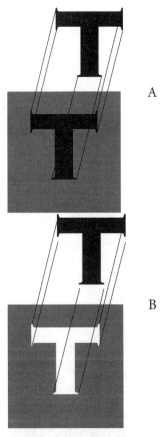

A

B

▼ *Figure 18.2 Overprint vs. Knockout*
This figure shows the difference between an overprint and a knockout. In the overprint (A) the black T is printed directly on top of the lighter cyan area without removing any of the cyan. In the knockout, the cyan area under the black T is removed or knocked out from behind the T. Overprinting is the safest way to trap because there are few alignment problems. However, overprinting will usually result in darker objects and color alterations of the overprinted object unless it is very dark (>95 grayscale value).
To trap this pair, would you spread the black "T" or choke the cyan background?
Note: A color version of this image can be found on page C-10 in the color plate section of this book (see Fig. C.16).

Who should trap?

There is a long term and ongoing debate over who should be responsible for trapping. In the best of all possible worlds clients would perform all the trapping chores because a file is most easily trapped when it is created. Then the printing company would not have to worry about it. In the real world, however, clients do not have the technical knowledge or skills necessary to assign traps correctly, and a poorly trapped file is more difficult to deal with than one with no trapping assigned at all. I come down in the middle of the debate. In general, I think it is best to let the output service bureau or printing company define the traps on files they will be printing. However, as a creator of files you should be knowledgeable enough about trapping to avoid creating difficult trapping problems. If you are not trap savvy, especially for process color traps, you will need to consult with the production staff of your printing company to determine some preferred ways of constructing your file. It's easy to construct absolutely beautiful color graphics files which are nearly impossible to trap and RIP. Consult with your printing company during the design and construction phase of your documents to avoid the biggest problems. Also check to make sure that your printing company will be trapping your file. Some companies have a policy of outputting your files without making any adjustments whatsoever. Following are some tips on avoiding trapping problems in the files you construct.

TIP

It is generally a good idea to leave trapping chores to the printing company who will be outputting your documents and images. The amount of trap which needs to be set between objects is very dependent upon the press on which the document will be printed and therefore specific to a specific printing press at a specific printing company. Furthermore most of the desktop page layout applications have limitations to their trapping functions. Print companies often have sophisticated trapping software which can applying trapping on the fly, even during the RIPing process.

TRAPPING TIPS

As mentioned, it is generally best to leave the trapping to your printing company. However, if you are the one who will be performing the trapping function, here are some tips for you.

➤ You can avoid the need for trapping between adjacent colored areas when you are working with process colors if you build adjacent touching elements with colors which have at least 15 percent of one dominant common color. Use cyan (C), magenta (M), or black (K) for your common color. Avoid using yellow (Y) as it is too weak a color to serve as an effective trap mask. Doing this will eliminate the need for trapping. For instance, if two touching elements contain at least 15 percent cyan, these two elements will not need to be trapped because the cyan plate will apply color across the trap boundary. Sharing two or more colors in adjacent colors will reduce the need for trapping at their boundary even more.

▼ **Figure 18.3 Trap Example**
Different applications use different methods for applying trap, but they all spread, choke, knock out, and overprint in one way or another. The FreeHand trap dialog box shows the foreground T being spread by 1 pt. If the reversed button were activated, then the background would choke. Note: A color version of this image can be found on page C-10 in the color plate section of this book (Fig. C.17).

- As a general rule, expand lighter colors into darker colors when you trap. This creates fewer noticeable problems in the overlap area or trap zone. (See Figures 18.3 and 18.4)

- If you do trap, note it on the document information sheet. You can print the window of a file job as a check disk content list.

- If you intend to apply trapping to a file, be aware of which portions of your document can be trapped by the application in which you are working. Most page layout applications such as QuarkXpress and PageMaker will not allow you to trap imported graphics. Also, you will generally not be able to trap page elements created in a page layout application such as type on top of an imported element such as an EPS graphic. Assign traps for EPS graphics in the original drawing program (ie., FreeHand, Illustrator, or CorelDraw). A good rule of thumb to know is that you can apply traps only to those items which are created in the application in which you are working.

- If you set chokes and spreads in a drawing application, be aware that most drawing applications **stroke** lines and outlines symmetrically; that is, they put half the stroke on either side of the line or outline. If you assign a 1 pt stroke to line in your drawing application, you are really creating only a .05 pt overlap or trap.

- Note the trapping capability of your program to flag those areas which may require or be favorable to traditional methods. Some examples of trouble traps: trapping on top of indeterminate (multiple) background colors; trapping on top of color TIFFs in a page layout application.

- Avoid spreading type, especially small serif type faces, because the enlargement will ruin the geometry of the typeface. In fact, it is a good idea to try and avoid either spreading or choking small type at all. Overprint dark type on top of lighter backgrounds whenever possible to retain the typeface's original geometric integrity.

- Design with trapping requirements and challenges in mind. Avoid, if you can, the creation of elements which are difficult to trap. Designs which include multiple overlapping blends are examples of designs to be avoided if possible.

- Note that trapping amounts are press-sensitive. A successful trap setting on one press may not work on another. Check with the production staff at your print company.

- Always consult with your printer for the preferred trap values before you start assigning trap values. Ask the printer if trapping is even necessary. Some single cylinder digital presses don't require trap creation.

- Ask your printer about an automatic trapping application. If the printer uses one, you may be wasting your time assigning traps because the automatic trapping application will probably just overwrite your trapping assignments.

- Be wary of sending PostScript files instead of a document files. PostScript files are unalterable and therefore fixed. Fonts and graphics are embedded, but this fact makes for a much larger file, so be careful. Also, be aware that text embedded in the included EPS file may not print. There is no room for error when you send PostScript files; what you send is what you get.

▼ *Figure 18.4 Trap Palette*
This closeup of the FreeHand trap palette indicates an application of a .25 pt trap. In addition, a trap nuance called tint reduction is also being applied. The tint reduction will decrease the screen value of the overlapping colors within the trap zone, or area of overlap to decrease the darkening which occurs where the two colors overlap.

TIP

Even if you do not perform the object trapping chores yourself, there are some document construction choices you can make which will minimize and often eliminate trapping problems altogether. When building objects with four color process, if you assign colors so that overlapping objects have at least two strong, common colors of at least 15% both objects will print on at least two plates, thereby minimizing the likelihood of a trapping problem occurring. The common color should be either cyan, black, or magenta but *not* yellow, as yellow is too weak to fill in a trap zone.

- Never set white to Overprint. White background areas should knock out to show the color of the underlying medium, usually paper.

- Take a field trip to your favorite printing company and have the folks there walk you through the printing process. Be sure to visit the stripping room to see how film is composited and discuss trapping with one of the strippers. Such a field trip will enlighten you in many ways about the printing process.

CHAPTER SUMMARY

There are two types of trapping, ink trapping and object trapping. Object trapping addresses how touching or overlapping objects which are assigned different colors, and print on separate press cylinders, will be aligned during the printing process. Due to slight shifts in paper alignment during the printing process, touching objects which are printed from different cylinders may become slightly misaligned during printing. When this happens, unsightly paper-colored lines may show up between objects which should be touching. To prevent these open spaces between objects we slightly overlap, or trap, these objects. When we discuss object trapping, to avoid confusion, we always refer to foreground objects and background colors. This overlap or trap can be accomplished in several way. Objects can be spread into their backgrounds, choked by their backgrounds, overprinted on top of their backgrounds, or even knock out an area in their backgrounds. Which techniques are used depends upon the objects and color involved. In general, in order to preserve the integrity of the size and shape of objects, light colors are moved into darker colors.

While applying trapping values to objects as we created them is a good idea in theory, trapping values are very specific to individual presses, and proper trapping technique requires a fair amount of skill and experience. So it is usually best to leave the trapping chores to the printing company who will be printing the job. But even if you do not perform most of the trapping functions, you can help mitigate trapping problems by using trapping savvy object creation and color assignment techniques, such as assigning strong (≥15%) common colors to touching objects which are built out of process colors.

PAULINE'S DIGITAL IMAGING TIPS

Pauline's Tip 18.1

You can avoid the need for trapping between adjacent colored areas when you are working with process colors if you build adjacent, touching elements with colors which have at least 15 percent of at least one dominant common color, either cyan or magenta.

Pauline's Tip 18.2

As a general rule, expand lighter colors into darker colors when you trap. This creates fewer noticeable problems in the overlap area or trap zone.

Pauline's Tip 18.3

When using chokes or spreads in drawing programs, be aware that most drawing applications stroke lines symmetrically, that is, half the stroke goes on either side of the line or outline. If you assign a 1 pt stroke to a line in your drawing application, you are really creating only a 0.5 pt overlap or trap.

Pauline's Tip 18.4

Note the trapping capability of your program to flag those areas which may require or may prefer traditional methods. Some examples of trouble traps: trapping on top of indeterminate (multiple) background colors; trapping items such as type on top of color imported graphics in a page layout application.

Pauline's Tip 18.5

Avoid spreading type, especially small serif type faces, as the enlargement of the characters will ruin the geometry of the typeface. In fact, it is a good idea to avoid spreading or choking small type at all. Overprint type whenever possible to retain the typeface's geometric integrity.

Pauline's Tip 18.6

In general, you will probably want to leave the trapping chores to your printing company, but some of these guidelines will help you avoid trapping problems. Always consult your printing company prior to building in traps to make sure you know to build them properly and that you use trap values appropriate for the printer's film and presses. Improperly assigned traps can be more of a problem than assigning no traps at all.

CHAPTER REVIEW

Check Your Comprehension

Multiple Choice Questions

To help you review the topics covered in this chapter, answer the following multiple choice questions.

1. Which type of trapping is involved with touching or overlapping color items on a printed page?

   A. Ink trapping

   B. Object trapping

   C. Fur trapping

   D. None of the above

2. Why do we need to worry about object trapping?

   A. Positions of objects on a page can shift during the printing process

   B. Inks may not stick properly when printed

   C. Objects may get trapped in the printing device and not get out

   D. We need fur for winter clothing :-)

3. Who should be responsible for applying the proper trapping values for a specific press?

   A. The document creator

   B. The ad agency

   C. The printing company

   D. Any of the above is fine

4. Which of the following trapping techniques involves moving a foreground object into its background color?

   A. Spreading

   B. Choking

   C. Overprint

   D. Knockout

5. What is the best way to handle trapping small solid type?

   A. Spread the type

   B. Choke the background

   C. Overprint the type

   D. Knock out the type

6. _____ is what happens when a color is entirely removed from behind an object.

   A. Spreading

   B. Choking

   C. Overprint

   D. Knockout

7. _____ can be used to prevent trapping problems with process colored items.

   A. Spreading type

   B. Knocking out

   C. Common colors

   D. All of the above

8. Which of the following generally should not be overprinted?

   A. White

   B. Type

   C. Solid colored objects

   D. All of the above

9. Which of the following objects should you avoid spreading?

   A. Lighter colored backgrounds

   B. Large objects

   C. Light colored objects

   D. Small serif type

10. Which of the following is a good general rule for trapping?

    A. Expand darker colors into lighter colors

    B. Expand lighter colors into darker colors

    C. Dark colors should choke light colors

    D. Light colors should overprint dark colors

11. What is a good minimum percentage of common color overlap?

    A. 5%

    B. 15%

    C. 25%

    D. 35%

12. Which of the following is a good reason to let your printing company perform trapping chores?

    A. Trapping values will be specific to their presses

    B. Accurate trapping requires considerable skill and experience

    C. Application trapping often leaves something to be desired

    D. All of the above

Check Your Understanding

Concept Questions

To help you review and expand your thinking on the topics covered in this chapter, answer the following questions.

1. Briefly explain the difference between ink trapping and object trapping.

2. What happens on a printing press which requires object trapping to be applied?

3. Why do you think we generally observe the trapping rule of expanding lighter colors into darker ones?

4. What kind of foreground objects should we nearly always overprint and why?

5. Describe the difference between a spread and a choke. Describe object/background circumstances under which you would use each one.

6. What is the difference between a knockout and an overprint? Describe object/background circumstances under which you would use each one.

7. What is meant by the concept of common color trap? When would you use this and how does this prevent trapping problems?

8. What is the difference between a multipurpose document and a repurposed document?

9. If we had light blue type object on a dark green background, explain the trapping issues involved with trapping this object successfully.

10. In general, who should perform trapping and why?

PROJECTS

1. In a page layout application document such as QuarkXpress or PageMaker set a lightly colored type object on top of a dark background. Now do the following:

A) Explain the foreground object to background object relationships here.

B) Set the type to knock out and print separations and a color composite.

C) Set the type to overprint and print separations and a color composite.

D) Set the type to spread and print separations and a color composite.

E) Set the background to choke and print separations and a color composite.

Which of the settings (A–E) gave the best result, and why?

19

The Proof Is
in the Separations

As the Byte Turns continues…

After all the PostScript heartaches, can Pauline E. Prepress and Danny D'Ziner endure the challenge of separation?

My print job looks different from the file I sent you. I didn't send a proof, but what difference does that make?

I'll check to see what happened.

Oh dear, not again. Why do I always get stuck in the middle??

Why can't she print Danny's file correctly?

GOOD GRIEF! I can't look at a disk and tell what's on it. Even when we launch a document, we cannot be sure that it is correct without the most recent proof!

Chapter Objectives

In this chapter you will learn:

- ◆ **Why we need separations**
- ◆ **Kinds of separations**
- ◆ **How to define spots and process separation**
- ◆ **The need for simplified documents**
- ◆ **Where, when, and how to perform**
  RGB to CMYK conversions
- ◆ **Proofing checklist**
- ◆ **Separation tips**
- ◆ **Key Terms**
  - • Separation
  - • RGB separation
  - • Spot color separation
  - • Process color separation
  - • Coats and finish separations
  - • SWOP
  - • UCR
  - • GCR
  - • Custom color profile

INTRODUCTION

In order for us to edit and output digital images we need to recreate these images in a form which allows us to manipulate them. Since computers only understand 0s and 1s we separate our images into grayscale valued building blocks. The grayscale values then control the application color values which are supplied by output devices. There are two fundamental **separations** which occur in the digital imaging process. The first separation occurs when we capture a color image with a scanner or digital camera. This separation converts a single color contone image into three (red, green, and blue) grayscale channels. The second major separation involves the reseparation of our three channel RGB images into four (CMYK) grayscale channels for printing. Color separation can also be created through the simple assignment of colors. There are two basic color systems which we use for printing, spot colors and process colors. Each spot color requires its own separation, its own ink color, and its own cylinder on a printing press. Process color separations create a wide range of colors by combining various percentages of cyan, magenta yellow and black on four separations, one for each color.

RGB to CMYK conversion can occur at many places in the production process; Also, there is an infinite number of RGB to CMYK conversion values. For commercial print output it is best to acquire RGB-CMYK setup values from your service provider. For desktop printers either manual setup or color profiles can be used. Before you send out files to be printed, be sure to proof your work. Part of this proofing process should involve printing separations to check for proper color assignments.

SEPARATIONS

Why separations?

Separations are required for both image capture and for multicolor printing. In order for us to capture and edit and then print a digital image, our images need to be separated into their basic color components. Since our scanners and computers are digital devices, they only work with digital data, that is data which is broken down into 0s and 1s. These 0s and 1s can be thought of as black and white values. As explained earlier in this book, in Chapters 6, 9, and 14, we combine multiple bits of information to capture and reproduce grayscale values. Grayscale values control color values, which are supplied by output devices. So the process of capturing an image with a scanner or digital camera, and then outputting that image to monitors or printing devices, involves a process of converting our color images into digitally generated grayscale values which in turn control the color values provided by various output devices. Scanners produce RGB color separated grayscale image. Monitors apply RGB values to produce color images whose values are controlled by the RGB grayscale values in an RGB image. These **RGB separations** are then reseparated into four (CMYK) grayscale separations (see Fig. 19.4). Color is then applied to each of these separations during the color printing process.

In commercial offset printing, each color is printed to a two tone (usually black and white) plate which then has color has applied to it on the various cylinders on a printing press. Each cylinder requires a separate black and white plate which carries a specific portion of the print image to be printed in that specific color. The image on each plate is created by exposure of light which shines through a separate piece of film created specifically for that plate. Increasingly, the film portion of this process, and in some cases even the plate portion, is being eliminated in favor of direct imaging on plates and press cylinders. But whether an image goes through a film-to-plate-to-press cylinder process or is directly imaged on cylinders, color images need to be separated into their component parts so that separate inks can be applied to the proper portions of an image in order to build the image properly on press.

Types of separations

There are basically four kinds of common separations: RGB, spot, process, and finishes. When you prepare a file for output, you need to make sure that all elements on your page are assigned the proper color separation values. Colors which are used in images, such as photographs, or assigned to objects can be found in color palettes in applications (see Fig. 19.1). Once a color is part of an application color palette it can be used to assigned to other objects in that document. Objects which are assigned the same colors will be separated to and printed on the same plates and cylinders on an offset commercial printing press (see Figs. 19.2 and 19.3).

RGB separation

The first separation to occur in the electronic publishing process occurs during the digitizing process, when an original contone color image is separated into three grayscale image channels. This digitizing is typically accomplished by a scanner or

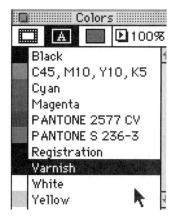

▼ *Figure 19.1 Color Palette*
This is the color palette from QuarkXPress showing the four process colors, a Pantone process color, a custom process color build using the four process colors, one Pantone spot color, and a varnish. There will be six individual separations printed on individual pieces of film from this list of ten colors. RGB colors should not be used in the printing process and should be removed. The varnish will be applied and separated, like a spot color. The process colors will be combined to create built process colors such as the Pantone process color and the custom process color, as well as any contone color images existing in the document. The registration color should be applied only to items such as crop, trim, registration, and fold marks which need to be placed on each separation. Note: A color version of this image can be found on page C-14 in the color plate section of this book (Fig. C.28).

▼ *Figure 19.2 Separation Setup*
This is the Print dialog box
with separation setup. Note
that only six separations will
be printed from the ten colors
listed in the color palette in
Figure 19.1. Here the SEPARA-
TION submenu choice is activated. This in turn activates
the list of separations shown
in the PLATE submenu.

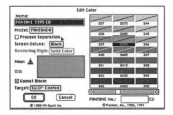

▼ *Figure 19.3 Spot Color
Separation*
This QuarkXPress edit color
dialog box demonstrates how
to designate a spot color to
separate as a spot color. Here
the spot color 3395 is assigned
from the Pantone spot color
swatch chart mode. Note that
the Process Separation check
box near the upper left hand
corner is *not* checked. If this
box is checked, QuarkXPress
will separate all items assigned
to this color on the four
process color plates. (see page
C-10, Fig. C.18 for a color version of this figure).

digital camera. The grayscale values in the three individual channels control the RGB values on an output device like a monitor. This RGB image is then reseparat-ed into a CMYK image for printing (see Fig 19.4).

Process color separations

The traditional process color system includes only four colors: cyan (C), magenta (M), yellow (Y), and black (K). These four process colors are used together in many different combinations to create a wide spectrum of colors. Unlike the spot color system where each spot color is applied independently of other colors, process colors are designed to work or build together to create other colors. So each color built with process colors will contain a combination of percentages of C, M, Y, and K. CMYK builds are particularly useful for recreating continuous tone color images like color photographs. If we tried to reproduce a color contone image with spot colors it would take thousands of colors, and therefore press cylinders, and would be astronomically expensive. Using the process color system, we need to use only the four process colors to recreate a continuous tone color image. Figures 19.5a and 19.5b show a demonstration of an image constructed two different ways: one with spot colors and one with process colors.

Spot colors separations

Spot colors are usually composed of specific mixtures of three ink colors. Each color is applied by its own cylinder on a printing press. The spot color gamut is very large. Spot colors are used when you want a very specific and usually bright color to print (see Chapter 14, "Color Me Right," for a detailed description of color systems). For each spot color which you want to print, a separate press cylinder will be required. This can become an expensive printing proposition in a hurry. If you print fewer than four colors, the use of spot color can be more cost effective than the four color process. Spot colors are most commonly used to print solid area line art and logo images, although they can also used to create multitonal contones such as duo-, tri- and quadtone images. Figures 19.5 a and 19.5b show a demon-stration of an image constructed two different ways: one with spot colors and one with process colors.

Coats and finishes

Although they are not colors, finishes, like varnishes, will be applied on a printing press just like colors are. In terms of how they will be applied and separated, fin-ishes should be thought of and treated just like spot colors. **Coats** and **finishes** are assigned to their own separations and therefore press cylinders, just like spot col-ors. Those areas of an image which need to have finish applied should be selected and designated for application just like a spot color. A finish is assigned a label just like a color and applied as a top layer on whichever items require a coating. Figure 19.2 shows an example of a finish item added to a color list.

Figure 19.5 shows an example of a seven-color chicken built out of both spot and process colors. While the spot color chicken will provide us with a more vivid chicken, the process color chicken will be a great deal less expensive to print.

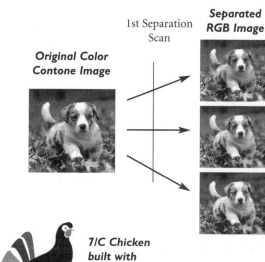
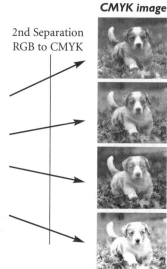
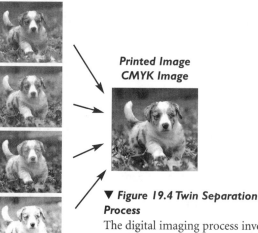

1st Separation Scan

Original Color Contone Image

Separated RGB Image

2nd Separation RGB to CMYK

Separated CMYK image

Printed Image CMYK Image

▼ *Figure 19.4 Twin Separation Process*

The digital imaging process involves two different separation events on the way to creating a printed image. The first separation is from color contone image to RGB. If your final output device is a monitor, you will stop here. If printing is your final destination a second separation is required converting from RGB to CMYK. (see page C-11, Fig. C.19 for a color version).

7/C Chicken built with 7 Spot Colors

Pantone 213 Plate

Pantone 2726 Plate

Pantone 389 Plate

Pantone Black Plate

Pantone 252 Plate

•

Pantone 3395 Plate

•

Pantone 486 Plate

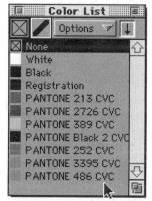

▼ *Figure 19.5a Spot Color Palette*

Each of the assigned spot colors seen in this palette will be printed on its own plate. Each differently colored portion of the image is separated and has a specific spot color applied to it from a different press cylinder. Note that all the extraneous colors have been removed from this palette. While multicolor spot color printing like this allows you to use vivid custom colors, it is far more expensive than using combinations of process colors to produce the many color variations. (See color plate section page C-11, Fig. C.20a for a color version).

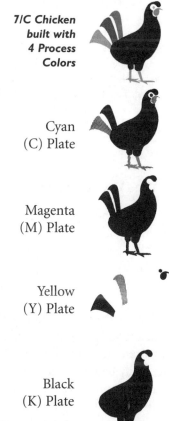

7/C Chicken built with 4 Process Colors

Cyan (C) Plate

Magenta (M) Plate

Yellow (Y) Plate

Black (K) Plate

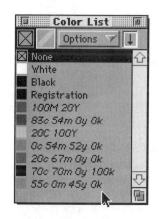

▼ *Figure 19.5b Process Color Palette*

All seven of the colors used here are created from various combinations of CMYK. Since only four sets of separations, film, plates, and cylinders are required to print this image, it is much less expensive to print than its spot color equivalent. Note that all the extraneous colors have been removed from this pallet to avoid confusion. (see page C-11, Fig. C.20b for a color version.)

Separations 393

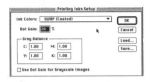

Before converting from RGB to CMYK, you should pay close attention to: 1) the ink color set chosen, and 2) the dot gain percentage. Contact your printer to obtain both. The dot gain percentage should be for the dot gain at 50%. The values set here will affect the appearance of the Separation Setup dialog box shown below. Note: This dialog box is from Photoshop 4.0. See Fig. 19.9 for the combined (Printing Ink and Separation) CMYK Setup dialog box found in Photoshop 5.0 and 5.5.

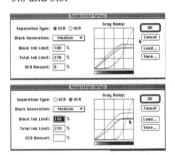

▼ *Figure 19.7 Separation Setup*

The values set in the Printing Inks setup dialog box above affect the curves shown here. Your choice of UCR or GCR will also affect the separation curves. The black generation begins at the three quarter tone for the UCR and at the quarter tone for the UCR curve. The overall placement of the UCR curve is lower due to the differences in the beginning of the black generation. Compare and contrast these curves with those used for other types of printing devices. See page C-12, Fig. C.22. Note: This dialog box is from Photoshop 4.0. See Fig. 19.9 for the combined (Printing Ink and Separation) CMYK Setup dialog box found in Photoshop 5.0/5.5.

How many and which colors to assign?

The number of colors which can be printed at any one time is limited by the number of print heads or cylinders which a printing device has. Most commercial printing companies have presses which have four, five, or six cylinders. Seven color presses are relatively uncommon, and eight are found even less frequently. Most desktop printing devices are limited to four print heads (usually CMYK). So it is very important to know how many final colors can actually be printed before we go off merrily assigning colors. It should also be reemphasized that objects that are assigned spot colors, which are frequently brighter and more highly saturated than process colors, which are then subsequently printed as CMYK process colors will rarely look the same as the original spot colors. Process simulations of spot colors are often darker and less saturated than their spot color originals. So if know that you will ultimately be printing a job on a desktop or commercial printing device using four color process, do not assign spot colors to begin with. Finally remember that every coat or finish which you apply will require its own cylinder on a commercial press. And while sheets can be run through a printing press more than once , this is usually much more costly than a single run printing.

Separations can occur at any of several steps in the electronic publishing process, including at the scanner, in Photoshop, through a page layout application, in a dedicated separation program or even during the RIPing process. The image created by separation at each of these devices is likely to be different. You will want to know where your separations are occurring. Choose the separation tool which gives you the best results and the most flexibility. If you are multipurposing images you may not want to convert to CMYK during the scanning process, but rather convert a copy of the original scanned image to CMYK to preserve the high color saturation of the original RGB image. Don't be shy about asking your service providers about the best conversion tool for their output devices.

SEPARATE WHERE?

A file may be separated into its various color components in any of several places including: during the scanning process, the original graphics application where a graphic was created such as Adobe Photoshop; from a page layout application which has separation capabilities such as QuarkXPress and PageMaker; from a dedicated separation application such as Adobe separator; or even at the RIP.

The first step in performing a separation is to decide who will perform the separation and then determine where. If your printer or service bureau is performing your high resolution scans for you and creating all of the original artwork, then they will generally be responsible for performing the separation. If you are doing your own scanning and art generation, then you may want to be responsible. In any case, have a discussion with your printer or separator to determine responsibility. If you will be performing the separation, seek your printer's advice on the best separation application and setting to be used for printing your files with their system.

Separating spot colors

The generation of spot and varnish separations is very straightforward and will often occur from the application where the page composition is occurring. This is often a page layout application such as QuarkXPress or PageMaker but may also be from a drawing program such as Illustrator or FreeHand if the page layout is performed there. The main problem to look out for with spot separations is to be sure that each spot color is set to print out on its on individual piece of film and that none of the spot colors is designated to be separated as a process color. Each application has its own way of indicating whether a color is destined to print as a spot or a process process color. Figure 19.3 shows how to designate a spot color in QuarkXPress. Note that you always want to make sure that the "Make Process" designation is never applied to a spot color. And just a reminder from the color chapter: Always choose your spot colors from a spot color swatch book. Don't depend upon the screen look of the colors, when you are choosing colors as the screen view is often unreliable.

Built process colors

Graphic, text, and other document elements which are assigned built process color values are some of the easiest images to separate. They are easy to separate if you have constructed the color values using color names from a process color swatch book such as the TruMatch or Pantone Process colors swatch books. With built process colors, there is never any question as to whether the colors will be on separate spot plates or on the process plates; they will always separate on the process plates. Always choose your built process colors from a color swatch book. Your monitor display of color is rarely dependable. And if you are trying to simulate a spot color, meaning get as close as as possible to a specific spot color while printing with the four (CMYK) process colors, be sure to use the Solid to Process swatch book for judging and assignment of your color, in order to assign the best combination of process colors (see Chapter 14, "Color Me Right," for a full discussion of this issue).

SEPARATIONS FROM PHOTOSHOP

The separation of process colors used to reproduce color contone images originally created in RGB color space (such as scanned or any digitally created images) is more complicated and demands much more attention than do **spot color separations**. The heart of the RGB contone separation problem centers on the difference in color gamuts which exists between RGB and CMYK color spaces. The separation of an RGB image into a CMYK image always involves a gamut compression (see Chapter 14 for a full discussion of this problem). The best rendition of RGB color into CMYK color space will occur if we map the original RGB image to the gamut of the specific CMYK device on which the image will be printed. This process is known as device-specific gamut mapping. Device-specific gamut mapping is accomplished through the creation and use of **custom color profiles.** Although this type of device-specific gamut mapping occurs infrequently today with our open DTP system, it will become more common in the future (see

▼ **Figure 19.8 RGB Setup**
Here the RGB Setup is being set for matching with commercial printing. It is important to set this RGB setting properly as it will dramatically affect the results of the RGB to CMYK conversion. sRGB should be avoided here if you are printing.

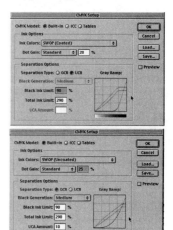

▼ **Figure 19.9 CMYK Setup**
These curves show the Separation Setup curves applied to an image to be color separated for printing on a SWOP commercial printing press. Note the difference in the starting positions and the effects of the black generation curves in the UCR and GCR variations. Obtain values for Ink colors, Dot gain, Black ink limit and Total ink limit from your printer. These curves will be applied to an RGB file when it is converted to a CMYK image, so be sure to make and set the correct choices and values in both dialog boxes prior to performing that conversion.
See color plate section page C-12, Fig. C.24 for color version.

▼ Figure 19.10 UCR Separations

Four separations are created here. Top to bottom, C, M, Y, and K using UCR black generation. Note how the black plate does not have as much tonal range as does the GCR black separation in Fig. 19.11. Also note how the C, M, and Y plates are darker than their GCR counterparts. See Color Plate section C-13 for a color version of this figure.

Chapter 14, "Color Me Right," for a more detailed treatment of color profiles). But even if you cannot choose a device-specific gamut mapping, you can at least apply some industry standard settings which will place your image well within the ballpark of where you need to be, and maybe even in the infield. We will use the settings and dialog boxes in Photoshop to demonstrate the process of properly converting an RGB image to a CMYK file. In Photoshop 5.5 there are two dialog boxes which are particularly important to the process of creating separations. These are the RGB Setup and CMYK Setup dialog boxes, both of which are found as submenu choices under the Preferences choice of the File menu. Be sure that you correctly configure these preferences prior to performing an RGB to CMYK conversion; these controls will be applied only during the gamut conversion and will have no effect after the conversion is complete. Call your printing company and ask for suggestions on the ink choices and specific values which you should enter into the following variables.

RGB Setup

Your monitor is a critical part of your publishing system, and controlling the way your monitor displays colors is key to obtaining high quality CMYK separations in Photoshop. Figure 19.8 shows the RGB Setup dialog box in Photoshop 5.5. This dialog box should be set up to match the final output device to which you will be outputting. In Fig. 19.8 the RGB Setup is configured for commercial printing. The values used in this dialog will dramatically affect the CMYK values and gamut of the final printed piece. If you are printing, sRGB should be avoided as a choice in the RGB menu, as this will severely restrict the color gamut of your image which can be reproduced. Ask your service bureau or printing company for which choices and values they recommend for use in this RGB Setup dialog box.

Printing ink setup/ink colors

The Printing Ink Setup dialog box (Photoshop 4.0) (Fig. 19.6) or the CMYK Setup (Photoshop5.0+) (Fig 19.8) is used to assign two key parameters of a color separation: 1) the ink set used, and 2) the dot gain. In the Printing Ink Setup/Ink Colors

IIII▶ TIP

If your are sending your files out to a commercial printing company, be sure to ask them for instructions on the best way to convert your RGB image to CMYK images. Some printing companies prefer UCR and others prefer GCR conversions. You may discover that it is best for the printing company to perform the conversion. For performing RGB to CMYK conversions for printing on desktop printers, consider using the color profile method. Color conversion profiles for a wide variety of devices come packaged with many applications, including Photoshop. While these generic profiles are not as precise as custom profiles, they can often get you in the close. Also remember that some desktop printers will automatically perform the RGB to CMYK conversion during the RIPing process, and your preconversion to CMYK may just confuse the issue. Be sure you know where and when your gamut conversion is happening.

menu you should choose the device which most closely matches the device on which you will be printing. Many printing companies use the **SWOP** (Specifications for Web Offset Press) Coated and SWOP Uncoated ink sets as defaults, but ask your printing company to be sure. The ink set choices you make here will affect the position and relationship of the curves in the Separation Setup dialog box. Note the difference between the two sets of curves shown in Figs. 19.6 and 19.9 which, respectively, correspond to the selection of SWOP Coated Printing Ink selections seen in Figs. 19.6 and 19.9. The differences between the two curves in these dialog boxes result in the different CMYK percentages which will be created when using **UCR** vs. **GCR** assigned for the separations. The positions and shapes of these curves will vary widely depending upon the inkset chosen due to differences in the colorants used, such as ink vs. toner, impurities, and behaviors which exist between the transparent inks used in SWOP printing and the thermoplastic toners used in color laser printing and the colorants used by other devices.

Dot gain

Dot gain is a measure of the amount by which a halftone dot of ink will grow when it is applied by a printing press (see Chapters 12 and 17, "Taming Your Scanner" and "Screening Your Images," for more complete discussions of dot gain). When you perform an RGB to CMYK conversion in Photoshop, the program will automatically apply the dot gain percentage entered into the Printing Ink Setup/CMYK Setup dialog box. For the SWOP setup shown in Figs. 19.6 and 19.9 the default dot gain is 20%. The dot gain of 20% refers to the dot gain which will be applied to a 50% halftone dot. A 50% dot will therefore be reduced to 30% and be expected to grow to 50% when printed on a printing press. Since the dot gain for most images is generally at a maximum around the 50% dot, a symmetrically decreasing dot gain curve is applied to dots as they approach the highlight and shadow points.

Dot gain varies with paper, ink, screen technology and frequency, and press conditions. Ask your printing company what dot gain percentage they recommend you assign for the press, paper, screen, and ink conditions which will be used for your job.

Using the dot gain function in the Photoshop Printing Ink Setup/CMYK dialog box will provide you with some generalized controls for dot gain. While this general control is much better than ignoring this setting, more precise control over dot gain can be achieved. If you want to gain more precise control dot gain, you can construct your own dot gain transfer curves and save them with the file (see Chapter 17, "Screening Your Images").

Separation setup

Configuring the Separation Setup/CMYK dialog boxes (Figs. 19.7 and 19.9) is the second step in preparing an RGB image for conversion and separation into a CMYK image. The curves you see in the Separation Setup/CMYK Setup dialog box are controlled partially by the choices you make in the Printing Ink Setup/Ink Colors dialog box and partially to the choices you make and values you assign in this Separation Setup/CMYK Setup dialog box. Figs. 19.7 and 19.9 would look very different if the SWOP ink settings were changed to a Color Laser Printer. The dif-

▼ *Figure 19.11 GCR Separations*
Four separations created, top to bottom, C,M,Y & K using GCR black generation. Note how the black plate has a much broader tonal range compared with the UCR black separation in Figure 19.9. Also note how the C,M, and Y plates are lighter than their UCR counterparts.
See Color Plate section C-13 for a color version of this figure.

ference between the two curves is primarily due to the different color characteristics of the transparent SWOP inks and the opaque thermoplastic toners used in the Canon Color Laser. You should notice that in the SWOP ink curves, the Cyan curve is much higher than the magenta and yellow curves. This disparity in curve strength is constructed to compensate for the impurity and therefore relative weakness of the cyan ink due to its contamination with yellow and magenta inks (see Chapter 12, "Taming Your Scanner," for a discussion of this phenomenon).

Besides selecting a UCR and GCR mode, you should pay close attention to the Black Ink Limit and Total Ink Limit assignments. These numbers affect the amount of ink which will be applied to the paper by the press. The Black Ink Limit will generally vary between 90 percent and 100 percent. The Total Ink Limit will generally range from 230 to 320 depending upon paper stock and press conditions. Again, it is prudent to call your printing company and ask them for the values you should use.

UCR and GCR

An obvious difference between an RGB file and a CMYK file is that the CMYK image has four colors and therefore channels, while the RGB image has only three. A simple gamut conversion from additive color space to subtractive color space involves a three-color conversion from RGB to CMY. When a CMY image is printed on an offset printing press using conventional inks, images tend to be murky and lack contrast, especially in the shadow areas. The transparent and impure nature of process inks makes it difficult to create high contrast images with them. Black shadow areas tend to look muddy brown. In addition to the low contrast issue, when printing with high percentages of all three CMY inks in shadow areas the three inks tend to merge, destroying shadow details.

The time honored solution to both the contrast and shadow detail challenges in process printing has been to substitute black or K for various portions of CMY ink percentages. (By the way, K stands for key color, because black is the color to which printers have traditionally keyed the placement of all the other color inks during the printing process.) The substitution of black for CMY works because in subtractive color space equal portions of cyan, magenta, and yellow create black.

There are two basic options we can choose for accomplishing this black substitution for CMY. The first option is called Under Color Removal, or UCR, and the second option is known as Gray Component Replacement, or GCR. The effects of both methods on the separation curves for SWOP conditions can be seen in Fig. 19.7. The top curve is the UCR curve and the bottom, the GCR built curve. The fundamental difference between UCR and GCR separations is the grayscale percentage where black substitution begins. In UCR-separated images the substitution of K for C, M, and Y does not begin in earnest until the three quarter tone. In GCR-separated images the substitution of K for C, M, and Y begins at the quarter tone. Look at the black generation curves in Fig. 19.7 to confirm this. Consequently, UCR images have most of their black substitution in the shadow regions of the image, while GCR images have black substitution throughout the tonal range from the quarter tone through the shadow region. Each method has its uses and proponents. Both methods will reduce ink volumes and provide better contrast and detail in the shadows. I generally prefer GCR for contone photographs because GCR provides improved contrast and reduces the total ink throughout the entire tonal range of the image. This tends to brighten and sharpen up the midtone areas of images which can easily become muddy. Be sure to ask your printer which method would be most appropriate for your images. Some printers use only one method and do not like to print images separated with the other. The difference between the effects of UCR and GCR can be seen in the separations shown in Figures 19.10 and 19.11. Note how the black plate generated with GCR shows density all the way down to the quarter tone, while the UCR-generated black plate displays most of its density from the three quarter tone through the shadow. You can also see less density displayed in the GCR-generated cyan, magenta, and yellow printing plates.

UCA

One often unknown and overlooked section of the Separation Setup/CMYK Setup dialog box is the area labeled UCA (short for Under Color Addition). UCA is available only when you choose the GCR black generation method. UCA is used when you are trying to produce a solid cover of a shadow region rather than preserve contone image detail. UCA is the opposite of and has the opposite effect of UCR. Applying a UCA percentage will increase the C, M, Y colors in the shadows in addition to the black being applied by the GCR. Adding more ink will, of course, tend to plug up the shadows and reduce shadow detail. With most contone images this is a disadvantage, but when the shadow region is dominated by solid areas instead of image detail, UCA can be an advantage. All the process colors including the black K are transparent, so they are not able to provide rich, high density blacks to cover solid areas. Solid black areas created with process black tend to look anemic compared with regions covered by spot color black inks containing more pigment and are more opaque. Through the use of UCA, all four process colors are bumped up in the shadow region to provide richer blacks for area coverage. Use this feature carefully; a little bit goes a long way. UCA should be used selectively on an image-by-image basis.

SOME SEPARATION TIPS

➤ Remove unnecessary color from color palettes both in original graphic documents and page layout documents. This will prevent confusion and extra plates from printing out during the final creation of film separations. Removing unused colors is also a good way to check your color assignments to see if you have assigned some colors you did not intend or if you have goofed up some reassignment of colors during a design or editing change. It is a good idea to remove RGB from your color palette for all your print jobs.

➤ Make sure that all colors on your color palette are properly designated as spot or process colors. Also be sure that each element has the proper spot or process color value assigned to it. The only way to be sure is to print your own set of process separations on your proof printer. For long documents, it is not necessary to print out color separations of every single page. Choose a couple of representative pages which contain all of the colors used in that document and print separations of them. If they separate properly on those pages, they will likely separate properly on the other pages. We can again see the value of using standardization tools such as Master Pages and Style Sheets. If most elements are created as Master Page and Style Sheet items, then they will be consistent throughout the document.

- Avoid assigning spot color values to elements and then asking your printer to match them with process color values. It rarely works. If you want an element to be printed with process colors, assign it process color values to begin with.

- Note spot and process colors carefully and choose separations instead of composite files if you want to print separations.

- Don't rename DCS files after they are created. Master DCS will not recognize renamed versions of its separate files.

- Do not set the line screen information in Photoshop (File—Page Setup) for Photoshop files exported from Photoshop for placement in another application such as QuarkXpress or PageMaker. Photoshop settings will override the importing program settings. Do not check Save Halftone Screen when saving a Photoshop file for this purpose.

- Pay attention to the Separation and Printing Inks (Photoshop 4.0)/RGB and CMYK Setup (Photoshop 5.0+) dialog boxes in Photoshop (under File: Preferences) prior to converting any RGB image to a CMYK image.

- Be sure to apply dot gain correction manually to your grayscale contone image using the Curves dialog box, or save your grayscale image as an EPS with a dot gain transfer curve.

- Blends created between two spot colors in the same area will be separated as process colors. But blends between tints of the same Pantone spot color will be printed as a spot plate. If you want to create a blend between two different overlapping spot colors, you must do two things: 1) clone and identically overlap the area into which you want the overlapping blend to occur and, 2) assign the separate spot color gradations to each overlapping area. Be sure that the gradations you create are constructed entirely out of the spot color. Do not blend a spot color into black or white. Use 100 percent or 0 percent of the spot color instead.

- When creating EPS files out of Photoshop, do not save the line screen and frequency information along with the file unless you want that information to override the screening information set in the output application or the RIP software. If you are sending your files out to be processed, it is best to let the output bureau set the screening information.

- The registration color (generally black) included on many color palettes should be applied only to items such as crop, trim, registration, and fold marks which will occur on each separation. The registration color should not be applied to regular text and graphic items used to construct documents.

- To perform RGB to CMYK conversions for printing on desktop printers, consider using the color profile method. Color conversion profiles for a wide variety of devices come packaged with many applications, including Photoshop. While these generic profiles are not as precise as custom profiles, they can often get close.

❥ Be aware of where your RGB to CMYK conversion is occurring. Choose the best place to make your conversion and be consistent about how you convert your images. Ask your service provider for guidance on the best way to convert your images for output on their devices.

PROOFING YOUR PRINTS

Why proof?

Prior to the age of electronic publishing, we as clients produced full scale mechanical artboards to deliver to a printer. Proofing was done by printers because they were the first ones to actually produce a composite print. Now, however, with computer-based document creation, the compositing is being done as we create the file. The good news is that by creating a digital file we have reduced the number of steps that we go through. The bad news is that by removing the mechanical art boards that we deliver to the printer, we remove the only complete hard copy that the printer could look at to see what we had created.

As nifty and wonderful as computers are, they also have their own set of challenges. One of those challenges is that we cannot see digital files. Another challenge is that once a file leaves one computer and is opened up on another computer, the nature and structure of that file may be altered. Sometimes these changes are significant and obvious, like a missing graphic or a major change in the display of a font in a headline. Other changes may be more subtle, like a few shifts in line breaks or a change in the font of a caption or footnote. In either case, your printer will not know if what is on the screen and what prints off of the printers is correct or not unless an actual hard copy proof printed by you from the file you have goes with the disk. Your hard copy proof replaces the mechanical art boards of old in terms of a visual check of what you expect.

Quality proofs checklist

Producing good quality, accurate proofs is key to making your job run smoothly. Here is a checklist of some features and characteristics of a good quality proof:

❑ Laser proof should be the most recent version of a file. Don't make changes to a file after you have created your final proof. If you make changes to a file, plan on creating another set of proofs.

❑ Make a composite of the entire file.

❑ Print color separations as well so you can check your color breaks and see how your separations will print (see Figure 19.2).

❑ Color breaks should be noted on composite, at least on simple files.

❑ Delete colors which will not be used from the file. Otherwise, the unused colors will still print out as separate plates when separations are printed.

❑ Indicate spot and process colors clearly.

❑ Note crop mark creation and location using the proper page size and bleeds. Make sure crops and separation descriptions are on the proof.

❑ Indicate bleeds. These should be *at least* 1/8" past the page trim size as determined by crop or cut marks. (Check with your printer for their bleed values.)

❑ Note percentage (%) of reduction.

❑ Send a marked up laser for changes after the initial blueline has been received and corrected.

❑ Edit graphics files properly. Don't add lines to fill in spaces between two boxes which are supposed to touch.

❑ Creating a proof or a set of proofs should not be a last minute affair. Leave some time to check your proofs for mistakes or any corrections/additions/changes. The creation of proofs is an aid to you and your output service company. Creating proofs allows you to check carefully what the final product will look like. Very often you will find mistakes in how color breaks have been assigned when you create color separations on a laser.

❑ Using your own electronic publishing system to create your files is a great boon to you in terms of the freedom and control it allows you over the creation and production processes. But with this freedom comes responsibility. Since you are creating the files, you are primarily responsible for creating and preparing those files correctly. Creating complete proofs is one of the best tools to help you prepare your file correctly for print production.

CHAPTER SUMMARY

There are two fundamental separations which occur in the digital imaging process. The first separation occurs when we capture a color image with a scanner of a digital camera. This separation converts a single color contone image into three (red, green, and blue) grayscale channels. The second major separation involves the reseparation of our three channel RGB images into four (CMYK) grayscale channels for printing. Color separation can also be created through the simple assignment of colors. There are two basic color systems which we use for printing, spot colors and process colors. Each spot color requires its own separation and its own cylinder on a printing press. **Process color separations** create a wide range of colors by combining various percentages of cyan, magenta yellow and black on four separations, one for each color.

RGB to CMYK conversion can occur at many places in the production process. There are also an infinite number of RGB to CMYK conversion values. For commercial print output it is best to acquire RGB-CMYK setup values from your service provider. For desktop printers either manual setup or color profiles can be used. Before you send out files to be printed, be sure to proof your work Part of this proofing process should involve printing separations to check for proper color assignments.

PAULINE'S DIGITAL IMAGING TIPS

Pauline's Tip 19.1

Create composite and color separated laser proofs of the most recent version of your documents. Use these lasers as your proofing tool. Your proofs replace the mechanical boards of old as visual guides for how you want your jobs to print. The proofs you send to your printer should be of the final corrected versions because they will be used to proof screen and film versions of your files.

Pauline's Tip 19.2

Plan time in your production schedule for proofing. No one can proof his own work, so provide time for others to proof the jobs. Use a proofing checklist so that a complete job is done.

Pauline's Tip 19.3

The Registration color is a composite black composed of all the colors used in your document. This black should be assigned only to document elements which should appear on all separations such as crop, trim, fold, and registration marks.

Pauline's Tip 19.4

For publications which will be reused with only type changes, consider designing with replaceable type areas and assigning a separate color to changeable text which will print on its own separation. This approach reduces the need to reprint all plates for a copy-only change.

Pauline's Tip 19.5

Create printer spreads on separate pages. Do not create side-by-side pages on a single sheet, like two 8.5" x 11" pages on an 11" x 17" sheet. Create two separate 8.5" x 11" sheets. A single 11" x 17" sheet cannot be imposed, while individual 8.5" x 11" can be positioned independently of each other and therefore imposed.

PAULINE'S DIGITAL IMAGING TIPS

Pauline's Tip 19.6

Mark up your proofs. Indicate bleeds, FPO and live images, and the percentage of scaling at which the proof was printed, if any, as well as crop, trim, fold, and registration marks. If you have any questions about colors or images, note them on your proofs.

Pauline's Tip 19.7

Prior to converting an RGB image to a CMYK in Photoshop, you need to first configure the Printing Ink setup and Separation (Photoshop 4.0)/RGB and CMYK (Photoshop 5.0+) setup dialog boxes. It is imperative to choose the correct set of inks, and the appropriate dot gain values for the inks, paper, and press with which your documents will be printed. Also, prior to the gamut conversion, you need to designate which kind of black generation curve will be used—UCR or GCR—as well as assigning ink percent values. Call your printing company for guidance in configuring these two dialog boxes and configure them before you complete the mode/gamut change. You may discover that it is best for the printing company to perform the conversion.

Pauline's Tip 19.8

It is extremely important to fill out your EFIS prior to sending your file out to be processed. Your EFIS contains crucial information about what your file contains and how it was constructed. This information is an important aid in helping your service bureau output your document. Remember, no one can see what is on your disk and your proofs. An EFIS provides the service company with the guidelines and information needed to process your files properly. When you fill out your EFIS, be sure to indicate the number of colors/separations which you expect. Indicate whether you have a spot color job, a four-color job, or a combination of four-color plus spot colors. Always clearly indicate the spot colors to be used.

Pauline's Tip 19.9

For performing RGB to CMYK conversions for printing on desktop printers, consider using the color profile method. Color conversion profiles for a wide variety of devices come packaged with many applications, including Photoshop. While these generic profiles are not as precise as custom profiles, they can often get you close. Also remember that some desktop printer will automatically perform the RGB to CMYK conversion during the RIPing process, and your preconversion to CMYK may just confuse the issue. Be sure you know when and where your gamut conversion is happening.

CHAPTER REVIEW

Check Your Comprehension

Multiple Choice Questions

To help you review the topics covered in this chapter, answer the following multiple choice questions.

1. Which of the following can be described as separations?
   A. RGB colors
   B. CMYK colors
   C. Spot colors
   D. All of the above

2. _____ always require a separate cylinder on an offset press in order to print.
   A. RGB colors
   B. CMYK colors
   C. Spot colors
   D. All of the above

3. A minimum of how many separations must occur when you start with a scan and finish with a CMYK image?
   A. One
   B. Two
   C. Three
   D. Four

4. Scanning divides a color contone image into how many separations?
   A. One
   B. Two
   C. Three
   D. Four

5. Four color process color printing divides a color contone image into how many separations?
   A. One
   B. Two
   C. Three
   D. Four

6. How many separations would a four color process image with two spots colors and a varnish produce?

   A. Two

   B. Four

   C. Six

   D. Seven

7. Which of the following should be considered when converting RGB values into CMYK?

   A. Print ink setup

   B. Separation setup

   C. Dot gain

   D. All of the above

8. UCR and GCR control which of the following?

   A. The generation of CMYK ink values

   B. The generation of RGB monitor values

   C. Dot gain values

   D. Printing ink setup

9. When setting up an RGB to CMYK conversion in Photoshop, we should consider

   A. Monitor or RGB setup

   B. Printing ink setup

   C. Separation setup

   D. All of the above

10. When you create a proof, which of the following should be indicated?

    A. Bleeds

    B. FPO images

    C. Scaling

    D. All of the above

11. From where should you get the RGB–CMYK setup values for commercial printing?

    A. In the Photoshop manual

    B. From your printing company

    C. Guess

    D. None of the above

12. Where can an RGB to CMYK color conversion take place?

    A. During the scanning process

    B. In Photoshop

    C. At a RIP

    D. All of the above

Check Your Understanding

Concept Questions

To help you review and expand your thinking on the topics covered in this chapter, answer the following questions.

1. Briefly explain why we need separations when we scan and print.

2. Explain why "color" scanning is essentially a separation process.

3. Explain the difference between spot and process print separations.

4. Describe the various places in a production process where RGB to CMYK conversion can take place.

5. Explain the statement: "If you intend to multipurpose an image it is generally a bad idea to perform the RGB to CMYK conversion during the scan."

6. What do UCR and GCR control? How are UCR and GCR similar and different?

7. What is the difference between a generic and a custom profile?

8. Detail the elements which should be shown on a proof you are sending to a printing company along with a file which you want them to print.

9. Explain why it is important to print color separated proofs as well as a composite proof when you are preparing a document to be sent out to print.

10. What are the components of the color named *registration*? Why should this color never be assigned to type?

PROJECTS

1. For an 8.5" x 11" document which you have previously created print a composite as well as color separated proofs on a black and white laser at 100%.

2. Print the document you used in Question 1 above with crop marks.

3. Add a bleeding element to your document, and position the bleeding element so that it extend at least 1/8" beyond the crop marks. Print both sets of lasers once more. Does the bleeding element bleed off the end of the laser printed page when printed at 100%? Explain why not. Mark the lasers up to indicate which element should bleed.

4. Figure out how you can show the element bleeding properly while printing it on your laser printer. Hint: Try printing the page so that the crop marks as well as the entire document will print on your laser output.

20
Managing the Mess

As the Byte Turns continues…

Oh, what a mess Danny D'Ziner and Pauline E. Prepress find themselves in…with all those fonts and graphics to collect.

What do you mean, some of my fonts are missing? I'm sure I sent them all. Did you lose them?

Ah… well, that's what they told me in production.

I hate being in the middle!

Are you sure we don't have them?

Read my lips, Sammy baby; WE DO NOT HAVE ALL OF THE FONTS! AND NO, WE DID NOT LOSE THEM!

Chapter Objectives

In this chapter you will learn:

- ◆ **Organizing your document and components**
- ◆ **Taz's four-folder technique**
- ◆ **Organizing Mac and Windows font files**
- ◆ **Maintaining links**
- ◆ **Graphic construction checklist**
- ◆ **Creating and using EFISs**
- ◆ **Matching proofs and files**
- ◆ **Key Terms**
  - • Collection
  - • Native files
  - • Flattening
  - • Flatness
  - • EFIS
  - • Font suitcase
  - • Screen fonts and printer fonts
  - • .pfm and .pfb fonts
  - • PostScript files
  - • Dry run technique

INTRODUCTION

When you are getting ready to print the final version of your documents, and particularly if you are preparing your files to send out to a service bureau or printing company for them to output, the most important task you can accomplish is to make sure all of the document components are available and working together. Organization of your document components, including page layout document, linked graphics files, and used font files, is the key to getting your documents ready to output.

The two keys to having complete working documents is to 1) make sure that your external high resolution graphics are indeed linked to your page layout document, and 2) make sure that all the font files which are used by the document are arranged properly and available to your document. I recommend a four-folder system for organizing your files. This system includes a **collection** folder, a document and graphics folder, a font folder and a native file folder. Font files need to be properly paired and graphics need to be simplified. PostScript and PDF files can be a useful way to collect all your document components in one large document. However, special care must be taken during file construction, as missing components are not easily replaced and mistakes are difficult to correct in these files. Sending along an **EFIS** which includes complete document component and characteristics information is a big help to your service bureau. I use the **dry run technique** to make sure that my documents are complete and that my final proofs match my final documents.

FILE HANDLING GUIDELINES

Gathering file components

The four-folder system

In Chapter 13, "Document Construction," we explored how an electronic file is put together. When a page is constructed in a page layout application like QuarkXpress or PageMaker, most of the actual printing data (the high resolution graphics and fonts) is located outside of the page layout document. In the case of graphics, only low resolution proxy files are resident in the page layout document. With fonts, both the low and high resolution files (screen and print fonts for Mac PostScript fonts, and **.pfb** and **.pfm** files for Windows PostScript fonts) are external to the page layout document. It is due to this multifile nature of most electronic documents that file gathering and organization is a critical and often laborious task. If any of the external files are missing, the page layout document will not print properly. It is important that all of the original graphic and font files actually used to construct the document are sent along with the document which is to be printed. It is not acceptable to ask your printer if he has fonts with the same name as your fonts and then expect the printer to use them to print your file. Remember, fonts are just special preformed versions of graphics. Name similarity is no guarantee that the printer's fonts will look or print the same as your fonts. Different versions of the same font may have different kerning pair information and even different character stroke and counter shapes and sizes. Therefore, plan to send all of the components you used to construct your file. It is sometimes important to send along preference and tracking information files or extensions from the applications you used. Ask your printer what he requires for the specific applications you have used.

Organize your fonts and graphics for sending

I utilize a four folder system for organizing my files to send out to service companies. My first folder is the collection folder which contains all the document files for the job which I want my printing company to print, including the page layout document, all linked graphics, and all used font files into one collection folder labeled with the name of the project. This collection folder should contain *only* the files which are associated with the job which you want the printing company to output. Extraneous files confuse the preflighting and production process.

Inside this collection folder, I organize my files into three folders. I place the page layout document and its linked graphics in the same folder to facilitate keeping the document and linked graphics together and to promote linking each time the page layout document is launched. Most applications will automatically relink with graphics which are located in the same folder as the document. In a similar manner, I place the screen and printer font files (Mac) or .pfm and .pfb font files (Windows) in the same folder so that they will be easily linked for viewing and printing. On a Mac the **screen fonts** should be placed in a screen **font suitcase**. On Windows place the .pfm files in a separate folder. You also include preference and

Disk to Send Out
• Label disk with file and company names
• Write file and company name on disk
• Include your phone number
• Include an instruction sheet if you have any special instructions

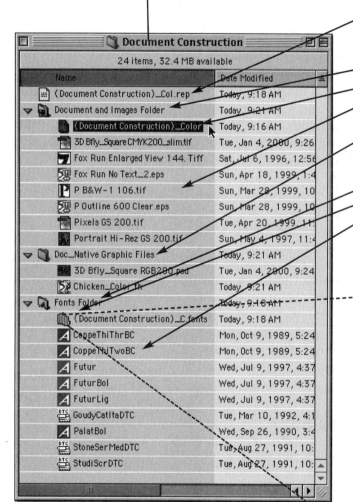

File Organization
•Docs and Graphics Folder
  - Document
  - All imported graphics: TIFFs and EPS preferably
  - Report document from collection utility
• Native Graphic files
  - Photoshop (.psd) files with editable layers and channels
  - Drawing documents (.fh or .il) with editable type and layers

• Font Folder (Preferably Type 1 fonts)
  - Screen Fonts/ .pfm (suitcase on Mac/ folder on Windows)
  - Printer Fonts/.pfb (matches to screen/.pfm fonts)

Notes: The composite page layout document and its associated imported graphics need to be in a common folder. Also place Screen and Printer / .pfm& .pfb font files in a common folder.

Screen Font Suitcase Content
All the screen fonts are placed in a suitcase instead of being loose. This helps keep the fonts organized and makes them much easier to activate and deactivate using font utilities. This organization also allows you to open the font suitcase and compare screen and printer fonts side by side.

▼ *Figure 20.1 Disk File Organization*
These illustrations show how a page layout document and its associated external linked files should be organized. The four folder technique works well. The first folder contains all the files you will be sending to the printing company, and *only* the files you want the printing company to print. One inside folder is for the page layout document along with all the linked high resolution graphics. Placing the page layout document and the linked graphics in the same folder will allow the high resolution graphics to automatically link to the document when it is launched. The same applies to the third, fonts, folder. Placing the screen/.pfm and printer fonts/.pfb files in the same folder allows the printer fonts to be linked when the screen fonts are accessed. The fourth folder is reserved for native graphic files such as Photoshop (.psd) files which contain layers and channels which will facilitate any editing which might have to be done to the graphic files.

data files for H&J and Kerning and tracking specifications, etc., with some versions of some applications. I also create a third folder in which I place editable native graphic files such as Photoshop (.psd) files with all their editable layers and channels. Having these **native files** will greatly facilitate their editing if that proves to be necessary (see Figs. 20.1 and 20.2 for examples of recommended file organization).

Fonts specifics

Macintosh fonts

If you work on a Mac, keep an empty font suitcase labeled *Screen Fonts* or labeled with your name in your screen fonts folder. This empty suitcase will be ready for you to copy onto your outgoing disk. On a Mac, using a font suitcase allows you to place all of your screen fonts into this one suitcase to keep them all together, organized, and easily accessible. This tidies up your screen fonts and even more importantly allows you and your printer to access all of your fonts at one time by just accessing this one screen font suitcase (see Fig. 20.2). On a Mac be sure to place all of your **printer fonts** in the same folder with your screen fonts or your screen fonts suitcase (Mac). Doing so will allow the automatic linking of your printer fonts to the screen fonts when the screen fonts are accessed. By labeling your screen font suitcase with your name, your service company can easily identify your fonts when accessing them. Refer to Chapter 11, "A Tale of True Typesetting," if you are having difficulty identifying screen and printer or .pfm and .pfb font files.

Windows fonts

If you work on a Windows OS-based machine, you also need to send the screen and printer font versions of your fonts. As described and shown in Chapter 11, the Windows versions of screen and printer fonts are .pfm and .pfb files located in the ps fonts folder (subdirectory). On Windows, the .pfm font files should be placed in their own folders which should in turn be placed in the folder which holds the .pfb font files (see Fig. 20.3). One of the greatest challenges of working with fonts on a

▼ *Figure 20.2 Empty Font Suitcase*
If you work on a Mac, keep an empty font suitcase in your fonts folder. This allows you always to have an empty font suitcase available to place screen fonts into when preparing a disk to send out. Before you place any fonts into it, copy the empty suitcase, either to a disk or to a folder on your desktop. This keeps the original empty suitcase free for future use. Windows does not utilize font suitcases.

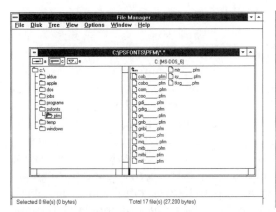 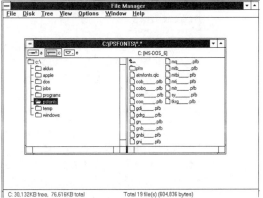

▼ *Figure 20.3 Windows Font Organization*
If you work PostScript fonts on a Windows machine you will be working with two font files, .pfb (outline and screen data) font file and .pfm (font metrics). These files should be organized as shown above. Place all .pfb (PostScript outlines) in one folder. Place all the matching .pfm (font metrics) files in their own folder. This font metrics (.pfm) folder should then be placed inside of the .pfb font file folder.

When organizing your document to send out to a service bureau or printing company for them to output, proper file organization can make everyone's life easier and results in faster service, better turnaround time and lower costs. Placing your page layout document in the same folder as the linked graphics will accomplish two things: 1) Your document and graphics will more likely remain together as they are moved from disk to disk, and 2) whenever your page layout document is launched, the linked graphics will automatically relink to the page layout document.

Windows machine is identifying them because they are limited to a three-character suffix on the end of the file to specify the font name. I highly recommend the use of ATM Deluxe as a font management tool for Windows. ATM Deluxe is a nearly indispensible utility which helps you easily identify, group, and manage your fonts.

Graphic specifics

Place all of your high resolution graphics along with the page layout document in a folder called Docs and Graphics or Documents and Images. Placing the layout document and graphics in the same folder will ensure that the high resolution graphics will link to the page layout document when it is launched. You may want to create a third folder called Native Graphic Files. In this folder you can place any Native Photoshop or drawing documents (Illustrator, FreeHand or CorelDraw documents) which are the parents to any complex images you have created. It is always a good idea to send along a fully editable parent document version of any TIFF or EPS print file you create. And the more complex your graphic, the more important it is to send along the parents (see EPS file preparation procedures below for a full checklist on producing printable EPS files while retaining the editability of the originals). See Fig. 20.1 for a native graphic file folder.

Vector and pixel graphic file preparation procedures

Both pixel and vector based images need to be simplified for RIPing. Combination pixel and vector graphic files are some of the most difficult and demanding files to RIP. Therefore, it is often wise to direct a little bit of extra attention toward the preparation of all of our graphic files. As we discussed in Chapter 9, "Grappling with Graphics," it is a good idea to perform certain file preparation functions in drawing application documents such as FreeHand, Illustrator, and CorelDraw files, and to Photoshop images as well, in order to make them easier to RIP. Performing vector-specific adjustments such as splitting long paths, converting type to graphics (a.k.a. convert into paths), and increasing path **flatness** ratios will go a long way toward satisfying our file prep battle of *reduce and simplify*. Removing layers and alpha channels from pixel-based Photoshop type graphics will make these types of images more RIPable as well. This type of output-specific file preparation will create a file which is very ready to print, but also ruins much of that file's editability. For example, splitting closed paths into segments makes them much more difficult to edit. When type is converted to outlines, the characters can no longer be edited as type: They must be edited as a graphic. If there is a change needed in the copy, it won't be editable. When constructing your initial drawing document, be sure to construct it in separate layers. This procedure not only makes the creation of the file easier but also makes any troubleshooting and editing of the file easier. Also be careful to limit the amount of type you set in any drawing document which you intend to export as an EPS. Converting large volumes of type to paths will create hundreds of individual paths. That situation can create output problems which are more daunting than the nested type problem you are trying to solve. Following is a suggested procedure for creating graphic files ready for printing and an original parent document file that remains fully editable.

Graphic construction checklist

❑ Construct the original drawing (vector) and photo (pixel) graphic document in separate layers.

❑ Perform a Save As and add Print to the end of the file's name, preserving the original file in its fully editable form.

❑ **Flatten** layers and remove alpha channels from Photoshop images.

❑ Limit the amount type set in the drawing application document if you intend to export the file as an EPS.

❑ Remove unnecessary items such as extra text boxes.

❑ Make sure colors are properly designated as spot or process.

❑ Remove unused colors.

❑ Simplify paths (reduce number of control points).

❑ Convert small amounts of type to paths. Most typesetting should be performed in a page layout application.

❑ Split paths.

❑ Set the vector path flatness ratios at between 2 and 5.

❑ Set the proper PPD and, if appropriate, line screen information for the printer (often an imagesetter) which will ultimately be used to output the file.

❑ Export the *Print* document as an EPS file; be sure to include the .eps suffix.

❑ Send in the editable native graphic files in a separate folder to facilitate editing.

Send the original fully editable parent document as well as the exported RIP-ready EPS to your printer or service bureau. This procedure will give you both a print version and a fully editable native or parent version of your drawing document. It is a good idea to send along both versions of the file—the print-ready EPS and the original drawing version—particularly if you think the printer may have to perform some editing on the file. This type of attention to technical detail goes a long way toward our general goal of *reduce and simplify*.

▼ Figure 20.4 PostScript File
Creating a PostScript file is an easy process to perform. The same Print dialog box is generally used as for normal printing. You are essentially printing your document to a disk instead of to a printer. In the above FreeHand Print dialog box, you just choose File instead of Printer in the Destination portion of the dialog box. While creating a PostScript file is easy, it is not always advisable to do so. A PostScript file is completely self contained and essentially uneditable. Always consult your printer before you send them a PostScript file, because you will want to set the proper print information before you create the file.

POSTSCRIPT AND PDF FILES

Two other options for saving your document are to save it as a PostScript file or as a PDF document. Creating a PostScript file means printing your file to disk, usually a local hard drive (see Fig. 20.4). Creating a PDF document involves processing your PostScript file through an application called Adobe Distiller. A PostScript file is a text file which contains a complete description of all of the elements which compose the document, including all the page geometry, copy and its placement, and formatting information, and all font and graphic files. The advantages of saving your final file as a PostScript file is that all of the information which you need for printing the file is automatically included in the PostScript file. The disadvantage of using a PostScript file format is that it is essentially locked; it cannot be altered. Unless the file is exactly correct, it will not print properly. Most service printing companies or service bureaus need to make minor corrections or at least setting alterations in the files you send them. The adjustment may be as minor as changing the printer description file or changing the line screen and separation information. But if your file is a PostScript file format, none of these instructions can be easily changed. If you use this file format, make sure that your file is complete and correct. PDF files have the advantage over PostScript of being viewable and somewhat editable, although not as editable as a standard application file like a QuarkXPress, PageMaker, or InDesign document. Communicate with your printing company to make sure that you have the most recent printer description files and that all of your color breaks, trapping, graphic resolutions, and graphic file formats and sizes have been set properly. Using PostScript file print utilities such as PS Express by Transoft can help speed up this process considerably. By the way, I always make a copy of my file by performing a Save As prior to creating a PostScript file or PDF document. If something happens to my file during the print-to-disk procedure, I still have a complete, undamaged version. (See Chapter 16, "Application-Specific Tips," for more detailed information on creating PostScript files and PDF documents.)

It is worth noting that the use of straight PostScript files is rapidly giving way to the use of PDF. This is due to PDF's smaller size, simpler PostScript and vastly improved editability over straight PostScript files.

PREPARING YOUR EFIS

What on earth is an *EFIS*? EFIS is short for Electronic File Information Sheet. These are the forms which your printing company asks you to fill out to help output your file. There is a number of items related to your electronic file which are not immediately obvious. The more your printer knows about your file, the easier the printer can output your job, and the faster and better quality job he can do. The EFIS serves as an important information sheet for the service company production staff. Keep in mind that the service production staff knows nothing about a file when they first receive it. The EFIS is your opportunity to inform the production staff about your file. Be sure to note any special instructions on the EFIS. Each job you send to an output service company should be accompanied by a separate EFIS. We know its takes a little time to fill it out, but doing so can save a great deal of

TIP

To make sure that your printing company knows exactly what to print, it is imperative that you send them a proof that exactly matches the document, font and linked graphics files you are sending them to print. The only sure-fire way to guarantee that the proofs you are sending match the file you are sending is to: 1) Perform a complete collection procedure with a dependable file collect utility like FlightCheck, 2) Activate only the font files you have collected (I make a temporary set), 3) Launch the document and graphics you have collected, 4) Make one last check for file completeness (used fonts and linked graphics), 5) print the final composite and color separated proof from this document. This will guarantee that your proof will match the document file you are sending to the printing company.

time and lots of heartache. A good EFIS serves as a checklist for you to use when you are preparing a file to send out. Below is a list of some of the essential items to tell your printer. Also see Appendix G for an example of a well designed EFIS.

EFIS checklist

Here are some items which will help your printer process your files:

❏ Your name
❏ Your company name
❏ Your phone and fax numbers (to contact you with questions and send you corrections)
❏ Job name
❏ Basic job characteristics: e.g., 4/c 25 pg. catalog
❏ Media delivered: e.g., 100MB Zip disk
❏ Page numbers or range of pages to be printed: pp. 1–4 and p. 15
❏ Page layout application used and especially the version number: e.g., XPress 3.31r5so Graphics applications used and their versions: e.g., Photoshop 3.01 and FreeHand 5.5
❏ Graphic file type present and the numbers: e.g., 25 TIFFs, 15 EPSs
❏ Typefaces (fonts) used and their style: e.g., B Helvetica bold Type 1
❏ Number of colors to be printed and their separation type and names. Clearly distinguish spot from process colors: e.g., 2 spot colors 256 and 3395; plus 4/c
❏ Send both composite and color separated proofs: composite for content and placement, color separations for color assignments
❏ On your proofs be sure to note bleeds, FPO graphics, color breaks, and the percentage reduction at which proof is printed
❏ Any special instructions or problem areas of which you are aware

Note for printing companies: Refer to Appendix G for an example of an EFIS sheet. This EFIS would be a good starting point if you work for a service bureau or printing company and you do not currently have an EFIS or you would like to upgrade yours. The two keys to an effective EFIS are simplicity and good design. A good EFIS should ask about all of the basic information in a file: applications/versions, fonts used, graphics, and colors. But it should avoid asking too much detail such as imagesetter output resolution or emulsion position. Too many technical details complicate the EFIS form, confuse your clients, and discourage them from filling out the EFIS sheet.

File preparation utilities

Because of the tediousness, opportunity for mistakes, and the possibility of forgetting components involved with the manual gathering of document components, I highly recommend the use of file gathering utilities.

If you use QuarkXPress, use the Collect for Output menu choice located under the File menu. Collect for Output will collect the page layout document itself and all of the linked graphics; then it will prepare a document report that lists all of the graphics, font, color, and other details associated with the document. Collect for Output does not collect fonts. If you are a PageMaker user, you can use the Save As and File for remote printing to help gather your document components. For gathering PageMaker document information, you can use the Document Info Addition/Plug-in which comes free with PageMaker, but I recommend the more complete plug-in, Save for Service Provider. Document Info is a bit confusing and not as complete as Save for Service Provider. Save for Service Provider also comes free with PageMaker 6.5 and above and will do a content preflight and collect the document components, including the fonts. FreeHand's Collect for Output will collect all the document components, document, graphics and font files, as well as prepare a document info sheet. (See Chapter 16, "Application-Specific Tips," for a view of the menu access and Appendix I: Utilities for a list of valuable DTP file prep utilities and brief description of their use.)

I highly recommend using preflight utilities, FlightCheck from Markzware or PreFlight Pro from Extensis. Both provide extensive troubleshooting of your files, collect documents, fonts and graphics, and include detailed document reports.

Dry run technique

I use this following Dry Run Technique procedure to test my file gathering for completeness, particularly with complex files. After I have completely preflighted my documents and printed a first set of proofs, edited them, and made my corrections, I am ready to gather and organize my files for final printing or for sending out to a service provider.

In the first step of the dry run technique, I create a collection folder (subdirectory in Windows) on my hard drive to collect all of the files I intend to send out (see Fig. 20.1). Then using a preflighting utility such as "FlightCheck" I collect all of my document components into my collect folder. Using a font management utility, such as ATM Deluxe, I deactivate all of my document construction font files. (This can be done on the same computer or a different computer.) I create a temporary font set from my collected document font files, and activate these font files. See

Chapter 11 for more specific information on font file management. Again, all this font management is accomplished using a font management utility. I then launch the document with the linked graphics I have collected and will be sending to the printer. When you launch your document, your application should link with its associated high resolution graphics. Access to your document fonts should be provided by the access you have established to your temporary set. I always check anyway for any missing fonts or graphics using a preflight utility to make sure all the fonts are available and that all the placed graphics are linked to their high resolution partners. I then print my final composite and color separated proofs from this document.

This process guarantees that your proofs will match the file you print and/or send to your service provider. This process also simulates what the printer will do. Any missing component problems should show up now. This procedure will allow you to test the completeness of your collection and print document accurate proofs. This easy-to-do dry run procedure will help guarantee at least that all the components needed for printing will be present. Missing pieces is still the number one complaint about customer files. By making sure that you send all the proper pieces, you will be making your printer happy and, as a consequence, even more cooperative.

CHAPTER SUMMARY

When preparing the final version of your documents for print and for preparing your files to send out to a service bureau or printing company for printing, the most important item on your to-do list is to make sure all of your document components are available and working together. Organizing your document components, page layout document, linked graphics files, and used font files is key to preparing your documents for output.

The two most important characteristics of complete working documents is to 1) make sure that your external high resolution graphics are linked to your page layout document, and 2) be certain that all the used font files are arranged properly and available to your document. I recommend a four-folder system for organizing your files. This includes 1) a collection folder, 2) a document and graphics folder, 3) a font files folder, and 4) a native file folder. Font files should be paired with screen and printer fonts (Mac) or .pfm and .pfb files (Windows). Graphics need to be simplified for small size and easy RIPing. Creating PostScript and PDF files can be a viable means of including all of your document components in one large document. Special care must be taken during file construction, missing components are not easily replaced and mistakes are difficult to correct in these PostScript and PDF files. Sending along an EFIS which includes complete document component and characteristics information is a big help to your service bureau. I am a big fan of the dry run technique to make sure that my documents are complete and that my final proofs match my final documents.

Note: See Chapter 11, "Tale of True Typesetting," for more specific information on font management, and Chapter 16, "Application-Specific Tips" for more details on document preflighting component collection.

Pauline's Digital Imaging Tips

Pauline's Tip 20.1

Organize the files you send out so that your page layout file and its associated graphics are in one folder and your fonts (both screen and printer) are in another. Place your screen fonts in a suitcase, if possible.

Pauline's Tip 20.2

Keep an empty suitcase labeled with your name in your fonts folder on your hard drive. This empty suitcase will be available to quickly and easily copy to your traveling disks and will serve as a readily available traveling font collection site during font gathering chores.

Pauline's Tip 20.3

Place original, fully editable parent files, such as un-split Illustrator documents with editable type and unflattened Photoshop format files, in a separate folder labeled Parent Documents. Place the original unaltered application documents in this folder. If text, path, or layer troubleshooting or editing needs to be performed on an image, the printer has the option of using these fully editable documents.

Pauline's Tip 20.4

To test and final proof your document, collect all document files (Doc. fonts and graphics) to a folder. Activate only the collected fonts. Launch your collected document with its linked graphics. Print your final proof from this document This simulates what your printer will do.

Pauline's Tip 20.5

Label your disks with your name, company, job ID, and your phone and fax number. Disks can get misplaced; make yours easy to identify.

Pauline's Tip 20.6

If you send a PostScript or PDF file to your printer, make very sure that it is well prepared and that no changes will be necessary. Select your printer's PPD instead of yours prior to creating the PostScript file. A PostScript file is essentially uneditable; what you send is what you get.

PAULINE'S DIGITAL IMAGING TIPS

Pauline's Tip 20.7

While it is better to work with uncompressed files, if you do send in compressed graphic files, be sure to indicate this on your EFIS and send in a decompression utility along with your disk.

Pauline's Tip 20.8

Create a separate Print file for complex drawing documents which you may want to edit later. Keep the original or parent document as is. Simplify, split paths, adjust flatness, and remove colors from the Print version before you export the EPS. Send all three files to the printer.

Pauline's Tip 20.9

Fill out your printer's EFIS (electronic file information sheet) completely and send it along with your job and proof prints. A properly completed EFIS greatly improves the chances that your file will print quickly and easily, thereby allowing your printer to get your job done on time and on budget.

Pauline's Tip 20.10

Develop a good working relationship with your printer or service bureau. The creation and printing of PostScript files is a joint effort between you and your printing company. It is better to establish a good relationship with one or two printers so that you each learn each other's requirements and characteristics. Negotiate year-long contracts at attractive prices. You will save money and so will the printer. Choose printing companies which have well trained digital and PostScript-savvy sales, customer service, and production staffs. Visit the company and tour the production facility.

Pauline's Tip 20.11

Use preflight utilities such as FlightCheck for Markzware or PreflightPro for Extensis to help troubleshoot your documents and collect and organize your page layout files and their associated fonts and graphics. Preflight utilities such as these are worth their weight in gold!

CHAPTER REVIEW

Check Your Comprehension

Multiple Choice Questions

To help you review the topics covered in this chapter, answer the following multiple choice questions.

1. Which of the following are required for your documents to print properly?
   A. Page layout document
   B. Linked graphics
   C. Availability of used font files
   D. All of the above

2. How many folders does the author recommend for organizing documents which are to be sent out for printing?
   A. One
   B. Two
   C. Three
   D. Four

3. High resolution external graphics need to be _____ to page layout documents in order for the graphic files to print properly but remain editable.
   A. Embedded
   B. Linked
   C. PostScripted
   D. Distilled into PDF

4. Which of the following pairs of files most resemble screen and printer font files?
   A. .tif and .eps
   B. .gif and .jpg
   C. .pfb and .pfm
   D. .sit and .doc

5. The most extensive and reliable preflight and document component collection will usually be performed by
   A. QuarkXPress
   B. PageMaker
   C. FlightCheck
   D. InDesign

6. _____ are known for their editability.

   A. TIFF files

   B. EPS files

   C. Native files

   D. PostScript files

7. Which of the following usually needs to be formed on a complex Photoshop image in order to make it more printable?

   A. Flattening

   B. Compression

   C. Save as a .psd file

   D. None of the above

8. Which of the following tools is necessary for the proper management of font files?

   A. Page layout application

   B. ATM Deluxe

   C. Stuffit Deluxe

   D. Norton Utilities

9. If properly constructed, PostScript and PDF files have this in common.

   A. Complete document, including fonts and graphics

   B. Very editable

   C. Not made good for printing

   D. Easier to edit than native application files.

10. _____ is made specifically for storing screen fonts on a Macintosh.

    A. Font folder

    B. System font folder

    C. Suitcase

    D. .pfb folder

11. Which of the following contains the font metric files on a Windows machine?

    A. Font suitcase

    B. Font folder in the Windows folder

    C. .pfb folder

    D. .pfm folder

12. Which describes the best technique for testing and proofing files?

    A. Dry run technique

    B. Print the file proof before the final file collection technique

    C. All fonts turned on technique

    D. Unlink the graphics technique

Check Your Understanding

Concept Questions

To help you review and expand your thinking on the topics covered in this chapter, please answer the following questions.

1. Describe the contents of a complete file which is ready to print.

2. Why are font management utilities like ATM deluxe so important to the file collection and proofing process?

3. Outline the basic similarities and differences between Macintosh and Windows font files.

4. Explain the four-folder technique and detail its advantages.

5. What is an EFIS sheet and why is it important? List the items which should be included on an EFIS sheet.

6. Outline the six important graphic simplification procedures.

7. Outline the basic advantages and disadvantages of PostScript and PDF files when compared with native application files such as QuarkXPress or InDesign documents.

8. Why is it true that the use of PDF files is rapidly replacing the use of straight PostScript files for printing?

9. Outline the steps you should take to establish a good working relationship with a printing company or other output service bureau.

10. Review the dry run technique, and explain how the it helps us test our document for completeness and create document accurate proofs.

PROJECTS

1. Use the four-folder technique to organize the components of an electronic file to send out to a service provider.

2. Create your own EFIS and fill it our using the same document in Question 1.

3. Use the dry run technique to test, collect and prepare accurate proofs for the document above. Be sure to use a font management utility to help out. You may want to review the concepts of font management developed in Chapter 11, with some special attention paid to isolating your document construction font files, and the creation of sets.

Appendices

APPENDIX A: BITS & BYTES

Review of bits, Bytes, bit depth and transfer speeds

bits and Bytes

bit (b): The smallest unit of the digital or binary computer language, restricted to either a 0 or a 1

Byte (B): A binary number which defines a computer character such as the number

      b   e   r

    1= 8 bits

Kilobit (Kb): One thousand (1,000) bits or 1000, 0s or 1s

Megabit (Mb): One million (1,000,000) bits =125,000 bytes (1,000,000 bits ÷ 8 bits/bytes = 125,000 bytes)

KiloByte (KB): One thousand (1,000) bytes or characters

MegaByte (MB): One million (1,000,000) bytes or characters

TerraByte (MB): One billion (1,000,000,000) bytes or characters

Bit depth: bits per pixel or bits per image

Number of bits per pixel (also known as bit depth, pixel depth or color depth)

1 bit image: 1 bit per pixel (b/p) = B&W (bitonal image)

8 bit image: 8 bits per pixel (b/p) = 256 shades of grayscale (or color) 2^8

10 bit image: 10 bits per pixel (b/p) = 1,024 shades of grayscale 2^{10}

12 bit image: 12 bits per pixel (b/p) = 4,096 shades of grayscale 2^{12}

14 bit image: 14 bits per pixel (b/p) = 16,384 shades of grayscale 2^{14}

24 bit image: 24 bits per image = three 8(b/p) channels (RGB color)

32 bit image: 32 bits per image = four 8(b/p) channels* (CMYK color)

Transfer speed: bits or Bytes per second

bits per second: b/s - Single bits per second transfer

Kilobits per second: Kb/s - Thousands of bits per second EG 28.8Kb/s modem

Megabits per second: Kb/s - Millions of bits per second EG 100Mb network

Bytes per second: B/s - Single Bytes per second transfer

KiloBytes per second: KB/s - Thousands of bits per second

MegaBytes per second: KB/s - Millions of Bytes per second: EG hard drive transfer

Remember: One Byte = 8 bits, 1B = 8b

Note: Confusing bits for Bytes or vice versa will result in a factor of eight error in any calculations you make

Note: bits are represented by a lower case b while Bytes are represented by upper case B

* Note: The channels referred to here are the building block channels which determine the mode of the image: B&W, GS, RGB, CMYK, Index, etc. Additional alpha channels can be added to images for storing selections, editing and controlling transparency, but these do not affect the mode of the image.

APPENDIX B: ASCII CODE CHART

American Standard Code for Information Interchange

A code which translates binary numbers into number, letter, symbol, or control characters: a = 01100001, 1 = 00110001 ASCII or text only files. A format in which text files can be saved and be nearly universally translated and read on a wide variety of computer platforms and operating systems and applications.

Binary	Char/Key	Binary	Char/Key	Binary	Char/Key	Binary	Char/Key
1000001 =	A	110101 =	5	1001110 =	N	1100111 =	g
1100001 =	a	110110 =	6	1001111 =	O	1101000 =	h
0110001 =	1	110111 =	7	1010000 =	P	1101001 =	i
0100001 =	!	111000 =	8	1010001 =	Q	1101010 =	j
100000=	space	111001 =	9	1010010 =	R	1101011 =	k
100001 =	!	111010 =	:	1010011 =	S	1101100 =	l
100010 =	"	111011 =	;	1010100 =	T	1101101 =	m
100011 =	#	111100 =	<	1010101 =	U	1101110 =	n
100100 =	$	111101 =	=	1010110 =	V	1101111 =	o
100101 =	%	111110 =	>	1010111 =	W	1110000 =	p
100110 =	&	111111 =	?	1011000 =	X	1110001 =	q
100111 =	'	1000000 =	@	1011001 =	Y	1110010 =	r
101000 =	(	1000001 =	A	1011010 =	Z	1110011 =	s
101001 =	)	1000010 =	B	1011011 =	[	1110100 =	t
101010 =	*	1000011 =	C	1011100 =	\	1110101 =	u
101011 =	+	1000100 =	D	1011101 =	]	1110110 =	v
101100 =	,	1000101 =	E	1011110 =	^	1110111 =	w
101101 =	-	1000110 =	F	1011111 =	`	1111000 =	x
101110 =	.	1000111 =	G	1100000 =	_	1111001 =	y
101111 =	/	1001000 =	H	1100001 =	a	1111010 =	z
110000 =	0	1001001 =	I	1100010 =	b	1111011 =	{
110001 =	1	1001010 =	J	1100011 =	c	1111100 =	l
110010 =	2	1001011 =	K	1100100 =	d	1111101 =	}
110011 =	3	1001100 =	L	1100101 =	e	1111110 =	~
110100 =	4	1001101 =	M	1100110 =	f	1111111=	delete

APPENDIX C: FILE FORMATS

Contents vs. containers

A good way to start to sort out the myriad, and continually increasing number of file formats, is to separate in your mind the difference between file contents (pixels and vectors) versus file containers (formats). There are basically two kinds of file contents or building blocks, pixels and vectors. All graphic files contain one or the other, or sometimes both, of these basic contents. The file formats are the containers into which these pixel and/or vector contents are stored.

Different file formats are used for various purposes. When we change the use for which a graphic file is intended, we often change the file format. For instance the two preferred file formats used in PostScript printing are TIFF and EPS. If we change the use of these graphic files to use on the Web these same images may be resaved as GIF, JPEG, PNG, or WSF format.

File formats: use specific

Pixel and or vector-based images can be saved in many different file formats. As discussed, it is useful to think of a file format as a container into which image components, pixels and/or vectors are stored. The file format we choose for an image should be determined by how the image will be used. For example if we are to use our images for printing to a PostScript printer, then a pixel-based TIFF or EPS would be most appropriate. If, however, our images will be used for placement on a Web page, then a GIF, JPEG, PNG or SWF file format would be most appropriate. Some file formats such as PCX, PICT and WMF tend to be more platform specific and less flexible than TIFFs and are therefore less desirable for use as a standard file format. For print I recommend that you initially save your images in the TIFF format. The TIFF format is a flexible, pixel-based file format which is compatible with use on Mac, Windows, and UNIX systems for print. If you reuse and/or recreate your images for other purposes you may change the file format of an image. Below is a review of file formats, color spaces, resolutions and use.

TIFF: TIFF (Tagged Information File Format) is a general pixel-based format that is used in PostScript printing, for grayscale and CMYK, at 200–300ppi for desktop through commercial printing. The TIFF file format is a good one for going cross platform with pixel-based images. TIFFs can be saved in either Mac or PC format. I generally save mine in PC format, as a Mac can read either one. As with all print file formats I recommend that no compression be used when saving images to TIFF.

EPS (pixel-based): EPS (Encapsulated PostScript) is an alternative to the TIFF format for saving pixel-based images. While usually larger in file size than TIFFs (sometimes up to 30% larger), some RIPs, workflows, and applications prefer this format for printing pixel-based images. Pixel-based EPSs are typically used in grayscale and CMYK images at 200–300 ppi for desktop and commercial printing. EPS files are basically sealed and therefore require that a screen preview be saved along with the pixel image data. Other image-use information such as line screen, transfer function and color management data can be saved along with the actual

Figure AC.1 Creating TIFFs
TIFFs are used in printing pixel-based images, although TIFFs can contain vector paths as well. Using the Save As dialog box in Photoshop allows you to flatten and remove alpha channels on the fly as you save your image. I generally save my TIFFs in IBM PC format, to enhance cross platform compatibility, and without any compression to reduce printing problems.

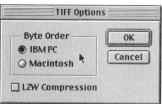

Figure AC.2 Creating EPSs
Like TIFFs, EPSs are used in printing. The EPS format can contain either pixel or vector components. EPS files require previews in order for them to be viewed in a page layout application. Choose either Mac (PICT) or PC (TIFF) headers. Most printing companies prefer binary encoding, although use of ASCII encoding may be preferable if you are working on a Windows network and are having problems transferring or printing binary files. Keep the Halftone Screen, Transfer Function and PostScript Color Management *unchecked* unless you are informed otherwise.

image information in an EPS. Only save this additional data if you are instructed by your printing company or other service bureau.

EPS (vector-based): EPS(Encapsulated PostScript) is the preferred format for vector-based images which will be printed on PostScript printers. Vector-based EPS files are, like pixel-based EPS, sealed and therefore require that a screen preview be saved along with the vector image data. This type of image file format is used for grayscale, spot colors or CMYK for desktop and commercial printing. Pixel-based TIFFs can be converted into vector-based EPSs through applications like Adobe® Streamline.

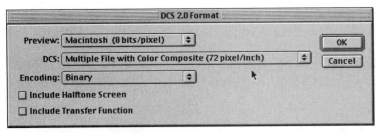

Figure AC.3 Creating DCSs

The DCS format is a special preseparated version of the EPS format, which is most commonly used for saving multicolored images. Like regular EPSs, DCSs are used in printing. And like regular EPSs DCS files require previews in order for them to be viewed in a page layout application. Choose either Mac or PC (TIFF) header.

When saving your image as a DCS file you will have several DCS options which will determine the number of files, and the type of composite file which will be created. Ask your printing company for specific instructions as to whether they use DCS files and how they prefer to have them set up.

As with other EPS graphic files, most printing companies prefer binary encoding. Use ASCII encoding if you are working on a Windows network and are have problems transferring/printing binary files. Keep the Halftone Screen, Transfer Function and PostScript Color Management unchecked unless you are informed otherwise.

DCS: DCS (Desktop Color Separations) is a special version of the EPS format. DSC is used for graphic images which will be separated during the printing process and can contain both process and spot color information. DCS files are preseparated, which usually makes for faster RIPing. There are two versions of DCS. DCS 1.0 supports four-color process separations, and DCS 2.0 will support four-color process and spot color separations. DCS files can be constructed as single or multiple files with or without separate low resolution composite screen preview images.

GIF: GIF (Graphic Interchange Format) is a common pixel-based image format used on the Web. GIF format supports 8 bit (or lower) grayscale, and index color images, typically at 72ppi.

JPEG: JPEG (Joint Photographic Expert Group) is a pixel-based format commonly used on the Web for viewing and image transfer. This type of image file format is used for mainly for grayscale, and 24 bit RGB images. JPEG can also be used in CMYK format for storage and printing of high resolution files, but a JPEG image should be converted into a CMYK, TIFF, or EPS prior to printing.

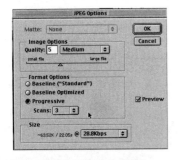

Figure AC.4 Creating JPEGs

JPEGs are used for Web images, for storage and sometimes printing. The quality of the image can be controlled through the amount of compression.

PNG: PNG (Portable Network Graphic) is a pixel-based format commonly used on the Web for viewing and image transfer. This type of image file format is used for mainly for grayscale, and 24 bit RGB images.

SWF: SWF (Shock Wave Format) is a vector-based format commonly used on the Web for animation graphics. This type of image file format can be grayscale, 8 or 24 bit RGB images. SWF can also be used for printing at high resolution, but should be converted into a spot or CMYK color space, TIFF, or EPS prior to printing.

PDF: Any graphic which you have created for print can be converted on the fly for use in a PDF file. Configure the Job Options in Distiller (Settings–Job Options). Set the image resolution to match the final output device, e.g., 72 ppi for WEB viewing, 125 ppi for 600 dpi laser, 200 ppi for printing at 150 lpi, and 300 ppi for printing at 200 lpi. I recommend turning off compression of your contone images to assure them highest possible quality printing.

STN: (STiNG) file format is a resolution independent file format for photographic images. Pixel-based contone images can be converted into .stn format with a program named GenuineFractals. The resolution independent file format allows for changing the size and resolution of contone photographic images while maintaining high image quality. This is a particularly useful format for multipurposing images.

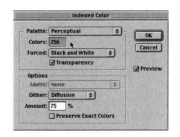

AC.5 Creating GIFs
GIFs are used for Web images, and support 8 bits or less of information. Image quality and load speed can be controlled through color and dithering choices.

FILE NAMING

For most flexible use, it is a good idea to place a proper three character, lowercase format identification extension or suffix at the end of your file names. Examples include: .tif for TIFF, .eps for EPS files, .gif for GIF files, and .jpg for JPEG files. This three character extension is not only important for the visual recognition of the file format, but is necessary for some computers to recognize the file format. Windows computers require the three character extension, and Macs do not. Regardless, it is useful to have that three character extension, as it helps to quickly and easily identify the file format of a graphic file at a glance. Photoshop provides you with the ability to automatically add this extension. I recommend using this capability. See the steps in Fig. AC.6.

If you are sharing your images with others on other platforms and/or across the Internet, it is good practice to get in the habit of limiting your file names to eight (8) characters. If you do not, the other platforms and/or Internet will do the limiting for you, indiscriminantly.

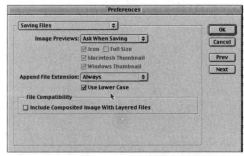

AC.6 Photoshop's file saving preferences
Photoshop can be configured to save a proper three character extension at the end of each file.

To configure Photoshop to do this, do the following:

1) Select the File Saving from the Preferences submenu under the File menu (File—Preferences—Saving Files).

2) Select Always from the Append File Extension pull down menu.

3) Place a check in the Use Lower Case box.

4) Click OK. Now Photoshop will add a proper three character lowercase extension to each file which is saved out of Photoshop.

APPENDIX D: FONT OVERVIEW

PostScript Type 1 Fonts
Screen   Printer

TrueType Fonts
Combined Screen and Printer

Characteristics

Screen	Printer
Bitmapped	Outline
Low resolution	High resolution
Specific point size	Scalable
For screen display	For printing

Characteristics

Bitmapped and outline

Low and high resolution

Scalable

For screen display and printing

Macintosh Font Files

Screen Font Files

- B Futura Bold 10
- B Futura Bold 12
- BO Futura BoldOblique 10
- BO Futura BoldOblique 12
- Futura 10
- Futura 12
- O Futura Oblique 10
- O Futura Oblique 12

Printer Font Files

- Futur   32K   PostScript™ font
- FuturBol   32K   PostScript™ font
- FuturBolObl   48K   PostScript™ font
- FuturObl   40K   PostScript™ font

TrueType Font Files Examples

- AppleGaramond Bd
- AppleGaramond BdIt
- AppleGaramond Bk
- AppleGaramond BkIt

Screen Font Icon View

Printer Font Icon View

FuturBolObl   FuturObl

Futur   FuturBol

TrueType Font Icon View

AppleGaramond Bd   AppleGaramond E

ppleGaramond BdIt   AppleGaramond Bl

Full Name With Point Size

- B Futura Bold 10
- B Futura Bold 12
- BO Futura BoldOblique 10
- BO Futura BoldOblique 12

Abbreviated Name

- FuturBol
- FuturBolObl

TrueType Font Naming
Full Name But With No Point Size

- AppleGaramond Bd
- AppleGaramond BdIt
- AppleGaramond Bk
- AppleGaramond BkIt

Note: Be careful of using icons for font identification. Printer font icons vary dramatically from one manufacturer to another, while the naming conventions discussed above remain the same

Windows Font Files

.pfm Outline Files

MOC____   MOCI____

MOBC____   MOBCI____

.pfb Font Metrics Files

Moc____   Moci____

Mobc____   Mobci____

Arial   Arial Black

Font Types and Their Characteristics

On a Mac PostScript screen fonts have point sizes included in their names because they are bitmapped graphic files and are specific sizes. PostScript printer fonts have abbreviated names with no point sizes because they are scalable PostScript files. TrueType font names have characteristics of both the screen and printer font names. They have full names like the screen fonts, but no point sizes because they are scalable like the printer fonts. Windows PostScript font files do not show point sizes in either font file.

WINDOWS POSTSCRIPT FONT FILES DETAILS

Windows Type 1 (.pfb) Font Files

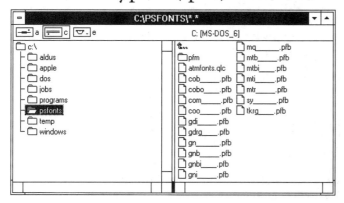

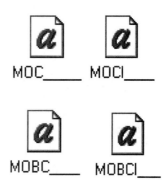

.pfm Outline Files

WINDOWS .PFB FILES

- Windows PostScript font files are stored in a separate folder called ps fonts. This also contains another folder which contains the .pfm files
- .pfb files contain both screen font data, as well as high resolution printer font information
- .pfb font files need to accompany the font metric (.pfm) files when you send a file to a service bureau or printing company.

Windows Type 1 Font Metric (.pfm) Font Files

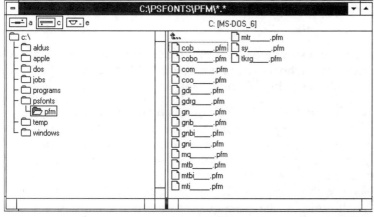

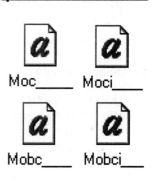

.pfb Font Metrics Files

WINDOWS .PFM FILES

- font metric files are stored in a separate subdirectory of the ps fonts directory, labeled .pfm
- .pfm files contain information which controls character spacing of text on a document page
- .pfm font files need to accompany the outline (.pfb) font files, shown above, when you send a file to a service bureau or printer. Collection of these font files can be aided by the use of file collection utilities like Marksware's FlightCheck.

APPENDIX E: TAZ'S TOP TWELVE QUESTIONS TO ASK YOUR PRINTING COMPANY

1. How many colors do their press print in one pass? (This will affect how suitable their press equipment is for your work. For instance, if you print primarily four color (4/c) process work you will generally want to have this work printed on presses which have at least four cylinders.)

2. What kind (sheet-fed, web, digital) and size presses does the company have? (This will affect how suitable their press equipment is for your work. If your print jobs are 40" across or are built in multipage signatures you will want to have your work printed on press which can handle press sheets of these sizes.)

3. At what lpi will your project be printed? (This will control the input resolution at which you create and/or scan or capture your images.)

4. What applications and versions do they support? If you are a PC/Windows user, ask if they are Windows savvy and if they can output your files from a Windows machine. (You want to know what your printing company is knowledgeable about and comfortable with.)

5. What file formats do they prefer: TIFF, EPS DCS? If you have larger project with many images, such as catalogs, do they offer low resolution swapouts? If so what kind do they use? Common ones include: OPI, DCS, or Dot E swapouts.

6. What kind of paper will be used to print your project? Coated or uncoated? (The kind of paper you use will affect image resolution, dot gain, and the look of your job, and in particular how images will reproduce. Discuss what kind of paper is best for your combination of job requirements and your budget.)

7. How much dot gain compensation will the specified paper have on images and screens? Who will do the dot gain on the grayscale images—you or them? (Without dot gain compensation, images tend to print darker than they should. Too much dot gain, and your image may print too light. Dot gain varies with paper.)

8. Who will be performing the RGB to CMYK conversion(and at what cost) on any scanned, captured or painted RGB images? (If the printing company wants you to perform this conversion, then Questions 9 and 10 below become crucial if you intent to make sure the quality and consistency of your color is maintained.)

9. Who should perform the scans or other image captures on your job. You? The printing company? A digital photographer? Who will be responsible for the final image color quality? (This responsibility and work flow should be established up front, especially when high quality color is concerned.)

10. How does the printing company suggest that the RGB to CMYK conversion be done? Are they using color management system, and do they use their own custom ICC color profiles? If so, will they provide you with those profiles and instruction on how to use them? If they are not using custom color profiles then ask your printing company for RGB to CMYK conversion value information for use in Photoshop. The critical values you will need include: 1) RGB setup values for your monitor, 2) ink set used, 3) dot gain number, 4) UCR or GCR, 5) total ink limit, 6) black ink limit, and 7) if GCR is being used A) Light or medium GCR and B) UCA values. (This discussion will critically affect the quality and predictability of your printed color.)

11. Who will perform trapping and imposition? (The printing company generally will be responsible.)

12. What proofs are available and will be provided? How close are these proofs to the press sheets they will be producing? (Have them show you samples. No proofs match the press sheets 100%! You want to know how close the proofs will be. As a general rule press sheets tend to be a bit darker than proofs, as they tend to have more dot gain. Conventional film based work flows use a different proofing system than direct to plate or press systems. Be sure you know what to expect!

APPENDIX F: DOCUMENT INFO AND INSTRUCTIONS

Following is an example of the type of information and instruction I send to a printing company to make sure my document will print correctly. Don't be shy about asking for or giving instructions!

Document info

1. Page layout performed in QXP (ver. 4.04)

2. Three (3) separate documents are provided: 1) Scanning manual (QXP doc. 85 pgs total without color signature); Document name: (Scanning manual)_Print, 2) Color signature (QXP doc 4 pgs; Document name: (Scanning manual)_Color sig (place in middle of book), 3) Cover (Illustrator document with placed CMYK TIFF); Document Name: WonderScan Cover.ai

3. Separate font files are supplied for each document (PostScript Type 1 fonts used exclusively)

4. RGB–CMYK conversion performed in Photoshop (ver. 5.02) with the following settings:
   - RGB setup = ColorMatch
   - SWOP Coated w/ 20% Dot gain (standard setting)
   - GCR = Light, black ink limit = 100%, total ink = 280, 10% UCA

5. *NO* Dot gain performed on included grayscale images. Dot gain adjustment on grayscale images must be performed during film output (see MatchPrints request below)

6. Color separated laser proofs provided.

7. Grayscale contones scanned at 200 ppi for printing at 150 lpi

8. Color contones scanned at 300 ppi for printing at 175 lpi

9. All pixel-based images provided as TIFFs

10. All vector-based images provided as EPSs

11. Preflight performed with FlightCheck V3.3r1

For questions contact: Taz Tally; ttallyphd@aol.com; 941.403.0000—Office, 472.526.7735—Cell

Instructions

1. Use current manual, with internal color signature, as construction guide for printing

2. Separate fonts are provided for each document. Please turn off/deactivate your fonts and load/activate mine. This is critical to maintaining my font integrity and proper flow and printing of type.

3. Printing company to perform dot gain correction on grayscale images

4. Please print black pages at 150 lpi: Please use 60lb Pressmaster text (or equivalent)

5. Color sig ok to print at 175 lpi: Please use 80lb Productolith gloss text (or equivalent)

6. Color cover print at 175 lpi: Please use 10pt C1S (coated one side) Carolina cover (or equivalent)

7. Printing company will perform trapping and imposition

8. I will need to see MatchPrints specific black-only pages and on color signature pages for sign off.
   - Black-only pages: pp. 1, 22, 26–27, 38, 40–45, 48–51
   - Color pages: All (pp. 79–72)

9. Color must be neutral and consistent on all three color image pages.

10. The Illustrator cover document will have to be adjusted for width to account for the thickness of the book.

11. Discuss print schedule and delivery date with

    Jazmine Saige
    Cybertime Scanning Corporation
    Kachemak Bay Drive, Homer, Alaska 99603
    TEL: 800-345-9987 (Ext. 2534)

APPENDIX G: EFIS EXAMPLE

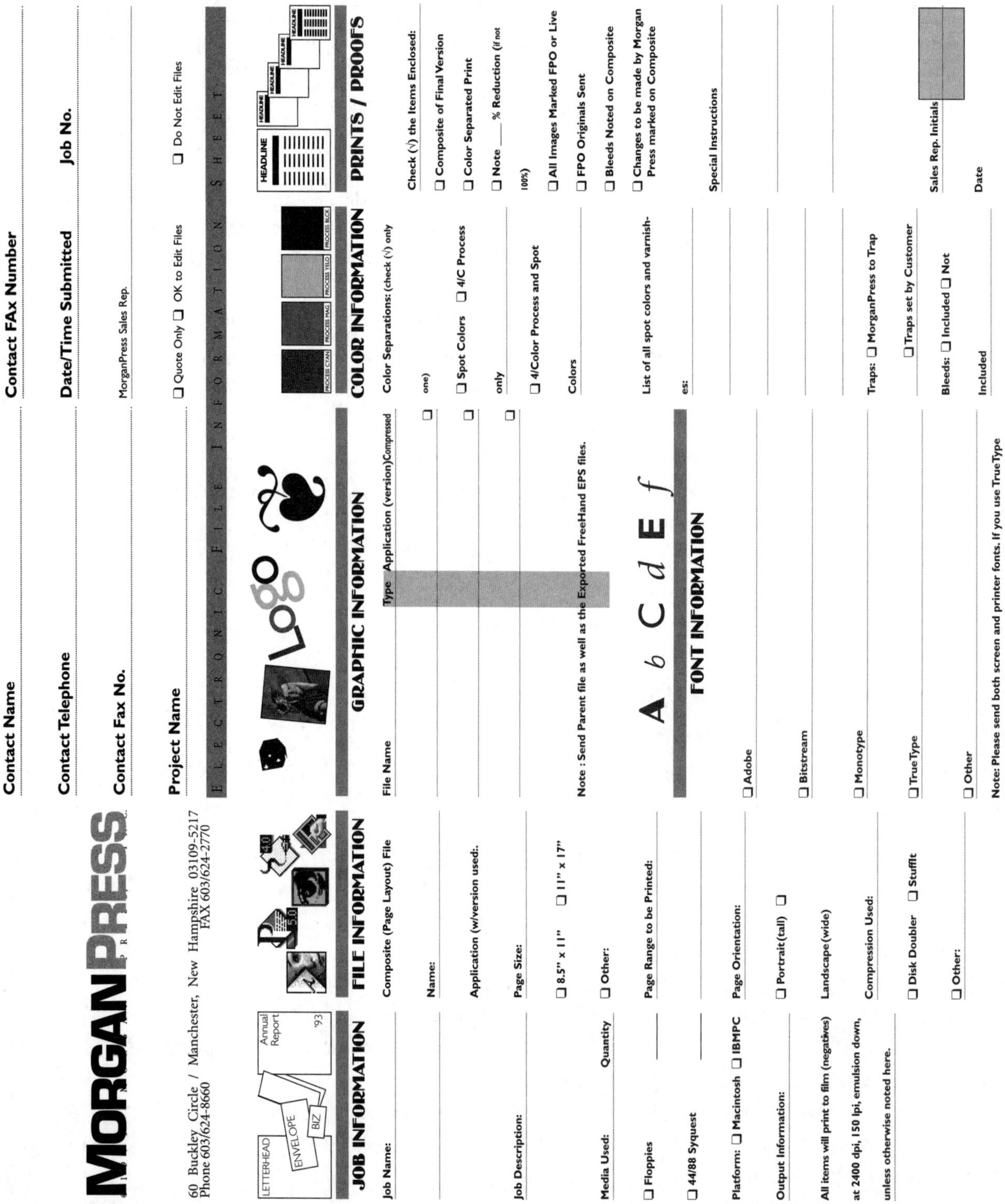

MORGAN PRESS

60 Buckley Circle / Manchester, New Hampshire 03109-5217
Phone 603/624-8660   FAX 603/624-2770

ELECTRONIC FILE INFORMATION SHEET

Contact Name _____   Contact FAx Number _____

Contact Telephone _____   Date/Time Submitted _____   Job No. _____

Contact Fax No. _____

Project Name _____   MorganPress Sales Rep. _____

☐ Quote Only ☐ OK to Edit Files   ☐ Do Not Edit Files

JOB INFORMATION

Job Name: _____

Quantity _____

Job Description: _____

Media Used: _____
☐ Floppies
☐ 44/88 Syquest

Platform: ☐ Macintosh ☐ IBMPC

Output Information:

All items will print to film (negatives) at 2400 dpi, 150 lpi, emulsion down, unless otherwise noted here.

FILE INFORMATION

Composite (Page Layout) File

Name: _____

Application (w/version used): _____

Page Size:
☐ 8.5" x 11"   ☐ 11" x 17"   ☐ Other: _____

Page Range to be Printed: _____

Page Orientation:
☐ Portrait(tall)   ☐ Landscape (wide)

Compression Used:
☐ Disk Doubler ☐ Stuffit   ☐ Other: _____

GRAPHIC INFORMATION

File Name / Type / Application (version) / Compressed
_____
_____
_____

Note : Send Parent file as well as the Exported FreeHand EPS files.

FONT INFORMATION

A b C d E f

☐ Adobe
☐ Bitstream
☐ Monotype
☐ TrueType
☐ Other

Note: Please send both screen and printer fonts. If you use TrueType fonts, use them exclusively or not at all.

COLOR INFORMATION

Color Separations: (check (√) only one)
☐ Spot Colors   ☐ 4/C Process only
☐ 4/Color Process and Spot Colors

List of all spot colors and varnishes:
_____
_____

Traps: ☐ MorganPress to Trap
       ☐ Traps set by Customer

Bleeds: ☐ Included ☐ Not Included

PRINTS / PROOFS

Check (√) the Items Enclosed:
☐ Composite of Final Version
☐ Color Separated Print
☐ Note ___ % Reduction (if not 100%)
☐ All Images Marked FPO or Live
☐ FPO Originals Sent
☐ Bleeds Noted on Composite
☐ Changes to be made by Morgan Press marked on Composite

Special Instructions
_____
_____

Sales Rep. Initials _____

Date _____

Electronic File Information Sheets (EFIS)

Electronic file information sheets are important to provide along with a complete set of your electronic files and proofs when you send your electronic documents out to a printing company or other service bureau. An EFIS provides a set of vital statistics about your documents including contact information and page layout document size, number of pages and the application and version used to create the printing document. In addition information about font and graphic files, and colors used in your document, should be included on this sheet. Many printing companies provide EFIS sheets such as this one, or you may use those created by Preflight programs such as FlightCheck, and/or one of your own such as the one show in here.

APPENDIX H: TAZ'S TOP TWELVE TIPS

Taz's File Prep Tip 1

Involve your printing company or output service bureau in the planning of your document. In fact it is an excellent idea to choose your printing company or output service bureau prior to beginning your document construction. Schedule a planning session where you will meet with the sales and production staff to discuss the construction and composition of your job. Be sure to discuss document sizes which print well on their presses, the lpi at which they will print your images, and at what resolution you should scan or create yours. Discuss who will do the scanning and what sort of proofing will be required. Is OPI appropriate for your job? Ask about how your paper will affect your document creation with such issues as dot gain and color. Send in test images for any items you have questions about, such as duotones, contone color, cross platform documents and complex images such as those with clipping paths.

Taz's File Prep Tip 2

Simplify your computer system as much as possible by removing any files, and especially from your operating system folder, which are not required or used. By reducing the number of unnecessary files from your computer you will not only free up valuable storage space but you will be reducing the possibility of potential crash causing file conflicts, and reducing the number of files of which your computer must keep track. As part of this process of simplification, any time you install new application or an update to a previous application, perform a custom, rather than a default installation, so that you can only install the files which you will need.

Taz's File Prep Tip 3

Your computer is not a typewriter; it is a sophisticated typesetting tool. Don't use multiple spaces and returns to control the horizontal and vertical placement of type. Use paragraph formatting and tabs to position type. Read Robin Williams' Book, *The Mac (or PC) Is Not A Typewriter*. I think this is the single best introduction to typesetting ever written.

Taz's File Prep Tip 4

Set your scanner up properly. Calibrate your scanner at the beginning of each scan session. For grayscale images, your scanner needs to be linear. For color contone scans, your scanner needs to be neutral as well as linear. Be sure to scan your images at the proper resolution (1.5 x lpi) and let your scanner perform any scaling functions for you. Discuss these scanning requirements with your printer.

Taz's File Prep Tip 5

Set up your RGB to CMYK conversion properly prior to making the conversion. Remember that each output device has its own gamut and therefore its own set of RGB to CMYK conversion criteria. I prefer to perform most of my image editing and basic color correction in RGB. I always save an archive RGB version of my image. I will convert a copy of the image to CMYK for use in print. Avoid going back to RGB from a CMYK file. Open and use the archive file instead.

Taz's File Prep Tip 6

Be careful with your color assignments. With print documents, if you assign a spot color, remember that each spot color will separate to its own piece of film, and will therefore require its own plate and cylinder on a press. So if you intend to print your document in process color only, do not assign spot colors. Also remember that spot colors will not separate on a composite desktop printer. When assigning colors to objects which will be displayed on the World Wide Web, assign one of the 216 Web-safe colors to help improve image redraw speed as well as color fidelity.

Taz's File Prep Tip 7

Do not embed one graphic file inside of another. Do not place one EPS graphic inside a vector graphics document and then save that graphic document as a second EPS graphic file. This will nest the first EPS image. RIPs have a very difficult time finding and RIPing the embedded graphic component files. Is there an easy way to tell if you have nested files? Yes! If all the vector graphic elements are selectable and editable, none are nested. Nested graphic files are not editable.

Taz's File Prep Tip 8

Use PostScript Type 1 rather than TrueType fonts. Using PostScript fonts will decrease the likelihood that you will have problems with your font files RIPing properly at high resolution. If you use TrueType fonts, use them exclusively; don't mix TrueType with Type 1 in the same document, and inform your printing company that you are using them.

Taz's File Prep Tip 9

When creating graphics for print your emphasis should be on image quality. Be sure that you create your graphic with enough resolution to be reproduced on the highest quality printing device to which you will print. Know and use the output resolution of the printing device as your guide to you image input resolution. Use the formula of 1.5-2.0 X lpi of your output device to determine your minimum and maximum resolution values.

When creating Web graphics, your emphasis should be more on speed than on maximum image quality. It is better to have thousands of viewers look at your good images than only a few look at at your perfect images. Use image resolution, compression, bit depth and image dimension to reduce the size of your Web-bound images.

Taz's File Prep Tip 10

Print accurate proofs of your documents before you send your files out to be printed. Send these accurate proofs along with your files to your service bureau or printing company. Your printing company will use these to check to see if their version of your document matches your version. Remember that an accurate proof is the only visual guide which your printing company has to help them print your file.

You should at least create composite proofs for checking composition. Better yet, prepare color separated proofs. Creating color separated proofs is the only foolproof way to check your color breaks, that is, to see if your colors are separating properly.

Taz's File Prep Tip 11

Get your document creation font files outside of your system/PS fonts folder. Test, sort, and organize your font files, and last but not least, use a font management tool such as Adobe ATM Deluxe to manage your font files. This one change in how you operate will significantly improve your productivity and dramatically decrease your font management problems. Remember that problems with font files continue to be the number one problem with customer files which arrive at printing companies.

Taz's File Prep Tip 12

Use Preflight utilities, such as MarkzWare's FlightCheck, to help you preflight your files and collect your file components. Your file preparation chores will be done more comprehensively, more consistently, faster, easier, and will be more foolproof. On top of that, these preflighting utilities will collect all your file components!

APPENDIX I: FILE PREP UTILITIES

Packing for traveling made easy

The following utilities will help simplify and/or facilitate your file creation and preparation chores. A brief description of the use of each application is included. The prices in parentheses are approximate.

- ATM (Adobe): a required utility which helps provide W.Y.S.I.W.Y.G. views and in the printing of scaled text characters
- ATM Deluxe (Mac and Windows) (Adobe): font management utility which helps organize and access large numbers of fonts
- PostScript Level 2 reference card (Merrit) : PostScript error code information
- PinPoint XT: for troubleshooting Quark Files
- LaserCheck (Merrit): file troubleshooting and imagesetter emulation utility
- PreFlight Pro (Extensis): preflight utility which troubleshoots as well as gathers all components
- Flight Check (Markzware): file prep utility which troubleshoots as well as gathers all components
- Bureau Manager: Quark extension for gathering file components, including fonts
- Collect for Output (Free): document and graphic file collection in Quark 3.2 and above
- Save for Service Provider (Free): PageMaker 6.5+ content preflight and collection utility
- QuarkPrint (Quark): expands Quark's print capabilities
- Display Pub Info (Free): document info; addition included with PageMaker 5.0 and above
- Blender (ZiffNet Mac): used to help calculate the number of blend steps required
- Suitcase (Extensis): Mac font management utility for organizing and accessing your fonts
- MasterJuggler (Symantic): Mac font management utility for organizing and accessing your fonts
- Streamline (Adobe): Pixel to vector conversion utility for creating scalable resolution independent line art graphics
- Font Chameleon ($125): allows you to change one font architecture into another
- Metamorphosis : allows you to change one font architecture into another
- Fontographer (Macromedia): the ultimate font creation and conversion tool
- ScanXpress Calculator (Express): helps to determine input scanning resolutions
- Color Compass (Praxisoft): color assignment and management utility
- The Fondler: font troubleshooting utility
- Font Reserve (Diamond Soft): Font management utility for the Macintosh
- DeBabelizer (Debabelizer): the ultimate file format conversion utility
- Intellihance (Extensis): photo enhancement plug-in for photoshop
- ScanPrep Pro: automated scanning application
- Binuscan ColorPro (Binuscan): comprehensive scanning, color correction, and separation suite of application.
- Pitstop (Enfocus): PDF editor
- Tailor (Enfocus): PostScript editor
- Genuine Fractal (Altimira): Graphic file scaling and resolution alteration

APPENDIX J: INFORMATION RESOURCES

BOOKS

Avoiding the Scanning Blues, Taz Tally, Prentice Hall, 2000, ISBN: 0-13-087322-5

Beyond the Mac Is Not a Typewriter, Robin Williams, Peachpit Press, 1996, 1-201-88598-0

CREF Computer Ready Electronic Files 2, Scitex Graphic Arts Users Association, Brentwood, TN

Design for Non-Designers, Robin Williams, Santa Fe NM, http://www.zumacafe.com

Getting It Printed, 3rd Edition, Mark Beach and Eric Kenly, North Light Books, 1999, ISBN: 0-89134-858-1

GRACOL General Requirements For Applications In Commercial Offset Lithography V. 2.0, Graphic Arts Communication Association, 1998, 703.519.8160

How to Make Sure What You See Is What You Get, Peter Fink, phone 800.551.5921

One-Minute Designer, Revised Edition, Roger C. Parker, MIS: Press, 1997, 1-55828-593-8

Photoshop in Black and White, 2nd Edition, Jim Rich and Sandy Bozek, Peachpit Press, 1995, 1-56609-189-6

Pocket Guide to Color Reproduction, Miles Southworth and Donna Southworth, Graphic Arts Publishing, 1994, 0-933600-09-7

Pocket Guide To Digital Prepress, Frank Romano, Delmar Publishers, 1996, 0-8273-7198-5

Pocket Guide To Digital Printing, Frank Cost, Delmar, 1997, 0-8273-7592-1

Pocket Pal: A Graphics Arts Production Handbook, International Paper, Memphis, TN

PostScript: A Visual Approach, Ross Smith, Peachpit Press, 0-938-151-12-6

QuarkXPress: Tips & Tricks, David Blatner and Eric Taub, Peachpit Press (for various versions for QuarkXPress)

Real World Photoshop, David Blatner and Bruce Fraser, Peachpit Press (for various versions for Photoshop)

Real World Scanning and Halftones, David Blatner and Steve Roth, Peachpit Press, 1995

The Art & Technology of Typography, Agfa Corp, 1988, Wilmington, MA

The Color Resource Complete Color Glossary, Miles Southworth, Thad McIlroy, and Donna Southworth, The Color Resource, 1992, 1-879847-01-9

The Color Scanning Success Handbook, Michael Kieran, Desktop Publishing Associates, 1997, 1-896097-01-4

The Complete Guide to Trapping, 2nd Edition, Brian Lawler, Hayden Books, 1995, 1-56830-098-0

The Mac (PC) Is Not A Typewriter, Robin Williams, Peachpit Press, 1990, 0-938151-31-2

The Photoshop WOW Book (series), Linnea Dayton and Jack Davis, Peachpit Press (for various versions of Photoshop)

Thinking in PostScript, Glenn C. Reid, Addison–Wesley, 1990, 0-201-52372-8

Understanding Desktop Color, 2nd Edition, Michael Kieran, Desktop Publishing Associates, 1994, 1-56609-164-0

How to Check and Correct Color Proofs, David Bann and John Gargan, North Light Books, ISBN 0-89134-350-4

PERIODICALS

Design Tools Monthly, Boulder, CO, 303.543.8300 (my favorite)

Step by Step Electronic Design, Dynamic Graphics, Peoria, IL, 800.255.8800

Dynamic Graphics, The Idea Guide to Quick Desktop Success, Dynamic Graphics, Peoria, IL, 800.255.8800

DTP Journal, Journal of the NADP (National Association of Desktop Publishers), 508.887.7900

Adobe Magazine, Adobe Systems, Mountain View, CA 415-961-4400, www.adobe.com

Graphic Arts Monthly, Graphic Arts Communication Association, Alexandria, VA

GATF: Graphic Arts Technical Foundation, various technical publications, Pittsburgh, PA

HOW: The Bottomline Design Magazine, Cincinnati, OH, 800.333.1115

Publish, Integrated Media, San Francisco, CA, 415.243.0600

Seybold Reports, Media, PA, 800.325.3830, www.seyboldreport.com

WEB RESOURCES

Viacom's Information Super Library: http://www.mcp.com—General, broad topics, electronic publishing information

Apple Computer: http://www.Apple.com—Apple computer information

Microsoft: http://www.microsoft.com—Microsoft information

Adobe Plug-in Source Catalog: http://www.imageclub.com/aps/—Plug-in resources for Adobe products

Extensis Phototools info: http://www.extensis.com—Extension technologies for many products

Macromedia: http://www.macromedia.com:—FreeHand and super Web-based product information and help

Netscape Color Info: http://www.connect.hawaii.com/hc/webmasters/—Web color information and resources

Pantone: http://www.pantone.com/whatsnew.html—Pantone-specific and general color information

Shareware: http://shareware.com—Wild and wooly world of shareware. Bring your virus protection

Design Tools Creaticity: http://www.creaticity.com—Wonderful update and problem solving information for wide variety of DTP issues

Amazon Books: http://www.amazon.com/exec/obidos/subst/home/home.html/002-0754583-8019430—Online book reviews and ordering

Adobe Publications: http://www.adobe.com/publications/adobemag—Access old versions of Adobe Magazine and other Adobe educational information

Apple Education Site: http://www.education.apple.com—Access Apple's extensive education; library

Apple Information/Support: http://info.apple.com—Apple troubleshooting infomation

Digital Media: http://www.digitalmedia.net—Excellent multimedia training

TazTally Seminars: http://www.tazseminars.com—Seminar training topics and schedules

Quark Updates: http://www.quark.com/files/update_select.html—Get Quark updates

For PDF files and Acrobat technology in general, consult these info sites:

• *PDF for Prepress:* www.prepress.ch/pdf_wp.pdf

• *PDF Bug List on Seybold Web site:* www.seyboldseminars.com. Includes a list of bugs and fixes and has an up-to-date list of PDF extensions

• *PDF devoted sites:* www.pdfzone.com

• *Adobe PDF info:* www.Adobe.com

Index

INDEX

P

Utility file, 56

V

Value, 20, 22, 24, 28, 32, 34, 37, 39–41, 43, 53, 68, 116, 122, 158, 177, 184, 192, 242, 247, 250–51, 253–54, 260, 291, 293, 296–98, 304, 307, 314–15, 346, 352, 363, 365, 368–69, 371–72, 379, 381–82, 384, 400–401, 435

Varnish, 31, 52, 392, 396, 407

Vector graphic, 46, 56, 167–68, 180–81, 258, 309, 415, 439

Vectors, 22, 24, 30, 34, 148, 156–57, 165–68, 171, 180–81, 189, 194–95, 206, 211, 255, 258, 270, 313, 316, 323, 355, 430

Video, 19, 23, 35, 47, 50, 56, 68–69, 76–79, 83, 85, 88, 97, 104, 114–15, 120, 130, 170, 175, 182, 186–187, 260, 299, 301, 325, back pages

Videoboard, 56

Virtual memory, 51, 56, 59, 127, 136–37, 140–41, 143

Virus, 56, 95, 102, 104, 106, 127, 133–35, 138–39, 141–43

Visualization scanning, 56, 237

W

WAN, 56

Web, 4, 9–11, 14–15, 19, 23–24, 27, 29, 36–37, 39–42, 45, 49–50, 54, 57, 69, 77–78, 88, 100–101, 104, 108, 114, 119–20, 124, 136, 145–46, 165, 168–70, 174–75, 179–81, 186–87, 189–90, 194, 258, 260, 262, 267, 269–70, 277, 283, 291, 293, 295, 297, 299–300, 304–5, 308–329, 349, 359, 398, 430–32, 435, 439–40, 443–46

Web safe color, 291, 295, 299, 308, 315, 322

Window, 29, 34, 57, 96, 98–99, 107–108, 123, 130, 209, 217, 223, 384

Windows, 29–30, 34–36, 39, 44, 47, 52, 54, 56–57, 76, 84–85, 94–104, 106, 108, 122, 127, 129–35, 138, 142–43, 146, 168, 171, 173, 175–76, 180–81, 215, 217, 219–21, 223–224, 227–28, 230–32, 277, 295, 299, 305, 315, 319, 323–24, 326, 328, 332, 334, 342, 347, 411–15, 419–20, 424–25, 430–35, 441

Windows-based, 39, 130–31, 314

Windows Operating System, 39, 57

Wmf, 166, 174–75, 180–82, 258, 349, 430

Workstation, 83, 86, 90, 174, 260

World Wide Web, 4, 10, 36–37, 42, 49–50, 57, 77, 88, 114, 168, 170, 175, 186–87, 267, 293, 297, 299, 305, 311–13, 325, 439

WYSIWYG, 30, 57, 220

X

XHTML, 9, 57

XML, 4, 9, 57

Y

YCC, 32, 39, 47, 260–61, 266, 302

Yellow, 8, 31–32, 38, 49, 56, 177, 243, 252, 292–94, 297, 367–68, 382–83, 385, 391, 393–94, 399–400, 403

Z

Zip, 43, 57, 75, 78–79, 82, 94, 136, 186, 418, back pages

Zip disk, 57, 418

Taz Tally Seminars
Electronic Publishing Educational Resources

Product & Price Form

PRODUCT	QTY	YOUR PRICE
Taz's BOOKS		
"Avoiding the Output Blues " (updated version)	___	$39.95
"Avoiding the Output Blues " (original version)	___	$25.00
"Avoiding the Scanning Blues "	___	$39.95
VIDEOS		
"Preparing Files for Print I"	___	$39.95
"Preparing Files for Print II"	___	$39.95
— or —		
Print Set for	___	$74.95
"Photoshop Techniques I"	___	$39.95
"Photoshop Techniques II"	___	$39.95
— or —		
Photoshop Set for	___	$74.95
"Taming Your Scanner I"	___	$39.95
"Taming Your Scanner II"	___	$39.95
— or —		
Scanning Set for	___	$74.95
"Keyboard Shortcuts"	___	$39.95
Calibration Targets		
Taz's Scanner Calibration Target	___	$25.00
Taz's Scanner Calibration Kit	___	$39.00
(Kit includes Target, and Taz's scanning tips and tricks)		

INTERACTIVE CDs

Font Management	__Mac only	___	$79.95
Scan & Photoshop	__Mac__Win	___	$79.95
PageMaker	__Mac___Win	___	$79.95
QuarkXPress	__Mac only	___	$79.95
Illustrator	__Mac___Win	___	$79.95
Acrobat	__Mac only	___	$79.95
FlightCheck	__Mac___Win	___	$79.95

Call for other available titles

    *Shipping and Handling $ _____
                 TOTAL $ _____

*Shipping & Handling charges are $5.00 for the first item and
$3.00 for each additional item. (A video set counts as one item.)

Order Form

PHONE ORDERS:

Please call
888-421-2103

FAX ORDERS:

Fax completed forms to:
816-471-4570

WEB ORDERS

Reach us at
WWW.TAZSEMINARS.COM

MAIL ORDERS

Mail to:
Taz Tally Seminars
3616 Heritage Lane
Ft. Myers, FL 33908

Ship To:

Name_____

Organization_____

Address_____

City_____State____Zip_____

Phone_____

Fax_____

eMail_____

Payment Method

❑ Check

❑ Money Order

❑ Credit Card

❑ MC ❑ Visa

Card #_____

Expiration date_____

Name on card_____

Signature _____

SPECIAL SCANNER CALIBRATION TARGET OFFER

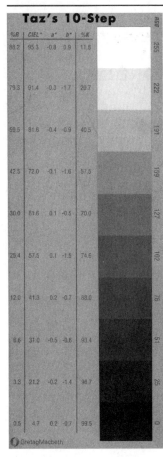

Improve the quality of your scanned images by calibrating your scanner. As discussed in Chapters 6 and 7, calibration of your scanner is one of the key variables to improving the quality and consistency of your scanned grayscale and color images.

Get your copy of Taz's calibration target specifically designed for use with desktop scanners.

Order your target today at a special book purchaser's discount price.

Calibration Target

Taz has created a special 10-step calibration target, made specifically for desktop scanners. It includes easy-to-read RGB and percent grayscale target values right on the target...No data sheets to lose!

Target list price $25.00
Your price: $21.95!

This target is the one used with the step-by-step procedure provided in Chapters 6 and 7 of this book.

Calibration Kit

This custom kit developed by Taz includes one of Taz's 10-step calibration targets as well as a complete step-by-step calibration procedure. Taz includes descriptions for using your calibration target with both your scanner and with Photoshop. Also includes Taz's favorite scanning tips and tricks.

Scanner Calibration Kit list price $39.00
Your price: $34.95!

Phone Orders: 941-433-0622   Fax Orders: 941-267-8389

Web Orders: www.tazseminars.com

Mail Orders: Taz Tally Seminars
3616 Heritage Lane
Ft. Myers, FL 33908

_____ Calibration Target $21.95 ea.   _____

_____ Calibration Kit $34.95 ea   _____

_____ Bulk order (10 minimum) $18.95 ea   _____ (includes a free Calibration Kit)

Shipping & Handling $3.00 _____

Total _____

Ship To: Name _____

Company _____

Address _____

City_____ State_____ Zip_____

Phone_____ Fax_____

Email_____

Payment Method: ❏ Check ❏ Money Order

Credit Card: ❏ MC ❏ Visa

Card #_____

Expiration date_____